GENDER
VIOLENCE

GENDER VIOLENCE

INTERDISCIPLINARY PERSPECTIVES

•

EDITED BY
Laura L. O'Toole AND Jessica R. Schiffman

NEW YORK UNIVERSITY PRESS
New York and London

NEW YORK UNIVERSITY PRESS
New York and London

Library of Congress Cataloging-in-Publication Data
Gender violence : interdisciplinary perspectives / edited by Laura L.
   O'Toole and Jessica R. Schiffman.
       p.   cm.
   Includes bibliographical references and index.
   ISBN 0-8147-8040-7 (cloth : alk. paper).—ISBN 0-8147-8041-5
   (pbk. : alk. paper)
       1. Women—Crimes against.   2. Violence.   3. Sex crimes.
4. Pornography—Social aspects.   5. Women—Crimes against—United
States.   6. Violence—United States.   Sex crimes—United States.
8. Pornography—United States—Social aspects.   I. O'Toole, Laura
L.   II. Schiffman, Jessica R.
   HV6250.4.W65G48   1997
   362.82'92—dc21   96-49903
                           CIP

New York University Press books are printed on acid-free paper,
and their binding materials are chosen for strength and durability.

Manufactured in the United States of America

To Lena and John O'Toole for their support and encouragement of my work; to Kathleen O'Toole for her example of commitment; and to Christian Meade, whose gentle spirit and compassion renews my faith in humanity and hope for a just world.

LOT

To Elizabeth and Joseph Schiffman, who encourage my questions; to the Women of Safeplace, who taught me what I needed to ask; and to Emma and Ethan Timmins-Schiffman, who give me every reason to believe in a brighter future.

JRS

And to Stephen Meade and Patrick Timmins, who demonstrate that nonviolence and true egalitarianism are possible in relationships between women and men.

LOT and JRS

Contents

Preface:
Conceptualizing Gender Violence

Think about the most consuming events of the last decade, those that grabbed the attention of the public through news headlines and court television and dominated daily conversation. A famed American sports hero is tried for the brutal murder of his ex-spouse and a companion, with the circumstantial case largely dependent upon his not-so-famous status as a former wife beater. Armies bent on "ethnic cleansing" during the devastating civil war in the former Yugoslavia slaughter rival men and use savage serial rapes to subdue and dehumanize women. Three U.S. servicemen are convicted of raping a twelve-year-old schoolgirl on the Japanese island of Okinawa, showing that military rape is not merely a strategy of war. A long-time and esteemed senator is compelled to resign in disgrace after dozens of women come forward with complaints of sexual harassment. Thousands of female children are sold into sexual slavery by impoverished families or kidnapped for sale in lucrative, government-sanctioned sex industries around the globe.

These diverse events have a common link: male perpetrators, acting alone or in groups, for whom violence and violation are rational solutions to perceived problems ranging from the need to inflate one's sexual self-esteem to denigrating rivals in war to boosting a country's GNP. They also demonstrate the real harm that women face on a daily basis in a world that views them sometimes as property, often as pawns, and usually as secondary citizens in need of control by men. These events are also similar in that they are not random. While several of these examples are deemed newsworthy on an international scale, given their political implications or the celebrity of perpetrators, they represent only a fraction of the violence against women and children that is committed on a daily basis across the world. If you read your community newspaper or scan local televised newscasts, you will find hundreds of similar events in any given month. These incidents, while often writ small, stand as clear testimony to the insidious problem of gender violence.

Acts of gender violence are similarly ubiquitous throughout history. Rape has been a tool of warriors for centuries. Working women experienced men's coercive sexual behaviors long before the term *sexual harassment* was coined. Gender violence often links divergent cultures as well. The incest taboo, so long identified by scholars as universal across cultures, appears to be more a taboo against speaking about incest than a successful mechanism of social control.

Violence at the end of the twentieth century extends from individual relationships, to the arrangement of power and authority in organizations, to the relations among countries of the world. Speaking broadly, violence is a mainstay in the entertainment and news media, in national and international politics, and in family dynamics, as well as in our social constructions of sexual desire. It simultaneously intrigues and repels us. Although most violence worldwide is male-on-male, the emergence of self-conscious women's political movements, combined with academic inquiry in women's studies, begs closer scrutiny of the patterns of male violence against women, both in intimate relationships and in public.

As a central organizing principle among human groups, gender is the constellation of personal attributes assigned to men and women in any culture. It is a primary character-istic by which we structure intimate relationships, divide labor, assign social value, and grant privilege. In most contemporary societies, dualistic gender systems endure, with clearly demarcated boundaries between what is considered masculine and what is con-sidered feminine—temperamentally, physically, sexually, and behaviorally. Gender is simultaneously a deeply embedded aspect of individual personalities and structural social arrangements; however, it is also contested social terrain. Gender relations at the end of the twentieth century are a complicated mix of congeniality and conflict; yet, in either case they are almost always imbued with an asymmetrical distribution of power. They are the product of social and cultural dynamics, historical forces, political struc-tures, and interpersonal chemistry. In many societies and for many individuals, however, it is the *conflicted* aspects of gender relations that are the most prominent.

We understand violence as the extreme application of social control. Usually under-stood as the use of physical force, it can take a psychological form when manifested through direct harassment or implied terroristic threats. Violence can also be structural, as when institutional forces such as governments or medical systems impinge upon individuals' rights to bodily integrity, or contribute to the deprivation of basic human needs. By our definition, gender violence is any interpersonal, organizational, or politi-cally oriented violation perpetrated against people due to their gender identity, sexual orientation, or location in the hierarchy of male-dominated social systems such as families, military organizations, or the labor force. Much of the violence in contempo-rary society serves to preserve asymmetrical gender systems of power. For example, compulsory aggression as a central component of masculinity serves to legitimate male-on-male violence, sexual harassment as a means of controlling the public behavior of women, gay and lesbian bashing, and rape as a standard tool in war, in prisons, and in too many intimate relationships.

Though gender violence is far from new, if we consider crime statistics, social science research, and media attention as indicators, the phenomenon appears to be escalating. Clearly and consistently documented throughout human history, the forms that such violence assumes—rape, battering, child abuse, and murder—comprise some of the most pressing social problems of our times. Given the centrality of gender and the ubiquity of violence, it is no wonder that the two are interwoven in our social systems. The systems in which they are embedded are complex; simplistic explanations or simple solutions will not suffice. Explicating the problem of gender violence demands a comprehensive and multifaceted analytical framework.

This volume attempts to provide such an interdisciplinary framework. It is the outgrowth of our personal and collegial efforts to understand the phenomenon of gender violence to a fuller extent than discipline-specific analysis currently allows. We are sociologists by training and continue to see the value of our discipline in explaining the significance of context in the study of gender violence—that is, the ways in which the organization of both interpersonal interaction and social institutions such as the law, economies, and religions contribute to the social construction of gender and to gender violence. As long-time participants in interdisciplinary women's studies programs, we have also been engaged by the important analyses of our colleagues in the social sciences and humanities that have enriched the study of gender relations, in many cases preceding sociology in uncovering significant social facts as well as the subdued or silenced voices of women. The poems and articles in this book have contributed to our own understanding of the interpersonal and structural dynamics of gender violence, as well as both the historical evolution and the contemporary manifestations of gender relations. We share that understanding here, weaving together the voices of analysts and artists with our own thoughts on how to best interpret the vast and ever-expanding literature on gender violence. We do this while acknowledging that the literature cannot completely represent the horrifying expanse of statistical evidence and personal experiences of rape, incest, domestic violence, sexual harassment, and murder.

So why have we called this book *Gender Violence* rather than *Violence against Women?* Although documenting and exploring the violation of women has been the primary focus of research and activism among feminist and profeminist analysts, we have chosen to include a broader set of questions that spring from the study of gender and violence: In what ways are ideas about gender and sexual identity used to legitimate violence against individuals and groups, regardless of their biological sex? To what extent does the social construction of gender facilitate male-on-male violence? Can and should men, at least in some cases, be acknowledged as passive victims of violence against women? By widening our analytical lens, we are able to incorporate important connections among violence against heterosexual women and men, lesbians and gay men, and children, and suggest important questions about structural and interpersonal violence for future analysis.

Gender Violence is organized into three parts. Part 1 contains a sociohistorical exploration of gender violence, focusing first across cultures, then more specifically on the conditions that give rise to gender violence in the United States. Part 2 examines the various forms of gender violence, from obscene phone calls to workplace harassment, rape, battering, and child abuse. Part 3 focuses on two currents that run strong within contemporary discourse on gender violence: the pornography debate and the dialogue around transforming gender relations. Each section of the book includes an introduction, suggested readings, and chapters that represent important contributions to the study of gender violence from a wide spectrum of academic and activist analysis. Although the chapters primarily address gender violence issues in the United States, we have integrated international perspectives into the analytical framework of the book. We include research-based articles, theoretical and critical analyses, and essays and first-person narratives.

The reader will notice that nearly every section is prefaced by a poem. We have organized the book this way in part to set the tone for the more scholarly analysis that follows, and in part to periodically break away from this analysis so as to hear women's voices unfettered by disciplinary jargon or academic theory. Understanding gender violence requires a merging of the analytical and experiential realms. Working toward a solution will ultimately require an understanding of both social dynamics and of the pain and tragedy that gender violence wreaks in the lives of women and men across the globe.

Among the anthologized works, the reader will note some inconsistency in terminology and capitalization in reference to racial/ethnic groups. These differences reflect the conventions and preferences of the different time periods when these chapters were originally crafted. In our introductory essays, we have chosen to capitalize all referents to racial or ethnic categories.

This volume is necessarily incomplete. There are many more insightful analyses and powerful voices than space permits. Many have yet to speak, and our search for solutions is far from complete. We hope this book will contribute to the dialogue among students, activists, and scholars concerned about understanding and eradicating gender violence. We believe such a dialogue is crucial, and we have attempted to design the book in a way that is accessible to all of these constituencies.

Many people have encouraged us to take on this project and have provided helpful commentary along the way. Colleagues and friends who have supported us in various ways include Suzanne Cherrin, Carol Clark, Kate Conway-Turner, Janeene Crook, Vernie Davis, Sandra Harding, John Linn, Rita Maloy, Carol Post, Carol Stoneburner, Donna Tuites, Kathleen Turkel, and Mary Ruth Warner. Kevin White provided us with many helpful suggestions in the early stages of the project. We appreciate the collegial encouragement of an even larger group of folks who comprise the women's studies faculties at the University of Delaware and Guilford College. We also sincerely appreciate the tenacity and courage of many current and former students at the University of Delaware and Guilford College who have confronted the difficult questions we have posed about gender and violence, often bearing the weight of great personal trauma. They have taught us a lot.

We have both been assisted by the institutions for which we work. In particular, we thank Mary Richards, dean of the College of Arts and Science at the University of Delaware, for supporting Jessica's sabbatical leave, and deans Kathy Adams and Cyril Harvey of Guilford College for providing research funds that facilitated Laura's long-distance collaboration. Eloise Barzcak, Amy Jasper, Kandra Strauss, Chandra Watson, and Kim Wunner have provided significant clerical assistance, enabling us to complete the project in a timely fashion. Our editor, Timothy Bartlett, believed in the project from its earliest inception. We thank him particularly for keeping us to task, as well as for his continued enthusiasm. We are both fortunate to have wonderfully supportive families, whose love and care have enabled us to produce this volume. Finally, we thank the contributors to this volume for their vision, with special gratitude to Larry Eldridge, Bill Gay, Demie Kurz, Kathleen O'Toole, and Claire Renzetti for contributing their new work to this project.

LAURA L. O'TOOLE
Greensboro, North Carolina

JESSICA R. SCHIFFMAN
Newark, Delaware

PART I

Roots of Male Violence and Victimization of Women

The two sections in this part explore the conditions that give rise to male violence against women. Section 1 takes a global perspective in analyzing widespread cultural and historical trends that are associated with patriarchal domination. In section 2, the United States is considered as a specific case to illustrate how unique sociocultural attributes can alter the terrain of gender relations, and thus, the nature and scope of gender violence. Taken together, these sections show that understanding gender violence requires generalized historical and theoretical knowledge, as well as smaller-scale case study analysis to capture the culture-specific contours that gender violence assumes. Readings in part 1 span the disciplines of anthropology, criminology, economics, history, political science, psychology, and sociology.

SECTION 1

The Roots of Male Violence
against Women

The roots of gender violence run deep in human history, and this depth makes attempts to trace them difficult. Male violence against women is so widespread that biological determinism has often dominated debates about its origins. In other words, gender violence is often explained as a natural and universal consequence of the biological difference between men and women. Age-old theories posit that superior strength and a variety of hormonal stimuli predispose men toward violent, controlling behavior. Such an amalgam of traits, juxtaposed against the purported natural passivity and compliance of the weaker female, it is argued, will likely produce violence in men, against women, in certain situations. One form of this argument suggests that the male's overwhelming urge to reproduce stimulates behavioral responses that lead to what we now define as rape.

Despite the overwhelming popularity and longevity of such explanations, other compelling theories have emerged. The influence of the contemporary feminist movement on academic inquiry has led to the reframing of central questions about gender relations. Deeply embedded intellectual traditions have been challenged by a social constructionist framework that suggests that *patriarchy*—the system of male control over women—is a human invention, not the inevitable outcome of biological characteristics. In order to denaturalize gender violence, then, one must uncover the *social* roots of institutionalized male dominance. This argument has important implications; if patriarchy is a social construction, then the violence that results from it becomes more problematic, less easy to dismiss as "human nature." Once an unfortunate, but taken-for-granted, aspect of the human condition, gender violence becomes a social problem with a beginning and, ostensibly, an end. In order to bring about its demise, however, we must take on the difficult challenge of discovering its origins.

The Contributions of Marx and Engels

Although the patriarchal family was not a central concern of Karl Marx's social theory, he did suggest that its modern form was a microcosm of the class antagonisms that later developed on a grand scale in society (Marx 1978). In the legal, monogamous family, women exchange their sexual and domestic services for economic security, and male sexual control of women in marriage is the equivalent of slave ownership. Applying the logic of Marxian economic theory more systematically to the condition of women, Friedrich Engels linked the "world-historic defeat of the female sex" to males' desire to circumvent their wives, passing private property (originally, herds of domesticated animals) on to their children. The emergence of the concept of private property and its appropriation by men, according to Engels (chapter 1 below), are the central historical events from which the modern social order and systematic gender violence have emerged. In this model, women are economic dependents; eventually defined as the property of fathers or husbands, they are subject to the violence that accompanies the status of slaves.

The Marx-Engels theory was the first to attribute women's deteriorated status to a sociological, rather than biological, source. Over one hundred years of social and economic analysis have not diminished the significance of economic arrangements in gender systems of power; however, economic determinism is no more satisfactory than biological determinism in explaining the origins of patriarchal domination. Given the complexity of human social life, any singular statement of cause and effect is doomed to fail. Although economic considerations remain salient to the analysis of gender violence, paradoxically, it is Marx's general theory of human social behavior, not his brief ruminations about gender relations in the family, that has been most helpful in elaborating contemporary theories of male dominance.

For Marx, the human capacity to labor is the essential building block of history; humans have created all the ideas, all the technologies, all the social structures that exist out of our own experiences in the material world. If all social systems are human creations, then patriarchy must be included in the inventory. Both Marx and Engels interpreted the anthropological record of their time to suggest that the earliest human groups were communitarian: nonhierarchical and reciprocal, with pooled resources and universal fulfillment of basic human needs. Some combination of subsequent social phenomena, therefore, must be responsible for the emergence of patriarchy and male violence. The physical potential for gender violence is presumed, but the requisite stimuli for its invention and the means through which it is institutionalized are necessarily social. Anthropologists, sociologists, and historians studying gender have built upon the framework provided by Marx and Engels, though in different ways, and each of these disciplines contributes significant analyses to our project.

The Significance of Sex/Gender Systems

Anthropological research is the source of most of the early evidence supporting a social, rather than biological, theory of gender. Researches such as those Margaret Mead (1935) conducted among peoples of New Guinea showed gendered behavior to be a relative concept: different cultures define masculinity and femininity according to their own social needs; indeed, cultures may have more than two gender categories. Men are not inherently aggressive, and women are not inherently passive and subordinate. The gender based division of labor, although apparently universal, takes many shapes and forms. Such findings have enabled social theorists to define sex (nature) and gender (culture) as mutually exclusive, though related, phenomena.

Studies of kinship systems in tribal social life provide a foundation for understanding early cultural definitions of gender, since all of early human social life was organized through these systems. The incest taboo is a particularly significant human invention, in that it allows for the exchange of women among men of different kin groups, which in turn facilitates trade and alliances. Eventually, however, it also contributes to the ascension of men into roles of social power (Levi-Strauss 1969). Some analysts suggest that the practice of exchanging women transforms them over time into tribal resources—commodities, rather than self-determined individuals.

Gayle Rubin's classic essay "The Traffic in Women: Notes on the Political Economy of Sex" (1976) called into question many of the key assumptions about kinship and gender that had dominated anthropology prior to the modern feminist movement. Rubin uses the works of Marx, Engels, and Claude Levi-Strauss in a fundamentally different frame of analysis: a feminist critique that reconceptualizes the essence of early kinship systems and links them to contemporary gender relations of power.

The crux of Rubin's argument is that the construction of sexual meaning, not the commodification of women per se, is the hallmark of early kinship structures. Given the elaborate differences among kinship systems historically and cross-culturally, Rubin replaces the notion of emergent patriarchy with the concept of sex/gender systems. All cultures have sex/gender systems in which a socially constructed set of relations that define and regulate sexuality, masculinity, and femininity emerge. These relations, though initially kin-centered, also serve as the framework for creating increasingly elaborate economic and political systems. In contemporary cultures, kinship exists within highly complex institutional structures. What is crucial for feminist scholarship is this: in the earliest human groups, the exchange (and oppression) of women did not exist for its own sake; it fulfilled central functions for group survival. The contemporary sex/gender system, still replete with oppressive sexual meaning and regulation, does not fulfill the same economic and political function that kinship once did. Kinship has been stripped of all its early functions, save reproduction and the socialization of individuals. Following this logic, according to Rubin, the contemporary sex/gender system seems to exist only to organize and reproduce itself (1976, 199) rather than all of human activity. Contemporary sex/gender systems therefore serve no necessary functions by reproducing oppressive and repressive gender relations.

Patriarchy and Women's Agency

Scholarly writing has traditionally viewed sex/gender systems as restrictions imposed upon women by men. Whether we study the work of Marxian scholars, mid–twentieth-century anthropologists, or contemporary feminists, we find a strong tendency to portray women as passive victims of male-dominated cultures. This is not hard to understand because academic literature has been researched and written from within male-dominated social systems, in which women have had little access to political-legal, economic, or familial power. Given that patriarchy predates recorded history, however, it is difficult to trace its origins to a single causal factor, such as physical force or economic exchange. What if its *origins* were relatively benign?

Historian Gerda Lerner (1986) has proposed a theory that uses a materialist conceptualization of history (in the tradition of Marx) as a starting point for understanding the origins of patriarchy. Combining her own exhaustive study of historical artifacts from the earliest human communities with a fresh interpretation of the academic literature, Lerner builds a scenario that depends upon women as cocreators of history. According to Lerner, patriarchy is initially the unintended consequence of human social organization, a process that most probably emerged out of the negotiated labor of males and females interested in mutual survival and the continuation of the species. Human biological difference does not predict or determine male dominance, but it is certainly a major factor in the elaboration of a rudimentary division of labor. Given extremely short life spans and the vulnerability of human infants, women probably would have chosen to engage in labor that involves less risk in order to heighten the chances that their offspring would survive. The gathering and child-rearing work that was predominantly, although not exclusively, performed by women was highly valued and central to early cultural production. It is only through the lens of modern, predominantly male interpreters that such work is devalued relative to the hunting of men.

According to Lerner (1986, 53), "Sometime during the agricultural revolution, relatively egalitarian societies with a sexual division of labor based on biological necessity gave way to more highly structured societies in which both private property and the exchange of women based on incest taboos and exogamy were common." In Lerner's formulation, women may have viewed their procreative abilities initially as tribal resources independent of coercion on the part of male kin. A complex combination of ecological, climatic, and demographic changes probably intervened to produce a scarcity of women in some kin groups, which eventually gave rise to the idea and practice of exchange. Although patriarchy clearly was formally established by the beginning of recorded history, it probably took centuries for any concise, systematic patriarchy to emerge. By the time women became consciously aware of the emergent power relations that formed early patriarchal systems, they were hardly in a position to do much about it. Once male control was identified, Lerner's research suggests, individual women chafed under its bonds and used various forms of resistance to secure status for themselves and their children; thus, while women may have been active agents in the creation of cultural arrangements that eventually limited their freedom, and may even be complicit in maintaining their personal power rather than pursuing collective rights for women, there is also a long historical record of active agents in protofeminist resistance to patriarchal control.

Violence and Male Power

The use of force to maintain privilege is a significant characteristic of male behavior in patriarchal societies. It contributes to the development of elaborate systems of economic and social inequality within and across gender. A central fact acknowledged by historians but generally underanalyzed is that women were the first slaves (Lerner 1986). In the quest for women, invading clans would kill adult males on the spot and enslave women and their children. Rape and other forms of physical and psychological violence were used to control women in their new communities. It was through mastering techniques of violent coercion on female captives that men eventually learned how to dominate and control other men without killing them. Both violence toward women and the elaborate social structures that develop around such practices serve to appropriate key aspects of women's independence and institutionalize patriarchy. Over time, overt and covert forms of violence come to characterize "normal" gender relations, institutionally and interpersonally.

Male control of women in families, which has endured the "progress" of centuries, is certainly not the only manifestation of androcentric sex/gender systems. Just as the construction of gender differs across cultures, gender violence takes many cultural forms: ten centuries of foot binding in China; witch burning in sixteenth-century Europe; female genital mutilation in Africa; female castration by physicians in the late nineteenth and early twentieth century in the United States; and bride burning in contemporary India. Demographers suspect that female infanticide has skewed male-to-female population ratios in many areas across the world. As these examples illustrate,

TABLE 1. LOCUS AND MANIFESTATIONS OF GENDER VIOLENCE

Locus and Agent	The Family	The "Community"	The State
Forms of Gender Violence	Physical Aggression 　Murder (dowry/other) 　Battering 　Genital mutilation 　Foeticide 　Infanticide 　Deprivation of food 　Deprivation of medical 　　care 　Reproductive coercion/ 　　control	*Social Reference Group* (Cultural, religious, etc.) *Violence directed toward 　women within or outside 　the group. Physical Abuse* 　Battery 　Physical chastisement 　Reproductive coercion/ 　　control 　Witch burning 　Sati	Political Violence (Policies, laws, etc.) 　Illegitimate detention 　Forced sterilization 　Forced pregnancies 　Tolerating gender 　violence by nonstate 　agents
	Sexual Abuse 　Rape 　Incest	Sexual Assault* 　Rape	Custodial Violence (Military/police, etc.) 　Rape 　Torture
	Emotional Abuse 　Confinement 　Forced marriage 　Threats of reprisals	*Workplace* Sexual Aggression 　Harassment 　Intimidation Commercialized Violence 　Trafficking 　Forced prostitution	
		Media 　Pornography 　Commercialization of 　　women's bodies	

Source: Margaret Schuler *Freedom from Violence: Women's Strategies from Around the World* (New York: UNIFEM, 1992), 14.

gender violence is not just a feature of micro-level interactions among intimates, but is also deeply embedded at the levels of community and nation-state (see table 1). So universal and widespread are the institutionalized forms of violence against women that Jane Caputi and Diana Russell (1990) developed the concept of *femicide* to describe the systematic and global destruction of women. Although men are the primary perpetrators of gender violence, women are not only the victims but are often collusive in the creation and preservation of violent traditions such as female genital mutilation, in the protection of men involved in incestuous relationships, or in the perpetuation of rape myths by blaming women for their victimization. Similarly, men can also be victims of gender violence, in ways that are explored in this volume.

The Social Reproduction of Gender Violence

Gender relations and expectations are situated in the various social structures of societies: labor markets, political systems, families, schools, health care systems, and so on.

While we have thus far theorized gender as a set of social relationships, it is also important to underscore its centrality as a deeply felt aspect of each person's self-identity. Each of us develops a gender psychology as we interact with other people. Our awareness of what constitutes appropriate behavior, the patterns of interaction in our families and peer groups, our selection and observation of reference groups, and the structure of opportunities available to us all contribute to our evolution as gendered beings. The extent to which violence becomes embedded in our repertoire of behaviors is, in part, related to our individual propensities to accept and internalize aspects of socially prescribed gender roles and relationships.

R. W. Connell (1987) has developed the useful concepts of *hegemonic masculinity* and *emphasized femininity* to refer to the dominant, idealized notions of sexual character that exist in a society. These idealizations are accepted as "normal" by society, although they always exist in opposition to quite a range of "real" human personalities and behaviors. For example, the hegemonic—or controlling—form of masculinity in the late-twentieth-century United States requires the ability to be powerful, aggressive, rational, and invulnerable, to control oneself and others in a variety of social situations. This usually implies athleticism, financial success, and the heterosexual domination of women, as well as a sufficient distance from characteristics deemed feminine by the culture. The extent to which men and boys in the United States comply with this set of characteristics varies widely, but the manliness of most will be judged by their ability to measure up to this standard of masculinity.

For women, the ideal standard is clearly articulated, but it is not as controlling as the one prescribed for men. Emphasized femininity is constructed as a counterpoint to masculinity: emotional, nurturing, vulnerable, and dependent, sexually desirable and malleable, rather than controlling. There is a certain amount of ambivalence built into contemporary femininity, however, because these behaviors are idealized but at the same time are not highly valued by the culture. Women acting in stereotypically masculine ways have received a certain amount of social acceptance in some arenas (such as in corporate boardrooms, where the most successful women "act like men," or in sporting events such as women's boxing), but the drumbeat of popular culture continually presents the traditional roles of wife, mother, and sexual ornament as primary.

At various points in human history, and particularly in the present, hegemonic masculinity becomes a breeding ground for gender violence. It is reproduced generally through the early socialization of boys in families and schools, through mass media images, and in male-dominated institutions such as the military, sports teams, politics, and science. Adherence to traditional femininity can be, quite literally, a health hazard for women, as socially prescribed acquiescence to male dominance may be an open invitation to male aggression. The roots of male dominance may be relatively simple, but the elaborate psychological and institutional systems that have evolved and sustained it over time are exceedingly complex.

We can return to the anthropological record for a glimmer of hope, however. Among its many contributions to social science is the recognition that male violence against women, although widespread, is not universal (Sanday, this volume). Understanding the conditions under which nonviolent gender relations flourish provides a springboard for continued analysis from a variety of academic disciplines and activist locations.

Contributions to This Section

The chapters in this section are examples of systematic attempts to comprehend male dominance generally, and violence against women specifically. Friedrich Engels's critical essay (originally published in 1884) is included because of its centrality to most subsequent analyses of patriarchy in the social sciences. Using a Marxian framework that has since been elaborated by feminist theorists, Engels attempts to develop a conclusive argument that women's oppression is an outgrowth of the emergence of economies based upon the accumulation of private property.

Michael Kaufman continues the discussion of socially produced gender within the context of kin relationships, but from within a neo-Freudian psychoanalytic framework. His exploration of the embedded nature of violence in the male psyche and male behavior is strikingly different from the economic perspective elaborated by Engels, but it clearly presents a line of analysis that is central to understanding the scope of male violence.

Peggy Reeves Sanday confronts universalized notions of male violence by differentiating societies according to the existence and frequency of rape within them. Biological determinism does not withstand the test of cross-cultural applicability when the results of this analysis are taken into account. By distinguishing the characteristics of rape-prone and rape-free societies, we move closer to understanding some of the central problems that need to be addressed within myriad violent social systems across the globe.

SUGGESTIONS FOR FURTHER READING

R. W. Connell, *Gender and Power* (Stanford: Stanford University Press, 1987).

Jalna Hanmer and Mary Maynard (eds.), *Women, Violence and Social Control* (Atlantic Highlands, NJ: Humanities Press International, 1987).

Gerda Lerner, *The Creation of Patriarchy* (New York: Oxford University Press, 1986).

Carole Pateman, *The Sexual Contract* (Stanford: Stanford University Press, 1988).

Visit from the Footbinder

SARAH GORHAM

Little shoes sell quickly in shop
windows. Three-inch tracks peel
off garden sand. If too large, crop
or bandage your feet. Force heel
under instep to meet your bent
digits. Bind them like crescent
moons that peep into the night.
A mistress shouldn't stray. Slowly
she sways. She hovers and floats,
point dancer, Buddha on tiptoe.
Dab with your spirit, microscopic
drip by drip. As you walk, feel it
evaporate. Anything more is a lie.
There is no permanent I.

From The *Kenyon Review,* 1992, p. 35. Reprinted by permission.

1

The Origin of the Family, Private Property, and the State

FRIEDRICH ENGELS

The Family: Its Past, Present and Future

* * *

* * * The evolution of the family in prehistoric times consisted in the continual narrowing of the circle—originally embracing the whole tribe—within which marital community between the two sexes prevailed. By the successive exclusion, first of closer, then of ever remoter relatives; and finally even of those merely related by marriage; every kind of group marriage was ultimately rendered practically impossible; and in the end there remained only the one, for the moment still loosely united, couple, the molecule, with the dissolution of which marriage itself completely ceases. This fact alone shows how little individual sex love, in the modern sense of the word, had to do with the origin of monogamy. The practice of all peoples in this stage affords still further proof of this. Whereas under previous forms of the family men were never in want of women but, on the contrary, had a surfeit of them, women now became scarce and were sought after. Consequently with pairing marriage begins the abduction and purchase of women—widespread *symptoms*, but nothing more of a much more deeply-rooted change that had set in. * * *

The pairing family, itself too weak and unstable to make an independent household necessary, or even desirable, did not by any means dissolve the communistic household transmitted from earlier times. But the communistic household implies the supremacy of women in the house, just as the exclusive recognition of a natural mother, because of the impossibility of determining the natural father with certainty, signifies high esteem for the women, that is, for the mothers. That woman was the slave of man at the commencement of society is one of the most absurd notions that have come down to us from the period of Enlightenment of the eighteenth century. Woman occupied not only a free but also a highly respected position among all savages and all barbarians of the lower and middle stages and partly even of the upper stage. Let Arthur Wright, missionary for many years among the Seneca Iroquois, testify what her place still was in the pairing family: "As to their family system, when occupying the old long houses [communistic households embracing several families] . . . it is probable that some one

Reprinted from *The Marx-Engels Reader*, 2d ed., edited by Robert C. Tucker, by permission of W. W. Norton and Company, Inc. Copyright © 1978, 1972 by W. W. Norton and Company, Inc.

clan [gens] predominated, the women taking husbands from other clans [gentes]. . . . Usually the female portion ruled the house; the stores were in common; but woe to the luckless husband or lover who was too shiftless to do his share of the providing. No matter how many children or whatever goods he might have in the house, he might at any time be ordered to pack up his blanket and budge; and after such orders it would not be healthful for him to attempt to disobey. The house would be too hot for him; and he had to retreat to his own clan [gens]; or, as was often done, go and start a new matrimonial alliance in some other. The women were the great power among the clans [gentes], as everywhere else. They did not hesitate, when occasion required, to knock off the horns, as it was technically called, from the head of the chief and send him back to the ranks of the warriors." * * *

*   *   *

* * * As wealth increased, it, on the one hand, gave the man a more important status in the family than the woman, and, on the other hand, created a stimulus to utilise this strengthened position in order to overthrow the traditional order of inheritance in favour of his children. But this was impossible as long as descent according to mother right prevailed. This had, therefore, to be overthrown, and it was overthrown; and it was not so difficult to do this as it appears to us now. For this revolution—one of the most decisive ever experienced by mankind—need not have disturbed one single living member of a gens. All the members could remain what they were previously. The simple decision sufficed that in future the descendants of the male members should remain in the gens, but that those of the females were to be excluded from the gens and transferred to that of their father. The reckoning of descent through the female line and the right of inheritance through the mother were hereby overthrown and male lineage and right of inheritance from the father instituted. We know nothing as to how and when this revolution was effected among the civilised peoples. It falls entirely within prehistoric times. That it was actually *effected* is more than proved by the abundant traces of mother right which have been collected, especially by Bachofen. How easily it is accomplished can be seen from a whole number of Indian tribes, among whom it has only recently taken place and is still proceeding, partly under the influence of increasing wealth and changed methods of life (transplantation from the forests to the prairies), and partly under the moral influence of civilisation and the missionaries. Of eight Missouri tribes, six have male and two still retain the female lineage and female inheritance line. Among the Shawnees, Miamis and Delawares it has become the custom to transfer the children to the father's gens by giving them one of the gentile names obtaining therein, in order that they may inherit from him. "Innate human causuistry to seek to change things by changing their names! And to find loopholes for breaking through tradition within tradition itself, wherever a direct interest provided a sufficient motive!" (Marx.) As a consequence, hopeless confusion arose; and matters could only be straightened out, and partly were straightened out, by the transition to father right. "This appears altogether to be the most natural transition." (Marx) As for what the experts on comparative law have to tell us regarding the ways and means by which this transition was effected among the civilised peoples of the Old World—almost mere hypotheses, of course—see M. Kovalevsky, *Outline of the Origin and Evolution of the Family and Property*, Stockholm, 1890.

The overthrow of mother right was the *world-historic defeat of the female sex*. The man seized the reins in the house also, the woman was degraded, enthralled, the slave of the man's lust, a mere instrument for breeding children. This lowered position of women, especially manifest among the Greeks of the Heroic and still more of the Classical Age, has become gradually embellished and dissembled and, in part, clothed in a milder form, but by no means abolished.

The first effect of the sole rule of the men that was now established is shown in the intermediate form of the family which now emerges, the patriarchal family. Its chief attribute is not polygamy—of which more anon—but "the organisation of a number of persons, bond and free, into a family under the paternal power of the head of the family. In the Semitic form, this family chief lives in polygamy, the bondsman has a wife and children, and the purpose of the whole organisation is the care of flocks and herds over a limited area." The essential features are the incorporation of bondsmen and the paternal power; the Roman family, accordingly, constitutes the perfected type of this form of the family. The word *familia* did not originally signify the ideal of our modern Philistine, which is a compound of sentimentality and domestic discord. Among the Romans, in the beginning, it did not even refer to the married couple and their children, but to the slaves alone. *Famulus* means a household slave and *familia* signifies the totality of slaves belonging to one individual. Even in the time of Gaius the *familia, id est patrimonium* (that is, the inheritance) was bequeathed by will. The expression was invented by the Romans to describe a new social organism, the head of which had under him wife and children and a number of slaves, under Roman paternal power, with power of life and death over them all. "The term, therefore, is no older than the ironclad family system of the Latin tribes, which came in after field agriculture and after legalised servitude, as well as after the separation of the Greeks and (Aryan) Latins." To which Marx adds: "The modern family contains in embryo not only slavery *(servitus)* but serfdom also, since from the very beginning it is connected with agricultural services. It contains within itself in *miniature* all the antagonisms which later develop on a wide scale within society and its state."

Such a form of the family shows the transition of the pairing family to monogamy. In order to guarantee the fidelity of the wife, that is, the paternity of the children, the woman is placed in the man's absolute power; if he kills her, he is but exercising his right.

We are confronted with this new form of the family in all its severity among the Greeks. While, as Marx observes, the position of the goddesses in mythology represents an earlier period, when women still occupied a freer and more respected place, in the Heroic Age we already find women degraded owing to the predominance of the man and the competition of female slaves. One may read in the *Odyssey* how Telemachus cuts his mother short and enjoins silence upon her. In Homer the young female captives become the objects of the sensual lust of the victors; the military chiefs, one after the other, according to rank, choose the most beautiful ones for themselves. The whole of the *Iliad*, as we know, revolves around the quarrel between Achilles and Agamemnon over such a female slave. In connection with each Homeric hero of importance mention is made of a captive maiden with whom he shares tent and bed. These maidens are taken back home, to the conjugal house, as was Cassandra by Agamemnon in Aeschylus. Sons born of these slaves receive a small share of their father's estate and are regarded as freemen. Teukros was such an illegitimate son of Telamon and was permitted to adopt his father's name. The wedded wife is expected to tolerate all this, but to maintain strict chastity and conjugal fidelity herself. True, in the Heroic Age the Greek wife is more respected than in the period of civilisation; for the husband, however, she is, in reality, merely the mother of his legitimate heirs, his chief housekeeper, and the superintendent of the female slaves, whom he may make, and does make his concubines at will. It is the existence of slavery side by side with monogamy, the existence of beautiful young slaves who belong to the *man* with all they have, that from the very beginning stamped on monogamy its specific character as monogamy *only for the woman*, but not for the man. And it retains this character to this day.

*   *   *

* * * In Euripides, the wife is described as *oikurema*, a thing for housekeeping (the word is in the neuter gender), and apart from the business of bearing children, she was nothing more to the Athenian than the chief housemaid. The husband had his gymnastic exercises, his public affairs, from which the wife was excluded; in addition, he often had female slaves at his disposal and, in the heyday of Athens, extensive prostitution, which was viewed with favour by the state, to say the least. It was precisely on the basis of this prostitution that the sole outstanding Greek women developed, who by their *esprit* and artistic taste towered as much above the general level of ancient womanhood as the Spartiate women did by virtue of their character. That one had first to become a *hetaera* in order to become a woman is the strongest indictment of the Athenian family.

In the course of time, this Athenian family became the model upon which not only the rest of the Ionians, but also all the Greeks of the mainland and of the colonies increasingly moulded their domestic relationships. But despite all seclusion and surveillance the Greek women found opportunities often enough for deceiving their husbands. The latter, who would have been ashamed to evince any love for their own wives, amused themselves with *hetaerae* in all kinds of amours. But the degradation of the women recoiled on the men themselves and degraded them too, until they sank into the perversion of boy-love, degrading both themselves and their gods by the myth of Ganymede.

This was the origin of monogamy, as far as we can trace it among the most civilised and highly-developed people of antiquity. It was not in any way the fruit of individual sex love, with which it had absolutely nothing in common, for the marriages remained marriages of convenience, as before. It was the first form of the family based not on natural but on economic conditions, namely, on the victory of private property over original, naturally developed, common ownership. The rule of the man in the family, the procreation of children who could only be his, destined to be the heirs of his wealth—these alone were frankly avowed by the Greeks as the exclusive aims of monogamy. For the rest, it was a burden, a duty to the gods, to the state and to their ancestors, which just had to be fulfilled. In Athens the law made not only marriage compulsory, but also the fulfillment by the man of a minimum of the so-called conjugal duties.

Thus, monogamy does not by any means make its appearance in history as the reconciliation of man and woman, still less as the highest form of such a reconciliation. On the contrary, it appears as the subjection of one sex by the other, as the proclamation of a conflict between the sexes entirely unknown hitherto in prehistoric times. In an old unpublished manuscript, the work of Marx and myself in 1846,[1] I find the following: "The first division of labour is that between man and woman for child breeding." And today I can add: The first class antagonism which appears in history coincides with the development of the antagonism between man and woman in monogamian marriage, and the first class oppression with that of the female sex by the male. Monogamy was a great historical advance, but at the same time it inaugurated, along with slavery and private wealth, that epoch, lasting until today, in which every advance is likewise a relative regression, in which the well-being and development of the one group are attained by the misery and repression of the other. It is the cellular form of civilised society, in which we can already study the nature of the antagonisms and contradictions which develop fully in the latter.

* * * With the rise of property differentiation—that is, as far back as the upper stage of barbarism—wage labour appears sporadically alongside of slave labour; and simultaneously, as its necessary correlate, the professional prostitution of free women appears side by side with the forced surrender of the female slave. Thus, the heritage bequeathed to civilisation by group marriage is double-sided, just as everything engendered by civilisation is double-sided, double-tongued, self-contradictory and antagonistic: on the one hand, monogamy, on the other, hetaerism, including its most extreme form, prostitution. Hetaerism is as much a social institution as any other; it is a continuation of the old sexual freedom—in favour of the men. Although, in reality, it is not only tolerated but even practised with gusto, particularly by the ruling classes, it is condemned in words. In reality, however, this condemnation by no means hits the men who indulge in it, it hits only the women: they are ostracised and cast out in order to proclaim once again the absolute domination of the male over the female sex as the fundamental law of society.

A second contradiction, however, is hereby developed within monogamy itself. By the side of the husband, whose life is embellished by hetaerism, stands the neglected wife. And it is just as impossible to have one side of a contradiction without the other as it is to retain the whole of an apple in one's hand after half has been eaten. Nevertheless, the men appear to have thought differently, until their wives taught them to know better. Two permanent social figures, previously unknown, appear on the scene along with monogamy—the wife's paramour and the cuckold. The men had gained the victory over the women, but the act of crowning the victor was magnanimously undertaken by the vanquished. Adultery—proscribed, severely penalised, but irrepressible—became an unavoidable social institution alongside of monogamy and hetaerism. The assured paternity of children was now, as before, based, at best, on moral conviction; and in order to solve the insoluble contradiction, Article 312 of the *Code Napoléon* decreed: *"L'enfant conçupendant le mariage a pour père le mari,"* "a child conceived during marriage has for its father the husband." This is the final outcome of three thousand years of monogamy.

Thus, in the monogamian family, in those cases that faithfully reflect its historical origin and that clearly bring out the sharp conflict between man and woman resulting from the exclusive domination of the male, we have a picture in miniature of the very antagonisms and contradictions in which society, split up into classes since the commencement of civilisation, moves, without being able to resolve and overcome them. Naturally, I refer here only to those cases of monogamy where matrimonial life really takes its course according to the rules governing the original character of the whole institution, but where the wife rebels against the domination of the husband. That this is not the case with all marriages no one knows better than the German Philistine, who is no more capable of ruling in the home than in the state, and whose wife, therefore, with full justification, wears the breeches of which he is unworthy. But in consolation he imagines himself to be far superior to his French companion in misfortune, who, more often than he, fares far worse.

*   *   *

Although monogamy was the only known form of the family out of which modern sex love could develop, it does not follow that this love developed within it exclusively, or even predominantly, as the mutual love of man and wife. The whole nature of strict monogamian marriage under male domination ruled this out. Among all historically active classes, that is, among all ruling classes, matrimony remained what it had been since pairing marriage—a matter of convenience arranged by the parents. And the first form of sex love that historically emerges as a passion, and as a passion in which any person (at least of the ruling classes) has a right to indulge, as the highest form of the sexual impulse—which is precisely its specific feature—this, its first form, the chivalrous love of the Middle Ages, was by no means conjugal love. On the contrary, in its classical form, among the Provençals, it steers under full sail towards adultery, the praises of which are sung by their poets. The *"Albas,"* in German *Tagelieder,* are the flower of Provençal love poetry. They describe in glowing colours how the knight lies with his love—the wife of another—while the watchman stands guard outside, calling him at the first faint streaks of dawn *(alba)* so that he may escape unobserved. The parting scene then constitutes the climax. The Northern French as well as the worthy Germans, likewise adopted this style of poetry, along with the manners of chivalrous love which corresponded to it; and on this same suggestive theme our own old Wolfram von Eschenbach has left us three exquisite Songs of the Dawn, which I prefer to his three long heroic poems.

Bourgeois marriage of our own times is of two kinds. In Catholic countries the parents, as heretofore, still provide a suitable wife for their young bourgeois son, and the consequence is naturally the fullest unfolding of the contradiction inherent in monogamy—flourishing hetaerism on the part of the husband, and flourishing adultery on the part of the wife. The Catholic Church doubtless abolished divorce only because it was convinced that for adultery, as for death, there is no cure whatsoever. In Protestant countries, on the other hand, it is the rule that the bourgeois son is allowed to seek a wife for himself from his own class, more or less freely. Consequently, marriage can be based on a certain degree of love which, for decency's sake, is always assumed, in accordance with Protestant hypocrisy. In this case, hetaerism on the part of the men is less actively pursued, and adultery on the woman's part is not so much the rule. Since, in every kind of marriage, however, people remain what they were before they married, and since the citizens of Protestant countries are mostly Philistines, this Protestant monogamy leads merely, if we take the average of the best cases, to a wedded life of leaden boredom, which is described as domestic bliss. The best mirror of these two ways of marriage is the novel; the French novel for the Catholic style, and the German novel for the Protestant. In both cases "he gets it": in the German novel the young man gets the girl; in the French, the husband gets the cuckold's horns. Which of the two is in the worse plight is not always easy to make out. For the dullness of the German novel excites the same horror in the French bourgeois as the "immorality" of the French novel excites in the German Philistine, although lately, since "Berlin is becoming a metropolis," the German novel has begun to deal a little less timidly with hetaerism and adultery, long known to exist there.

In both cases, however, marriage is determined by the class position of the participants, and to that extent always remains marriage of convenience. In both cases, this marriage of convenience often enough turns into the crassest prostitution—sometimes on both sides, but much more generally on the part of the wife, who differs from the ordinary courtesan only in that she does not hire out her body, like a wage-worker, on piecework, but sells it into slavery once for all. And Fourier's words hold good for all marriages of convenience: "Just as in grammar two negatives make a positive, so in the morals of marriage, two prostitutions make one virtue." Sex love in the relation of husband and wife is and can become the rule only among the oppressed classes, that is, at the present day, among the proletariat, no matter whether this relationship is officially sanctioned or not. But here all the foundations of classical monogamy are removed. Here, there is a complete absence of all property, for the safeguarding and inheritance of which monogamy and male domination were established. Therefore, there is no stimulus whatever here to assert male domination. What is more, the means, too, are absent; bourgeois law, which protects this domination, exists only for the propertied classes and their dealings with the proletarians. It costs money, and therefore, owing to the worker's poverty has no validity in his attitude towards his wife. Personal and social relations of quite a different sort are the decisive factors here. Moreover, since large-scale industry has transferred the woman from the house to the labour market and the factory, and makes her, often enough, the bread-winner of the family, the last remnants of male domination in the proletarian home have lost all foundation—except, perhaps, for some of that brutality towards women which became firmly rooted with the establishment of monogamy. Thus, the proletarian family is no longer monogamian in the strict sense, even in cases of the most passionate love and strictest faithfulness of the two parties, and despite all spiritual and worldly benedictions which may have been received. The two eternal adjuncts of monogamy—hetaerism and adultery—therefore, play an almost negligible role here; the woman has regained, in fact, the right of separation, and when the man and woman cannot get along they prefer to part. In short, proletarian marriage is monogamian in the etymological sense of the word, but by no means in the historical sense.

Our jurists, to be sure, hold that the progress of legislation to an increasing degree removes all cause for complaint on the part of the woman. Modern civilised systems of law are recognising more and more, first, that, in order to be effective marriage must be an agreement voluntarily entered into by both parties; and secondly, that during marriage, too, both parties must be on an equal footing in respect to rights and obligations. If, however, these two demands were consistently carried into effect, women would have all that they could ask for.

This typical lawyer's reasoning is exactly the same as that with which the radical republican bourgeois dismisses the proletarian. The labour contract is supposed to be voluntarily entered into by both parties. But it is taken to be voluntarily entered into as soon as the law has put both parties on an equal footing on *paper*. The power given to one party by its different class position, the pressure it exercises on the other—the real economic position of both—all this is no concern of the law. And both parties, again, are supposed to have equal rights for the duration of the labour contract, unless one or the other of the parties expressly waived them. That the concrete economic situation compels the worker to forego even the slightest semblance of equal rights—this again is something the law cannot help.

As far as marriage is concerned, even the most progressive law is fully satisfied as soon as the parties formally register their voluntary desire to get married. What happens behind the legal curtains, where real life is enacted, how this voluntary agreement is arrived at—is no concern of the law and the jurist. And yet the simplest comparison of laws should serve to show the jurist what this voluntary agreement really amounts to. In countries where the children are legally assured of an obligatory share of their parent's property and thus cannot be disinherited—in Germany, in the countries under French law, etc.—the children must obtain their parents' consent in the question of marriage. In countries under English law, where parental consent to marriage is not legally requisite, the parents have full testatory freedom over their property and can, if they so desire, cut their children off with a shilling. It is clear, therefore, that despite this, or rather just because of this, among those classes which have something to inherit, freedom to marry is not one whit greater in England and America than in France or Germany.

The position is no better with regard to the juridical equality of man and woman in marriage. The equality of the two before the law, which is a legacy of previous social conditions, is not the cause but the effect of the economic oppression of women. In the old communistic household, which embraced numerous couples and their children, the administration of the household, entrusted to the women, was just as much a public, a socially necessary industry as the providing of food by the men. This situation changed with the patriarchal family, and even more with the monogamian individual family. The administration of the household lost its public character. It was no longer the concern of society. It became a *private service*. The wife became the first domestic servant, pushed out of participation in social production. Only modern large-scale industry again threw open to her—and only to the proletarian woman at that—that avenue to social production; but in such a way that, when she fulfils her duties in the private service of her family, she remains excluded from public production and cannot earn anything; and when she wishes to take part in public industry and earn her living independently, she is not in a position to fulfil her family duties. What applies to the woman in the factory applies to her in all the professions, right up to medicine and law. The modern individual family is based on the open or disguised domestic enslavement of the woman; and modern society is a mass composed solely of individual families as its molecules. Today, in the great majority of cases the man has to be the earner, the bread-winner of the family, at least among the propertied classes, and this gives him a dominating position which requires no special legal privileges. In the family, he is the bourgeois; the wife represents the proletariat. In the industrial world, however, the specific character of the economic oppression that weighs down the proletariat stands out in all its sharpness only after all the special legal privileges of the capitalist class have been set aside and the complete juridical equality of both classes is established. The democratic republic does not abolish the antagonism between the two classes; on the contrary, it provides the field on which it is fought out. And, similarly, the peculiar character of man's domination over woman in the modern family, and the necessity, as well as the manner, of establishing real social equality between the two, will be brought out into full relief only when both are completely equal before the law. It will then become evident that the first premise for the emancipation of women is the reintroduction of the entire female sex into public industry; and that this again demands that the quality possessed by the individual family of being the economic unit of society be abolished.

*   *   *

We have, then, three chief forms of marriage, which, by and large, conform to the three main stages of human development. For savagery—group marriage; for barbarism—pairing marriage; for civilisation—monogamy, supplemented by adultery and prostitution. In the upper stage of barbarism, between pairing marriage and monogamy, there is wedged in the dominion exercised by men over female slaves, and polygamy.

As our whole exposition has shown, the advance to be noted in this sequence is linked with the peculiar fact that while women are more and more deprived of the sexual freedom of group marriage, the men are not. Actually, for men, group marriage exists to this day. What for a woman is a crime entailing dire legal and social consequences, is regarded in the case of a man as being honourable or, at most, as a slight moral stain that one bears with pleasure. The more the old traditional hetaerism is changed in our day by capitalist commodity production and adapted to it, and the more it is transformed into unconcealed prostitution, the more demoralising are its effects. And it demoralises the men far more than it does the women. Among women, prostitution degrades only those unfortunates who fall into its clutches; and even these are not degraded to the degree that is generally believed. On the other hand, it degrades the character of the entire male world. Thus, in nine cases out of ten, a long engagement is practically a preparatory school for conjugal infidelity.

We are now approaching a social evolution in which the hitherto existing economic foundations of monogamy will disappear just as certainly as will those of its supplement—prostitution. Monogamy arose out of the concentration of considerable wealth in the hands of one person—and that a man—and out of the desire to bequeath this wealth to this man's children and to no one else's. For this purpose monogamy was essential on the woman's part, but not on the man's; so that this monogamy of the woman in no way hindered the overt or covert polygamy of the man. The impending social revolution, however, by transforming at least the far greater part of permanent inheritable wealth—the means of production—into social property, will reduce all this anxiety about inheritance to a minimum. Since monogamy arose from economic causes, will it disappear when these causes disappear?

One might not unjustly answer: far from disappearing, it will only begin to be completely realised. For with the conversion of the means of production into social property, wage labour, the proletariat, also disappears, and therewith, also, the necessity for a certain—statistically calculable—number of women to surrender themselves for money. Prostitution disappears; monogamy, instead of declining, finally becomes a reality—for the men as well.

At all events, the position of the men thus undergoes considerable change. But that of the women, of *all* women, also undergoes important alteration. With the passage of the means of production into common property, the individual family ceases to be the economic unit of society. Private housekeeping is transformed into a social industry. The care and education of the children becomes a public matter. Society takes care of all children equally, irrespective of whether they are born in wedlock or not. Thus, the anxiety about the "consequences," which is today the most important social factor—both moral and economic—that hinders a girl from giving herself freely to the man she loves, disappears. Will this not be cause enough for a gradual rise of more unrestrained sexual intercourse, and along with it, a more lenient public opinion regarding virginal honour and feminine shame? And finally, have we not seen that monogamy and prostitution in the modern world, although opposites, are nevertheless inseparable opposites, poles of the same social conditions? Can prostitution disappear without dragging monogamy with it into the abyss?

Here a new factor comes into operation, a factor that, at most, existed in embryo at the time when monogamy developed, namely individual sex love.

No such thing as individual sex love existed before the Middle Ages. That personal beauty, intimate association, similarity in inclinations, etc., aroused desire for sexual intercourse among people of opposite sexes, that men as well as women were not totally indifferent to the question of with whom they entered into this most intimate relation is obvious. But this is still a far cry from the sex love of our day. Throughout antiquity marriages were arranged by the parents; the parties quietly acquiesced. The little conjugal love that was known to antiquity was not in any way a subjective inclination, but an objective duty; not a reason for but a correlate of marriage. In antiquity, love affairs in the modern sense occur only outside official society. The shepherds, whose joys and sorrows in love are sung by Theocritus and Moschus, or by Longus's *Daphnis and Chloë* are mere slaves, who have no share in the state, the sphere of the free citizen. Except among the slaves, however, we find love affairs only as disintegration products of the declining ancient world; and with women who are also beyond the pale of official society, with *hetaerae*, that is, with alien or freed women; in Athens beginning with the eve of its decline, in Rome at the time of the emperors. If love affairs really occurred between free male and female citizens, it was only in the form of adultery. And sex love in our sense of the term was so immaterial to that classical love poet of antiquity old Anacreon, that even the sex of the beloved one was a matter of complete indifference to him.

Our sex love differs materially from the simple sexual desire, the *eros*, of the ancients. First, it presupposes reciprocal love on the part of the loved one; in this respect, the woman stands on a par with the man; whereas in the ancient *eros*, the woman was by no means always consulted. Secondly, sex love attains a degree of intensity and permanency where the two parties regard non-possession or separation as a great, if not the greatest, misfortune; in order to possess each other they take great hazards, even risking life itself—what in antiquity happened, at best, only in cases of adultery. And finally, a new moral standard arises for judging sexual intercourse. The question asked is not only whether such intercourse was legitimate or illicit, but also whether it arose from mutual love or not. It goes without saying that in feudal or bourgeois practice this new standard fares no better than all the other moral standards—it is simply ignored. But it fares no worse, either. It is recognized in theory, on paper, like all the rest. And more than this cannot be expected for the present.

Where antiquity broke off with its start towards sex love, the Middle Ages began, namely, with adultery. We have already described chivalrous love, which gave rise to the Songs of the Dawn. There is still a wide gulf between this kind of love, which aimed at breaking up matrimony, and the love destined to be its foundation, a gulf never completely bridged by the age of chivalry. Even when we pass from the frivolous Latins to the virtuous Germans, we find, in the *Nibelungenlied,* that Kriemhild—although secretly in love with Siegfried every whit as much as he is with her—nevertheless, in reply to Gunther's intimation that he has plighted her to a knight whom he does not name, answers simply: "You have no need to ask; as you command, so will I be forever. He whom you, my lord, choose for my husband, to him will I gladly plight my troth." It never occurs to her that her love could possibly be considered in this matter. Gunther seeks the hand of Brunhild without ever having seen her, and Etzel does the same with Kriemhild. The same occurs in the *Gudrun,* where Sigebant of Ireland seeks the hand of Ute the Norwegian, Hetel of Hegelingen that of Hilde of Ireland; and lastly, Siegfried of Morland, Hartmut of Ormany and Herwig of Seeland seek the hand of Gudrun; and here for the first time it happens that Gudrun, of her own free will, decides in favour of the last named. As a rule, the bride of a young prince is selected by his parents; if these are no longer alive, he chooses her himself with the counsel of his highest vassal chiefs, whose word carries great weight in all cases. Nor can it be otherwise. For the knight, or baron, just as for the prince himself, marriage is a political act, an opportunity for the accession of power through new alliances; the interests of the *House* and not individual inclination are the decisive factor. How can love here hope to have the last word regarding marriage?

It was the same for the guildsman of the medieval towns. The very privileges which protected him—the guild charters with their special stipulations, the artificial lines of demarcation which legally separated him from other guilds, from his own fellow guildsmen and from his journeymen and apprentices—considerably restricted the circle in which he could hope to secure a suitable spouse. And the question as to who was the most suitable was definitely decided under this complicated system, not by individual inclination, but by family interest.

Up to the end of the Middle Ages, therefore, marriage, in the overwhelming majority of cases, remained what it had been from the commencement, an affair that was not decided by the two principal parties. In the beginning one came into the world married, married to a whole group of the opposite sex. A similar relation probably existed in the later forms of group marriage, only with an ever-increasing narrowing of the group. In the pairing family it is the rule that the mothers arrange their children's marriages; and here also, considerations of new ties of relationship that are to strengthen the young couple's position in the gens and tribe are the decisive factor. And when, with the predominance of private property over common property, and with the interest in inheritance, father right and monogamy gain the ascendancy, marriage becomes more than ever dependent on economic considerations. The *form* of marriage by purchase disappears, the transaction itself is to an ever-increasing degree carried out in such a way that not only the woman but the man also is appraised, not by his personal qualities but by his possessions. The idea that the mutual inclinations of the principal parties should be the overriding reason for matrimony had been unheard of in the practice of the ruling classes from the very beginning. Such things took place, at best, in romance only, or—among the oppressed classes, which did not count.

This was the situation found by capitalist production when, following the era of geographical discoveries, it set out to conquer the world through world trade and manufacture. One would think that this mode of matrimony should have suited it exceedingly, and such was actually the case. And yet—the irony of world history is unfathomable—it was capitalist production that had to make the decisive breach in it. By transforming all things into commodities, it dissolved all ancient traditional relations, and for inherited customs and historical rights it substituted purchase and sale, "free" contract. And H. S. Maine, the English jurist, believed that he made a colossal discovery when he said that our entire progress in comparison with previous epochs consists in our having evolved from status to contract, from an inherited state of affairs to one voluntarily contracted—a statement which, in so far as it is correct, was contained long ago in the *Communist Manifesto*.

But the closing of contracts presupposes people who can freely dispose of their persons, actions and possessions, and who meet each other on equal terms. To create such "free" and "equal" people was precisely one of the chief tasks of capitalist production. Although in the beginning this took place only in a semiconscious manner, and in religious guise to boot, nevertheless, from the time of the Lutheran and Calvinistic Reformation it became a firm principle that a person was completely responsible for his actions only if he possessed full freedom of the will when performing them, and that it was an ethical duty to resist all compulsion to commit unethical acts. But how does this fit in with the previous practice of matrimony? According to bourgeois conceptions, matrimony was a contract, a legal affair, indeed the most important of all, since it disposed of the body and mind of two persons for life. True enough, formally the bargain was struck voluntarily; it was not done without the consent of the parties; but how this consent was obtained, and who really arranged the marriage was known only too well. But if real freedom to decide was demanded for all other contracts, why not for this one? Had not the two young people about to be paired the right freely to dispose of themselves, their bodies and its organs? Did not sex love become the fashion as a consequence of chivalry, and was not the love of husband and wife its correct bourgeois form, as against the adulterous love of the knights? But if it was the duty of married people to love each other, was it not just as much the duty of lovers to marry each other and nobody else? And did not the right of these lovers stand higher than that of parents, relatives and other traditional marriage brokers and matchmakers? If the right of free personal investigation unceremoniously forced its way into church and religion, how could it halt at the intolerable claim of the older generation to dispose of body and soul, the property, the happiness and unhappiness of the younger generation?

These questions were bound to arise in a period which loosened all the old social ties and which shook the foundations of all traditional conceptions. At one stroke the size of the world had increased nearly tenfold. Instead of only a quadrant of a hemisphere the whole globe was now open to the gaze of the West Europeans who hastened to take possession of the other seven quadrants. And the thousand-year-old barriers set up by the medieval prescribed mode of thought vanished in the same way as did the old, narrow barriers of the homeland. An infinitely wider horizon opened up both to man's outer and inner eye. Of what avail were the good intentions of respectability, the honoured guild privileges handed down through the generations, to the young man who was allured by India's riches, by the gold and silver mines of Mexico and Potosi? It was the knight-errant period of the bourgeoisie; it had its romance also, and its love dreams, but on a bourgeois basis and, in the last analysis, with bourgeois ends in view.

Thus it happened that the rising bourgeoisie, particularly in the Protestant countries, where the existing order was shaken up most of all, increasingly recognized freedom of contract for marriage also and carried it through in the manner described above. Marriage remained class marriage, but, within the confines of the class, the parties were accorded a certain degree of freedom of choice. And on paper, in moral theory as in poetic description, nothing was more unshakably established than that every marriage not based on mutual sex love and on the really free agreement of man and wife was immoral. In short, love marriage was proclaimed a human right; not only as man's right *(droit de l'homme)* but also, by way of exception, as woman's right *(droit de la femme)*.

But in one respect this human right differed from all other so-called human rights. While, in practice, the latter remained limited to the ruling class, the bourgeoisie—the oppressed class, the proletariat, being directly or indirectly deprived of them—the irony of history asserts itself here once again. The ruling class continues to be dominated by the familiar economic influences and, therefore, only in exceptional cases can it show really voluntary marriages; whereas, as we have seen, these are the rule among the dominated class.

Thus, full freedom in marriage can become generally operative only when the abolition of capitalist production, and of the property relations created by it, has removed all those secondary economic considerations which still exert so powerful an influence on the choice of a partner. Then, no other motive remains than mutual affection.

Since sex love is by its very nature exclusive—although this exclusiveness is fully realised today only in the woman—then marriage based on sex love is by its very nature monogamy. We have seen how right Bachofen was when he regarded the advance from group marriage to individual marriage chiefly as the work of the women; only the advance from pairing marriage to monogamy can be placed to the men's account, and, historically, this consisted essentially in a worsening of the position of women and in facilitating infidelity on the part of the men. With the disappearance of the economic considerations which compelled women to tolerate the customary infidelity of the men—the anxiety about their own livelihood and even more about the future of their children—the equality of woman thus achieved will, judging from all previous experience, result far more effectively in the men becoming really monogamous than in the women becoming polyandrous.

What will most definitely disappear from monogamy, however, is all the characteristics stamped on it in consequence of its having arisen out of property relationships. These are, first, the dominance of the man, and secondly, the indissolubility of marriage. The predominance of the man in marriage is simply a consequence of his economic predominance and will vanish with it automatically. The indissolubility of marriage is partly the result of the economic conditions under which monogamy arose, and partly a tradition from the time when the connection between these economic conditions and monogamy was not yet correctly understood and was exaggerated by religion. Today it has been breached a thousandfold. If only marriages that are based on love are moral, then, also, only those are moral in which love continues. The duration of the urge of individual sex love differs very much according to the individual, particularly among men; and a definite cessation of affection, or its displacement by a new passionate love, makes separation a blessing for both parties as well as for society. People will only be spared the experience of wading through the useless mire of divorce proceedings.

Thus, what we can conjecture at present about the regulation of sex relationships after the impending effacement of capitalist production is, in the main, of a negative character, limited mostly to what will vanish. But what will be added? That will be settled after a new generation has grown up: a generation of men who never in all their lives have had occasion to purchase a woman's surrender either with money or with any other means of social power, and of women who have never been obliged to surrender to any man out of any consideration other than that of real love, or to refrain from giving themselves to their beloved for fear of the economic consequences. Once such people appear, they will not care a rap about what we today think they should do. They will establish their own practice and their own public opinion, conformable therewith, on the practice of each individual—and that's the end of it.

*   *   *

The Origin of the State

* * * Above we discussed separately each of the three main forms in which the state was built up on the ruins of the gentile constitution. Athens represented the purest, most classical form. Here the state sprang directly and mainly out of the class antagonisms that developed within gentile society. In Rome gentile society became an exclusive aristocracy amidst numerous plebs, standing outside of it, having no rights but only duties. The victory of the plebs burst the old gentile constitution asunder and erected on its ruins the state, in which both the gentile aristocracy and the plebs were soon wholly absorbed. Finally, among the German vanquishers of the Roman Empire, the

state sprang up as a direct result of the conquest of large foreign territories, which the gentile constitution had no means of ruling. As this conquest did not necessitate either a serious struggle with the old population or a more advanced division of labour, and as conquered and conquerors were almost at the same stage of economic development and thus the economic basis of society remained the same as before, therefore, the gentile constitution could continue for many centuries in a changed, territorial form, in the shape of a Mark constitution, and even rejuvenate itself for a time in enfeebled form in the noble and patrician families of later years, and even in peasant families, as in Dithmarschen.[2]

The state is, therefore, by no means a power forced on society from without; just as little is it "the reality of the ethical idea," "the image and reality of reason," as Hegel maintains. Rather, it is a product of society at a certain stage of development; it is the admission that this society has become entangled in an insoluble contradiction with itself, that it is cleft into irreconcilable antagonisms which it is powerless to dispel. But in order that these antagonisms, classes with conflicting economic interests, might not consume themselves and society in sterile struggle, a power seemingly standing above society became necessary for the purpose of moderating the conflict, of keeping it within the bounds of "order"; and this power, arisen out of society, but placing itself above it, and increasingly alienating itself from it, is the state.

In contradistinction to the old gentile organisation, the state, first, divides its subjects *according to territory*. As we have seen, the old gentile associations, built upon and held together by ties of blood, became inadequate, largely because they presupposed that the members were bound to a given territory, a bond which had long ceased to exist. The territory remained, but the people had become mobile. Hence, division according to territory was taken as the point of departure, and citizens were allowed to exercise their public rights and duties wherever they settled, irrespective of gens and tribe. This organisation of citizens according to locality is a feature common to all states. That is why it seems natural to us; but we have seen what long and arduous struggles were needed before it could replace, in Athens and Rome, the old organisation according to gentes.

The second is the establishment of a *public power* which no longer directly coincided with the population organising itself as an armed force. This special public power is necessary, because a self-acting armed organisation of the population has become impossible since the cleavage into classes. The slaves also belonged to the population; the 90,000 citizens of Athens formed only a privileged class as against the 365,000 slaves. The people's army of the Athenian democracy was an aristocratic public power against the slaves, whom it kept in check; however, a gendarmeric also became necessary to keep the citizens in check, as we related above. This public power exists in every state; it consists not merely of armed people but also of material adjuncts, prisons and institutions of coercion of all kinds, of which gentile society knew nothing. It may be very insignificant, almost infinitesimal, in societies where class antagonisms are still undeveloped and in out-of-the-way places as was the case at certain times and in certain regions in the United States of America. It grows stronger, however, in proportion as class antagonisms within the state become more acute, and as adjacent states become larger and more populated. We have only to look at our present-day Europe, where class struggle and rivalry in conquest have screwed up the public power to such a pitch that it threatens to devour the whole of society and even the state.

In order to maintain this public power, contributions from the citizens become necessary—*taxes*. These were absolutely unknown in gentile society; but we know enough about them today. As civilisation advances, these taxes become inadequate; the state makes drafts on the future, contracts loans, *public debts*. Old Europe can tell a tale about these, too.

In possession of the public power and of the right to levy taxes, the officials, as organs of society, now stand *above* society. The free, voluntary respect that was accorded to the organs of the gentile constitution does not satisfy them, even if they could gain it; being the vehicles of a power that is becoming alien to society, respect for them must be enforced by means of exceptional laws by virtue of which they enjoy special sanctity and inviolability. The shabbiest police servant in the civilised state has more "authority" than all the organs of gentile society put together; but the most powerful prince and the greatest statesman, or general, of civilisation may well envy the humblest gentile chief for the uncoerced and undisputed respect that is paid to him. The one stands in the midst of society, the other is forced to attempt to represent something outside and above it.

As the state arose from the need to hold class antagonisms in check, but as it arose, at the same time, in the midst of the conflict of these classes, it is, as a rule, the state of the most powerful, economically dominant class which, through the medium of the state, becomes also the politically dominant class, and thus acquires new means of holding down and exploiting the oppressed class. Thus, the state of antiquity was above all the state of the slave owners for the purpose of holding down the slaves, as the feudal state was the organ of the nobility for holding down the peasant serfs and bondsmen, and the modern representative state is an instrument of exploitation of wage labour by capital. By way of exception, however, periods occur in which the warring classes balance each other so nearly that the state power, as ostensible mediator, acquires, for the moment, a certain degree of independence of both. Such was the absolute monarchy of the seventeenth and eighteenth centuries, which held the balance between the nobility and the class of burghers; such was the Bonapartism of the First, and still more of the Second French Empire, which played off the proletariat against the bourgeoisie and the bourgeoisie against the proletariat. The latest performance of this kind, in which ruler and ruled appear equally ridiculous, is the new German Empire of the Bismarck nation: the capitalists and workers are balanced against each other and equally cheated for the benefit of the impoverished Prussian cabbage Junkers.

In most of the historical states, the rights of citizens are, besides, apportioned according to their wealth, thus directly expressing the fact that the state is an organisation of the possessing class for its protection against the non-possessing class. It was so already in the Athenian and Roman classification according to property. It was so in the mediaeval feudal state, in which the alignment of political power was in conformity with the amount of land owned. It is seen in the electoral qualifications of the modern representative states. Yet this political recognition of property distinctions is by no means essential. On the contrary, it marks a low stage of state development. The highest form of the state, the democratic republic, which under our modern conditions of society is more and more becoming an inevitable necessity, and is the form of state in which alone the last decisive struggle between proletariat and bourgeoisie can be fought out—the democratic republic officially knows nothing any more of property distinctions. In it wealth exercises its power indirectly, but all the more surely. On the one hand, in the form of the direct corruption of officials, of which America provides the classical example; on the other hand, in the form of an alliance between government and Stock Exchange, which becomes the easier to achieve the more the public debt increases and the more joint-stock companies concentrate in their hands not only transport but also production itself, using the Stock Exchange as their centre. The latest French republic as well as the United States is a striking example of this; and good old Switzerland has contributed its share in this field. But that a democratic republic is not essential for this fraternal alliance between government and Stock Exchange is proved by England and also by the new German Empire, where one cannot tell who was elevated more by universal suffrage, Bismarck or Bleichröder. And lastly, the possessing class rules directly through the medium of universal suffrage. As long as the oppressed class, in our case, therefore, the proletariat, is not yet ripe to emancipate itself, it will in its majority regard the existing order of society as the only one possible and, politically, will form the tail of the capitalist class, its extreme Left wing. To the extent, however, that this class matures for its self-emancipation, it constitutes itself as its own party and elects its own representatives, and not those of the capitalists. Thus, universal suffrage is the gauge of the maturity of the working class. It cannot and never will be anything more in the present-day state; but that is sufficient. On the day the thermometer of universal suffrage registers boiling point among the workers, both they and the capitalists will know what to do.

The state, then, has not existed from all eternity. There have been societies that did without it, that had no conception of the state and state power. At a certain stage of economic development, which was necessarily bound up with the cleavage of society into classes, the state became a necessity owing to this cleavage. We are now rapidly approaching a stage in the development of production at which the existence of these classes not only will have ceased to be a necessity, but will become a positive hindrance to production. They will fall as inevitably as they arose at an earlier stage. Along with them the state will inevitably fall. The society that will organise production on the basis of a free and equal association of the producers will put the whole machinery of state where it will then belong: into the Museum of Antiquities, by the side of the spinning wheel and the bronze axe.

Thus, from the foregoing, civilisation is that stage of development of society at which division of labour, the resulting exchange between individuals, and commodity production, which combines the two, reach their complete unfoldment and revolutionise the whole hitherto existing society.

Production at all former stages of society was essentially collective and, likewise, consumption took place by the direct distribution of the products within larger or smaller communistic communities. This production in common was carried on within the narrowest limits, but concomitantly the producers were masters of their process of production and of their product. They knew what became of the product: they consumed it, it did not leave their hands; and as long as production was carried on on this basis, it could not grow beyond the control of the producers, and it could not raise any strange, phantom powers against them, as is the case regularly and inevitably under civilisation.

But, slowly, division of labour crept into this process of production. It undermined the collective nature of production and appropriation, it made appropriation by individuals the largely prevailing rule, and thus gave rise to exchange between individuals—how, we examined above. Gradually, the production of commodities became the dominant form.

With the production of commodities, production no longer for one's own consumption but for exchange, the products necessarily pass from hand to hand. The producer parts with his product in the course of exchange; he no longer knows what becomes of it. As soon as money, and with it the merchant, steps in as a middleman between the producers, the process of exchange becomes still more complicated, the ultimate fate of the product still more uncertain. The merchants are numerous and none of them knows what the other is doing. Commodities now pass not only from hand to hand, but also from market to market. The producers have lost control of the aggregate production of the conditions of their own life, and the merchants have not acquired it. Products and production become the playthings of chance.

But chance is only one pole of an interrelation, the other pole of which is called necessity. In nature, where chance also seems to reign, we have long ago demonstrated in each particular field the inherent necessity and regularity that asserts itself in this chance. What is true of nature holds good also for society. The more a social activity, a series of social processes, becomes too powerful for conscious human control, grows beyond human reach, the more it seems to have been left to pure chance, the more do its peculiar and innate laws assert themselves in this chance, as if by natural necessity. Such laws also control the fortuities of the production and exchange of commodities; these laws confront the individual producer and exchanger as strange and, in the beginning, even as unknown powers, the nature of which must first be laboriously investigated and ascertained. These economic laws of commodity production are modified at the different stages of development of this form of production; on the whole, however, the entire period of civilisation has been dominated by these laws. To this day, the product is master of the producer; to this day, the total production of society is regulated, not by a collectively thought-out plan, but by blind laws, which operate with elemental force, in the last resort in the storms of periodic commercial crises.

We saw above how human labour power became able, at a rather early stage of development of production, to produce considerably more than was needed for the producer's maintenance, and how this stage, in the main, coincided with that of the first appearance of the division of labour and of exchange between individuals. Now, it was not long before the great "truth" was discovered that man, too, may be a commodity; that human power may be exchanged and utilised by converting man into a slave. Men had barely started to engage in exchange when they themselves were exchanged. The active became a passive, whether man wanted it or not.

With slavery, which reached its fullest development in civilisation, came the first great cleavage of society into an exploiting and an exploited class. This cleavage has continued during the whole period of civilisation. Slavery was the first form of exploitation, peculiar to the world of antiquity; it was followed by serfdom in the Middle Ages, and by wage labour in modern times. These are the three great forms of servitude, characteristic of the three great epochs of civilisation; open, and, latterly, disguised slavery, are its steady companions.

The stage of commodity production, with which civilisation began, is marked economically by the introduction of 1) metal money and, thus, of money capital, interest and usury; 2) the merchants acting as middlemen between producers; 3) private ownership of land and mortgage; 4) slave labour as the prevailing form of production. The form of the family corresponding to civilisation and under it becoming the definitely prevailing form is monogamy, the supremacy of the man over the woman, and the individual family as the economic unit of society. The cohesive force of civilised society is the state, which in all typical periods is exclusively the state of the ruling class, and in all cases remains essentially a machine for keeping down the oppressed, exploited class. Other marks of civilisation are; on the one hand fixation of the contrast between town and country as the basis of the entire division of social labour; on the other hand, the introduction of wills, by which the property holder is able to dispose of his property even after his death. This institution, which was a direct blow at the old gentile constitution, was unknown in Athens until the time of Solon; in Rome it was introduced very early, but we do not know when.[3] Among the Germans it was introduced by the priests in order that the good honest German might without hindrance bequeath his property to the Church.

With this constitution as its foundation civilisation has accomplished things with which the old gentile society was totally unable to cope. But it accomplished them by playing on the most sordid instincts and passions of man, and by developing them at the expense of all his other faculties. Naked greed has been the moving spirit of civilisation from the first day of its existence to the present time; wealth, more wealth and wealth again; wealth, not of society, but of this shabby individual was its sole and determining aim. If, in the pursuit of this aim, the increasing development of science and repeated periods of the fullest blooming of art fell into its lap, it was only because without them the ample present-day achievements in the accumulation of wealth would have been impossible.

Since the exploitation of one class by another is the basis of civilisation, its whole development moves in a continuous contradiction. Every advance in production is at the same time a retrogression in the condition of the oppressed class, that is, of the great majority. What is a boon for the one is necessarily a bane for the other; each new emancipation of one class always means a new oppression of another class. The most striking proof of this is furnished by the introduction of machinery, the effects of which are well known today. And while among barbarians, as we have seen, hardly any distinction could be made between rights and duties, civilisation makes the difference and antithesis between these two plain even to the dullest mind by assigning to one class pretty nearly all the rights, and to the other class pretty nearly all the duties.

But this is not as it ought to be. What is good for the ruling class should be good for the whole of the society with which the ruling class identifies itself. Therefore, the more civilisation advances, the more it is compelled to cover the ills it necessarily creates with the cloak of love, to embellish them, or to deny their existence; in short, to introduce conventional hypocrisy—unknown both in previous forms of society and even in the earliest stages of civilisation—that culminates in the declaration: The exploiting class exploits the oppressed class solely and exclusively in the interest of the exploited class itself; and if the latter fails to appreciate this, and even becomes rebellious, it thereby shows the basest ingratitude to its benefactors, the exploiters.[4]

And now, in conclusion, Morgan's verdict on civilisation: "Since the advent of civilisation, the outgrowth of property has been so immense, its forms so diversified, its uses so expanding and its management so intelligent in the interests of its owners that it *has become*, on the part of the people, *an unmanageable power. The human mind stands bewildered in the presence of its own creation.* The time will come, nevertheless, when human intelligence will rise to the mastery over property, and define the relations of the state to the property it protects, as well as the obligations and the limits of the rights of its owners. The interests of society are paramount to individual interest, and the two must be brought into just and harmonious relation. A mere property career is not the final destiny of mankind, if progress is to be the law of the future as it has been of the past. The time which has passed away since civilisation began is but a fragment of the past duration of man's existence; and but a fragment of the ages yet to come. The dissolution of society bids fair to become the termination of a career of which property is the end and aim, because such a career contains the elements of self-destruction.

Democracy in government, brotherhood in society, equality in rights and privileges, and universal education, foreshadow the next higher plane of society to which experience, intelligence and knowledge are steadily tending. *It will be a revival, in a higher form, of the liberty, equality and fraternity of the ancient gentes."* (Lewis Henry Morgan, *Ancient Society,* 1877, p. 552.)

NOTES

1. The reference is to *The German Ideology.*

2. The first historian who had at least an approximate idea of the nature of the gens was Niebuhr, thanks to his knowledge of the Dithmarschen families—to which, however, he also owes the errors he mechanically copied from there. *[Engels]*

3. Lassalle's *Das System der erworbenen Rechle (System of Acquired Rights)* turns, in its second part, mainly on the proposition that the Roman testament is as old as Rome itself, that in Roman history there was never "a time when testaments did not exist": that the testament arose rather in pre-Roman times out of the cult of the dead. As a confirmed Hegelian of the old school, Lassalle derived the provisions of the Roman law not from the social conditions of the Romans, but from the "speculative conception" of the will, and thus arrived at this totally unhistoric assertion. This is not to be wondered at in a book that from the same speculative conception draws the conclusion that the transfer of property was purely a secondary matter in Roman inheritance Lassalle not only believes in the illusions of Roman jurists, especially of the earlier period, but he even excels them. *[Engels]*

4. I had intended at the outset to place the brilliant critique of civilisation, scattered through the works of Fourier, by the side of Morgan's and my own. Unfortunately, I cannot spare the time. I only wish to remark that Fourier already considered monogamy and property in land as the main characteristics of civilisation, and that he described it as a war of the rich against the poor. We also find already in his work the deep appreciation of the fact that in all imperfect societies, those torn by conflicting interests, the individual families *(les families incohérentes)* are the economic units. *[Engels]*

2

The Construction of Masculinity and the Triad of Men's Violence

MICHAEL KAUFMAN

The all too familiar story: a woman raped, a wife battered, a lover abused. With a sense of immediacy and anger, the women's liberation movement has pushed the many forms of men's violence against women—from the most overt to the most subtle in form— into popular consciousness and public debate. These forms of violence are one aspect of our society's domination by men that, in outcome, if not always in design, reinforce that domination. The act of violence is many things at once. At the same instant it is the individual man acting out relations of sexual power; it is the violence of a society— a hierarchical, authoritarian, sexist, class-divided, militarist, racist, impersonal, crazy society—being focused through an individual man onto an individual woman. In the psyche of the individual man it might be his denial of social powerlessness through an act of aggression. In total these acts of violence are like a ritualized acting out of our social relations of power: the dominant and the weaker, the powerful and the powerless, the active and the passive . . . the masculine and the feminine.

For men, listening to the experience of women as the objects of men's violence is to shatter any complacency about the sex-based status quo. The power and anger of women's responses force us to rethink the things we discovered when we were very young. When I was eleven or twelve years old a friend told me the difference between fucking and raping. It was simple: with rape you tied the woman to a tree. At the time the anatomical details were still a little vague, but in either case it was something "we" supposedly did. This knowledge was just one part of an education, started years before, about the relative power and privileges of men and women. I remember laughing when my friend explained all that to me. Now I shudder. The difference in my responses is partially that, at twelve, it was part of the posturing and pretense that accompanied my passage into adolescence. Now, of course, I have a different vantage point on the issue. It is the vantage point of an adult, but more importantly my view of the world is being reconstructed by the intervention of that majority whose voice has been suppressed: the women.

This relearning of the reality of men's violence against women evokes many deep feelings and memories for men. As memories are recalled and recast, a new connection becomes clear: violence by men against women is only one corner of a triad of men's

From *Beyond Patriarchy: Essays by Men on Pleasure, Power, and Change,* Oxford University Press, 1987, pp. 1–29. Reprinted by permission.

violence. The other two corners are violence against other men and violence against oneself.

On a psychological level the pervasiveness of violence is the result of what Herbert Marcuse called the "surplus repression" of our sexual and emotional desires.[1] The substitution of violence for desire (more precisely, the transmutation of violence into a form of emotionally gratifying activity) happens unequally in men and women. The construction of masculinity involves the construction of "surplus aggressiveness." The social context of this triad of violence is the institutionalization of violence in the operation of most aspects of social, economic, and political life.

The three corners of the triad reinforce one another. The first corner—violence against women—cannot be confronted successfully without simultaneously challenging the other two corners of the triad. And all this requires a dismantling of the social feeding ground of violence: patriarchal, heterosexist, authoritarian, class societies. These three corners and the societies in which they blossom feed on each other. And together, we surmise, they will fall.

The Social and Individual Nature of Violence and Aggression

Origins of Violence

The most vexing question in the matter of men's violence is, of course, its biological roots. It would be very useful to know whether men in particular, or humans in general, are biologically (for example, genetically or hormonally) predisposed to acts of violence against other humans.

From the outset, feminism has been careful to draw a distinction between sex and gender. The strictly biological differences between the sexes form only the substrate for a society's construction of people with gender. Indeed, the appeal of feminism to many men, in addition to the desire to ally ourselves with the struggle of our sisters against oppression, has been to try to dissociate "male" from "masculine." While many of the characteristics associated with masculinity are valuable human traits—strength, daring, courage, rationality, intellect, sexual desire—the distortion of these traits in the masculine norm and the exclusion of other traits (associated with femininity) are oppressive and destructive. The process of stuffing oneself into the tight pants of masculinity is a difficult one for all men, even if it is not consciously experienced as such.

But the actual relation of sex and gender is problematic. For one thing, what might be called the "gender craft" of a society does its work on biological entities—entities whose ultimate source of pleasure and pain is their bodies.[2] What makes the relationship between sex and gender even more difficult to understand is that the production of gender is itself an incredibly complex and opaque process. As Michele Barrett and Mary McIntosh point out, although stereotypical roles do exist, each individual is not "the passive victim of a monolithically imposed system."[3]

In recent years there has been a major attempt to reclaim for biology the social behaviour of human beings. Sociobiology aims at nothing less than the reduction of human social interaction to our genetic inheritance. The study of apes, aardvarks, and tapeworms as a means of discerning the true nature of humans is almost surprising in its naivete, but at times it is socially dangerous in its conception and execution. As many critics have pointed out, it ignores what is unique about human beings: our construction of ever-changing social orders.

Indeed, humans are animals—physical creatures subject to the requirements of genes, cells, organs, and hormones of every description. Yet we do not have a comprehensive understanding of how these things shape behavior and, even if we did, behavior is just a small, fragmented moment to be understood within the larger realm of human desire and motivation. Even if we did have a more comprehensive knowledge, what is important is that humans, unlike apes or even the glorious ant, live in constantly evolving and widely differing societies. Since the era when humans came into existence, our history has been a movement *away* from an unmediated, "natural," animal existence.

Even if we could ascertain that humans in general, or men in particular, are predisposed to building neutron bombs, this does not help us answer the much more important question of how each society shapes, limits, or accentuates this tendency. To take only the question of violence, why, as societies develop, does violence seem to move from something isolated and often ritualistic in its expression to a pervasive feature of everyday life? And why are some forms of physical violence so widely accepted (corporal punishment of children, for example) while others are not (such as physical attacks on pharaohs, presidents, and pontiffs)?

That much said let us also say this: there is no psychological, biological, or social evidence to suggest that humans are *not* predisposed to aggression and even violence. On the other hand, a predisposition to cooperation and peacefulness is also entirely possible. It is even possible that men—for reasons of hormones—are biologically more aggressive and prone to violence than women. We do not know the answer for the simple reason that the men we examine do not exist outside societies.

But in any case, the important question is what societies do with the violence. What forms of violence are socially sanctioned or socially tolerated? What forms of violence seem built into the very structure of our societies? The process of human social development has been one of restraining, repressing, forming, informing, channeling, and transforming various biological tendencies. Could it not be that this process of repression has been a very selective one? Perhaps the repression of certain impulses and the denial of certain needs aggravate other impulses. I think of the man who feels he has no human connections in his life and who goes out and rapes a woman.

In spite of a general feminist rejection of sociobiology, this pseudoscience receives a strange form of support among some feminists. In her book, *Against Our Will: Men, Women and Rape*, Susan Brownmiller argues, not only that violent, male aggression is psychologically innate, but that it is grounded in male anatomy. And conversely, the view of female sexuality appears to be one of victimization and powerlessness. She argues, "By anatomical fiat—the inescapable construction of their genital organs—the human male was a natural predator and the human female served as his natural prey."[4] Alice Echols suggests that many cultural feminists also tend to repeat many traditional, stereotypical images of men and women.[5]

The essential question for us is not whether men are predisposed to violence, but what society does with this violence. Why has the linchpin of so many societies been the manifold expression of violence perpetrated disproportionately by men? Why are so many forms of violence sanctioned or even encouraged? Exactly what is the nature of violence? And how are patterns of violence and the quest for domination built up and reinforced?

THE SOCIAL CONTEXT

For every apparently individual act of violence there is a social context. This is not to say there are no pathological acts of violence, but even in that case the "language" of the violent act, the way the violence manifests itself, can only be understood within a certain social experience. We are interested here in the manifestations of violence that are accepted as more or less normal, even if reprehensible: fighting, war, rape, assault, psychological abuse, and so forth. What is the context of men's violence in the prevalent social orders of today?

Violence has long been institutionalized as an acceptable means of solving conflicts. But now the vast apparati of policing and war making maintained by countries the world over pose a threat to the future of life itself.

"Civilized" societies have been built and shaped through the decimation, containment, and exploitation of other peoples: extermination of native populations, colonialism, and slavery. "I am talking," writes Aimé Césaire, "about societies drained of their essence, cultures trampled underfoot, institutions undermined, lands confiscated, religions smashed, magnificent artistic creations destroyed, extraordinary possibilities wiped out. . . . I am talking about millions . . . sacrificed."[6]

Our relationship with the natural environment has often been described with the metaphor of rape. An attitude of conquering nature, of mastering an environment waiting to be exploited for profit, has great consequences when we possess a technology capable of permanently disrupting an ecological balance shaped over hundreds of millions of years.

The daily work life of industrial, class societies is one of violence. Violence poses as economic rationality as some of us are turned into extensions of machines, while others become brains detached from bodies. Our industrial process becomes the modern-day rack of torture where we are stretched out of shape and ripped limb from limb. It is violence that exposes workers to the danger of chemicals, radiation, machinery, speedup, and muscle strain. It is violence that condemns the majority to work to exhaustion for forty or fifty years and then to be thrown into society's garbage bin for the old and used-up.

The racism, sexism, and heterosexism that have been institutionalized in our societies are socially regulated acts of violence.

Our cities themselves are a violation, not only of nature, but of human community and the human relationship with nature. As the architect Frank Lloyd Wright said, "To look at the plan of a great City is to look at something like the cross-section of a fibrous tumor."[7]

Our cities, our social structure, our work life, our relation with nature, our history, are more than a backdrop to the prevalence of violence. They are violence; violence in an institutionalized form encoded into physical structures and socioeconomic relations. Much of the sociological analysis of violence in our societies implies simply that violence is learned by witnessing and experiencing social violence: man kicks boy, boy kicks dog.[8] Such experiences of transmitted violence are a reality, as the analysis of wife battering indicates, for many batterers were themselves abused as children. But more essential is that our personalities and sexuality, our needs and fears, our strengths and weaknesses, our selves are created—not simply learned—through our lived reality. The violence of our social order nurtures a psychology of violence, which in turn reinforces the social, economic and political structures of violence. The ever-increasing demands of civilization and the constant building upon inherited structures of violence suggest that the development of civilization has been inseparable from a continuous increase in violence against humans and our natural environment.

It would be easy, yet ultimately not very useful, to slip into a use of the term "violence" as a metaphor for all our society's antagonisms, contradictions, and ills. For now, let us leave aside the social terrain and begin to unravel the nature of so-called individual violence.

The Triad of Men's Violence

The longevity of the oppression of women must be based on something more than conspiracy, something more complicated than biological handicap and more durable than economic exploitation (although in differing degrees all these may feature.)

JULIET MITCHELL [9]

It seems impossible to believe that mere greed could hold men to such a steadfastness of purpose.

JOSEPH CONRAD [10]

The field in which the triad of men's violence is situated is a society, or societies, grounded in structures of domination and control. Although at times this control is symbolized and embodied in the individual father—patriarchy, by definition—it is more important to emphasize that patriarchal structures of authority, domination, and control are diffused throughout social, economic, political, and ideological activities and in our relations to the natural environment. Perhaps more than in any previous time during the long epoch of patriarchy, authority does *not* rest with the father, at least in much of the advanced capitalist and noncapitalist world. This has led more than one author to question the applicability of the term patriarchy.[11] But I think it still remains useful as a broad, descriptive category. In this sense Jessica Benjamin speaks of the current reign of patriarchy without the father. "The form of domination peculiar to this epoch expresses itself not directly as authority but indirectly as the transformation of all relationships and activity into objective, instrumental, depersonalized forms."[12]

The structures of domination and control form not simply the background to the triad of violence, but generate, and in turn are nurtured by, this violence. These structures refer both to our social relations and to our interaction with our natural environment. The relation between these two levels is obviously extremely complex. It appears that violence against nature—that is, the impossible and disastrous drive to dominate and conquer the natural world—is integrally connected with domination among humans. Some of these connections are quite obvious. One thinks of the bulldozing of the planet for profit in capitalist societies, societies characterized by the dominance of one class over others. But the link between the domination of nature and structures of domination of humans go beyond this. Various writers make provocative suggestions about the nature of this link.

Max Horkheimer and T. W. Adorno argue that the domination of humans by other humans creates the preconditions for the domination of nature.[13] An important sub-theme of Mary O'Brien's book *The Politics of Reproduction* is that men "have understood their separation from nature and their need to mediate this separation ever since that moment in dark prehistory when the idea of paternity took hold in the human mind. Patriarchy is the power to transcend natural realities with historical, man-made realities. This is the potency principle in its primordial form."[14] Simone de Beauvoir says that the ambivalent feelings of men toward nature are carried over onto their feelings toward women, who are seen as embodying nature. "Now ally, now enemy, she appears as the dark chaos from whence life wells up, as this life itself, and as the over-yonder toward which life tends."[15] Violence against nature, like violence against women, violence against other men, and violence against oneself, is in part related to what Sidney Jourard calls the lethal aspects of masculinity.[16]

The Individual Reproduction of Male Domination
No man is born a butcher.
BERTOLT BRECHT[17]

In a male-dominated society men have a number of privileges. Compared to women we are free to walk the streets at night, we have traditionally escaped domestic labor, and on average we have higher wages, better jobs, and more power. But these advantages in themselves cannot explain the individual reproduction of the relations of male domination, that is, why the individual male from a very early age embraces masculinity. The embracing of masculinity is not only a"socialization" into a certain gender role, as if there is a pre-formed human being who learns a role that he then plays for the rest of his life. Rather, through his psychological development he embraces and takes into himself a set of gender-based social relations: the person that is created through the process of maturation becomes the personal embodiment of those relations. By the time the child is five or six years old, the basis for lifelong masculinity has already been established.

Two factors, intrinsic to humans and human development, form the basis for the individual acquisition of gender. These conditions do not explain the existence of gender: they are simply preconditions for its individual acquisition.

The first factor is the malleability of human desires. For the infant all bodily activities—touch, sight, smell, sound, taste, thought—are potential sources of sexual pleasure. Or rather, they *are* sexual pleasure in the sense of our ability to obtain pleasure from our bodies. But this original polysexuality is limited, shaped, and repressed through the maturation process that is necessary to meet the demands of the natural and social world. Unlike other animals our sexuality is not simply instinct: it is individually and socially constructed. It is because of this, and because of the human's capacity to think and construct societies and ideologies, that gender can exist in differentiation from biological sex.

As Herbert Marcuse and, following him, Gad Horowitz have pointed out, the demands of societies of domination—of "surplus-repressive" societies—progressively narrow down sexuality into genital contact, with a heterosexual norm. (Marcuse argues that a certain "basic repression"—a damming up or deflection—of human desires is necessary for any conceivable human association. But in addition to this, hierarchical and authoritarian societies require a "surplus repression" to maintain structures of domination.)[18]

This narrowing down onto genital contact is not simply a natural genital preference but is the blocking of energy from a whole range of forms of pleasure (including "mental" activities). And for reasons discussed elsewhere by Horowitz and Kaufman, the acquisition of the dominant form of masculinity is an enhancement of forms of pleasure associated with activity and the surplus repression of our ability to experience pleasure passively.

We try to compensate for this surplus repression with the pleasures and preoccupations of work, play, sports, and culture. But these are not sufficient to offset the severe limits placed on love and desire. To put this crudely, a two-day weekend cannot emotionally compensate for five days of a deadening job. And what is more, these social activities are themselves sources of struggle and tension.

The second factor that forms the basis for the individual's acquisition of gender is that the prolonged period of human childhood results in powerful attachments to parental figures. The passionate bonding of the young child to the primary parental figures obtains its particular power and salience for our personal development in societies where isolated women have the primary responsibility for nurturing infants and children, where the child's relation with the world is mediated most strongly through a small family rather than through a small community as a whole, and in which traits associated with the "opposite" sex are suppressed.

This prolonged period of human childhood is a prolonged period of powerlessness. The intense love for one or two parents is combined with intense feelings of deprivation and frustration. This natural ambivalence is greatly aggravated in societies where the attention parents are able to provide the young is limited, where social demands place additional frustrations on top of the inevitable ones experienced by a tiny person, and where one or two isolated parents relive and repeat the patterns of their own childhood. As will be seen, part of the boy's acquisition of masculinity is a response to this experience of powerlessness.

By the time children are sufficiently developed physically, emotionally, and intellectually at five or six to have clearly defined themselves separately from their parents, these parental figures have already been internalized within them. In the early years, as in later ones, we identify with (or react against) the apparent characteristics of our love objects and incorporate them into our own personalities. This is largely an unconscious process. This incorporation and internalization, or rejection, of the characteristics of our love objects is part of the process of constructing our ego, our self.

This internalization of the objects of love is a selective one, and it is a process that takes place in specific social environments. The immediate environment is the family, which is a "vigorous agency of class placement and an efficient mechanism for the creation and transmission of gender inequality."[19] Within itself, to a greater or lesser extent, the family reflects, reproduces, and recreates the hierarchical gender system of society as a whole.[20]

As noted above, the child has ambivalent feelings toward his or her primary caring figures. Love combines with feelings of powerlessness, tension, and frustration. The child's experience of anxiety and powerlessness results not only from the prohibitions of harsh parents but also from the inability of even the most loving parents who cannot exist solely for their young, because of the demands of society, demands of natural reality, and demands of their own needs.

Both girls and boys have these ambivalent feelings and experiences of powerlessness. But the feelings toward the parents and the matter of power are almost immediately impregnated with social meaning. Years before the child can put words to it, she or he begins to understand that the mother is inferior to the father and that woman is inferior to man. That this inferiority is not natural but is socially imposed is beyond the understanding of the child and even beyond the understanding of sociobiologists, presidents, and popes. (Size itself might also feed into this perception of inferiority, or perhaps it is simply that in hierarchical, sexist society, size becomes a symbol of superiority.) In the end the biological fact of "otherness" becomes overlaced with a socially imposed otherness. The child is presented with two categories of humans: males, who embody the full grandeur and power of humanity, and females, who in Simone de Beauvoir's words, are defined as "other" in a phallocentric society.[21]

The human's answer to this powerlessness and to the desire to find pleasure is to develop an ego and a superego, that is, a distinct self and an internal mechanism of authority. An important part of the process of ego development is the identification with the objects of love. Progressively both sexes discover and are taught who the appropriate figures of identification are. But the figures of identification are not equal.

Society presents the young boy with a great escape. He may feel powerless as a child, but there is hope, for as an adult male he will have privilege and (at least in the child's imagination) he will have power. A strong identification—that is, an incorporation into his own developing self—of his image of his father in particular and male figures in general is his compensation for his own sense of powerlessness and insecurity. It is his compensation for distancing himself from his first love, his mother.

In this process the boy not only claims for himself the activity represented by men and father. At the same time he steps beyond the passivity of his infantile relationship to the mother and beyond his overall sense of passivity (passivity, that is, in the sense of feeling overwhelmed by desires and a frustrating world). He embraces the project of controlling himself and controlling the world. He comes to personify activity. Masculinity is a reaction against passivity and powerlessness and, with it comes a repression of all the desires and traits that a given society defines as negatively passive or as resonant of passive experiences. The girl, on the other hand, discovers she will never possess men's power, and henceforth the most she can aspire to is to be loved by a man—that is, to actively pursue a passive aim.

Thus the achievement of what is considered the biologically normal male character (but which is really socially created masculinity) is one outcome of the splitting of human desire and human *being* into mutually exclusive spheres of activity and passivity. The monopoly of activity by males is not a timeless psychological or social necessity. Rather, the internalization of the norms of masculinity require the surplus repression of passive aims—the desire to be nurtured. The repression of passivity and the accentuation of activity constitute the development of a "surplus-aggressive" character type. Unfortunately, such a character type is the norm in patriarchal societies, although the degree of aggressiveness varies from person to person and society to society.

Part of the reason for this process is a response to the fear of rejection and of punishment. What does one fear? Loss of love and self-esteem. Why, in the child's mind, would it lose love and self-esteem? Because it does what is prohibited or degraded. In order to not do what is prohibited or degraded, during this process of identification the child internalizes the values and prohibitions of society. This is the shaping of the superego, our conscience, sense of guilt, and standards of self-worth. Through the internalization of social authority, aggressiveness is directed against oneself.[22]

This whole process of ego development is the shaping of a psychic realm that mediates between our unconscious desires, the world, and a punishing superego. But as should now be clear, the development of the ego is the development of masculine or feminine ego. In this sense, the ego is a definition of oneself formed within a given social and psychological environment and within what Gayle Rubin calls a specific sex-gender system.[23]

The boy is not simply *learning* a gender role but is becoming *part* of that gender. His whole self, to a greater or lesser extent, with greater or lesser conflict, will be masculine. Ken Kesey magnificently captured this in his description of Hank, a central character in *Sometimes a Great Notion:* "Did it take that much muscle just to walk, or was Hank showing off his manly development? Every movement constituted open aggression against the very air through which Hank passed."[24]

The Reinforcement of Masculinity

Masculinity is unconsciously rooted before the age of six, is reinforced as the child develops, and then positively explodes at adolescence. Beauvoir's comment about girls is no less true for boys: "With puberty, the future not only approaches; it takes residence in her body; it assumes the most concrete reality."[25]

It is particularly in adolescence that masculinity obtains its definitive shape for the individual. The masculine norm has its own particular nuances and traits dependent on class, nation, race, religion, and ethnicity. And within each group it has its own personal expression. Adolescence is important because it is the time when the body reawakens, when that long-awaited entrance into adulthood finally takes place, and when our culture makes the final socio-educational preparations for adult work life. In adolescence the pain and fear involved in repressing "femininity" and passivity start to become evident. For most of us, the response to this inner pain is to reinforce the bulwarks of masculinity. The emotional pain created by obsessive masculinity is stifled by reinforcing masculinity itself.

The family, school, sports, friends, church, clubs, scouts, jobs, and the media all play a role as the adolescent struggles to put the final touches on himself as a real man. The expression of male power will be radically different from class to class. For the middle class adolescent, with a future in a profession or business, his own personal and social power will be expressed through a direct mastering of the world. Workaholism or at least a measuring of his value through status and the paycheck might well be the outcome. Fantasies of power are often expressed in terms of fame and success.

For a working class boy, the avenue of mastering the world of business, politics, the professions, and wealth is all but denied. For him male power is often defined in the form of working class machismo. The power to dominate is expressed in a direct physical form. Domination of the factors of production or of another person is achieved through sheer bravado and muscle power. In an excellent examination of the development of white male, working class identity in Britain, Paul Willis demonstrates that the acquisition of a positive working class identity is coterminous with the development of a particular gender identity. Though stigmatized by society as a whole, manual labor becomes the embodiment of masculine power. "Manual labor is suffused with masculine qualities and given certain sensual overtones for 'the lads.' The toughness and awkwardness of physical work and effort . . . takes on masculine lights and depths and assumes a significance beyond itself."[26]

Adolescence is also the time of our first intense courtships. Although so much of pre- and early-adolescent sexual experience is homosexual, those experiences tend to be devalued and ignored. Relations with young women are the real thing. This interaction furthers the acquisition of masculinity for boys because they are interacting with girls who are busy acquiring the complementary femininity. Each moment of interaction reinforces the gender acquisition of each sex.

THE FRAGILITY OF MASCULINITY

Masculinity is power. But masculinity is terrifyingly fragile because it does not really exist in the sense we are led to think it exists, that is, as a biological reality—something real that we have inside ourselves. It exists as ideology; it exists as scripted behavior; it exists within "gendered" relationships. But in the end it is just a social institution with a tenuous relationship to that with which it is supposed to be synonymous: our maleness, our biological sex. The young child does not know that sex does not equal gender. For him to be male is to be what he perceives as being masculine. The child is father to the man. Therefore, to be unmasculine is to be desexed—"castrated."

The tension between maleness and masculinity is intense because masculinity requires a suppression of a whole range of human needs, aims, feelings, and forms of expression. Masculinity is one half of the narrow, surplus-repressive shape of the adult human psyche. Even when we are intellectually aware of the difference between biological maleness and masculinity, the masculine ideal is so embedded within ourselves that it is hard to untangle the person we might want to become (more "fully human," less sexist, less surplus-repressed, and so on) from the person we actually are.

But as children and adolescents (and often as adults), we are not aware of the difference between maleness and masculinity. With the exception of a tiny proportion of the population born as hermaphrodites, there can be no biological struggle to be male. The presence of a penis and testicles is all it takes. Yet boys and men harbor great insecurity about their male credentials. This insecurity exists because maleness is equated with masculinity; but the latter is a figment of our collective, patriarchal, surplus-repressive imaginations.

In a patriarchal society being male is highly valued, and men value their masculinity. But everywhere there are ambivalent feelings. That the initial internalization of masculinity is at the father's knee has lasting significance. Andrew Tolson states that "to the boy, masculinity is both mysterious and attractive (in its promise of a world of work and power), and yet, at the same time, threatening (in its strangeness, and emotional distance). . . . It works both ways; attracts and repels in dynamic contradiction. This simultaneous distance and attraction is internalized as a permanent emotional tension that the individual must, in some way, strive to overcome."[27]

Although maleness and masculinity are highly valued, men are everywhere unsure of their own masculinity and maleness, whether consciously or not. When men are encouraged to be open, as in men's support and counselling groups, it becomes apparent that there exists, often under the surface, an internal dialogue of doubt about one's male and masculine credentials.

One need think only of anxieties about the penis, that incomparable scepter, that symbol of patriarchy and male power. Even as a child the boy experiences, more or less consciously, fearful fantasies of "castration." The child observes that the people who do not have penises are also those with less power. In the mind of a four- or five-year-old child who doesn't know about the power of advertising, the state, education, interactive psychological patterns, unequal pay, sexual harassment, and rape, what else can he think bestows the rewards of masculinity than that little visible difference between men and women, boys and girls?

Of course at this early age the little penis and testicles are not much defense against the world. Nor can they measure against the impossibly huge genitals of one's father or other men. I remember standing in the shower when I was five or six years old, staring up in awe at my father. Years later I realized a full circle had turned when I was showering with my five-year-old son and saw the same crick in his neck and the same look in his eyes. This internalized image of the small, boyish self retains a nagging presence in each man's unconscious. This is so much so that, as adults, men go to war to prove themselves potent, they risk their lives to show they have balls. Expressions such as these, and the double meaning of the word impotent, are no accident.

Just the presence of that wonderfully sensitive bit of flesh, as highly valued as it is in patriarchal culture, is not enough to guarantee maleness and masculinity. But if there are indeed such great doubts in adolescence and beyond about one's masculine credentials, how is it that we combat these doubts? One way is by violence.

MEN'S VIOLENCE AGAINST WOMEN

> In spite of the inferior role which men assign to them, women are the privileged objects of their aggression.
>
> SIMONE DE BEAUVOIR[28]

Men's violence against women is the most common form of direct, personalized violence in the lives of most adults. From sexual harassment to rape, from incest to wife battering to the sight of violent pornographic images, few women escape some form of male aggression.

My purpose here is not to list and evaluate the various forms of violence against women, nor to try to assess what can be classed as violence per se.[29] It is to understand this violence as an expression of the fragility of masculinity and its place in the perpetuation of masculinity and male domination.

In the first place, men's violence against women is probably the clearest, most straightforward expression of relative male and female power. That the relative social, economic, and political power can be expressed in this manner is, to a large part, because of differences in physical strength and in a lifelong training (or lack of training) in fighting. But it is also expressed this way because of the active/passive split. Activity as aggression is part of the masculine gender definition. That is not to say this definition always includes rape or battering, but it is one of the possibilities within a definition of activity that is ultimately grounded in the body.

Rape is a good example of the acting out of these relations of power and of the outcome of fragile masculinity in a surplus-repressive society. In the testimonies of rapists one hears over and over again expressions of inferiority, powerlessness, anger. But who can these men feel superior to? Rape is a crime that not only demonstrates physical power, but that does so in the language of male-female sex gender relations. The testimonies of convicted rapists collected by Douglas Jackson in the late 1970s are chilling and revealing.[30] Hal: "I felt very inferior to others. . . . I felt rotten about myself and by committing rape I took this out on someone I thought was weaker than me, someone I could control." Carl: "I think that I was feeling so rotten, so low, and such a creep . . ." Len: "I feel a lot of what rape is isn't so much sexual desire as a person's feelings about themselves and how that relates to sex. My fear of relating to people turned to sex because . . . it just happens to be the fullest area to let your anger out on, to let your feelings out on."

Sometimes this anger and pain are experienced in relation to women but just as often not. In either case they are addressed to women who, as the Other in a phallocentric society, are objects of mystification to men, the objects to whom men from birth have learned to express and vent their feelings, or simply objects with less social power and weaker muscles. It is the crime against women par excellence because, through it, the full weight of a sexually based differentiation among humans is played out.

This anger and pain are sometimes overlayed with the effects of a class hierarchy. John: "I didn't feel too good about women. I felt that I couldn't pick them up on my own. I took the lower-class woman and tried to make her look even lower than she really was, you know. 'Cause what I really wanted was a higher-class woman but I didn't have the finesse to actually pick these women up."

Within relationships, forms of male violence such as rape, battering, and what Meg Luxton calls the "petty tyranny" of male domination in the household[31] must be understood both "in terms of violence directed against women as women and against women as wives."[32] The family provides an arena for the expression of needs and emotions not considered legitimate elsewhere.[33] It is the one of the only places where men feel safe enough to express emotions. As the dams break, the flood pours out on women and children.[34] The family also becomes the place where the violence suffered by individuals in their work lives is discharged. "At work men are powerless, so in their leisure time they want to have a feeling that they control their lives."[35]

While this violence can be discussed in terms of men's aggression, it operates within the dualism of activity and passivity, masculinity and femininity. Neither can exist without the other. This is not to blame women for being beaten, nor to excuse men who beat. It is but an indication that the various forms of men's violence against women are a dynamic affirmation of a masculinity that can only exist as distinguished from femininity. It is my argument that masculinity needs constant nurturing and affirmation. This affirmation takes many different forms. The majority of men are not rapists or batterers, although it is possible that the majority of men have used superior physical strength or physical coercion or the threat of force against a woman at least once as a teenager or an adult. But in those who harbor great personal doubts or strongly negative self-images, or who cannot cope with a daily feeling of powerlessness, violence against women can become a means of trying to affirm their personal power in the language of our sex-gender system. That these forms of violence only reconfirm the negative self-image and the feeling of powerlessness shows the fragility, artificiality, and precariousness of masculinity.

VIOLENCE AGAINST OTHER MEN

At a behavioral level, men's violence against other men is visible throughout society. Some forms, such as fighting, the ritualized display violence of teenagers and some groups of adult men, institutionalized rape in prisons, and attacks on gays or racial minorities are very direct expressions of this violence. In many sports, violence is incorporated into exercise and entertainment. More subtle forms are the verbal putdown or, combined with economic and other factors, the competition in the business, political, or academic world. In its most frightening form, violence has long been an acceptable and even preferred method of addressing differences and conflicts among different groups and states. In the case of war, as in many other manifestations of violence, violence against other men (and civilian women) combines with autonomous economic, ideological, and political factors.

But men's violence against other men is more than the sum of various activities and types of behavior. In this form of violence a number of things are happening at once, in addition to the autonomous factors involved. Sometimes mutual, sometimes one-sided, there is a discharge of aggression and hostility. But at the same time as discharging aggression, these acts of violence and the ever-present potential for men's violence against other men reinforce the reality that relations between men, whether at the individual or state level, are relations of power.[36]

Most men feel the presence of violence in their lives. Some of us had fathers who were domineering, rough, or even brutal. Some of us had fathers who simply were not there enough; most of us had fathers who either consciously or unconsciously were repelled by our need for touch and affection once we had passed a certain age. All of us had experiences of being beaten up or picked on when we were young. We learned to fight, or we learned to run; we learned to pick on others, or we learned how to talk or joke our way out of a confrontation. But either way these early experiences of violence caused an incredible amount of anxiety and required a huge expenditure of energy to resolve. That anxiety is crystallized in an unspoken fear (particularly among heterosexual men): all other men are my potential humiliators, my enemies, my competitors.

But this mutual hostility is not always expressed. Men have formed elaborate institutions of male bonding and buddying: clubs, gangs, teams, fishing trips, card games, bars, and gyms, not to mention that great fraternity of Man. Certainly, as many feminists have pointed out, straight male clubs are a subculture of male privilege. But they are also havens where men, by common consent, can find safety and security among other men. They are safe houses where our love and affection for other men can be expressed.

Freud suggested that great amounts of passivity are required for the establishment of social relations among men but also that this very passivity arouses a fear of losing one's power. (This fear takes the form, in a phallocentric, male-dominated society, of what Freud called "castration anxiety.") There is a constant tension of activity and passivity. Among their many functions and reasons for existence, male institutions mediate this tension between activity and passivity among men.

My thoughts take me back to grade six and the constant acting out of this drama. There was the challenge to fight and a punch in the stomach that knocked my wind out. There was our customary greeting with a slug in the shoulder. Before school, after school, during class change, at recess, whenever you saw another one of the boys whom you hadn't hit or been with in the past few minutes, you'd punch each other on the shoulder. I remember walking from class to class in terror of meeting Ed Skagle in the hall. Ed, a hefty young football player a grade ahead of me, would leave a big bruise with one of his friendly hellos. And this was the interesting thing about the whole business; most of the time it was friendly and affectionate. Long after the bruises have faded, I remember Ed's smile and the protective way he had of saying hello to me. But we couldn't express this affection without maintaining the active/passive equilibrium. More precisely, within the masculine psychology of surplus aggression, expressions of affection and of the need for other boys had to be balanced by an active assault.

But the traditional definition of masculinity is not only surplus aggression. It is also exclusive heterosexuality, for the maintenance of masculinity requires the repression of homosexuality.[37] Repression of homosexuality is one thing, but how do we explain the intense fear of homosexuality, the homophobia, that pervades so much male interaction? It isn't simply that many men may choose not to have sexual relations with other men; it is rather that they will find this possibility frightening or abhorrent.

Freud showed that the boy's renunciation of the father—and thus men—as an object of sexual love is a renunciation of what are felt to be passive sexual desires. Our embrace of future manhood is part of an equation:

male = penis = power = active = masculine.

The other half of the equation, in the language of the unconscious in patriarchal society, is

female = castrated = passive = feminine.

These unconscious equations might be absurd, but they are part of a socially shared hallucination of our patriarchal society. For the boy to deviate from this norm is to experience severe anxiety, for what appears to be at stake is his ability to be active. Erotic attraction to other men is sacrificed because there is no model central to our society of active, erotic love for other males. The emotionally charged physical attachments of childhood with father and friends eventually breed feelings of passivity and danger and are sacrificed. Horowitz notes that the anxiety caused by the threat of losing power and activity is "the motive power behind the 'normal' boy's social learning of his sex and gender roles." Boys internalize "our culture's definition of 'normal' or 'real' man: the possessor of a penis, therefore loving only females and that actively; the possessor of a penis, therefore 'strong' and 'hard,' not 'soft,' 'weak,' 'yielding,' 'sentimental,' 'effeminate,' passive. To deviate from this definition is not to be a real man. To deviate is to arouse [what Freud called] castration anxiety."[38]

Putting this in different terms, the young boy learns of the sexual hierarchy of society. This learning process is partly conscious and partly unconscious. For a boy, being a girl is a threat because it raises anxiety by representing a loss of power. Until real power is attained, the young boy courts power in the world of the imagination (with superheroes, guns, magic, and pretending to be grown-up). But the continued pull of passive aims, the attraction to girls and to mother, the fascination with the origin of babies ensure that a tension continues to exist. In this world, the only thing that is as bad as being a girl is being a sissy, that is, being like a girl.[39] Although the boy doesn't consciously equate being a girl or sissy with homosexual genital activity, at the time of puberty these feelings, thoughts, and anxieties are transferred onto homosexuality per se.

For the majority of men, the establishment of the masculine norm and the strong social prohibitions against homosexuality are enough to bury the erotic desire for other men. The repression of our bisexuality is not adequate, however, to keep this desire at bay. Some of the energy is transformed into derivative pleasures—muscle building, male comradeship, hero worship, religious rituals, war, sports—where our enjoyment of being with other men or admiring other men can be expressed. These forms of activity are not enough to neutralize our constitutional bisexuality, our organic fusion of passivity and activity, and our love for our fathers and our friends. The great majority of men, in addition to those men whose sexual preference is clearly homosexual, have, at some time in their childhood, adolescence, or adult life, had sexual or quasi-sexual relations with other males, or have fantasized or dreamed about such relationships. Those who don't (or don't recall that they have) invest a lot of energy in repressing and denying these thoughts and feelings. And to make things worse, all those highly charged male activities in the sportsfield, the meeting room, or the locker room do not dispel eroticized relations with other men. They can only reawaken those feelings. It is, as Freud would have said, the return of the repressed.

Nowhere has this been more stunningly captured than in the wrestling scene in the perhaps mistitled book, *Women in Love,* by D. H. Lawrence. It was late at night. Birkin had just come to Gerald's house after being put off following a marriage proposal. They talked of working, of loving, and fighting, and in the end stripped off their clothes and began to wrestle in front of the burning fire. As they wrestled, "they seemed to drive their white flesh deeper and deeper against each other, as if they would break into a oneness." They entwined, they wrestled, they pressed nearer and nearer. "A tense white knot of flesh [was] gripped in silence." The thin Birkin "seemed to penetrate into Gerald's more solid, more diffuse bulk, to interfuse his body through the body of the other, as if to bring it subtly into subjection, always seizing with some rapid necromantic foreknowledge every motion of the other flesh, converting and counteracting it, playing upon the limbs and trunk of Gerald like some hard wind. . . . Now and again came a sharp gasp of breath, or a sound like a sigh, then the rapid thudding of movement on the thickly-carpeted floor, then the strange sound of flesh escaping under flesh." [40]

The very institutions of male bonding and patriarchal power force men to constantly reexperience their closeness and attraction to other men, that is, the very thing so many men are afraid of. Our very attraction to ourselves, ambivalent as it may be, can only be generalized as an attraction to men in general.

A phobia is one means by which the ego tries to cope with anxiety. Homophobia is a means of trying to cope, not simply with our unsuccessfully repressed, eroticized attraction to other men, but with our whole anxiety over the unsuccessfully repressed passive sexual aims, whether directed toward males or females. But often, Otto Fenichel writes, "individuals with phobias cannot succeed in avoiding the feared situations. Again and again they are forced to experience the very things they are afraid of. Often the conclusion is unavoidable that this is due to an unconscious arrangement of theirs. It seems that unconsciously they are striving for the very thing of which they are consciously afraid. This is understandable because the feared situations originally were instinctual aims. It is a kind of 'return of the repressed.' " [41]

In the case of homophobia, it is not merely a matter of an individual phobia, although the strength of homophobia varies from individual to individual. It is a socially constructed phobia that is essential for the imposition and maintenance of masculinity. A key expression of homophobia is the obsessive denial of homosexual attraction; this denial is expressed as violence against other men. Or to put it differently, men's violence against other men is one of the chief means through which patriarchal society simultaneously expresses and discharges the attraction of men to other men.

The specific ways that homophobia and men's violence toward other men are acted out varies from man to man, society to society, and class to class. The great amount of *directly expressed* violence and violent homophobia among some groups of working class youth would be well worth analyzing to give clues to the relation of class and gender.

This corner of the triad of men's violence interacts with and reinforces violence against women. This corner contains part of the logic of surplus aggression. Here we begin to explain the tendency of many men to use force as a means of simultaneously hiding and expressing their feelings. At the same time the fear of other men, in particular the fear of weakness and passivity in relation to other men, helps create our strong dependence on women for meeting our emotional needs and for emotional discharge. In a surplus-repressive patriarchal and class society, large amounts of anxiety and hostility are built up, ready to be discharged. But the fear of one's emotions and the fear of losing control mean that discharge only takes place in a safe situation. For many men that safety is provided by a relationship with a woman where the commitment of one's friend or lover creates the sense of security. What is more, because it is a relationship with a woman, it unconsciously resonates with that first great passive relation of the boy with his mother. But in this situation and in other acts of men's violence against women, there is also the security of interaction with someone who does not represent a psychic threat, who is less socially powerful, probably less physically powerful, and who is herself operating within a pattern of surplus passivity. And finally, given the fragility of masculine identity and the inner tension of what it means to be masculine, the ultimate acknowledgement of one's masculinity is in our power over women. This power can be expressed in many ways. Violence is one of them.

Violence against Oneself

When I speak of a man's violence against himself I am thinking of the very structure of the masculine ego. The formation of an ego on an edifice of surplus repression and surplus aggression is the building of a precarious structure of internalized violence. The continual conscious and unconscious blocking and denial of passivity and all the emotions and feelings men associate with passivity—fear, pain, sadness, embarrassment—is a denial of part of what we are. The constant psychological and behavioral vigilance against passivity and its derivatives is a perpetual act of violence against oneself.

The denial and blocking of a whole range of human emotions and capacities are compounded by the blocking of avenues of discharge. The discharge of fear, hurt, and sadness, for example (through crying or trembling), is necessary because these painful emotions linger on even if they are not consciously felt. Men become pressure cookers. The failure to find safe avenues of emotional expression and discharge means that a whole range of emotions are transformed into anger and hostility. Part of the anger is directed at oneself in the form of guilt, self-hate, and various physiological and psychological symptoms. Part is directed at other men. Part of it is directed at women.

By the end of this process, our distance from ourselves is so great that the very symbol of maleness is turned into an object, a thing. Men's preoccupation with genital power and pleasure combines with a desensitization of the penis. As best he can, writes Emmanuel Reynaud, a man gives it "the coldness and the hardness of metal." It becomes his tool, his weapon, his thing. "What he loses in enjoyment he hopes to compensate for in power; but if he gains an undeniable power symbol, what pleasure can he really feel with a weapon between his legs?"[42]

Beyond Men's Violence

Throughout Gabriel Garcia Marquez's *Autumn of the Patriarch*, the ageless dictator stalked his palace, his elephantine feet dragging forever on endless corridors that reeked of corruption. There was no escape from the world of terror, misery, and decay that he himself had created. His tragedy was that he was "condemned forever to live breathing the same air which asphyxiated him."[43] As men, are we similarly condemned, or is there a road of escape from the triad of men's violence and the precarious structures of masculinity that we ourselves recreate at our peril and that of women, children, and the world?

Prescribing a set of behavioral or legal changes to combat men's violence against women is obviously not enough. Even as more and more men are convinced there is a problem, this realization does not touch the unconscious structures of masculinity. Any man who is sympathetic to feminism is aware of the painful contradiction between his conscious views and his deeper emotions and feelings.

The analysis in this article suggests that men and women must address each corner of the triad of men's violence and the socioeconomic, psycho-sexual orders on which they stand. Or to put it more strongly, it is impossible to deal successfully with any one corner of this triad in isolation from the others.

The social context that nurtures men's violence and the relation between socioeconomic transformation and the end of patriarchy have been major themes of socialist feminist thought. This framework, though it is not without controversy and unresolved problems, is one I accept. Patriarchy and systems of authoritarianism and class domination feed on each other. Speaking of the relation of capitalism and the oppression of women, Michele Barrett says that male-female divisions

> are systematically embedded in the structure and texture of capitalist social relations . . . and they play an important part in the political and ideological stability of this society. They are constitutive of our subjectivity as well as, in part, of capitalist political and cultural hegemony. They are interwoven into a fundamental relationship between the wage-labour system and the organization of domestic life and it is impossible to imagine that they could be extracted from the relations of production and reproduction of capitalism without a massive transformation of those relations taking place.[44]

Radical socioeconomic and political change is a requirement for the end of men's violence. But organizing for macrosocial change is not enough to solve the problem of men's violence, not only because the problem is so pressing here and now, but because the continued existence of masculinity and surplus aggressiveness works against the fundamental macrosocial change we desire.

The many manifestations of violence against women have been an important focus of feminists. Women's campaigns and public education against rape, battering, sexual harassment, and more generally for control by women of their bodies are a key to challenging men's violence. Support by men, not only for the struggles waged by women, but in our own workplaces and among our friends is an important part of the struggle. There are many possible avenues for work by men among men. These include: forming counselling groups and support services for battering men (as is now happening in different cities in North America); championing the inclusion of clauses on sexual harassment in collective agreements and in the constitutions or by-laws of our trade unions, associations, schools, and political parties; raising money, campaigning for government funding, and finding other means of support for rape crisis centers and shelters for battered women; speaking out against violent and sexist pornography; building neighborhood campaigns on wife and child abuse; and personally refusing to collude with the sexism of our workmates, colleagues, and friends. The latter is perhaps the most difficult of all and requires patience, humor, and support from other men who are challenging sexism.

But because men's violence against women is inseparable from the other two corners of the triad of men's violence, solutions are very complex and difficult. Ideological changes and an awareness of problems are important but insufficient. While we can envisage changes in our child-rearing arrangements (which in turn would require radical economic changes) lasting solutions have to go far deeper. Only the development of non-surplus-repressive societies (whatever these might look like) will allow for the greater expression of human needs and, along with attacks on patriarchy per se, will reduce the split between active and passive psychological aims.[45]

The process of achieving these long-term goals contains many elements of economic, social, political, and psychological change each of which requires a fundamental transformation of society. Such a transformation will not be created by an amalgam of changed individuals; but there *is* a relationship between personal change and our ability to construct organizational, political, and economic alternatives that will be able to mount a successful challenge to the status quo.

One avenue of personal struggle that is being engaged in by an increasing number of men has been the formation of men's support groups. Some groups focus on consciousness raising, but most groups stress the importance of men talking about their feelings, their relations with other men and with women, and any number of problems in their lives. At times these groups have been criticized by some antisexist men as yet another place for men to collude against women. The alternatives put forward are groups whose primary focus is either support for struggles led by women or the organization of direct, antisexist campaigns among men. These activities are very important, but so too is the development of new support structures among men. And these structures must go beyond the traditional form of consciousness raising.

Consciousness raising usually focuses on manifestations of the oppression of women and on the oppressive behavior of men. But as we have seen, masculinity is more than the sum total of oppressive forms of behavior. It is deeply and unconsciously embedded in the structure of our egos and superegos; it is what we have become. An awareness of oppressive behavior is important, but too often it only leads to guilt about being a man. Guilt is a profoundly conservative emotion and as such is not particularly useful for bringing about change. From a position of insecurity and guilt, people do not change or inspire others to change. After all, insecurity about one's male credentials played an important part in the individual acquisition of masculinity and men's violence in the first place.

There is a need to promote the personal strength and security necessary to allow men to make more fundamental personal changes and to confront sexism and heterosexism in society at large. Support groups usually allow men to talk about our feelings, how we too have been hurt growing up in a surplus-repressive society, and how we, in turn, act at times in an oppressive manner. We begin to see the connections between painful and frustrating experiences in our own lives and related forms of oppressive behavior. As Sheila Rowbotham notes, "the exploration of the internal areas of consciousness is a political necessity for us."[46]

Talking among men is a major step, but it is still operating within the acceptable limits of what men like to think of as rational behavior. Deep barriers and fears remain even when we can begin to recognize them. As well as talking, men need to encourage direct expression of emotions—grief, anger, rage, hurt, love—within these groups and the physical closeness that has been blocked by the repression of passive aims, by social prohibition, and by our own superegos and sense of what is right. This discharge of emotions has many functions and outcomes: like all forms of emotional and physical discharge it lowers the tension within the human system and reduces the likelihood of a spontaneous discharge of emotions through outer- or inner-directed violence.

But the expression of emotions is not an end in itself; in this context it is a means to an end. Stifling the emotions connected with feelings of hurt and pain acts as a sort of glue that allows the original repression to remain. Emotional discharge, in a situation of support and encouragement, helps unglue the ego structures that require us to operate in patterned, phobic, oppressive, and surplus-aggressive forms. In a sense it loosens up the repressive structures and allows us fresh insight into ourselves and our past. But if this emotional discharge happens in isolation or against an unwitting victim, it only reinforces the feelings of being powerless, out of control, or a person who must obsessively control others. Only in situations that contradict these feelings—that is, with the support, affection, encouragement, and backing of other men who experience similar feelings—does the basis for change exist.[47]

The encouragement of emotional discharge and open dialogue among men also enhances the safety we begin to feel among each other and in turn helps us to tackle obsessive, even if unconscious, fear of other men. This unconscious fear and lack of safety are the experience of most heterosexual men throughout their lives. The pattern for homosexual men differs, but growing up and living in a heterosexist, patriarchal culture implants similar fears, even if one's adult reality is different.

Receiving emotional support and attention from a group of men is a major contradiction to experiences of distance, caution, fear, and neglect from other men. This contradiction is the mechanism that allows further discharge, emotional change, and more safety. Safety among even a small group of our brothers gives us greater safety and strength among men as a whole. This gives us the confidence and sense of personal power to confront sexism and homophobia in all its various manifestations. In a sense, this allows us each to be a model of a strong, powerful man who does not need to operate in an oppressive and violent fashion in relation to women, to other men, or to himself. And that, I hope, will play some small part in the challenge to the oppressive reality of patriarchal, authoritarian, class societies. It will be changes in our own lives inseparably intertwined with changes in society as a whole that will sever the links in the triad of men's violence.

Notes

My thanks to those who have given me comments on earlier drafts of this paper, in particular my father, Nathan Kaufman, and to Gad Horowitz. As well I extend my appreciation to the men I have worked with in various counselling situations who have helped me develop insights into the individual acquisition of violence and masculinity.

1. Herbert Marcuse, *Eros and Civilization* (Boston: Beacon Press, 1975; New York: Vintage, 1962); Gad Horowitz, *Repression* (Toronto: University of Toronto Press, 1977).

2. Part of Freud's wisdom was to recognize that, although the engendered psychology of the individual was the product of the maturation of the individual within an evolving social environment, the body was in the last analysis the subject and the object of our desires.

3. Michele Barrett and Mary McIntosh, *The Anti-Social Family* (London: Verso/New Left Books, 1982). 107.

4. Susan Brownmiller, *Against Our Will: Men, Women and Rape* (New York: Bantam Books, 1976), 6.

5. Alice Echols, "The New Feminism of Yin and Yang" in Ann Snitow *et al.*, eds., *Powers of Desire* (New York: Monthly Review Press, 1983) 439–59, and Alice Echols, "The Taming of the Id: Feminist Sexual Politics, 1968–83," in Carol Vance, ed., *Pleasure and Danger* (London: Routledge and Kegan Paul, 1984), 50–72. The two articles are essentially the same.

6. Aimé Césaire, *Discourse on Colonialism* (New York: Monthly Review Press, 1972), 21–2, first published in 1955 by Éditions Présence Africaine.

7. C. Tunnard, *The City of Man* (New York: Scribner, 1953), 43. Quoted in N. O. Brown, *Life Against Death* (Middletown: Wesleyan University Press, 1959), 283.

8. This is the approach, for example, of Suzanne Steinmetz. She says that macrolevel social and economic conditions (such as poverty, unemployment, inadequate housing, and the glorification and acceptance of violence) lead to high crime rates and a tolerance of violence that in turn leads to family aggression. See her *Cycle of Violence* (New York: Praeger, 1977), 30.

9. Juliet Mitchell, *Psychoanalysis and Feminism* (New York: Vintage, 1975), 362.

10. Joseph Conrad, *Lord Jim* (New York: Bantam Books, 1981), 146; first published 1900.

11. See for example Michele Barrett's thought-provoking book, *Women's Oppression Today* (London: Verso/New Left Books, 1980), 10–19, 250–1.

12. Jessica Benjamin, "Authority and the Family Revisited: or, A World Without Fathers?", *New German Critique* (Winter 1978), 35.

13. See *ibid.*, 40, for a short discussion of Adorno's and Horkheimer's *Dialectic of Enlightenment*.

14. Mary O'Brien, *The Politics of Reproduction* (London: Routledge and Kegan Paul, 1981), 54–5.

15. Simone de Beauvoir, *The Second Sex* (New York: Vintage, 1974), 162; first published 1949. Dorothy Dinnerstein pursues a similar line of argument but, in line with the thesis of her book, points to mother-raised-children as the source of these ambivalent feelings toward women. See Dinnerstein, *op. cit.*, especially, 109–10.

16. Sidney Jourard, "Some Lethal Aspects of the Male Role" in Joseph H. Pleck and Jack Sawyer, eds., *Men and Masculinity* (Englewood Cliffs: Prentice-Hall, 1974), 21–9.

17. Bertolt Brecht, *Threepenny Novel*, trans. Desmond I. Vesey (Harmondsworth: Penguin, 1965), 282.

18. Marcuse, *op. cit.*, and Horowitz, *op. cit.*

19. Barrett and MacIntosh, *op. cit.*, p. 29.

20. This is true not only because each socioeconomic system appears to create corresponding family forms, but because in turn, that family structure plays a large role in shaping the society's ideology. In Barrett's and McIntosh's words, in our society a family perspective and family ideology have an "utterly hegemonic status" within society as a whole. And there is a dialectical interaction between family form and the organization of production and paid work (*ibid.*, 78, 130).

21. De Beauvoir, *op. cit.*, *passim*.

22. Sigmund Freud, *Civilization and Its Discontents* (New York: W. W. Norton, 1962), 70, 72.

23. Gayle Rubin, "The Traffic in Women: Notes on the 'Political Economy' of Sex" in Rayna R. Reiter, ed., *Toward an Anthropology of Women* (New York: Monthly Review Press, 1975), 157–210.

24. Ken Kesey, *Sometimes a Great Notion* (New York: Bantam, 1965), 115. (One is eerily reminded of St. Augustine's statement, "Every breath I draw in is a sin." Quoted in Horowitz, *op. cit.*, 211.)

25. De Beauvoir, *op. cit.*, 367.

26. Paul Willis, *Learning to Labor* (New York: Columbia University Press, 1981), 150. And see Stan Gray, "Sharing the Shop Floor," in M. Kaufman, ed., *Beyond Patriarchy* (Toronto: Oxford University Press, 1987).

27. Andrew Tolson, *The Limits of Masculinity* (London: Tavistock, 1977), 25.

28. Simone de Beauvoir, in the *Nouvel Observateur*, Mar. 1, 1976. Quoted in Diana E. H. Russell and Nicole Van de Ven, eds., *Crimes Against Women* (Millbrae, Calif.: Les Femmes, 1976), xiv.

29. Among the sources on male violence that are useful, even if sometimes problematic, see Lenore E. Walker, *The Battered Woman* (New York: Harper Colophon, 1980); Russell and Van de Ven *op. cit.*; Judith Lewis Herman, *Father-Daughter Incest* (Cambridge, Mass.: Harvard University Press, 1981); Suzanne K. Steinmetz, *The Cycle of Violence* (New York: Praeger, 1977), Sylvia Levine and Joseph Koenig, *Why Men Rape* (Toronto: Macmillan, 1980); Susan Brownmiller, *op. cit.*, and Connie Guberman and Margie Wolfe, eds., *No Safe Place* (Toronto: Women's Press, 1985).

30. Levine and Koenig, *op. cit.*, pp. 28, 42, 56, 72.

31. Meg Luxton, *More Than a Labour of Love* (Toronto: Women's Press, 1980), 66.

32. Margaret M. Killoran, "The Sound of Silence Breaking: Toward a Metatheory of Wife Abuse" (M.A. thesis, McMaster University, 1981), 148.

33. Barrett and MacIntosh, *op. cit.*, 23.

34. Of course, household violence is not monopolized by men. In the United States roughly the same number of domestic homicides are committed by each sex. In 1975, 8.0% of homicides were committed by husbands against wives and 7.8% by wives against husbands. These figures, however, do not indicate the chain of violence, that is, the fact that most of these women were reacting to battering by their husbands. (See Steinmetz, *op. cit.*, p. 90.) Similarly, verbal and physical abuse of children appears to be committed by men and women equally. Only in the case of incest is there a near monopoly by men. Estimates vary greatly, but between one-fifth and one-third of all girls experience some sort of sexual contact with an adult male, in most cases with a father, stepfather, other relative, or teacher. (See Herman, *op. cit.*, 12 and *passim.*)

35. Luxton, *op. cit.*, p. 65.

36. This was pointed out by I. F. Stone in a 1972 article on the Vietnam war. At a briefing about the U.S. escalation of bombing in the North, the Pentagon official described U.S. strategy as two boys fighting: "If one boy gets the other in an arm lock, he can probably get his adversary to say 'uncle' if he increases the pressure in sharp, painful jolts and gives every indication of willingness to break the boy's arm" ("Machismo in Washington," reprinted in Pleck and Sawyer, *op. cit.*, 131). Although women are also among the victims of war, I include war in the category of violence against men because I am here referring to the casualty of war.

37. This is true both of masculinity as an institution and masculinity for the individual. Gay men keep certain parts of the self-oppressive masculine norm intact simply because they have grown up and live in a predominantly heterosexual, male-dominated society.

38. Horowitz, *op. cit.*, 99.

39. This formulation was first suggested to me by Charlie Kreiner at a men's counselling workshop in 1982.

40. D. H. Lawrence, *Women in Love* (Harmondsworth: Penguin, 1960), 304–5; first published 1921.

41. Fenichel, *op. cit.*, 212.

42. Emmanuel Reynaud, *Holy Virility*, translated by Ros Schwartz (London: Pluto Press, 1983), 41–2.

43. Gabriel Garcia Marquez, *Autumn of the Patriarch*, trans. Gregory Rabassa (Harmondsworth: Penguin, 1972), III: first published 1967.

44. Barrett, *op. cit.*, pp. 254–5. Willis follows a similar line of thought in his discussion of the development of the male working class. He says that patriarchy "helps to provide the real human and cultural conditions which . . . actually allow subordinate roles to be taken on 'freely' within liberal democracy" (Willis, *op. cit.*, 151). But then in turn, this reinforces the impediments to change by the maintenance of a division within the working class. As an article in the early 1970s in *Shrew* pointed out, "the tendency of male workers to think of themselves as men (i.e., powerful) rather than as workers (i.e., members of an oppressed group), promotes a false sense of privilege and power, and an identification with the world of men including the boss," Kathy McAfee and Myrna Wood, "Bread and Roses," quoted by Sheila Rowbotham, *Woman's Consciousness, Men's World* (Harmondsworth: Penguin, 1973).

45. For a discussion of non-surplus-repressive societies, particularly in the sense of being complementary with Marx's notion of communism, see Horowitz, *op. cit.*, particularly chapter 7, and also Marcuse, *op. cit.*, especially chaps. 7, 10, and 11.

46. Rowbotham, *op. cit.*, 36.

47. As is apparent, although I have adopted a Freudian analysis of the unconscious and the mechanisms of repression, these observations on the therapeutic process—especially the importance of a supportive counselling environment, peer-counselling relations, emotional discharge, and the concept of contradiction—are those developed by forms of co-counselling, in

particular. Reevaluation Counselling. But unlike the latter, I do not suppose that any of us can discharge all of our hurt, grief, and anger and uncover an essential self simply because our "self" is created through that process of frustration, hurt, and repression. Rather I feel that some reforming of the ego can take place that allows us to integrate more fully a range of needs and desires, which in turn reduces forms of behavior that are oppressive to others and destructive to ourselves. Furthermore, by giving us greater consciousness of our feelings and the means of discharge, and by freeing dammed-up sources of energy, these changes allow us to act more successfully to change the world.

3

The Socio-Cultural Context of Rape: A Cross-Cultural Study

PEGGY REEVES SANDAY

In her comprehensive and important analysis of rape, Susan Brownmiller says that "when men discovered that they could rape, they proceeded to do it" and that "from prehistoric times to the present rape has played a critical function" (1975, 14–15). The critical function to which Brownmiller refers has been "to keep all women in a constant state of intimidation, forever conscious of the knowledge that the biological tool must be held in awe for it may turn to weapon with sudden swiftness borne of harmful intent" (1975, 209).

Brownmiller's attribution of violence to males and victimization to females strums a common theme in Western social commentary on the nature of human nature. Most of the popularizers of this theme present what amounts to a socio-biological view of human behavior which traces war, violence, and now rape to the violent landscape of our primitive ancestors, where, early on, the male tendency in these directions became genetically programmed in the fight for survival of the fittest. Human (viz. male) nature is conceived as an ever present struggle to overcome baser impulses bequeathed by "apish" ancestors. (For examples of this general theme, see Ardrey 1966; Lorenz 1966; Tiger 1969.)

The research described in the present paper departs from the familiar assumption that male nature is programmed for rape, and begins with another familiar, albeit less popular, assumption that human sexual behavior, though based in a biological need "is rather a sociological and cultural force than a mere bodily relation of two individuals" (Malinowski 1929, xxiii). With this assumption in mind, what follows is an examination of the socio-cultural context of sexual assault and an attempt to interpret its meaning. By understanding the meaning of rape, we can then make conjectures as to its function. Is it, as Susan Brownmiller suggests, an act that keeps all women in a constant state of intimidation, or is it an act that illuminates a larger social scenario?

This paper examines the incidence, meaning, and function of rape in tribal societies. Two general hypotheses guided the research: first, the incidence of rape varies cross-culturally; second, a high incidence of rape is embedded in a distinguishably different

From the *Society for the Psychological Study of Social Issues, Journal of Social Issues* 37 (1981): 5–27 (edited). Reprinted by permission. Tables deleted in this volume can be found in the original.

cultural configuration than a low incidence of rape. Using a standard cross-cultural sample of 156 tribal societies, the general objectives of the paper are:

1. to provide a descriptive profile of 'rape prone' and 'rape free' societies;
2. to present an analysis of the attitudes, motivations, and socio-cultural factors related to the incidence of rape.

Description of the Evidence

In most societies for which information on rape was available, rape is an act in which a male or a group of males sexually assaulted a woman. In a few cases, descriptions of women sexually assaulting a male or homosexual rape are reported. This study, however, was oriented exclusively to the analysis of rape committed by males against women.

The standard cross-cultural sample published by Murdock and White (1969) formed the basis for this research. This sample offers to scholars a representative sample of the world's known and well-described societies. The complete sample consists of 186 societies, each 'pinpointed' to an identifiable sub-group of the society in question at a specific point in time. The time period for the sample societies ranges from 1750 B.C. (Babylonians) to the late 1960s. The societies included in the standard sample are distributed relatively equally among the following six major regions of the world: Sub-Saharan Africa, Circum-Mediterranean, East Eurasia, Insular Pacific, North America, South and Central America.

This analysis of rape was part of a larger study on the origins of sexual inequality (see Sanday 1981a). Due to the amount of missing information on the variables included in this larger study, thirty of the standard sample societies were excluded, reducing the final sample size to 156. Since many of the variables included in the larger study were pertinent to the analysis of the socio-cultural context of rape, the same sample was employed here.

The information for coding the variables came from codes published in the journal *Ethnology;* library materials; and the Human Relations Area Files. The data obtained from the latter two sources were coded by graduate students in anthropology at the University of Pennsylvania using codes developed by me on one-third of the standard sample societies. When the coding was completed, a random sample of societies was selected for checking. The percentage of items on which coders and checkers agreed averaged 88 percent of the 21 variables checked for each society. Disagreements were resolved either by myself or still another coder after rechecking the material.

There was a significant discrepancy between the number of societies for which information was obtained on rape for this study and that obtained by other authors employing the same sample. Broude and Greene (1976) were able to find information on the frequency of rape in only 34 of the standard sample societies, whereas for this study information was obtained for 95 of these societies. This discrepancy raises questions about the operational definitions of rape employed in the coding.

Although the codes used in the two studies were similar, my definition of "rape prone" included cases in which men rape enemy women, rape is a ceremonial act, and rape may be more a threat used by men to control women in certain ways than an actuality. Broude and Greene appear to have excluded such incidents from their coding and to have focused only on the intra-societal incidence of uncontrolled rape. The

TABLE 1. COMPARISON OF TWO CODES FOR RAPE

Society No.[a]	Society Name	Sanday Code[b]		Broude & Greene Code[b]
		Rape Code	Type of Rape[c]	
11	Kikuyu	3	Ceremonial rape	No information
19	Ashanti	1	Rape is rare or absent	No information
13	Mbuti	1	Rape is rare or absent	Agrees with Sanday Code
14	Mongo	1	Rape is rare or absent	Agrees with Sanday Code
28	Azande	3	Rape of enemy women Rape cases reported	Disagrees (Rape rare)
41	Tuareg	1	Rape is rare or absent	No information
60	Gond	1	Rape is rare or absent	No information
66	Mongols	1	Rape is rare or absent	No information
70	Lakher	1	Rape is rare or absent	Agrees with Sanday Code
91	Arunta	3	Ceremonial rape	No information
108	Marshallese	3	Gang rape is accepted	Agrees with Sanday Code
127	Saulteaux	3	Rape used as threat	No information
143	Omaha	3	Rape used as punishment	Disagrees (Rape absent)
158	Cuna	1	Rape is rare or absent	Agrees with Sanday Code
163	Yanomamo	3	Rape of enemy women	Agrees with Sanday Code
166	Mundurucu	3	Rape used as punishment	Agrees with Sanday Code
169	Jivaro	1	Rape is rare or absent	No information
179	Shavante	3	Rape used as punishment	No information

[a] Refers to standard sample number listed by Murdock and White (1969).
[b] See Table 2 for the two rape codes.
[c] For each of the societies listed, the ethnographic descriptions of the incidence of rape are presented later in this paper.

differences in these operational definitions are apparent from the information presented in Table 1.

A sub-sample of societies are listed in Table 1 along with the codes used in this study and the code given by Broude and Greene (1976). Broude and Greene report no information in nine societies where information on the incidence of rape was recorded in this study. The two codes agree in seven out of the remaining nine and disagree in two cases. Broude and Greene report that among the Azande rape is a rare occurrence while in this study the Azande were classified as rape prone due to the practice of raiding for wives. Broude and Greene report that rape is absent among the Omaha, whereas I found evidence from several sources that rape is present. The ethnographic descriptions which led to my rape codes for the eighteen societies listed in Table 1 can be found in the following sections profiling 'rape prone' and 'rape free' societies.

Broude and Greene (1976) find that rape is absent or rare in 59 percent of the 34 societies for which they found information on the frequency of rape (see Table 2). They say that rape is "common, not atypical" in the remaining 41 percent. In this study, forty-seven percent of the societies were classified as 'rape free'; 35 percent were classified in an intermediate category; and 18 percent were classified as 'rape prone' (see Table 2). Thus both studies support the first general hypothesis of this study: sexual assault is *not* a universal characteristic of tribal societies. The incidence of rape varies cross-culturally.

TABLE 2. CROSS-CULTURAL INCIDENCE OF RAPE

Sanday Code	No. and % of Societies		Broude & Greene (1976:417) Code	No. and % of Societies	
Incidence of Rape (RA4)—	N	%	Frequency of Rape	N	%
1. *Rape Free.* Rape is reported as rare or absent.	45	47%	1. Absent	8	24%
2. Rape is reported as present, no report of frequency, or suggestion that rape is not atypical.	33	35%	2. Rare: isolated cases	12	35%
3. Rape Prone. Rape is accepted practice used to punish women, as part of a ceremony, or is *clearly* an act of moderate to high frequency carried out against own women or women of other societies.	17	18%	3. Common: not atypical	14	41%
Total	95	100%		34	100%

Profiles of 'Rape Prone' Societies

In this study a 'rape prone' society was defined as one in which the incidence of rape is high, rape is a ceremonial act, or rape is an act by which men punish or threaten women.

An example of a 'rape prone' society is offered by Robert LeVine's (1959) description of sexual offenses among the Gusii of southwestern Kenya. In the European legal system which administers justice in the District where the Gusii live, a heterosexual assault is classified as rape when a medical examination indicates that the hymen of the alleged victim was recently penetrated by the use of painful force. When medical evidence is unobtainable, the case is classified as "indecent assault." Most cases are of the latter kind. The Gusii do not distinguish between rape and indecent assault. They use the following expressions to refer to heterosexual assault: "to fight" (a girl or woman); "to stamp on" (a girl or woman); "to spoil" (a girl or woman); "to engage in illicit intercourse." All of these acts are considered illicit by the Gusii. LeVine uses the term rape "to mean the culturally disvalued use of coercion by a male to achieve the submission of a female to sexual intercourse" (1959, 965).

Based on court records for 1955 and 1956 LeVine estimates that the annual rate of rape is 47.2 per 100,000 population. LeVine believes that this figure grossly underestimates the Gusii rape rate. During the same period the annual rape rate in urban areas of the United States was 13.85 per 100,000 (13.1 for rural areas). Thus, the rate of Gusii rape is extraordinarily high.

Normal heterosexual intercourse between Gusii males and females is conceived as an act in which a man overcomes the resistance of a woman and causes her pain. When a bride is unable to walk after her wedding night, the groom is considered by his friends "a real man" and he is able to boast of his exploits, particularly if he has been able to make her cry. Older women contribute to the groom's desire to hurt his new wife. These women insult the groom, saying:

"You are not strong, you can't do anything to our daughter. When you slept with her you didn't do it like a man. You have a small penis which can do nothing. You should grab our daughter and she should be hurt and scream—then you're a man" (LeVine 1959, 969).

The groom answers boastfully:

"I am a man! If you were to see my penis you would run away. When I grabbed her she screamed. I am not a man to be joked with. Didn't she tell you? She cried—ask her!" (LeVine 1959, 969).

Thus, as LeVine says (1959, 971), "legitimate heterosexual encounters among the Gusii are aggressive contests, involving force and pain-inflicting behavior." Under circumstances that are not legitimate, heterosexual encounters are classified as rape when the girl chooses to report the act.

LeVine estimates that the typical Gusii rape is committed by an unmarried young man on an unmarried female of a different clan. He distinguishes between three types of rape: rape resulting from seduction, premeditated sexual assault, and abduction (1959).

Given the hostile nature of Gusii sexuality, seduction classifies as rape when a Gusii female chooses to bring the act to the attention of the public. Premarital sex is forbidden, but this does not stop Gusii boys from trying to entice girls to intercourse. The standard pose of the Gusii girl is reluctance, which means that it is difficult for the boy to interpret her attitude as being either willing or unwilling. Misunderstandings between girl and boy can be due to the eagerness of the boy and his inability to perceive the girl's cues of genuine rejection, or to the girl's failure to make the signs of refusal in unequivocal fashion. The boy may discover the girl's unwillingness only after he has forced himself on her.

Fear of discovery may turn a willing girl into one who cries rape. If a couple engaging in intercourse out of doors is discovered, the girl may decide to save her reputation by crying out that she was being raped. Rape may also occur in cases when a girl has encouraged a young man to present her with gifts, but then denies him sexual intercourse. If the girl happens to be married, she rejects the boy's advances because she is afraid of supernatural sanctions against adultery. Out of frustration, the boy (who may not know that the girl is married) may resort to rape and she reports the deed.

In some cases one or more boys may attack a single girl in premeditated sexual assault. The boys may beat the girl badly and tear her clothing. Sometimes the girl is dragged off to the hut of one of them and forced into coitus. After being held for a couple of days the girl is freed. In these cases rupture of the hymen and other signs of attack are usually present.

The third type of rape occurs in the context of wife abduction. When a Gusii man is unable to present the bridewealth necessary for a normal marriage and cannot persuade a girl to elope, he may abduct a girl from a different clan. The man's friends will be enlisted to carry out the abduction. The young men are frequently rough on the girl, beating her and tearing her clothes. When she arrives at the home of the would-be lover, he attempts to persuade her to remain with him until bridewealth can be raised. Her refusal is ignored and the wedding night sexual contest is performed with the clansmen helping in overcoming her resistance.

Of these three types of rape, the first and third are unlawful versions of legitimate patterns. Seduction is accepted when kept within the bounds of discretion. Abduction is an imitation of traditional wedding procedures. Abduction lacks only the legitimizing bridewealth and the consent of the bride and her parents. In both of these cases LeVine says, "there is a close parallel between the criminal act and the law-abiding culture pattern to which it is related." Seduction and abduction classify as rape when the girl chooses to report the incident.

Data collected from the standard cross-cultural sample allows us to place the hostility characterizing Gusii heterosexual behavior in cross-cultural perspective. Broude and Greene (1976), who published codes for twenty sexual practices, find that male sexual advances are occasionally or typically hostile in one-quarter (26%) of the societies for which information was available. They found that males were typically forward in verbal (not physical) sexual overtures in forty percent of the societies, that females solicited or desired physical aggression in male sexual overtures in eleven percent of the societies, and that males did not make sexual overtures or were diffident or shy in twenty-three percent of the societies.

Examination of a variety of 'rape prone' societies shows that the Gusii pattern of rape is found elsewhere but that it is by no means the only pattern which can be observed. For example, in several societies the act of rape occurs to signal readiness for marriage and is a ceremonial act. Since this act signifies male domination of female genitals, its occurrence was treated as a diagnostic criterion for classification as 'rape prone.'

Among the Kikuyu of East Africa it is reported that in former times, as part of initiation, every boy was expected to perform the act of ceremonial rape called *Kuihaka muunya* (to smear oneself with salt earth) in order to prove his manhood. It was thought that until a boy had performed the act of rape he could not have lawful intercourse with a Kikuyu woman and hence could not marry. During the initiation period boys would wander the countryside in bands of up to 100 in number. The object of each band was to find a woman on whom to commit the rape. The ideal woman was one from an enemy tribe who was married. In practice it appears that the ceremonial rape consisted of nothing more than masturbatory ejaculation on the woman's body or in her presence. Immediately after the act the boy was able to throw away the paraphernalia which marked him with the status of neophite (Lambert 1956).

Rape marks a girl as marriageable among the Arunta of Australia. At age 14 or 15 the Arunta girl is taken out into the bush by a group of men for the vulva cutting ceremony. A designated man cuts the girl's vulva after which she is gang raped by a group of men which does not include her future husband. When the ceremony is concluded the girl is taken to her husband and from then on no one else has the right of access to her. (Spencer and Gillen 1927).

In other rape prone societies, rape is explicitly linked to the control of women and to male dominance. Among the Northern Saulteaux the assumption of male dominance is clearly expressed in the expectation that a man's potential sexual rights over the woman he chooses must be respected. A woman who turns a man down too abruptly insults him and invites aggression. There is a Northern Saulteaux tale about a girl who was considered too proud because she refused to marry. Accordingly, a group of medicine men lured her out into the bush where she was raped by each in turn (Hallowell 1955). Such tales provide women with a fairly good idea of how they should behave in relation to men.

The attitude that women are "open" for sexual assault is frequently found in the societies of the Insular Pacific. For example, in the Marshall Islands one finds the belief that "every woman is like a passage." Just as every canoe is permitted to sail from the open sea into the lagoon through the passage, so every man is permitted to have intercourse with every woman (except those who are excluded on account of blood kinship). A trader, well acquainted with the language and customs of one group of Marshall Islanders, reported the following incident. One day while standing at the trading post he saw 20 young men enter the bushes, one after another. Following the same path, he discovered a young girl stretched out on the ground, rigid and unconscious. When he accused the young men of cruel treatment they replied: "It is customary here for every young man to have intercourse with every girl" (Erdland 1914, 98–99).

In tropical forest societies of South America and in Highland New Guinea it is fairly frequent to find the threat of rape used to keep women from the men's houses or from viewing male sacred objects. For example, Shavante women were strictly forbidden to observe male sacred ceremonies. Women caught peeking are threatened with man handling, rape, and disfigurement (Maybury-Lewis, 1967).

Perhaps the best known example of rape used to keep women away from male ritual objects if found in the description of the Mundurucu, a society well known to anthropologists due to the work of Robert and Yolanda Murphy. The Mundurucu believe that there was a time when women ruled and sex roles were reversed with the exception that women could not hunt. During that time, it is said, women were the sexual aggressors and men were sexually submissive and did women's work. Women controlled the "sacred trumpets" (the symbols of power) and the men's houses. The trumpets are believed to contain the spirits of the ancestors who demand ritual offering of meat. Since women did not hunt and could not make these offerings, men were able to take the trumpets from them, thereby establishing male dominance. The trumpets are secured in special chambers within the men's houses and no woman can see them under penalty of gang rape. Such a threat is necessary because men believe that women will attempt to seize from the men the power they once had. Gang rape is also the means by which men punish sexually "wanton" women (Murphy and Murphy 1974).

Another expression of male sexual aggressiveness, which is classified as rape in this study, is the practice of sexually assaulting enemy women during warfare. The Yanomamo, described by Napoleon Chagnon and Marvin Harris, are infamous for their brutality toward women. The Yanomamo, according to Harris (1977), "practice an especially brutal form of male supremacy involving polygyny, frequent wife beating, and gang rape of captured enemy women." The Yanomamo, Harris says, "regard fights over women as the primary causes of their wars" (1977, 69). Groups raid each other for wives in an area where marriageable women are in short supply due to the practice of female infanticide. The number of marriageable women is also affected by the desire on the part of successful warriors to have several wives to mark their superior status as "fierce men." A shortage of women for wives also motivates Azande (Africa) warfare. Enemy women were taken by Azande soldiers as wives. Evans-Pritchard calls these women "slaves of war" and says that they were "not regarded very differently from ordinary wives, their main disability being that they had no family or close kin to turn to in times of trouble" (1971, 251). The absence of close kin, of course, made these women more subservient and dependent on their husbands.

Another source on the Azande discusses how the act of rape when committed against an Azande woman is treated. If the woman is not married, this source reports, the act is not treated as seriously. If the woman is married, the rapist can be put to death by the husband. If the rapist is allowed to live, he may be judged guilty of adultery and asked to pay the chief 20 knives (the commonly used currency in marriage exchanges) and deliver a wife to the wronged husband. This source indicates that the rape of a woman is not permitted but the punishments are established, suggesting that rape is a frequent occurrence (Lagae 1926).

Among some American Indian buffalo hunters, it is not uncommon to read that rape is used as a means to punish adultery. There is a practice among the Cheyenne of the Great Plains known as "to put a woman on the prairie." This means that the outraged husband of an adulterous woman invites all the unmarried members of his military society to feast on the prairie where they each rape the woman (Hoebel 1960). Among the Omaha, a woman with no immediate kin who commits adultery may be gang raped and abandoned by her husband (Dorsey 1884). Mead reports that the Omaha considered a "bad woman" fair game for any man. No discipline, no set of standards, other than to be cautious of an avenging father or brother and to observe the rule of exogamy, Mead says, kept young men from regarding rape as a great adventure. Young Omaha men, members of the Antler society, would prey upon divorced women or women considered loose (Mead 1932).

Summarizing, a rape prone society, as defined here, is one in which sexual assault by men of women is either culturally allowable or, largely overlooked. Several themes interlink the above descriptions. In all, men are posed as a social group against women. Entry into the adult male or female group is marked in some cases by rituals that include rape. In other cases, rape preserves the ceremonial integrity of the male group and signifies its status vis-à-vis women. The theme of women as property is suggested when the aggrieved husband is compensated for the rape of his wife by another man, or when an adulterous woman is gang raped by her husband and his unmarried compatriots. In these latter cases, the theme of the dominant male group is joined with a system of economic exchange in which men act as exchange agents and women comprise the medium of exchange. This is not to say that rape exists in all societies in which there is ceremonial induction into manhood, male secret societies, or compensation for adultery. For further illumination of the socio-cultural context of rape we can turn to an examination of rape free societies.

Profiles of 'Rape Free' Societies

Rape free societies are defined as those where the act of rape is either infrequent or does not occur. Forty-seven percent of the societies for which information on the incidence or presence of rape was available (see Table 2) were classified in the rape free category. Societies were classified in this category on the basis of the following kinds of statements found in the sources used for the sample societies.

Among the Taureg of the Sahara, for example, it is said that "rape does not exist, and when a woman refuses a man, he never insists nor will he show himself jealous of a more successful comrade" (Blanguernon 1955, 134). Among the Pygmies of the Ituri forest in Africa, while a boy may rip off a girl's outer bark cloth, if he can catch her, he may never have intercourse with her without her permission. Turnbull (1965), an anthropologist who lived for some time among the Pygmies and became closely identified with them, reports that he knew of no cases of rape. Among the Jivaro of South America rape is not recognized as such, and informants could recall no case of a woman violently resisting sexual intercourse. They say that a man would never commit such an act if the woman resisted, because she would tell her family and they would punish him. Among the Nkundo Mongo of Africa it is said that rape in the true sense of the word—that is, the abuse of a woman by the use of violence—is most unusual. If a woman does not consent, the angry seducer leaves her, often insulting her to the best of his ability. Rape is also unheard of among the Lakhers, and in several villages the anthropologist was told that there had never been a case of rape.

Other examples of statements leading to the classification of rape free are listed as follows:

> Cuna (South America), "Homosexuality is rare, as is rape. Both . . . are regarded as sins, punishable by God" (Stout 1947, 39).

> Khalka Mongols (Outer Mongolia), "I put this question to several well-informed Mongols: —what punishment is here imposed for rape? . . . one well-educated lama said frankly: "We have no crimes of this nature here. Our women never resist" (Maiskii 1921, 98).

> Gond (India), "It is considered very wrong to force a girl to act against her will. Such cases of ghotul-rape are not common . . . If then a boy forces a girl against her will, and the others hear of it, he is fined" (Elwin 1947, 656).

The above quotes may obscure the actual incidence of rape. Such quotes, leading to the classification of societies as 'rape free', achieve greater validity when placed within the context of other information describing heterosexual interaction.

There is considerable difference in the character of heterosexual interaction in societies classified as 'rape prone' when compared with those classified as 'rape free'. In 'rape free' societies women are treated with considerable respect, and prestige is attached to female reproductive and productive roles. Interpersonal violence is minimized, and a people's attitude regarding the natural environment is one of reverence rather than one of exploitation. Turnbull's description of the Mbuti Pygmies, of the Ituri forest in Africa, provides a prototypical profile of a 'rape free' society (1965).

Violence between the sexes, or between anybody, is virtually absent among the net hunting Mbuti Pygmies when they are in their forest environment. The Mbuti attitude toward the forest is reflective of their attitude toward each other. The forest is addressed as "father," "mother," "lover," and "friend." The Mbuti say that forest is everything—the provider of food, shelter, warmth, clothing, and affection. Each person and animal is endowed with some spiritual power which "derives from a single source whose physical manifestation is the forest itself." The ease of the Mbuti relationship to their environment is reflected in the relationship between the sexes. There is little division of labor by sex. The hunt is frequently a joint effort. A man is not ashamed to pick mushrooms and nuts if he finds them, or to wash and clean a baby. In general, leadership is minimal and there is no attempt to control, or to dominate, either the geographical or human environment. Decision-making is by common consent; men and women have equal say because hunting and gathering are both important to the economy. The forest is the only recognized authority of last resort. In decision making, diversity of opinion may be expressed, but prolonged disagreement is considered to be "noise" and offensive to the forest. If husband and wife disagree, the whole camp may act to mute their antagonism, lest the disagreement become too disruptive to the social unit (see Turnbull 1965).

The essential details of Turnbull's idyllic description of the Mbuti are repeated in other 'rape free' societies. The one outstanding feature of these societies is the ceremonial importance of women and the respect accorded the contribution women make to social continuity, a respect which places men and women in relatively balanced power spheres. This respect is clearly present among the Mbuti and in more complex 'rape free' societies.

In the West African kingdom of Ashanti, for example, it is believed that only women can contribute to future generations. Ashanti women say:

> I am the mother of the man. . . . I alone can transmit the blood to a king. . . . If my sex die in the clan then that very clan becomes extinct, for be there one, or one thousand male members left, not one can transmit the blood, and the life of the clan becomes measured on this earth by the span of a man's life (Rattray 1923, 79).

The importance of the feminine attributes of growth and reproduction are found in Ashanti religion and ritual. Priestesses participate with priests in all major rituals. The Ashanti creation story emphasizes the complementarity and inseparability of male and female. The main female deity, the Earth Goddess, is believed to be the receptacle of past and future generations as well as the source of food and water (Rattray 1923, 1927). The sacred linkage of earth-female-blood makes the act of rape incongruous in Ashanti culture. Only one incident of rape is reported by the main ethnographer of the Ashanti. In this case the man involved was condemned to death (Rattray 1927, 211).

In sum, rape free societies are characterized by sexual equality and the notion that the sexes are complementary. Though the sexes may not perform the same duties or have the same rights or privileges, each is indispensable to the activities of the other (see Sanday 1981a for examples of sexual equality). The key to understanding the relative absence of rape in rape free as opposed to rape prone societies is the importance, which in some cases is sacred, attached to the contribution women make to social continuity. As might be expected, and as will be demonstrated below, interpersonal violence is uncommon in rape free societies. It is not that men are necessarily prone to rape; rather, where interpersonal violence is a way of life, violence frequently achieves sexual expression.

Approaches to the Etiology of Rape

Three general approaches characterize studies of the etiology of rape. One approach focuses on the broader sociocultural milieu, another turns to individual characteristics. The first looks at how rapists act out the broader social script, the second emphasizes variables like the character of parent-child interaction. A third approach, which may focus on either individual or social factors, is distinguishable by the assumption that male sexual repression will inevitably erupt in the form of sexual violence. These approaches, reviewed briefly in this section, guided the empirical analysis of the socio-cultural context of rape in tribal societies.

Based on his study of the Gusii, LeVine (1959) hypothesizes that four factors will be associated with the incidence of rape cross-culturally:

1. severe formal restrictions on the nonmarital sexual relations of females;
2. moderately strong sexual inhibitions on the part of females;
3. economic or other barriers to marriage that prolong the bachelorhood of some males into their late twenties;
4. the absence of physical segregation of the sexes.

The implicit assumption here is that males who are denied sexual access to women, will obtain access by force unless men are separated from women. Such an assumption depicts men as creatures who cannot control their sexual impulses, and women as the unfortunate victims.

LeVine's profile of the Gusii suggests that broader social characteristics are related to the incidence of rape. For example, there is the fact that marriage among the Gusii occurs almost always between feuding clans. The Gusii have a proverb which states "Those whom we marry are those whom we fight" (1959, 966). The close correspondence between the Gusii heterosexual relationship and intergroup hostilities suggests the hypothesis that the nature of intergroup relations is correlated with the nature of the heterosexual relationship and the incidence of rape.

The broader approach to the etiology of rape is contained in Susan Brownmiller's contention that rape is the means by which men keep women in a state of fear. This contention is certainly justified in societies where men use rape as a threat to keep women from viewing their sacred objects (the symbol of power) or rape is used to punish women. In societies like the Mudurucu, the ideology of male dominance is upheld by threatening women with rape. Just as the quality of intergroup relations among the Gusii is reflected in heterosexual relations, one could suggest that the quality of interpersonal relations is reflected in the incidence of rape. In societies where males are trained to be dominant and interpersonal relations are marked by outbreaks of violence, one can predict that females may become the victims in the playing out of the male ideology of power and control.

A broader socio-cultural approach is also found in the work of Wolfgang and Ferracuti (1967) and Amir (1971). Wolfgang and Ferracuti present the concept of the subculture of violence which is formed of those from the lower classes and the disenfranchised. The prime value is the use of physical aggression as a demonstration of masculinity and toughness. In his study of rape, Amir placed the rapist "squarely within the subculture of violence" (Brownmiller 1975, 181). Rape statistics in Philadelphia showed that in 43 percent of the cases examined, rapists operated in pairs or groups. The rapists tended to be in the 15–19 age bracket, the majority were not married, and 90 percent belonged to the lower socio-economic class and lived in inner city neighborhoods where there was also a high degree of crime against the person. In addition, 71 percent of the rapes were planned. In general, the profile presented by Amir is reminiscent of the pattern of rape found among the Kikuyu, where a band of boys belonging to a guild roamed the country side in search of a woman to gang rape as a means of proving their manhood and as a prelude to marriage. Brownmiller summarizes Amir's study with the following observations:

> Like assault, rape is an act of physical damage to another person, and like robbery it is also an act of acquiring property: the intent is to "have" the female body in the acquisitory meaning of the term. A woman is perceived by the rapist both as hated person and desired property. Hostility against her and possession of her may be simultaneous motivations, and the hatred for her is expressed in the same act that is the attempt to "take" her against her will. In one violent crime, rape is an act against person and property.

The importance of the work of Wolfgang and Ferracuti, Amir, and Brownmiller's observations lies in demonstrating that rape is linked with an overall pattern of violence and that part of this pattern includes the concept of woman as property. From the short descriptions of rape in some of the societies presented above, it is clear rape is likely to occur in what I would call, to borrow from Wolfgang, cultures of violence. Rape prone societies, as noted, are likely to include payment to the wronged husband, indicating that the concept of women as property also exists. This concept is not new to anthropology. It has been heavily stressed in the work of Levi-Strauss who perceives tribal women as objects in an elaborate exchange system between men.

The second type of approach to the understanding of rape focuses on the socialization process and psychoanalytic variables. This approach is reflected in the following quote from the conclusions of David Abrahamsen who conducted a Rorschach study on the wives of eight convicted rapists in 1954. Abrahamsen (1960, 165) says:

> The conclusions reached were that the wives of the sex offenders on the surface behaved toward men in a submissive and masochistic way but latently denied their femininity and showed an aggressive masculine orientation; they unconsciously invited sexual aggression, only to respond to it with coolness and rejection. They stimulated their husbands into attempts to prove themselves, attempts which necessarily ended in frustration and increased their husbands' own doubts about their masculinity. In doing so, the wives unknowingly continued the type of relationship the offender had had with his mother. There can be no doubt that the sexual frustration which the wives caused is one of the factors motivating rape, which might be tentatively described as a displaced attempt to force a seductive but rejecting mother into submission.

Brownmiller (1975, 179) includes this quote in her analysis of policeblotter rapists and her reaction to it is rather interesting. She rejects Abrahamsen's conclusions because they place the burden of guilt not on the rapist but on his mother and wife. The fact of the matter is that dominance cannot exist without passivity, as sadism cannot exist without masochism. What makes men sadistic and women masochistic, or men dominant and women passive, must be studied as part of an overall syndrome. Abrahamsen's conclusions certainly apply to Gusii males and females. With respect to the way in which Gusii wives invite sexual aggression from their husbands consider the following description of various aspects of Gusii nuptials:

> ... the groom in his finery returns to the bride's family where he is stopped by a crowd of women who deprecate his physical appearance. Once he is in the house of the bride's mother and a sacrifice has been performed by the marriage priest, the women begin again, accusing the groom of impotence on the wedding night and claiming that his penis is too small to be effective. ... When the reluctant bride arrives at the groom's house, the matter of first importance is the wedding night sexual performance. ... The bride is determined to put her new husband's sexual competence to the most severe test possible. She may take magical measures which are believed to result in his failure in intercourse. ... The bride usually refuses to get onto the bed: if she did not resist the groom's advances she would be thought sexually promiscuous. At this point some of the young men may forcibly disrobe her and put her on the bed. ... As he proceeds toward sexual intercourse she continues to resist and he must force her into position. Ordinarily she performs the practice known as *ogotega*, allowing him between her thighs but keeping the vaginal muscles so tense that penetration is impossible. ... Brides are said to take pride in the length of time they can hold off their mates (LeVine 1959, 967–969).

The relations between parents and children among the Gusii also fit Abrahamsen's conclusions concerning the etiology of rape. The son has a close and dependent relationship with his mother. The father is aloof from all his children, but especially his daughters. The father's main function is to punish which means that for the Gusii girl, her early connection with men is one of avoidance and fear. On the other hand, the relationship of the Gusii boy with his mother is characterized by dependence and seduction.

Studies of the etiology of rape suggest several hypotheses that can be tested cross-culturally. These hypotheses are not opposed; they are stated at different explanatory levels. One set phrases the explanation in socio-cultural terms, the other in psycho-cultural terms. Still another, only touched on above, suggests that male sexuality is inherently explosive unless it achieves heterosexual outlet. This latter assumption, implicit in LeVine's hypotheses mentioned above, also draws on the notion, most recently expressed in the work of Stoller (1979), that sexual excitement is generated by the desire, overt or hidden, to harm another. If the latter were the case, we would be led to believe that rape would exist in all societies. The argument presented here, however, suggests that rape is an enactment not of human nature, but of socio-cultural forces. Thus, the prevalence of rape should be associated with the expressions of these forces. Some of these expressions and their correlation with the incidence of rape are examined in the next section.

Socio-Cultural Correlates of Rape

Four general hypotheses are suggested by the work of LeVine, Brownmiller, Abrahamsen, Wolfgang and Amir. These hypotheses are:

1. Sexual repression is related to the incidence of rape;
2. intergroup and interpersonal violence is enacted in male sexual violence;
3. the character of parent-child relations is enacted in male sexual violence;
4. rape is an expression of a social ideology of male dominance.

These hypotheses were tested by collecting data on: variables relating to childrearing; behavior indicating sexual repression; interpersonal and intergroup violence; sexual separation; glorification of the male role and an undervaluation of the female role.

All but the first of the general hypotheses listed above were supported. There is no significant correlation between variables measuring sexual repression and the incidence of rape. Admittedly, however, sexual repression is very difficult to measure. The variables may not, in fact, be related to sexual abstinence. These variables are: length of the post-partum sex taboo (a variable which indicates how long the mother abstains from sexual intercourse after the birth of a child); attitude toward premarital sex (a variable which ranges between the disapproval and approval of premarital sex); age at marriage for males; and the number of taboos reflecting male avoidance of female sexuality.

The correlations support the hypothesis that intergroup and interpersonal violence is enacted in sexual violence against females. Raiding other groups for wives is significantly associated with the incidence of rape. The intensity of interpersonal violence in a society is also positively correlated with the incidence of rape, as is the presence of an ideology which encourages men to be tough and aggressive. Finally, when warfare is reported as being frequent or endemic (as opposed to absent or occasional) rape is more likely to be present.

The character of relations between parents and children is not strongly associated with the incidence of rape. When the character of the father-daughter relationship is primarily indifferent, aloof, cold and stern, rape is more likely to be present. The same is true when fathers are distant from the care of infants. However, there is no relationship between the nature of the mother-son tie (as measured in this study) and the incidence of rape.

There is considerable evidence supporting the notion that rape is an expression of a social ideology of male dominance. Female power and authority is lower in rape prone societies. Women do not participate in public decision making in these societies and males express contempt for women as decision makers. In addition, there is greater sexual separation in rape prone societies as indicated by the presence of structures or places where the sexes congregate in single sex groups.

The correlates of rape strongly suggest that rape is the playing out of a socio-cultural script in which the expression of personhood for males is directed by, among other things, interpersonal violence and an ideology of toughness. If we see the sexual act as the ultimate emotional expression of the self, then it comes as no surprise that male sexuality is phrased in physically aggressive terms when other expressions of self are phrased in these terms. This explanation does not rule out the importance of the relationship between parents and children, husbands and wives. Raising a violent son requires certain behavior patterns in parents, behaviors that husbands may subsequently act out as adult males. Sexual repression does not explain the correlations. Rape is not an instinct triggered by celibacy, enforced for whatever reason. Contrary to what some social scientists assume, men are not animals whose sexual behavior is programmed by instinct. Men are human beings whose sexuality is biologically based and culturally encoded.

Conclusion

Rape in tribal societies is part of a cultural configuration that includes interpersonal violence, male dominance, and sexual separation. In such societies, as the Murphys (1974, 197) say about the Mundurucu: "men ... use the penis to dominate their women." The question remains as to what motivates the rape prone cultural configuration. Considerable evidence (see Sanday 1981) suggests that this configuration evolves in societies faced with depleting food resources, migration, or other factors contributing to a dependence on male destructive capacities as opposed to female fertility.

In tribal societies women are often equated with fertility and growth, men with aggression and destruction. More often than not, the characteristics associated with maleness and femaleness are equally valued. When people perceive an imbalance between the food supply and population needs, or when populations are in competition for diminishing resources, the male role is accorded greater prestige. Females are perceived as objects to be controlled as men struggle to retain or to gain control of their environment. Behaviors and attitudes prevail that separate the sexes and force men into a posture of proving their manhood. Sexual violence is one of the ways in which men remind themselves that they are superior. As such, rape is part of a broader struggle for control in the face of difficult circumstances. Where men are in harmony with their environment, rape is usually absent.

The insights garnered from the cross-cultural study of rape in tribal societies bear on the understanding and treatment of rape in our own. Ours is a heterogeneous society in which more men than we like to think feel that they do not have mastery over their destiny and who learn from the script provided by nightly television that violence is a way of achieving the material rewards that all Americans expect. It is important to understand that violence is socially and not biologically programmed. Rape is not an integral part of male nature, but the means by which men programmed for violence express their sexual selves. Men who are conditioned to respect the female virtues of growth and the sacredness of life, do not violate women. It is significant that in societies where nature is held sacred, rape occurs only rarely. The incidence of rape in our society will be reduced to the extent that boys grow to respect women and the qualities so often associated with femaleness in other societies—namely, nurturance, growth, and nature. Women can contribute to the socialization of boys by making these respected qualities in their struggle for equal rights.

Section 2

Gender Violence in the United States

As in any society, social relations in the United States have been influenced by the cultural, political, and economic conditions within which they have emerged. Gender, as a central organizing principle in societies, has mediated the distribution of power and the division of labor throughout U.S. history. In the early colonial period, for example, households and communities were the primary institutions operating in the lives of European settlers. The political sphere was governed from afar and politics, in general, were experienced less directly by Americans than is the case today.

In European American families, gender relations were determined in part by traditional relations in the family's country of origin, as well as by the specific experiences of being bound together in an economy where households were the central producing and consuming units. In some communities, they were also affected by collective acceptance or abhorrence of the sex/gender systems of native peoples with whom settlers came into contact. In Free Love and other utopian experiments of the early colonial period, for example, European colonists experimented with radical sexual and familial practices such as interracial marriages, multiple-partner unions, and nonsexual companionable communities (D'Emilio and Freedman 1988), based in some cases as much upon their observations of native groups as upon their collective sense that these alternative patterns were liberating for males and females.

By and large, however, gender was organized around the division of labor in what was an agricultural-based subsistence economy, although mediating relationships such as those formed in churches and communities provided significant contributions. For example, monogamous, heterosexual families were specified and blessed by Christian churches, and communities regulated sanctions regarding the use of force and violence in the context of daily relationships. There is evidence that women had more decision-making power, relative to men, in the household-based economy of the colonial period than in any other period in American history. There is also evidence that women were seen as autonomous sexual beings rather than merely the object possessions of men. Nevertheless, domestic violence, rape, incest, and various other forms of sexual coercion are documented in the personal and public records that have been preserved from the early colonial period (D'Emilio and Freedman 1988).

Large-scale economic change in any social system has profound repercussions in the various other institutions that comprise the system. In the nineteenth-century United

States, the slow but steady evolution from a predominantly agrarian subsistence economy to an industrial capitalist structure had profound concomitant effects on the social organization of gender in families, in the political sphere, and in the cultural meanings and artifacts of the society. For one thing, wage earning replaced home manufacture as the driving force behind a family's acquisition of durable goods. Wage earners became increasingly central in the household, and from the late 1700s to the close of the nineteenth century men became increasingly associated with wage earning in the industrial economy (Pleck and Pleck 1980). Although women continued to labor in and out of the industrial economy, they were increasingly associated with a supposedly nonproductive family sphere, and this association contributed to a decline in their economic and social power relative to men. It was during this period that womanhood came to be associated with frailty, domestic subservience, and romantic love; men's familial and emotional attachments to women, on the other hand, became increasingly invisible as men were defined more and more by their work outside of the home (Cancian 1989).

Changes in the organization of the family alter not only social definitions of masculinity and femininity, but also the regulation of sexuality. In the early industrial period, the transition of the family from a productive to a primarily consuming economic unit was accompanied by an overall shift in the family's functions as a social unit. Family became associated with intimacy and privacy, juxtaposed against an ever-expanding public sphere of formal organizations. Sexuality became increasingly less public as it was situated in the ideal, self-contained nuclear family unit. Neighbors and extended family members lost their powers over the regulation of community behavior. Culturally, the nineteenth century is often depicted as a time of repressed sexuality; indeed, the privatization of family, and the situation of sexuality within its boundaries, contributed to the lessening of public discourse about and public displays of sexuality.

As suggested in the preceding section, the exploitation of women by men in both intimate relationships and institutional contexts quite often exists simultaneously with economic systems that are exploitative and hierarchically organized. As the United States industrialized, conditions emerged within which violating women was more easily rationalized, given their perceived status as weak, intellectually inferior, and less central to the productive sphere of society. Contributing to women's vulnerability was the invisibility of this exploitation in the privatized family—in spite of the fact that in the United States family is culturally defined as a haven of nurturing and love.

The sexual and feminist revolutions of the 1960s profoundly challenged the ideal depictions of masculinity, femininity, family, and sexuality in ways that affect both private and public activity. Sexuality increasingly has been cast as a public issue, sparking more than twenty-five years of sexual exploration, as well as heated debate regarding nature, morality, and cultural values. Changes in sexual practice have been evolving simultaneously with changes in work roles and, indeed, the very structure of the U.S. economy. The current postindustrial service economy is still organized around a dual labor market in which women's labor is valued and compensated less than men's. As the industrial labor market has been replaced by a primarily service-oriented labor market, more women have entered the work force, usually in jobs earmarked specifically for them.

The convergence of deindustrialization, an expanding female labor market, and an increasing cultural preoccupation with sexuality have altered the prevailing social conditions, and hence, gender relations. One result of this convergence is that much of women's work is sexualized—that is, women's sexuality is a crucial part of the actual labor process. "Hooters girls," exotic dancers, and cheerleaders for professional sports teams are but the most obvious examples of sexualized occupations. In addition, sexual meanings are often scripted into the provision and marketing of goods and services that are presumably nonsexual (Tancred-Sheriff 1989), from the expectations for behavior in "women's occupations" such as receptionist and flight attendant to the car advertisements that feature women in semi-erotic poses. Even though many women have benefited economically and professionally from challenges to these images by the contemporary women's movement and the incremental changes in women's legal rights, the majority of women still labor in low-paid, sex-typed jobs and are made more vulnerable still by their limited access to social power.

Citizenship, Masculinity, and Violence

While gender violence is personally experienced first and foremost in the context of intimate relationships, it would be wrong to present the family as the central locus and agent of violence. Indeed, violence in intimate contexts can only exist in communities that condone it. Community acquiescence to gender violence certainly varies; in some settings the support is more overt than in others, yet, analysts continue to show the ways in which larger cultural contexts shape and reproduce the meanings and practices that hold sway in the most basic relationships we form.

It is crucial to bear in mind that a great deal of the world's violence—including gender violence—is institutional (Connell 1995). For example, the military and military-style institutions such as the police play a substantial role in both shaping violent masculinity and socializing male members to distance themselves from femininity. Attempts by organizations to maintain internal continuity, as well as to legitimate their socialization rituals, often result in institutional tolerance for the violent behavior of members: thus, gay bashing, sexual harassment of female working peers, and rape in the context of war are tolerated, and often rewarded. Programs for male athletes provide a training ground, generally, for social and political leadership in the United States; they figure prominently in recruitment for, and daily routines within, military-style organizations. Sports events are replete with militaristic metaphor and pageantry. Woven together as primary contexts for the formation of male identity, militarism and sports form a well-integrated system for shaping men for life in civil society. Such institutions shape the behavior patterns and worldview that men take into their intimate relationships with women and other men.

In the United States, the social construction of citizenship has included a double standard of strong gender-related assumptions. Historically, the right to own property, vote, and participate in the occupation of one's choice have all been regulated by the government in ways that have included gender restrictions. Similarly, the responsibility to join the armed services of the country and the ability to engage in combat have been delegated in response to social expectations about gender-appropriate behavior.

The United States' system of adversarial internal politics and penchant for involvement in global conflicts have contributed to the male-centeredness of its political and military institutions. The ever-increasing significance of these related institutions in everyday life contribute to a civic culture that not only tolerates violence, but also teaches it as a skill (Ewing 1982). This is particularly true for men, for whom the civic advocacy of violence is strong. R. W. Connell (1995) even theorizes that the hegemonic masculine ideal incorporates key aspects of militarism, and that in many cultures, war is the true test of masculinity. Males in the United States are targeted for team sports, adventure and war toys, and influenced by media role models, so that the internalization of militaristic tendencies is most strongly associated with masculinity. The culture normalizes militarism through the celebration of military holidays and heroes and through legitimating the unconscious use of military metaphors in our daily communications: we attack a problem, are under the gun to find a solution, and frequently beat an idea to death (Ewing 1982). All of us, male and female, participate in these cultural and linguistic celebrations of war.

Sex, Markets, and "Normal" Violence in the United States

Much gender violence takes place in the context of sexual relationships; thus, it is important to understand the social construction of dominant sexual practices. Infusing sexual relationships with violence is not by any means limited to the United States. Edwin Schur (1988) suggests, however, that globally sex has been increasingly "Americanized," taking on distinct cultural forms as sexual meanings emerge in conjunction with gender and economic inequality, consumerism, and the larger U.S. culture of violence.

Schur's ideas are consistent with those of others who see clear correlations between economic stratification and gender inequality. From this perspective, contemporary capitalist market economies provide the context for an increasingly complex commodification of sexuality. In a culture that promotes the belief that basic human needs can be met by purchasing the right products, it is no surprise that a huge sex entertainment industry emerges. The buying and selling of sex through prostitution, sex toys, manuals, videos—and now, the emergence of computer programs that produce "virtual sex"—are logical outgrowths of a profit-oriented market economy in a society that is preoccupied with sex.

Treating sex as a commodity, in conjunction with the system of gendered behaviors and expectations that comprise our ideals of masculinity and femininity, produces a distinctly American brand of sexuality. In the United States, sexuality is a desired product in and of itself, rather than primarily a component of committed relationships. It has been largely disassociated from procreation; we can be treated by medical specialists if we perceive ourselves as sexually abnormal; and increasingly it is seen as both normal and desirable to achieve orgasm without benefit of contact with another human being. In addition, American media depictions of sexuality frequently "eroticize dominance" (Schur 1988). Sex and violence are both dominant components of American cultural experience, and they are often fused in the same film, television, advertising, and literary packages. Given the massive exportation of U.S. media products, this Americanized conception of sex is heavily marketed worldwide by the entertainment industry.

The more sexual needs can be fulfilled by using products, rather than relating to people in love-based relationships, the more depersonalized sexuality becomes. The more depersonalized and isolated our notions of sexuality become, the less we value partners as individuals. In a consumer-oriented society, even partners can become means to achieving a sexual end. Some critics suggest that depersonalized and commodified sexuality opens the door to gender violence through the objectification and dehumanization of women. This process is exacerbated by the sex industry; the more women are seen as things—sex toys, or tools, or machines—the easier it is to violate them. The frequent portrayal of coerced sexuality in mainstream movies, music videos, television, and pornographic materials provides a backdrop for rationalizing gender violence in everyday interactions.

Race, Class, and Gender: Dimensions of Power

Power, financial success, and physical strength define the ideal man in the United States, but these attributes are not distributed evenly among the male population. Socioeconomic strata exist among women; similarly, men are differentially ranked and rewarded across a number of social and economic dimensions. For both sexes, race, class, age, and sexual orientation are among the most significant stratifying characteristics. Given the competitive and consumption-oriented nature of U.S. society, both economic and social mobility are desirable, and our routes to mobility may include physical force and coercion—taking power when it is not offered for the sake of personal social gain.

Social psychologists use the concept of relative deprivation to help explain class conflict and racial unrest. When social and economic affluence are characteristic of a society, but are unevenly distributed in visible ways, conflict is likely to emerge; this is particularly true in societies like the United States where equality is often raised as a social ideal. We can apply the concept of relative deprivation to the study of gender violence as well. When ideal masculinity involves possession of certain characteristics that are unevenly distributed (such as "Whiteness," success with women, athleticism, and money), men who are deficient in one or more of these central areas may become frustrated and angry. One way that men who experience relative deprivation compensate for real or perceived deficiencies is through the use of their physical strength to gain power. Such a route to power is more likely to be taken in a society where economic resources are shrinking and Whiteness is overvalued. This by no means suggests that gender violence is confined to lower-class men or to men of color, although relative deprivation may be helpful in understanding some of the motivations to violence among these groups. Relative deprivation, however, cuts across race and class boundaries and is experienced by men from all sectors of U.S. society. Rich and politically powerful men may feel relative deprivation when gauging their athleticism or communicative abilities against the masculine ideal; they may also use domestic violence or rape as a way to compensate for perceived deficiency in their relationships with women. Male college students may engage in gay-bashing to compensate for perceived inadequacies in successfully attracting and courting women. Measuring up to the ideal standard is difficult in a performance-oriented, market-driven, and highly stratified culture. In such a context, men seek and use power over women and other men to access rewards in social institutions (Pleck 1980). Taking power in the cultural context of the United States often involves the use of violence as a substitute for culturally legitimate means.

Contributions to This Section

We have briefly outlined the sociohistorical foundations of the contemporary American sex/gender system. The United States is only one of a number of case studies we could have selected to illustrate the fluidity of cultural definitions about gender and sexuality;

indeed, culturally specific social conditions provide the basis for the great variation that still exists in gender relations worldwide. Economy, state, and media are central institutions in constructing and enforcing gender relations. We can situate our understanding of both gender and violence by analyzing the social evolution of these institutions in the United States.

We have already discussed some of Edwin Schur's general propositions regarding the social construction of sex in contemporary U.S. society, which he developed in his book *The Americanization of Sex*. We include portions of a chapter that focuses specifically upon the institutionalization of sexual coercion in the United States. This sociological perspective contextualizes sexual violence in a set of sociohistorical conditions and contributes significantly to a macro-level analysis that is so often lost in public discussions of gender violence. We are often most comfortable with an analysis that sees perpetrators of gender violence as deviants in a just society. Schur begs the question of whether we must rather theorize a pathological society that requires large-scale social change if we are to eliminate gender violence.

Criminologist James Messerschmidt has developed the first systematic analysis of male crime to integrate a gender perspective. His work draws connections between masculinity and crime across the spectrum of illegal activities in which men engage. His analysis dovetails nicely with the feminist and profeminist analyses that see race, class, and gender intersecting to produce various forms of social behavior. In "Varieties of 'Real Men,'" Messerschmidt paints a picture of the varying contours of masculinity in the United States, focusing in turn on the specific social landscapes where these variations manifest themselves: the street, the workplace, and the family. Messerschmidt peels back the layers of the hegemonic masculine ideal to bring race and class considerations into his analysis, with specific reference to crimes of violence against women.

Carol J. Sheffield's classic article "Sexual Terrorism" extends our conceptualization of gender violence by introducing the concept of terrorism into our analytical lexicon. Terrorism is generally understood as a form of political violence that frequently involves the use of symbolism. The word "terrorism" generally conjures up images of plane hijackings, heroic suicides in fundamentalist holy wars, or the shards of bombed-out buildings such as the federal office building in Oklahoma City. Sheffield reminds us that violation takes many forms, and that fear of violence is itself a violation, as well as a powerful mechanism of social control in the lives of women. Women in the United States experience a deep fear of violation. Real sexual danger—exemplified in escalating rates of rape, domestic violence, incest, and sexual harassment—provides the backdrop for women's rational fear. The seemingly indiscriminate nature of sexual violence provides the terroristic element that renders women continuously self-conscious and fearful in contemporary society. Beyond its theoretical contribution, Sheffield's article functions as a substantive preface for the next section of this volume, weaving the inventory of violent acts together into a sociopolitical frame of analysis.

SUGGESTIONS FOR FURTHER READING

John D'Emilio and Estelle B. Freedman, *Intimate Matters: A History of Sexuality in America* (New York: Harper & Row, 1988).

Clyde W. Franklin II, *Men and Society* (Chicago: Nelson-Hall, 1988).

Michael S. Kimmel and Michael A. Messner, *Men's Lives*, 3d ed. (Boston: Allyn and Bacon, 1995).

James Messerschmidt, *Masculinities and Crime: Critique and Reconceptualization of Theory* (Lanham, MD: Rowman and Littlefield, 1993).

Michael A. Messner, *Power At Play: Sports and the Problem of Masculinity* (Boston: Beacon Press, 1992).

Joseph Pleck, *The Myth of Masculinity* (Cambridge: MIT Press, 1981).

Edwin Schur, *The Americanization of Sex* (Philadelphia: Temple University Press, 1988).

Need: A Chorale for Black Woman Voices

AUDRE LORDE

For Patricia Cowan[1] and Bobbie Jean Graham[2] and the hundreds of other mangled Black Women whose nightmares inform these words.

> *tattle tale tit.*
> *your tongue will be slit*
> *and every little boy in town*
> *shall have a little bit.*
> —NURSERY RHYME

I

(Poet)
This woman is Black
so her blood is shed into silence
this woman is Black
so her blood falls to earth
like the droppings of birds
to be washed away with silence and rain.

(Pat)
For a long time after the baby came
I didn't go out at all
and it got to be pretty lonely.
Then Bubba started asking about his father
made me feel
like connecting to the blood again
maybe I'd meet someone
we could move on together
help make the dream real.

An ad in the paper said
  "Black actress needed
   to audition in a play by Black Playwright."
I was anxious to get back to work
and this was a good place to start
so Monday afternoon
on the way home from school with Bubba
I answered the ad.

In the middle of the second act
he put a hammer through my head.

(Bobbie)
If you're hit in the middle of Broadway
by a ten-ton truck
your caved-in chest bears the mark of a tire
and your liver pops like a rubber ball.
If you're knocked down by a boulder
from a poorly graded hill
your dying is stamped with the print of rock.

But when your boyfriend methodically
beats you to death
in the alley behind your apartment
while your neighbors pull down their window shades
because they don't want to get involved
the police call it a crime of "passion"
not a crime of hatred.

Yet I still died
of a lacerated liver
and a man's heelprint
upon my chest.

II

(Poet)
Dead Black women haunt the black maled streets
paying our cities' secret and familiar tithe of blood
burn blood   beat blood   cut blood
seven-year-old-child rape-victim   blood
of a sodomized grandmother   blood
on the hands of my brother
as women we were meant to bleed
but not this useless blood
each month a memorial
to my unspoken sisters   fallen
red drops upon asphalt.

(All)
We were not meant to bleed
a symbol for no one's redemption
Is it our blood
that keeps these cities fertile?

(Poet)
I do not even know all their names.
Black women's deaths are not noteworthy
not threatening or glamorous enough
to decorate the evening news
not important enough to be fossilized
between right-to-life pickets
and a march against gun-control
we are refuse in this city's war
with no medals   no exchange of prisoners
no packages from home   no time off
for good behavior
no victories. No victors.

(Bobbie)
How can I build a nation
afraid to walk out into moonlight
lest I lose my power
afraid to speak out
lest my tongue be slit
my ribs kicked in
by a brawny acquaintance
my liver bleeding life onto the stone.

(All)
How many other deaths
do we live through daily
pretending
we are alive?

III

(Pat)
What terror embroidered my face
onto your hatred
what unchallenged enemy
took on my sweet brown flesh
within your eyes
came armed against you
with only my laughter   my hopeful art
my hair catching the late sunlight
my small son eager to see his mama work?

On this front page
My blood stiffens in the cracks of your fingers
raised to wipe a half-smile from your lips.
Beside you a white policeman
bends over my bleeding son
decaying into my brother
who stalked me with a singing hammer.

I need you. For what?
Was there no better place
to dig for your manhood
except in my woman's bone?

(Bobbie)
And what do you need me for, brother,
to move for you   feel for you   die for you?
We have a grave need for each other
but your eyes are thirsty
for vengeance
dressed in the easiest blood
and I am closest.

(Pat)
When you opened my head with your hammer
did the boogie stop in your brain
the beat go on
did terror run out of you like curdled fury
a half-smile upon your lips?
And did your manhood lay in my skull
like a netted fish
or did it spill out like milk or blood
or impotent fury off the tips of your fingers
as your sledgehammer clove my bone
to let the light out
did you touch it as it flew away?

(Bobbie)
Borrowed hymns veil a misplaced hatred
saying you need me   you need me   you need me
a broken drum
calling me   Black goddess   Black hope   Black
strength   Black mother
yet you touch me
and I die in the alleys of Boston
my stomach stomped through the small of my back
my hammered-in skull in Detroit
a ceremonial knife
through my grandmother's used vagina

the burned body hacked to convenience
in a vacant lot
I lie in midnight blood like a rebel city
bombed into submission
while our enemies still sit in power
and judgment
over us all.

(Bobbie & Pat)
Do you *need* me submitting to terror   at nightfall
to chop into bits and stuff warm into plastic bags
near the neck of the Harlem River
they found me   eight months swollen
with your need
do you need me to rape in my seventh year
bloody semen in the corners of my childish mouth
as you accuse me of being seductive.

(All)
Do you need me imprinting upon our children
the destruction our enemies print upon you
like a Mack truck or an avalanche
destroying us both
carrying their hatred back home
you relearn my value
in an enemy coin.

IV
(Poet)
I am wary of need that tastes like destruction.

(All)
I am wary of need
that tastes like destruction.

(Poet)
Who learns to love me
from the mouth of my enemies
walks the edge of my world
a phantom in a crimson cloak
and the dreambooks speak of money
but my eyes say death.

The simplest part of this poem
is the truth in each one of us
to which it is speaking.

How much of this truth can I bear
to see

and still live
unblinded?
How much of this pain can I use?

"We cannot live without our lives."

(All)
*"We cannot live
without our lives."*[3]

(1979, 1989)

NOTES

1. Patricia Cowan, 21, bludgeoned to death in Detroit, 1978.
2. Bobbie Jean Graham, 34, beaten to death in Boston, 1979. One of twelve Black women murdered within a three-month period in that city.
3. "We cannot live without our lives." From a poem by Barbara Deming.

4

Sexual Coercion in American Life

EDWIN SCHUR

An Epidemic of Forced Sex

Appraisers of the current sexual "scene" rarely discuss sexual victimization. Yet intimidation, coercion, and violence are key features of sexual life in America today. We may profess to view coercive sexuality as deviant. But, actually, it is in many respects the norm.[1] To be sure, we are not all rapists, sexual harassers, or child abusers. However, these behaviors are extremely widespread and may well be increasing. They are not isolated departures from some benign patterning of our sexual activities. On the contrary, they constitute important indicators of where our current value priorities and socioeconomic structures are leading us sexually.

We do not know, and indeed cannot know, precisely how much sexual coercion there is. But the estimates are daunting. In recent years, the Federal Bureau of Investigation has been reporting close to 80,000 rapes a year, and estimating that one forcible rape occurs somewhere in the United States every seven minutes. It is widely recognized that even these figures greatly understate the problem. Rape is known to be one of the most underreported crimes. Victimization surveys, in which sampled members of the general population are queried about all crimes committed against them (including those they did not report to the police), show rates of rape four times as high as the official ones.[2]

Sexual abuse of children—we are just beginning to realize—is also extremely widespread, and may be growing. In the Russell study, 16 percent of the women reported at least one incident of incestuous abuse before the age of eighteen (12 percent before age fourteen), and 31 percent reported some sexual abuse by a nonrelative before they had reached eighteen (20 percent before age fourteen). Combining the two categories of abuse (when actual physical contact of some kind was involved) produced overall figures of 38 percent (before age eighteen) and 28 percent (before fourteen). When noncontact experiences (exhibitionism, advances not acted upon) were added the totals were, respectively, 54 percent and 48 percent. Only 2 percent of incest cases and 6 percent of other cases had ever been reported to the police. Rate comparisons for different time periods and between age cohorts, furthermore, convinced Russell that both incest and sexual abuse of children outside the family may have "quadrupled since the early 1900s."[3]

From *The Americanization of Sex*, Temple University Press, 1988, pp. 139–93 (edited). Reprinted by permission.

Sexual harassment of working women is another highly prevalent yet officially "invisible" pattern in present-day American life. Here again, the proportion of incidents that is reported and acted upon is extremely low. But surveys among the general female population, and also in particular work settings or occupational categories, have disclosed very high rates of sexual intimidation and exploitation by male employers, supervisors, and fellow workers. For example, in a 1976 *Redbook* magazine survey, 88 percent of the 9,000 readers who responded reported having experienced some form of sexual harassment at work, and 92 percent considered the problem serious. Surveys of workers at the United Nations, middle management workers in large corporations, and students at major universities have likewise produced evidence of extensive sexual intimidation and exploitation.[4]

The behaviors I have mentioned so far are not, of course, the only types of sexual coercion that Americans experience. Relatively few prostitutes or other sex workers sell their sexuality by free choice. Even where they have not been directly coerced into such work, we might well conclude that some degree of indirect and broadly social coercion has shaped their decision. Nor are noncommercial sexual relations necessarily free of coercion. I discuss below the (far from infrequent) occurrence of wife rape. But short of such outright assault, a subtle coercion exists whenever an individual feels pressured into undesired sexual activity.

It is true that virtually all social relations display a certain amount of coercion in this very broad sense. Yet we do not have to apply the term that expansively to see that coercive sexuality is an alarming presence in our society. The major types of direct and severe coercion that I have noted constitute, in themselves, a national disgrace. Nor is it the case that all modern societies exhibit similar patterns. At least with respect to rape, it continues to be true that "the United States shows a significantly higher rate than most, if not all, European jurisdictions."[5] Such conclusions are based on the necessarily limited—and, as between countries, not always fully comparable—official statistics. Nonetheless, the differences have tended to be too great (American rates running from five to thirty times those of various other Western countries) to be accounted for on that basis alone.

Given the sketchy character of available evidence, similar cross-national comparisons regarding child abuse and sexual harassment would have to be even more tentative. Yet one suspects that America—in these as in so many sexual matters—might again be in the lead. In any case, whether we top other countries in these respects or not, the figures we do have for our own society give cause for great concern. There are, admittedly, no scientific criteria by which to prove what constitutes a high rate of sexual coercion. But the statistics I have cited should speak for themselves. The magnitude of coercive sexuality in America today greatly exceeds what one should expect to find in a humane and liberated society.

Feminists sometimes assert that rape is not really "sexual" behavior. In arguing that its essence is violence and hostility, they seek to underscore the coerciveness of rape—to depict it as being totally unlike lovemaking. However, they usually do go on to point up the links between rape and certain approved outlooks on sex. We should not assume it is only by chance that male hostility and aggression often take this particular form. Rape not only tells us something about male attitudes toward women. It also tells us something about men's ideas about sexuality.

A common defence against charges of sexual harassment (at least in its milder forms) emphasizes the sexual aspect but denies the coercion. The supposedly offending behaviors, it is claimed, merely reflect normal sexual interaction in the workplace. We should see this argument not as a defense of harassment, but rather as an indictment of normal outlooks. However, even if it provides no excuse for sexually offensive acts, the very making of this argument does usefully highlight the systemic aspect of sexual coercion. As in the case of rape as well, this particular form of coercive sexuality bears a close connection to approved scenarios of male-female interaction. I am going to discuss these links extensively throughout this chapter. In such instances, the combination of sexuality and coercion constitutes both the offense and the "normality." As regards sexual abuse of children, the influence of approved interaction scenarios may be less evident. But with the growing sexualization of children in our society, the line between normative behavior and sexual offense may, in this case too, be growing hazier.

How successful have feminists and other activists been in alerting us to these problems of sexual victimization? There have been, during the past two decades, efforts to kindle public concern on each of them. First the cause for greatest alarm was rape, then worker harassment; now the "hot issue" is child abuse. Yet one has the impression that, despite these successive eruptions of activist effort and media attention, the public's understanding of coercive sexuality remains shallow.

The very fact that these issues seem to come and go suggests that people approach them piecemeal. In addition, the individualizing tendency I mentioned earlier interferes with thinking systematically about sexual coercion. And it is characteristic of moral crusades to focus on specific categories of individual offenders. Thus, much of the public alarm has been directed toward "rapists," "child molesters," and sexist employers. In terms of short-run policy measures, this may not be too bad. Yet it distracts us from the full dimensions and sociocultural groundings of the problems.

Perhaps only in the current attention to pornography is there any focus on coercive sexuality as a key feature of modern American life. And even there, the inferences about connections may be misguided. Pornography, for example, is taken to be *the* cause of rape, without regard for the attitudinal and structural factors that may underlie both rape and pornography. Then too, except on this one matter, the New Right (with its heavy concentration on such issues as abortion, homosexuality, and sex education) has most likely diverted attention away from the overall relation between sexuality and coercion.

One suspects, indeed, that many Americans continue to view acts of sexual coercion as pathological violations of our society's norms. Some probably believe that the frequency of these behaviors has been exaggerated. Others may become concerned about one type of sexual offense, without ever placing it as part of a more general pattern. From the standpoint of systematically reducing sexual coercion in American life, these views are not very helpful. The offenses are not, in fact, unrelated to each other. And we cannot simply attribute them to individual wrongdoers. In fact, we cannot appreciate them apart from the normal workings of our sexual system or our social system. To a considerable extent they are integral to those systems, rather than departures from them.

The Context of Coercion

SEXUALITY AND INDIFFERENCE

There are, indeed, many good reasons for expecting to find a close link between sex and coercion in modern American society. Coercive sexuality is a predictable corollary of American outlooks on sex. In particular, sexist attitudes and habits, a misguidedly mechanistic approach to the question of what sex is, and the commercializing instinct encouraged under modern capitalism combine to shape our sexual thinking and sexual goals. All these tendencies (and the general cultural values that they reflect) push us in the direction of sexual indifference and insensibility. When one adds the pervasive socioeconomic inequality that depresses and diminishes the lives of so many Americans, the stage is well set for sexual coercion to be widespread.

Under the general conditions of modern life, Toffler and other critics warned, people become disposable. Our distorted thinking about sexuality and the tenacious hold on us of sexist outlooks only serve to exacerbate this broad tendency. Virtually all the aspects of social and sexual relations are conducive to sexual intimidation and victimization. In an era of secondary relations (to recall Kingsley Davis's term), the other person tends to be seen as a means of achieving our own purposes. He or she is not valued intrinsically. Even in the context of supposedly intimate relationships, using the other person may become the actual norm. The prospect of that happening in other situations, then, must be extremely high.

How is this general tendency affected by our more specific ideas regarding sex? The modernization of sex has contributed to an objectified and scientized conception of sexual acts. Sex came to be seen largely as the production of orgasms and the satisfaction of biological needs. It was studied primarily as a matter of physiological capacity and measurable results. From that standpoint, the way in which sexual needs were satisfied was not deemed terribly important. Nor was there much emphasis, really (despite the usual humanistic call for it), on mutuality in sexual relations. Rather, the focus was on sex as something the individual got, or gave. In addition, the positive valuation of sexuality as natural led the biologically oriented sexual modernizers to develop a quantitative theme. They seemed to imply that as regards sexuality (and as Americans tended to assert in so many areas), more is better. High total sexual outlet it seemed, was good, and low total outlet bad.

When applied in a context of mutual "pleasuring," and as an antidote to long-standing sexual repression, these new ideas had considerable value. But as I have already suggested, they produced distortion as well. There has been relatively little discussion of their possible bearing on sexual coercion and violence. It seems clear, however, that thinking of sex in this way—particularly when social relations of all kinds tend to be depersonalized anyway—might facilitate sexual abuse. The individual is encouraged to view sex not only as a need that must be satisfied but also as a "thing" that should be sought and obtained. If it can not be gotten in more acceptable ways, then perhaps it should be taken—by force, if necessary.

Such a conception of one's sexuality meshes well with the contemporary decline in ability to really see the other person. This ability is impaired by the widespread dissemination of unreal sexual imagery, as well as by the general depersonalization in American life. When such imagery triggers abstracted sexual response, there is a sense in which the actual person on the receiving end of that response isn't really there at all. In addition, the fact that many people in our society are routinely selling their sexual services must also contribute to a dulling of sexual sensitivity. When sexuality can be bought and sold so readily, and treated as a mere service, how much attention must be paid to the person with whom one "has" sex?

That these types of response may make it easier to abuse people sexually should be obvious. A psychological distancing from the other person enables the abuser to disregard the latter's wishes and feelings. (The same basic point has been made regarding the relative ease of killing people through high-altitude bombing and other even more detached techniques of modern warfare.) Such distanced others are more readily conceived of as being there to be used. They can do things for us, or we can with seeming impunity do things to them.

Let me reiterate that, while coerced sex is totally unlike lovemaking, the abuser may nonetheless think that what he (or she) is "getting" is "sex." (Indeed, it is the modernized conception of sexuality just commented on that makes such a belief possible. Only with an orgasm-preoccupied view of sex could coerced sex acts be held to produce "satisfaction.") Based on their interviews with over a hundred convicted rapists, two researchers insist on "the part that sex plays in the crime. The data clearly indicate that from the rapists' point of view rape is in part sexually motivated." They go on to describe rape as "a means of sexual access," and to comment that "when a woman is unwilling or seems unavailable for sex, the rapist can seize what isn't volunteered."[6] In a similar vein, another writer—who interviewed a general sampling of men regarding their attitudes toward rape—states: "In the conception of sex as a commodity, sex is something a man can buy, sell, get for free, or steal (rape)."[7]

DISPOSABLE WOMEN

Sexual indifference within our society provides a general impetus for the use of coercion. Distribution of the results, however, is highly skewed. At least with respect to adults (and it might also be true of child abuse, though at present we cannot be sure) most sexual victimizers are male and most of the victims are female. This is not just due to average disparities in physical strength. As writers on rape and sexual harassment—and on the situation of women more generally—have frequently noted, it reflects the overall social dominance of males and subordination of females. The power that is involved in this patterning of coercion is not just physical. It is social, psychological, economic, and—in the broadest sense—political.

Sexual objectification exhibits this skewed distribution. In our society, it is primarily women who are presented as sex objects. They are presented in that way for—and (the idea lingers) they exist for—the sexual pleasure of men. (In that not-yet-dispelled conception, they also exist to service men in other ways—primarily as housekeepers and childrearers.) When the general status of females is limited (in large measure) to their sexuality, men are likely to see every specific woman primarily as a potential source of sexual satisfaction. The object-like status of women, furthermore, is closely tied up with ideas of sexual property.

Equating women with their sexuality (the process Firestone called "sex privatization") and restricting them in other spheres are two sides of the same (sexist) coin. This extreme sexualization implies limiting women's access to, and not taking them seriously in, nonsexual roles. If they are to be kept in their place, women's freedom of choice must be restricted and their economic dependence on men preserved. Social stigmatization of women, whenever and wherever they step out of line, helps to sustain these limitations.[8]

Much like the alleged pedestal, which in fact helps keep women down, thinking of women as "the sex" helps to ensure their control by men. In this conception their primary use is sexual, and they are all too easily seen as being sexually usable. Presumably, one can conceive of a situation in which men were socially and economically dominant and yet not sexually coercive. However, the trivialization and sexualization of women are highly conducive to such coercion—at least in a society such as ours in which a general pattern of sexual indifference prevails. Furthermore, forced sex is in a way the ultimate indicator, and preserver, of male dominance. Its occurrence and even the perception that it may at any time occur reassure males of their power and help to keep women subordinate.

These conceptions of their dominance, and of woman's secondary (and largely sexual) status, are—as feminists have been insisting—heavily built into the basic socialization of males in our society. Men have learned to respond to women—at least initially, and sometimes more lastingly—not as individuals but in category terms. And, to a large extent, it is a woman's sexual presence that overwhelms other bases for response. In addition, the socialization of most males has strongly endorsed the idea that it is normal for males to be sexually aggressive. This fact lay behind Susan Griffin's claim, in an already-classic discussion of "Rape: The All-American Crime," that "in our society, it is rape itself that is learned." [9]

It should be emphasized here how very closely male conceptions of sexual satisfaction have been tied to images of conquest. Most American men, it is reasonable to believe, still tend to think in terms of "making out" and "scoring." Add the counterpart term for anticipated female acquiescence, "putting out," and one has a capsule summary of culturally approved male outlooks on sex. The crucial point, of course, is that men are *supposed to* try to coerce women into sexual activity.

To the extent this scenario embodied the traditional double standard, "good" women were supposed to say no (however much they desired sexual relations) and to put up resistance by fending off advances. In general, the socialization counterpart of male sexual aggression was female sexual passivity. Citing this theme, feminists depicted women as having been socialized to be victims. In some ways, both sexes were learning their roles in the rape scenario. And this basic learning, we can be fairly certain, continues to be reinforced through pornographic depictions of rape—in which, characteristically, both persons are portrayed as (eventually) enjoying the action.

The most insidious aspect of these learned conceptions is that they are so closely linked to our general ideas concerning masculinity and femininity. As Diana Russell has aptly suggested, a "virility mystique" inclines men to associate sex with coercion and violence. Real men are supposed "to be able to separate their sexual responsiveness from their needs for love, respect, and affection." They are expected to respond, not to specific female persons, but to the presence or depiction of any sexy woman. They are supposed to be able to perform sexually in each and every such instance. Russell concludes, I think sensibly, that "if men were not taught to separate sexual feelings from feelings of warmth and caring, rape would be unthinkable, and fewer men would impose their sexuality on unwilling women in other less extreme ways too." [10]

The other side of this equation has been the female's induced submissiveness and absorption in fantasies of romance. Germaine Greer argued, in *The Female Eunuch*, that the masculine-feminine distinction in modern society rests on a "castration" of women: "Men have commandeered all the energy and streamlined it into an aggressive conquistadorial power, reducing all heterosexual contact to a sadomasochistic pattern." [11] Sexual autonomy and assertiveness are not, in this pattern, open to women. As a recent analysis of mass-marketed romances brought out, these popular depictions reinforce the belief that "pleasure for women is men." [12] Attracting them, arousing their lust, and perhaps being overwhelmed by them is what women are for.

By no means do I wish to imply that giving women equal opportunity with respect to sexual coercion would be a good thing. Free choice to formulate one's own sexual desires, and the ability to pursue them actively, ought to be maximized. But this must be done without encouraging victimization. The equalizing of a sexual distortion cannot be viewed as a social gain. My comments here are intended only to underscore the key role our prevailing gender system plays in perpetuating and shaping coercive sexuality. There is little doubt that that role is substantial. The individual (male as well as female) becomes "disposable" under conditions of social modernity. But for women this situation has long obtained—not just as a vague threat, but as a recurring feature of their daily lives.

Inequality and Violence

Modern American society is characterized by high levels of socioeconomic inequality and interpersonal violence. These conditions, separately and in combination, help to determine present-day patterns of sexual victimization. The reference to combined (or additive) effects is important, for most experts are agreed that a great deal of the violence in our society is due to the inequality. One of the major theories about the occurrence of large-scale violence attributes it to "relative deprivation." As the term relative deprivation indicates, you don't have to be in absolutely dire straits to feel deprived—and, as a consequence, frustrated, resentful, and hostile. This helps to explain how there can be such high levels of violence in a society that many think of as being extremely affluent.

Actually, as economists and sociologists frequently point out, that affluence has been much exaggerated. One recent textbook summary cites 1984 Census figures in noting that "many Americans can barely make ends meet or are living in poverty. Over 15 percent of all American families have incomes below the official poverty level, and over half have incomes below $25,000." The same writers go on to comment that "although America's poor people seldom die of starvation and generally have more than the hopelessly poor of the third world, they lead lives of serious deprivation compared not only with the wealthy but with the middle class as well. This relative deprivation profoundly affects the style and quality of their lives."[13]

In our media-saturated society, the constant depiction of affluent lifestyles—to which almost all Americans are exposed—can only increase a poor person's feelings of frustration and resentment. Author Charles Silberman has aptly noted that "the poor may be invisible to the rest of us, but we are not invisible to them; their television sets thrust them inside our homes every day of the week. For members of the lower class, consequently, life is a desperate struggle to maintain a sense of self in a world that offers little to nourish, and much to destroy, it."[14] To the extent feelings of relative deprivation lie behind some acts of sexual coercion, these media presentations may have special significance.

The playboy mentality, much routine advertising, and perhaps even the basic conception of women as objects to be appropriated and displayed convey the message that sexuality is linked to affluence. As I mentioned earlier, the poor person therefore feels doubly deprived. Among males, there must be a nagging realization that one is not going to be able to get either the affluence or the women who are depicted as most desirable. (And, though its influence on sexual coercion is not as great, poor women must have a sense that achieving the pinnacle of sexual desirability is probably beyond them.)

For the man especially—given our culture's definition of masculinity—taking sex through force or violence may be one kind of response. It may represent an eruption of general and pent-up frustration and hostility. Yet it may also sometimes be seen as a "solution" of sorts to the perceived sexual deprivation. (In this regard, I would stress once more that our mechanistic conception of sexuality allows the belief that what one is getting through such acts is "sex.") We know, of course, that not all poor people commit acts of sexual coercion. And, if we had complete information about those incidents of coercive sexuality that are not currently recorded, we might well find that middle-class rates exceed those of the lower classes.

However, that is no reason to doubt that poverty and the attitudes it engenders help to determine the extent of sexual coercion in our society. Researchers often want to test formal theories quantitatively, to determine the main cause of rape, or child abuse, or harassment. Given our tendency to individualize, especially, it is understandable that "cause" might be thought of in terms of supposed differences between offenders and nonoffenders. The question "Why do some persons do this, while others do not?" is certainly a legitimate one to pursue. On the other hand, when a behavior pattern becomes endemic to the entire society, the very issue of widespread prevalence becomes at least as important as that of individual differentiation.

From that standpoint, statistical comparison studies of individuals tend to be inadequate. A less rigorous but more far-reaching examination of multiple factors that may contribute to the overall situation may be appropriate. I think that is true in this case. Some instances of sexual coercion may be traceable primarily to poverty and its frustrations, others primarily to the depersonalizing and sexist outlooks that affect all of us. Often, some combination of these influences may be involved. Statistical tabulations and correlations are not going to enable us to isolate a single primary cause of a pattern that is this pervasive. Depersonalization, sexism, and inequality all help to shape it.

So too does the violence that suffuses American life. Since the 1960s, several national commission reports (on crime, civil disorders, and violence) have documented and publicized the prevalence of interpersonal violence in our society. It has come to be recognized that violence has had a central place in our history,[15] and hence cannot be viewed as some contemporary aberration. Criminologists frequently note that violent crimes comprise only a small proportion of all criminal offenses. Yet it is generally agreed that the United States exhibits extremely high rates of crimes of violence. A recent summary of data available in the early 1980s, for example, showed that if one combined cases (for 1981) of homicide, forcible rape, robbery, and aggravated assault, one found a recorded total of 1,321,910 such offenses. If one considered instead "personal victimizations" (which included rape, robbery, assault, and theft) reported in a national victimization survey (for 1980) one came up with a total of 21,642,000 offenses.[16]

Crime rates do fluctuate over time, for a number of reasons. For example, the age structure of the population (proportion in the most crime-prone categories), the extent to which people are concentrated in urban settings, and (as regards officially recorded statistics) the level of police resources and activity can all affect crime rates. However, nobody disputes that there is a great deal of violent crime in America today. Nor that fear of being a victim of such violence is widespread.[17] Even though, statistically, the probability of such victimization is lower than that of being killed or injured accidentally, such fear is understandable and its personal impact all too real.

If Americans are highly fearful of violence, they may nonetheless become inured to it. The greatest danger from television depictions of violence, I believe, comes through an indirect and long-term impact of that sort. There is much less likelihood of specific crimes being caused by direct imitation of fictional enactments of violence than of the audience developing a general sense that violent behavior is now routine. If and when such a feeling does develop, then people—in all kinds of situations—may be more likely to resort to violence than they would have been otherwise. The daily litany of local killings reported on the evening news may, in that sense, be at least as consequential as more lurid, but fictional, portrayals of crime and violence.

For our purposes here, media (and pornographic) depictions of sexuality are, obviously, of special relevance. Wide exposure to depictions that link sex and violence can— again, more probably through subtle attitudinal change than by direct example—lead people increasingly to associate the two. As I mentioned earlier, the likelihood is not great that an individual will immediately go out and commit a rape following a specific exposure to pornography. But if Americans are fed a steady diet of such depictions it could, more generally, erode those sensibilities that should help to deter sexual coercion. Extensive use of sadomasochistic imagery in the highly popular rock music videos is one sign that this diet is growing. Violent pornography readily and inexpensively available on videocassettes is another.

If we go beyond sheer physical violence to consider the more general question of coercion, we again find ample supporting "tradition" in our culture. Americans place a high value on results, and have not always been too scrupulous regarding the means used to achieve them. Notwithstanding our alleged disposition to support the underdog, we are quick to exploit personal advantage. Our culture's approval, or at the very least acceptance, of "cutthroat competition"—whether in business, athletics, or elsewhere— enables Americans to disregard the costs to others of their efforts to get ahead. And, similarly, pressuring other people to do things they might not want to do is in the vaunted tradition of American salesmanship.

I have suggested four general factors that may contribute to the prevalence of sexual coercion: depersonalization, leading to sexual indifference; the persisting devaluation (and sexualization) of women; pervasive socioeconomic inequality; and culturally induced habituation to force and violence. My emphasis, in these comments, has been on features of our culture and social system that are conducive to people's committing acts of sexual victimization. But the same sociocultural factors produce victims as well as offenders. Inequality, especially, contributes to both sides of the victimization process, but in an interestingly unbalanced way.

Given the current feminization of poverty (in which females represent a large proportion of those below the official poverty line),[18] we would expect many women, too, to develop feelings of relative deprivation that could lead to violent behavior. Presumably some instances of maternal child abuse reflect such a situation. Generally speaking, however, felt deprivation does not drive women into becoming sexual victimizers. Here we see the combination of inequality and basic socialization coming into play. It is men whose status has rested on demonstrating (along with financial success) their aggressiveness through sexual conquest and control. Women have been socialized to be relatively passive, and to play the sexual object role. Sexual aggressiveness, at least until very recently, has been deemed inappropriate—indeed unfeminine—behavior.

When women have experienced feelings of sexual deprivation, they have tended to internalize them rather than to try by aggressive means to assuage them. And by the same token the frustrations of economic deprivation have pushed women in different directions from those characteristically taken by men. The latter are much more likely to become sexually coercive in such situations. And when they adopt illicit means of alleviating their financial plight, men will tend toward methods we define as masculine—for example, armed robbery, which women as well would be perfectly capable of in physical terms. Women will deal with the situation in ways more consistent with approved female roles. Thus, their major cash-producing deviance will involve selling their sexuality. (Among men, but on a considerably smaller scale, homosexual prostitution represents a similar adaptation to economic insufficiency.)

THE BALANCE OF POWER

As regards situations of direct sexual coercion, economic dependency may, again, contribute to women's victimization. Power, we must remind ourselves, is central to the entire phenomenon of coercive sexuality. Equality and coercion are mutually exclusive concepts; one can only be coerced by someone who has greater power. This power is not only physical, though physical power may indeed sometimes be involved. (Thus, depending on their strength relative to that of a male attacker, some women may be at a physical disadvantage when assaulted sexually. Weak and unaggressive males in prison may be especially vulnerable to "homosexual" rape—usually carried out, in fact, by heterosexuals. The vulnerability to abuse by adults of young children of either sex also is, in part, physical.)

But more significant, overall, are disparities in social (perhaps also psychological) and economic power. The widespread subjection of women to sexual victimization is part and parcel of their general subordination and devaluation in our society. That women's claims of victimization are not often enough taken seriously, nor the offenders severely punished, are further indicators of women's relatively low social power. This general condition is regularly seen in the high vulnerability to coercion of specific women—especially in certain key situations.

Marriage is one of these, and employment another. (A third area—less significant because of its more limited social class distribution and because the woman's financial independence is likely to be greater—is psychotherapy. Recent disclosures of sexual abuse of female patients by male therapists have highlighted the power disparity and authority-dependency aspects of this relationship.) [19] In both of these crucial life situations, financial and social dependency frequently mean that a woman has extremely limited freedom of action. She cannot easily walk away from the situation, if equally secure alternatives are not available to her. This helps to explain the high vulnerability of women to abuse by their husbands. It also highlights the predicament of women workers who are being subjected to sexual harassment.

Reducing Sexual Coercion

America did not invent sexual coercion. But its current cultural priorities and system of social stratification certainly encourage its prevalence. No doubt some amount of forced sex has existed in most societies. Yet ours seems unusually coercion-prone. It is important to recognize this as a general state of affairs. We are not going to alter the situation very much by doing something to (or "for") individual rapists, harassers, and child abusers. For coercion to be significantly reduced, our cultural priorities and approved behavior patterns—as well as the distribution of income and opportunity—are going to have to change.

Actually, in this area more than on other sexual issues, law enforcement does have a role to play. These situations are very different from the victimless crime ones. As regards some potential rapists, for example—especially the more affluent ones (who have more to lose by being caught and punished)—stringent laws may have some real deterrent effect. Then, too, these offenses are so horrendous that a strong symbolic statement (through law) condemning them seems warranted. Even so, and however just we may find it to punish the violators, we need to recognize that the effects of such measures can only be limited ones.

Ultimately, the root conditions themselves will have to be confronted. This means an all-out attack on sexism and depersonalization. But it also means that we must reduce the inequities and priorities that our form of capitalism sustains. Based in part on data drawn from anthropology, Julia and Herman Schwendinger assert that a society's "mode of production" is the most basic determinant of the prevalence of rape. They state further that "the exploitative modes of production that have culminated in the formation of class societies have either produced or intensified sexual inequality and violence."[20]

The problem in applying this to modern societies is that virtually all of them (socialist societies included) are class societies of some sort. Modern capitalism has no monopoly on exploitation or violence, nor on sexism. On the other hand, our particular no-holds-barred version of capitalism does seem to provide special encouragement of coercion. Whether uniquely or not, it does I believe promote the "amoral individualism" and "callous and instrumental indifference to suffering"[21] that the Schwendingers cite as major factors in our rape situation. Whatever one thinks, overall, about the relative merits of socialism and capitalism, the fact remains that rape (and other sexual coercion) will not be significantly reduced if the present systematic inequality is allowed to persist. As the Schwendingers note, such a reduction requires addressing the economic underpinnings of violence and violent crime in general.[22] On this point, at the very least, their argument seems unassailable.

Notes

1. For a discussion of this matter, see Edwin M. Schur, *Labeling Women Deviant* (New York: Random House, 1984), especially chap. 4, "Victimization of Women: Deviance or Conformity?"

2. An overview and analysis of the different kinds of rape statistices can be found in Diana E. H. Russell, *Sexual Exploitation* (Beverly Hills, CA: Sage Publications, 1984), 29–65.

3. Diana E. H. Russell, *The Secret Trauma: Incest in the Lives of Girls and Women* (New York: Basic Books, 1986), 60–62, 84, 78.

4. See Alliance Against Sexual Coercion, *Fighting Sexual Harassment* (Boston: Alyson, 1981); Lin Farley, *Sexual Shakedown* (New York: Warner Books, 1978); Eliza G. C. Collins and Timothy B. Blodgett, "Sexual Harassment: Some See It, Some Won't," *Harvard Business Review,* March–April 1981, 77–95; Donna J. Benson and Gregg E. Thomson, "Sexual Harassment on a University Campus," *Social Problems* 29 (February 1982):236–51; and Bernice Lott, Mary Ellen Reilly, and Dale R. Howard, "Sexual Assault and Harassment: A Campus Community Case Study," *Signs* 8 (Winter 1982):296–319.

5. Gilbert Geis, "Forcible Rape: An Introduction," in Duncan Chapell, Robley Geis, and Gilbert Geis (eds.), *Forcible Rape* (New York: Columbia University Press, 1977), 31; see also Russell, *Sexual Exploitation,* 30–31.

6. Diana Scully and Joseph Marolla, "Riding the Bull at Gilley's: Convicted Rapists Describe the Rewards of Rape," *Social Problems* 32 (February 1985):257.

7. Timothy Beneke, *Men on Rape* (New York: St. Martin's Press, 1982), 26.

8. See Schur, *Labeling Women Deviant,* on the reproduction of gender in everyday interaction. See also Nancy Henley and Jo Freeman, "The Sexual Politics of Interpersonal Behavior," in Jo Freeman, ed., *Women: A Feminist Perspective,* 2d ed. (Palo Alto, CA: Mayfield, 1979).

9. Susan Griffin, "Rape: The All-American Crime," *Ramparts,* September 1971, as reprinted in Chappell, Geis, and Geis (eds.), *Forcible Rape,* 50.

10. Diana E. H. Russell, *The Politics of Rape* (New York: Stein and Day, 1975), 263–64.

11. Germaine Greer, *The Female Eunuch* (New York: Bantam, 1972), 7.

12. Ann Barr Snitow, "Mass Market Romance: Pornography for Women Is Different," in Ann Snitow, Christine Stansell, and Sharon Thompson (eds.), *Powers of Desire* (New York: Monthly Review Press, 1983), 253.

13. Joseph Julian and William Kornblum, *Social Problems*, 5th ed. (Englewood Cliffs, N.J.: Prentice-Hall, 1986), 201–2.

14. Charles E. Silberman, *Criminal Violence, Criminal Justice* (New York: Random House, 1978), 110.

15. Hugh Davis Graham and Ted Robert Gurr, *The History of Violence in America* (New York: Bantam, 1969).

16. As summarized in Joseph F. Sheley, *America's "Crime Problem"* (Belmont, CA: Wadsworth, 1985), 90.

17. See the discussion in Silberman, *Criminal Violence, Criminal Justice*, 3–20; see also John E. Conklin, *The Impact of Crime* (New York: Macmillan, 1975).

18. For a concise discussion, see Barbara Ehrenreich, *The Hearts of Men* (Garden City, NY: Doubleday Anchor Books, 1983), 172–82.

19. See Joanna Bunker Rohrbaugh, *Women: Psychology's Puzzle* (New York: Basic Books, 1979), 393–95; and Phyllis Chesler, *Women and Madness* (New York: Avon, 1972).

20. Julia R. Schwendinger and Herman Schwendinger, *Rape and Inequality* (Beverly Hills, CA: Sage, 1983), 179.

21. Ibid., 204.

22. Ibid., 220.

5

Varieties of "Real Men"

JAMES MESSERSCHMIDT

It was a theoretical breakthrough in social theory when the family came to be recognized generally as both gendered and political. Feminist work has now begun to reveal theoretically what we have known for some time in practice — that other social milieux, such as the street and workplace, are not only political but also gendered (Acker 1990; Connell 1987; Cockburn 1983). I extend this theoretical insight through an analysis of how the social structures of labor, power, and sexuality constrain and enable social action within three specific social settings: the street, the workplace, and the family. I focus on how some men, within particular social situations, can make use of certain crimes to construct various public and private adult masculinities.

Research reveals that men construct masculinities in accord with their position in social structures and, therefore, their access to power and resources. Because men situationally accomplish masculinity in response to their socially structured circumstances, various forms of crime can serve as suitable resources for doing masculinity within the specific social contexts of the street, the workplace, and the family. Consequently, I emphasize the significant differences among men and how men utilize different types of crimes to situationally construct distinct forms of masculinities. We begin with the street and an examination of pimping.

The Street

Middle-class, working-class, and lower–working-class young men exhibit unique types of public masculinities that are situationally accomplished by drawing on different forms of youth crime. Moreover, class and race structure the age-specific form of resources employed to construct the cultural ideals of hegemonic masculinity. Such public arenas as the school and street are lush with gendered meanings and signals that evoke various styles of masculinity and femininity. Another type of public masculinity found in the social setting of the street is that of the adult pimp. This particularized form of masculinity is examined here within the context of "deviant street networks."

From *Masculinities and Crime: Critique and Reconceptualization of Theory*, Rowman and Littlefield Publishers, 1993, pp. 119–53 (edited). Reprinted by permission.

THE PIMP AND HIS NETWORK

Eleanor Miller's (1986, 35–43) respected work *Street Woman* reports that in Milwaukee, Wisconsin, African American men in their mid to late twenties and early thirties dominate what she calls "deviant street networks." Deviant street networks are groups of men and women assembled to conduct such illegal profit-making ventures as prostitution, check and credit-card fraud, drug trafficking, burglary, and robbery. Although both men and women engage in various aspects of these "hustling activities," gender relations are unequal, reflecting the social structures of labor, power, and normative heterosexuality. Miller (p. 37) found that a major source of continuous income in these networks "derives from the hustling activity of women who turn their earnings over to the men in exchange for affection, an allowance, the status of their company, and some measure of protection." Commonly referred to as "pimps," the men act as agents and/ or companions of these women, substantially profiting from their labor. Miller found that to work as street hustlers, it is essential that women have a "male" sponsor and protector. However, this "essential" has not always existed in the history of prostitution.

Throughout the 1800s, U.S. prostitution was condemned but not classified as a criminal offense, and was conducted primarily under the direction of a "madam" in brothels located in specific red-light districts (Rosen 1982, 27–30). In an attempt to halt prostitution, state legislatures enacted laws in the early 1900s in order to close down these red-light districts and, contemporaneously, women-controlled brothels. Predictably, rather than halting prostitution, new forms of prostitution emerged from this attempt at legislating morality. As Rosen (p. 32) shows in *The Lost Sisterhood*, the closing of the brothels simply increased streetwalking for women; because prostitutes could no longer receive "johns" "in the semiprotected environment of the brothel or district, . . . they had to search for business in public places—hotels, restaurants, cabarets, or on the street." This search for customers in public places exposed prostitutes to violent clients and police harassment. Consequently, these women turned to men for help in warding off dangers, providing legal assistance, and offering some emotional support. Eventually, the overall prostitution business came to be dominated by individual pimp entrepreneurs or masculine-dominated syndicated crime.

In today's deviant street network, the pimp usually controls two to three women (labeled "wives-in-law") on the street (Miller 1986, 37–38). The women turn over their earnings to the pimp and he decides how it will be spent. The disciplinarian of the network, the pimp also "decides upon and metes out the punishment" (Romenesko and Miller 1989, 120). Indeed, as Romenesko and Miller (p. 117) show in their interviews with street hustlers, the pimp demands unquestioned respect:

> Showing respect for "men" means total obedience and complete dedication to them. Mary reports that in the company of "men" she had to "talk mainly to the women—try not to look at the men if possible at all—try not to have conversations with them." Rita, when asked about the rules of the street, said, "Just basic, obey. Do what he wants to do. Don't disrespect him. . . . I could not disrespect him in any verbal or physical way. I never attempted to hit him back. Never." And, in the same vein, Tina said that when her "man" had others over to socialize, the women of the family were relegated to the role of servant. "We couldn't speak to them when we wasn't spoken to, and we could not foul up on orders. And you cannot disrespect them."

This authority and control exercised by pimps over women is also clearly exemplified in biographies of pimp life (Malcolm X 1965; Slim 1967). Christina Milner and Richard

Milner (1972, 52–53) reported a similar form of gendered power in their study of African American pimps in San Francisco:

> First and foremost, the pimp must be in complete control of his women; this control is made conspicuous to others by a series of little rituals which express symbolically his woman's attitude. When in the company of others she must take special pains to treat him with absolute deference and respect. She must light his cigarettes, respond to his every whim immediately, and never, never, contradict him. In fact, a ho [prostitute] is strictly not supposed to speak in the company of pimps unless spoken to.

Gender is a situated accomplishment in which we produce forms of behavior seen by others in the same immediate situation as masculine or feminine. Within the confines and social setting of the street, economically marginal men and women create street networks for economic survival, yet simultaneously "do gender" in the process of surviving. In this manner, deviant street networks become the condition that produces material survival as well as the social setting that reaffirms one's gender. The result is a gendered, deviant street network in which men and women do masculinity and femininity, albeit in a distinct manner.

In short, the division of street network labor is concerned both with rationally assigning specific tasks to network members and with the symbolic affirmation and assertion of specific forms of masculinity and femininity (discussed further below). Consequently, pimps simultaneously do pimping and masculinity. As marginalized men, street pimps choose pimping in preference to unemployment and routine labor for "the man." Lacking other avenues and opportunities for accomplishing gender, the pimp lifestyle is a survival strategy that is exciting and rewarding for them as men. The deviant street network provides the context within which to construct one's "essential nature" as a man and to survive as a human being.

THE COOL POSE OF THE BADASS

African American street pimps engage in specific practices (constrained by class and race) intended to construct a specific "cool pose" as an important aspect of their specific type of masculinity (Majors 1986; Majors and Billson 1992). In the absence of resources that signify other types of masculinity, sex category is held more accountable and physical presence, personal style, and expressiveness take on an increased importance (Messner 1989, 82). Consequently, as Richard Majors (1986, 5) argues, many "black males have learned to make great use of 'poses' and 'postures' that connote control, toughness and detachment," adopting a specific carriage that exemplifies an expressive and distinct assertion of masculinity.

The often flamboyant, loud, and ostentatious style of African American pimps signifies aspects of this cool pose. The exaggerated display of luxury (for example, in the form of flashy clothing) is also a specific aspect of the cool pose distinctively associated with African American pimps. Majors and Billson (1992, 81–84) argue that the "sharp" and "clean" look of pimps is intended to upstage other men in the highly competitive arena of the street where they earn street applause for their style, providing an "antidote to invisibility." Pimps literally prance above their immediate position in the class and race divisions of labor and power, thereby constructing a specific masculine street upper-crust demeanor.

Notwithstanding, this cool presence complements an intermittent and brutal comportment to construct masculinity and, in the process, show that the pimp means business. In other words, the African American pimp must always be prepared to employ violence both for utilitarian reasons and for constructing and maintaining a formidable, portentious profile (Katz 1988, 97). The following account by Milner and Milner (1972, 232) illustrates this unpredictable use of violence:

> One ho known as Birthday Cake said she worked for a pimp for four years, gave him a new Cadillac every year, and one night came home from work with her money "funny" and got the beating of her life. She walked in and handed over the money; he counted it and said, "That's all right, honey," drew her a bath, laid her down afterwards on the bed, went to the closet and got a tire iron and beat her senseless with it. She showed us the long scars which required hundreds of stitches and demonstrated her permanent slight limp.

This "badass" form of masculinity (Katz 1988, 80–113) is also publicly displayed for, and supported by, other pimps. Milner and Milner (1972, 56) discuss how a pimp took one of "his" prostitutes (who was also a dancer) into the dancer's dressing room and "began to shout at her and slap her around" loud enough for everyone in the bar to hear. "The six pimps sitting at the back of the bar near the dressing room began to clap and whistle loudly," seemingly for the current dancer, "but in reality to cover the noise of the beating from the ears of the straight customers" (p. 56). Emerging from the dressing room and joining the others, the pimp exclaimed, "Well, I took care of that bitch." Then they all began to "joke around." In contrast, when the prostitute emerged, not "one of them (pimps) felt it proper to comfort her in any way" (p. 56). Such violence, neither out-of-control nor ungovernable, is situationally determined and regulated. Thus, pimp violence becomes a means of disciplining the prostitute and of constructing a badass public masculinity.

The combined cool pose and badass identity of African American pimps clearly represent a specialized means with which to transcend class and race domination. Yet, it also demonstrates the socially constrained nature of social action, and how African American pimps rework the ideals of hegemonic masculinity as a vehicle for achieving that transcendence. Pimping, then, is a resource for surmounting oppressive class and race conditions and for reasserting the social dominance of men. Moreover, like other men, pimps associate masculinity with work, with authority and control, and with explicit heterosexuality.

Within deviant street networks, the prostitute/pimp relationship represents a reworking of these hegemonic masculine ideals under specifically structured social possibilities/constraints. Through their authority and control within deviant street networks, pimps create a class- and race-specific type of masculine meaning and configuration, resulting in a remodeling of heterosexual monogamy in which the pimp provides love, money, and an accompanying sense of security for his "wives-in-law" (Romenesko and Miller 1989, 123).

Normative heterosexuality is the major focus of activities: wives-in-law are expected to be sexually seductive to men, receptive to the sexual "drives" and special "needs" of men (including the pimp), and to work for men who "protect" them and negotiate the "rough spots."[1] Pimping, as a resource for demonstrating that one is a "real man," distinguishes pimps from prostitutes in a specific way. Within the social context of the deviant street network, this pimp type of masculinity is sustained by means of collective and gendered practices that subordinate women, manage the expression of violence against women, and exploit women's labor and sexuality. Indeed, the individual style of the pimp is somewhat meaningless outside the group (Connell 1991, 157); it is the deviant street network that provides meaning and currency for this type of masculinity.[2] Pimping, in short, is a practice that facilitates a particular gender strategy.

In spite of the above, in attempting to transcend oppressive social structures, African American pimps ultimately reproduce them. Their masculine style is at once repugnant to "conventionality"—their source of wealth anathema to traditional morality (Katz 1988, 97)—yet simultaneously reactionary and reproductive of the gendered social order. In other words, African American pimps respond in a gender-specific manner to race and class oppression, which in turn locks them into the very structured constraints they attempt to overcome. Thus, pimping becomes a form of social action that ultimately results in the reproduction of the gender divisions of labor and power as well as normative heterosexuality.

The following section examines two distinct types of masculinity constructed in the workplace.

The Workplace

The gender divisions of labor and power and normative heterosexuality structure gender relations in the workplace. The workplace not only produces goods and provides services but is the site of gendered control and authority. Because women historically have been excluded from paid work or segregated within it, today the gender division in the workplace is both horizontally and vertically segregated (Walby 1986; Reskin and Roos 1987; Game and Pringle 1984).[3] The result is that women are concentrated overwhelmingly at the lower levels of the occupational hierarchy in terms of wages and salary, status, and authority. Indeed, a recent study of nearly four hundred firms revealed that the vast majority of women were either completely or nearly completely segregated by gender (Bielby and Baron 1986). Consequently, gender relations through-out much of the paid-labor market—like gender relations in schools, youth groups, and deviant street networks—embody relations of power: the domination of men and the subordination of women. Moreover, the creation of "male" and "female" jobs helps to maintain and reproduce this power relationship. Accordingly, gender differences are maintained through gender segregation, and occupational segregation is born of prac-tices ultimately based on conceptions of what constitutes the "essential" natures of men and women.

In addition, the concepts "worker" and "a job" are themselves gendered. As Joan Acker (1990) recently demonstrated, these concepts embody the gender divisions of labor and power. Historically, the idea of a job and who works it has assumed a specific gendered organization of public and private life: a man's life centers on full-time work at a job outside the household; a woman's life focuses on taking care of all his other needs. Consequently, as the abstract worker is masculinized (p. 152):

> it is the man's body, his sexuality, minimal responsibility in procreation, and conventional control of emotions that pervades work and organizational processes. Women's bodies— female sexuality, their ability to procreate and their pregnancy, breast feeding, childcare, menstruation, and mythic "emotionality"—are suspect, stigmatized, and used as grounds for control and exclusion.

Because organization and sexuality occur simultaneously, the workplace is sexualized and normative heterosexuality actually conditions work activities (Hearn and Parkin

1987). As Rosemary Pringle (1989, 162) recently reported, heterosexuality in the workplace is actively perpetuated in a range of practices and interactions exemplified in "dress and self-presentation, in jokes and gossip, looks and flirtations, secret affairs and dalliances, in fantasy and in the range of coercive behaviors that we now call sexual harassment."

Within the social situation of gendered segregation, power, and normative heterosexuality, men and women in the paid-labor market actively construct specific types of masculinity and femininity, depending upon their position in the workplace. In other words, social action is patterned in the workplace in terms of a distinction between masculine and feminine. Regarding men specifically, a power hierarchy exists in the workplace among men and, not surprisingly, different forms of masculinity correspond to particular positions in this hierarchy.

Let us now look at two differing forms of masculinity in the workplace: (1) workers and their relation to a specific type of sexual harassment and (2) corporate executives and their involvement in a variant form of sexual harassment. In each case, I demonstrate how specific crimes are a resource for constructing particularized representations of private masculinity—those that are occluded from the vision, company, or intervention of outsiders.

Workers and Sexual Harassment

Studies highlight the persistence and dominance of normative heterosexuality on the shop floor—such practices as exhibiting men's sexuality as biologically driven and perpetually incontinent, whereas women are the objects of a sexuality that precipitates men's "natural urges" (Willis 1979; Cockburn 1983; Hearn 1985; Gray 1987). This macho sexual prowess, mediated through bravado and sexist joking, is constructed and encouraged on the shop floor (Collinson and Collinson 1989, 95–98). Moreover, failure to participate in this specific interaction raises serious questions about one's masculinity. In this way, situationally specific notions of heterosexuality are reproduced through the construction of shop-floor masculinity and center on men's insistence on exercising power over women.

Under such conditions, when women enter the shop floor as coworkers, a threatening situation (for the men, that is) results. In this situation, some shop-floor men are likely to engage in forms of interaction quite different from their interaction with women outside the workplace. Not surprising, sexual harassment is more prevalent in this type of social setting. For example, one study of a manufacturing firm (in which the vast majority of manual laborers were men) found (DiTomaso 1989, 81):

> the men in the plant acted differently than they would if they interacted with these women in any other context. Their behavior, in other words, was very much related to the work context itself. It appeared to provide a license for offensive behavior and an occasion for attempting to take advantage of many of the women in the plant.

In DiTomaso's study, the younger women on the shop floor were perceived by the men as the most threatening because they were competing directly for the same kinds of jobs as were the men. Consequently, these women were more likely than other women to be subjected to demeaning forms of social interaction: the men's behavior was more likely to exceed simple flirtation and to involve specific forms of sexual harassment. The following are comments from several women in the plant (pp. 80–81):

"The men are different here than on the street. It's like they have been locked up for years."

"It's like a field day."

"A majority of the men here go out of their way to make you feel uneasy about being inside the plant and being a female; nice guys are a minority."

Research reveals that sexual harassment occurs at all levels in the workplace—from shop floor to management. However, sexual harassment by men on the shop floor generally is twice as serious and persistent, and is different from sexual harassment by managers (Hearn 1985, 121). In the shop-floor setting (where men are the majority), sexual harassment is "a powerful form of economic protection and exclusion from men's territory. Women workers are perceived as a threat to solidarity between men" (pp. 121–122). Studies of shop-floor sexual harassment suggest that 36 to 53 percent of women workers report some type of sexual harassment (Gruber and Bjorn 1982); furthermore, a recent study of workplace sexual assault suggests that manual workers (as opposed to other men in the firm) committed the overwhelming majority of both attempted and completed assaults within the entire firm (Schneider 1991, 539).

Notwithstanding, the most common types of sexual harassment on the shop floor involve such demeaning acts as sexual slurs, pinches or grabs, and public displays of derogatory images of women (Schneider 1991, 539; Carothers and Crull 1984, 222). Perceptively, women shop-floor coworkers are more likely than women coworkers in other occupational settings to describe this sexual harassment as designed to label them as "outsiders." The "invasion" of women on the shop floor poses a threat to men's monopoly over these jobs, and one way to discourage women from attempting to compete in this domain is to remind them, through remarks and behavior, of their "female fragility" (Carothers and Crull 1984, 224). In this way, then, shop-floor men attempt to secure the "maleness" of the job by emphasizing the "femaleness" of women coworkers (DiTomaso 1989, 88).

Although most shop-floor workers clearly do not engage in sexual harassment, the unique social setting of the shop floor increases the likelihood that this particular type of sexual harassment will occur. Indeed, this specific shop-floor sexual harassment must be seen as a practice communicating anger against women for invading a "male" bastion and for threatening the economic and social status of men (Carothers and Crull 1984, 224). In addition, however, the shop floor is an ideal arena for differentiating between masculinity and femininity—performing manual labor demonstrates to others that such workers are "real men." The presence of women on the shop floor dilutes this gender distinction: if women can do what "real men" do, the value of the practice for accomplishing masculinity is effectively challenged. Because "doing gender" means creating differences between men and women, by maintaining and emphasizing the "femaleness" of women coworkers, shop-floor men are attempting to distinquish clearly between women and men manual laborers, thus preserving the peculiar masculinity of the shop floor. This type of sexual harassment serves as an effective (albeit primitive) resource for solidifying, strengthening, and validating a specific type of heterosexual shop-floor masculinity, while simultaneously excluding, disparaging, and ridiculing women (Segal, 1990: 211).[4]

Moving from shop floor to boardroom, we will next consider how a different type of sexual harassment provides certain white corporate executives with resources for constructing a specific form of private masculinity.

White Corporate Executives and Sexual Harassment

Sexual harassment is a resource available to corporate executives for constructing a specific type of masculinity. Because of their subordinate position in the corporation, women "are vulnerable to the whim and fancy of male employers or organizational superiors, who are in a position to reward or punish their female subordinate economically" (Box 1983, 152). In other words, corporate-executive men are in a unique position to sexually exploit, if they desire, women subordinates. Executive exploitation of sexuality is often a means of reinforcing men's power at the same time as making profits. For example, secretaries frequently are treated as conspicuous "possessions"; therefore, by hiring the "best looking" instead of the most competent secretary, managers exploit secretarial sexuality to "excite the envy of colleagues, disarm the opposition and obtain favors from other departments" (Hearn 1985, 118). Thus, as Jeff Hearn (p. 118) points out, exploitation of secretarial sexuality is not only a matter of directly objectifying women but also of using their sexuality for the eyes of other men. Economic and gender relations are produced simultaneously through the same ongoing sexual practices.

In addition to this direct exploitation of secretarial sexuality, corporate executives sometimes engage in specific types of sexual harassment. While shop-floor men who engage in sexual harassment are more likely to undertake practices that create a sexually demeaning work environment characterized by slurs, pictures, pinches, and grabs, white corporate-executive men are more likely to threaten women workers and lower-level managers who refuse to comply with demands for sexual favors with the loss of their jobs (Carothers and Crull 1984, 222). One secretary described this type of sexual harassment from a corporate executive as follows (cited in Carothers and Crull 1984, 222):

> He always complimented me on what I wore. I thought he was just being nice. It got to the place that every time he buzzed for me to come into his office for dictation, my stomach turned. He had a way of looking at me as if he were undressing me. This time as his eyes searched up and down my body and landed on my breast, he said. "Why should your boyfriend have all the fun. You could have fun with me *and* it could pay off for you. *Good* jobs are really scarce these days."

The harassment of women in subordinate positions by an executive man more likely involves hints and requests for dates or sexual favors, which, when rejected, are likely followed by work retaliation (p. 224). Essentially, this particular type of sexual harassment involves economic threats by white, corporate-executive men such that if a woman employee or would-be employee refuses to submit, she will, on the one hand, not be hired, retained, or promoted or, on the other hand, will be fired, demoted, or transferred to a less-pleasant work assignment. Assuming that the woman employee or potential employee does not desire a sexual relationship with the executive, such threats are extremely coercive. Given the economic position of many of these women, termination, demotion, or not being hired is economically devastating. When women depend on men for their economic well-being, some men take advantage of their economic vulnerability and engage in this particular practice of sexual harassment.

Although the imbalance of corporate gender power can be exercised coercively, sexual harassment is by no means automatic. Women often enter into genuine and humane relationships with men in the workplace, notwithstanding the fact that these men may be in supervisory positions vis-à-vis the woman.[5] Nevertheless, the general power imbalance within the corporation often creates conditions such that men in supervisory positions may exercise economic coercion to gain sexual access without genuine overt consent. Indeed, the corporate structural position of white executive men ensures that such exploitation will more likely be manipulative than violent.

One recent study of workplace assaults found that shop-floor workers utilized physical force more often than other forms of coercion because they lack the institutionalized economic means with which to force compliance. Corporate executives are much more likely to use economic coercion than physical force as a means with which to obtain sexual access to women subordinates (Schneider 1991). Two women who experienced this type of sexual assault stated in part (cited in MacKinnon 1979, 32):

> "If I wasn't going to sleep with him, I wasn't going to get my promotion."

> "I was fired because I refused to give at the office."

When women refuse to "give at the office," some corporate executives retaliate by exercising their power over women's careers. In one case, an executive, "following rejection of his elaborate sexual advances, barraged the woman with unwarranted reprimands about her job performance, refused routine supervision or task direction, which made it impossible for her to do her job, and then fired her for poor work performance" (MacKinnon 1979, 35).

The social construction of masculinity/femininity in the executive/secretary relationship shows clearly how this specific type of sexual harassment comes about. A secretary is often expected to nurture the executive by stroking his ego, making his coffee, cleaning the office, and ensuring he is presentable (Sokoloff 1980, 220). Secretaries are often symbolically hired as "office wives." In one case, an executive had his secretary do all his grocery shopping and even go to his home and take his washing off the line! (Pringle 1989, 169–170).

Rosabeth Moss Kanter (1977, 88) noted some time ago that a "tone of emotional intensity" pervades the relationship between secretary and executive. The secretary comes to "feel for" the executive, "to care deeply about what happens to him and to do his feeling for him." In fact, according to Kanter (p. 88), secretaries are rewarded for their willingness "to take care of bosses' personal needs." In other words, women subordinates construct a specific type of femininity by performing an extensive nurturing service for the executive.[6] Women do in the workplace what they traditionally have done in the home. It should come as no surprise that some executives come to expect such nurturance from women subordinates, just as they do from their wives, and that some take this nurturance further to include sexual nurturing. The result is that some women are coerced to exchange sexual services for material survival. As Carothers and Crull (1984, 223) observe in their important study of sexual harassment:

> The male boss can use his power over women within the organizational structure to impose sexual attentions on a woman, just as he can coerce her into getting his coffee. They both know that if she does not go along, she is the one who will lose in terms of job benefits.

Corporate-executive harassment and sexual coercion are practices that simultaneously construct a specific form of masculinity. This type of sexual harassment arrogantly celebrates hegemonic masculinity, its presumed heterosexual urgency, and the "normality" of pursuing women aggressively. In an attempt to "score" with his secretary, the corporate-executive sexual harasser strengthens gender hierarchy, thereby "affirming in men a shared sense of themselves as the dominant, assertive and active sex" (Segal 1990, 244). The corporate executive enjoys an immediate sensation of power derived from this practice, power that strengthens his masculine self-esteem.

In this way, in addition to normative heterosexuality, white, corporate-executive sexual harassers attempt to reproduce their gender power. Through the practice of corporate sexual harassment, executives exhibit, as MacKinnon (1979, 162) argues, "that they can go this far any time they wish and get away with it." White, corporate-executive sexual harassment, constructed differently than by shop-floor men, provides a resource for constructing this specific type of heterosexual masculinity that centers on the "driven" nature of "male" sexuality and "male" power.

Although clearly most corporate executives do not engage in sexual harassment, the social setting of the executive/secretary relationship increases the probability that this specific form of sexual harassment will occur. Corporate executives engage in sexual harassment to reinforce their power by sexualizing women subordinates, creating "essential" differences between women and men by constructing this particular type of masculinity.

The Family

In addition to the street and the workplace, the divisions of labor and power frame social interactions and practices in the contemporary nuclear family where, for example, women remain responsible primarily for unpaid housework and child care while men remain responsible primarily for paid labor. Indeed, the gender division of household labor defines not only who does most of the unpaid household labor but also the kind of household labor assigned to men and women. Moreover, the sociological evidence indicates clearly that in Western industrialized societies gender asymmetry in the performance of household labor continues to exist (Andersen 1988, 141–145; Messerschmidt 1986, 74; Hartmann 1981; Berk 1985; Hochschild 1989, 1992) and women share less in the consumption of household goods (from food to leisure time) than do men (Walby 1989, 221).

It is true that barely 10 percent of all U.S. heterosexual households consist of a husband and wife with two children living at home, where the husband is the sole breadwinner (Messerschmidt 1986, 74). Further, as fertility is delayed or declines, and with more and more women working during pregnancy and child-rearing years, active motherhood is shrinking as a component of most women's lives (Petchesky 1984, 246). Nevertheless, evidence indicates that women continue to perform most of the household labor, even as these demographic changes occur and women's participation in the paid-labor market increases dramatically. Indeed, Arlie Hochschild (1992, 512) concluded in her study of fifty-two heterosexual couples over an eight-year period that just as "there is a wage gap between men and women in the work place, there is a 'leisure gap' between them in the home. Most women work one shift at the office or factory and a 'second shift' at home."

This gender division of labor embodies the husband's power to define the household setting in his terms. While conscious efforts are being made in many households to dismantle familial power relations (Connell 1987, 124), especially in the middle class (Ehrenreich 1983), for most couples the capacity of each spouse to determine the course of their shared life is unequal: men alone make the "very important" decisions in the household; women alone make few "important" decisions (Komter 1989). In many dual-career families, men's power is deemed authentic and an acceptable part of social relations. This legitimized power in the family provides men with considerably greater authority (Komter 1989; Pahl 1992; Bernard 1982). Concomitantly, the marital sexual relationship, as with other aspects of marriage, likely embodies power, unless consciously dismantled, and "in most cases it is the husband who holds the initiative in defining sexual practice" (Connell 1987, 123).

The concept of patriarchy has lost its strength and usefulness as a theoretical starting point for comprehending gender inequality in Western industrialized societies. Nevertheless, the concept is helpful to describe a certain type of masculinity that persists today: some men are simply *patriarchs* in the traditional sense. Patriarchs fashion configurations of behavior and pursue a gender strategy within the family setting that control women's labor and/or sexuality. Moreover, these men will most likely use violence against women in the family. In the final section of this chapter, the discussion focuses on two forms of violence against women in the family—wife beating and wife rape—and analyzes how these crimes serve as a resource for the construction of specific types of patriarchal masculinities.

WIFE BEATING AND BATTERING RAPE

Victimization surveys indicate that in the home, wives are assaulted much more often by their husbands than husbands are by their wives (less than 5 percent of domestic violence involves attacks on husbands by their wives) and women are much more likely than men to suffer injury from these assaults (Dobash, Dobash, Wilson, and Daly 1992).[7] Wife beating also develops within a setting of prolonged and persistent intimidation, domination, and control over women (Dobash et al. 1992; Dobash and Dobash 1984; Pagelow 1984). Accordingly, wife beating is the "chronic battering of a person of inferior power who for that reason cannot effectively resist" (Gordon 1988, 251).

Violence by men in the household derives from the domestic authority of men and is intimately linked to the traditional patriarchal expectation (1) that men are the credible figures within monogamous relationships and (2) that men possess the inherent right to control those relationships. As Susan Schechter (1982, 222) argues, "a man beats to remind a woman that the relationship will proceed in the way he wants or that ultimately he holds the power."

Katz's (1988, 18–31) discussion of "righteous slaughter"—killing among family members, friends, and acquaintances—by men aids in understanding how this focus on household authority and control results in wife beating as a resource for masculine construction. Katz argues that for the typical killer, murder achieves *Good* by obliterating *Bad*. Moreover, the killer has no capacity to "ignore a fundamental challenge" to his self-worth and identity. From the killer's perspective, the victim teases, dares, defies, or pursues the killer. Accordingly, the killer sees himself as simply "defending his rights." In other words, the killer's identity and self-worth have been taken away—by an insult, losing an argument, an act of infidelity—and such events attack an "eternal human value" that calls for a "last stand in defense of his basic worth." The "eternally humiliating situation" is transformed into a blinding rage and the compulsion to wipe away the stigmatizing stain through the act of murder. And the rage is not random and chaotic but, rather, "coherent, disciplined action, cunning in its moral structure" (p. 30). The killer "does not kill until and unless he can fashion violence to convey the situational meaning of defending his rights" (p. 31).

Investigations of wife beating indicate further the application of the notion "defending his rights." Violence is regarded by the husband as achieving *Good* by pulverizing *Bad;* such men engage in a coherent and disciplined rage to defend what they consider to be their rights. According to interviews with wife beaters, their wife is perceived as not "performing well," not accomplishing what her "essential nature" enjoins and stipulates. Women are beaten for not cooking "up to standards," for not being obeisant and deferential, and for not completing or performing housework sufficiently—for not being a "good wife" (Ptacek 1988, 147). According to the offender, the "privileges of male entitlement have been unjustly denied" because the wife is not submissive and, therefore, not conforming to his standards of "essential femininity" (p. 148). Irene Frieze's (1983, 553) interviews with wife beaters found that they believe "it is their right as men to batter wives who disobey them."

Dobash and Dobash (1984, 274) similarly found that most wife beating is precipitated by verbal confrontations centering on possessiveness and jealousy on the part of the husband and a husband's demand concerning domestic labor and services. During an argument over such issues, "the men were most likely to become physically violent at the point when the woman could be perceived to be questioning his authority or challenging the legitimacy of his behavior or at points when she asserted herself in some way" (p. 274). In other words, wife beating arises not solely from gendered subordination but also from women actively contesting that subordination (Gordon 1988, 286). In such situations, the wife beater is punishing "his wife" for her failure to fulfill adequately her "essential" obligations in the gender division of labor and power and for her challenge to his dominance. The wife beater perceives that he has an inherent patriarchal right to punish "his woman" for her alleged wrongdoing.

Wife beaters are piously sure of their righteousness, and thus fashion their violence to communicate the situational meaning of defending their patriarchal rights. Indeed, the more traditional the gender division of labor (regardless of class and race position) the greater the likelihood of wife beating (Edleson, Eisikovits, and Guttman 1986; Messerschmidt 1986; Smith 1990a). In such traditional patriarchal households, both husband and wife tend to perceive the lopsided gender division of labor and power as "fair" (Berk 1985). Linda Gordon's (1988, 260–261) historical study of family violence found that in households where wife beating is prevalent:

> Women as well as men professed allegiance to male-supremacist understandings of what relations between the sexes should be like. These shared assumptions, however, by no means prevented conflict. Women's assumptions of male dominance did not mean that they quit trying to improve their situations.

The wife beater attempts to resolve in *his* way what he regards as a conflict over this "fair" arrangement, even when the wife is not actively or consciously contesting that "fair" household organization.[8] Accordingly, as West and Zimmerman (1987, 144) argue, "It is not simply that household labor is designated as 'women's work,' but that for a woman to engage in it and a man not to engage in it is to draw on and exhibit the 'essential nature' of each." By engaging in practices that maintain gender divisions of labor and power, husbands and wives do not simply produce household goods and services, but also produce gender. Indeed, husbands and wives develop gendered rationalizations and justifications for this asymmetrical household labor. What follows are selected but representative examples (Komter 1989, 209):

By wives:
"He has no feeling for it."
"He is not born to it."
"It does not fit his character."

By husbands:
"She has more talent for it."
"It is a woman's natural duty."

When this asymmetry is questioned (whether consciously or not), the wife beater assumes that his "essential rights" are being denied—an injustice has occurred, a violation of the "natural" order of things. The "essential nature" of wife beaters is that they control familial decision making and thus dominate the family division of labor and power. When wives "question" this decision making, through words or actions, they threaten their husband's control of the gender division of labor and power. In other words, the husband interprets such behavior as a threat to his "essential nature"— control and domination of the household. Because spousal domestic labor is a symbolic affirmation of a patriarch's masculinity and his wife's femininity, such men are extremely vulnerable to disappointment when that labor is not performed as they expect (Gordon 1988, 268).

According to the wife beater, it is his duty to determine, for example, what constitutes a satisfactory meal, how children are cared for, when and how often sexual relations occur, and the nature of leisure activities (Ferraro 1988, 134). Women are beaten for some of the most insignificant conduct imaginable: for example, preparing a casserole instead of a meat dish for dinner, wearing their hair in a ponytail, or remarking that they do not like the pattern on the wallpaper. Kathleen Ferraro (p. 135) discusses a case in which even the issue of wearing a particular piece of clothing was perceived by the husband as a threat to his control:

> On her birthday, she received a blouse from her mother that she put on to wear to a meeting she was attending without Steven. He told her she could not wear the blouse, and after insisting that she would, Steven beat her. It was not only her insistence on wearing the blouse that evening that triggered Steven's abuse. It was the history of his symbolic control, through determining her appearance that was questioned by wearing the new blouse.

Wife beaters (regardless of class and race position) presume they have the patriarchal right—because it is part of their "essential nature"—to dominate and control their wives, and wife beating serves both to ensure continued compliance with their commands and as a resource for constructing a "damaged" patriarchal masculinity. Thus, wife beating increases (or is intended to do so) their control over women and, therefore, over housework, child care, and sexual activity.

Yet wife beating is related not only to the husband's control over familial decision making, but also develops from another form of control, possessiveness. For some wife beaters, spousal demonstration of loyalty is a focal concern and is closely monitored. For instance, time spent with friends may be interpreted by a wife beater simply as disloyalty. Indeed, sexual jealousy of friends is a common theme in the literature on wife beating (Dobash and Dobash 1979, 1984; Ferraro 1988; Frieze 1983), and indicates the importance of the social structure of normative heterosexuality to understanding wife beating. The wife's uncommitted wrong is the potential to be unfaithful, which to her husband is not only a serious challenge to his patriarchal ideology, but his very real fear that his wife will choose another man and, thereby, judge him less "manly" than his "competitor." Thus, because time spent with friends endangers his ongoing interest in heterosexual performance, wife beating reassures him that his wife is his to possess sexually.

Moreover, not only potential sexual competitors can threaten a patriarchal husband, but relatives may also pose threats to a wife's loyalty. Pregnancy, for example, is closely associated with wife beating, and reflects the husband's resentment of the fetal intruder (Ferraro 1988). Walker (1979, 83–84) offers an example of a husband and wife who planned to spend the day together, but the wife broke off the plans, choosing instead to baby-sit her three-year-old granddaughter. Her husband (Ed) seems to have interpreted this choice as disloyal behavior and a challenge to his ultimate control:

> Ed became enraged. He began to scream and yell that I didn't love him, that I only loved my children and grandchildren. I protested and said, "Maybe you would like to come with me," thinking that if he came, he might feel more a part of the family. He just became further enraged. I couldn't understand it. . . . He began to scream and yell and pound me with his fists. He threw me against the wall and shouted that he would never let me leave, that I had to stay with him and could not go. I became hysterical and told him that I would do as I saw fit. . . . Ed then became even further enraged and began beating me even harder.

Thus, under conditions where labor services are "lacking" and possessiveness is "challenged," a wife beater's masculinity is threatened. In such a scenario, predictably, the wife beater attempts to reestablish control by reconstructing his patriarchal masculinity through the practice of wife beating.

Approximately 30 to 40 percent of battered women are also victims of wife rape (Walker 1979; Russell 1982b; Frieze 1983). These "battering rapes," as Finkelhor and Yllö (1985) describe them, do not result from marital conflicts over sex; rather, the rape is an extension of other violence perpetrated on the victim. The wife beating/rape represents punishment and degradation for challenging his authority and, thus, the traditional division of labor and power. In fact, although wife beating and battering rapes extend across all classes and races (for the reasons discussed above), they occur most frequently in working-class and lower–working-class households wherein the traditional patriarchal gender division of labor and power—husband decision maker and wife caretaker—is strongest (Straus, Gelles, and Steinmetz 1980; Finkelhor and Yllö 1985; Smith 1990b; Walker 1977–78; Messerschmidt 1986, 144). Research consistently shows that class conditions are associated with wife beating: for example, low-income (Straus et al. 1980; DeKeseredy and Hinch 1991) and working-class wives are approximately twice as likely as middle-class wives to experience wife beating (Smith 1990a; Stets and Straus 1989). Moreover, among couples in which the husband is unemployed or employed part-time, the level of husband-to-wife violence is three times as high as the level among couples in which the husband is fully employed (Straus et al. 1980; DeKeseredy and Hinch 1991).

Finally, Michael Smith's (1990b, 49) study of risk factors in wife beating found that "the lower the income, the higher the probability of abuse." This same study went on to report that the chances of a low-income woman being severely battered during marriage exceed those of a middle-class woman by a factor of ten. Smith's (1990b, 267) data reveals that "men with relatively low incomes, less educated men, and men in low-status jobs were significantly more likely than their more privileged counterparts to subscribe to an ideology of familial patriarchy. These men were also more likely to have beaten their wives."

Although at work he is individually powerless, at home the working-class battering rapist is a patriarch endowed with individual authority. His ability to earn money (if available) "authorizes" his patriarchal power as husband/father. But his masculine identity depends on the demarcation of public and private responsibility; consequently, any challenge to the status quo in the home is taken personally as a confrontation (Tolson 1977, 70). In seeking to sustain this specific type of patriarchal masculinity, working-class men develop an intense emotional dependency on the family/household (Donaldson 1987), demanding nurturance, services, and comfort on their terms when at home. As Lynne Segal (1990, 28) points out, "the sole site of authority" for such men is in the home. And when their power and authority are threatened or perceived to be threatened at home, working-class men are more likely than other men to employ battering rapes to accomplish gender and reestablish their control. As Harris and Bologh (1985, 246) point out in their examination of "blue collar battering," "If he can establish an aura of aggression and violence, then he may be able to pass as a 'real man,' for surely it is admirable to use violence in the service of one's honor."

Battering in this sense is a resource for affirming "maleness." Because of their structural position in the class division of labor, working-class men—in particular, lower–working-class men—lack traditional resources for constructing their masculinity and, as a result, are more likely than are middle-class men to forge a particular type of masculinity that centers on ultimate control of the domestic setting through the use of violence. Moreover, unemployment and low occupational status undermine the patriarchal breadwinner/good provider masculinity: he cannot provide for his wife and children. Such men are more likely than are economically advantaged husbands to engage in wife beating and battering rapes to reestablish their masculinity. As Kathleen Ferraro (1988, 127) puts it, "for men who lack any control in the civil realm, dominance within the private realm of the home becomes their sole avenue for establishing a sense of self in control of others." [9]

In sum, most working- and lower–working-class husbands do not abuse their wives, nor is this particular type of abuse limited to this class of men. Nevertheless, the peculiar social conditions prevalent in working- and lower–working-class families increase the incidence of this type of abuse. For these men, power is exercised in the home in ways that hegemonic masculinity approves: men are allowed to be aggressive and sexual. Lacking dominance over others at work or the ability to act out a breadwinner (or even economic contributor) masculinity, sex category is particularly important, and working- and lower–working-class men are more likely to express their masculinity as patriarchs, attempting to control the labor and sexuality of "their women." Consequently, when patriarchal relations are "challenged," their taken-for-granted "essential nature" is undermined and, accordingly, doing masculinity requires extra effort. Wife beating/rape is a specific practice designed with an eye to one's accountability as a "real man" and, therefore, serves as a suitable resource for simultaneously accomplishing gender and affirming patriarchal masculinity.

FORCE-ONLY RAPE

However, wife rape is not limited to the victims of wife beating. Indeed, in Finkelhor and Yllö's (1985) study, 40 percent of their sample were "force-only rapes"—situations in which husbands use only the force necessary to coerce their wives into submission.

The perpetrators and victims of force-only rapes were significantly more educated than those of battering rapes, more often middle-class, and almost half held business- or professional-level jobs.[10] Moreover, the perpetrators and victims of force-only rapes were much less likely to have been in a relationship based on the traditional gender divisions of labor and power. Sex was usually the issue in force-only rapes, and the offenders were "acting on some specifically sexual complaint," such as how often to have sex or what were acceptable sexual activities (p. 46).

In some sectors of the "progressive" middle class, there have been serious attempts to become truly equal marriage partners, where the wife has a career and where the husband participates equally in child care and housework. However, the greater the income differential between husbands and wives, the less involved some husbands are in parenting and housework, and there exists greater equality in dual-career families than in dual-income families (Segal 1990, 38). Consequently, as Barbara Ehrenreich (1989, 218–220; see also 1983, 1984) argues, a new heterosexual masculinity on the part of certain progressive, middle-class men has emerged, consisting of choosing a mate who can "pull her own weight" economically and who is truly committed to sharing household labor equally.

Notwithstanding, this progressive "dual-career" relationship is not supplemented, in many cases, by a progressive sexual relationship. As Andrew Tolson (1977, 121) argued as early as 1977, for many progressive, middle-class men, sexual passion is "still acted out in familial terms of masculine 'conquest'—to which women could only 'respond.' " Although many progressive, middle-class men seriously seek "free women" who live for themselves and their careers (Ehrenreich 1984), in bed they continue to demand submission and the affirmation of masculinity through heterosexual performance (Tolson 1977, 121). That is, many progressive, middle-class men continue to adhere to the hegemonic masculine ideology that "entitles" them to sex with their wives whenever they want it. For example, Finkelhor and Yllö (1985, 62–70) discuss the case of Ross, a middle-class businessman who somewhat represents this progressive middle class, yet who frequently raped his wife. Ross describes below how one such rape occurred during an argument over sex that his wife was winning (p. 66):

> She was standing there in her nightie. The whole thing got me somewhat sexually stimulated, and I guess subconsciously I felt she was getting the better of me. It dawned on me to just throw her down and have at her . . . which I did. I must have reached out and grabbed at her breast. She slapped my hand away. So I said, "Lay down. You're going to get it." She replied, "Oh, no, you don't," so I grabbed her by the arms and she put up resistance for literally fifteen seconds and then just resigned herself to it. There were no blows or anything like that. It was weird. I felt very animalistic, and I felt very powerful. I had the best erection I'd had in years. It was very stimulating. . . . I walked around with a smile on my face for three days.

Ross believed his wife not only controlled the sexuality in their lives, but that she had "completely and totally emasculated" him (p. 68). The rape was both a way to overcome that loss of power in his life and a means to construct a specific type of patriarchal masculinity centering on heterosexual performance and the domination and control of women's sexuality.

Another businessman, Jack, stated to Finkelhor and Yllö (p. 72), "When she would not give it freely, I would take it." He felt that his wife did not have the right to deny sex, he had the right to sex when he pleased, and it was her duty to satisfy his sexual needs. Similarly, in Irene Frieze's (1983, 544, 553) study of wife rape, the vast majority of wife rapists engaged in this form of violence in order to prove their "manhood," believing "that their wives were obligated to service them sexually in whatever ways they desired."

Thus, in force-only rapes, the assaults are practices of masculine control based on expectations that sex is a right. Both battering and force-only rapists consciously choose such violent action to facilitate a patriarchal gender strategy and to protect what they view as their "essential" privileges. The resulting masculine construction is not only an exhibition of their "essential nature," but also illustrates the seductive quality of violence for displaying that "essential nature." For these men, masculine authority is quite simply expressed through the violent control of women.

Nevertheless, such personal choices become enigmatic when detached from social structures. In battering rapes, because the traditional division of labor and power is prevalent and the struggle is over authority and control of that division, these men construct a patriarchal form of masculinity that punishes and degrades the wife for deviating from her "essential" duties. In force-only rapes, however, the gender division of labor is not the issue: this is the classic, middle-class, dual-career family in which both partners participate in decision making and household tasks, and in which the husband accepts, in a general way, his wife's autonomous right to develop her own interests. However, the force-only rapist feels specifically wronged, cheated, and deprived in the sexual realm. Some progressive, middle-class men simply adhere to the hegemonic masculine ideology that entitles them to sex whenever they want it. Sex is considered a marriage right by which gender is accomplished through effective performance in the sexual realm. Like sexual harassment, a similar type of crime, wife rape can be a resource for accomplishing masculinity differently. And as the social setting within the nuclear family changes, so does the conceptualization of what is normative masculine behavior. Different social settings generate different masculinities, even when the particular resource (crime) is similar.

In sum, the structure of the gender division of labor and power and normative heterosexuality impinges on the construction of masculinity. These structural features both preclude and permit certain forms of crime as resources that men may use to pursue a gender strategy and construct their masculinity. Although both battering and force-only rapists try to control their wives, they do so in qualitatively different ways. The social relations extant within their respective gender divisions of labor and power are different, and different options exist for maintaining their control. The choices made by each type of rapist, and the resources available to carry out those choices, develop in response to the specific social circumstances in which they live. For these reasons, then, these men employ different forms of violence to construct different types of private masculinities.

This chapter has attempted to demonstrate that men produce specific configurations of behavior that can be seen by others within the same immediate social setting as "essentially male." These different masculinities emerge from practices that utilize different resources, and class and race relations structure the resources available to construct specific masculinities. Pimps, workers, executives, and patriarchs generate situationally accomplished, unique masculinities by drawing on different types of crime indigenous to their distinct positions within the structural divisions of labor and power. Because men experience their everyday world from a uniquely individualistic position in society, they construct the cultural ideals of hegemonic masculinity in different ways.

Social structures are framed through social action and, in turn, provide resources for constructing masculinity. As one such resource, specific types of crime ultimately are based on these social structures. Thus, social structures both enable and constrain social action and, therefore, masculinities and crime.

NOTES

1. Prostitutes, or "wives-in-law," are constructing a femininity that both confirms and violates stereotypical "female" behavior. In addition to the conventional aspects of femininity just mentioned, prostitute femininity also ridicules conventional morality by advocating sex outside marriage, sex for pleasure, anonymous sex, and sex that is not limited to reproduction and the domesticated couple. This construction of a specific type of femininity clearly challenges, in certain respects, stereotypical femininity. Nevertheless, the vast majority of prostitutes do not consider themselves feminists: they know very little about the feminist movement, do not share its assumptions, and believe men and women are "naturally" suited for different types of work (Miller 1986, 160).

2. The masculinity constructed by African American pimps is fittingly comparable to the masculinity associated with men (usually from working-class backgrounds) who are members of white motorcycle gangs. The men in such groups act extremely racist and similarly exploit the sexuality and labor of "biker women." However, biker men do not display a "cool pose" with an accompanying show of luxury in the form of flashy clothing and exotic hairstyles. On the contrary, a biker usually has long unkempt hair, a "rough" beard, and his "colors" consist of black motorcycle boots, soiled jeans, and a simple sleeveless denim jacket with attached insignia (see Hopper and Moore 1990; Willis 1978).

3. Horizontal segregation allocates men and women to different types of jobs; vertical segregation concentrates men and women in different occupations at different steps in an occupational hierarchy.

4. Nevertheless, it should be pointed out that increasing numbers of men are attempting to counter sexism on the shop floor and, therefore, reconstruct shop-floor masculinity. For an excellent example, see Gray 1987.

5. Indeed, office romances seem to be flourishing because women more routinely work beside men in professional and occupational jobs (Ehrenreich 1989, 219).

6. This particular form of femininity has been explored by Pringle (1988).

7. Despite devastating criticisms of the Conflict Tactics Scale as a methodological tool (Dobash, Dobash, Wilson, and Daly 1992), some researchers (remarkably) continue to use it to guide their work, concluding that women are about as violent as men in the home (Straus and Gelles 1990) or even, in some cases, that more men are victimized in the home than are women (McNeely and Mann 1990).

8. Unfortunately, there is scant research on wife beating in racial-minority households. Nevertheless, what evidence there is on African American households suggests that when violence does occur, both husband and wife are likely to accept the traditional patriarchal division of labor and power as natural and that complete responsibility for the battering, when questioned, "lies with white society" (Richie 1985, 42; see also Asbury 1987). Consequently, I am forced to concentrate solely on class and wife beating.

9. This is not to deny that many middle-class men engage in wife beating for the reasons discussed earlier in this section. What I suggest, following Segal (1990, 255) and others, is that it is clearly less common in middle-class households because such men have access to other resources, possibly more effective resources, through which they exert control over women without employing violence.

10. Because Finkelhor and Yllö (1985, 9) found no significantly higher rate of marital rape among African Americans than among whites, I do not distinguish by race.

6

Sexual Terrorism

CAROLE J. SHEFFIELD

> No two of us think alike about it, and yet it is clear to me, that question underlies the whole movement, and our little skirmishing for better laws, and the right to vote, will yet be swallowed up in the real question, viz: Has a woman a right to herself? It is very little to me to have the right to vote, to own property, etc., if I may not keep my body, and its uses, in my absolute right. Not one wife in a thousand can do that now.
>
> —LUCY STONE, *in a letter to Antoinette Brown, July 11, 1855*

The right of men to control the female body is a cornerstone of patriarchy. It is expressed by their efforts to control pregnancy and childbirth and to define female health care in general. Male opposition to abortion is rooted in opposition to female autonomy. Violence and the threat of violence against females represent the need of patriarchy to deny that a woman's body is her own property and that no one should have access to it without her consent. Violence and its corollary, fear, serve to terrorize females and to maintain the patriarchal definition of woman's place.

The word *terrorism* invokes images of furtive organizations of the far right or left, whose members blow up buildings and cars, hijack airplanes, and murder innocent people in some country other than ours. But there is a different kind of terrorism, one that so pervades our culture that we have learned to live with it as though it were the natural order of things. Its target is females—of all ages, races, and classes. It is the common characteristic of rape, wife battery, incest, pornography, harassment, and all forms of sexual violence. I call it *sexual terrorism* because it is a system by which males frighten and, by frightening, control and dominate females.

The concept of terrorism captured my attention in an "ordinary" event. One afternoon I collected my laundry and went to a nearby laundromat. The place is located in a small shopping center on a very busy highway. After I had loaded and started the machines, I became acutely aware of my environment. It was just after 6:00 P.M. and dark, the other stores were closed, the laundromat was brightly lit, and my car was the only one in the lot. Anyone passing by could readily see that I was alone and isolated. Knowing that rape is often a crime of opportunity, I became terrified. I wanted to leave and find a laundromat that was busier, but my clothes were well into the wash cycle, and, besides, I felt I was being "silly," "paranoid." The feeling of terror persisted, so I sat in my car, windows up and doors locked. When the wash was completed, I dashed in, threw the clothes into the dryer, and ran back out to my car. When the clothes were dry, I tossed them recklessly into the basket and hurriedly drove away to fold them in the security of my home.

From Jo Freeman, editor, *Women: A Feminist Perspective,* 5th ed. (Mountain View, CA: Mayfield Press, 1994). Reprinted by permission of author.

Although I was not victimized in a direct, physical way or by objective or measurable standards, I felt victimized. It was, for me, a terrifying experience. I felt controlled by an invisible force. I was angry that something as commonplace as doing laundry after a day's work jeopardized my well-being. Mostly I was angry at being unfree: a hostage of a culture that, for the most part, encourages violence against females, instructs men in the methodology of sexual violence, and provides them with ready justification for their violence. I was angry that I could be victimized by being "in the wrong place at the wrong time." The essence of terrorism is that one never knows when is the wrong time and where is the wrong place.

Following my experience at the laundromat, I talked with my students about terror- ization. Women students began to open up and reveal terrors that they had kept secret because of embarrassment: fears of jogging alone, shopping alone, going to the movies alone. One woman recalled feelings of terror in her adolescence when she did child care for extra money. Nothing had ever happened, and she had not been afraid of anyone in particular, but she had felt a vague terror when being driven home late at night by the man of the house.

The male students listened incredulously and then demanded equal time. The harder they tried, the more they realized how very different—qualitatively, quantitatively, and contextually—their fears were. All agreed that, while they experienced fear in a violent society, they did not experience terror, nor did they experience fear of rape or sexual mutilation. They felt more in control, either from a psychophysical sense of security that they could defend themselves or from a confidence in being able to determine wrong places and times. All the women admitted feeling fear and anxiety when walking to their cars on the campus, especially after an evening class or activity. None of the men experienced fear on campus at any time. The men could be rather specific in describing where they were afraid: in Harlem, for example, or in certain parts of downtown Newark, New Jersey—places that have a reputation for violence. But either they could avoid these places or they felt capable of self-protective action. Above all, male students said that they *never* feared being attacked simply because they were male. They *never* feared going to a movie or to a mall alone. Their daily activities were not characterized by a concern for their physical integrity.

The differences between men's and women's experiences of fear underscore the meaning of sexual terrorism: that women's lives are bounded by both the reality of pervasive sexual danger and the fear that reality engenders. In her study of rape, Susan Brownmiller argues that rape is "nothing more or less than a conscious process of intimidation by which all men keep all women in a state of fear."[1] In their study *The Female Fear*, Margaret T. Gordon and Stephanie Riger found that one-third of women said they worry at least once a month about being raped. Many said they worry daily about the possibility of being raped. When they think about rape, they feel terrified and somewhat paralyzed. A third of women indicated that the fear of rape is "part of the background" of their lives and "one of those things that's always there." Another third claimed they never worried about rape but reported taking precautions, "sometimes elaborate ones," to try to avoid being raped.[2] Indeed, women's attempts to avoid sexual intrusion take many forms. To varying degrees, women change and restrict their behavior, life-styles, and physical appearances. They will pay higher costs for housing and transportation and even make educational and career choices to attempt to minimize sexual victimization.

Sexual terrorism includes nonviolent sexual intimidation and the threat of violence as well as overt sexual violence. For example, although an act of rape, an unnecessary hysterectomy, and the publishing of *Playboy* magazine appear to be quite different, they are in fact more similar than dissimilar. Each is based on fear, hostility, and a need to dominate women. Rape is an act of aggression and possession. Unnecessary hysterectomies are extraordinary abuses of power rooted in men's concept of women as primarily reproductive beings and in their need to assert power over that reproduction. *Playboy*, like all forms of pornography, attempts to control women through the power of definition. Male pornographers define women's sexuality for their male customers. The basis of pornography is men's fantasies about women's sexuality.

Components of Sexual Terrorism

The literature on terrorism does not provide a precise definition.[3] Mine is taken from Hacker, who says that "terrorism aims to frighten, and by frightening, to dominate and control."[4] Writers agree more readily on the characteristics and functions of terrorism than on a definition. This analysis will focus on five components to illuminate the similarities and distinctions between sexual terrorism and political terrorism. The five components are ideology, propaganda, indiscriminate and amoral violence, voluntary compliance, and society's perception of the terrorist and the terrorized.

An *ideology* is an integrated set of beliefs about the world that explains the way things are and provides a vision of how they ought to be. Patriarchy, meaning the "rule of the fathers," is the ideological foundation of sexism in our society. It asserts the superiority of males and the inferiority of females. It also provides the rationale for sexual terrorism. The taproot of patriarchy is the masculine/warrior ideal. Masculinity must include not only a proclivity for violence but also all those characteristics claimed by warriors: aggression, control, emotional reserve, rationality, sexual potency, etc. Marc Feigen Fasteau, in *The Male Machine*, argues that "men are brought up with the idea that there ought to be some part of them, under control until released by necessity, that thrives on violence. This capacity, even affinity, for violence, lurking beneath the surface of every real man, is supposed to represent the primal untamed base of masculinity."[5]

Propaganda is the methodical dissemination of information for the purpose of promoting a particular ideology. Propaganda, by definition, is biased or even false information. Its purpose is to present one point of view on a subject and to discredit opposing points of view. Propaganda is essential to the conduct of terrorism. According to Francis Watson, in *Political Terrorism: The Threat and the Response*, "Terrorism must not be defined only in terms of violence, but also in terms of propaganda. The two are in operation together. Violence of terrorism is a coercive means for attempting to influence the thinking and actions of people. Propaganda is a persuasive means for doing the same thing."[6] The propaganda of sexual terrorism is found in all expressions of the popular culture: films, television, music, literature, advertising, pornography. The propaganda of sexual terrorism is also found in the ideas of patriarchy expressed in science, medicine, and psychology.

The third component, which is common to all forms of political terrorism, consists of "indiscriminateness, unpredictability, arbitrariness, ruthless destructiveness and amorality."[7] Indiscriminate violence and amorality are also at the heart of sexual terrorism. Every female is a potential target of violence—at any age, at any time, in any place. Further, as we shall see, amorality pervades sexual violence. Child molesters, incestuous fathers, wife beaters, and rapists often do not understand that they have done anything wrong. Their views are routinely shared by police officers, lawyers, and judges, and crimes of sexual violence are rarely punished in American society.

The fourth component of the theory of terrorism is voluntary compliance. The institutionalization of a system of terror requires the development of mechanisms other than sustained violence to achieve its goals. Violence must be employed to maintain terrorism, but sustained violence can be costly and debilitating. Therefore, strategies for ensuring a significant degree of voluntary compliance must be developed. Sexual terrorism is maintained to a great extent by an elaborate system of sex-role socialization that in effect instructs men to be terrorists in the name of masculinity and women to be victims in the name of femininity.

Sexual and political terrorism differ in the final component, perceptions of the terrorist and the victim. In political terrorism we know who is the terrorist and who is the victim. We may condemn or condone the terrorist, depending on our political views, but we sympathize with the victim. In sexual terrorism, however, we blame the victim and excuse the offender. We believe that the offender either is "sick" and therefore in need of our compassion or is acting out normal male impulses.

Types of Sexual Terrorism

While the discussion that follows focuses on four types of sexual terrorism—rape, wife abuse, sexual abuse of children, and sexual harassment—recent feminist research has documented other forms of sexual terrorism, including threats of violence, flashing, street hassling, obscene phone calls, stalking, coercive sex, pornography, prostitution, sexual slavery, and femicide. What women experience as sexually intrusive and violent is not necessarily reflected in our legal codes, and those acts that are recognized as criminal are often not understood specifically as crimes against women—as acts of sexual violence.

Acts of sexual terrorism include many forms of intrusion that society accepts as common and are therefore trivialized. For example, a recent study of women's experiences of obscene phone calls found that women respondents overwhelmingly found these calls to be a form of sexual intimidation and harassment.[8] While obscene phone calls are illegal, only in rare cases do women report them and the police take them seriously. In contrast, some forms of sexual terrorism are so extraordinary that they are regarded not only as aberrant but also as incomprehensible. The execution of fourteen women students at the University of Montreal on December 6, 1989, is one example of this. Separating the men from the women in a classroom and shouting, "You're all fucking feminists," twenty-five-year-old Marc Lepine systematically murdered fourteen women. In his suicide letter, claiming that "the feminists have always enraged me," Lepine recognized his crime as a political act.[9] For many women, this one act of sexual terrorism galvanized attention to the phenomenon of the murder of women because they are women. "Femicide," according to Jane Caputi and Diane E. H. Russell, describes "the murders of women by men motivated by hatred, contempt, pleasure, or a sense of ownership of women."[10] Most femicide, unlike the Montreal massacre, is committed by a male acquaintance, friend, or relative. In *Surviving Sexual Violence*, Liz Kelly argues that sexual violence must be understood as a continuum—that is, "a continuous series of events that pass into one another" united by a "basic common character."[11] Viewing sexual violence in this way furthers an understanding of both the "ordinary" and "extraordinary" forms of sexual terrorism and the range of abuse that women experience in their lifetimes.

Many types of sexual terrorism are crimes, yet when we look at the history of these acts, we see that they came to be considered criminal not so much to protect women as to adjust power relationships among men. Rape was originally a violation of a father's or husband's property rights; consequently, a husband by definition could not rape his wife. Wife beating was condoned by the law and still is condemned in name only. Although proscriptions against incest exist, society assumes a more serious posture toward men who sexually abuse other men's daughters. Sexual harassment is not a crime, and only recently has it been declared an actionable civil offense. Crimes of sexual violence are characterized by ambiguity and diversity in definition and interpretation. Because each state and territory has a separate system of law in addition to the federal system, crimes and punishments are assessed differently throughout the country.

RAPE

Rape statutes have been reformed in the past decade, largely to remove the exemption for wife rape and to use gender-neutral language. The essence of the definition of rape, however, remains the same: sexual penetration (typically defined as penile-vaginal, but may include oral and anal sodomy or penetration by fingers or other objects) of a female by force or threat of force, against her will and without her consent.[12]

Traditional views of rape are shaped by male views of sexuality and by men's fear of being unjustly accused. Deborah Rhode argues, in *Justice and Gender,* that this reflects a "sexual schizophrenia." That is, forced sexual intercourse by a stranger against a chaste woman is unquestionably regarded as a heinous crime, whereas coercive sex that does not fit this model is largely denied.[13] Since most women are raped by men they know, this construction excludes many forms of rape.

Because rape is considered a sexual act, evidence of force and resistance is often necessary to establish the nonconsent needed to convict rapists. Such proof is not demanded of a victim of any other crime. If females do not resist rape as much as possible, "consent" is assumed.

By 1990, forty-two states had adopted laws criminalizing rape in marriage: sixteen states recognize that wife rape is a crime and provide no exemptions; twenty-six states penalize wife rape but allow for some exemptions under which husbands cannot be prosecuted for raping their wives. Eight states do not recognize wife rape as a crime.[14] In spite of statutory reform, wife rape remains a greatly misunderstood phenomenon, and the magnitude of sexual abuse by husbands is not known. In Diana E. H. Russell's pioneering study on rape in marriage, 14 percent of the female respondents reported having been raped by their husbands.[15] The prevalence of wife rape, however, is believed to be much higher; approximately 40 percent of women in battered women's shelters also report having been raped by their husbands.[16] Victims of wife rape, according to one study, are at a greater risk of being murdered by their husbands, or of murdering them, than women who are physically but not sexually assaulted.[17]

WIFE ABUSE

For centuries it has been assumed that a husband had the right to punish or discipline his wife with physical force. The popular expression "rule of thumb" originated from English common law, which allowed a husband to beat his wife with a whip or stick no bigger in diameter than his thumb. The husband's prerogative was incorporated into

American law. Several states once had statutes that essentially allowed a man to beat his wife without interference from the courts.[18]

In 1871, in the landmark case of *Fulgham v. State*, an Alabama court ruled that "the privilege, ancient though it be, to beat her with a stick, to pull her hair, choke her, spit in her face or kick her about the floor or to inflict upon her other like indignities, is not now acknowledged by our law."[19] The law, however, has been ambiguous and often contradictory on the issue of wife abuse. While the courts established that a man had no right to beat his wife, it also held that a woman could not press charges against her abusive husband. In 1910, the U.S. Supreme Court ruled that a wife could not charge her husband with assault and battery because it "would open the doors of the court to accusations of all sorts of one spouse against the other and bring into public notice complaints for assaults, slander and libel."[20] The courts virtually condoned violence for the purpose of maintaining peace.

Laws and public attitudes about the illegality of wife abuse and the rights of the victim have been slowly evolving. During the 1980s, there was a proliferation of new laws designed to address the needs of victims of domestic violence and to reform police and judicial responses to wife abuse. These measures include temporary or permanent protection orders, state-funded or state-assisted shelters, state-mandated data collection, and proarrest or mandatory arrest policies.[21] Most states, however, continue to define domestic violence as a misdemeanor crime, carrying jail sentences of less than one year. Felony crimes are punishable by more than one year in jail, and police officers tend to arrest more often for felony offenses. The distinction between misdemeanor and felony crimes is also based on the use of weapons and the infliction of serious injuries.[22] While wife abuse is still considered a misdemeanor crime, a National Crime Survey revealed that at least 50 percent of the domestic "simple assaults" involved bodily injury as serious as or more serious than 90 percent of all rapes, robberies, and aggravated assaults.[23]

Sexual Abuse of Children

Defining sexual abuse of children is very difficult. The laws are complex and often contradictory. Generally, sexual abuse of children includes statutory rape, molestation, carnal knowledge, indecent liberties, impairing the morals of a minor, child abuse, child neglect, and incest. Each of these is defined, interpreted, and punished differently in each state.

The philosophy underlying statutory-rape laws is that a child below a certain age— arbitrarily fixed by law—is not able to give meaningful consent. Therefore, sexual intercourse with a female below a certain age, even with consent, is rape. Punishment for statutory rape, although rarely imposed, can be as high as life imprisonment. Coexistent with laws on statutory rape are laws on criminal incest. Incest is generally interpreted as sexual activity, most often intercourse, with a blood relative. The difference, then, between statutory rape and incest is the relation of the offender to the child. Statutory rape is committed by someone outside the family; incest, by a member of the family. The penalty for incest, also rarely imposed, is usually no more than ten years in prison. This contrast suggests that sexual abuse of children is tolerated when it occurs within the family and that unqualified protection of children from sexual assault is not the intent of the law.

SEXUAL HARASSMENT

Sexual harassment is a new term for an old phenomenon. The research on sexual harassment, as well as the legal interpretation, centers on acts of sexual coercion or intimidation on the job and at school. Lin Farley, in *Sexual Shakedown: The Sexual Harassment of Women on the Job,* describes sexual harassment as "unsolicited nonreciprocal male behavior that asserts a woman's sex role over her function as a worker. It can be any or all of the following: staring at, commenting upon, or touching a woman's body; requests for acquiescence in sexual behavior; repeated nonreciprocated propositions for dates; demands for sexual intercourse; and rape."[24]

In 1980 the Equal Employment Opportunity Commission issued federal guidelines that defined sexual harassment as any behavior that "has the purpose or effect of unreasonably interfering with an individual's work performance or creating an intimidating or hostile or offensive environment." Such behavior can include "unwelcome sexual advances, requests for sexual favors, and other verbal or physical conduct of a sexual nature."[25] It was not until six years later, however, that the Supreme Court, in *Meritor Savings Bank FSB v. Vinson,* ruled that sexual harassment was a form of sex discrimination under Title VII of the Civil Rights Act of 1964.[26]

In October 1991 national attention was focused on the issue of sexual harassment as a result of allegations made against Supreme Court Justice nominee Clarence Thomas by Professor Anita Hill. (Thomas was subsequently confirmed as a Supreme Court justice by a vote of fifty-two to forty-eight.) While there was a blizzard of media attention about sexual harassment, what emerged most clearly from the confirmation hearings was that the chasm between women's experiences of sexual harassment and an understanding of the phenomenon by society in general had not been bridged. Perhaps most misunderstood was the fact that Professor Hill's experience and her reaction to it were typical of sexually harassed women.[27]

Characteristics of Sexual Terrorism

Those forms of sexual terrorism that are crimes share several common characteristics. Each will be addressed separately, but in the real world these characteristics are linked together and form a vicious circle, which functions to mask the reality of sexual terrorism and thus to perpetuate the system of oppression of females. Crimes of violence against females (1) cut across socioeconomic lines; (2) are the crimes least likely to be reported; (3) when reported, are the crimes least likely to be brought to trial or to result in conviction; (4) are often blamed on the victim; (5) are generally not taken seriously; and (6) fuse dominance and sexuality.

VIOLENCE AGAINST FEMALES CUTS ACROSS SOCIOECONOMIC LINES

The question "Who is the typical rapist, wife beater, incest offender, etc?" is raised constantly. The answer is simple: men. Female sexual offenders are exceedingly rare. The men who commit acts of sexual terrorism are of all ages, races, and religions; they come from all communities, income levels, and educational levels; they are married, single, separated, and divorced. The "typical" sexually abusive male does not exist.

One of the most common assumptions about sexual violence is that it occurs primarily among the poor, uneducated, and predominately nonwhite populations. Actually, violence committed by the poor and nonwhite is simply more visible because of their lack of resources to secure the privacy that the middle and upper classes can purchase. Most rapes, indeed, most incidents of sexual assault, are not reported, and therefore the picture drawn from police records must be viewed as very sketchy.

The data on sexual harassment in work situations indicates that it occurs among all job categories and pay ranges. Sexual harassment is committed by academic men, who are among the most highly educated members of society. In a 1991 *New York Times* poll, five out of ten men said they had said or done something that "could have been construed by a female colleague as harassment." [28]

All the studies on wife abuse testify to the fact that wife beating crosses socioeconomic lines. Wife beaters include high government officials, members of the armed forces, businessmen, policemen, physicians, lawyers, clergy, blue-collar workers, and the unemployed. [29] According to Maria Roy, founder and director of New York's Abused Women's Aid in Crisis, "We see abuse of women on all levels of income, age, occupation, and social standing. I've had four women come in recently whose husbands are Ph.D.s — two of them professors at top universities. Another abused woman is married to a very prominent attorney. We counseled battered wives whose husbands are doctors, psychiatrists, even clergymen." [30]

Similarly, in Vincent De Francis's classic study of 250 cases of sexual crimes committed against children, a major finding was that incidents of sexual assault against children cut across class lines. [31] Since sexual violence is not "nice," we prefer to believe that nice men do not commit these acts and that nice girls and women are not victims. Our refusal to accept the fact that violence against females is widespread throughout society strongly inhibits our ability to develop meaningful strategies to eliminate it. Moreover, because of underreporting, it is difficult to ascertain exactly how widespread it is.

CRIMES OF SEXUAL VIOLENCE ARE THE LEAST LIKELY TO BE REPORTED

Underreporting is common for all crimes against females. There are two national sources for data on crime in the United States: the annual Uniform Crime Reports (UCR) of the Federal Bureau of Investigation, which collects information from police departments, and the National Crime Survey (NCS), conducted by the U.S. Department of Justice, which collects data on personal and household criminal victimizations from a nationally representative sample of households.

The FBI recognizes that rape is seriously underreported by as much as 80 to 90 percent. According to FBI data for 1990, 102,555 rapes were reported. [32] The FBI Uniform Crime Report for 1990 estimates that a forcible rape occurs every five minutes. [33] This estimate is based on reported rapes; accounting for the high rate of underreporting, the FBI estimates that a rape occurs every two minutes. The number of forcible rapes reported to the police has been increasing every year. Since 1986, the rape rate has risen 10 percent. [34]

The National Crime Survey (renamed in 1991 as the National Crime Victimization Survey) data for 1990 reports 130,260 rapes. [35] This data is only slightly higher than FBI data; researchers argue that NCS data has serious drawbacks as well. [36] Just as victims are reluctant to report a rape to the police, many are also reluctant to reveal their victimization to an NCS interviewer. In fact, the NCS does not ask directly about rape (although it will in the future). A respondent may volunteer the information when asked questions about bodily harm. The NCS also excludes children under twelve, thus providing no data on childhood sexual assault.

In April 1992 the National Victim Center and the Crime Victims Research and

Treatment Center released a report entitled "Rape in America," which summarized two nationwide studies: the National Women's Study, a three-year longitudinal survey of a national probability sample of 4,008 adult women, and the State of Services for Victims of Rape, which surveyed 370 agencies that provide rape crisis assistance.[37] The National Women's Study sought information about the incidence of rape and information about a number of health issues related to rape, including depression, posttraumatic stress disorder, suicide attempts, and alcohol- and drug-related problems.

The results of the National Women's Study confirm a belief held by many experts that the UCR and NCS data seriously underrepresents the occurrence of rape. According to the National Women's Study, 683,000 adult women were raped during a twelve-month period from the fall of 1989 to the fall of 1990.[38] This data is significantly higher than UCR and NCS data for approximately the same period. Moreover, since rapes of female children and adolescents under the age of eighteen and rapes of boys or men were not included in the study, the 683,000 rapes of adult women do not reflect an accurate picture of all rapes that occurred during that period. The data in this study also confirms the claim that acquaintance rape is far more pervasive than stranger rape. While 22 percent of victims were raped by someone unknown to them, 36 percent were raped by family members: 9 percent by husbands or ex-husbands, 11 percent by fathers or stepfathers, 16 percent by other relatives. Ten percent were raped by a boyfriend or ex-boyfriend and 29 percent by nonrelatives such as friends or neighbors (3 percent were not sure or refused to answer).[39]

Perhaps the most significant finding of the National Women's Study is that rape in the United States is "a tragedy of youth."[40] The study found that 29 percent of rapes occurred to female victims under the age of 11, 32 percent occurred to females between the ages of eleven and seventeen, and 22 percent occurred to females between the ages of eighteen and twenty-four.[41] Other research suggests that one in four women will be the victim of rape or an attempted rape by the time they are in their midtwenties, and at least three-quarters of those assaults will be committed by men known to the victims.[42] Lifetime probability for rape victimization is as high as 50 percent; that is, one out of two women will be sexually assaulted at least once in her lifetime.[43]

The FBI's Uniform Crime Report indexes 10 million reported crimes a year but does not collect statistics on wife abuse. Since statutes in most states do not identify wife beating as a distinct crime, incidents of wife abuse are usually classified under "assault and battery" and "disputes." Estimates that 50 percent of American wives are battered every year are not uncommon in the literature.[44] Recent evidence shows that violence against wives becomes greatest at and after separation.[45] Divorced and separated women account for 75 percent of all battered women and report being battered fourteen times as often as women still living with their partners.[46] These women are also at the highest risk of being murdered by their former husbands. Thirty-three percent of all women murdered in the United States between 1976 and 1987 were murdered by their husbands.[47]

"The problem of sexual abuse of children is of unknown national dimensions," according to Vincent De Francis, "but findings strongly point to the probability of an enormous national incidence many times larger than the reported incidence of the physical abuse of children."[48] He discussed the existence of a wide gap between the reported incidence and the actual occurrence of sexual assaults against children and suggested that "the reported incidence represents the top edge of the moon as it rises over the mountain."[49] Research definitions as to what constitutes sexual abuse and research methodologies vary widely, resulting in reported rates ranging from 6 percent to 62 percent for female children and 3 percent to 31 percent for male children.[50] David Finkelhor suggests that the lowest figures support the claim that child sexual abuse is far from a rare occurrence and that the higher reported rates suggest a "problem of epidemic proportions."[51]

In a study of 126 African-American women and 122 white women in Los Angeles County, 62 percent reported at least one experience of sexual abuse before the age of eighteen.[52] The same men who beat their wives often abuse their children. Researchers have found that "the worse the wife-beating, the worse the child abuse."[53] It is estimated that fathers may sexually abuse children in 25 percent to 33 percent of all domestic abuse cases. There is also a strong correlation between child abuse and the frequency of marital rape, particularly where weapons are involved.[54]

Incest, according to author and researcher Florence Rush, is the *Best Kept Secret.*[55] The estimates, however speculative, are frightening. In a representative sample of 930 women in San Francisco, Diana E. H. Russell found that 16 percent of the women had been sexually abused by a relative before the age of eighteen and 4.5 percent had been sexually abused by their fathers (also before the age of eighteen).[56] Extrapolating to the general population, this research suggests that 160,000 women per million may have been sexually abused before the age of eighteen, and 45,000 women per million may have been sexually abused by their fathers.[57]

Accurate data on the incidence of sexual harassment is impossible to obtain. Women have traditionally accepted sexual innuendo as a fact of life and only recently have begun to report and analyze the dimensions of sexual coercion in the workplace. Research indicates that sexual harassment is pervasive. In 1978 Lin Farley found that accounts of sexual harassment within the federal government, the country's largest single employer, were extensive.[58] In 1988 the U.S. Merit Systems Protection Board released an updated study that showed that 85 percent of working women experience harassing behavior at some point in their lives.[59]

In 1976 over nine thousand women responded to a survey on sexual harassment conducted by *Redbook* magazine. More than 92 percent reported sexual harassment as a problem, a majority of the respondents described it as serious, and nine out of ten reported that they had personally experienced one or more forms of unwanted sexual attentions on the job.[60] The Ad Hoc Group on Equal Rights for Women attempted to gather data on sexual harassment at the United Nations. Their questionnaire was confiscated by UN officials, but 875 staff members had already responded; 73 percent were women, and more than half of them said that they had personally experienced or were aware of incidents of sexual harassment at the UN.[61] In May 1975, the Women's Section of the Human Affairs Program at Cornell University in Ithaca, New York, distributed the first questionnaire on sexual harassment. Of the 155 respondents, 92 percent identified sexual harassment as a serious problem, 70 percent had personally experienced some form of sexual harassment, and 56 percent reported incidents of physical harassment.[62] A 1991 *New York Times*/CBS poll found that four out of ten women experienced sexual harassment at work, yet only 4 percent reported it.[63]

In *The Lecherous Professor*, Billie Wright Dziech and Linda Weiner note that the low reportage of sexual harassment in higher education is due to the victims' deliberate avoidance of institutional processes and remedies.[64] A pilot study conducted by the National Advisory Council on Women's Educational Programs on Sexual Harassment in Academia concluded:

The sexual harassment of postsecondary students is an increasingly visible problem of great, but as yet unascertained, dimensions. Once regarded as an isolated, purely personal problem, it has gained civil rights credibility as its scale and consequences have become known, and is correctly viewed as a form of illegal sex-based discrimination.[65]

CRIMES OF VIOLENCE AGAINST FEMALES HAVE THE LOWEST CONVICTION RATES

The common denominator in the underreporting of all sexual assaults is fear. Females have been well trained in silence and passivity. Early and sustained sex-role socialization teaches that women are responsible for the sexual behavior of men and that women cannot be trusted. These beliefs operate together. They function to keep women silent about their victimization and to keep other people from believing women when they do come forward. The victim's fear that she will not be believed and, as a consequence, that the offender will not be punished is not unrealistic. Sex offenders are rarely punished in our society.

Rape has the lowest conviction rate of all violent crimes. The likelihood of a rape complaint ending in conviction is 2 to 5 percent.[66] While the intent of rape reform legislation was to shift the emphasis from the victim's experiences to the perpetrator's acts,[67] prosecutions are less likely to be pursued if the victim and perpetrator are acquainted, and juries are less likely to return a conviction in cases where the victim's behavior or *alleged behavior* (emphasis mine) departed from traditional sex-role expectations.[68]

Data on prosecution and conviction of wife beaters is practically nonexistent. This is despite the fact that battery is, according to the U.S. Surgeon General, the "single largest cause of injury to women in the U.S." and accounts for one-fifth of all emergency room visits by women.[69] Police departments have generally tried to conciliate rather than arrest. Guided by the "stitch rule," arrests were made only when the victim's injuries required stitches. Police routinely instructed the parties to "break it up" or "talk it out" or asked the abuser to "take a walk and cool off." Male police officers, often identifying with the male abuser, routinely failed to advise women of their rights to file a complaint.[70]

As a result of sustained political activism on behalf of abused women, many states have revised their police training and have instituted pro- or even mandatory arrest policies. In 1984 the Attorney General's Task Force on Family Violence argued that the legal response to such violence be predicated on the abusive act and not on the relationship between the victim and the abuser.[71] A key issue, however, is the implementation of such reform. The record shows that the criminal justice system has responded inconsistently.[72]

Studies in the late 1970s and 1980s showed that batterers receive minimal fines and suspended sentences. In one study of 350 abused wives, none of the husbands served time in jail.[73] And while the result of pro- and mandatory arrest policies is a larger number of domestic violence cases entering the judicial system,[74] "there is considerable evidence that judges have yet to abandon the historical view of wife abuse."[75] In 1981, a Kansas judge suspended the fine of a convicted assailant on the condition that he buy his wife a box of candy.[76] In 1984 a Colorado judge sentenced a man to two years on work release for fatally shooting his wife five times in the face. Although the sentence was less than the minimum required by law, the judge found that the wife had "provoked" her husband by leaving him.[77] Recent task force reports on gender bias in the courts reveal a pattern of nonenforcement of protective orders, trivialization of complaints, and disbelief of females when there is no visible evidence of severe injuries.[78] In 1987 a Massachusetts trial judge scolded a battered women for wasting his time with her request for a protective order. If she and her husband wanted to "gnaw" on each other, "fine," but they "shouldn't do it at taxpayers' expense." The husband later killed his wife, and taxpayers paid for a murder trial.[79]

The lack of support and protection from the criminal justice system intensifies the double bind of battered women. Leaving the batterer significantly increases the risk of serious injury or death, while staying significantly increases the psychological terrorism and frequency of abuse. According to former Detroit Police Commander James Bannon, "You can readily understand why the women ultimately take the law into their own hands or despair of finding relief at all. *Or why the male feels protected by the system in his use of violence*" (emphasis mine).[80]

In his study of child sexual abuse, Vincent De Francis found that plea bargaining and dismissal of cases were the norm. The study sample consisted of 173 cases brought to prosecution. Of these, 44 percent (seventy-six cases) were dismissed, 22 percent (thirty-eight cases) voluntarily accepted a lesser plea, 11 percent (six cases) were found guilty of a lesser charge, and 2 percent (four cases) were found guilty as charged. Of the remaining thirty-five cases, they were either pending (fifteen) or terminated because the offender was committed to a mental institution (five) or because the offender absconded (seven), or no information was available (eight). Of the fifty-three offenders who were convicted or pleaded guilty, thirty offenders escaped a jail sentence. Twenty-one received suspended sentences and were placed on probation, seven received suspended sentences without probation, and two were fined a sum of money. The other 45 percent (twenty-three offenders) received prison terms from under six months to three years; five were given indeterminate sentences—that is, a minimum term of one year and a maximum term subject to the discretion of the state board of parole.[81]

In Diana E. H. Russell's study of 930 women, 648 cases of child sexual abuse were disclosed. Thirty cases—5 percent—were reported to the police; four were cases of incestuous abuse, and twenty-six were extrafamilial child sexual abuse. Only seven cases resulted in conviction.[82]

Most of the victims of sexual harassment in the Cornell University study were unwilling to use available procedures, such as grievances, to remedy their complaints, because they believed that nothing would be done. Their perception is based on reality; of the 12 percent who did complain, over half found that nothing was done in their cases.[83] The low adjudication and punishment rates of sexual-harassment cases are particularly revealing in light of the fact that the offender is known and identifiable and that there is no fear of "mistaken identity," as there is in rape cases. While offenders accused of familial violence—incest and wife abuse—are also known, concern with keeping the family intact affects prosecution rates.

BLAMING THE VICTIM OF SEXUAL VIOLENCE IS PERVASIVE

The data on conviction rates of men who have committed acts of violence against females must be understood in the context of attitudes about women. Our male-dominated society evokes powerful myths to justify male violence against females and to ensure that these acts will rarely be punished. Victims of sexual violence are almost always suspect. We have developed an intricate network of beliefs and attitudes that perpetuate the idea that "victims of sex crimes have a hidden psychological need to be victimized."[84] We tend to believe either that the female willingly participated in her victimization or that she outright lied about it. Either way, we blame the victim and excuse or condone the offender.

Consider, for example, the operative myths about rape, wife battery, incest, and sexual harassment.

RAPE
All women want to be raped.
No woman can be raped if she doesn't want it (you-can't-thread-a-moving-needle argument).
She asked for it.
She changed her mind afterward.
When she says no, she means yes.
If you are going to be raped, you might as well relax and enjoy it.

WIFE ABUSE
Some women need to be beaten.
A good kick in the ass will straighten her out.
She needs a punch in the mouth every so often to keep her in line.
She must have done something to provoke him.

INCEST
The child was the seducer.
The child imagined it.

SEXUAL HARASSMENT
She was seductive.
She misunderstood. I was just being friendly.

Underlying all the myths about victims of sexual violence is the belief that the victim causes and is responsible for her own victimization. In the National Women's Study, 69 percent of the rape victims were afraid that they would be blamed for their rape, 71 percent did not want their family to know they had been sexually abused, and 68 percent did not want people outside of their family knowing of their victimization.[85] Diana Scully studied convicted rapists and found that these men both believed in the rape myths and used them to justify their own behavior.[86] Underlying the attitudes about the male offender is the belief that he could not help himself: that is, he was ruled by his biology and/or he was seduced. The victim becomes the offender, and the offender becomes the victim. These two processes, blaming the victim and absolving the offender, protect the patriarchal view of the world by rationalizing sexual violence. Sexual violence by a normal male against an innocent female is unthinkable; therefore, she must have done something wrong or it would not have happened. This view was expressed by a Wisconsin judge who sentenced a twenty-four-year-old man to ninety days' work release for sexually assaulting a five-year-old girl. The judge, claiming that the child was an "unusually promiscuous young lady," stated that "no way do I believe that [the defendant] initiated sexual contact."[87] Making a victim believe she is at fault erases not only the individual offender's culpability but also the responsibility of the society as a whole. Sexual violence remains an individual problem, not a sociopolitical one.

One need only read the testimony of victims of sexual violence to see the powerful effects of blaming the victim. From the National Advisory Council on Women's Educational Programs Report on Sexual Harassment of Students:

> I was ashamed, thought it was my fault, and was worried that the school would take action against me (for "unearned" grades) if they found out about it.

> This happened seventeen years ago, and you are the first person I've been able to discuss it with in all that time. He's still at _____, and probably still doing it.

> I'm afraid to tell anyone here about it, and I'm just hoping to get through the year so I can leave.[88]

From *Wife-Beating: The Silent Crisis,* Judge Stewart Oneglia comments,

> Many women find it shameful to admit they don't have a good marriage. The battered wife wraps her bloody head in a towel, goes to the hospital, and explains to the doctor she fell down the stairs. After a few years of the husband telling her he beats her because she is ugly, stupid, or incompetent, she is so psychologically destroyed that she believes it.

A battered woman from Boston relates,

> I actually thought if I only learned to cook better or keep a cleaner house, everything would be okay. I put up with the beating for five years before I got desperate enough to get help.[89]

Another battered woman said,

> When I came to, I wanted to die, the guilt and depression were so bad. Your whole sense of worth is tied up with being a successful wife and having a happy marriage. If your husband beats you, then your marriage is a failure, and you're a failure. It's so horribly the opposite of how it is supposed to be.[90]

Katherine Brady shared her experience as an incest survivor in *Father's Days: A True Story of Incest.* She concluded her story with the following:

> I've learned a great deal by telling my story. I hope other incest victims may experience a similar journey of discovery by reading it. If nothing else, I would wish them to hear in this tale the two things I needed most, but had to wait years to hear: "You are not alone and you are not to blame."[91]

SEXUAL VIOLENCE IS NOT TAKEN SERIOUSLY

Another characteristic of sexual violence is that these crimes are not taken seriously. Society manifests this attitude by simply denying the existence of sexual violence, denying the gravity of these acts, joking about them, and attempting to legitimate them.

Many offenders echo the societal norm by expressing genuine surprise when they are confronted by authorities. This seems to be particularly true in cases of sexual abuse of children, wife beating, and sexual harassment. In her study of incest, Florence Rush found that child molesters very often do not understand that they have done anything wrong. Many men still believe that they have an inalienable right to rule "their women." Batterers, for example, often cite their right to discipline their wives; incestuous fathers cite their right to instruct their daughters in sexuality. These men are acting on the belief that women are the property of men.

The concept of females as the property of men extends beyond the family unit, as the evidence on sexual harassment indicates. "Are you telling me that this kind of horsing around may constitute an actionable offense?" queried a character on a television special on sexual harassment.[92] This represents the typical response of a man accused of sexual harassment. Men have been taught that they are the hunters, and women—all women—are fair game. The mythology about the workaday world abounds with sexual innuendo. Concepts of "sleazy" (i.e., sexually accessible) nurses and dumb, big-breasted, blond secretaries are standard fare for comedy routines. When the existence of sexual violence can no longer be denied, a common response is to joke about it in order to belittle it. "If you are going to be raped, you might as well enjoy it" clearly belittles the violence of rape. The public still laughs when Ralph threatens Alice with "One of these days, POW—right in the kisser." Recently, a television talk-show host remarked that "incest is a game the whole family can play." The audience laughed uproariously.

SEXUAL VIOLENCE IS ABOUT VIOLENCE, POWER, AND SEX

The final characteristic common to all forms of violence against females is perhaps the most difficult to comprehend. During the past decade, many researchers argued (as I did in earlier versions of this article) that sexual violence is not about sex but about violence. I now believe, however, that the "either-or" dichotomy—either sexual violence is about sex or it's about violence—is false and misleading. Male supremacy identifies females as having a basic "flaw"—a trait that distinguishes males and females and legitimates women's inferior status. This "flaw" is female sexuality: it is tempting and seductive and therefore disruptive, capable of reproducing life itself and therefore powerful.[93] Through sexual terrorism men seek to bring this force under control. The site of the struggle is the female body and female sexuality.

Timothy Beneke, in *Men on Rape*, argues that "not every man is a rapist but every man who grows up in America and learns American English learns all too much to think like a rapist" and that "for a man, rape has plenty to do with sex."[94] Twenty years of research and activism have documented that women largely experience rape, battery, incest, and sexual harassment as violence. That women and men often have vastly different experiences is not surprising. Under patriarchy men are entitled to sex; it is a primary vehicle by which they establish and signal their masculinity. From the male perspective, female sexuality is a commodity, something they must take, dominate, or own. Our popular culture routinely celebrates this particular notion of masculinity. Women are permitted to have sex, but only in marriage (the patriarchal ideal), or at least in love relationships. Women earn their femininity by managing their sexuality and keeping it in trust for a potential husband. The double standard of sexuality leads inevitably to coercion and sexual violence.

Many believe that re-visioning rape as violence not only accurately reflects many women's experiences but also is a more productive strategy for reforming legislation and transforming public attitudes. While arguing that "theoretically and strategically" the "rape as violence" position is the better one, attorney and author Susan Estrich points out that such an approach obscures the reality that the majority of rapes are coerced or forced but unaccompanied by conventional violence.[95] In fact, one consequence of this approach is that it precludes protest from women who experience sexual intrusions in ways not typically seen as violent.

It is argued that in sexual harassment the motive is power, not sex. There is a wide consensus that sexual harassment is intended to "keep women in their place." Yet, the means by which this is attempted or accomplished are sexual: rude comments about sex or about a woman's body, pornographic gestures or posters, demands for sexual favors, rape, etc. Clearly, to the harassers, a woman's place is a largely sexual one; her very presence in the workplace sexualizes it. In the accounts of women's experiences with sexual harassment in *Sexual Harassment: Women Speak Out*,[96] themes of sexual power and sexual humiliation resonate in each essay.

In wife battery the acts of violence are intended to inflict harm on the woman and ultimately to control her, but the message of the violence is explicitly sexual. For example, the most common parts of a woman's body attacked during battering are her face and her breasts—both symbols of her sexuality and her attractiveness to men. During pregnancy, the focus of the attack often shifts to the abdomen—a symbol of her reproductive power. In addressing the "either-or" debate in the sexual abuse of children, David Finkelhor points out "sex is always in the service of other needs. Just because it is infused with nonsexual motives does not make child sexual abuse different from other kinds of behavior that we readily call 'sexual'."[97]

Conclusion

The dynamic that underscores all manifestations of sexual terrorism is misogyny—the hatred of women. Violence against women is power expressed sexually. It is violence eroticized. Diana E. H. Russell argues that "we are socialized to sexualize power, intimacy, and affection, and sometimes hatred and contempt as well."[98] For women in the United States, sexual violence and its threat are central issues in their daily lives. Both violence and fear are functional. Without the power to intimidate and punish women sexually, the domination of women in all spheres of society—political, social, and economic—could not exist.

NOTES

1. Susan Brownmiller, *Against Our Will: Men, Women and Rape* (New York: Simon and Schuster, 1975), 5.

2. Gordon and Riger, 22.

3. Yonah Alexander, "Terrorism and the Mass Media: Some Considerations," in Yonah Alexander, David Carlton, and Paul Wilkinson (eds.), *Terrorism: Theory and Practice* (Boulder, CO: Westview Press, 1979), 159; Ernest Evans, *Calling a Truce to Terrorism: The American Response to International Terrorism* (Westport, CT: Greenwood Press, 1979), 3; Charmers Johnson, "Perspectives on Terrorism," in Walter Laquer (ed.), *The Terrorism Reader* (Philadelphia: Temple University Press, 1978), 273; Thomas P. Thornton, "Terror as a Weapon of Political Agitation," in Harry Eckstein (ed.), *The Internal War* (New York: Free Press, 1964), 73; Eugene Walter, *Terror and Resistance* (New York: Oxford University Press, 1969), 6; Francis M. Watson, *Political Terrorism: The Threat and the Response* (Washington, DC: R. B. Luce Co., 1976), 15; Paul Wilkinson, *Political Terrorism* (New York: John Wiley and Sons, 1974), 11.

4. Frederick F. Hacker, *Crusaders, Criminals and Crazies: Terrorism in Our Time* (New York: W. W. Norton and Co., 1976), xi.

5. Marc Feigen Fasteau, *The Male Machine* (New York: McGraw-Hill Book Co., 1974), 144.

6. Watson, 15.

7. Wilkinson, 17.

8. Sheffield, "Obscene Phones Calls," 487.

9. Malette and Chalouh, 100.

10. Caputi and Russell, 34.

11. Kelly, 76.

12. Estrich, 8; UCR, 43; Koss and Harvey, 4.

13. Rhode, 245.

14. Russell, *Rape in Marriage*, 21–22.

15. Ibid., xxii.

16. Ibid., xxvi.

17. Campbell, 340.

18. *Bradley v. State, I Miss.* (7 Walker) 150 (1824); *State v. Block*, 60 N.C. (Win.) 266 (1864).

19. *Fulgham v. State*, 46 Ala. 143 (1871).

20. *Thompson v. Thompson*, 218 U.S. 611 (1910).

21. Schweber and Feinman, 30.

22. *Arrest in Domestic Violence Cases: A State by State Summary* (New York: National Center on Women and Family Law, Inc., 1987), 1.

23. Langan and Innes, 1.

24. Lin Farley, *Sexual Shakedown: The Sexual Harassments of Women on the Job* (New York: McGraw-Hill Book Co., 1978), 14–15.

25. U.S. House of Representatives, 1980: 8.

26. *Mentor Savings Bank FSB v. Vinson*, 477 U.S. 57 (1986).

27. Lewin, A22; *Sexual Harassment: Research and Resources. A Report in Progress* (New York: The National Council for Research on Women, 1991), 10–13.

28. Kolbert, 1.

29. Roger Langley and Richard C. Levy, *Wife-Beating: The Silent Crisis* (New York: E. P. Dutton, 1977), 43.

30. Ibid., 44.

31. Vincent De Francis, *Protecting the Child Victim of Sex Crimes Committed by Adults* (Denver: American Humane Society, 1969), vii.

32. UCR, 1991, 16.

33. Ibid., 7.

34. Ibid., 16.

35. U.S. Department of Justice, *Criminal Victimization in the United States*, 1990, 5.

36. Koss and Harvey, 11–17.

37. National Victim Center, *Rape in America*, 1.

38. Ibid., 2.

39. Ibid., 4.

40. Ibid., 3.

41. Ibid.

42. Parrot and Bechofer, ix.

43. Crites, 36.

44. Langley and Levy, 3.

45. Zorza, 423.

46. Harlow, 5.

47. Caputi and Russell, 35.

48. De Francis, vii.

49. Ibid.

50. Finkelhor, *Sourcebook*, 19.

51. Ibid.

52. Russell, *Secret Trauma*, 69.

53. Bowker et al., 164.

54. Ibid.

55. Florence Rush, *The Best Kept Secret* (Englewood Cliffs, NJ: Prentice-Hall, 1980), 5.

56. Russell, *Secret Trauma*, 10.

57. Ibid.

58. Farley, 31.

59. Rhode, 232.

60. Ibid., 20.

61. Ibid., 21.

62. Ibid., 20.

63. Kolbert, A17.

64. Dziech and Weiner, xxi.

65. Frank J. Till, *Sexual Harassment: A Report on the Sexual Harassment of Students* (Washington, DC: National Advisory Council on Women's Educational Programs, 1980), 3.

66. Rhode, 246.

67. Koss and Harvey, 5.

68. LaFree, 240.

69. Zorza, 243.

70. Rhode, 239.

71. *Attorney General's Task Force*, 4.

72. Ibid.

73. Rhode, 241.

74. Goolkasian, 3.

75. Crites, 41.

76. Ibid., 45.

77. Ibid.

78. Schafran, 280, 283–84.

79. Goodman, 13.

80. James Bannon, quoted in Del Martin, *Battered Wives* (New York: Pocket Books, 1977), 115.

81. De Francis, 190–91.

82. Russell, *Secret Trauma*, 85.

83. Farley, 22.

84. Georgia Dullea, "Child Prostitution: Causes Are Sought" (*New York Times*, Sept. 4, 1979), p. C11.

85. *Rape in America*, 4.

86. Scully, 58.

87. Stanko, 95.

88. Till, 28.

89. Ibid., 115.

90. Ibid., 116.

91. Katherine Brady, *Father's Days: A True Story of Incest* (New York: Dell Publishing Co., 1981), 253.

92. Till, 4.

93. Sheffield, "Social Control," 172.

94. Timothy Beneke, *Men on Rape: What They Have to Say About Sexual Violence* (New York: St. Martin's Press, 1982), 16.

95. Estrich, 83.

96. Sumrall and Taylor.

97. Finkelbor, *New Theory*, 34.

98. Russell, *Secret Trauma*, 393.

PART II

Forms of Sexual Coercion and Violence

Part 2 consists of four sections, each of which explores a specific form of gender violence. Each section includes a historical sketch of the phenomenon studied, as well as a discussion of legal remedies that have been available to address the violence. Multiple causes and effects of various forms of gender violence are explored, drawing attention to the similarities that exist among them. Section 1 discusses sexual harassment as a widely experienced form of gender violence that is often trivialized in public discourse relative to other types of sexual coercion. Section 2 explores rape from multiple perspectives, drawing on writings that are both analytical and experiential in their treatment of the phenomenon. In section 3, partner battering is analyzed across a range of intimate relational contexts. The effects of gender violence upon children, as both victims and observers, is explored in section 4. In addition to articles that represent history and the social sciences, part 2 includes critical essay, folklore, literary analysis, and first-person narrative.

SECTION 1
Sexual Harassment

By now we are all familiar with stories of sexual harassment in and out of the workplace: the woman who quits her job to escape unwanted sexual advances from her boss; the jogger who faces catcalls from men on her morning run; the army officer forced to "run the gamut" by the men in her unit; the young boy teased relentlessly by classmates for "acting like a girl." Until recently few people have linked sexual harassment to the larger problem of gender-related power inequities in our society.

The hearing over Clarence Thomas's alleged harassment of Anita Hill and Bob Packwood's forced resignation from the Senate after years of harassing his female staff members have brought the subject of sexual harassment into the consciousness of U.S. citizens as never before. These cases are only the tip of the iceberg; yet they forced the public to awaken to a problem that had been previously thought of as sexual banter, inconsequential for either perpetrators or victims.

Sexual harassment was initially conceptualized to describe the unwanted sexual advances and requests for sexual favors experienced by women at work. Over the last two decades, however, gender studies has expanded the range of contexts and experiences that constitute the scope of sexual harassment. Catharine MacKinnon (1979) was one of the first scholars to theorize the unfavorable conditions that so many women had experienced but had found perplexing to identify. MacKinnon presented the case for a widespread phenomenon that was particularly prevalent among women working outside the home, and she countered skeptics with the simultaneous recognition that it is difficult for victims to articulate or report that which has no name. The fact that sexual harassment was not legally defined until 1980 made gathering "official data" on the problem difficult until quite recently. In addition, the general public did not consider sexual harassment a pervasive problem until after the Clarence Thomas debacle thrust it into the political spotlight. The dual structural problems of no legal recourse and lack of public recognition combine with situational factors (such as victims' fear of reprisal) to produce relatively few reports of harassment. Studies show that many women experience some form of harassment at work or in school, although no more than 5 percent of victims ever report their experiences to public authorities or their employing institutions (Fitzgerald and Shulman 1993).

The invisibility of sexual harassment until so recently is very likely the consequence of two significant sociological phenomena: the social construction of sexuality and the organization of human activities into public and private spheres. As we have seen, the emergence of sex/gender systems has been accompanied by sexual definition and regulation in which, in a predominance of cultures, sexuality is "normal" when it is exercised in heterosexual relationships featuring male dominance and female passivity. Widespread acceptance of polarized gender roles, subsumed in the rhetoric of biological determinism, has allowed behaviors we now define as harassment to be explained uncritically as nature taking its course. While human "progress" is ultimately defined as our ability to transcend the natural, innate sexual urges have consistently been viewed as some of the more difficult impulses to control—particularly in men.

The organization of human activities into public and private spheres, though it has its roots in the gender-based division of labor, is a fairly modern phenomenon. Modern societies increasingly organize activity into these spheres and conceptualize sexuality as belonging to the personal and private domain; yet the fact remains that a great deal of what we understand about sexuality is constructed in the public sphere and a good deal of sexual interaction occurs in public places (Hearn and Parkin 1987). Our intellectual frame of reference, until quite recently, assumed that sexuality was safely tucked away in the private sphere, thus veiling the extent to which sexuality pervades our activities in the public sphere.

Contemporary feminism provided a context within which sexual harassment *could* be named. By questioning biological determinism, and indeed, the very social structures within which gender relations take shape, scholars and activists could begin to theorize sexual harassment as a condition shaped by the distribution and mobilization of social power. Claiming the personal as political, feminists at the forefront of the contemporary movement threw conventional sexual regulations and definitions into the boiling cauldron of dissent. Once sexuality resurfaced in public discourse and was increasingly exposed as both a social construction and locus of power relations, the "discovery" of sexual harassment was inevitable.

Identifying Sexual Harassment

The second-class status of women was identified simultaneously by contemporary feminists sharing experiences in informal consciousness-raising groups and through the work of more formal inquiries, such as that conducted by the Presidential Commission on the Status of Women in the United States in the early 1960s (Freeman 1984). Sexual harassment was one of the common threads of experience that women began to weave into an analysis of male power in patriarchal societies. Women shared experiences of intimidation, unwanted sexual advances, intrusive touching, and sexually charged innuendo—a seemingly endless litany of offensive and controlling behaviors that pervaded the public sphere and often shattered the privacy that women expected in the home. Women were harassed by strangers in the street, superiors in the workplace, professors in their college classrooms, and faceless voices over the telephone. The earliest research on sexual harassment focused on the experiences of women at work. Given that work-related issues dominated the agenda of mainstream feminist organizations in the 1970s, this is not surprising. Work had been conceptualized as the primary route to financial independence and self-worth for women. That the organizations within which women labored were potentially fraught with intimidation was of immense concern to activists and scholars in the emergent field of women's studies. One of the first large-scale surveys of working women found that 70 percent of respondents had experienced some form of harassment at work (Farley 1978), and studies since consistently find large majorities of women who claim victimization. MacKinnon (1979) stretched the definitional boundaries of harassment by introducing the notion of a sexualized environment—a workplace in which the "white noise" is focused on sexual innuendo, causing many women significant anxiety and discomfort that ultimately affects their capacity to work.

In 1980, the U.S. government specified sexual harassment in the Code of Federal Regulations (No. 1604.11, 925), adopting a broad-ranging definition that included quid pro quo forms of harassment (requests for sexual favors where submission is linked to conditions of employment), unwanted sexual advances, and the existence of hostile working conditions. By 1982, the Association of American Colleges was documenting systematic harassment of women in institutions of higher education through its Project on the Status and Education of Women. Within these institutions, female students, faculty members, and administrators were routinely faced with both a "chilly climate" and direct forms of sexual intimidation (Hall and Sandler 1982; Hughes and Sandler 1986, 1988).

Explaining Harassment at Work

The early 1980s saw an explosion of research focused on the sexual harassment of women at work. While many sought only to calculate the extent of the problem, scholars began to develop and test various theories to explain harassment. Initially, theoretical work revolved around three potential explanatory models: the natural/biological model, the organizational model, and the sociocultural model (Tangri, Burt, and Johnson 1982). Conventional wisdom favors the natural/biological model, which sees sexual harassment as an outgrowth of the natural attraction between men and women being played out in public contexts. Those who subscribe to the biological model generally accept the corollary that the naturally aggressive sexuality of men contributes to the phenomenon, but that only "sick" men escalate from normal sexual banter to sexual harassment.

Early feminist theory had generally rejected the premises of the biological model. In adopting a more structural approach that focused on the distribution of power and the division of labor in organizations, feminist research on harassment has contributed much to the development of what is known as the organizational model. In this model, the hierarchical nature of modern organizations provides a clear framework within which to take account of women's location in organizational structures relative to men, the nature of women's work, and eventually, the social construction of gender in organizational contexts. Sociological research on the blocked mobility of women in corporations (Kanter 1977), as well as the treatment of token women in nontraditional occupations (Kanter 1977; Zimmer 1988; Yoder 1991), and the gendered discourses of power in bureaucracies (Ferguson 1984) set the stage for the integration of harassment into a more general theory of gender exploitation in workplaces.

The organizational power perspective is probably best articulated by MacKinnon, who described sexual harassment as occurring when "a man in the position of authority, whether a supervisor or teacher, uses his hierarchically superordinate role to place conditions of sexual compliance on his female subordinate's access to the benefits of her job or her educational program" (1979, 235). This perspective derives strength from the gender demography of modern organizations, in which the majority of women workers are segregated into low-wage, sex-typed jobs with less access to organizational power than men. Indeed, a significant number of women who have experienced harassment have been victimized by superiors or other powerful men in their schools or workplaces.

While useful in explaining the harassment experiences of many women, organizational power is not the only dynamic operating to facilitate harassment in organizations. Enough research established the existence of harassment by working peers and subordinates to suggest that the work roles and occupations of women were significant per se, regardless of the distribution of organizational power (Gutek and Morasch 1982; Tangri, Burt, and Johnson 1982; Gutek 1985). In particular, the concept of *sex-role spillover* provided an important lens through which to view harassment (Gutek and Morasch 1982). This concept refers to the extent that general cultural ideals and expectations about women pervade the workplace and shape the expectations about women workers. While organizations are presumably gender-neutral environments, sex-role spillover occurs when women at work are expected to be nurturers, mediators, and/or sexually available in accordance with the "natural" roles that women fill in the home. Gutek and Morasch suggest that sex-role spillover is most likely to be experienced by women in traditionally female occupations, such as clerical work, where the association of job to gender is strong. The combination of sex-role spillover, and the sheer numbers of women in clerical occupations, produce high victimization rates among women in sex-typed jobs.

While the concept of sex-role spillover adds a significant dimension to the organizational model of harassment, women in nontraditional occupations also experience sexual harassment. In fact, research suggests that women in male-dominated professions and male-dominated institutions suffer higher rates of victimization than women in socially sanctioned female occupations (Padavic and Reskin 1990; Mansfield et al. 1991). Among nontraditional occupational categories, women in the trades are most likely to experience sexual harassment, and women of color face both racial and sexual harassment in their jobs. Women who step beyond the boundaries of women's work in male-dominated institutions such as military and athletic organizations also face hostility, intimidation, and harassment. Is has been suggested that women's intrusion into the formerly homosocial worlds of these institutions threatens both male solidarity and male social privilege (Yoder 1991); thus, both male power and the perceived occupational inappropriateness of women in male fields are significant factors motivating men who harass.

Research on organizational cultures has facilitated our understanding of how organizations become sexualized. Organizations are increasingly recognized as social systems with their own cultures that shape both organizational goals and interpersonal relations at work. In addition to company guidelines that enforce sexual regulations in organizations (such as no dating between employees), there are value systems, communicative processes, rituals, and organizational symbols that tell employees how they may behave as sexual beings at work. Some organizations, such as pornographic bookstores, "gentlemen's clubs," and stores that specialize in intimate apparel and sex toys, have explicit sexual goals and concomitant sexualized cultures (Hearn and Parkin 1987). Most organizations, however, have ostensibly suppressed sexuality; their goals are explicitly nonsexual. Though sexuality appears suppressed, however, many of these organizations may tacitly encourage oppressive male sexuality among employees through exploitative ad campaigns, company rituals at events such as employee picnics and holiday parties, or through the frequent use of sexual metaphor in communicative processes. The experience of female employees of the Strohs Brewing Company provides a case in point. While Strohs is in the business of manufacturing and marketing beer, female employees brought a sexual harassment suit against the company, charging that, among other things, the company's Swedish Bikini Team advertising campaign in the early 1990s contributed to a sexualized work environment in which women were subjected to a daily barrage of demeaning, degrading, and often physically intrusive behaviors from male employees.

Traditional organizational cultures are often sexually charged, but this charge is largely heterosexual in nature. This frequently contributes to the harassment and intimidation of lesbians and gay men. Research on lesbians in the workplace indicates patterns of harassment similar to those experienced by heterosexual women (Schneider 1982; Taylor 1986). Heterosexist work environments are also settings where hegemonic masculinity must be proved by men on the shop floor (Collinson and Collinson 1989; Messerschmidt 1993) or on the drill field (Eisenhart 1975). Martin P. Levine (1979) reports that many gay men experience harassment or intimidation that leads them to divert their career goals to find more hospitable environments. Verta Taylor and Nicole C. Raeburn (1995) found that gay and lesbian sociologists who are activists in identity politics face discrimination and harassment in their places of employment. It is also important to recognize that straight men who abhor the exploitation of women and the marginalization of gays and lesbians in both organizations and the larger culture are affected negatively by aggressively (hetero) sexist environments. Taken together, research shows that organizational structures, cultures, and work roles, while analytically distinct, are not mutually exclusive; thus, harassment is a pervasive and multifaceted organizational problem for women, as well as for some men.

The third dominant model of harassment, the sociocultural model, posits that sexual harassment is not peculiar to organizations or their structures, but rather is a manifestation of patriarchy and male dominance in the larger sociocultural system. Male sexual aggression is not viewed as a natural attribute, but as part of a social script that boys and men are socialized to accept and girls and women are taught to expect. Men are socially rewarded for their sexual and occupational dominance, which serves collective and personal interests. It is therefore theorized that the influence of external cultural demands, rather than organizational factors, predisposes men to harass. The organizational and sociocultural models have both been supported by organizational research. The latter, however, provides an important link between the harassment of women at work and that which occurs in other public and private contexts.

Harassment outside the Workplace

While most harassment research has focused on work and occupations, important discussions about the phenomenon of street harassment (Bernard and Schlaffer 1983; Gardner 1995) show that harassment is not only a vehicle through which individual men exercise power over women, but it also often functions as a ritual of male bonding for participants. Cheryl Bernard and Edit Schlaffer's (1983) early research among street harassers found that few men engaged in solitary harassment—catcalls, whistles, and groping behaviors were viewed as group activities. Public harassments, including those children frequently engage in at school (see section 4 below), are simultaneously expressions of male solidarity and bravado and mechanisms for the social control and intimidation of females and males who don't conform to expectations of masculinity. In the case of sexual harassment of children by their peers, efforts to deal effectively with the problem are muddied by the fact that teachers and parents tacitly accept behaviors that are often antecedent to harassment, such as teasing and bullying (Stein 1995).

The maintenance of the patriarchal social system and male privilege, emphasized in the sociocultural model of harassment, is equally applicable to harassment that occurs in the private sphere, whether the perpetrator is a stranger or an intimate. Domestic terrorism, which is discussed in section 3, is frequently an exercise of male dominance, often triggered by men's perceptions of impotence in the public sphere. Similarly, the obscene or threatening phone call functions to fill a psychological need of the male caller and the collective social need of men to keep women self-conscious and in their proper place.

The Consequences of Sexual Harassment

Sexual harassment in all its forms has been found to have deleterious effects upon its victims. Some victims of sexual harassment have described their experiences as psychological rape; indeed, the literature suggests that the physical, psychological, and economic consequences of sexual harassment are similar to those experienced by victims of other forms of trauma.

Physical ailments reported by victims of sexual harassment include gastrointestinal disorders, headaches, anxiety attacks, insomnia, and other problems associated with high levels of stress (Crull 1982; Salisbury et al. 1986). Most sexually harassed women exhibit an immediate distress response following their victimizations that psychologists describe as a state of psychological shock (Koss 1990, 78). Other emotional responses include anger, depression, feelings of vulnerability, humiliation, and alienation (Working Women's Institute 1979; Gutek 1981).

The ubiquity of sexual harassment and its after-effects means that women are controlled economically and socially. In 1981, the U.S. Merit Systems Board found that one in ten women had quit her job in response to sexual harassment, and a more recent two-year study found that sexual harassment had led to the transfer, termination, or reassignment of more than 36,000 federal employees (U.S. Merit Systems Protection Board 1987). It is also estimated that at least 20 percent of women students drop a class in response to harassment (Fitzgerald 1982), and others may alter their career goals by changing majors to avoid specific harassers or hostile environments. Due to the scope and severity of harassment, women are frequently put in the position of reevaluating educational and career decisions. It is also the case that the comfort of daily routines, which are usually taken for granted by men, may be altered for women by the threat of harassment. How many women have changed their jogging routes or parking patterns to avoid a construction site or the front porch of a fraternity house? To what extent do personal tastes in clothing or entertainment preferences become issues given their perceived correlation to harassment? The victim-blaming atmosphere surrounding sexual harassment seems to have life-altering consequences for women in all realms of their daily experience. Sexual harassment, in all its forms, has been metaphorically described as the "dripping tap" of sexual violence and exploitation (Wise and Stanley 1987)—a constant and strong reminder of the status of women and sexual minorities in contemporary cultures.

Contributions to This Section

The articles in this section attempt to both document and explain a range of sexual harassment experiences. Michael D. Smith and Norman N. Morra have researched the nature and extent of telephone harassment in Canada. In "Obscene and Threatening

Telephone Calls to Women" they present data from a national survey that illustrate the similarities between women's responses to harassment and the responses of victims to other forms of gender violence. Their findings beg more analysis of this under-studied phenomenon and its inclusion into theoretical work on gender violence.

Carol Burke provides a portrait of life in the military in "Dames at Sea." Drawing from her experience as an instructor at the U.S. Naval Academy, Burke shows how *little* damaging public exposés, such as the 1991 Tailhook scandal in the U.S. Navy, change the daily life of military women. Burke's article is a prime illustration of the coexistence of sexualized environments and sexual harassment.

In "Changed Women and Changed Organizations," Barbara A. Gutek and Mary P. Koss review research on the sexual harassment of women at work from an organizational perspective. Moving beyond the consequences of sexual harassment for individual victims, the authors discuss the ways in which sexual harassment should be problematized from the standpoint of organizational effectiveness.

Finally, Kathryn Quina uses case studies from women in higher educational institutions to show the similarity between sexual harassment and rape on a variety of levels. Recognizing that rape and sexual harassment are closely situated on the continuum of sexual exploitation, Quina makes a strong case for more serious consideration of sexual harassment as a social problem and the development of more comprehensive healing strategies for victims.

Suggestions for Further Reading

Louise F. Fitzgerald, *Sexual Harassment in Higher Education: Concepts and Issues* (Washington, D.C.: National Education Association of the United States, 1992).

Carol Brooks Gardner, *Passing By: Gender and Public Harassment* (Berkeley: University of California Press, 1995).

Jeff Hearn and Wendy Parkin, *"Sex" at "Work": The Power and Paradox of Organization Sexuality* (New York: St. Martin's Press, 1987).

Anita Faye Hill and Emma Coleman Jordan (eds.), *Race, Gender, and Power in America: The Legacy of the Hill–Thomas Hearing* (New York: Oxford University Press, 1995).

Michele A. Paludi (ed.), *Ivory Power: Sexual Harassment on Campus* (Albany: State University of New York Press, 1990).

Dale Spender, *Nattering on the Net: Women, Power, and Cyberspace* (North Melbourne: Spinfex Press, 1995).

Anatomy Lesson

CHERRÍE MORAGA

A black woman and a small beige one talk about their bodies.
About putting a piece of their anatomy in their pockets
upon entering any given room.

When entering a room full of soldiers who fear hearts,
you put your heart in your back pocket,
the black woman explains. It is important, not to intimidate.
The soldiers wear guns, *not* in their back pockets.

You let the heart fester there. You let the heart seethe.
You let the impatience of the heart build and build
until the power of the heart hidden begins to be felt in the room.
Until the absence of the heart begins to take on the shape
of a presence.
Until the soldiers look at you and begin to beg you
to open up your heart to them, so anxious are they to see
what it is they fear they fear.

Do not be seduced.

Do not forget for a minute that the soldiers wear guns.
Hang onto your heart.
Ask them first what they'll give up to see it.
Tell them that they can begin with their arms.

Only then will *you* begin to negotiate.

From *Loving in the War Years,* South End Press, 1983, p. 68. Reprinted by permission.

7

Obscene and Threatening Telephone Calls to Women: Data from a Canadian National Survey

MICHAEL D. SMITH AND NORMAN N. MORRA

Women experience a broad range of physical or sexual violence by men or the threat of such violence. One of the most common of these intrusions is the obscene[1] or threatening telephone call—what Stanko (1990) calls the "the background noise of sexual intimidation for most women in modern life" (p. 98). Ironically, researchers have paid little systematic attention to this particular manifestation of violence against women.

This study adds to the meager store of existing information on obscene and other types of threatening phone calls to women.[2] Using quantitative and qualitative data from a survey on the sexual harassment of women in Canada, we sought answers to the following questions:

1. How prevalent are obscene and threatening telephone calls to women?
2. Are some women more at risk than others?
3. In what circumstances do such calls occur?
4. Who are the callers?
5. How do obscene and threatening phone calls affect the women who receive them?
6. What are the implications of the findings for theorizing about violence, fear, and the social control of women?

Method

SAMPLE AND INTERVIEWS

The sample was designed to represent the population of women between the ages of eighteen and sixty-five who live in Canada, spoke English or French, and (because the survey focused mainly on sexual harassment in the workplace) worked, or had worked during the last year, at a paid job outside the home.

A two-stage probability sampling process was employed. In the first stage, households were selected using random digit dialing (RDD) of residential telephone numbers on a province-by-province basis. Over ninety-seven percent of Canadian households have at least one telephone. The second stage entailed the random selection of a respondent

From *Gender and Society,* vol. 8, no. 4, pp. 584–96. Sage Publications, 1994 (edited). Reprinted by permission of Sage Publications. Tables deleted in this volume may be found in the original.

from each household contacted. If only one eligible woman resided in the household (the case of nine out of every ten households), she became the respondent; otherwise, the respondent was selected from among the eligible respondents using the most-recent-birthday method. These procedures resulted in a geographically representative sample of Canadian women, based on the 1986 census of Canada (Northrup 1992).

Using computer-assisted telephone interviewing (CATI), women interviewers working for the Institute of Social Research (ISR), located at York University, conducted interviews with 1,990 respondents. On average, the interviews took thirty minutes to complete, but many lasted an hour or more. All interviewing took place between April and August 1992.

The survey response rate, defined as the number of completed interviews divided by the estimated number of eligible households (times 100) was sixty-five percent. An ISR report provides details regarding the calculation of this rate and other technical aspects of the study (Northrup 1992).

MEASURES

The questions on obscene, threatening, and silent phone calls appeared at about the three-quarters mark of the questionnaire, following an extensive section on sexual harassment at work. After a brief introduction that referred to "unwanted phone calls," the interviewer asked the respondent if she had "ever received an obscene or threatening phone call." If the answer was yes, the interviewer asked, "How many obscene or threatening phone calls have you received in the past twelve months?" She then asked the respondent if she had ever received "silent phone calls that made you feel uneasy?" and, if yes, how many in the past twelve months? An affirmative response to any of these items resulted in an invitation to describe "the call, or series of calls, that disturbed you the most." A series of closed and open questions about the most disturbing calls — their characteristics, the characteristics of the callers, police and telephone company responses to complaints, emotional impact on the recipients — followed. Respondents were also asked about how they dealt with obscene and threatening calls generally.

Results

PREVALENCE AND FREQUENCY

Table 1 reveals lifetime prevalence rates of 66.5 percent for obscene or threatening phone calls and 64.1 percent for silent calls that made the respondent feel "uneasy." Put

TABLE 1. PREVALENCE AND FREQUENCY OF PHONE CALLS

	Prevalence				*Frequency of Calls*		
	Calls, Ever		*Calls, Past Year*		*Past Year, %*		
Type of Call	*Number of Women*	*%*	*Number of Women*	*%*	*1*	*2–5*	*6>*
Obscene/threatening	1,323	66.5	469	23.6	34.5	47.1	18.3
Silent	1,275	64.1	701	35.2	14.4	49.1	36.5
Either/both	1,656	83.2					

Note: $N = 1,990$ respondents.

differently, two-thirds of the women interviewed reported ever having received at least one obscene or threatening phone call, and almost two-thirds of the respondents reported ever having received at least one upsetting silent call. In the last year, 23.6 percent received obscene or threatening calls and 35.2 percent received silent calls.

Most of the women who were victimized during the survey years were victimized frequently. Among those who received silent calls, for example, almost eighty-six percent got more than one, and thirty-six percent got six or more.

SOCIAL-DEMOGRAPHIC RISK FACTORS ASSOCIATED WITH VICTIMIZATION IN THE PAST YEAR

Are some women more vulnerable than others to getting obscene, threatening, and silent phone calls? To examine this question, we first computed bivariate relationships between sociodemographic risk factors associated with the respondent and past-year victimization rates. These analyses showed that marital status, age, region, and community size were significantly related to victimization during the survey year; education, income, and occupational status were not. (These data are not shown.)

We then computed a series of logistic multiple regression analyses, which assessed the extent to which the statistically significant sociodemographic variables together predicted the occurrence of calls. In each analysis, variables were entered using a stepwise procedure in which the most significant variables enter first. Employing a likelihood ratio chi-square test, each step significantly improved the fit of the models. In short, being divorced or separated, being young, living in Ontario, and living in a major metropolitan area were independent, statistically significant predictors of whether or not a respondent received one or more obscene, threatening, or silent phone calls during the survey year.[3]

MOST DISTURBING CALLS EVER RECEIVED

Characteristics of Calls

Table 2 presents some basic descriptive characteristics of the calls, or series of calls, that recipients found most disturbing. (Henceforth, all data refer to calls *ever* received.) The bulk of these calls were of the obscene or threatening (78 percent), as opposed to the silent (22 percent) variety. Typically, they came after dark (61.2 percent), although a significant number of series calls occurred both during the day and after dark (16.5 percent). More often than not, the woman was either alone (50.1 percent) or sometimes alone (15.7 percent). Almost always she was at home (89 percent). It seems that respondents tended to define most disturbing calls as those in which the women felt especially vulnerable to further, more terrible intrusions.

Characteristics of Callers

Who makes these calls? Not surprisingly, the typical obscene or threatening caller was male (84.5 percent), adult (86.8 percent), and, unlike most men who abuse women, apparently a total stranger (73.8 percent).

A significant number of women (almost one in ten) said they were not sure if they knew the caller. As Stanko (1990) notes, wondering if someone who treats you normally in public is trying to intimidate you anonymously in private is disquieting, to say the least.

TABLE 2. MOST DISTURBING CALLS: CHARACTERISTICS OF CALLS

Characteristic	Number of Cases[a]	%
Total	1,618	100.0
Type of Call		
Obscene/threatening	1,262	78.0
Silent	356	22.0
When received		
During the day	357	22.4
After dark	977	61.2
Both	263	16.5
Alone/other adult present		
Alone	797	50.1
Other adult	544	34.2
Both	249	15.7
Where received		
Home	1,430	89.0
Work	84	5.2
Home and work	52	3.2
Somewhere else	41	2.6

[a] Columns may not add to 1,618 owing to deletion of missing cases.

Reporting to Police and Phone Company

Well over 1,600 women described a "most" disturbing call or series of calls; yet, only 218 of these women reported the calls to the police, and only 314 women complained to the telephone company. Of the police and telephone company responses, roughly three in ten were in the form of advice, much of which (if followed) would cost the woman money (e.g., change your number, get call display) or, for most women, is simply not practical (e.g., do not answer, get an unlisted number). The other most frequent answer? Nothing can be done. Smaller numbers of complainants got emotional support (mainly from the police) or action designed to catch the caller (mainly from the telephone company).

Emotional Effects

The question, "How did receiving these [most disturbing] calls make you feel?" precipitated an avalanche of responses. What follows conveys in the respondents' own words the range and intensity of their emotional reactions to the calls.

Fear.   Almost three out of every four women (74.5 percent) indicated they experienced some degree of fear, ranging from uneasiness or nervousness to outright terror. We coded these responses into two categories, labeled fear one and fear two, based on the severity of the fear described.

Respondents in fear one used words such as *uneasy, nervous, powerless, vulnerable, defenseless, helpless, trapped, insecure,* and *panicky.* Some examples are given below.

- I felt uneasy, very uneasy, you know, creepy. I would like to know who it is and why.
- It almost made me feel like someone outside was watching me . . . vulnerable.
- Upset, I was paranoid when I walked to my car, thinking that someone was watching me, going to do something to me.

- These silent calls bother me the most because they are coming at work. I'm alone for the most part at work and I get the impression that someone is coming in and casing the place.

The second fear category contains responses that explicitly describe, or at least strongly suggest, fear at a visceral level. Key words are, for example, *scared, frightened, terrified.*

- I was frightened. It went on for months. Nobody ever said anything, just silence.
- I was really scared. He called many times and even talked to my kids about me, asking them questions about me.
- Scared, really scared. It happened right after my husband left for work, at 6:20 in the morning, and it came as he was leaving the driveway, which made me think someone was watching.
- Frightened. It was as if they were right outside my door. One of them said he could see me. I was in the office and the lights were on in other office buildings. I was worried what his next move might be. It was at night.

Anger. Approximately 19 percent of the women said they felt anger, ranging from *annoyed* and *irritated* to *mad* and *outraged:*

- Angry. But then I figured it was someone without a life.
- I guess if I had been alone I would have been scared, but I wasn't so I was just mad.
- I was angry at the person who was doing it. How dare he talk to me in this way. I slammed the phone so hard I was surprised it didn't break.
- Angry, very angry. The last time I told him he was a coward.

Felt nothing. Despite the fact they were answering a question about "disturbing" telephone calls, 8 percent of the recipients indicated that the calls did not upset them, at least not significantly.

- They didn't upset me.
- I laughed.
- Nothing. I know people are crazy. I don't take it seriously.
- I wasn't upset. I just brushed it off.

Repulsion, violation, shock. We coded most of the remaining responses under three headings: *repulsion* ("Sick, really sick. The things he said were things I had never heard before"); *violation* ("I felt invaded. Here I am in my own home and someone is phoning me. Is it a joke? Is someone angry at me? I'm supposed to feel safe in my own home, but I went around and made sure all the doors were locked"); and *shock* ("First I was stunned, then I was scared after I hung up, scared that they knew my phone number and my house").

Coping Strategies

In an effort to determine how women attempt to avoid or otherwise deal with these calls, we asked all respondents who had received at least one call if they had ever changed their phone number as a result. Approximately 16 percent said yes. We then inquired about telephone answering machines and call-identification or "display" systems that display the caller's number (and, in some newer versions, name). Slightly over 21 percent of the 902 women who had an answering machine said they used it to avoid obscene and threatening calls. Of the 157 women who had call display, 56.7 percent indicated that they used it to fend off such calls, typically by screening them ("If I don't recognize the number, I don't pick it up"), calling back to confront the caller ("If I don't recognize the number, I still answer, but if the person doesn't say anything at the other end, I call them back to see who they are"), recording the caller's number ("I write down the number and go to the phone company and find out who the number belongs to"), or telling the caller that she has a call display ("I let the caller know that I have his number"). Clearly, however, many women cannot afford these services.

Theoretical and Practical Implications

Kate Millett laid the groundwork for a feminist analysis of threatening telephone calls when she wrote briefly about men's "bullying, obscene, or hostile remarks" as "psychological gestures[s] of ascendancy." Such gestures, she maintained, were backed up by the use of force as an "ever present instrument of intimidation" (Millett 1990, 36). Feminists subsequently elaborated the argument that men's control over women rests as much on threat and fear as it does on actual violence. Today most view obscene and threatening phone calls as expressions of violence in their own right as well as intrusions that lead to fear of "real" violence, physical and sexual.

The present findings provide strong support for the cornerstone of this argument, namely, that violence against women is widespread and systemic. Most women have suffered some form of men's violence. No sphere of women's lives is completely safe. The high levels of obscene and other types of threatening phone calls uncovered in this study, together with their distribution across all social and demographic lines, point to a social, not an individual, phenomenon; a pervasive, gender-based pattern of behavior, not the work of psychologically deranged individuals.

It goes without saying that women experience a wide range of men's physical, visual, and verbal intrusions as violence. These behaviors vary in the degree of direct physical harm they produce, but physical harm is only one dimension of victimization; getting an obscene phone call can be as traumatic as being hit. What connects what Wise and Stanley (1987) call the "dripping tap" forms of men's violence, such as obscene phone calls, and the "sledgehammer" forms, such as rape, is the capacity of all such forms to terrorize, to intimidate, to coerce, and to control (pp. 98–122).

The present results show clearly that obscene and threatening phone calls have harmful effects on women. In describing their emotional reactions to the calls that disturbed them most, almost three out of every four respondents said they felt a degree of fear, mixed, more often than not, with a sense of powerlessness over what might happen next. Such calls have material consequences, as well; for instance, about 16 percent of all women who reported receiving one or more obscene or threatening calls changed their phone number as a result.

Some charge that the state, while openly condemning violence against women, in effect condones it by acting inconsistently, in contradictory ways, or not at all. The criminal justice system, for example, still fails to grasp fully what sexual violence means from women's perspectives. With regard to obscene and threatening telephone calls, this appears to be the case, although limitations of the data allow only a partial exploration of this claim.[4]

In the first place, few respondents sought assistance from either the police or the telephone company. Whether they considered the calls too trivial to report, thought that their complaints would not be taken seriously, or believed that nothing could be done, we do not know. In any event, most of those who did complain were told that nothing could be done or received largely impractical advice.

To be sure, the very nature of these intrusions renders them difficult to combat. Most calls are made in private and leave no physical trace behind them. Even if a woman has call display, an obscene caller can subscribe to a free service that "blocks" the display of his number. (One telephone company offers a "call return" feature that negates the blocking function.) Another device, "call trace" (which enables the police to trace a threatening caller), appears to be an effective weapon, but it is expensive and available only in some areas. Also, a determined caller can always use a public telephone with little fear of being caught.

Section 372 of the Criminal Code on "indecent" and "harassing" telephone calls states that it is an offense to (1) convey to another person "with intent to injure or alarm" information that the caller knows is false, (2) make an "indecent" call "with intent to alarm or annoy," and (3) make "repeated" calls "without lawful excuse" and "with intent to harass" (Watt and Fuerst 1992, 567–8). In each case, the prosecution must prove that the defendant did indeed make the calls (or caused them to be made) and did indeed intend to "injure," "alarm," "annoy," or "harass." In the absence of physical evidence, this becomes nearly impossible. The gender-neutral phrasing of the law also diverts attention from the fact that the vast majority of the recipients of such calls appear to be women.

Of all the manifestations of men's violence against women, obscene and threatening phone calls may be the most pervasive. Certainly they are the most insidious. Without question, technological and legal means to protect women from this verbal violence are within reach. What remains is for the law and other arms of the state to take seriously what women say about how such calls affect them.

Notes

1. From women's perspective, obscene calls are threatening by definition, for a woman has no way of knowing that an obscene caller may be motivated purely by sex and poses no threat of an actual physical assault.

2. For a much fuller rendition of this article, please contact the second author.

3. The overrepresentation of divorced or separated and young women suggests that callers, to the extent they know the identity of their victims, perceive such women as especially fitting targets. As for women living in metropolitan areas, perhaps the men who harass them disproportionately reside in such places. Or perhaps the anonymity of big cities gives men who call known women confidence that their voices will not be recognized. Why living in Ontario should present an additional risk remains an open question.

4. The Canadian Radio-Television and Telecommunications Commission is the quasi-federal government agency responsible for regulating the telephone industry.

8

Dames at Sea: Life in the Naval Academy

CAROL BURKE

Reflecting on the much publicized Tailhook scandal, in which naval officers allegedly assaulted twenty-six women (several of them fellow officers), I recalled a lovely cool September morning in 1984 during the first semester of my seven-year tenure teaching at the Naval Academy. To a civilian whose only connection to the military was an old photograph of my father in a World War II uniform, the place was spectacularly impressive: the Severn in the distance, glassy and still; the gray stone buildings, massive and proud; the grounds a deep green even after a dry summer; and the orderly rows of ginkgoes fanning their gold leaves in unison. As I walked to Sampson Hall, the oldest building on the yard, I heard the approach of a group of midshipmen, running in formation and chanting in guttural tones: "Rape, Maim, Kill Babies. Rape, Maim, Kill Babies, Oorah!"

Marching chants ("cadence calls," as they are referred to in the Navy, "jodies" in the Army), along with the drill they accompany, help inculcate—often with a dose of irony—a strong, corporate identity. Typically, they oppose the longing for loved ones with the celebration of a new life as a member of the group. In cadence calls, a kind of early white version of rap music, trainees sing of the unfaithful girls they've left behind: "Ain't no use in goin' home,/Jody's got your girl and gone." But they also talk of compensation for such loss: "I don't want no teenage queen./I just want my M-16." Cadence calls not only instill mutual solidarity but resurrect the Casey Jones of American ballad tradition as a brave fighter pilot who survives the crash of his plane only to subdue women with greater ferocity.

> Climbed all out with his dick in his hand.
> Said, "Looky here, ladies, I'm a hell of a man."
>
> Went to his room and lined up a hundred . . .
> Swore up and down he'd fuck everyone.
>
> Fucked ninety-eight till his balls turned blue.
> Then he backed off, jacked off, and fucked the other two.

From *The New Republic*, August 17 and 24, 1992, pp. 16, 18, 20. Reprinted by permission.

Sadomasochistic cadence calls have increased since women entered the brigade of midshipmen in 1976. A version of the traditional song "The Prettiest Girl" portrays a woman appreciative of the violence she receives at the hands of a midshipman:

> The ugliest girl I ever did see
> was beatin' her face against a tree.
>
> I picked her up; I punched her twice.
> She said, "Oh, Middy, you're much too nice."

In the necrophilic chant "My Girl Is a Vegetable," midshipmen celebrate sex with a comatose girlfriend:

> My girl's a vegetable
> She lives in a hospital.
>
> (chorus)
>
> I'll do most everything
> To keep her alive.
>
> My girl's a paraplegic.
> Making love is so strategic.
>
> (chorus)
>
> My girl ain't got no eyes,
> Just two sockets full o' flies.
>
> (chorus)
>
> Sometimes I even play a joke,
> Pull the plugs and watch her choke.

Other Naval Academy practices celebrate violence toward women with the same gusto. Members of the Male Glee Club, a group of ambassadors for the Naval Academy, entertain themselves on bus trips home with a lurid variation of the popular song "The Candy Man":

> The S&M Man
>
> Who can take a chain saw,
> Cut the bitch in two,
> Fuck the bottom half
> and give the upper half to you . . .
>
> The S&M Man, the S&M Man
> The S&M Man cause he mixes it with love
> and makes the hurt feel good!

> Who can take a bicycle,
> Then take off the seat,
> Set his girlfriend on it
> Ride her down a bumpy street . . .
>
> Who can take an ice pick
> Ram it through her ear
> Ride her like a Harley,
> As you fuck her from the rear . . .

Although a large number of commissioned officers receive their training at Officer Candidate School and at several naval ROTC programs on college campuses, the midshipmen, the faculty, and the administration of the Naval Academy generally believe that it is the academy that "sets the standard for the Fleet." The institution's undergraduate regimen of rigorous academic studies, strenuous athletics, and confrontational leadership training produces, according to most members of the academy community, officers best qualified to assume the Navy's top positions, as indeed most of them do.

In the 1870s Congress condemned as hazing the assumption of authority on the part of upper-classmen at the Naval Academy to physically abuse or verbally humiliate underclassmen. Despite congressional condemnation, physical abuse continued in the form of ritual paddlings and demeaning practices like the game of "Cuckoo Clock," in which a plebe was ordered to crouch under a table and stick his head out as fast as he could saying, "Cuckoo," before being swatted with a newspaper by hovering upper-classmen.

A "no touching" rule was finally enacted two years ago, and physical abuse has dramatically lessened. But routine verbal insults continue through a system known as "Plebe Indoctrination." A freshman who has failed to memorize one item on the day's menu must submit to the public verbal abuse of an upperclassman. For example, the upperclassman may yell, "You aren't worth a piece of dirt on my shoe," to which the plebe will respond in one of only four permissible responses: Yes, Sir. No, Sir. No excuse, Sir. I'll find out, Sir. Those upperclassmen who delight in applying this humiliation day after day are known as "flamers"; their victims as "shit screens."

Women students at the Naval Academy face the same indignities during their plebe year as do their male counterparts. But they must learn to cope with more virulent forms of ridicule deeply rooted in Naval Academy traditions. On Sunday nights each company awards "the brick" to the midshipman whose date (or "drag," in academy jargon) is judged the ugliest of the weekend. After "Pig Pushes" (dances to which girls from private schools in the Baltimore and Philadelphia areas are bussed), the midshipman who dances with "the biggest pig" wins a pool of money collected from his fellow company members. On the dance floor, a midshipman may rub his fingers and thumb together behind the back of his partner, signifying his eagerness to claim the winnings at the end of the evening.

Periodically a "Hog Log" is maintained by midshipmen working in the main office where a visiting date checks in and awaits the midshipman who has invited her. Should a visitor be branded as unattractive, her name is entered in the "Hog Log." In recent years officials have banned such practices, yet many of them continue unofficially in the

Hall, where upperclassmen exercise casual intimidation and midshipmen are reluctant to incriminate one another.

Although upperclass male and female students may date during leave hours, a male midshipman known to be dating a female midshipman may be "branded" by the rest of his company. In this ceremony his pants are pulled down and a "W" (for WUBA) "branded" with boot blacking on his buttocks. The acronym WUBA was first used in 1976 to describe the freshly issued uniforms of the first female midshipmen: Women's Uniform Blue Alpha. The expression began to appear in misogynist graffiti ("WUBA Go Home!"); as jokes slipped into productions of The Masqueraders, the academy drama group; and as offensive catcalls. Although censored, the expression enjoys wide currency today at the Naval Academy, sometimes jokingly said to stand for "Women Used By All." WUBA jokes circulate quickly among the brigade of midshipmen:

> How are a WUBA and a bowling ball similar?
> You pick them up, put three fingers in them, and throw them in the gutter.

> What do you call a mid who fucks a WUBA?
> Too lazy to beat off.

> What's the difference between a WUBA and a warthog?
> About 200 pounds, but the WUBA has more hair.

The majority of the male student body stigmatizes women midshipmen as overweight and promiscuous. Ironically, with the intensive physical regimen required of all students, an overweight midshipman, male or female, is rare. When any students exceed their approved weight by a few pounds, they find their names and excess pounds posted on company bulletin boards. To many civilian faculty and outsiders, female midshipmen seem underweight.

Male midshipmen learn early that there are two sets of insignia to be earned: one based on military performance, the other on masculine prowess. They sport Chiquita and Dole banana stickers on the insides of their hats to mark each time they have had sex with a date on academy grounds. The Chiquita sticker signifies "scoring" in one's room; the Dole sticker, anywhere on the grounds.

Earning one's "brown wings" is common parlance for having engaged in anal intercourse with a woman. One female freshman complained of the sexist E-mail she and other women received almost nightly by anonymous midshipmen, including verses like the following:

> I love my woman dearly
> We get together yearly
> And although she said it stings
> I still earned my brown wings.

Women at the Naval Academy learn to accept silently what many view as intimidation. Like their male counterparts, they quickly learn that complaining of mistreatment is viewed as a sign of weakness and draws unwanted attention to them. Their immediate supervisors, upperclassmen who have themselves withstood humiliating abuse and whose job it is to test these recruits daily, favor those who stoically withstand interrogation and intimidation.

An informal group calling themselves "Webbites" shamelessly practices bigotry. Adherents of James Webb, former secretary of the Navy who in a visit to the Naval Academy several years ago referred to female midshipmen as "Thunder Thighs," this group has evolved over the past decade from a collection of outspoken critics of women in the military to a secret society, one that in 1991 referred to itself as the "WUBA KLUX KLAN" and solicited new members to further its goal of ridding the Naval Academy of women. Female midshipmen know that they may someday be required to serve under a former "Webbite" or that their commanding officer may be a member of the last class at the Naval Academy to graduate with no women, a class in which several members inscribed on their class rings "LCWB" (Last Class With Balls).

In response to widely publicized discrimination, the Navy has adopted the philosophy that although it cannot change the way people think, it can regulate behavior by identifying and proscribing all forms of sexist and racist behavior. There is little evidence that such regulations have produced the desired effect. As long as high-ranking officers wink at humiliating rituals and spontaneous acts of debasement, as long as they accept these as inevitable pranksterism (or "high jinks," as Admiral Virgil Hill referred to the handcuffing of a female midshipman to a urinal), such behavior will continue, if not as an expression of the fighter/jock ethos fueled at the Tailhook convention, then as other forms of abjection. We have a right to demand of the Navy and of its premier institution, the Naval Academy, a basic standard of decency, one we expect of all public institutions in a democratic society.

In a recent interview, J. Daniel Howard, undersecretary of the Navy, declared, "Americans don't want a naval officer to behave like just any person in society. They expect a higher standard of behavior." In fact, when we insist that assailants be prosecuted, we invoke no "higher standard of behavior." When we condemn those who witness a crime but fail even to notify police, we demand no superior moral standard than the decency and responsibility that come with citizenship. What happened at the Tailhook reunion was both traditional and criminal. Although a thorough criminal investigation may identify the perpetrators and others who sought to inhibit an investigation, the deep-rooted misogynistic traditions that breed such behavior will be harder to uproot.

9

Changed Women and Changed Organizations: Consequences of and Coping with Sexual Harassment

BARBARA A. GUTEK AND MARY P. KOSS

In the 1944 film *Gaslight* starring Ingrid Bergman and Charles Boyer, the husband slowly drives his wife toward insanity by causing the gaslights to flicker all the while claiming that the lights are perfectly fine (Hamilton and Dolkart 1991). The metaphor of gaslighting communicates the psychological torture inherent in sexual harassment. A woman who is harassed may be unsure at first if what she is experiencing really is harassment, may be unsure what to do about it, and may not receive support from others when she enlists assistance in stopping the harassment. Consider the following scenario.

> When Jane Doe took a job with a major hotel chain, her new boss promised that the job had "unlimited potential" for a bright, ambitious person. Jane, an ambitious young woman, liked almost everything about her job except the frequent sexist joking and sexual innuendos that pervaded the work place. Others went along with the jokes, but Jane complained. In response, her boss pressed her for details of her private life, dating behavior, and sexual preferences. He told her that in the "family atmosphere" of the organization, this was normal and expected. When she complained to her boss' boss, she was assured that she did not need to disclose any personal information. Yet, nothing changed in her department. Her increasing discomfort led her to talk to her boyfriend about the behavior that she now labeled sexual harassment. Her boyfriend asked her what she did to encourage her boss to make these comments and urged her to behave in a more professional manner. Jane then went to the human resources department with the intention of lodging a sexual harassment complaint against her boss. The HR specialist told her that she was responsible for handling her boss, and that the organization did not have a sexual harassment policy because it never needed one. In the meantime, her boss' comments took on an increasingly hostile tone and on her next performance appraisal, Jane received a rating of poor for "attitude." Devastated, she decided to seek help from a therapist, who gave her a battery of tests, informed her that she was suffering from a mild case of depression, and was unduly obsessed about her work. He suggested she come in twice a week in order to learn to deal with her feelings about work in a "constructive and empowering way." Still there was no change at work except the frequency and hostility of the comments which were increasingly directed specifically at Jane. She also felt a new sense of isolation. Some workers who formerly were friendly

From *Journal of Vocational Behavior*, vol. 42, no. 1, pp. 136–52. Copyright © 1993 by Academic Press, Inc. Reprinted by permission.

began to treat Jane in a hostile manner. Jane began thinking about quitting her job, but she didn't have another job lined up and the therapy was expensive. She felt depressed about being diagnosed as mildly depressed, a label she had never previously used to describe herself. Her boyfriend complained that she wasn't much fun anymore. Shortly thereafter, in casual conversation with a woman who worked in the same building, Jane discovered the woman had formerly worked for Jane's boss. Her experiences with Jane's boss were amazingly parallel to Jane's own experiences with him. She told Jane she eventually quit the organization. A few days later, when her boss made an unusually crude comment, Jane turned to him and slapped him across the face. He walked out of the room, came back with his supervisor, and together they told Jane she was fired for unprofessional behavior. As a last resort, Jane went to see an attorney who advertised in the newspaper that he would help people who had been wrongfully terminated. When she told him her story, he told her she probably could not win a sexual harassment case in court: she had hit her boss, and she wasn't sure that witnesses would corroborate her story. He did, however, suggest that she might be able to get her job back if they argued that she hit her boss because she was suffering from PMS.

This report, a composite of real experiences encountered by one of the authors in cases brought to court, represents a worst case scenario of the unfolding of a sexual harassment case and shows how sexual harassment can confront a victim with perceptions that are often invalidated by those around her. The more she seeks validation for her view, the more hostile and rejecting her world becomes, until she feels she is failing in her most important life roles. How different this scenario would be if Jane worked in an organization that was sensitive to sexual harassment, valued its female employees, had a sexual harassment policy and procedures, and enforced them. How different too the scenario might be if Jane's boyfriend and therapist offered constructive suggestions for altering the situation rather than blaming her.

This article focuses on some consequences of sexual harassment of women. How does sexual harassment affect a female victim and the organization for which she works? How does she attempt to cope with harassment when she is confronted with it? These topics are interconnected because the responses of victims will be influenced by the amount of support and understanding received from significant others and employers. Likewise, the extent of emotional, physical, and psychological damage a woman experiences from harassment also depends on the responsiveness of other people and the organization for which she works.

Sexual harassment has been conceptualized as part of a spectrum of gender-based abuses that all involve exploitation and physical or sexualized violence (Hamilton, Alagna, King, and Lloyd 1987; Russell 1984), and the sexual victimization literature has served as a model for responses to harassment (Koss 1990; Quina and Carlson 1989). The parallels between sexual harassment and childhood sexual abuse, particularly incest, are many (Hamilton et al. 1987; Salisbury, Ginorio, Remick, and Stringer 1986). Like the victim of incest, the sexually harassed woman is economically if not emotionally dependent on the aggressor. The abuse is humiliating so there is motivation to keep it a secret. It often continues for a long time and is experienced as an abuse of power and a betrayal of trust. Finally, retraumatization by the legal system is likely if redress from responsible authorities is sought. Sexual harassment differs from other forms of sexual victimization primarily in its direct impact on economic status and career well-being, which are only affected indirectly by other forms of victimization (Salisbury et al. 1986).

Empirical documentation of the psychological impact of harassment is difficult to obtain because the symptomatology is multiply determined. In addition to the impact of the sexual harassment itself, the aftereffects are influenced by disappointment in the way others react; the stress of harassment-induced life changes such as moves, loss of income, and disrupted work history; the triggering of unresolved issues from previous victimizations sustained by the woman; and finally, the trauma of litigation. Measuring the impact of harassment involves outcomes within three domains, which include somatic health, psychological health, and work variables including attendance, morale, performance, and impact on career track. In short, there is no single impact of sexual harassment. Instead, there are many different impacts depending on the domain examined and point in the process where the assessments are made.

It is unfortunate that there is a catch-22 quality inherent in research on the psychological and somatic reactions to sexual harassment. To show that harassment is harmful to the victim requires the demonstration that it has caused physical and emotional distress. Yet, evidence of breakdown in the victim undermines her credibility and competence as a person and as an employee (Gutek, forthcoming; Hamilton and Dolkart 1991; Jensvold 1991). Clinicians who evaluate victims of sexual harassment need to be aware that they are evaluating someone undergoing multiple abnormal stressors (Brown 1991). They must also be mindful of the ways in which mental health practitioners become tools of the harasser or institution including forced psychotherapy and illegal forced fitness-for-duty examinations (Jensvold 1991).

Effects on the Harassed Woman

Carefully controlled studies of effects of harassment have not been done. Information about impacts comes primarily from self-reported effects included in prevalence studies, convenience samples, specialized populations such as victims who have filed complaints or visited a counseling center, and anecdotal accounts of harassment. Thus, a review of outcomes yields a list of possible effects but does not allow conclusions about their prevalence or the conditions under which any particular effect will occur.

WORK OUTCOMES

Nearly one in ten women reported that they left their jobs as a result of sexual harassment in the original U.S. Merit Systems Protection Board (1981) study and in three separate studies of employed people in Los Angeles (Gutek, Nakamura, Gahart, Handschumacher, and Russell 1980; Gutek 1985). During a recent two-year period, over 36,000 federal employees quit their jobs, were transferred or reassigned, or were fired because of sexual harassment (U.S. Merit Systems Protection Board 1987). Among eighty-eight cases filed with the California Department of Fair Employment and Housing, almost half had been fired and another quarter had quit out of fear or frustration (Coles 1986). Some of the women who are fired or quit their jobs are unable to find or unwilling to take another job in the same field or occupation. Thus, sexual harassment can derail a career or lead or force a woman into an occupation which pays less well and/or offers fewer opportunities for advancement.

Among other negative work-related outcomes that have been reported is deterioration of interpersonal relationships at work (Bandy 1989; Culbertson, Rosenfeld, Booth-Kewley, and Magnusson 1992; DiTomaso 1989; Gutek 1985). Harassment can constrain the potential for forming friendships or work alliances with male co-workers (Schneider 1982). As a result of harassment university students report that they dropped courses and changed majors, academic departments and programs, and career intentions (Adams, Kottke, and Padgitt 1983; Benson and Thomson 1982; Fitzgerald, Schullman, Bailey, Richards, Swecker, Gold, Ormerod, and Weitzman 1990; Lott, Reilly, and Howard 1982). Lowered self-esteem and decreased feelings of competence may follow the realization that rewards may have been based on sexual attraction rather than ability (McCormack 1985).

Sexual harassment also affects women's satisfaction with the job and commitment to the organization (Culbertson et al. 1992). Among women who were harassed in Los Angeles County, 38% said the harassment affected the way they thought about their jobs (Gutek 1985). O'Farrell and Harlan (1982) reported that harassment had a strong negative impact on a woman's satisfaction with co-workers and supervisors in their study of women in blue collar jobs. It was less strongly related to satisfaction with promotions and satisfaction with work content. Negative affect such as anger or disgust at being harassed has been associated with loss of motivation, distraction, and dreading work (Jensen and Gutek 1982). General hostility toward women, which seems especially prevalent in some blue collar jobs, is often expressed in a sexually harassing manner (Carothers and Crull 1984; DiTomaso 1989; Wolshok 1981).

The impact of sexual harassment on women's job performance is less clear. According to Martin (1978; 1980), the exclusion of policewomen from informal social interaction networks which results from sexual harassment denies them the feedback that is necessary for successful job performance. But Gruber and Bjorn (1982) found that women auto-workers reported that sexual harassment had relatively little effect on their work behavior or sense of competence. Sexual harassment may not affect the diligence or effort a woman puts into her work, but lack of access to information and support from others in the work environment may well have an indirect effect on her work performance (see DiTomaso 1989; Collinson and Collinson 1989).

Sexual harassment and sex discrimination appear to go together. Women who report a lot of sexual harassment in their organization also tend to believe the organization is discriminatory in its treatment of women (DiTomaso 1989; Ragins and Scandura 1992). A study in Finland (Högbacka, Kandolin, Haavio-Mannila, and Kauppinen-Toropainen 1987) also showed that women who had encountered sexual harassment in their work group were more likely than other women to experience sex discrimination. Harassment and discrimination were not related for men.

Psychological and Somatic Outcomes

Beyond work outcomes, sexual harassment has been associated with a variety of negative effects on the victim. For example, Gruber and Bjorn (1982) found that in their sample of 138 women in mostly unskilled jobs in the auto industry, sexual harassment negatively affected self-esteem and life satisfaction. It was unrelated to family/home satisfaction, political efficacy, or personal control. Benson and Thomson (1982) found that sexual harassment was associated with a low sense of self-confidence, and Gutek (1985) found that sexual harassment sometimes affected the woman's relationship with other men.

Depending on the severity of the abuse, between 21 and 82% of women indicated that their emotional or physical condition worsened as a result of harassment (U.S. Merit Systems Protection Board 1981). In a sample of 92 women who had requested assistance for sexual harassment, virtually all reported debilitating stress reactions affecting work performance and attitudes, psychological health, and physical health

(Crull 1982). The physical symptoms frequently reported by victims include gastrointestinal disturbances, jaw tightness and teeth grinding, nervousness, binge-eating, headaches, inability to sleep, tiredness, nausea, loss of appetite, weight loss, and crying spells (Crull 1982; Gutek 1985; Lindsey 1977; Loy and Stewart 1984; Safran 1976; Salisbury et al. 1986). Among the emotional reactions reported by victims of sexual harassment were anger, fear, depression, anxiety, irritability, loss of self-esteem, feelings of humiliation and alienation, and a sense of helplessness and vulnerability (Gutek 1985; Safran 1976; Silverman 1976–77; Tong 1984; Working Women's Institute 1979).

Many writers have speculated that gender-based abuse is related to the high rates of depression among women compared to men (Hamilton et al. 1987; McGrath, Keita, Strickland, and Russo 1990). More recently similarities have been noted between the symptoms seen in the aftermath of sexual harassment and the symptoms characteristic of post-traumatic stress disorder (PTSD) as defined in the American Psychiatric Association's (1987) *Diagnostic and Statistical Manual* (Hamilton and Dolkart 1991; Jensvold 1991; Koss 1990). The PTSD diagnosis conceptualizes the symptoms seen in the aftermath of severe stressors as normal responses to abnormal conditions (APA 1987). Considerable evidence suggests that PTSD can and does develop in persons with no history of psychopathology prior to the stressor.

Four criteria are required to qualify for the PTSD diagnosis: exposure to a stressor outside the realm of normal human experience, re-experiencing of the trauma, heightened arousal, and avoidance of people and interests that remind the victim of the trauma. The hallmark of PTSD is intrusive re-experiencing of the trauma, which may not occur until months or years following the trauma when recollections are triggered by some actual or symbolic reminder of the trauma. Recollections are in the form of daytime memories or nightmares and are accompanied by intense psychological distress. One victim of sexual harassment described her re-experiences as follows. "Memories of my intimate experiences with him continued to plague me. At unexpected moments, particularly when I was alone in my car, I would suddenly feel him there with me. His fingertips would draw my face toward his, and I would again feel his kiss, catching me unaware and sending a jolt of anxiety through my body" (Anonymous 1991, 506). As this excerpt illustrates, re-experiencing is more than a visual phenomenon; physical reactions associated with the trauma re-occur as well. To reduce the distress of re-experiencing, trauma victims often go to great lengths to avoid reminders of the trauma.

A recent survey of 3,020 women provides prevalence data for sexual harassment in a nationally representative sample of women of whom 2,720 had been employed at some point in their lives (Kilpatrick, June 30, 1992). Data were collected by a random-digit-dial telephone survey. Measurement included standard questions to assess both major depression and PTSD as defined by the DSM-III-R. The findings are provocative and are presented here to apprise readers of the most recent research. However, the study has not yet been published and the material that follows is taken from brief oral testimony before congress that precluded examination of methodology and data analysis (Kilpatrick 1992) and a conference presentation (Saunders 1992).

Women suffering from PTSD and depression were more likely to have been sexually harassed than women who have never experienced PTSD or depression, suggesting that sexual harassment may contribute to depression and PTSD. Women who were diagnosed as having PTSD or depression reported more of each of seven types of harassment than did employed women in general. For example, 37% of women suffering from PTSD and 31% of women currently suffering from depression reported that they had been told sex stories by a supervisor, compared to 17% of the whole sample of employed women; 16 and 14% of women suffering from PTSD and depression respectively, compared to 7% of women in general, said they were touched sexually by a supervisor; and 17 and 15% of PTSD and depressed women, respectively, compared to 6% of employed women in general, reported that they were kissed or fondled by a supervisor.

Among women who reported that they felt sexually harassed, women suffering from PTSD or depression appeared to have more negative beliefs about the effects of sexual harassment than other women who reported that they felt sexually harassed. For example, among the 488 women in the survey who felt sexually harassed, 57% of women in general, but 62% of women suffering from PTSD and 65% of women suffering depression thought their career would be hurt if they complained about the harassment. In addition, although 35% of the harassed women said the harassment interfered with their job, 43% of women with PTSD and 45% of depressed women said that sexual harassment interferes with their job. In general, the harassed women suffering from PTSD and depression were as likely as women in general to tell their boss to stop the offensive behavior, 74% of women in general, and 77 and 69% of women diagnosed as having PTSD and depression, respectively, said they told their bosses to stop the offensive behavior. Women suffering from PTSD were less likely, however, than other harassed women to file a formal complaint: 6% of women with PTSD, 13% of depressed women, and 12% of employed women who were harassed filed a formal complaint about the harassment.

More definitive consideration of these results must await publication of a comprehensive report of the project. If the initial results hold, they suggest researchers might pay more attention to the role of sexual harassment in a variety of psychological and somatic problems encountered by women. Sexual harassment might well contribute to both PTSD and depression in women.

Effects on the Organization

Although relatively little research has addressed the effects of harassment on women victims, even less has focused on the effects on the organization. In general, the scant literature available is highly speculative and anecdotal. According to one form of logic, sexual harassment has no effects on the organization, at least no negative effects. If it were counterproductive or hurt the organization's effectiveness, it would have been sanctioned a long time ago. One perspective that views sexual harassment as relatively benign is the natural/biological view in which sexual harassment is seen as an expression of natural, biological attraction between men and women (Tangri, Burt, and Johnson 1982). In fact, many managers and workers think the seriousness and frequency of sexual harassment is overrated. For example, among readers of *Harvard Business Review* responding to a questionnaire about sexual harassment (Collins and Blodgett 1981), two-thirds of the men and about half of the women agreed or partly agreed with the statement: "The amount of sexual harassment at work is greatly exaggerated." In a systematic sample of employed people in Los Angeles County, less than 5% of either sex said sexual harassment was a major problem at their workplace (Gutek 1985). Other studies yield much higher figures. A recent study involving a stratified random sample of Navy enlisted personnel and officers found that over 60% of women and over 30% of men said sexual harassment is a problem in the Navy (Culbertson et al. 1992). Among a random sample of adults in Connecticut, 56% of men and 72% of women indicated that sexual harassment was either a "serious" or "very serious" problem (Loy and Stewart 1984).

Rather than being benign, sexual harassment has no doubt had negative effects on organizations all along, but these effects were invisible because sexual harassment itself was invisible, unnamed, and unreported. In its assessment of the magnitude of sexual harassment in the federal workforce, the U.S. Merit Systems Protection Board (1981) sought to assign a dollar figure to sexual harassment, estimating the cost of absenteeism, medical costs, and turnover attributable to harassment. Since, as noted above, about 10% of women have quit a job because of sexual harassment, turnover costs alone are substantial. The direct costs in absenteeism, medical expenses and indirect costs in the form of loss of motivation, distraction at work, and loss of commitment to the organization are also likely to be substantial, given the magnitude of harassment. Unfortunately, solid research on these effects is lacking.

Today, most large corporations do have sexual harassment policies and procedures for dealing with allegations of harassment. According to a recent report (Bureau of National Affairs 1987), 97% of the companies in their study had sexual harassment policies, but the majority of these policies were established well after 1980, the year the EEOC published guidelines on sexual harassment. Indeed when the *Harvard Business Review* conducted its survey in 1981 (Collins and Blodgett 1981), only 29% of respondents said they worked in companies where top executives had issued statements to employees disapproving of sexual conduct. Even where policies are in place today, the procedures which support the policies leave much to be desired, e.g., they advise victims to seek help from a supervisor when the supervisor is the harasser in up to half of incidents of harassment (Gutek 1985). Research on the effectiveness of various types of procedures for handling sexual harassment is yet to be conducted (but see Rowe 1981).

Another area where there is very little evidence is in the response of organizations to charges of harassment. The temptation to ignore the complaint or put it off until later is great (Gutek 1985; Biaggio, Watts, and Brownell 1990). Many managers and administrators are uncomfortable dealing with sensitive issues like harassment, and even well-meaning ones may handle the situation badly. Finally, finding instances of sexual harassment in the organization is disconcerting and embarrassing. "It must be recognized that harassment charges are embarrassing to institutions, and administrators may wish to suppress reports even though such suppression potentially places institutions in greater legal jeopardy than a direct response to complaints" (Biaggio et al. 1990, 216).

Workers who allege harassment are whistleblowers (Miceli and Near 1988; Near and Miceli 1987) and, as the carrier of bad news, may be blamed for "causing trouble." The effects on any workplace caught in the throes of an investigation into an allegation of sexual harassment or divided by a court case of harassment may be more visible to management than the effects of harassment itself. This is especially likely if harassment victims do not report the harassment. While there are anecdotal reports of managers' resentment at having to deal with sexual harassment allegations and male employees' fears that they will be unjustly accused, the topic has not been addressed in research.

Victims' Responses to Sexual Harassment

When a sample of employees is surveyed about what they would do if they were harassed, most say they would tell the person to stop (Dunwoody-Miller and Gutek 1985). In a Finnish study, 53% of both sexes said they would "have a talk" with the harasser (Högbacka et al. 1987). In addition, many men and women believe women should be able to handle sexual harassment themselves (Benson and Thomson 1982;

Gutek 1985, chap. 4; Sheppard 1989; Collins and Blodgett 1981). In a random sample survey of Los Angeles County workers, 79% of the women who had received at least one sexual overture from a man at work reported that they were confident they could handle future overtures (Gutek 1985). Thus, the majority of people apparently believe that sexual harassment is something that can and should be handled individually, i.e., by the person who is harassed.

A review of the literature on responses to harassment suggests that they fit into a two-by-two table: One axis consists of individual attempts to cope with harassment and coping responses involving another party such as a supervisor, therapist, physician, spouse, co-worker, or an outside agency or institution, e.g., the Equal Employment Opportunity Commission, a law firm, or a state agency. The second axis consists of indirect (e.g., ignoring, avoiding, evading) versus direct (e.g., confronting) responses. As will be noted below, individual, indirect coping responses (e.g., ignore the incident, avoid the perpetrator) are more common than responses that fit into the other three quadrants.

Individual Responses to Harassment

Real victims do not usually tell the harasser to stop. Their initial attempts to manage the initiator are rarely direct: typically, harassers are more powerful, physically and organizationally, than the victims, and sometimes the perpetrator's intentions are unclear. The first or the first several harassing events are often ignored (Benson and Thomson 1982; Dunwoody-Miller and Gutek 1985; MacKinnon 1979; Lindsey 1977; Loy and Stewart 1984). In their study of women automobile assembly workers, Gruber and Bjorn (1982) found that 23% of women said they ignored the harassment and 22% responded "mildly" (by telling the man, "I've heard all that before," or "I'm not your type" [p. 286]). A woman may be especially likely to ignore the behavior or respond mildly if she can ascribe the man's behavior to some extenuating circumstance (e.g., "It had to do with the pair of pants I was wearing. He thought they were nice" [Gutek 1985, 79]. "At the time he had been feeling lonely. He had left his wife" [Gutek 1985, 86]). She may also interpret or reinterpret the situation so that the incident is not defined as sexual harassment (Rabinowitz 1990). Interpreting the situation as "horseplay" or "laughing it off" is common (e.g., Gutek 1985; Ragins and Scandura 1992). "There were a lot of men where I worked. A lot of horseplaying." "It was not really serious. He is a very young man and I think he was just joking or playing around." (Gutek 1985, 83). Gruber and Bjorn (1982) also found that making light of the harassment was a fairly common response (reported by 10% of the women autoworkers they studied.)

Sometimes the woman tries to avoid the man, an indirect strategy reported by 51% of women officers and 68% of enlisted women in a recent U.S. Navy study (Culbertson et al. 1992; see also Loy and Stewart 1984, Table 3). Benson and Thomson (1982) found that female students try to avoid taking classes from male professors known to harass students. Given the differential in power (Zalk 1990), it certainly seems easier for students to avoid a potential harasser than to confront him. The ultimate step in avoiding the harasser is to quit the job, a common response of women who confront serious harassment (Loy and Stewart 1984).

Direct strategies (confronting the harasser) are less often used but are reported to be effective. Rowe (1981), for example, found the following direct response to be quite effective: Write a letter to the harasser, describing explicitly what is objectionable and outline a proper working relationship. Hand deliver the letter to the harasser and wait while he reads it. A letter has several advantages over a verbal request that the harassment cease. A written response shows that the victim felt strongly enough about the matter to write the letter, and allows the woman to deliberate in choice of words. Perhaps most importantly, the letter serves as a record that the victim confronted the perpetrator, copies of which can be sent to various administrators in the organization and can be shown in a court of law, should the harassment continue or should the perpetrator retaliate.

Other forms of direct response include hitting or insulting the harasser, tactics that are not commonly tried. In their study of automobile workers, Gruber and Bjorn (1982) found that 15% of women auto workers verbally "attacked" the harasser and 7% physically attacked or stopped the harasser.

COPING RESPONSES INVOLVING OTHERS

Individual responses to harassment are considerably more common than responses involving a third party or another institution, perhaps because most of the options involving other people are also direct (i.e., confrontational). When they could not avoid the harasser, Benson and Thomson (1982) found that students reported the following kind of indirect strategy involving others: bringing a friend along whenever they were forced to interact with the harasser.

Direct responses involving others are used by a minority of women victims and the more formal forms of protest (filing a grievance or lawsuit) are less common than simply reporting the harassment to someone in authority (Grauerholz 1989). In a survey of workers in Finland, only 20% of women (and 5% of men) said they would report harassment to a supervisor if they were harassed. In the random sample survey of workers in Los Angeles, 18% of women who were harassed actually did report the harassment to someone in authority (Gutek 1985). Comparable figures for a random sample of Navy personnel were 24% for enlisted women and 12% for women officers (Culbertson et al. 1992). Gruber and Bjorn (1982) found that 7% of the harassed automobile workers they studied reported the matter to someone in authority (see also Loy and Stewart 1984, Table 3).

Only 5% of women victims responding to the 1987 U.S. Merit Systems Protection Board study either filed a formal complaint or requested an investigation. In the 1989 Navy study, among those women who were harassed, 12% of enlisted women and 5% of female officers filed a grievance. The Women's Legal Defense Fund (1991) concluded that in the civilian work force between 1 and 7% of women who are harassed file a formal complaint or seek legal help. Available evidence suggests that less than half are decided in favor of the woman alleging harassment (Terpstra and Baker 1988, 1992). According to the first U.S. Merit Systems Protection Board study of the federal workforce (1981), only 2% of the people harassed took official action; half that number won their cases. The court cases discussed in the media constitute a very small percentage of cases of sexual harassment.

In general, harassment victims do not make official complaints either to their organization or to another agency for several reasons: they feel that making a complaint will not accomplish anything, they are concerned about retaliation for complaining (Culbertson et al. 1992; Gutek 1985), and often they do not want to hurt the harasser and they fear that complaining might negatively affect his job and/or family (Gutek 1985). Women who blame themselves for the harassment are especially concerned about protecting "the person who bothered" her (Jensen and Gutek 1982). Some women also report that they were too embarrassed or afraid to report the harassment (Culbertson et al. 1992). In the U.S. Navy study, the most common negative reaction reported by women who did complain about harassment was "I was humiliated in front of others" (reported by 33% of enlisted women and 34% of officers).

THE EFFECTIVENESS OF DIFFERENT COPING STRATEGIES

The available research suggests that the indirect strategies of coping with harassment by reinterpreting, ignoring, and avoiding are very common, but not particularly effective. Quitting a job or leaving school may be effective in stopping the immediate harassment of that person, but it has other consequences for the person who leaves, and it is unlikely to stop the harasser from harassing other women (Rabinowitz 1990). If they are not particularly effective, why then are the indirect responses so commonly tried? Gruber and Bjorn (1982) suggested three reasons why individual, indirect methods may be so common. First, indirect methods such as reinterpreting the situation or avoiding the harasser may allow a woman to "manage" the situation without disrupting the work setting or her relationship with other people at work (Benson and Thomson 1982; Collins and Blodgett 1981; Gutek 1985; Sheppard 1989).

Second, women may perceive the direct methods as riskier and less certain in their outcomes than the indirect methods. Avoiding the perpetrator may seem safer than confronting him or filing a complaint against him. Although there is some evidence that fear of retaliation is a realistic fear (Coles 1986), there is no evidence that direct methods of coping with harassment are necessarily riskier than indirect methods, particularly if riskiness is equated with effectiveness of stopping the harassment. While they appear to be more effective in stopping the harassment than indirect methods of coping with sexual harassment, it is possible to make a case that direct attempts at dealing with harassment may be problematic for women as a group. By forcing the perpetrator and/or the organization to deal with the issue, the woman making the complaint may be viewed as disrupting the workplace and she may well engender hostile reactions (DiTomaso 1989; Biaggio et al., 1990). Unfortunately, the topic of riskiness of various types of responses to harassment has not been studied.

Third, Gruber and Bjorn (1982) suggested that some harassment is ambiguous because it combines a degree of sexual interest with offensive behavior. "This ambiguity may reduce a woman's ability to respond in an assertive or direct manner" (p. 276; see also Gutek 1985, chap. 4). Along similar lines, in a scenario study, Williams and Cyr (1992) found that male (but not female) students rated the perpetrator's behavior as less harassing if the women target had made a prior commitment to a friendly relationship with the harasser.

CONTINGENCIES IN RESPONSE TO HARASSMENT

Although the individual, indirect responses to sexual harassment are common, it makes sense to ask whether some women or some situations encourage women to respond directly or to involve other people or institutions. For example, a victim of harassment might more readily employ a direct response to harassment if she has a supportive supervisor and works in an organization having a sexual harassment counselor or prominently displayed posters forbidding sexual harassment. Unfortunately, few of the circumstances under which women victims use different kinds of coping responses are known and data suggest only one tentative conclusion. Women who were more severely harassed tended to respond in a more assertive and direct manner than those who were not severely harassed (Gruber and Bjorn 1982; Loy and Stewart 1984). Victims are more likely to ignore the harassment, joke about it, or evade the harasser when the harassment is mild. A recent scenario study showed that student respondents thought the victim would be more likely to report the incident if she had not previously been friendly toward the perpetrator (Williams and Cyr 1992), but, as noted above, existing research of inexperienced raters shows that their reactions are not always consistent with the behaviors of real victims.

Characteristics of the woman victim might also affect how she responds to harassment. Gruber and Bjorn (1986) tested three hypotheses about coping with sexual harassment. They found support for the hypothesis that women with less organizational power would respond less actively and directly than women with some organizational power. (They defined power as having high job skills, having high job status, and/or not being at a lower organizational level than the harasser). They also found some support for a second hypothesis, namely that women with fewer personal resources (i.e., those having low self-esteem, low personal control, strong sense of being trapped in their job) would respond in an indirect manner more often than women with more personal resources. Similar findings were reported by Jensen and Gutek (1982) who found that women who tended to exhibit behavioral self-blame (i.e., felt their own behavior contributed to the harassment) were less likely than other women victims to discuss the harassment with others or report it to others. They also found that women who had traditional sex-role attitudes were less likely than other women to report the harassment to someone. Finally, Gruber and Bjorn (1986) found no support for their third hypothesis that black women, representing people who have low "sociocultural power," would respond less assertively than white women (see also Culbertson et al. 1992 for consistent findings.)

It should be noted that both Gruber and Bjorn's (1986) and Jensen and Gutek's (1982) studies were cross-sectional and, thus, it is not possible to draw definitive causal relationships from the data. Although it is appealing to assume that failing to report the harassment led to lower self-esteem and/or behavioral self-blame, it is also possible that low self-esteem and/or self-blame prevented victims from directly dealing with the harassment in some manner.

Stages of Response to Harassment

Another approach to the study of responses to harassment, illustrated by the scenario described at the beginning of the paper, is a stage model. Most harassment is not a one-time occurrence, but unfolds over time. How a woman responds probably depends on the progression of the harassment. Has she already tried ignoring, evading, or joking? Is the harassment continuing, escalating, becoming more hostile or threatening? The progressive reactions to harassment observed among women in psychotherapy document a sequence of changes in the victim's central beliefs about herself, her co-workers, and the work world (Salisbury et al. 1986). Four stages of response can be identified.

(1) Confusion/Self-Blame. The sexual harassment was a series of events. After each incident, the victim believed that the harassment was going to level off or eventually stop. When the harasser's behavior escalated, which it did in virtually all of the cases studied, the victim felt out of control and helpless.

(2) Fear/Anxiety. Subsequent to the harasser's continuing behavior, the victim felt

trapped and became "paranoid." She feared potential retaliation at work, the future of her career, and potential financial ruin. Outside of work, she feared being called on the phone in the early morning, having her home watched, or being followed in a car. Concentration, motivation, work performance, and attendance were adversely affected and self-esteem declined.

(3) Depression/Anger. Once the woman recognized that she was a legitimate victim who was not to blame for her harassment, anxiety often shifted to anger. Often this shift occurred when she decided to leave her job or was fired. This anger about being treated unfairly was a prime motive to file charges. While filing charges may have represented a positive step by the victim to take control of her destiny, it often led to a decided deterioration in the work situation.

(4) Disillusionment. The organizational response to sexual harassment was often hurtful and disappointing. By speaking up, the woman encountered a whole new set of institutional abuses. Often, the woman eventually realized that she had been naive about getting help in the system. She then questioned her expectations about fairness, loyalty, and justice. These ingenuous beliefs gradually become replaced by the insight that justice doesn't always prevail.

Discussion

This review of the clinical and empirical literature on the outcomes of sexual harassment shows that the topic has received very little attention, especially in comparison to the abundance of research that has been devoted to the definition of harassment and to the frequency of its occurrence (Gutek and Dunwoody 1988). What is available tends to be anecdotal, case studies, or nonrepresentative self-reports. Relatively little has made its way into journals but has been confined to conference presentations, books, and book chapters. Furthermore, the body of studies fails to do justice to the complexity of the outcome questions. Thus the literature allows us to list categories of outcomes, but does not allow us to draw conclusions about the frequency of different outcomes or the conditions leading to the various outcomes. The review suggests that sexual harassment is hardly benign—either for the individual or the organization. It raises three questions: why is there so little research, what kind of research is needed, and what are the pros and cons of researching outcomes?

WHY SO LITTLE RESEARCH ON OUTCOMES AND REACTIONS?

In general, this review reveals an appalling lack of empirical data on outcomes, especially in comparison to research on other forms of gender-based sexual exploitation. There are several possible explanations for the lack of data on the impact of harassment. The primary one is that the topic is embraced by none of the major funding agencies. It is illegal but is not viewed as a serious crime by justice authorities, and it is a victimization but viewed as a minor one in terms of psychological adjustment by mental health agencies. As a consequence, much more is known about the impacts of rape or child sexual abuse than is known about sexual harassment. Almost all the research on sexual harassment has been done without funding and it suffers for it. Much of the research is opportunistic, uses students, and focuses on issues easy to study without funding (e.g., how students respond to various sexual harassment scenarios.) The data reviewed here suggest that sexual harassment may be a far more significant contributor to women's distress than has been acknowledged; funds for in-depth, controlled studies should be made available.

What Kinds of Research Are Needed?

The widespread prevalence of sexual harassment demands that future research include studies in which victims are followed prospectively in time from the point of victimization and administered standardized measurements across the three domains of outcome: psychological distress, somatic effects, and work-related changes. Also important are the development of measures of responses to harassment, as exemplified by recent work by Fitzgerald and Brock (1992) and studies of the variables that mediate or moderate the impact of harassment. These should include *person variables* (e.g., age, demographic characteristics, pre-existing personality functioning, perception of the meaning of the trauma, and qualities assigned to the self and others post-harassment), *event variables* (e.g., severity, duration, frequency of abuse, degree of personal violation, and whether victimization was shared with others or suffered alone), *organization variables* (e.g., policies in place, response to the harassment, quality and availability of resources to assist victims, and degree of physical and emotional safety ensured post-trauma), and *environment variables* (e.g., immediate response of significant others, quality and continuity of social support, and community and company attitudes and values about harassment, corporate climate).

Samples of women from general populations (e.g., college students, employed women) as well as specific populations (e.g., victims who have filed law suits, victims who have sought help from counseling centers) should be followed over time to gain a better understanding of the development of work outcomes as well as somatic and psychological outcomes. The inclusion of the mediating and moderator variables discussed above will elucidate the conditions under which sexual harassment leads to the various outcomes that have been identified in this review. In doing so, the research may suggest strategies for minimizing negative outcomes for victims of harassment. While minimizing negative outcomes is less desirable than eliminating sexual harassment altogether, it helps.

Finally, an understanding of the true costs of sexual harassment borne by organizations and their employees, as well as the more visible costs of dealing with charges of harassment, investigations, and lawsuits, may encourage organizations to provide a more supportive environment for female employees who encounter harassment.

The Pros and Cons of Focusing on Outcomes

A focus on outcomes suggests a linear sequence in which some stimulus (sexual harassment in this case) necessarily leads to one or more outcomes. Undoubtedly there are women who are sexually harassed by a legal or standardly accepted lay definition of harassment but who may experience few or none of the outcomes discussed in this chapter. Does the failure to exhibit outcomes negate the person's experience of harassment, i.e., will the presence of outcomes be taken as a necessary condition for the existence of harassment? Will a woman be able to successfully allege harassment if she keeps her job, receives a positive performance evaluation, or gets a raise? Will she be able to successfully charge harassment if she does not need a therapist, has no physical symptoms, and sleeps and eats well? Will it be necessary to show adverse impacts including somatic and psychological effects in order to have one's charge of harassment taken seriously? In the formal complaint process, a reliance on the existence of negative outcomes as proof of the allegation of harassment has contributed to the retraumatization of harassment victims. Women who allege harassment may be required by their own attorneys or counselors in their companies to undergo fitness-for-duty examinations or psychotherapy (Jensvold 1991). One problem with a reliance on negative effects as an indicator of harassment is that they contribute to a common stereotype of woman, namely, the "sick woman" syndrome. Sexual harassment made her sick.

Unfortunately, the charge that the woman has been psychically or physically damaged by the harassment leaves open an alternate interpretation of her "sickness," namely that she has always been emotionally or physically fragile or damaged. Thus, by coming forth and complaining about harassment or filing a sexual harassment lawsuit, a woman runs the risk of being portrayed either as a person made sick by harassment or worse, a person who has always had physical and/or psychological problems (Gutek, forthcoming). Prospective studies and archival research may be possible in settings such as the military to allow comparison of pre- and post-trauma psychological status and health care utilization. Sustained research on the conditions under which any particular effect occurs should provide valuable information in court cases and alleviate the double bind now faced by many women who take their cases to court.

10

The Victimizations of Women

KATHRYN QUINA

In the comic strip *Beetle Bailey*, common forms of sexual harassment are carried out by harmless characters whom we are supposed to love, or at least feel a kind of charitable forgiveness toward. General Halftrack is the archetypic older gentleman whose dowdy wife starves him for affection. His secretary Miss Buxley—who can't type—drives him wild with her sexy figure and short skirts. "Killer" (short for "lady-killer," a curiously violent name) is always whistling at "chicks" (who love it), accompanied by Beetle, who is equally aggressive but not as successful. Zero just stares at women's bodies.

Played out in the real world, these scenarios are not funny. The similarity of a university department to a comic strip seems especially incongruous, yet many of us have had to cope with Generals, Killers, Beetles, and Zeros in our professional as well as personal lives. In my first five years as an academic, I had an older professor literally chase me around a desk, similar-aged colleagues determined to bed me, and a dean who simply could not stop staring at my chest (and I'm not Miss Buxley!). Sadly, I am not the only one to relate these experiences. In most of the instances described above, I learned about other victims of the same offenders; in my research on sexual harassment and rape, I have met many more victims of other offenders.

The striking thing about sexual harassment is that it is almost never harmless. In this paper, I will argue that sexual harassment is a sexual assault which shares important commonalities with rape, an offense few of us today believe is harmless. While harassment is less physically intrusive and usually less violent or life-threatening, it is not substantially different structurally or socially from rape. In this view, the burgeoning literature on the issues of rape victimization allows important insight and understanding of the sexual harassment situation and survivor reactions.

The conceptual framework for this position is that rape and harassments are both sexual assaults which lie on a continuum of sexual exploitation, varying primarily in degree of physical intrusion and potential physical injury to the victim.[1] On the least physically violent pole, this continuum begins with verbal assaults, including sexually offensive jokes or degrading comments. At the most violent pole are rape-murder and femicide. On this scale, sexual harassment and rape are relatively close together. In fact, many assaults now called harassment—those involving sexual contact—are legally the equivalent of rape.

Six major commonalities underlying this continuum are discussed here, illuminated with stories from students and colleagues and from my own life to provide a glimpse of the reality of these sexual assaults.[2] These areas of commonality are: (1) power dynamics; (2) gender roles and relationships; (3) offender characteristics; (4) cultural stereotyping; (5) emotional reactions of survivors; and (6) paths to resolution.

Power Dynamics

Researchers have now clearly established that rape is not sexually motivated, but is a violent way to achieve a sense of power (Groth 1979). Case studies support a similar psychological mechanism among sexual harassers. The rapist is likely to use his physical strength advantage over his victim, or to wield a gun or knife. The sexual harasser uses his age or social position, or wields economic power and authority as his weapons (Alliance Against Sexual Coercion 1981; Fitzgerald, Gold, Ormerod, and Weitzman 1987; Hall and Sandler 1982). Both clearly rely on the fear and vulnerability of their victims.

Ann was a new assistant professor, the only woman in a large department. Only one colleague, Ed, had welcomed her arrival. Late one night, Ed called her to "discuss a problem." He began talking about her future tenure decision and her need to be more "friendly." He also suggested they have dinner to discuss their relationship, since he knew it would "help her get ahead." At the same time, he warned her not to associate with students (the only other women) or any of the women's groups on campus, because such associations would "look bad" in the eyes of her colleagues. Already isolated, she now avoided him as well as the women.

Gender Roles and Relationships

By far, the sexual offender is most likely to be a male: an estimated 99 percent of rapists (Groth 1979) and 75–90 percent of sexual harassers (Reilly, Lott, and Gallogly 1986) are men. The victim is most likely to be female and young (Finkelhor 1979; Reilly et al. 1986). Cultural gender roles are also important to rape and harassment. By their own admission, rapists believe in, and attempt to act out, extreme versions of the cultural stereotype of masculinity as dominance over women (Beneke 1982). There is evidence that sexual harassers hold the same stereotypes and desire the same macho image (Dziech and Weiner 1990). Furthermore, both kinds of offender hold extreme stereotypes of women, including the mythical images described later in this paper of women as masochistic and secretly desiring their "attentions." Finally, cultural demands on women to be "feminine"—that is, to be passive, submissive, helping, and nurturant— probably increase the likelihood of being victims of rape or harassment (Bart 1985b).

For several months, Beth remained silent about her major professor's sexual comments and the way he touched her whenever they were alone. She tried to be nice, partly to avoid his wrath and partly because she didn't know what else to do. Meanwhile, other graduate students were beginning to tease her about him. One day, as she described it, she "freaked out." She yelled at him to get out of her office and quit bothering her. Not only did his abuse stop, but the other students, who overheard the interaction, began to treat her with greater respect. Until she spoke up, they had assumed she was "using her femininity."

Characteristics of the Abuser

Sexual abusers, from harassers to rapists, from child molesters to murderers, are "habitual" offenders, many assaulting hundreds of women, children, and men (Rosenfeld 1985; Freeman-Longo and Wall 1986). Furthermore, these offenders carry out their repeated assaults in a highly stereotypical fashion, or *modus operandi*. Even those who claim to be in love with their victims are likely to have a characteristic pattern of behaviors leading up to, during, and following the assault (Holroyd and Brodsky 1977).

Cindy, a student tutor, was assaulted by a client, who accused her of "exuding sexuality all over the place." She remained silent, embarrassed by the experience and frightened by the powerful message she felt she must be projecting. A month later, a coworker filed a complaint of sexual assault against the same man, and Cindy spoke up. In the ensuing legal proceedings, another student victim came forward, and records revealed that several previously reliable tutors had resigned after working with this client.

This has important implications for any victim: someone else probably has a similar story to tell. Unfortunately, we have a tendency to view each assault as an isolated incident, attributing the cause to the victim's character or behavior (Cann, Calhoun, Selby, and King 1981), and fail to look for a pattern. The legal implications are also important: it may be possible to identify others who have shared the experience and to pursue a group grievance.

Cultural Images and Mythologies

Brownmiller (1975) provided an excellent review of the cultural mythologies surrounding rape, and the images of rape victims, extending back to Biblical writings. Thanks to extensive educational efforts and willingness of survivors to speak up, these attitudes have become less prevalent with respect to rape (Kanarian and Quina-Holland 1981). However, stereotypes and misinformation continue to be applied to sexual harassment. These mythologies consistently blame the victim for sexual abuse, and on a larger scale, act to keep women "in their place" (MacKinnon 1979). The most common attributions about sexual harassment fall into three categories:

(1) Sexual assault is a form of seduction. In history (e.g., Homer's sirens) and in our contemporary culture (e.g., Cindy's case), sex is imbued with images of women as temptresses and men as helpless slaves to powerful sexual drives. MacDonald (1971) wrote a handbook for police officers describing twenty-seven ways in which women "precipitated" rape. While his data were seriously flawed (Hursch 1977), similar warnings are now being given with respect to sexual harassment. Meyer (1981) suggested that women in the workplace must be careful about the way they dress and talk, because it could cause their coworkers to harass them. Fitzgerald et al. (1987) found that professors, who dated students were more likely (than non-dating professors of the same students) to perceive that women students had approached them. These ideas are summed up by the classic first response to all victims of sexual assault: What were YOU doing, and what were YOU wearing?

(2) Women secretly need/want to be forced into sex. Not long ago, masochism was considered an essential element of women's personality (Deutsch 1944). Young men learn from an early age that women like to be forced into sex (Malamuth and Briere

1986), and that they "say no but mean yes."[3] It is not surprising, then, that harassment usually continues or escalates when the victim has given no positive response, or a negative response (Alliance Against Sexual Coercion 1981). Harassers offer such excuses as "I know her better than she knows herself," while onlookers—like Beth's fellow graduate students—may suspect the victim really enjoys the attention.

(3) Women do not tell the truth. The historical distrust of women's words influenced legal statutes and practices concerning sexual assault until the 1970s, and still affects attitudes towards survivors. For example, charges of rape had to be corroborated by a witness in some states, and the judge's instructions to the jury included a warning that rape is easy to accuse, and hard to prove (Brownmiller 1975). Such suspicion clouds survivors of sexual harassment as well. The first concern is often whether she or he had any reason to harm the alleged offender. At a conference I attended last year, a university counsel (a woman!) recommended that *any* time a sexual harassment case ended in acquittal, the university should consider bringing charges of perjury (for false accusation) against the alleged victim.

Survivor Reactions

Individual responses to rape and sexual harassment, of course, vary widely as a function of the severity of the assault, the victim's personal style, and the availability of social support afterward. However, survivors of all the sexual assaults on our continuum have described long-term emotional aftereffects: grief, anger, fear, lowered self-esteem, helplessness, guilt and shame, body image distortion, sexual dysfunction, and problems in other relationships. Underlying these survivor reactions are three common features of the victimization experience.

(1) Sexual assault is a severe trauma. Even when harassment is not physically violent, survivors report strong fear reactions (Alliance Against Sexual Coercion 1981), loss of control, and disruption of their lives—experiences shared with survivors of more physically dangerous assaults such as rape, accidents, or natural disasters.

"Looking back, I don't know what I was afraid of," mused Deborah some years after her experience as a student worker fondled by a professor, "but I was terrified each time this man came toward me." At the end of the semester, Deborah wrote a short note about the professor's advances, gave it to her dorm advisor, and left school. She gave up her ambitions to become a scientist, and didn't return to college for many years.

(2) Sexual assault is a violation. Physical contact is not necessary to create a feeling of being violated, as noted in the reactions of intense disgust by women who receive obscene phone calls or street harassment. Since in sexual harassment the victim frequently knows the offender, a violation of trust is almost always experienced. Most survivors also report feeling degraded by the experience, stripped of their dignity by the abuser.

When a nationally known scholar asked her to participate in his research project, Ellen was thrilled. Flattered by his attentiveness and excited by promises of a letter of recommendation to top graduate schools, she worked long hours, collecting data and writing up a paper herself. Shortly before it was to be sent for publication, Dr. X delivered his ultimatum: no sex, no authorship. Ellen submitted, although disgusted by him physically, because she was so invested in the project. After they had sex, he laughed at her tears. The next day, he told her he did not consider her contributions very thoughtful or important, certainly not sufficient to deserve authorship; and that he had only allowed her to work on these projects because he knew how much she wanted to be near him. Ellen lost a year of work and a publication. More importantly, she lost her confidence. Dr. X's comments were emotionally devastating, and ultimately more degrading than the sexual act.

(3) Sexual assault causes secondary social losses. Too often, survivors find no social comfort and support after rape or harassment. Those who remain silent, like Ann, often become increasingly isolated and begin to view themselves as deviant. To those who tell, family and friends often offer rejection, blame, or disbelief, rather than the support and comforting they need. Employees who file charges of sexual harassment face a range of harmful social responses, including being demoted or fired (Farley 1978). These secondary betrayals increase the severity of long-term emotional reactions, and interfere with healthy resolution.

At first, Faye didn't tell her mother about the abuse she was experiencing at work, or about the charges she had filed against the department chair. Unfortunately, a local newspaper picked up the story, and her mother learned about the case when a friend who lived near the university called her. Faye's mother, embarrassed by the publicity, accused Faye of "bringing shame upon the family," and said "a lady would never have gotten herself into a mess like this!" Soon after, Faye dropped the case, too emotionally exhausted to continue.

Paths to Resolution

Individual resolution needs are as varied as the emotional responses to sexual assault. Many emotional responses, such as stress behaviors and fear, reduce with time and distance from the trauma. Others, notably guilt, depression, helplessness, and relationship problems, may continue or grow worse with time, and may need more direct intervention. However, some paths to resolution have been found to help survivors of any sexual assault. For those wishing further information, specific counseling approaches and guidance are offered in a forthcoming book by Quina and Carlson.

(1) Cast the experience as a sexual assault, and recognize its effects. Survivors frequently use terminology that does not include the word "rape" (Russell 1984), and until recently we didn't even have a term for "harassment." Thus many have difficulty recognizing their experience as victimization. It is helpful to use the words that fit the experience, validating the depth of the survivor's feelings, and allowing her to feel her experience was serious. In some cases, the terminology of sexual assault can help a person recognize the relationship among victimizations, as in Ellen's case.

After her professor's sudden change of behavior, Ellen found herself mistrusting everyone. Her relationships with men, including other professors, became more sexual, although she didn't want to have sex with anyone. Finally, through counseling, she was able to describe for the first time a sexual assault by a favorite uncle during her childhood. As she told of growing up with her uncle's praise and the devastating reversal of feelings she experienced after he assaulted her, she began to see both incidents clearly as sexual assaults rather than seductions. She recognized that she had begun to respond to all men with a sense of resigned dread, anticipating a sexual assault. In fact, she interpreted any compliment from a man as a signal he wanted to have sex with her, since that was where kindness had led in the past.

(2) Find others with similar experiences and share stories. It is essential to know that we are not alone. In therapy groups or just in self-disclosing conversations, or even in reading the stories of others, the sexual assault survivor can discover she is rational, her reactions are normal, and that others have overcome this trauma. Furthermore, as stories are compared, the cultural and social pattern emerges, and victim blame becomes more difficult to maintain.

Eventually, Ann went to a campus professional women's function, sitting quietly in the back of the room. A woman faculty member from another department came over to talk, and befriended her. In their discussion, Ann's new friend disclosed that one of Ann's colleagues—the same man who had approached Ann—had acted very strangely toward her. She described a conversation much like Ann's. Suddenly, Ann felt relieved of all her self-doubts about her situation. She also realized that sexual harassment was a serious problem on campus. She became active in the organization, and helped organize a campus "speak-out" on harassment.

(3) Recognize the personal losses of sexual assault, and allow a grieving process. In addition to betrayals and life changes such as being fired or rejected by friends, the experience of sexual assault constitutes a major personal loss. Recovery from sexual assault often follows the analytic grief process, described by Rando (1984). The mourning process takes time, perhaps a year or more, and involves stages of acute stress, denial, depression, and anger prior to achieving peace with the reality of the loss. Survivors need to appreciate the depth of their feelings of loss, and to allow themselves to mourn, in order to achieve that peace.

Faye spent months being "tough" about her lawsuit—she described it as having to block out all emotions in order to survive (denial). When her mother called and accused her of shaming the family, her well-crafted armor came crashing down. She found herself unable to get up and get dressed in the morning, and had to seek therapy. Her therapist wisely recognized the signs of mourning and the reasons for Faye's grief, and eased her fears about her normalcy. When Faye did not feel strong enough to pursue the lawsuit, her therapist helped her mourn that loss as well, appreciating that she had done all she could, and helping her feel like a survivor rather than a victim.

(4) Join or form a feminist network and support group, to prevent future traumas for others as well as oneself. In addition to rich friendships and the feelings of mutual caring in such a group, self-esteem can be raised by helping others, and a good strong feminist support group can provide real empowerment. Some campuses have formed casual support groups for women in general, where sexual harassment might be discussed (e.g., first year graduate student women, women in science); some counseling and women's centers provide facilitators for sexual assault survivors' groups. Any format is possible.

I finally left my first job, where I was the only woman, and moved to a department with three faculty women. We started meeting for lunch regularly, just to touch base about ongoing events and to do problem solving when necessary. At least once a semester we went to dinner with the women secretaries, and had an evening of fun, support, empathy, and genuine mutual admiration. Now the number of women faculty in our department has grown to six, our dinners have expanded to include women from related departments, and our empowerment—as well as our deep friendships—are extraordinary. Recently a male colleague told us he envied our relationship, because it allowed us to disclose and discuss our *problems* as well as our successes. We helped him form his own support group of gentle men!

NOTES

1. This framework is laid out in the student/staff handbook on sexual harassment and assault distributed at the University of Rhode Island, coauthored by Quina, Carlson, and Temple (1984), and fully described in the guide for counseling sexual assault survivors by Quina and Carlson (1989). Other support for this view is found in Chapman and Gates (1978) and in Stanko (1985).

2. All stories in this paper are based on true situations. The names are fictitious, and details of the stories have been altered slightly, to protect the identities of the victims and perpetrators. I am grateful to these women for sharing their deep personal pain with me. I have chosen to use the term "victim" to refer to the dynamic, and survivor to refer to the individual after the assault.

3. Several male friends have described the early inculcation of these images of women—and of what "real men" do to women—especially through peer pressure during adolescence. I appreciate their honesty, and their efforts to overcome their own sexism.

SECTION 2
Rape

In the last quarter of the twentieth century, rape—and especially how we define it and prosecute those guilty of it—has been frequently disputed. Particularly in North America, where feminists have defined rape as both a symbol and an explanation of the position of women in the social structure, the subject is a flashpoint of debates. In the spring of 1991 the William Kennedy Smith rape trial, covered extensively by the media, brought many of the elements of the discussion into America's living rooms. The accused was privileged, a member of a celebrated family, who was about to begin a medical career. The complainant was a single mother, from an ordinary background. He said she consented to sex on the lawn at the Kennedy's Palm Beach estate after an evening of drinking. She claimed he assaulted her after inviting her back to his home. Was he the target of an unscrupulous woman seeking notoriety or fortune? Was she the victim of a man accustomed to getting what he wanted, a woman who had no chance against the reputation and resources of her adversary? The problem of teasing the truth out of an event so steeped in conflicting values and beliefs reflects the polarities inherent in most debates about rape.

Overwhelming evidence supports the contention that rape and coercive sexual intercourse occur frequently and are, in fact, a common experience for women in our culture. One sample of 930 randomly selected women, taken from a probability survey of households in San Francisco, found that 44 percent of those who completed the in-person interview had experienced rape or attempted rape. Of these, 50 percent had been raped more than once (Russell 1982a). In a random probability sample of 481 college women who were mailed a questionnaire that asked them to comment on any undesirable sexual experiences, more than 25 percent reported being coerced to perform a sexual act at least once during their college years, many on more than one occasion, with 7 percent of the incidents classifiable as felony sex offenses (Fenstermaker 1989). In a national representative random sample, more than three thousand college women were asked to complete a lengthy survey about themselves, including information about sexual experiences. Fifty-four percent of the women had experienced sexual victimization; 12 percent had experienced attempted rape; and 15 percent had been raped (Koss, Gidycz, and Wisniewski 1987). Despite the variance in research methods, populations studied, and findings, the picture that emerges from these and many other studies is that rape is a frequent occurrence in the United States.

The Debates over What Constitutes Rape

How we define and view rape very much depends, of course, on the culture in which our beliefs are formed. In the contemporary United States we have no universal understanding of what constitutes rape; thus a patriarchal definition has usually prevailed, centering on the danger to men of seductive, ensnaring, and vindictive women, and marginalizing the effects of sexual abuse on women. In *The Morning After: Sex, Fear, and Feminism on Campus,* Katie Roiphe contributes to the heated discussion about rape through her claim that feminists obscure true rape by defining the term too broadly. Roiphe asserts that women are being convinced to define sexual experience as sexual abuse. In counterpoint to Roiphe's argument, many feminists claim that rape is the ultimate form of gender violence, the most intimate touch turned perverse, in which the power that men have over women is acted out in the assaultive behavior of men who seek to control and dominate women's bodies. In this view, the traditional definition of rape is so narrow as to preclude the punishment of most rapists.

Rape and the Law

Punishment for rape has traditionally had little to do with compensating the raped person, particularly if that person is a woman. Instead, the most severe punishment has been meted out in response to a perception of damage to male property. Ancient Judaic law, for example, specified punitive fees to be paid to fathers or husbands for the loss of virginity or exclusive sexual access to a raped woman (Porter 1986). Under Roman law in the early Christian era both the rapist and the victim suffered the death penalty if she was "willing" (Bryson 1986). Punishment for rape has often been a reflection of class or race bias. During the early Renaissance in Italy, for example, punishment varied with the social status of the victim. Among the most heinous examples of socially stratified responses were the numerous death sentences and lynchings of African American men who were accused of raping White women from Reconstruction through the early half of the twentieth century in the American South (Pleck 1990; Davis 1983). There is convincing evidence that many of the rape charges leveled against African American men were politically motivated (Pleck 1990). During the same time period, White men who raped African American women never received severe punishment if they received any at all (Edwards n.d.). During the time of slavery, the racial double standard ensured that the sexual abuse of enslaved African women was not legally classified as rape. Even today the press "prefers [rapes] against White victims while ignoring those against Blacks" (Benedict 1992, 251). At issue are the relative value of sexual property to those men who hold power, and the ability of those in power to use accusations of rape to teach a lesson. Although rape clearly has been a public issue at certain times in history, it is only recently that the focus has shifted away from concerns about damage to male property and the threat to the male-dominated social order, and turned instead toward a discourse of power and politics played out in gender relations.

One of the most tangible effects of the feminist movement's attention to rape has been an unprecedented rewriting of rape laws. The intention of the reforms has been to remove the barriers to "legal protection to female victims who failed to adhere to conventional standards of propriety, for disregarding women's experience of sexual violation, and for inflicting emotional distress on rape victims who report and prosecute rape charges" (Goldberg-Ambrose 1992, 173). Some reforms have focused on altering the legal definition of who qualifies as a victim. In Mexico, for instance, prior to 1991 "the law stated that women had to be 'chaste and honest' to qualify as rape victims" (de la Luz Lima 1992, 19). Efforts to enable married women to bring rape charges against abusive husbands have been another focus of reform in both the United States (Russell 1990) and England (Hall, James, and Kertesz 1984). Gender-neutral laws, widely adopted in the United States, have redefined rape so that the sex of the victim and offender are immaterial. Although these changes have enabled male victims of male rape to come forward, few have, due in part to social stigma about homosexuality. Male victims of female rape and female victims of female rape are still extremely rare. Other reforms have attempted to change rules of evidence in order to reflect new attitudes about rape. One such effort has been the institution of "rape shield" laws, which prohibit the introduction of a victim's past sexual history in court except under specific conditions. In some parts of the world, women who bring rape charges can still be executed as "adulterers" for permitting the violation to occur. In Pakistan, for example, "no distinction is made between rape . . . and extra-marital intercourse," with punishment for the latter ranging up to "stoning to death for married persons and 100 lashes for unmarried persons" (Shaheed 1994, 216, 217).

Although there have been well-intentioned efforts, and some successes, victims' continued lack of power is still evidenced by the difficulty of obtaining justice in cases of rape. Studies from England, Scotland, Australia, Canada, and Scandinavia report mishandling of rape victims by the criminal justice system (Temkin 1986). Despite reforms, the police, the courts, and the public in general often blame victims for their victimization, an attitude even more pronounced for male victims.

Most rapes are never reported to law enforcement officials. Surveys in England and New Zealand have found low rates of reporting (Temkin 1986), and it is estimated that as many as 83 percent of rapes go unreported in the United States (U.S. Department of Justice 1988). Failure to report a crime that the victim often perceives to be life-threatening and that results in a host of long-lasting and serious effects deserves explanation.

Increasing Scope of the Problem

Despite low rates of reporting, the number of rapes reported continues to rise. Official statistics from Canada reveal that the sexual assault rate almost doubled between 1983 and 1988. In the United States, rape continues to be the fastest growing felony crime. There are two widely accepted explanations for the dramatic increase in reported rapes. The first suggests that more women are raped due to a backlash against the advances in women's rights over the past several decades. There is some historical evidence to support this thesis; available records indicate that rape may have been relatively rare in the preindustrial era (Porter 1986). Accordingly, rape may be on the increase, particularly in North America, as gender relations are destabilized in response to the gains of the women's movement. This theory claims that as the grasp of patriarchal control over women weakens, men who are threatened by women's increasing power may respond by exerting more brutal control. When male dominance is legitimated by the social order, the threat of rape as an instrument of social control is unnecessary. The second explanation claims that the increase in reported rapes stems from an increase in supportive services for victims and lessened public stigma associated with victimization. Since the early 1970s, when virtually no services were available for victims of rape, rape crisis centers and hotlines have opened up in most communities in the United States. It is now common for police departments and court personnel to have received specific training in assisting rape victims. Elements of both explanations have most likely contributed to the tremendous increase in reported rapes of women in the United States.

Reports of rape, however, continue to be discounted by police and prosecutors, and convictions are rare. Of those rape trials that do result in the conviction of an offender for rape, almost all represent approximations of the stereotypical heterosexual stranger rape (Estrich 1987). If the victim and offender are acquainted, others are less likely to judge the event to be a legitimate rape (Bourque 1989). Since some studies have found that as many as 85 percent of rape or attempted rape victims know their attackers (Koss, Dinero, and Seibel 1988), it is no wonder that rape convictions are so rare. In fact, a correlation can likely be drawn between the degree of acquaintance, public perception of the legitimacy of a rape charge, and the response of the criminal justice system. At one end of the continuum, stranger rape of a woman by a man is associated with public sympathy for the victim and a higher likelihood of conviction. At the other end of the continuum, marital rape is associated with lack of public recognition and laws defined in such a way that few cases can be prosecuted. In practice, married women and prostitutes have abridged rights to sexual self-determination: Married women are presumed to have permanently agreed to the sexual demands of their spouses, and prostitutes are effectively denied the legal right to refuse sexual access to their bodies. This has led some feminist critics to claim that rape appears to be regulated rather than prohibited (MacKinnon 1983), and that husbands, neighbors, acquaintances, and "johns" have been assured sexual access to women through "the protection of being excluded from rape prohibitions" (Estrich 1987, 4).

In what appears to be an almost universal silence on the issue, male rape victims have virtually no protection. Public awareness is limited to a casual acceptance of the brutality of prison rape, while rape of men by other men outside of prisons is barely acknowledged. In fact, male rape may be neither regulated nor prohibited.

Causes of Rape

Prior to recent scholarly attention, rape was generally perceived to be caused by the overwhelming and uncontrollable sexual passion of men, stirred to life by teasing women who flaunted their sexual availability and did not take responsibility for the outcome. Alternatively, a claim of rape was thought to be the delayed reaction of a woman to fear about her reputation after participating in sexual activity, or retribution against a boyfriend or husband for a perceived wrong. Women cried rape when it served their purposes.

In the earlier part of the twentieth century, psychoanalytic theories of rape causality centered around Freudian concepts of female masochism. Although Freud himself had almost nothing to say about rape (Forrester 1986), it was not uncommon for his followers to hear in women's tales of sexual abuse an unconscious desire for seduction. This was the familiar "no means yes" writ large: rapes happened because women really wanted them to. More recently, neo-Freudians such as Nancy Chodorow (1978) have seen the difference in social status of men and women as an outcome of their expected roles in the social structure. In this view, young girls gain identity through dependence, attachment, and self-denial, qualities deemed necessary for the socially prescribed role of mothering. These same traits may make women more vulnerable to abuse.

An alternative and widely popular perception of rape causality focuses on the mentally ill rapist. The "disease model of rape" (Scully 1990, 161), consistent with a larger cultural trend of medicalizing deviance, attributes rape to the out-of-control behavior of sick individuals. This explanation for rape has a tenacious hold and continues to be reflected in public policies that suggest that counseling is the preferred mode of treatment for sexually violent men. More violent sex offenders with additional behavioral problems are also perhaps most likely to be arrested and prosecuted, while men who exhibit more socially acceptable behavior, but are sexually violent with their intimates, are less likely to be labeled as rapists.

The sociobiological explanation of rape claims that men and women have evolved differing investments in sexual behavior. Human reproductive behavior is driven by the desire to transmit genetic material. Women have a high investment in a long gestational period and prolonged infant care, which demand a sizable allocation of time and energy, and thus want to control the selection of who they mate with in order to assure that the male will help care for any offspring. Men are concerned with increasing their chances to inseminate as many females as possible in order to pass on their genes. The time economy of reproduction thus enables men to spend their reproductive energies on other reproductive activities, such as copulating with as many females as possible. Natural selection may thus have favored forced copulation (Ellis 1989). Much of the evidence for the sociobiological theory of rape comes from the study of animals and insects (see Angier 1995) and rests on the arguable premise that human behavioral traits are based on evolutionary selection and are genetically programmed (Ellis 1989).

More recently, social science has taken the lead in theorizing about the causes of rape. These theories see social arrangements and cultural learning as central to shaping incidents of rape. Anthropologists have looked at the varieties of cultural traditions and behavior to explain why rape is not the same everywhere. Sociologists have studied the effect of sexual stratification and socialization on rape. For many social scientists, rape is seen as the result of disparities between masculinity and femininity within a culture. In cultures where rape occurs frequently, the supply and demand for rape is seen as a result of women's socialization into passivity and restraint and men's socialization into aggressiveness and domination. Ideals about masculinity and femininity also promote a sexual double standard that applies differing social consequences to the sexual activity of men and women. Sexual activity enhances men's social position and self-esteem while multiple sexual relationships diminish women's social status. Women are therefore held responsible for maintaining sexual boundaries that men are expected to threaten. Women must defend their sexual integrity; yet when a rape occurs, fear of social censure prevents many women from reporting it.

Peggy Reeves Sanday claims that "rape is the playing out of a socio-cultural script in which the expression of personhood for males is directed by interpersonal violence and an ideology of toughness" (1986, 85). Other social theorists emphasize the political and economic structures that support rape. As long as women are excluded from sharing political and economic power with men, any interaction between them is fraught with power dynamics. Sexuality and how individuals express it reflect social expectations, what people believe their needs to be, and the interplay of social constraints and social privilege. As Hannah Feldman notes, "Intimidation, force, and predetermined gender roles—the tools of rape—are established by societal norms before rape happens" (1993, 18). Sexual intercourse becomes a "dense transfer point" for acting out the power dynamics between men and women (Foucault 1980a, 130). Rape is seen as an expression of the power that men have to control the lives of individual women. The fear of rape serves to perpetuate the inequality of the sexes by preventing women from moving freely in society.

Psychology has added to the contemporary understanding of the causes of rape through studies that attempt to define what beliefs men and women hold about rape and how such beliefs affect behavior. When the ability of sexual activity to "gratify both sexual and power needs" (Burkhart and Stanton 1988, 54) is linked to a misogynistic attitudinal structure, rape is a logical outcome. Neil M. Malamuth (1981) found that 35 percent of college males in his sample indicated some likelihood that they would rape a woman if they could be assured of not being caught. Like actual rapists, these men believed in rape myths and demonstrated sexual arousal at depictions of rape. In other studies, men who were sexually responsive to depictions of rape were also found to be more willing than the control group to act aggressively toward women in a laboratory setting (Malamuth 1986, 1983). Other studies have found that men who claim a high likelihood of raping (Check and Malamuth 1983; Tieger 1981) or are highly sex-role stereotyped (Burt 1980) also hold beliefs that minimize the serious effects and negative impact rape has on victims. Kathryn M. Feltey, Julie J. Ainslie, and Aleta Geib found that men and women have been socialized to hold different values about sex and therefore develop differing models of sexual behavior: men develop "prorape attitudes," while women feel that they "have relinquished their right to withdraw consent" (1991, 245). Interestingly, men who hold nontraditional attitudes about male and female behavior have also been found to hold victim-supportive attitudes (Williams 1984).

One very widely debated topic has been the role that pornography may play in promoting and encouraging rape. Some characterize pornography as "pro-rape propaganda" (Funk 1993, 51). Others point to the 1970 President's Commission on Obscenity and Pornography, which found that there is no link between the consumption of pornography and sexual violence. The discussion is an important one because in the United States pornography serves as sex education for many young men; the average age for first viewing printed pornography is thirteen, and the average age for first viewing a pornographic film is fourteen (*NFD Journal* 1989). With increasing access to explicit cable television programs, the Internet, and videos, pornography is increasingly available to young people. Issues surrounding the pornography debate will be presented in greater detail in section 1 of part 3.

Little has been written about the causes of male-on-male rape, but what we know about why men rape women may offer some clues. If masculinity is equated with power and dominance, and sexual activity gratifies both sexual and power needs, a man who rapes another man may be doubly asserting his manhood.

Effects of Sexual Aggression

For women, sexually coercive experiences are associated with high levels of anxiety, guilt in combination with sexual activity, and poor social and familial adjustment (Rogers 1984); depression and hostility (Check, Elias, and Barton 1988); alienation (Williams 1984); suicide attempts (Weis and Borges 1973; Warshaw 1988); feelings of diminished self-worth, depressed expectations for the future, eating disorders, lack of concentration, and sleep disorders (Warshaw 1988); phobias and delayed traumatic response (Burgess and Holmstrom 1974); and circumscribed activity (thereby affecting educational and work opportunities) (Hall 1985; Association of American Colleges 1978). In addition, women who have been sexually assaulted by acquaintances may suffer more complicated effects (Hall 1985) and show a slower degree of recovery than women who are raped by strangers (Warshaw 1988). The looming threat of contracting AIDS as the result of rape has increased the psychological trauma as well as the very real physical risk for victims (see Roberts 1993; Koss et al. 1994; Carillo 1992). Rape appears to be a life-altering event with very serious consequences.

Living in a culture where the threat of sexual attack is pervasive shapes and constrains the lives even of those women who have not directly experienced sexual assault (see Sheffield, this volume). Although the threat of rape poisons the atmosphere in which women live, it is also becoming apparent that public attention to the issue may plant fears and therefore contribute to a sense of threat that is both real and cautionary. It is urgent that we find a balance between adequate information about the threat of rape to provide self-protection and an awareness of the power women hold to experience their strength and autonomy.

Information on how rape affects male victims is sparse. The tremendous stigma attached to the victim of male-on-male rape, redolent of homophobia, has contributed to an apparent absence of knowledge about the effects of rape victimization. The little information available indicates that, whether victimized in prison or out, male victims of rape experience a diminishment of manhood—a reduction to the status of women. What consequences ensue for the victim remain to be discovered.

We know somewhat more about the effects of sexual aggression on the perpetrators. Scully and Marolla (1985) found that convicted rapists perceive rape as a rewarding experience for a variety of reasons, including feelings of power, sexual gratification, recreation and adventure, enhanced self-esteem, an added bonus to another activity (such as theft), and retribution and punishment for perceived wrongs. For other convicted rapists, rape is sex; it is the norm for their sexual behavior (Scully 1990). While rape has proven to have a strongly negative effect on the victims, it appears to be rewarding for rapists.

Gang Rape and Male Bonding

In recent years scholars have addressed the connection between gang rape and male bonding. Patricia Yancey Martin and Robert A. Hummer addressed the "group and organizational context of fraternities" (1989, 115) and its connection to the sexual abuse of women. Sanday (1990) presented an anthropological case study of gang rape as a ritual of male bonding in fraternity culture. Although the authors of both studies acknowledge that not all fraternities or all fraternity members participate in such activities, the findings were "that fraternities are a physical and sociocultural context that encourages the sexual coercion of women" (Martin and Hummer 1989, 115) and that they foster "a sexual discourse that rationalizes male sexual aggression against women by defining it as a necessary, indeed natural, ingredient of male sexual expression and heterosexual masculine identity" (Sanday 1990, 73).

Highly publicized cases of sexual abuse involving athletes have spurred others to investigate connections between athletics and sexual abuse. They have found that "dominant institutional forms of sport have made men's power and privilege over women seem natural" (Messner and Sabo 1994, 5). These authors have found that "nothing inherent in sports makes athletes especially likely to rape women. Rather, it is the way sports are organized to influence developing masculine identities and male peer groups that leads many male athletes to rape" (1994, 34).

Male athletes and fraternity members may be predisposed to sexually abusive behavior of women due to adherence to a narrow and stereotypical practice of masculinity shared by both groups (Martin and Hummer 1989). Research into the practices of other male membership groups could further our understanding of the relationships among male bonding, the development of an aggressive masculinity, and the sexual abuse of women (see O'Toole, this volume).

Acquaintance Rape

It is through acquaintance rape that the interconnectedness of power dynamics and sexual activity becomes most apparent. The social conditions under which young men and women interact are rife with potential for abuses. Particularly in the United States, current social norms empower young people to spend a great deal of unsupervised time together. In addition, alcohol and drugs are readily available disinhibitors that contribute to sexual abuse. Young people frequently have access to cars and apartments, both of which afford privacy, and both of which are often the sites of sexual aggression. When these enabling conditions are combined with the power differential between men and women, and the resultant sexual aggressiveness of men and sexual passivity of women, the frequency of rape among dating partners should be no surprise.

The system of heterosexual dating in the United States is stratified so that men are virtually in control. From the initial request for a date to the specific plans, mode of transportation, and financial outlay, the man is traditionally the initiator. The power to initiate is related to the social ability to dominate; in hierarchical relationships the initiator is the person who holds more social status (Lewin 1985). This hierarchical system presents women as sexual commodities. By arranging, controlling, and paying for a date, men expect to be rewarded sexually. At least one study (Muehlenhard and Linton 1987) has found a correlation between sexual aggression and a man's initiation of a date, paying of all expenses on the date, and driving. In addition, studies in high schools and on college campuses continue to reveal that many men and women believe that a man is entitled to force a date to have sexual intercourse if he has spent money on her (Mahoney 1981; Lewis 1988).

Contributions to This Section

The contributors to this section represent a variety of approaches to the study of rape. In a field where history and the social sciences have dominated the discussion, we include literary commentary and the first-person narrative of a rape survivor. Read together, these authors provide an understanding of the history and causes of rape, as well as its personal and social consequences.

Patricia Donat and John D'Emilio, in "A Feminist Redefinition of Rape and Sexual Assault: Historical Foundations and Change," offer a concise history of rape in the United States from colonial times to the 1990s. They explore the meanings of sexual assault and women's sexuality and point to changes in social attitudes, behavior, and definitions over time. Their work illustrates both the changing value of women in society and how those changes are reflected in beliefs regarding rape.

In "Undeclared War: African-American Women Writers Explicating Rape," Opal Palmer Adisa explores the writings of African American women and finds a common thread. According to Adisa, rape is conceptualized by these writers as a battle, with women's bodies as the contested territory. The authors she includes share an understanding of rape as a mechanism to oppress, suppress, and deny humanity to Black women and thus undermine their independence. These writers create a revolutionary body of work that attempts to reclaim the power to define experience and simultaneously provide inspiration for resistance and change.

In "Raped: A Male Survivor Breaks His Silence," Fred Pelka reveals his rape victimization and explores the factors that ensured his fifteen-year silence about the event. He points out that men who are raped experience suspicion and trivialization similar to women victims, with the added issues of having their sexuality and masculinity questioned. Pelka claims that men who are raped are feminized in the eyes of other men and lose what (White, heterosexual) men have always taken for granted in this culture: the authority to define and control sexual behavior.

In "Subcultural Theory of Rape Revisited," Laura L. O'Toole draws on theories of masculinity and recent empirical studies of rape among fraternity members and athletes to develop a theory of masculinist subcultures in which rape is acceptable behavior. The author concedes that although not all rapes take place within an identifiable male group, the large number of rapes that do occur within such contexts requires that we further explore subcultures of violent heterosexual masculinity.

Mary P. Koss, Lori Heise, and Nancy Felipe Russo look at the effects of rape on the health of women around the world. They compile information from a broad range of international resources to contribute to a changing focus on rape as an issue of criminal justice to one of human rights. While data are sparse due to limited resources and training for researchers on gender violence, what the authors find is compelling. Rape appears to be a major factor in the health and well-being of women around the globe.

Suggestions for Further Reading

Barbara Baynton, "The Chosen Vessel," Laurie Hergenhan (ed.), *The Australian Short Story: An Anthology from the 1890s to the 1980s* (New York: University of Queensland Press, 1986).

Linda Brookover Bourque, *Defining Rape* (Durham, NC: Duke University Press, 1989).

Susan Estrich, *Real Rape* (Cambridge: Harvard University Press, 1987).

Diana Russell, *Rape in Marriage* (Bloomington: Indiana University Press, 1990).

Peggy Reeves Sanday, *Fraternity Gang Rape: Sex, Brotherhood, and Privilege on Campus* (New York: New York University Press, 1990).

Diana Scully, *Understanding Sexual Violence: A Study of Convicted Rapists* (Cambridge: Unwin Hyman, 1990).

Patricia Searles and Ronald Berger (eds.), *Rape and Society: Readings on the Problem of Sexual Assault* (Boulder, CO: Westview Press, 1995).

Sylvana Tomaselli and Roy Porter (eds.), *Rape* (Cambridge: Basil Blackwell, 1986).

Robin Warshaw, *I Never Called It Rape: The Ms. Report on Recognizing, Fighting and Surviving Date and Acquaintance Rape* (New York: Harper & Row, 1988).

The Rape

JEANNE MURRAY WALKER

So I can never forget, I've kept one small glove.
My husband, Wilfred, had the most delicate hands.
In Pittsburgh during that winter
the wind raged like a criminal
come to finish us off. I sang hymns,
"Leaning On The Everlasting Arms,"
and lay all night awake in Wilfred's embrace.
To stay warm enough to live—that became our religion.
One morning on the doorstep of our apartment house
we saw a frozen baby, a plucked chicken, blue as steel.
The next week Wilfred found work stoking the furnace
in a garment factory—twenty-seven men applied.
I thought they'd chosen Wilfred
because love conquers all,
and I was right. Oh, I was right.
The boss gave Wilfred leather gloves
and sent him every night back home
from their hot furnace, florid as a rose.
I could smell the boss in Wilfred's hair.
When we lay down on our narrow bed,
the boss smiled at me out of Wilfred's eyes.

In what part of me did I understand?
I knew it in my arms. I could feel
that man's hot shadow shouldering up
at night when I held Wilfred,
but my tongue had turned to stone.

One Saturday afternoon when I was asleep alone,
the boss's boots hammered up our stairs.

From *The Midwest Quarterly*, 1980, pp. 316–17. Reprinted by permission.

He wanted me, it turns out. Wilfred
was a corridor between us. Wilfred
is an opening in both directions,
I thought, as I heard the man unlock the door
with Wilfred's key. He was wearing
a double breasted suit and Wilfred's gloves.
He laid the gloves on the radiator. He said, "Sing."

Slowly I started the old music
he never had a right to hear:
  Take my hand and let it move
  At the impulse of thy love,
  At the impulse of thy love.
That afternoon I thought I hated all of them.
I thought I hated Jesus.

11

A Feminist Redefinition of Rape and Sexual Assault: Historical Foundations and Change

PATRICIA L. N. DONAT AND JOHN D'EMILIO

The issues of rape and sexual assault have been major concerns of the feminist movement since its revival in the late 1960s. Because of the work of feminists, the contemporary understanding of rape and sexual assault, and the social response to sexual violence, have undergone significant revision. This chapter examines the feminist response to traditional conceptualizations of rape and the impact it has had. It begins by presenting some historical background to set a context for understanding more recent events.

The Colonial Era

During the colonial period, settlers in the English colonies were influenced strongly by the church, which prescribed the behavior of its congregation. The family was defined as the central unit in society and sex roles were differentiated rigidly. Men were dominant and women were submissive. The woman was regarded "not as a person . . . but as a sexual 'type'—an inferior, a receptacle, . . . or a simple answer to his needs" (Koehler 1980, 93). Sexuality was channeled into marriage for the procreation of legitimate offspring. Nonmarital sexual intercourse was immoral, an offense against both family and community (D'Emilio and Freedman 1988).

In order to regulate deviance, the church, courts, and community joined to monitor private sexual behavior and to limit sexual expression to marriage. Colonial society held the entire community responsible for upholding morality, and sexual crimes were punished severely. Women bore the heaviest responsibility for regulating premarital sexual contact. "Church and society dealt more harshly with women . . . [because] female chastity and fidelity assured men of the legitimacy of their children" (D'Emilio and Freedman 1988). The integrity of the family was critical to the development of community and was guarded with care. For men, the integrity of the family rested on female purity and monogamy.

A woman's value within society was based on her ability to marry and to produce legitimate heirs. The ability to attract a spouse was influenced by the woman's perceived purity. The rape of a virgin was considered a crime against the father of the raped

From *Society for the Psychological Study of Social Issues, Journal of Social Issues* 48, no. 1 (1992):9–22. Reprinted by permission.

woman rather than against the woman herself. A raped woman could not expect to marry into a respectable family and might very well remain the economic liability of the father.

During the colonial period, the rape cases most likely to come to court were those in which the perpetrator was from a lower social class than the victim or in which the victim was a married woman who physically resisted. "When men of the lower order raped women of a higher social standing, they threatened the prerogatives of other men" (Lindemann 1984, 81).

Women were dependent on the courts and community (i.e., men) for their protection. In order to ensure her safety, a woman who was sexually attacked needed to comply with male standards for her behavior by proving her nonconsent through physical and verbal resistance, and through immediate disclosure of the attack to both family and neighbors. Proof of nonconsent was necessary to verify that the woman had not voluntarily engaged in sexual acts outside of marriage. If a woman could not prove nonconsent, she might be punished for the assault (D'Emilio and Freedman 1988). Rape was therefore "an expression of male control over women, regulated by law in a way that serves the men who hold political power more than it protects women" (Lindemann 1984, 81).

The Nineteenth Century

Toward the end of the eighteenth century, sexual meanings began to change. Sexuality no longer was tied so closely to reproductive intentions, and more emphasis was placed on courtship and individual choice rather than on community and family control. The subsequent decline in traditional church and state regulation of morality loosened constraints on nonmarital sex.

During the nineteenth century, young women from the countryside and from immigrant families began to enter the paid work force and earn their livings outside the family household. Patriarchal controls over women's time, behavior, and sexuality weakened (Stansell 1986). With increased freedom, however, also came increased vulnerability. Previously, "courtship was one part of a system of barter between the sexes, in which a woman traded sexual favors for a man's promise to marry. Premarital intercourse then became a token of betrothal" (Stansell 1986, 87). Women, however, no longer could assume that a pregnancy would lead to marriage.

Female virtue continued to be important for finding a spouse. In the nineteenth century women were viewed as pure and virtuous by nature, and as disinterested in sex. Women of all classes were expected to use their natural purity and superior morality to control men's innate lust. The impure woman threatened the delicate moral balance and suggested the "social disintegration that sexuality symbolized" (Freedman 1981, 20). A woman who engaged in sexual intercourse, even against her will, was considered to be depraved—a "fallen" woman—and was often blamed for the man's crime and socially stigmatized as a result of the attack. "As woman falls from a higher point of perfection, so she sinks to a profounder depth of misery than man" (Freedman 1981, 18).

The Twentieth Century

During the twentieth century, the writings of Sigmund Freud and other psychologists and sexologists provided the foundation for reconceptualizing sexual behavior and categorizing sexual deviations. One emerging concern was an interest in understanding the causes of sexual aggression. Many hypotheses were developed, but most theories included the belief that rape was a perversion and that rapists were mentally ill (Amir 1971). One theory of sexual aggression suggested that the rapist's behavior was the result of socialization by a strong maternal figure and a weak paternal figure. Another theory proposed that the rapist's behavior was the result of a defective superego that left the individual unable to control his sexual and aggressive impulses. Therefore, the rapist was considered to have a "character disorder" and was classified as a "sick" individual. Other theories to explain the rapist's behavior included castration fears, feelings of sexual inferiority and inadequacy, homosexual tendencies, organic factors, and mental deficiencies (Amir 1971). All of these theories reduced the rapist's responsibility for his actions since he was considered unable to control his pathological impulses. In other words, rape was reconceptualized from the perpetrator's point of view. The focus was on understanding the plight of the man, not the woman. Her victimization was simply a by-product of his pathology.

During the 1930s, the public increasingly became interested in sex crimes committed by men against women. In 1937, the *New York Times* created a new index category of sex crimes, which included 143 articles published that year (Freedman 1989). Due to the influence of psychoanalytic theories, sex offenders began to be considered more as deviants than as criminals. Between 1935 and 1965, several state commissions to investigate sex crimes were formed; in many places, authority for the treatment and rehabilitation of the sex offender shifted away from the penal system and toward the mental health system (Freedman 1989). Psychiatrists began to carry more influence concerning treatment of the sex offender. The label "sexual psychopath" was used to describe the violent male offender who was unable to control his sexual impulses and attacked the object of his frustrated desires. Thus rape was conceptualized primarily as an act of sex rather than an act of violence.

As awareness of sex crimes increased, public concern also escalated. Several "sex psychopath laws" were passed that permitted offenders to receive indefinite commitment to state mental hospitals rather than jail sentences. This law reform, initiated by male legislators, was opposed by many women who endorsed stronger criminal penalties for rape and sexual assault. Although sexual psychopath laws were promoted as a measure to protect women, in reality these laws often resulted in White men being labeled as mentally ill and sent to state hospitals, and Black men being found guilty of a crime and sent to jail (Freedman 1989).

Racial Aspects of Rape

In addition to oppressing women, rape served as a method of racial control. The sexual assault of minority women maintained the supremacy of White men. The experience of the Black female victim was virtually ignored. White men used

> women as verbs with which to communicate with one another (rape being a means of communicating defeat to the men of a conquered tribe). . . . Rape sent a message to black men, but more centrally, it expressed male sexual attitudes in a culture both racist and patriarchal. (Hall 1983, 322)

In the post-Reconstruction South, White men used the myth of the Black man as sexually uncontrollable and as a threat to all White women as an excuse for violence toward Black men and as a means to control women through fear. Black men who were accused of sexually attacking White women received the harshest penalties. A Black man convicted of rape often was executed or castrated (D'Emilio and Freedman 1988; Jordon 1968). In the 1930s the Association of Southern Women for the Prevention of Lynching stated that the traditions of chivalry and lynching were a form of sexual and racial intimidation rather than protection.

> Lynching, it proclaimed, far from offering a shield against sexual assault, served as a weapon of both racial and sexual terror, planting fear in women's minds and dependency in their hearts. It thrust them in the role of personal property or sexual objects, ever threatened by black men's lust, ever in need of white men's protection. (Hall 1983, 339)

The myth of the Black rapist still lingers in more severe sentencing penalties for Black offenders (Hall 1983). Thus rape and its legal treatment can be seen as the ultimate demonstration of power in a racist and patriarchal society.

Perceptions of the Rape Victim

In addition to changes in the conceptualization of male offenders, society's perception of the victim's role in the assault also changed during the twentieth century. As female nature became sexualized and female desire for sexuality legitimated, rape became redefined as "not only a male psychological aberration, but also an act in which women . . . contributed to their victimization" (Freedman 1989, 211). Many people became skeptical that a woman could be raped if she did not consent. A well-known attorney once began a rape trial by placing a coke bottle on a table, spinning it, and demonstrating to the jury his difficulty in forcing a pencil into the opening (Margolin 1972). The implication was that a woman would be able to fend off a man attempting to rape her (Schwendinger and Schwendinger 1983). Therefore, if a woman was raped, she must have "asked for it."

Laws requiring physical evidence of penetration, the need for corroboration, and allowing testimony about the victim's sexual history in court trials had the effect of placing the victim on trial. In addition, juries often still received the traditional instruction that an accusation of rape "is one which is easily made and, once made, difficult to defend against, even if the person accused is innocent" (Berger 1977, 10). The jury was cautioned to be suspicious of the victim's testimony, much more so than in other criminal cases. As a result, prosecution rates for rape remained low.

> In 1972, 3,562 rapes were reported in Chicago: 833 arrests were made, 23 defendants pleaded guilty: and 8 were found guilty and sentenced after a trial . . . fewer than 1 percent of rapes resulted in jail sentences. (Deckard 1983, 433)

The Feminist Redefinition of Sexual Assault

During the 1960s, increasing numbers of women were employed. As the decade began, approximately 36 percent of women worked outside the home; by its end, over 50 percent of women were in the paid labor force (Deckard 1983). Although women's presence in the public sphere was increasing, they rarely held decision and policy-making positions.

With women's increasing involvement in activities outside the home, the opportunity for a woman to be victimized increased (Gardner 1980). A few men viewed women's new-found assertiveness and involvement in the public sphere as an attack on traditional roles and a defiance of chivalry. To such men, the woman who did not conform to traditional roles was relegated to the role of the "loose woman" and was not entitled to protection under the traditional guidelines for male–female relationships (Griffin 1971). The following description of rape in the nineteenth century still applied:

> sexual assault could be conceived of . . . as an exploitation of women's presumed dependence on men. If a woman had herself violated patriarchal norms by straying out of her dependent position—if she had fought off her attacker, asserted her rights alone in court, or behaved in too self-reliant a manner more generally—the term "rape" no longer applied, no matter how forceful the attack visited on her. (Arnold 1989, 49)

Societal definitions of rape demanded adherence to traditionally defined feminine roles and behaviors. The implicit warning to women was to behave (e.g., accept traditional feminine roles) or to suffer the consequence—rape.

Women, however, began to resist traditional definitions of appropriate feminine behavior and expressed their dissatisfaction. Betty Friedan (1963), in *The Feminine Mystique,* and the National Organization for Women (NOW), founded in 1966, expressed women's changing views and interest in public reform. Women's liberationists also began to work toward changing social policies. A process called consciousness raising was used in informal women's groups to begin to empower women and to help them identify sources of sisterhood and oppression. As women began to meet, they realized that individual concerns (e.g., sexual harassment, fear of walking the streets at night) were widely shared. As a result, many women questioned the reasons for their oppression, and they began to recognize that "the personal is political." The dilemmas women were experiencing were not idiosyncratic, but were constructed socially as a result of the hierarchial gender system in our culture (D'Emilio and Freedman 1988). Kate Millet (1970) in her landmark book, *Sexual Politics,* concluded that within our patriarchal system, force takes "a form of violence particularly sexual in nature and realized most completely in the act of rape" (p. 69).

During the 1970s, rape became an important issue within the feminist movement. Sexual assault was redefined from the victim's perspective. A woman's victimization was an "experience of helplessness and loss of control, the sense of one's self as an object of rage" (Hall 1983, 342). The act of rape was seen not as an end in itself, but as a means of enforcing gender roles in society and maintaining the hierarchy in which men retained control. Feminists refuted the long-held belief that rapists were men who were helplessly controlled by their overwhelming sexual impulses. Rape was recognized as an act of violence, *not* of sex as psychoanalytic theorists had previously held. Rape was a form of domination and control, a weapon used to enforce women's subordinate role to men.

In 1971, an article by Susan Griffin described rape as the "All-American crime." She reported that "forcible rape is the most frequently committed violent crime in America today," and emphasized that all women are victims even if they are not the direct targets of the attack because "rape and the fear of rape are a daily part of every woman's consciousness" (p. 27). She held that women's behavior is shaped by their fear of attack, and as a result, women's movements are restricted. They fear to live alone, walk outside at night, smile at strangers, and leave their windows open. Psychological research has found that women's perceptions of their vulnerability to attack and their fear of being a victim of a violent crime are related to the amount of precautionary behaviors in which they engage. Women, especially those unsure of their ability to protect themselves physically, engage in isolating behavior, such as not going out at night or visiting friends (Riger and Gordon 1981). This limits women's opportunities to be active participants in the public sphere.

The first rape crisis center was founded in Washington, D.C., in 1972, and the number of centers has increased steadily since that time (Deckard 1983). Now there are more than 550 rape crisis centers across the country, some helping as many as 1,100 victims annually (King and Webb 1981). Rape crisis centers and rape hotlines provide valuable assistance to victims of sexual assault and rape. Victims are provided with information and escorted to the police station and the hospital, and volunteers serve as advocates for the victim after the attack. Many of these centers also have educational programs in the community to help dispel rape myths and change public attitudes about rape (Deckard 1983). Cuts in governmental funding during the Reagan administration, however, have resulted in the closing of some centers, and in an increased need for volunteers and private funding.

Susan Brownmiller (1975), in her bestselling book, *Against Our Will: Men, Women, and Rape*, reaffirmed the relationship between sexual aggression and women's fear, defining rape as "a conscious process of intimidation by which all men keep all women in a state of fear" (p. 5). Her book was crucial in the definition of rape from a feminist perspective. Brownmiller's analysis formed the foundation for numerous theoretical papers and psychological research. Her book detailed the evolution of rape in our culture and the role it has played throughout history.

Brownmiller began her analysis by considering biology. Women are physiologically vulnerable to sexual attack, and once "men discovered that they could rape, they proceeded to do it" (1975, 6). Rape served a critical function of domination and intimidation in primitive societies. "His forcible entry into her body, despite her physical protestations and struggle, became the vehicle of his victorious conquest over her being, the ultimate test of his superior strength, the triumph of his manhood" (p. 5). Rape, therefore, was a purposeful act of control. In some cases, rape was an act of manhood, a rite of passage, or a form of male bonding. This male bonding, on occasion, is exhibited in the form of gang rape. Examining gang rape, Brownmiller concluded that " 'sharing the girl among us fellows' strengthens the notion of group masculinity and power" (p. 28). This bond between men results from their "contempt for women" and thrives in a culture of "forced and exaggerated male/female polarities" (p. 211).

The victims of rape often are portrayed as secretly enjoying their victimization—a depiction particularly common in the media. Movie images often present the woman as resisting only initially and eventually becoming overwhelmed by sexual desire despite her original protests. These images reinforce rape myths, and they prompted many feminists to speak out against the way women are portrayed in the media (Jozsa and Jozsa 1980; Read 1989). The images themselves represent women as inferior and as victims rather than agents in their own sexuality. Groth and Birnbaum (1979, 27) stated that "pornography is a media equivalent to the crime of rape. It is the sexual expression of power and anger." Women began to speculate about the relationship between the way women were portrayed in the media and the prevalence of rape and sexual assault. As a result, the phrase "pornography is the theory, rape is the practice" became a rallying cry for some radical feminists (Morgan 1980, 134).

The use of coercive authority also is a component of sexual assaults in our culture. Sometimes a mere difference in status provides the necessary tool to force intercourse on an unwilling partner. Date rape, homosexual rape in prisons, and rape by police are just a few examples of this form of manipulation. In reality, however, all rapes involve status differences due to the gender-based distribution of power in our society (Box 1983, 150). A woman's resistance within a dependent relationship often is weakened and she becomes vulnerable to being victimized. In addition, victimization may be facilitated by the institutional structure, which often places men in positions of authority and power over women. "Rape by an authority figure can befuddle a victim who has been trained to respect authority so that she believes herself complicitous. Authority figures emanate an aura of rightness: their actions cannot be challenged" (Brownmiller 1975, 300). The victim is left with feelings of guilt and powerlessness, while the aggressor's behavior is left undisputed. For years, many women blamed themselves and did not define their sexual victimization as rape. Since the advent of feminism, and with increased research and public education, women have begun to define unwanted sexual intercourse, even contact between acquaintances, as rape (Warshaw 1988).

ACQUAINTANCE RAPE

As public discourse on sexual violence continued, it became increasingly evident that rapists were not only strangers behind bushes, but also might be dates, acquaintances, neighbors, husbands, friends, and relatives. Feminists made the case that every man is a potential rapist and all women are potential victims. Due to this reconceptualization, date rape became an area of concern. In 1972, *Ms.* magazine discussed the issue of date rape on college campuses across the country. Initial research indicated that rape between acquaintances was much more common than previously believed. Kanin and Parcell (1977) found that approximately 83 percent of college women had experienced male sexual aggression while dating. Research a decade later confirmed this incidence rate. Koss, Gidycz, and Wisniewski (1987) found that 27.5 percent of college women reported being victims of rape or attempted rape; 53.7 percent of women, including those who reported being raped, had experienced some form of unwanted sexual contact and/or sexually assaultive behavior. These results suggest that sexually aggressive behavior is experienced by the majority of women in "normal" dating relationships. This high incidence rate gives credence to the feminist conceptualization of rape as being supported by our culture.

Psychological Research on Rape

The views of feminists, in particular the work of Susan Brownmiller, sparked research within psychology to examine the "rape-supportive culture" that provides the context for sexual assault. Researchers made empirical studies of feminist ideas and combined these feminist views into a theoretical framework to understand and predict sexual aggression. Martha Burt (1980) hypothesized that our culture and the status of women within that culture play a significant role in the attitudes toward sexual violence held by persons, particularly rapists. She hypothesized that myths about rape (e.g., "women ask for it") might act as releasers or facilitators of sexual aggression. These rape myths were proposed as part of a larger attitudinal structure that serves to facilitate sexually aggressive acts in our culture. Attitudinal factors that were found by Burt to predict rape-supportive myths were (a) sex role stereotyping, (b) adversarial sexual beliefs, and (c) acceptance of interpersonal violence.

Sex role stereotyping refers to the appropriateness of familial, work, and social roles being based on the sex of the individual being considered (e.g., "It is acceptable for a woman to have a career, but marriage and family should come first"; Burt 1980, 222). Adversarial sexual beliefs refers to the view that male–female relationships are naturally filled with conflict and competition (e.g., "Most women are sly and manipulating when they are out to attract a man"—p. 222). Acceptance of interpersonal violence refers to the belief that violence is an appropriate way of interacting with others, particularly in male–female relationships (e.g., "Sometimes the only way to get a cold woman turned on is to use force"—p. 222). These attitudes were studied by researchers (Burt and Albin 1981; Check and Malamuth 1983; Malamuth 1983) as a means to understand sexual aggression using a feminist framework.

Koss, Leonard, Beezley, and Oros (1985) developed a theoretical model for characterizing nonstranger sexual aggression that incorporated Burt's findings and feminist views. They proposed a social control/social conflict model of date rape:

> Culturally transmitted assumptions about men, women, violence, sexuality, and myths about rape constitute a rape-supportive belief system. Furthermore, stratified systems such as the American dating situation may legitimate the use of force by those in power and weaken resistance of the less powerful. Finally, acquisition of stereotyped myths about rape may result in a failure to label as rape sexual aggression that occurs in dating situations. (Koss et al. 1985, 982)

This view of a culturally based belief system that perpetuates violence against women and oppresses women has been endorsed by several feminist writers (Brownmiller 1975; Griffin 1971; Johnson 1980).

Rape within the Legal System

In the colonial period, the law conceptualized rape as the violation of a man's property. It was a man's personal privilege to have access to a woman's body. Feminist theorists have rejected traditional legal conceptualizations, which often blame the woman for her own victimization, and have refuted rape myths that women enjoy being raped, and ask and deserve to be raped by dressing provocatively. They refuse to allow women to be blamed for their own victimization. Instead, blame is placed squarely on the attacker.

Feminists have lobbied for changes in rape legislation. Previous laws considered rape an all-or-nothing crime, in which convicted offenders received sentences that ranged from 5 years to life depending on the particular state's statutes. Maximum sentences of 30–50 years in prison were not uncommon for convicted rapists (Babcock, Freedman, Norton, and Ross 1975). Prior to the 1972 case of *Furman v. Georgia*, which "invalidated arbitrary capital punishment laws, sixteen states permitted imposition of death for rape" (Berger 1977, 8). Some writers hypothesized that the severe penalties for rape may have discouraged juries from convicting a defendant because of a "perceived sense of disproportion between culpability and the prescribed sentence" (Andenaes 1966, 970). Now most states have revised their laws to include several levels of sexual assault with a broader range of penalties. A perpetrator may be charged with first-, second-, or third-degree rape, with each charge varying in the maximum sentence following conviction. First-degree rape is defined as forced sexual intercourse under aggravated circumstances. Second-degree rape is described as forced sexual intercourse. Third-degree rape is defined as nonconsensual intercourse or intercourse with threat to self or property. This calibrated system of offenses and penalties has increased conviction rates, and may therefore enhance the effectiveness of prosecution as a deterrent (Andenaes 1966, 970).

In addition, the criterion of force was determined in the past by examining the victim's behavior rather than the offender's behavior. In the 1970s, women in New York needed the corroboration of a witness who saw or heard the assault to verify that it had indeed been rape, and that the woman had resisted the attack. In addition, some states viewed "no resistance" as consensual intercourse, and required the victim to have verbally said "no" or forcibly resisted or screamed (Margolin 1972). Unless the woman exhibited these behaviors, the man's behavior was not considered rape.

In 1974, Michigan passed the first comprehensive rape reform legislation in the country (Loh 1981). Since that time, most states have enacted similar changes. These reforms have focused on the perpetrator's behavior (e.g., use of physical force or threat of force) as the legal criterion rather than the victim's behavior alone. The context of the assault and the interaction between the victim and assailant are becoming increasingly important.

Although rape legislation has changed a great deal, many changes are still sought (see Goldberg-Ambrose 1992). In about half of the states a man cannot be charged with sexually assaulting his wife unless they are separated legally. In six states, a husband can never be charged with raping his wife (Searles and Berger 1987). Recently a North Carolina woman was kidnapped and raped by her husband, but since they had been separated less than one year, the separation was not yet legal and she was unable to charge him with rape. In one-fourth of the states, a man cannot be the victim of rape (Searles and Berger 1987). In states with progressive statutes, sex-neutral terminology is used for both offender and victim. In approximately 70 percent of states, a victim's past sexual behavior with persons other than the defendant is admissible for determining consent, while only six states prohibit the introduction of the victim's sexual history (Searles and Berger 1987).

Criticism of Radical Feminist Reconceptualizations

Some feminists have criticized Brownmiller's (1975) conceptualization of rape. Rather than placing all the blame on women as in the past, Brownmiller counterblamed, condemning all men for their innate violence (Benjamin 1983). In addition, radical feminists have ignored the "history of women's resistance to oppression" and focused on sexuality itself as the enemy—"an unchanging, aggressive male sexuality of which women have been eternally the victims" (Arnold 1989, 36). Brownmiller's book also has been faulted as "supporting a notion of universal patriarchy and timeless sexual victimization; it leaves no room for understanding the reasons for women's collaboration, their own sources of power, . . . the class and racial differences in their experience of discrimination and sexual danger" (Hall 1983, 341). The radical feminist view also focuses exclusively on the negative. Some writers believe that in order for feminism to persist, women must use their own strength as an energy source for reform.

> Social movements, feminism included, move toward a vision; they cannot operate solely on fear. It is not enough to move women away from danger and oppression; it is necessary to move toward something: toward pleasure, agency, self-definition. Feminism must increase women's pleasure and joy, not just decrease our misery, (Vance 1984, 24)

Areas of Action and Change: Then and Now

Education is still needed to help change society's attitudes about rape. In the recent past, women have been the target for increased awareness, but now men also are being included in the process of consciousness raising (Walsh 1990). "The anti-rape movement must not limit itself to training women to avoid rape or depending on imprisonment as a deterrent, but must aim its attention at changing the behavior and attitudes of men" (Hall 1983, 346). For example, the University of Florida has introduced a program called FARE (Fraternity Acquaintance Rape Education) to educate men in fraternities and on athletic teams (Walsh 1990).

Education of women also is needed to empower them to action. In our culture, women are socialized to be submissive, but some feminists have challenged this role. "To be submissive is to defer to masculine strength: is to lack muscular development or any interest in defending oneself" (Griffin 1971, 33). Women can take courses in self-defense to strengthen their bodies, and to gain the ability and the confidence to defend themselves should they be attacked. Ann Sheldon (1972) felt this solution to rape was inescapable: "there is no other way except resistance to be free" (p. 23).

Feminists clearly have made a major difference in the way sexual assault and rape are understood in our culture. Yet considering the long historical tradition of women bearing the guilt for sexual victimization, it is not surprising that much still needs to change. Over 15 years ago, Brownmiller called for action, saying, "the purpose in this book has been to give rape its history. Now we must deny it a future" (1975, 454). That need is still true today.

12

Undeclared War: African-American Women Writers Explicating Rape

OPAL PALMER ADISA

Preamble

Slavery was a war, and the bodies of Africans were the battle field. African women, men, and children were held captive in the holds of ships when brought to these shores. Stripped, poked, fondled, and teeth-counted, they were sold on auction blocks. They worked from sunrise to sunset in the cotton and cane fields of the Americas, were tied to stakes, and had designs beaten into their bodies. African people were lynched for plotting to escape, for insubordination, for asserting their humanity.

The war waged against African women under slavery was particularly insidious because, in addition to other forms of physical abuse, rape was used as the major means of control. This manifestation of white men's misogynistic attitude towards slave women resulted in miscegenation. In addition, slave women, although clearly the victims of this abuse, were labelled promiscuous and salacious. However, contrary to what scholars like Eugene D. Genovese (1974) have suggested about the great love affair between masters and their slave women, there is little tangible evidence to support such a claim. Angela Davis (1983) notes how some scholars have ignored the testimonies of slave women.

> Despite the testimonies of slaves about the high incidence of rape and sexual coercion, the issue of sexual abuse has been all but glossed over in the traditional literature on slavery. It is sometimes even assumed that slave women welcomed and encouraged the sexual attention of white men. What happened between them, therefore, was not sexual exploitation, but rather "miscegenation." (Davis 1983, 25)

What power did a slave woman have to voice her abuse? Who would have listened to her? What laws were there to protect her? Slave women were muted by their debased social status.

The two freest people in America are the white man and the black woman. (Anonymous)

From *Women's Studies International Forum* 15, no. 3 (1992): 363–74. Elsevier Science Ltd., Pergamon Imprint, Oxford, England. Reprinted by permission.

The above statement represents an attempt to obfuscate and demean the suffering that African-American women have had and continue to experience as second class citizens of the United States. Freedom was never something for which a slave woman could barter, for even when she was granted a modicum of mobility, she was still subjected to the sexual will of any white man. The Black woman's "freer" status is based on a myth which we must reject in order to understand more fully the true circumstances in which she lives. From the moment a woman was captured on the coast of West Africa, her body became a battlefield that she constantly tried to wrest from the master's control.

One need only read *Incidents in the Life of a Slave Girl* (1861), the autobiography of Linda Brent, to understand the precarious fate of most female slaves. Brent writes, "But I now entered on my fifteenth year—a sad epoch in the life of a slave girl. My master began to whisper foul words in my ear. Young as I was, I could not remain ignorant of their import" (p. 26). The fact that Brent was only 15, and her master, an established medical doctor with a wife, did not prevent him from wielding his power over her, stalking her and making it clear to her how completely powerless she was: "My master met me at every turn, reminding me that I belonged to him, and swearing by heaven and earth that he would compel me to submit to him" (p. 27). Brent's experience illustrates how the majority of African-American women were thrust into battle with few weapons. They not only relied upon resilience and cunning to avoid their masters for as long as possible, but also to stay clear of jealous mistresses who took every opportunity to vent their anger and frustration on hapless slaves.

Given the context of slavery, a war in which the targeted group was forcibly removed from its home, thrust into a foreign environment, forced to learn a new language, and forbidden to use arms in its defense, rape was, as Angela Davis puts it, "an unveiled element of counter-insurgency" (1971, 12). For slaves, to organize openly was tantamount to signing one's death warrant. By raping the Black woman, not only did the white master violate her in the most devastating way, he also revealed the impotency of the entire slave community. "Rape is the act of the conqueror," Susan Brownmiller (1975, 35) asserts. But the significance of the act extends past sheer aggression because it was intended not only to assert control over Black women, but also to dehumanize and reduce them to the level of animals.

Realizing that it would be cheaper and more convenient to "breed" one's own slave rather than rely on the dying slave trade, plantation owners further reduced slave women to the status of breeders. Brownmiller (1975) reviews the historical context.

> Since it was the slaveholding class that created the language and wrote the laws pertaining to slavery, it was not surprising that legally the concept of raping a slave simply did not exist. One cannot rape one's own property. The rape of one man's slave by another white man was considered a mere "trespass" in the eyes of the plantation law. The rape of one man's slave by another slave had no official recognition in law at all. (pp. 162–163)

After 200 years of continuous abuse, African-American women became adept at spotting a rapist. Although they could not always circumvent being raped, they devised ways to endure it, and they hemmed alertness into their skirts.

As with the slave woman, rape remained one of life's hazards for the emancipated African-American woman. The short-lived political and economic gains of Reconstruction were countered by the tyranny of the Ku Klux Klan that burned homes, lynched men, and raped women of the African-American community. Testimonies gathered from African-American men and women after the Memphis Riots, 1865, dramatically reveal the inextricable linking of lynching, home burning, and raping of women. Frances Thompson, testifying in 1865 before the Chairman appointed to investigate the damage done to the community after the riots, reports thus:

> They drew their pistols and said they would shoot us and fire the house if we did not let them have their way with us. All seven of the men violated us two. Four of them had to do with me, and the rest with Lucy. (Thompson 1973, 174)

Earlier in her testimony to the Chairman, Frances Thompson testified that two of the seven men were police; she saw their stars. Even after slavery, African-American people had little or no protection under the law and were subject to the most debasing kinds of abuse. Past and present analysis shows that rape is not a crime of uncontrollable sexual passion, but one used to vent misogyny and to exert physical, political, and economic control.

FBI statistics indicate that one out of three women will be raped in her lifetime, one out of four before the age of 18. Shocking as these figures are, African-American women are more likely to be raped than any other women, are least likely to be believed, and must often watch their rapists treated with impunity or mild punishment. Brownmiller (1975) cites from a study of rape convictions conducted in the city of Baltimore in 1967, which highlights this phenomenon:

> Of the four categories of rapist and victim in a racial mix, blacks [men] received the stiffest sentences for raping white women and the mildest sentence for raping black women. Of the 26 blacks convicted in Baltimore of raping white women, only one got less than five-to-ten years. Of the five white men convicted in Baltimore of raping black women, one received a sentence of from 15 to 20 years, three received less than five years, and one received a suspended sentence. (p. 216)

Statistics such as these prove that Black women's bodies have historically provided the battlefield, as well as the reward for victory, in a continuing war on the African-American community.

From this historical context, a body of work has emerged which, I believe, is an attempt by African-American women to heal their wounds and garner strength. The preponderance of works by African-American writers in which rape is the direct subject or is used as a metaphor, a figurative way of talking about the abuses that African-American women have and continue to suffer, is by no means surprising. Some of the poets draw from their own experiences as survivors of rape. Others draw upon cultural paradigms that promote the subjugation of women and vindicate the acts of abusive men. Whatever their inspiration, these poets all realize that every woman is vulnerable in a society that allows, and sometimes even encourages, their physical abuse. African-American poets illustrate how rape has been, and remains, the most lethal weapon used to oppress, suppress, and dehumanize Black women in order to subvert their struggles to lead independent lives.

From Ann Petry's *The Street* (1946), Dorothy West's *The Living Is Easy* (1982), Pauline Hopkins' *Contending Forces* (1978), Margaret Walker's *Jubilee* (1967), to Toni Morrison's *The Bluest Eye* (1970), Alice Walker's *The Color Purple* (1982), and Gayle Jones' *Corregidora* (1975), the brutal rape of Black women is recounted in painful detail. But it is in the works of poetry—from that of Frances E. W. Harper (1969), to Jayne

Cortez (1983), Sonia Sanchez (1981), Ntozake Shange (1979)—that the bestiality of such an act is rendered raw by metaphor and imagery, and the terror that it produces is most graphically recounted. Rape stalks African-American women's lives, and the poets, in particular, have turned their most potent weapon, their pen, to their defense.

From the very beginning, African-Americans writing about slavery and the post-slavery years have described the plight of the Black woman in an attempt to solicit the pathos of the wider community. Their artistic endeavors were limited, however, since their primary goal was to assert the humanity of the slave woman and to establish her virtue. Francis Harper, the nineteenth-century African-American poet, abolitionist, and anti-lynching crusader, euphemized the horrors of rape for moral reasons. She writes in the sixth stanza of "Bury Me in a Free Land":

> If I saw young girls from their mothers' arms
> Bartered and sold for their youthful charms,
> My eye would flash with a mournful flame,
> My death-paled cheek grow red with shame. (Harper 1969, p 36)

Harper, undoubtedly aware of the commonly held perception of slave women as immoral, refrains from using the word "rape," yet her meaning is clear. Harper relies on words like "charm," "mournful flame," and "shame," to convey the crime, her revolt and the dishonor which she shares with her less fortunate sisters. The poem ends triumphantly and the priority is clear, the zeal for freedom and dignity.

> I ask no monument, proud and high,
> To arrest the gaze of the passers-by;
> All that my yearning spirit craves,
> Is bury me not in a land of slaves. (Harper 1969, 37)

In their efforts to garner sympathy for slave women, writers like Harper faced a major difficulty in attempting to impugn the patriarchal structure of society with its double code for women. Paternalistic conceptions of women are rooted in Judeo-Christian ethics which espouse the idea that woman, Eve, is the temptress who causes man's fall and eviction from paradise. Hazel Carby (1987) examines the implications of this notion:

> The institutionalized rape of black women has never been as powerful a symbol of black oppression as the spectacle of lynching. Rape has always involved patriarchal notions of women being, at best, not entirely unwilling accomplices, if not outwardly inviting a sexual attack. (p. 39)

Thus the rape of slave women, and later the freed African-American woman, was indirectly condoned by society. Most recently, however, contemporary African-American poets have fought back without hesitating to name the crime, point to the accuser, and take up arms in defense of their bodies and personage.

Present in the work of many African-American poets is the historical antecedent— the unacknowledged suffering of their foremothers. Their poetry forges the link between the exploitation in their and their ancestors' lives, simultaneously commenting on the precarious position that African-American women still occupy in this society. Amina Baraka's "Soweto Song" (1983) is particularly effective because its subject, speaking in the first person, becomes all African women who were taken as slaves, and all women reading this poem become the warrior preparing for battle. Moreover, Soweto, the physical place, is viewed as an extension of the southern United States. The poet suggests that the same war which began in slavery is continuing:

> i come from the womb of Africa
> to praise my black diamond
> to shine my black gold
> to fight my people enemies
> to stand on my ancestors shoulders
> to dance in the hurricane of revolution
>   Soweto, Soweto, Soweto,
> i come with my hammer & sickle
> i come with bullets for my gun
> to fire on my enemies
> to stab the savages that sucked my breast
> to kill the beast that raped my belly
> i come painted red in my peoples blood
> to dance on the wind of the storm
> to help sing freedom songs
>   Soweto, Soweto, Soweto, (p. 70)

A striking feature of this poem is that Baraka uses the lower case form of the character "i." Since capitalization is used throughout the remainder of the poem in a conventional manner, we are left to surmise the significance of the lower case "i." While the "i" in the poem admits to the singularity of the persona's struggle, the poet also infuses the subject with a great deal of power. After a while the "i" no longer reads as first person singular, but rather as the collective "we." Moreover, the poem's tone seems to declare: I'm prepared; I know this is a war; therefore I am armed and ready to do battle. The simple, repetitive refrain, "i come/to" functions as an evocation, a war chant to boost the spirit and inspire the warriors.

The poem's structure forces us to pause at the lines: "To stab the savages that sucked my breast/to kill the beast that raped my belly." Baraka turns the tables upside down by taking the terms historically used to refer to African-Americans and hurls them at the former masters. The racist epithets "savage" and "beast" become accusations exposing the rapist aggressor's true nature.

Although the momentum of the poem remains active until the end, the focus shifts, the tone is softened, and the emphasis is on rebuilding and moving forward. The repetitive structure and the deliberate slowness of the language are done to highlight the determined move toward freedom.

> i come to carve monuments in the image of my people
> i come to help hold the flag of freedom
> i come to bring my tears to wash your wounds
> i come to avenge slavery
> i come to claim by blood ties
> i come to help free my people
>   Soweto, Soweto, Soweto, (p. 70)

Connected with the freedom of the people is the need to "avenge slavery." Slavery is the war that must be acknowledged; due compensation must be paid.

The works of African-American female poets are like a broken record trapped in the groove on the issues of rape and slavery. The poems can be interpreted as ritual baths performed to cleanse them, rid them of this desecration. The proliferation of female body imagery and the control and restrictions imposed on African-American women's reproductive rights are evident in the poems. Akua Lezli Hope's "Lament" (1983) makes vivid this point.

> my contraceptive history
> pregnant with pain
> the breech birth of clashing cultures
>
> forced cervical dilation
> snake steel rods
> insidious constraint and rape
>
> sometimes i bear mulattoes
> strangers to my skin
> strongwilled aliens
> strangers to my heart (p. 141)

Hope introduces a sentiment not often, in fact seldom, expressed by African-American women writers. The poem's persona, through abortion, rejects those offspring forced on her as a result of being raped. The clear distancing between the mother and her children, expressed in the third stanza, represents the woman's protest against her rape, her refusal to accept the product of her violation. Her mulatto children remain aliens, "strangers to my heart," perhaps because it is easier to kill an intruder, or stranger.

In the next stanza of "Lament," Hope makes no attempt to justify the act of infanticide; it is not done out of love, but rather rejection. Although the decision causes anguish, there is no indication that the persona feels remorse, nor does she oscillate because she has no other alternative.

> i remove rods
> to early brand or slay them
> each choice conceives anguish
> capitulation harkens suffering
> rebellion beckons despair
>   upon my womb
>   upon my womb (p. 141)

Since a woman's body is the battlefield, she must make it the source of her resistance: "upon my womb/i swear silent oaths/razor-toothed and lockjawed..." (p. 141). The passion and force embedded in these three lines is unquestionable. The womb, considered a sacred part of a woman's femininity, becomes her armor.

Wars, no matter how long they last, change over a period of time. Poets Abbey Lincoln and June Jordan transport us to the present and demonstrate how rape continues to be ubiquitous as well as intimate. More African-American women are being raped by their "brothers," often a male disguised as their "friend." The war has spread and there are no clear demarcations to distinguish battlefield or safe zone. Even though slaves were granted freedom, the African-American woman is still not free, not even in her home that she works to secure. The fact is that no place is safe; all are suspect.

Abbey Lincoln's "On Being High" (1983) explores date rape under the rubric of the African-American female as a bitch, a woman who is open to all sexual advances. The poem's theme is that African-American women's pursuit of love is thwarted.

> On a date, I thought, with somebody I thought I knew,
> bursting with blooming love songs,
> I was raped . . . While terror ran rampant in a tearful face, the lawful sheriff,
> investigating, questioned him first . . .
> Then, securing me alone to talk, leered and said
> I oughta drop the case.
> Unsure of my rights, I sent my head on higher
> and dropped the case. (p. 187)

Lincoln makes it blatantly evident that the law offers no protection for African-American women, an injustice heightened by the fact that many African-American women are unsure of their rights. It is not because they are ignorant. They know instinctively that the books are stacked against them, and they have little to no recourse. So the phrase, "I sent my head higher" is perplexing because while it could suggest pride, or refusal to be defeated, the act is merely a gesture in the face of the reality: Her rapist is exonerated. She remains as defenseless as her slave sister whose only weapon was her guile.

June Jordan, the poet/activist who has been raped on two occasions, divides "Rape Is Not a Poem" (1980a) into four sections. The first section serves as a prelude, a metaphorical analogy to the rape that comes later. Her matter-of-fact tone heightens the anger, the utter contempt and betrayal that she feels.

> One day she saw them coming into the garden
> where the flowers live.
> They
> found the colors beautiful and
> they discovered the sweet smell
> that the flowers held
> so
> they stamped upon and tore apart
> the garden
> just because (they said)
> those flowers?
> They were asking for it. (p. 79)

While it can be argued that the reference to a woman's sexual anatomy as a flower is cliché, the comparison nonetheless illustrates the destruction of an organic thing by those who plunder simply to make a point. Moreover, the men's entrance into the garden is clearly an invasion. The act of rape that they commit is to assuage their fear, their feeling of impotence. Rape confirms their power to dominate what is "discovered," to seize what is "held," to destroy by right of conquest.

The poem then moves from the metaphorical into the realm of reality. The setting is clear, the people are tangible, the dialogue appears civil, bordering on mundane. Before the dialogue collapses into triteness, however, there appears dissonance, conflict, a suppressed war.

> I let him into the house to say hello.
> "Hello," he said.
> "Hello," I said.
> "How are you?" he asked me.
> "Not bad," I told him.
> "You look great," he smiled.
> "Thanks; I've been busy: I am busy."
> "Well, I guess I'll be heading out, again," he said.
> "Okay," I answered and, "Take care," I said.
> "I'm gonna do just that," he said.
> "No!" I said: "No! Please don't. Please leave me alone. Now. No.
>   Please!" I said.
> "I'm leaving," he laughed: "I'm leaving you alone; I'm going now!"
> "No!" I cried: "No. Please don't do this to me!" But he was not
>   talking anymore and there was nothing else that I could say to
>   make him listen to me. (p. 79–80)

Surprisingly, the persona does not identify the act, does not cry rape. Instead she begs, "Please don't do this to me!" Why the restraint? Does the persona acquiesce because she knows ultimately that she must yield to the stronger, brutal force? Dialogue is aborted. Even the tone of the third section, while it names her anger, is intellectual, an attempt to place the act within a larger historical context.

> And considering your contempt
> And considering my hatred consequent to that
> And considering the history
> that leads us to this dismal place where
> (your arm
> raised
> and my eyes
> lowered)
> there is nothing left but the drippings
> of power and
> a consummate wreck of tenderness/I
> want to know:
> Is this what you call
> Only Natural? (p. 80)

In the last two lines the question the persona poses, "Is this what you call/Only Natural?" is sardonic, but her disillusionment is apparent. In section four of this poem, Jordan flings the adage, "Men are dogs" out the window. She describes her dog in a gentle manner, then ends the poem, "You should let him teach you how/to come down." (p. 81). The implication is clear: a dog is or can be more appropriate than the man who violated her, and can in fact teach her persecutor restraint.

In yet another poem, "The Rationale, or She Drove Me Crazy" (1980b), Jordan assumes the voice of a rapist who goes before the judge and in his defense pleads, "Then I lost control; I couldn't resist./What did she expect? . . ." (p. 11). The rapist is portrayed as a man driven out of control by an apparently sexy woman walking on the streets alone. As in the other poem, the irony of the situation, and the innate contradiction of society with its blatant disregard for women is revealed in a tag that Jordan saves for the end: "third time apprehended/for the theft of a Porsche" (p. 12). Once again the rapist is not punished for his assault of a woman, but rather for his theft of a car officially deemed more valuable than women.

With the invention of the pill and the widespread advocacy of other forms of birth control, women have supposedly been liberated, at least sexually. The idea that women own their own bodies because they are allowed to make decisions about conception, along with the notion that men's deeply ingrained prejudices against women have changed, if not false, is overly optimistic. The reality does not substantiate this propaganda. The truth is that incidents of rape continue to escalate, while undisguised misogyny is a constant and reoccurring blitz in all forms of media.

A close look at social dynamics reveals that as a result of women being granted apparent sexual "freedom," people appear to be less sensitive to incidents of rape. Sexual liberation allows for different classifications of rape and, implicitly, different levels of abuse—some violations may appear less horrendous than others. Both of these facts combine to make it just as difficult now as in the past for women to prove rape, much less receive justice.

Yet another damaging effect of women's sexual "freedom" is the fact that women often buy into this advocacy of sexual promiscuity and so dismiss, or downplay, being raped. Bell Hooks (1989), the African-American feminist, examines this trend as it is depicted in the movie, "She's Gotta Have It," produced and directed by an independent African-American male filmmaker, Spike Lee. Lee says his intention for the movie is "to portray a radical new image of black female sexuality." However, Bell Hooks asserts that the portrayal of Nola Darling in "She's Gotta Have It" reinforces and perpetuates old norms overall" (Hooks 1989, 141). In her essay, "whose pussy is this: a feminist comment," Hooks demonstrates how the movie makes rape palatable and "is perfectly compatible with sexist pornographic fantasies about rape to show a woman enjoying violation" (p. 139). In the scene where the rape occurs (the scene is not identified as such), Nola Darling, the sexually liberated protagonist, invites one of her beaus, her rapist, over. The implication is that Nola complied with the actions of the rapist, that she was "ravished." She is reduced to not even owning her most private part. As her "lover"/assailant is ramming her from the rear, as if she is a bitch in heat, he demands of her, "whose pussy is this?" She submits, "Yours." And as Hooks rightly notes, "It is difficult for anyone who has fallen for the image of her as sexually liberated to not feel let down, disappointed both in her character and in the film" (p. 139).

What has contributed to the all too frequent portrayal of rape in the electronic media as an act enjoyed by women? How has this image contributed to women's confusion over their own rights, and the ability to differentiate between rape versus pleasure? How has this portrayal contributed to making women believe that they are accomplices in their own violation and are responsible for men's actions toward them? Bell Hooks postulates that the scene in "She's Gotta Have It"

impresses on the consciousness of black males, and all males, the sexist assumption that rape is an effective means of patriarchal social control, that it restores and maintains male power over women. It simultaneously suggests to black females, and all females, that being sexually assertive will lead to rejection and punishment. (Hooks 1989, 139)

This indicates that the war, which began for African-American women in slavery, continues just as dangerously as before. Now, however, not only do we have to be vigilant before the known rapist but before those pretending to be friends who would use our professed sexual liberation as a weapon to disarm and silence us like Nola Darling in "She's Gotta Have It."

Ntozake Shange (1979) demonstrates in a prose/poem the extent to which rape is intended to implant in a woman's mind the idea that she is defenseless. If she fails to conform to patriarchal dictates her actions will be viewed as subversive, and violence may be used to force her to submit. Shange points out the pervasiveness of rape, and how it affects females all over the world.

> I'm so saddened that being born a girl makes it dangerous to attend midnight mass unescorted. Some places if we're born girls & some one else who's very sick & weak & cruel/attack us & break our hymen/we have to be killed/sent away from our families/ forbidden to touch our children. These strange people who wound little girls are known as attackers, molesters, & rapists. They are known all over the world & are proliferating at a rapid rate. To be born a girl who will always have to worry not only about the molesters, the attackers & the rapist/but also about their peculiarities/does he stab too/or shoot/does he carry an ax/does he spit on you/does he know if he doesn't drop sperm we can't prove we've been violated/those subtleties make being a girl too complex/for some of us & we go crazy/or never go anyplace. (Shange 1979, 28)

This prose/poem successfully conveys the message that rape is international, and that in some societies, rape victims are not only blamed for their victimization, but are further punished by being killed, ostracized, and/or banished. However, Shange does not conclude that the threatened female must withdraw inward, resort to madness or reclusiveness, for safety. She, like Jordan, knows that there is no safe place, not even in one's home.

> some of us have never had an open window or a walk alone/but sometimes our homes are not safe for us either/rapist attackers & molesters are not strangers to everyone/they are related to somebody/ & some of them like raping & molesting their family members better than a girl-child they don't know yet/ (Shange 1979, 28)

Shange offers no resolution to the problem, but she does assert, that as women ". . . we owe no one anything/not our labia, not our clitoris, not our lives." In a triumphant note, with a voice that shoves away the hand that would silence our voices, Shange demands that we have "our lives/ to live" (p. 29).

In another prose/poem, "otherwise i would think it odd to have rape prevention month," Shange seems to adopt a snide posture at rape prevention month. She is suggesting that rape is so pervasive, and has become so much a part of patriarchal domination that to set aside only a month to deal with this cancerous disease is to fail to comprehend truly the enormity of the situation or appreciate the plight of women. Yet, Shange offers nine alternatives, in which she points out the ludicrousness and futility of the program. In Alternative No. 8, however, she seems to suggest a means for women to empower themselves:

> unless the streets are made safe for us/we shall call a general strike/in factories/at home/at school. We shall say we cannot come to work/it is not safe. (Shange 1979, 30)

Shange apparently forgets her message, conveyed in her other poem: home is not safe; no place is. Nonetheless, she focuses in this poem on the need for women to organize and demand that their collective voices be heard.

The poet who is most unflinching on the subject of rape, who dramatizes it and renders it in explicit war terminology, is Jayne Cortez (1983). In her poem, "Rape," Cortez uses graphic language to shock out of its complacency a society that habitually victimizes women. Cortez's outrage over injustice is vociferous, and her alliance with her sisters is uncompromising. Just as significant as her dedication to this alliance is her willingness to name the rapists for what they are: vicious, ruthless, fascist, and racist. The rapist is not made a figurative beast, or a misdirected man out of control. She portrays a rapist who is unquestionably human, rational, and culpable for the terror that he engenders in women.

Cortez writes about women who seem to recognize and accept the fact that they are at war with a society that allows men to assert their dominance by subjugating and demoralizing women's bodies. "Rape" got its impetus from two much publicized cases that occurred in the mid-70s: the cases of Inez Garcia, a Native American woman, and Joanne Little, an African-American woman. These women's stories are significant because they both refused to submit, play dead, pick themselves up after the ordeal, and continue on with their lives as if they had not been abused. Inez Garcia and Joanne Little encouraged all women not to submit, to fight back. Both cases generated support from women's groups around the country, and after much networking, letter writing, protesting, both women were acquitted of their rapists' deaths. Cortez writes:

> What was Inez supposed to do for
> the man who declared war on her body
> the man who carved a combat zone between her breasts
> was she supposed to lick crabs from his hairy ass
> kiss every pimple on his butt
> blow hot breath on his big toe
> draw back the corners of her vagina and
> hee haw like a Calif. burro
>
> This being war time for Inez
> she stood facing the knife
> the insults and
> her own smell drying on the penis of
> the man who raped her
>
> She stood with a rifle in her hand
> doing what a defense department will do in times of war
> And when the man started grunting and panting and
>   wobbling forward like
> a giant hog
> She pumped lead into his three hundred pounds of
>   shaking flesh
> Sent it flying to the virgin of Guadeloupe
> then celebrated day of the dead rapist punk
> and just what the fuck else was she suppose to do? (p. 89)

Cortez establishes the war motif from the beginning. She makes it clear that the man instigates the violence and emphasizes the logical necessity of the woman's response to his threat. Thus, Inez is likened to a defense department that has but two options under fire. Her shooting the rapist empowers all women who have been made to feel responsible for their violation.

In the second half of the poem, which is dedicated to Joanne Little's victory, Cortez repeats the war imagery, and poses the same rhetorical question. By explicitly describing the details that took place during the events leading up to both women's retaliation, Cortez forces the reader to experience their violation vicariously. We, faced with the graphic reality of the violence and humiliation perpetrated on Garcia and Little, understand how a woman can be provoked enough to take up the rifle or the ice pick in her defense.

> And what was Joanne supposed to do for
> the man who declared war on her life
> Was she supposed to tongue his encrusted toilet stool
> > lips
> suck the numbers off his tin badge
> choke on his clap trap balls
> squeeze on his nub of rotten maggots and
> sing god bless america thank you for fucking my life
> > away
>
> This being wartime for Joanne
> she did what a defense department will do in times of war
> and when the piss drinking shift sniffing guard said
> I'm gonna make you wish you were dead black bitch come
> > here
> Joanne came down with an ice pick in
> the swat freak mother fucker's chest
> yes in the fat neck of the racist policeman
> Joanne did the dance of the ice pick and once again
> from coast to coast
> house to house
> we celebrate day of the dead rapist punk
> and just what the fuck else were we supposed to do (pp. 89–90)

The poet does not distinguish the persona from the general pool of women. Her affinity is clear. She understands that in another place and time she could be either Inez or Joanne; in fact any female could. That is why we, all women, celebrate the "day of the dead rapist punk." While the focus of the poem is on the women, and recounting the ordeals that led to their victory, Cortez reminds us of the larger political context under which we live. Her indictment is clear in the line, "sing god bless america thank you for fucking my life away." She reminds us that the fate of these women is implicitly condoned by the white, racist, misogynist system that regards females as commodities, garbage dumps on which to heap its waste.

The historical and political context inserted in many of these poets' works demonstrates their commitment to making a tangible contribution to the African-American community. In choosing to write about the issue of rape, they automatically participate in both the fictional and real worlds. Furthermore, writers like Jayne Cortez use factual events to heighten the poignancy and sense of urgency in their work, and to emphasize the seriousness of their artistic mission. By uncovering and dismantling the social paradigms that work to oppress women, they hope to present a model and a means with which women can fight back.

Alice Walker uses the same techniques as Cortez—the use of factual evidence—to shed light on the system of abuse used to put down Black women who have increasingly refused to be passive victims, have taken courage from their other sisters and are fighting back with all they have. In an essay entitled "Trying to See My Sister" (1989), Walker discusses how this African-American woman's refusal to be raped resulted in unreasonable and excessive punishment. She uses the case of Dessie Woods, which generated much protest in the 70s (1975), but with a less successful outcome than those of Inez Garcia and Joanne Little. Walker notes, "The woman who saved her life, and saved them both from rape, was given twenty-two years, later reduced to twelve." Dessie Woods served 6 years before being released from jail on July 9, 1981. Walker recounts how all her attempts to see Dessie Woods were met with stumbling blocks. She also records that Dessie Woods was kept in solitary confinement for extended periods of time and regularly given Prolixin.

The incidents leading up to the conviction of Dessie Woods are not particularly unusual given the historical abuse of Black women. Woods had accompanied another African-American woman to visit the friend's brother in prison in Lyons, Georgia. After the visit they discovered that there was no bus to get back home to Atlanta, so they hitchhiked a ride from a white man in a police uniform. The man bought them lunch in a restaurant before driving them into the woods under the pretense of taking them to the bus station. He said he intended to have sex with both of them and they protested, but to no avail. When he stopped the car, Dessie Woods' friend jumped out and ran. In her essay, Alice Walker recounts the events that led Dessie Woods to kill her attempted rapist.

> The man drew his gun and pointed it after her. The other woman (Dessie) threw her five feet two inches against the five-foot-nine, 215 pound man and struggled to take his gun. In the process of that struggle, the gun went off twice. The man was killed by two bullet shots to the head.

Dessie Woods' friend was given a 5-year sentence, with 3 1/2 years on probation, but for "slaying the dragon," as Walker puts it, Dessie Woods was given 22. What does this incident teach us? That the woman who defends herself and/or another woman from rape will be punished; her mobility will be restricted; she will be isolated lest she evoke others to be like her; and she will be experimented on with drugs in an attempt to squash her spirit and/or make her dysfunctional. Dessie Woods' case teaches us the painful lesson that to defend oneself in this war that women face daily is to take on the most brutal battalion. Current events seem to point towards the more pessimistic possibility in Jordan's declaration in "Against the Wall:" ". . . if you undertake to terrorize and to subjugate and to stifle even one moment more of these, our only lives, we will take yours, or die trying" (Jordan 1978, 149). While Dessie Woods ultimately did not die as a result of defending her life, society punished this "insignificant" African-American woman for daring to refuse the sexual advances of a law-enforcing, southern white man. As Walker concludes, "It is obvious that Black women do not have the right to self-defense against racist and sexist attacks by white men. I realize I am in prison as well" (pp. 23–24). All women are in prisons as long as society continues its overt and covert racist and chauvinistic practices.

Cortez, Walker, and Jordan are among those who understand the political implications of rape. They show that the subjugation of Black women results from their, and their community's, systematic disempowerment. In her essay "Against the Wall" (1978), June Jordan makes this comparison clear. Jordan begins with the personal, the individual woman, to emphasize the historical antecedents—slavery and the perilous role of slave women—which still informs the assault to which African-American women continue to be prey. Jordan writes of the African-American woman's need to assert her right to be, to go where she pleases when she pleases, and declares that no man has the right to attack her because she insists on her autonomy.

> The writer is a woman, and Black, besides. Consequently the act of taking a walk means that she, this writer, will be perceived as a provocative/irresponsible/loose/insubordinate creature on the streets, by herself, moving along as though she had a natural right to wander around, after dark. (Jordan 1978, 147)

Notice the restrictions imposed on her mobility; women's place has been defined, and even the time of the day when women can occupy this place has been stipulated. Obedience is demanded in exchange for "protection." Independence results in castigation and the burden of shouldering the responsibility for her own victimization.

> If she's raped, if guys on the corners molest her innate sovereignty by making obscene remarks and noises as she passes by, if a bunch of punks decide to mug and mutilate her person, people will say: But why was she there? And I will answer: Why in the world should she be anywhere else? . . . Of course, rape is not new. In a way, that is the meaning of my identity: I have been raped. Somebody stronger than I am will attempt, yet again, and again, to maim and to desecrate my inalienable right to self-determination . . . Or he will claim that he had to invade and conquer my home because I was friendly with Cubans or other kinds of problematic types who were misleading my infantile mentality . . . (Jordan 1978, 148–149)

In the above passage, Jordan draws a link between the rape of a woman and the rape of a nation because they are both part of the same phenomenon. Both originate within the same paradigm: Colonialism equals oppression. Imbedded in this matrix is the general notion that women and developing nations are child-like, infants who need the tyrannical guidance of men—the patriarchal syndrome at work. Jordan condemns the system that allows for the exploitation of women and developing countries to be so easily justified. Her appeal is not only to women, but to all conscious humans to stop and evaluate their actions. The rape of a woman—or a country—cannot be dismissed and explained away.

Jordan and Ntozake Shange are representative of poets who introduce the international perspective, and demonstrate the commonality of women's struggle, These writers assert that the liberation of women is inextricably connected to the sovereignty of developing nations throughout the world. The rape of their individual bodies parallels the rape of their communities, and in a wider political context, exemplifies the same power game at work in the rape of so called "Third World" countries by the West. The intention is the same: to make women/developing countries feel small, inferior, afraid to act on their own behalf, withdraw inside themselves, accept the abuse, and nod thanks.

> Because all of us who are comparatively powerless, because we have decided that if you interfere, if you seek to intrude, if you undertake to terrorize and to subjugate and to stifle even one moment more of these, our only lives, we will take yours, or die trying. (Jordan 1978, 149)

Statements such as this voice an otherwise silent pain. These poets' works allow women to throw off the guilt of perceiving themselves as accomplices in their own oppression; they inform women that we are not alone in facing the same daily bombardment of life in a combat zone. They insist that women can and must fight back, must refuse to surrender our lives to oppression. As June Jordan advises those who rape the lives of women and nations, "We will take yours, or die trying" (1983, 70).

For African-American women, rape continues as an ever present threat to their particular bodies. It is as June Jordan says, "the meaning of her identity." To be an African-American woman in this society is to be subject to rape. As such, rape is not a trope in the works of African-American women writers and poets; it is a lived experience that has left many scars, and is still the source of much suffering. Thanks to the heroic efforts of women such as Inez Garcia, Joanne Little, and Dessie Woods, and the careful articulation of women poets and writers, most women can now identify the war and name the battle. As a result, women have taken up arms in their own defense and will not be disarmed, except by death. While society refuses to acknowledge that women are at war for the right to be independent humans in charge of our own bodies, we no longer need to wait for society to acknowledge this fact and grant us the right to bear arms. We are beyond the point where we need to have our reality defined for us. We will not turn back. We will not shut up. We will not be shoved in some corner. And, we will not submit to rape.

13

Raped: A Male Survivor Breaks His Silence

FRED PELKA

The man who raped me had a remarkable self-assurance which could only have come from practice. He picked me up just outside Cleveland, heading east in a van filled with construction equipment. That early morning in May I'd already spent a sleepless twenty-four hours trying to hitchhike from Oxford, Mississippi, to Buffalo, New York, so it felt good when I was offered a ride through the western fringe of Pennsylvania. First, though, the driver told me he needed to stop along the way, to pick up some building supplies. We drove to a country club undergoing renovation, where I hung out with his co-workers while he signed for several boxes of equipment which we carried back to his van. Getting back onto the turnpike he told me about one more stop he had to make.

As a man, I've been socialized never to admit to being vulnerable, to discuss those moments when I wasn't in control. I know also how women and children are routinely punished when they speak out about abuse, how they are blamed for their own victimization. The examples are endless: Witness the contempt with which Anita Hill was treated. For these reasons and more I'm still reticent, years after it happened, to recount what happened to me that day in Ohio. This chapter marks the first time in fifteen years I have publicly discussed it under my own name.

The second building seemed deserted. We went up a flight of stairs, down a corridor into a side room. I looked around for the equipment he'd mentioned, and noticed him locking the door behind us. He slugged me before I could react, forced me down with his hands around my throat. As I began to lose consciousness I heard him say, "If you scream, if you make one wrong move, I'll kill you."

The police told me later that the man who raped me was a suspect in the rapes of at least six other young men. During the assault his mood swung from vicious, when he promised to strangle me or break my neck, to self-pity, when he wept because we were both among "the wounded ones." In that enormous calm that comes after the acceptance of death, I wondered who would find my body.

Most rapes don't happen like this. Most victims know their attacker(s)—he is a

From *On the Issues* 22 (spring 1992): 8–11, 40. Reprinted by permission.

neighbor, friend, husband, or father, a teacher, minister or doctor. The vast majority of rapes are committed by men against women and children, and the FBI estimates that anywhere from 80 to 90 percent go unreported. Rape is an integral part of our culture, and fully one third of all women in this country will be raped at some point in their lives. But this sexist violence does occasionally spill over onto boys and men. The National Crime Survey for 1989 estimated that one in twelve rape survivors is male.

For all this, nobody really knows how many men are raped each year, or how many boys are sexually abused. One study at the University of New Hampshire found that one in eleven young men surveyed had been sexually abused before their eighteenth birthday. I've seen articles which speculate that anywhere from one in nine to one in seven men will be raped or sexually abused in their lifetime, most often by other males, but these are little more than guesses.

"Since rape is generally misconstrued to be a sexually motivated crime," writes Dr. A. Nicholas Groth and Anne Wolbert Burgess, "it is generally assumed that males are unlikely targets of such victimization, and then when it does occur, it reflects a homosexual orientation on the part of the offender. However, the causes of male rape that we have had an opportunity to study do not lend much support to either assumption." Groth and Burgess interviewed men in the community who had been raped, and men who admitted to raping other men, and published their findings in the *American Journal of Psychiatry*. In half the cases they studied, the gender of the victim "did not appear to be of specific significance" to the rapist. "Their victims included males and females, adults and children," and "may symbolize . . . something they want to conquer or defeat. The assault is an act of retaliation, an expression of power, and an assertion of their strength or manhood."

In their article, Burgess and Groth dispute some of the prevalent myths about male rape. The first is that men simply don't get raped, at least not outside prison. Of course, if men don't get raped then what happened to me either wasn't rape (the police asking, "Did you come?"), or I'm not a man (my male friends wanting to know how I could "let something like this" happen to me). The second myth—that all men who are raped or rape other men are gay—is a product of our culture's homophobia, and our ignorance of the realities of sexual violence. Most people find it difficult to understand why a straight man would rape another straight man. But if you see rape as a way of exerting control, of confirming your own power by disempowering others, then it makes perfect sense. If it makes you feel powerful and macho to force sex on a woman or child, think of how much more powerful you feel raping another man.

"I have a special place," the man who raped me said after a long while. "It's out in the country, where we can make all the noise we want." It seemed obvious what would happen to me once we arrived at "his special place," but I knew there was no hope for my survival as long as we stayed in that room. So I agreed to go with him to "the country." I promised not to try to escape. It is perhaps an indication of his fragile hold on reality that he believed me.

We walked back to his van and drove away. I waited until I saw some people, then jumped as we slowed to make a turn, rolling as I hit the pavement. I ran into the nearest building—a restaurant—just as patrons were finishing their lunch. Conversation stopped, and I was confronted by a roomful of people, forks raised in mid-bite, staring.

"I think you'd better call the police," I told the waitress. This was all I could say, placing my hands flat on the counter between us to control their trembling. She poured me a cup of black coffee. And then the police arrived.

The two detectives assigned to my case conformed to the standard good cop/bad cop archetype. The good cop told me how upset he'd seen "girls" become after being raped. "But you're a man, this shouldn't bother you." Later on he told me that the best thing to do would be to pull up my pants "and forget it ever happened." The bad cop asked me why my hair was so long, what was I doing hitchhiking at seven o'clock in the morning? Why were my clothes so dirty? Did I do drugs? Was I a troublemaker?

I used to be puzzled at how the bad cop obviously didn't believe me, in spite of the fact that, by his own account, in the months before my assault six other men had come to him with similar stories. Then I heard of the Dahmer case in Milwaukee, how in May 1991 Dahmer's neighbors saw him chasing a naked fourteen-year-old boy, bleeding from the anus, through the alley behind their building. The responding officers returned the boy to Dahmer's apartment, where Dahmer explained that this was just a lover's spat, which the police believed in spite of the youth's apparent age, and the photos scattered on Dahmer's floor of murdered and mutilated boys and men. The police reassured a neighbor who called again, saying that everything was all right—this at the very moment Dahmer was murdering Konerak Sinthasomphone. Afterwards Dahmer dismembered Sinthasomphone's body.

Sinthasomphone was one of at least seventeen boys and men raped and murdered by Dahmer, their body parts stored in vats and freezers in his apartment. It was reported that his first assaults were committed in Ohio, so I had to brace myself before I could look at Jeffrey Dahmer's photo in the paper. At first I was relieved to find that he was not the man who raped me. Then I thought how this meant my assailant is likely still out there, looking for more "wounded ones."

Because I gave them such detailed information—the country club, the name painted on the side of his van—the detectives were able to locate my assailant not too many hours after I was brought into their precinct. The good cop asked, after I identified the rapist, whether I wanted to press charges. He explained how I'd have to return to Ohio to appear before a grand jury, and then return again for the trial, how the newspapers would publish my name, how little chance there was of a conviction.

"He says you seduced him," the good cop said. "So it's your word against his."

The bad cop glared at me when I told them there was no way I wanted any of this to be made public. "You mean," he fumed, "I wasted my whole afternoon on this shit?" Standing in front of me with an expression of disgust, he asked, "How do you think this makes me feel?"

By then it was getting dark. I hitchhiked the remaining 200 miles home, studying every movement of every man who offered me a ride. I arrived at my apartment after midnight, walking the last ten miles.

In the weeks that followed the assault, every stupid, insensitive thing I'd ever said about rape came back to haunt me. A friend of mine had been attacked several months earlier, also while hitchhiking. She told me just a few hours after it happened how she'd missed her bus, and didn't want to be late to work. She said the man offering her a lift seemed normal enough, even "nice."

"You should've waited for the next bus," I lectured. Today I cringe at my arrogance. Hitchhiking, like walking alone after dark, or feeling safe on a date, at work, at home, is another perquisite to which only men are entitled. How dare she not understand the limits of her freedom?

While women tell me that the possibility of rape is never far from their minds, most men never give it a first, let alone a second, thought. This may explain why they react so negatively to accounts by male survivors. To see rape as "a women's issue" is a form of male privilege most men would prefer not to surrender. They would rather believe that they can move with immunity through the toxic atmosphere of violence and fear they and their compatriots create. Being a male survivor meant I'd lost some of that immunity. No wonder I felt as if I'd been poisoned, as if I were drowning.

For years I pretended, as per the good cop's recommendation, that nothing had happened, secretly feeling that I was somehow responsible, somehow less masculine. The turning point came with the media storm that swirled up around the Big Dan rape in New Bedford, Massachusetts. The movie "The Accused" is based on that incident — a woman assaulted in a bar while other men looked on and cheered. Naive as I was, I figured this was a pretty clear-cut case. Where the police might have doubted my will to resist (no broken bones, no massive lacerations), here was a victim overpowered by half a dozen men. How could anyone doubt that she had been brutalized? Yet, during the trial, *The Boston Herald* ran the front page headline "SHE LED US ON!" I realized then that, even had I been murdered, someone would have inevitably questioned my complicity: "He probably liked rough sex."

It's just this sort of victim-blaming that discourages survivors from reporting their trauma, or seeking treatment, but there are other factors which may discourage males in particular. Homophobia for one: The sort of gender McCarthyism that labels any man a faggot who cannot or will not conform to accepted norms of masculine feeling or behavior. Men who rape other men capitalize on this, knowing that straight victims don't want to appear gay, and gay victims might fear coming out of the closet. Groth and Burgess report, for instance, that "a major strategy used by some offenders . . . is to get the victim to ejaculate." This "strategy" was attempted in roughly half the cases they studied, and in half of those the rapist succeeded in ejaculating his victim. This confuses the victim, who often misidentifies ejaculation with orgasm. It confirms for the rapist the old canard about how victims "really want it." And, as Groth and Burgess say, it leaves the survivor "discouraged from reporting the assault for fear his sexuality may be suspect."

For male survivors of child sexual abuse there is also the unfortunate theory that boys who are abused inevitably grow up to be men who rape. One survivor told me it was for this reason he had decided never to be a father. Not that he'd ever wanted to abuse children, nor was there any evidence he ever would. He eventually came to realize that because some rapists are themselves survivors doesn't mean that all male survivors of child sexual abuse turn out to be rapists.

Finally, rape-crisis centers, the only institutions in our society founded expressly to help rape survivors, are identified by some men as hotbeds of feminism, and many men take "feminist" to mean "man-hating." It's true that the vast majority of rape crisis counselors are women, that the entire stop-rape movement is an extension of the women's movement. For the record, though, I have never felt any hostility in response when calling a rape-crisis center, this in spite of the fact that RCCs are often plagued by "hotline abusers" — men who call to masturbate to the sound of a female voice.

On the other hand, I've run across a good deal of hostility towards women from male survivors with whom I've talked. One man told me how certain he was that the counselors at his local RCC hated men, even though, by his own admission, he'd never called, and knew no one who had. A while back I attended a survivors' conference organized by a Boston women's group, attended by several hundred women and maybe a dozen men. One of these men stood up during a plenary session to shout at the women on the podium. As an incest survivor, he said, he felt "marginalized" and "oppressed" by the way the conference was run, despite the fact that a number of the workshops were specifically geared toward males, and that a keynote speaker received a standing ovation when he described his work with boys and men. Some male survivors even blame women for the denial and homophobia they encounter after their assault. They openly resent the (pitifully few) resources available to female survivors, as if any help women receive is at the expense of men. Even Geraldo has picked up this theme: His show on male survivors ended with an attack on rape crisis centers for their alleged refusal to acknowledge male victimization.

This hostility has been exacerbated by the so-called men's movement, the Robert Bly/mythopoetic crowd, with their "Wild Man" and "Inner Warrior" archetypes. These men say a lot of absurd things about sexual violence, not the least of which is that "just as many men get raped as women." This last statement is often repeated by Chris Harding, editor of *Wingspan,* which *The Boston Globe* calls "the bible of the new men's movement." Harding is generally quick to add that most of these rapes "occur in prison"—a statement which is as inaccurate as it is pernicious, assuming as it does that a disproportionate number of male rapes are committed by working-class and minority men. The men's movement claims that rape is a "gender-neutral issue," and thus has nothing to do with sexism.

What is ironic about all this is that what little acknowledgement there is of male victimization generally comes from the *women's* stop-rape movement. To the extent that male survivors *can* tell their stories, it is because of the foundation laid by feminists. So this woman-bashing is as ungrateful as it is gratuitous.

One source of confusion appears to be the distinction between victimization and oppression. Male survivors charge that feminists see rape as a "man vs. woman" issue, emphasizing the central role male violence plays in stunting and destroying women's lives, and they're right. The distinction is that while many women, and some men, are victimized by rape, all women are oppressed by it, and any victimization of women occurs in a context of oppression most men simply do not understand. Rape for men is usually a bizarre, outrageous tear in the fabric of reality. For women, rape is often a confirmation of relative powerlessness, of men's contempt for women, and its trauma is reinforced every day in a thousand obvious and subtle ways.

For myself, I don't need for rape to be gender neutral to feel validated as a male survivor. And I certainly don't need to denigrate women, or to attack feminists, to explain why I was abused by the (male) police, ridiculed by my (male) friends, and marginalized by the (male dominated) society around me. It is precisely because we have been "reduced" to the status of *women* that other men find us so difficult to deal with. It was obvious to me at the police station that I was held in contempt because I was a *victim*—feminine, hence perceived as less masculine. Had I been an accused criminal, even a rapist, chances are I would have been treated with more respect, because I would have been seen as more of a man. To cross that line, to become victims of the violence which works to circumscribe the lives of women, marks us somehow as traitors

214 I FRED PELKA

to our gender. Being a male rape survivor means I no longer fit our culture's neat but specious definition of masculinity, as one empowered, one always in control. Rather than continue to deny our experience, male survivors need to challenge that definition.

As Diana E. H. Russell says in *The Politics of Rape,* "Women must start talking about rape: Their experiences, their fears, their thoughts. The silence about rape must be broken."

The same must be true for men. And so I offer this article as my first contribution to that effort.

I've been back to northern Ohio exactly once in the fifteen years following that day. Seven years ago I was traveling from Boston to Chicago with a car full of friends. It was early morning, and I was sleeping in the back seat when we pulled off the highway, and steered onto a street that looked oddly, disturbingly familiar. Rubbing my eyes, I felt an unsettling sense of deja vu. And then I remembered.

"Time for some coffee," the driver said, and I wondered then if we would eat breakfast at that same restaurant, if I would meet that same waitress. We didn't, and I chose not to tell my companions what had happened to me all those years ago.

Today I think I might be less disconcerted. Today I think I just might have told them what happened.

14

Subcultural Theory of Rape Revisited

LAURA L. O'TOOLE

Identifying the conditions and causes of rape has been a major project of feminist scholars and criminologists across social science disciplines for the last twenty years. This project continues to command attention, as both total numbers of reported rapes and rape rates continue to skyrocket during the 1990s in the United States. In 1990, the number of reported rapes in the United States exceeded 100,000 for the first time, after a decade of steady increase. The U.S. rape rate rose from 33.6 per 100,000 persons in 1982 to 42.8 in 1992 (Federal Bureau of Investigation 1993); and there still is every indication that these numbers reflect but a small proportion of actual rapes.

Sociology has contributed to a number of important theoretical perspectives in the study of rape. Conceptualized until quite recently as a crime committed by psychologically impaired individuals, rape has been redefined as a crime that is most frequently committed by "everyman" (Russell 1984). Sociological research has been crucial in bringing about this redefinition. For example, surveys investigating the sexual behavior and attitudes of young men in college and university populations find that anywhere from one quarter to more than half of respondents report that they have forced women to engage in sex against their will (Kanin 1967, 1977, 1985; Koss, Gidycz, and Wisniewski 1987; Muehlenhard and Linton 1987; Warshaw 1988).

Two theoretical explanations for the epidemic of rape are most frequently validated in the literature. *Gender role socialization* theory focuses on the ways the dominant culture indoctrinates males to be sexual aggressors (Griffin 1971; Sanday 1981b; Beneke 1982), to expect sex on demand (Scully and Marolla 1985), to believe aggression is a normative component of heterosexual relationships (Berger and Searles 1985; Hennenberger and Marriott 1993), and to embrace victim-blaming myths about rape (Griffin 1971; Check and Malamuth 1983; Margolin, Miller, and Moran 1989; Feltey, Ainslee, and Geib 1991). This perspective is supported by a plethora of research that identifies the sources through which this information is communicated to males throughout the life cycle. These agents include the media, with particular emphasis on pornography (Longino 1980; MacKinnon 1984), R-rated Hollywood films (Donnerstein and Linz 1986), music videos (Shur 1988) and "gangsta rap" (hooks 1994), peers (Ageton 1983; Kanin 1985), and even religious dogma that supports female submissiveness and male control of female sexuality (Brownmiller 1975).

Political-economic theories of rape were developed based on women's historical powerlessness and their legal definition as the property of men (Russell 1982b; Schwendinger and Schwendinger 1983). Indeed, rape was originally considered a property crime against the father or husband of the victim. More recently, this perspective has analyzed the commodification of women's sexuality in advertising and the multibillion-dollar sex industry as a central aspect of rape. This commodification of sexuality, combined with the eroticization of dominance exemplified in many media portrayals of sexuality, contributes to escalating sexual violence (Schur 1988). The dehumanizing effects of commodification provide legitimacy for violence against categories of people defined as things or property. Thus, sexual violence results from both the dehumanization of women defined as sexual property, and the social definition of this violence as a source of erotic pleasure (Schur 1988).

Recently, attempts have been made to integrate aspects of these two dominant theoretical models with classical models of deviant behavior or biological sexuality. For example, in their analysis of rape and structural variables across the United States, Larry Baron and Murray A. Straus (1989) find relationships between rape rates and variables such as circulation rates of pornographic magazines and the legal status of women. They also implicate general conditions of social disorganization and the culturally legitimated use of violence in gender relationships in the escalation of rape. Lee Ellis (1989) employs an evolutionary model of human sexuality to suggest that natural selection has predisposed human males toward sexual aggression, which is manifested through operant conditioning and is perhaps indirectly influenced by the social learning process, including the use of pornographic materials. Of these two, the evolutionary model requires close scrutiny given its foundation in biological determinism. That, however, is not the intent of this chapter. Rather, it is to look more closely at another perspective developed in the 1970s, then critiqued and abandoned in the 1980s. This theory, based upon classic criminological evidence suggesting the existence of violent subcultures (Wolfgang and Feracuti 1967), has received primarily unfavorable treatment by scholars in the field.

Application of the violent subculture perspective to rape behavior has focused upon explaining higher rates of rape in lower-class and racial-ethnic communities. The main tenet of this perspective is that certain communities, with firmly established boundaries, adopt norms and lifestyle preferences that differ from those of the larger culture. In the case of rape, it has been suggested that norms and values that condone, and in some cases glorify, sexual violence are institutionalized in the subculture and subsequently passed on through the intergenerational transmission of knowledge. Menachem Amir's (1971) study of rape and rapists in Philadelphia was the first empirical application of this theory, and his work was used extensively by Susan Brownmiller, who further legitimated the rape subculture perspective in her classic feminist tome *Against Our Will: Men, Women and Rape* (1975).

Rape Subculture Theory: Controversy and Critique

Major critiques of the subcultural perspective revolve around its race and class bias. The literature that explores the prevalence of rape in various social categories finds that this crime cuts across race and class boundaries. This becomes particularly clear when the phenomena of acquaintance rape and rape in marriage are taken into account. Evidence from victimization studies supports a model of violent criminality in which race is significant; however, "conduct" variables such as previous criminal record account for more variance than "status" variables such as race (Hindelang 1981, 461). Although economic and social stressors contribute to the victimization process, sociologists have argued that the disproportionately higher rates of reported rapes in lower-class and racial-ethnic communities more likely indicate over-surveillance by criminal justice authorities, as well as underreporting among the middle and upper classes (Hindelang 1981). Moreover, by focusing on communities traditionally labeled deviant by dominant institutions, we obscure the levels of sexual violence in the larger society (Andersen 1993). This focus also serves to de-emphasize the significance of societally produced male gender role socialization and the societal commodification of female sexuality as major precipitators of rape. Thus, subculture of violence theories have been dismissed as insufficient at best, and biased at worst, in their capacity to explain the phenomenon of rape. Indeed, the only scenario in which the term subculture is used unabashedly to explain rape behavior is the prison world of male-on-male rape.

The controversial nature of the subcultural theory of rape has contributed to its inadequate scrutiny (Baron, Straus, and Jaffe 1988). Baron and Straus suggest that use of the term subculture is problematic both for measurement reasons and because the norms that legitimate violence are widely diffused (1989, 149). Although they suggest that certain groups may institutionalize cultural support for violence more than others, their efforts are applied toward a state-level, rather than micro-level, analysis.

Bringing Gender In

I would agree that we have not sufficiently tested rape subculture theory. I would argue, however, that we have cast it aside without realizing the major problem with its application to the study of rape. The problem is that we have taken a predominantly gender-neutral frame of reference and applied it unaltered to a gendered phenomenon. Classic deviant subculture theory has focused primarily on lower-class, urban, and often racial-ethnic males; yet, in applying this theory to rape, it is the class and ethnicity— not the maleness—of the perpetrators that have been most accountable for the behavior. The rape behavior itself is but one item on a laundry list of other criminal activities that characterize these groups.

It may be time to revisit rape subculture theory using the vehicle of gender analysis. Bombarded by images of women as toys and violence as erotic, "everyman" may indeed have the capacity to rape; but every man does not rape. Indeed, a spate of recent contextualized studies of rape suggest that there may be clusters of individuals whose in-group identification and ritual behaviors may fit the sociological definition of subculture, although the literature stops short of defining them as such. These are *masculinist* subcultures, which may cut across race and class but share the signatory characteristics of hypermasculinity and the glorification of coercive sexuality. Nestled within the sex/ gender system of the larger culture and specific patriarchal institutions, masculinist subcultures appear to flourish, even as the feminist movement, the U.S. Congress, local crime units, and college campuses focus increasingly on creating strategies to prevent rape.

Masculinity and Violence in Theory and Practice

Social scientists have long identified dichotomous sets of behavioral characteristics associated with masculinity and femininity that operate in instrumental and relational contexts. Shaped by conscious and unconscious learning processes, as well as the structure of institutions, traditional Western masculinity is constructed with heavy emphasis on rationality, competition, athleticism, financial success, aggression, control over emotion, and heterosexuality. Michael Kaufman (this volume) suggests that the requirements of masculinity reproduce and reinforce a "triad" of men's violence: against women, other men, and self.

Observable as these traits may be, however, there has been a problematic tendency to conceptualize masculinity as a rigid monolith. R. W. Connell's (1987) theory of masculinity is particularly useful for understanding both the social processes through which variant forms of masculinity are constructed and the ways in which violence becomes both an ideological and practical component of many—but not all—men's lives.

Connell suggests that at any given historical moment there exists at a societal level an ordering of masculinity and femininity that produces controlling conceptualizations for public consumption (1987, 183). This ordering is rooted in the structural dominance of men over women. The dominant, "stylized" prescriptions, while generally inconsistent with the observable variety of existent behaviors and beliefs, nonetheless serve as the ideological basis for social relations. The socially constructed ideal for men, *hegemonic masculinity*, is more rigid and controlling than what he refers to as *emphasized feminity*, which has a variety of acceptable forms. The various nonconformist and subordinated masculinities that exist are greatly devalued; thus, men in our culture, more so than women, have a stake in conformity to the dominant masculine ideal: to be perceived as less than a "real man" places one in the position of being equated with the globally subordinate female.

Peer pressure is a strong influence in the acquisition and display of masculinity. It is already operating in the sex talk and dirty play of preadolescent little-leaguers studied by Gary Alan Fine (1986) and the marauding school boys invading girls' turf in the schoolyards observed by Barrie Thorne (1992). Such youngsters are acting on their perceptions of the gender order; but as children, they lack many of the resources necessary to fully emulate the dominant model. Given that physical strength and prowess can be called upon to claim masculinity, however, violence is learned early and often retrieved from the tool kit of masculinity to prove manhood when social power or financial resources are inaccessible.

What the research literature on masculinity has yet to uncover are the events that may occur in the transition from exploratory peer group to full-blown masculinist subculture, and why some boys and men circumvent such groups in their selectively internalized construction of masculinity. Traditional deviant subculture theory has asked all the wrong questions about gender (Messerschmidt 1993), and rape subculture theory so far has asked too few.

Identifying Male Rape Subcultures

Over the years, studies of rape perpetrators have focused primarily on likelihood of raping, belief in rape myths, sexual history, attitudes toward women, motivation, race, and means of forcing sex (Bourque 1989). Associating peer-group pressure with coercive sexuality among males is not new, but until quite recently it has been underanalyzed. S. S. Ageton's (1983) three-year analysis of data from the National Youth Survey found that rapists in the sample were more likely than nonoffenders to be involved with delinquent peers. Offenders also differed from their nonoffending counterparts in their attitudes that legitimated rape and sexual assault. The extent to which the attitudes and behaviors associated with peer group affiliation may be directly related to rape behavior cannot be gauged. Eugene J. Kanin's (1985) analysis of date rapists shows that 41 percent of self-identified rapists participated in gang rapes and 85 percent reported considerable or great pressure from peers to be heterosexually active; yet, contextualized analysis that might dovetail with these findings in the development of a subcultural explanation for the proliferation of date and gang rapes in contemporary U.S. society has not emerged.

J. W. Messerschmidt (1993), in a groundbreaking profeminist analysis of masculinity and crime, has developed the first systematic criminological theory to extensively integrate an analysis of masculinity. He suggests that "because men situationally accomplish masculinity in response to their socially constructed circumstances, various forms of crime can serve as suitable resources for doing masculinity within the specific social contexts of the street, the workplace, and the family" (1993, 119). In looking at incidents such as the gang rape of a jogger in Central Park in 1989, Messerschmidt, using Connell's framework as a basis for his analysis, suggests that gang rapes are "simply resources for demonstrating essential 'male nature' when more conventional means are unavailable" (1993, 115). Although Messerschmidt provides significant insight by identifying the functions of group rape in solidifying alliances and facilitating intragroup masculinity contests, his examples focus primarily on the lower and working classes; thus, while he contends that such events are not race and class specific, his important work suffers due to the invisibility of privileged offenders in the sociological casebook. In addition, we still understand little about the peer-group affiliations of single-offender rapists through this analysis.

Recent social scientific studies and media accounts of sexual aggression in college fraternities and among members of male sports teams provide the first significant empirical examples from which we can begin to develop a gender-based, rather than class-based, subculture of rape theory. These studies identify groups with clear and defining boundary characteristics that have institutionalized normative systems and rituals prescribing sexual coercion as central aspects of subcultural identity and existence. Indeed, adherence to the norms and participation in the rituals are often qualifications for group initiation and ongoing membership.

THE FRATERNITY SUBCULTURE

Colleges and universities are the setting for an increasing number of sexual assaults: rapes by members of the campus community, rapes by strangers, date rapes, and gang or "party" rapes (Bohmer and Parrot 1993). While the likelihood of committing sexual assault increases among residents of various all-male housing units, research on assailants suggests that it is fraternity pledges who are most likely to rape on campus (Koss, cited in Bohmer and Parrot 1993, 21–22). Two in-depth studies of fraternity involvement in ritual gang rape behavior provide context for understanding this finding.

Patricia Yancey Martin and Robert A. Hummer (1989) formulate an organizational perspective for understanding rape in fraternities, within which the social construction of brotherhood involves value for traditional masculinity and a normative structure that promotes loyalty, secrecy, and group protection. During the pledge process, fraternities require recruits to participate in a variety of ritual practices, not unlike those used in military boot camps, that identify athletic masculinity and require subordination of self to the group. Pledges are also evaluated on their social ability with women, and sexual access to women is an advertised benefit of group membership in the recruitment process (1989, 468).

Once accepted into the brotherhood, a complex system of norms and rituals influences the behavior of members. Martin and Hummer suggest that secret rituals, handshakes, and mottoes function to maintain group boundaries and exemplify the expectation of loyalty among brothers (1989, 464). Norms defining women as servers and sexual prey become translated into sexual aggression when fused with those prescribing the use of alcohol, violent behavior, and competition.

Peggy Reeves Sanday's (1990) research characterizes the group rape as a ritual bonding activity of men in fraternities. The purpose of the activity is less to achieve sexual gratification than it is to affirm the shared masculinity and brotherhood of members. Men in Sanday's study considered "pulling train" or the "express," in which brothers line up to take their turn having sex with a (usually) intoxicated woman, a routine aspect of their "little sister" program (1990, 7).

Sanday describes the gang rape as a collective phenomenon, made possible by the loss of individual identity during initiation ritual. In citing the example of one male informant, she suggests, "The experiences [he] endured provide powerful evidence for the suggestion that personhood, in this case defined in terms of the brotherhood, is socially constructed" (1990, 137). Pledges are routinely ridiculed as sexually inadequate until admitted as members. They are treated as "despised women" and referred to in terms demeaning them as homosexuals. Many initiation rituals are designed to cleanse these inadequacies; thus, Sanday argues that the successful pledge is stamped with two collective images: the purified body accepted into brotherhood, and the despised and dirty feminine (1990, 155–56).

Both of these studies provide evidence of strong boundary maintenance, including hostility toward out-group members, secret rituals, "groupthink," and shared normative systems that are overtly and overwhelmingly preoccupied with hypermasculinity. Although the gang rape is conceptualized in these analyses as a logical outcome of the fraternity culture, Robin Warshaw (1988) emphasizes that more one-on-one rapes occur in fraternity houses than gang rapes. We can nonetheless hypothesize that the subcultural norms regarding masculinity and femininity in conjunction with the promise of secrecy and protection by brothers contribute to date rapes as well.

THE SPORT SUBCULTURE

With respect to campus rapes, the second most implicated category of assailants are college athletes (Bohmer and Parrot 1993). A recent report suggested that NCAA basketball and football players were reported to the police for committing sexual assaults 38 percent more than males in the general college population, averaging one report of an athlete for sexual assault every eighteen days between 1983 and 1986 (Hoffman 1986). In a study of locker-room discourse among members of two "big time" college sport teams, Curry (1991) identifies a pattern of fraternal bonding not unlike that characterizing the fraternities described above. A similar preoccupation with masculinity, defined rigidly through physical prowess and heterosexual performance, results in locker-room talk that dehumanizes women and promotes rape. Warshaw (1988, 112) similarly finds athletic teams to be "breeding grounds" for rape: "They are organizations which pride themselves on the physical aggressiveness of their members and which demand group loyalty and reinforce it through promoting the superiority of their members over outsiders." As with fraternities, the gang rape among athletes is conceptualized by Warshaw as "group sex," in effect a homoerotic bonding of members to each other where the woman involved is no more than an instrument through which the ritual activity is enabled.

Colleges are not the only contexts within which male sport subcultures can emerge. Examples abound from high school through the professional sports. The recent case of the "Spur Posse" in Lakewood, California, a predominantly White suburban area, exemplifies the ways in which sexual performance becomes a membership criterion for participants. The posse is a group of twenty to thirty Lakewood High School athletes, nine of whom were accused of raping and molesting girls as young as ten years old (Gross 1993). Although the gang had been involved in other delinquent behaviors, it came into the national spotlight when it was revealed that the sexual assaults were linked to an ongoing masculinity contest wherein each act of sexual intercourse—consensual or forced—resulted in a point in the tally (Mydans 1993). The self-proclaimed high-scorer of the group had accumulated sixty-six points by the time of the arrests (Gross 1993).

Fraternities and sports teams provide a starting point from which other male institutions can be explored. Each of the above examples provides insight into male groups with distinct boundaries, as well as value systems, ritual activities, and discourses that promote sexual aggression as a qualification of initiation and ongoing membership. Such characteristics are routinely analyzed in conjunction with subcultural affiliation in the sociological literature.

Another potential arena for applying a subcultural perspective is the U.S. military, which has received increasing public and governmental scrutiny since media exposure of the 1991 Tailhook assault of female Naval officers by their peers and superordinates. The extent to which such events are stimulated by the peer-group affiliation of assailants would be an interesting case to explore. The emergence of information about ritual sexual abuse in pseudoreligious contexts, for example, could also be analyzed from a subcultural perspective. Thus far, the academic discourse has been primarily restricted to the heated debates of psychotherapists over the reality of this phenomenon.

Other subcultures detached from such institutional frameworks, but equally dangerous, might be identified and analyzed. In her foreword to Sanday's *Fraternity Gang Rape*, Judge Lois G. Forer describes patterns across a number of multiple-offender rape cases that have come before her: all the participants could be said to be members of "gangs," all were operating on their own "turf," consumed large quantities of alcohol, and had sex with their victims in the presence of the group (1990, xiv). The gangs described ranged from unemployed inner-city youths to married buddies whose weekly "night out" was a ritual of rape in the park with a young woman picked up by a member for a date.

The increase of information about such cases strengthens the potential value of a subcultural perspective to inform future research on rape. Further support comes from the existence of "good guys." Martin and Hummer (1989) tell us that some fraternity pledges withdraw from fraternity recruitment drives by choice; not all team athletes become involved in subcultural bonding and ritual activities. Many other men show no preference for either activity. Presumably some of these men may become involved in coercive sexuality; some will not. It is the extent to which peers—and centrally, peers in close-knit, primary group contexts—develop a subcultural existence that highlights heterosexual and violent masculinity that needs to be further explored.

Methodological Implications of a Masculinist Rape Subculture Model

Sociological understanding of the subcultural groups specified, as well as the identification of other groups as subcultural entities, requires theoretical attention to the merits of subcultural theory when fused with the other existing and legitimated theories of rape. In addition, empirical testing of hypotheses about the correlation of male subcultures with the widespread proliferation of sexual violence requires important considerations with respect to research design and data analysis. The methodological implications of such a theoretical perspective, for example, beg us to question the usefulness of crime statistics, including demographic and geographical characteristics, in explaining rape. These statistics provide only surface information and are insufficient without being integrated with more micro-level contextual analyses. Baron and Straus (1989) suggest that a major failing of rape research has been the search for a single cause. A multicausal explanation might benefit strongly from inclusion of a masculinist subculture perspective with the dominant models of gender socialization and political-economic theory.

The plausibility of a gender-based subcultural analysis, teamed with the necessity of facilitating social change, requires more context-specific analysis of rape and the formulation of research questions about group affiliation and pressure. What conditions facilitate the emergence of rape subcultures and provide them with members? Why do some men resist such group affiliation? What normative patterns, rituals activities and discourses, boundary-maintenance mechanisms, and other group characteristics set these subcultures apart from conventional male friendship groups? How many rapes—stranger or acquaintance, single assailant or multiple offender—can we begin to attribute to the group affiliation of perpetrators? Where and under what conditions do such rapes occur? These questions conceivably can be integrated into survey research among victims and self-reported perpetrators, as well as in more qualitative analyses involving fieldwork; but they are questions that need to be asked and in a more systematic manner than we have asked them thus far.

Rape subculture theory deserves another round of exploratory research. Stripped from the controversial grip of race and class bias, we may come to learn important information about sexual violence that not only will enhance our sociological understanding of rape, but will be central in finding solutions to this escalating social problem.

15

The Global Health Burden of Rape

**MARY P. KOSS, LORI HEISE, AND
NANCY FELIPE RUSSO**

Almost everywhere in the world, the popular mythology surrounding rape is the same. Rape is perceived as a rare event, perpetrated by unknown assailants who are either unbalanced or who lose control of themselves in the face of female enticement. Over the past two decades, feminist scholars and activists have challenged this perception using research and women's experience to replace myth. The result has been a transformation in our understanding of the notion of rape. Research has helped reveal the alarming frequency of sexual coercion in women's lives and the various guises in which rape occurs. Research has likewise debunked the public's preoccupation with "stranger danger" by documenting the frequency of rape by acquaintances, intimates, and spouses. Feminist legal scholars have in turn won many changes in how rape is treated in law. Legal reforms have altered the very acts that are defined as rape, broadening the scope of the crime to include oral and anal penetration and a greater range of perpetrators (Estrich 1987). They have also sought to shift the burden of proof from the woman to the man, reducing the demand for evidence of physical injury to prove nonconsent. As these changes filter into the culture at large, women increasingly realize the applicability of the term rape to incidents that they have experienced.

Feminist scholarship has also helped transform rape from merely a social or criminal justice issue to an issue of health and human rights (Bunch 1991). Recent work conceptualizes rape as a violation of women's bodily integrity and therefore an abuse of their fundamental human rights. Other work has successfully reframed rape as a woman's health issue with long-term consequences for women's physical, psychological, and social health. Rape is now recognized as a risk factor for a range of diseases and reproductive health consequences. These consequences play a predominant role in determining women's quality of life. Today it is widely believed that multiple forms of men's violence against women have common roots and ultimately have to be understood as interrelated dimensions of women's experience (Koss, Goodman, Browne, Fitzgerald, Keita, and Russo 1994). This perspective is reflected in the United Nations (UN) recent "Declaration of the Eradication of Violence against Women," which characterizes rape as one of many forms of gender-based abuse (UN Resolution 48/104, December 1993).

From *Psychology of Women Quarterly,* 18 (1994):509–37. Reprinted with the permission of Cambridge University Press.

According to this declaration, violence against women includes, "Any act of gender-based violence that results in, or is likely to result in, physical, sexual, or psychological harm or suffering to women, including threats of such acts, coercion, or arbitrary deprivations of liberty, whether occurring in public or private life" (Economic and Social Council 1992, 5). The declaration specifically lists marital rape, sexual abuse of female children, sexual harassment, trafficking in women, forced prostitution, and violence perpetrated by the State among the many acts explicitly covered by the definition.

Although it is artificial to separate the forms of male-perpetrated violence that women cumulatively encounter across their lifespans, it is sometimes necessary. To give adequate consideration to existing scholarship within space limitations, we reluctantly limit the focus of this chapter to rape of adolescent and adult women globally. We have tried to avoid reiterating conclusions based on U.S. research that are available in reviews published elsewhere (see Foa, Rothbaum, and Steketee 1993; Koss et al. 1994; Koss 1993; Resick 1993). In addition to duplication, reliance on research findings from the United States risks inappropriate generalization to a global context. Instead, we have tried to emphasize the universality of the issues by using documentation from as many different nations as possible. This effort has required us to use information collected under the auspices of nongovernmental organizations that often lack the resources and training in methodology characteristic of academic researchers. The critical reader will notice multiple instances where documentation is sparse or weak. Each of these instances should be viewed as an idea for future research. We sincerely hope that this chapter will stimulate interest in the study of the health effects of rape beyond the boundaries of the United States.

Rape in Sociocultural Context

The defining characteristic of rape is lack of choice or consent by the woman to engage in sexual intercourse (Minturn, Grosse, and Haider 1969; Rozée 1993; Sanday 1981b). Rozée (1993) prefers the word choice to the word consent, because it avoids implicit acceptance of a male prerogative to initiate sexual intercourse. This prerogative is evident in most North American jurisdictions where rape is defined as penetration (oral, anal, or vaginal), against consent, through force, threat of bodily harm, or when the woman is unable to consent (Searles and Berger 1987).

The critical role that sociocultural supports play in defining and promoting rape as well as shaping its consequences is reflected in the categorization of rape into two major types: normative and non-normative (Rozée 1993). These distinctions mirror Heise's (1993b) conceptual distinction between tolerated and transgressive rape. Whatever rape's form, every society has mechanisms that "legitimize, obfuscate, deny, and thereby perpetuate violence" (Heise, Pitanguy, and Germain 1993, 1; also see LaFree 1989). These social processes prompted one feminist legal scholar to write that, "Rape, from a woman's point of view, is not prohibited, it is regulated" (MacKinnon 1983, 651).

Non-normative Rape

Rape that is non-normative is defined as "illicit, uncondoned genital contact that is both against the will of the woman and in violation of social norms for expected behavior" (Rozée 1993, 504). This definition depicts the stereotypical rape that consists of a surprise attack on a virtuous woman. In fact, the wrongness of rape is often determined not by the nature of the act committed but by the marital or moral status of the woman.

Cultural responses to rape reflect the attitude that only women of good character deserve protection from rape. This notion is codified in certain Latin American countries—including Costa Rica, Ecuador, and Guatemala—whose laws recognize rape of only honest and chaste women (Heise et al. 1993). The distinction between types of women may also be implied. In Pakistan, courts have ruled that testimony of women of easy virtue has less weight. To assess a woman's virtue, that court uses, among other things, a finger test to see if her vagina accommodates two fingers easily. If so, sex is said to be habitual, and a woman's testimony loses weight (Jahangi and Jalani 1990). In Sri Lanka, class and caste are additional considerations. Thus, virgins under eighteen years of age who are raped by a man of lesser class or caste are assured of a conviction. "But if you are an independent lower class woman, of middle age, raped by an acquaintance, then it is better that you nurse your wounds at home" (Coomaraswamy 1992, 51).

Such attitudes hearken back to the days when rape was first conceived of as a crime. For the first few thousand years in the development of Western civilization, the crime of rape appears to have consisted of defilement of a virgin. The legal recourse was to demand that the perpetrator compensate the girl's father for her lost value in the marriage market (Brownmiller 1975). Still in Peru, the penalty for rape decreases as the victim gets older and drops to virtually no punishment for raping a mature woman (Human Rights Watch 1992c). In Guatemala, Peru, and Chile, the law specifically exonerates a man who rapes a minor if he agrees to marry her and thus legitimizes the union (Heise et al. 1993). In the United States as well, criminal justice officials often fail to prosecute cases that fall outside their stereotypical notions of real rape, which in general involve a stranger brutally raping a respectable woman (Estrich 1987). Women who are sexually experienced, have been drinking, or who otherwise violate traditional gender norms find the justice system very reluctant to address their rapes.

Pakistan, however, earns the dubious distinction of having the legal system most biased against the victim. As part of a fundamentalist wave of reform in 1979, Pakistan passed the Zina Ordinance, which made all forms of sex outside of marriage—including rape, fornication, and adultery—crimes against the state. A new law of evidence also made women's testimony worth only half that of a man's, making it even more difficult for rape victims to prove their cases. Women who fail to meet Pakistan's high standard of proof for rape can be thrown in jail for adultery or fornication based on their own admission of intercourse. Others who become pregnant due to unreported rapes have likewise been charged, the pregnancy itself serving as evidence of illicit sex. Human rights activists estimate that upwards of 1,500 Pakistani women are in prison awaiting trial for *zina* (Human Rights Watch 1992a).

NORMATIVE RAPE

Normative rape is defined as "genital contacts that the female does not choose, but that are supported by social norms" (Rozée 1993, 503). It can be said that there are sociocultural supports for rape when "there is no punishment of the male or the female only is punished; if the rape itself is condoned as a punishment of the female; if the genital contact is embedded in a cultural ritual such as an initiation ceremony; or when refusal is disapproved or punished by the community" (Rozée 1993, 503).

Acquaintance rape including date and marital rape. The naming of forced genital contact by intimates, particularly spouses, as rape is a revolutionary transformation of the concept. Rapes in which the parties are friends, romantic partners, or spouses are still unlikely to be treated the same as rapes by total strangers, even in settings where the law makes no distinctions among rapes according to relationships. Women are least likely to have legal protection from marital rape. Outside North America there is no widely accepted legal concept of marital rape; only last year did the United Kingdom move to outlaw it (Human Rights Watch 1992c).

But many women worldwide are beginning to question the traditional notion that marriage represents tacit agreement to provide sexual services to the husband upon demand (Russell 1990). For example, Indian researcher Annie George (1993) speculates whether the notion of consent by virtue of marriage has any validity among lower caste Indian women who are married off at a very young age, have no say in whom they will marry, and have been given virtually no information about sex prior to their wedding night. Algerian gynecologist Malika Ben Baraka (1993) likewise observes that the consummation of marriage itself can constitute rape in her country, where very young girls are physically restrained and forced to submit to intercourse on their wedding night without any prior instruction in sexuality. The trauma of defloration can be even more excruciating in those countries where young girls are infibulated to preserve their virginity until marriage. Not infrequently, infibulated women must be cut open on their wedding nights so that intercourse can occur (Toubia 1993).

Punitive rape. Punitive rape is a category of normative rape that involves "any genital contact that is used in a disciplinary or punitive manner . . . occurs generally as a masculine response to women behaving in a way that is considered solely the prerogative of males . . ." (Rozée 1993, 507–8). In Latin America, for example, feminists contend that the aim of rape is to change women from "Madonna to whore" and to warn them that they must retreat to their traditional sphere (Bunster 1986, 307; quoted in Lykes, Brabeck, Ferns, and Radan 1993, 535). Rape as punishment often involves the violation of one woman by a series of men.

Rape as a mechanism of intentional social control of women leaders has been documented in Peru and in India (Human Rights Watch 1992c; Mathur 1992). In Rajasthan, India, for example, a woman leader of the highly successful Women's Development Programme was gang raped by male community members because they disapproved of her organizing effort against child marriage. The woman was raped in front of her husband, who was warned, "Keep your wife in line or we'll rape her again."

Another form of punitive rape is sexual torture of women by state security forces in their villages or while in detention (Blatt 1992; Lunde and Ortmann 1990). Sexual torture is a form of psychological manipulation that has the aim of depriving "the victim of his or her identity" (Agger 1989, 307). Amnesty International (1992) describes the ill-treatment of women in detention and documents hundreds of women worldwide who have been victims of state-sanctioned rapes. Human Rights Watch (1992b, 1992c) has recorded state-tolerated rape of women in detention both in Peru and Pakistan.

Rape as a weapon of war. Throughout history, rape has co-occurred with warfare and has involved the capture of women as slaves, prostitutes, concubines, and raiding for wives (Brownmiller 1975; Rozée 1993). In January, 1993, the United Nations Commission on Human Rights passed a resolution that for the first time identified rape as a war crime (United Nations 1993). Rape in war is designed to destroy the bonds of family and society and demoralize the enemy. Where there is ethnic conflict, rape is used to accomplish goals of both war and nationalism (Asia Watch 1992; United Nations 1993). Documented incidents of rape during wartime include:

1. Massive raping of women during recent conflicts in Liberia, Uganda, Peru, Cambodia, Somalia, and Bosnia (Goldfeld, Mollica, Pesavento, and Farone 1988; Human Rights Watch 1993b, 1993c; Swiss and Giller 1993).
2. An international team sent by the UN to investigate the former Yugoslavia in January 1993 estimated rapes on the basis of data on abortions, deliveries, pregnancies known to be due to rape, and sexually transmitted diseases. During their short 10-day mission, they documented 119 pregnancies at six hospitals in Bosnia, Croatia, and Serbia. Using estimates of a single act of intercourse resulting in pregnancy 1 to 4% of the time, they estimated that the 119 pregnancies alone represented 11,900 rapes (Swiss and Giller 1993; United Nations 1993). The use of rape appeared to be part of an "ethnic-cleansing strategy" because it was used with the expressed intent to impregnate (Thomas 1993).
3. In Bangladesh, estimates are that the 9-month war for independence in 1971 resulted in the rape of 250,000–400,000 women and led to an estimated 25,000 pregnancies according to International Planned Parenthood (attributed to Brownmiller 1975; cited in Swiss and Giller 1993).
4. The Japanese government recently acknowledged that during World War II, it forcibly conscripted 100,000–200,000 women (mostly Korean) into sexual slavery to serve as "comfort women" for the Japanese Army (Hearings before the United Nations Secretary-General, February 25, 1992, cited in Swiss and Giller 1993).
5. Recent reports indicate that Burmese government agents have been raping Muslim women to get them to move out of contested areas and over the border into Bangladesh (Human Rights Watch, 1993a).
6. Among women who lived in Cambodia under the Pol Pot reign who later immigrated to the United States and sought treatment for trauma, at least 53% had been raped or sexually assaulted in addition to other heinous tortures (Van Boemel and Rozée, 1992). Other practitioners working with this group have reported rates of rape as high as 95% (Mollica 1986).

Other forms of normative rape.   Other forms of normative rape include exchange rape, ceremonial rape, and status rape. "Exchange rape" involves the "male use of female genital contact as a bargaining tool, gesture of solidarity, or conciliation" (Rozée 1993, 507). Wyatt (1993) has suggested that the world community must address a form of exchange rape that she calls "survival rape." Here, young women living under economic deprivation involve themselves with older men to obtain goods or services that they need for survival. "Ceremonial rape" is a category of unchosen genital contact that occurs within the context of ceremonies including defloration rituals or virginity tests, where sexual intercourse is part of the ceremony and females are expected to participate whether they want to or not (Rozée 1993). "Status rape" occurs because of acknowledged differences in rank including master and slave, chief and clanswoman, nobleman and commoner, or priest and parishioner (Rozée 1993). Recent examples of status rapes include the treatment of Asian maids in Kuwait, where cultural expectations dictate that domestic servants be sexually available for their employers (Human Rights Watch 1992b).

The Prevalence of Rape Worldwide

Accurate estimates of the global health burden of sexual victimization are hampered by lack of data on the incidence and prevalence of rape in its various forms. Unfortunately, conclusions drawn from crime statistics are virtually useless for estimating the incidence of sexual assault because women are universally reluctant to report rape to authorities. Thus, community-based surveys reveal that less than 2% of rape victims informed the police in Korea (Shim 1992) and 12% did so in the United States (National Victim Center 1992). Crime statistics are also of limited utility in estimating the health burden of rape because they generally reflect only those rapes that occurred within the previous year, whereas the aftereffects of rape may extend for many years beyond the incident or series of incidences.

Measurement of rape prevalence faces a central methodological challenge—to overcome women's historic tendency to keep silent about rape. In addition, other compelling social forces complicate the collection of valid and reliable data, including: norms about discussing sexual matters, distrust of authorities, distrust of fellow citizens under conditions of social stress, and difficulty creating privacy and confidentiality in small, close-knit societies. Currently, there exists a small database on the prevalence of rape, most of which was developed in the United States. Koss (1993) recently reviewed and critiqued these studies. She concluded that estimates of rape or sexual assault prevalence among adult women range between 14% and 25% in the majority of sources. The major problem identified in this literature is that lack of comparability across studies in definitions and methodologies has precluded the accumulation of a cohesive database.

To begin constructing a global database on rape prevalence, we will review information drawn from three main sources: ethnographic records collected and catalogued by anthropologists, international crime survey data, and cross-national studies of rape prevalence among college-aged women.

ETHNOGRAPHIC STUDIES

Rape is found in 42% to 90% of nonindustrial societies, depending on how it is defined and on the cultural and geographic representativeness of sample of societies examined (Bart, Blumberg, Tombs, and Behan 1975; Broude and Greene 1976; Levinson 1989; Minturn et al. 1969; Sanday 1981b). Note that these figures refer to the proportion of societies in which rape occurs at some level, not to the magnitude of rape within any one society. Thus, Minturn and associates defined rapes as "sexual relations without the consent of the woman involved" (p. 303) and reported its occurrence in 90% of the societies studied. Sanday (1981b) coded 156 world societies on the basis of a similar definition. She included as rape unchosen sexual intercourse that occurred in the context of ceremonies and as part of warfare, but she excluded "sleepcrawling" (that is, surreptitious sex with a woman who is asleep in the same room as the remainder of her family; Rozée 1993, 509). Sanday reported rape in 53% of her sample of nonindustrial societies, partly because she classified as rape-free those societies where rape did occur but was extremely rare. Rozée (1993) likewise defined rape as lack of female choice and examined a sample of 35 nonindustrial societies. One or more forms of rape were found in all of the 35 societies she examined. Nearly all of the societies (97%) had normative rape, that is, structured ways of sexually abusing women that did not violate social norms, including marital rape (40% of societies), exchange rape (71%), punitive rape

(14%), theft rape (63%), ceremonial rape (49%), and status rape (29%). Non-normative rape was found in 63% of the societies studied.

It would be incorrect to conclude on the basis of these studies that the ethnographic record documents a universal male predilection, perhaps biologically based, to rape women (Sanday 1993). Rather, the data force the conclusions that rape takes multiple forms depending on the sociocultural context, and that in some societies, rape is far less common than in others. These societies warrant study so that the rest of the world may learn from them. Knowledge that can be gained from examination of relatively rape-free societies include how social organizations and customs minimize rape and how to socialize boys so that they learn to control aggressive tendencies and behave in nonaggressive ways (Miedzian 1993; Sanday 1993).

INTERNATIONAL CRIME SURVEY DATA

A question about sexual victimization was included in the International Crime Survey (van Dijk and Mayhew 1993). The text of the question was the following, "Firstly, a rather personal question. People sometimes grab, touch or assault others for sexual reasons in a really offensive way. This can happen either inside one's house or elsewhere, for instance in a pub, the street, at school, on public transport, in cinemas, on the beach, or at one's work place. Over the past five years has anyone done this to you?" (van Dijk and Mayhew 1993, 21). The results revealed that among industrial countries included in the sample, Australia ranked number one in affirmative responses (5.6%), Canada second (4.1%), and the United States third (3.7%). Data from nonindustrial nations are not yet publicly available.

Given the extensive sample included in the International Crime Survey and the expense of data collection, it is very unfortunate that the screening for sexual assault is both minimal and ambiguous. Although disaggregated figures are presented in the report for rape and molestation, this distinction cannot be made on the basis of the screening item alone, and the authors do not discuss their follow-up questioning. Use of a global screening item for all forms of sexual assault from which cases of rape can later be culled by further questioning has been shown in the United States to result in serious underestimation of rape (Koss 1993). More successful in obtaining disclosure of rape are multiple, behaviorally specific, culturally sensitive questions to jog respondents' recollection about the variety of guises in which rape may appear. A further problem with the approach toward rape in this survey is the unfortunate wording of the screening item. The use of the expression "in a really offensive way" describes an appropriate reaction to sexual crimes such as unwanted groping, pinching, or rubbing up against the victim. It clearly understates the typical reaction to rape. Coming as it does after questions about crimes such as pickpocketing, the item intended to identify the range of sexual assaults may instead favor recall of minor public molestations. Also suggestive of problems with the rape item are the ratings of severity that respondents ascribed to the sexual assault item. From country to country they varied greatly: some societies considered that the item described a serious violation, whereas others considered it a minor one. If the international crime survey screening for rape referred unambiguously to forcible rape, it would be difficult to find a society that considered the violation minor.

TABLE 1. PREVALENCE OF RAPE AMONG COLLEGE-AGED WOMEN

Country	Authors	Sample	Definition of Rape	Completed Rape	Completed and Attempts
Canada	DeKeseredy and Kelly 1993	1,853 women at 95 colleges and universities (national probability sample)	anal, oral, or vaginal intercourse by force or threat of force, SES #9, 10	8.1% (by dating partners since high school)	23.3% (rape or sexual assault by anyone ever)
New Zealand	Gavey 1991	347 female psychology students (convenience sample)	anal, oral, or vaginal intercourse by force or threat, or because a man gave alcohol or drugs, SES #8, 9, 10	14.1% (lifetime)	25.3% (lifetime)
United Kingdom	Beattie 1992	1,476 women at 22 universities (convenience sample)	anal, oral, or vaginal intercourse by force or threat, or when intoxicated, SES #8, 9, 10	11.7% (lifetime)	19.4% (lifetime)
United States	Koss et al. 1987	3,187 women at 32 colleges and universities (representative sample)	anal, oral, or vaginal intercourse by force or threat, or when intoxicated, SES #8, 9, 10	15.4% (since age 14)	27.5% (since age 14)
Seoul, Korea	Shim 1992	2,270 adult women (quota sample)	SES #9, 10	7.7% (lifetime)	21.8% (lifetime)

Note: These data have previously appeared in a report commissioned by the World Bank (1993).
Estimates of rape and attempted rape are based on different combinations of the following questions taken from the Sexual Experiences Survey (SES) (Koss et al. 1987):

8. Have you had sexual intercourse when you didn't want to because a man gave you alcohol or drugs?
9. Have you had sexual intercourse when you didn't want to because a man threatened or used some degree of physical force (twisting your arm, holding you down, etc.) to make you?
10. Have you engaged in sexual acts (anal or oral intercourse or penetration by objects other than a penis) when you didn't want to because a man threatened or used some degree of physical force (twisting your arm, holding you down, etc.) to make you?

CROSS-NATIONAL STUDIES OF COLLEGE STUDENTS

More or less directly comparable cross-national figures on rape prevalence come from a small number of studies that have administered the Sexual Experiences Survey (Koss, Gidycz, and Wisniewski 1987) to college students in several countries. This survey consists of 10 items to screen for a continuum of unwanted sexual behavior, including three items designed to measure rape as it is defined in most North American jurisdictions. Administrations of the survey to students in Canada, New Zealand, United Kingdom, United States, and Korea are summarized in Table 1. Individual authors have assembled their rape prevalence figures differently, depending on whether they wished to include or exclude unwanted sex while intoxicated as rape (item 8). In addition to differences in definition, other sources of variation include the researcher's choice of the age at which recall is to begin and whether focus is on all experiences or is limited to those incidents involving dating partners. Even with these sources of variation in mind, however, the data point to an impressive consistency in prevalence of rape among college students cross-nationally. Lifetime prevalence of completed and attempted rape combined among college women is universally above 20%.

High-risk groups. Also consistent are cross-national findings on the typical victims and perpetrators of rape. Table 2 contains figures from selected cities and countries that point to a sad global reality. The majority of perpetrators are people known to the victim, and a substantial subset of victims are very young girls. Across diverse continents and hemispheres, between one and two thirds of the victims are 15 years and younger.

The Effects of Rape

The effects of rape include psychological distress, sociocultural impacts, and somatic consequences. A large body of empirical literature exists to document these effects. (For

TABLE 2. STATISTICS ON SEXUAL CRIMES, SELECTED COUNTRIES[a]

City or Country	Percent of Perpetrators Known to Victim	Percent of Victims 15 Years and Under	Percent of Victims 10 Years and Under
Lima, Peru	60	—	18[c]
Malaysia	68	58	18[b]
Mexico City	67	36	23
Panama City	63	40	—
Papua New Guinea	—	47	13[d]
Santiago, Chile[e]	72	58	32[c]
United States	78	62[f]	29

Note: Data are from the following sources: Malaysia data (Consumer's Association 1988); Mexico City data (COVAC 1990 and *Carpeta Basica* 1991. Mexico City: Procurador de Justicia del Distrito Federal de Mexico); Panama City data (Perez 1990); Peru data (Portugal 1988); Papua New Guinea data (Riley 1985, as cited in Bradley 1990); Chile data (Avendano and Vergara 1992); United States data (National Victims Center 1992). These data have appeared previously in a report commissioned by the World Bank (1993).
[a] Studies include rape and sexual assaults such as attempted rape and molestation except for U.S. data which includes only completed rapes. [b] Percentage of survivors age 6 and younger. [c] Percentage of survivors age 9 and younger. [d] Percentage of survivors age 7 and younger. [e] Based on 5-year averages derived from crimes reported to the Legal Medical Service, 1987–1991; Anuario Estadistico del Servicio Medico Legal de Chile. [f] Percentage of survivors age 17 and younger.

reviews of psychological effects see Goodman, Koss, and Russo 1993a, 1993b; Hanson 1990; Lurigio and Resick 1990; McCann, Sakheim, and Abrahamson 1988; Resick 1987, 1990; Roth and Lebowitz 1988. For reviews of somatic effects see Council on Scientific Affairs 1992; Dunn and Gilchrist 1993; Hendricks-Mathews 1993; Koss and Heslet 1992.) However, most of the studies are based on Western women in peacetime, many of whom may have experienced a single episode of rape (Swiss and Giller 1993). Studies generally have not taken into account the cumulative impact of multiple traumas as commonly experienced by women in war and conflict situations, including death of loved ones, loss of home and community, dislocation, untreated illness, deprivation, and war-related injury (for exceptions see Bowen, Carscadden, Beighle, and Fleming 1992; Friedman 1992; Mollica and Son 1989; Mollica, Wyshak, and Lavelle 1987; Rozée and Van Boemel 1989; Sheperd 1992; Van Boemel and Rozée 1992).

PSYCHOLOGICAL DISTRESS

Given the nature of rape, it is not surprising that some symptoms are experienced by almost everyone in the immediate aftermath. However, approximately one quarter of women continue to experience negative effects several years after rape (Hanson 1990). Even when evaluated many years after sexual assault, survivors in the United States and New Zealand were more likely to have received several psychiatric diagnoses during their adult life, including major depression, alcohol abuse/dependence, drug abuse/dependence, generalized anxiety, obsessive-compulsive disorder, and post-traumatic stress disorder (Burnam et al. 1988; Kilpatrick, Saunders, Veronen, Best, and Von 1987; Winfield, George, Schwartz, and Blazer 1990; Mullen, Romans-Clarkson, Walton, and Herbison 1988). These effects may be more severe for younger victims. For example, Burnam et al. (1988) found that those who were sexually abused as children were more likely (59% vs. 24%) than those not abused to have at least one psychiatric diagnosis. Rape and other sexual abuse in childhood also creates a legacy of increased vulnerability to revictimization. Thus, child abuse victims are 2.4 times more likely to be raped as adults (Wyatt, Guthrie, and Notgrass 1992).

Many of the psychological effects of rape—including intrusive memories, attempts to avoid reminders of the trauma, depression, and anxiety—are conceptualized as post-traumatic stress disorder (PTSD) in North America (American Psychiatric Association 1994). Most rape victims who are evaluated at a trauma center in the immediate aftermath of rape meet symptom criteria for PTSD. For example, an average of 12 days following assault, 94% of rape victims met PTSD symptom criteria; 46% still met the criteria 3 months later (Rothbaum, Foa, Riggs, Murdock, and Walsh 1992). Rape is more likely to induce PTSD than a range of traumatic events affecting civilians, including robbery, tragic death of a close friend or family member, or natural disaster (Norris 1992).

However, the PTSD conceptualization has been severely critiqued, especially by Latin-American feminist psychologists. (Becker, Lira, Castillo, Ganez, and Kovalskys 1990; Martîn-Baró 1988; Rozée and Van Boemel 1989). Critics see the PTSD diagnosis as a conceptualization rooted in the medical model that ignores the gendered, structural, and social aspects of male violence against women. It also deflects attention from traumatized social relations and social systems by overemphasizing individual responses to male violence. These comments are well founded because none of the current models of PTSD address characteristics of the victim that may shape her response to rape, including ethnicity, class, and sexual orientation. Nor do they address the fact that the cultural context that spawned the violence may itself present an obstacle to recovery (Goodman, Koss, and Russo 1993a, 1993b).

Promising to ameliorate some of the shortcomings in conceptual models of PTSD are new developments linking specific aspects of the environment with emotions (Lazarus 1991). In this conceptualization a person's emotional response to an event is neither determined by the actual event nor by intrapsychic processes, but rather by a cognitive appraisal of the experience that arises out of a person–event interaction (Lazarus 1991). Cognitive appraisals are substantially influenced by both individual and sociocultural variables including family history, existence of prior trauma, personality, coping style, ethnicity, class, sexual orientation, community attitudes, and gender-based norms. The notion of cognitive appraisal suggests that understanding psychological responses to rape requires looking at both the trauma and the recovery process from the woman's point of view—in the context of her personal meanings.

SOCIOCULTURAL IMPACTS

One rape can affect many women when it leads nonvictimized women to change their behavior and to restrict their movements to avoid being raped. A range of findings suggest that women develop distrust of men and live their lives under the threat of sexual violation. For example:

1. Women in Seoul, Korea identified rape as the major stress in their lives (Korean Sexual Violence Relief Center 1991). A second survey of over 2,000 women found that 40% felt "extremely uneasy" about sexual violence and restricted their activities because of these fears (Shim 1992).
2. In Ethiopia, women refugees reduced the number of cooked meals they fed their children because they feared being raped while collecting firewood (LaPin 1992).
3. Female health workers in Gujurat, India, report being reluctant to travel alone between villages for fear of being raped (Khanna 1992, cited in Heise et al. 1993).
4. In a national telephone survey of 12,300 Canadian women conducted by Statistics Canada, 60% of women reported that they feared walking alone after dark, 81% feared using public transportation after dark, and 83% feared walking alone to their cars in a parking garage. Women who actually had been victims of violence were only slightly more likely to be fearful than women who had never been personally affected by violence (*The Daily Statistics Canada*, November 18, 1993, pp. 8–9).
5. For urban U.S. women younger than 35, rape is feared even more than murder (Warr 1985). In response to their fear about rape, over half of the women surveyed reacted with self-isolation, forgoing certain activities such as evening entertainment. In contrast, most men (90%) living in some neighborhoods denied taking steps to reduce their vulnerability to crime, even though statistics suggest that they are more likely to be victims of every violent crime with the exception of rape (Gordon and Riger 1989).

More dire social effects of rape occur in societies where the stigma of rape is pronounced. In parts of Asia and the Middle East, for example, these include being divorced by one's husband, being ostracized by one's family, and even being killed by family members to cleanse the family honor (Ben Baraka 1993). In Cambodian culture women are likened to cotton. "Once cotton has fallen in the soil, it can never be washed completely clean" (Van Boemel and Rozée 1992, 239; taken from Mollica 1986). In contrast, men are likened to diamonds, which can be washed if soiled. Whereas monks perform purification rituals for men, none are available for women who have been raped. These women must carry their sense of impurity for the remainder of their lives (Mollica 1986).

Somatic Effects

The somatic effects of rape can include injuries such as suicide and homicide, chronic illness, and a range of reproductive health consequences.

Intentional injuries including suicide and murder. Rape is associated with physical injury caused by the perpetrator (Beebe 1991; Koss, Woodruff, and Koss 1991; National Victims Center 1992). But in societies where victim-blaming is strong and the stain of sexual violation is considered permanent, rape also can become a significant risk factor for both suicide and murder. Although the majority of honor killings are against women suspected of adultery or fornication, one study of 72 honor murders among Arab Israelis notes that 5 were against women who had been raped (Kressel 1981). Likewise, in a study of women murdered in Alexandria, Egypt, 47% were victims of rape who had been killed by a relative (Graitcer and Youssef 1993). Some cultures place so much emphasis on virginity that the greatest preoccupation of victims in the aftermath of rape is seeking surgical reconstruction of their hymen. According to Eman Kandaloof, Palestinian Outreach Coordinator of Israel's Haifa Rape Crisis Center, "Women tend to fixate on getting their hymens reconstructed instead of dealing with the psychological aftermath of the rape (Kandaloof 1991).

Illnesses. A number of chronic conditions are diagnosed disproportionately among rape victims, including chronic pelvic pain, arthritis, gastrointestinal disorders, headaches, chronic pain disorders, psychogenic seizures, premenstrual symptoms, and substance use (Golding 1994; Koss and Heslet 1992). A number of potential mechanisms exist to account for the links between victimization and illness, and somatic symptoms may be multiply determined. Examples of somatic consequences of rape reported in various nations include:

1. In Bangladesh 84% of victims suffered injuries or unconsciousness, mental illness, or death following rape (Shamim 1985).
2. Among Ugandan rape victims, 53% described headaches, chest pain, and rashes, and 57% described gynecological symptoms including vaginal discharge or pelvic pain (Giller 1992).
3. U.S. women with a history of victimization by rape (and other crimes) report more symptoms of illness across virtually all body systems and perceive their health less favorably than nonvictimized women (Kimerling and Calhoun 1994; Koss, Koss, and Woodruff 1991).
4. Victimized women, compared to those free from male violence, are more likely to report negative health behaviors, including smoking, alcohol use, and failure to use seat belts (Koss, Koss, and Woodruff 1991).

REPRODUCTIVE HEALTH CONSEQUENCES

It is on the battleground of reproductive health that some of the fiercest struggles to realize women's rights are being waged. In the context of women's freedom to control their own bodies, "Rape is undoubtedly the most direct breach of choice that a woman can face" (Heise 1993b, 77). In the material that follows we address not only the direct consequences of rape on reproductive health but also the barriers to change in reproductive health behavior posed by women's fears of rape.

Pregnancy. Between 15 and 18% of rape victims who visited Mexican rape crisis centers reported they became pregnant as a result of rape (CAMVAC 1985; COVAC 1990), figures consistent with data from Thailand and Korea (Archavanitkui and Pramualratana 1990; Shim 1992). In the United States, pregnancy results from rape in approximately 5% of the cases (Beebe 1991; Koss; Woodruff, and Koss 1991). Forced impregnation takes on an additional horror where abortion is illegal, and the victim faces the prospect of bearing the rapist's child.

Rape also plays a causal role in pregnancy among teenagers (Boyer and Fine 1992). For example:

1. A study conducted in the maternity hospital of Lima, Peru revealed that 90% of young mothers 12–16 years of age delivered a child that resulted from rape (Rosas 1992). The vast majority were impregnated by their father, stepfather, or other close relative. An organization for adolescent mothers in Costa Rica reported similar findings: 95% of their clients under age 15 were victims of incest (Treguear and Carro 1991).
2. In Peru, where abortion is illegal even in the case of rape, a high percentage of abortions are performed on rape victims, many of whom are minors abused by fathers or other family members (Human Rights Watch 1992c). According to Peru's Health Ministry, 43% of all maternal hospitalizations in 1990 were due to botched abortions.
3. In the United States, women survivors of sexual assault in childhood were found to be three times more likely to become pregnant before age 18 compared to nonvictimized women (Zierler et al. 1991; also see Wyatt 1988).

High-risk sexual behaviors. In Barbados, a probability survey of 407 women and men revealed that sexual abuse was the single most powerful predictor of high-risk sexual activity during adolescence for both women and men (Handwerker 1991). After controlling for SES factors and home environment variables, sexual abuse remained linked to the age at first intercourse and the number of sexual partners. These effects remained significant until respondents reached their mid-30s. In the United States, a background of childhood or adolescent sexual abuse or rape is associated with a range of high-risk sexual behaviors (Boyer and Fine 1992; Finkelhor 1987; Paone, Chavkin, Willets, Friedman, and Des Jarlais 1992; Zierler et al. 1991). For example, abused girls began sex earlier, were more likely to use alcohol and drugs, were less likely to use birth control at first intercourse, and were more likely to be battered or to have traded sex for food, money, shelter, or drugs (Boyer and Fine 1992). Early sexual abuse raised the risk of entering prostitution (Finkelhor 1987; Meyerding 1977). In the United States, the chance of working in prostitution was four times greater among those forced to have sex in childhood or adolescence compared to nonabused (Zierler et al. 1991). Among crack cocaine users those sexually abused as children were more likely to engage in sex for drugs transactions (Paone et al. 1992).

Sexually transmitted disease including AIDS. In many parts of the world there appears to be a trend for men to seek younger and younger partners based on the belief that this behavior will protect them from exposure to HIV. Among women, sexual experience at very young ages is just as important as multiple sex partners in raising the risk for sexually transmitted diseases. It is well established that women have a much greater chance of being infected per coital act and have particularly vulnerable reproductive tracts at young ages (Ericksen 1994). Some examples of the severity of the problem include:

1. Ten percent of clients contact STDs from rape in Thailand (Archavanitkui and Pramu-alratana 1990).
2. In studies in Nigeria and Uganda, 16% of female patients seeking treatment for STDs were under 5 years of age and another 6% were between 6 and 15 years (Kisekka and Otesanya 1988).
3. Twenty-two percent of female patients attending an STD clinic in Nigeria were under 10 years of age (Sogbetun, Alausa, & Osoba, 1977).
4. Children in Nicaragua identified sexual abuse as the number one health priority facing children in their country (Rompiendo el Silencio, 1992).

In the United States, sexually transmitted diseases occur as a result of rape in 4 to 30% of victims (Koss and Heslet 1992). In addition to pain and stigmatization, untreated STDs can lead to pelvic inflammatory disease, which is a major cause of infertility. In societies where the role of women is closely identified with her ability to bear children, this rape-related consequence is psychologically and socially devastating.

Birth control use. In many countries, such as Mexico, wives' bargaining power in marriage is lowest in decisions about when and if sexual intercourse will occur (Beneria and Roldan 1987; Worth 1989). A major determinant of birth control use is partner approval in countries as diverse as Mexico, South Africa, and Bangladesh (Banwell 1990; Kincaid 1991). Fear of male reprisal limits the use of birth control (Dixon-Mueller 1992). In Mexico and Peru, women feared violence, desertion, or accusations of infidelity if they suggested birth control (Folch-Lyon, Macorra, and Schearer 1981; Fort 1989). Natural family planning in the Philippines, Peru, and Sri Lanka is undermined by the husband arriving home drunk and forcing his wife to have sex (Liskin 1981). Victimization can lower self-esteem and confidence and impede the ability to protect the self. Therefore, the ability to enforce condom use is influenced both by the aftereffects of earlier victimization and by direct threats of violence.

The Cumulative Health Burden

The burden of sexual violence on health can be calculated in terms of the additional costs to the health care systems to care for victimization-related health aftereffects and in terms of women's quality of life by examining the healthy years of life lost because of violence.

ECONOMIC COSTS

Victimized women in the United States receive significantly more medical care than nonvictimized women (Golding et al. 1988; Kimerling and Calhoun 1994; Koss, Koss, and Woodruff 1991). Thus, adult women who had been physically and sexually assaulted in their past visited their physician twice as often in an index year—an average of 6.9 visits per year, compared to 3.5 visits for nonvictimized women (Koss, Koss, and Woodruff 1991). Utilization data across 5 years preceding and following victimization ruled out the possibility that victims had been high utilizers of services from some earlier point preceding their victimization. The costs of providing a year of healthcare for the severely victimized women are 2.5 times higher than for nonvictimized women.

HEALTHY YEARS OF LIFE LOST

Estimates of the health burden of rape must take into account both its prevalence and the extent of disability that it creates. Perhaps the best attempt to quantify the health consequences appears in the *World Development Report 1993: Investing in Health*, the policy annual of the World Bank. For this exercise, Bank staff and outside experts attempted to estimate the healthy years of life lost to women and men from a variety of causes. The exercise counted every year lost due to premature death as one disability-adjusted life year or DALY and every year spent sick or incapacitated as a fraction of a DALY, depending on the severity of the disability. Neither rape nor domestic violence are diseases in and of themselves but they are risk factors that lead to a range of diseases including mental disorders such as PTSD, physical illnesses such as irritable bowel syndrome, and reproductive consequences such as sexually transmitted diseases, exposure to HIV, and pregnancy-related health consequences.

According to this analysis, rape and domestic violence both emerge as a significant cause of disability and death among women of reproductive age in both the industrialized and developing world. The estimates suggest that gender-based victimization accounts for almost 1 in every 5 healthy years of life lost to women ages 15 to 44 in established market economies. The health burden for rape and domestic violence is roughly the same in developing countries, but because of a greater overall burden of disease, the percentage attributable to gender-based victimization is smaller. Among demographically developing countries, estimates are that rape and domestic violence account for 5% of the healthy years of life lost to women of reproductive age. In developing countries where maternal mortality and poverty-related diseases have been brought under relative control, rape and domestic violence again account for a larger percentage, 16% of the total burden. On a global basis, the health burden from gender-based victimization (9.5 million DALY) is comparable to that posed by other diseases or risk factors already high on the world agenda such as HIV (10.6 million DALY), tuberculosis (10.9 million DALY), sepsis during childbirth (10 million DALY), all cancers (9.0 million DALY), and cardiovascular disease (10.5 million DALY).

Conclusions and Recommendations

The studies reviewed here reveal that rape is manifested in a variety of forms, supported by sociocultural norms, and is widespread around the globe. Although current data are sparse, they confirm that rape plays a significant role in women's physical and mental health. In addition, they substantiate the assertion made at the outset that women's rights with regard to their bodies do involve survival issues with widespread public impact. However, more and better research is needed to spur political action globally and to influence the ways in which physical, mental, and reproductive healthcare are delivered to women. In the following material we focus on applied research. We also consider intervention and prevention strategies of utmost importance but do not wish to duplicate Schuler's numerous recommendations for understanding, responding to, and preventing gender-based violence, including rape (1992; 22–23).

ASSEMBLING A GLOBAL DATABASE

Reliable and valid cross-national data on rape prevalence are an important priority because these numbers help raise awareness of the problem of sexual violence and justify allocation of resources for services and prevention. The reverse may also be true. That is, the minimal existing database may reflect the current priority placed on documenting this threat to women's health and quality of life. It is particularly pressing that changes be made in international crime surveys so that the rape is detected more fully. Emerging evidence from credible sources such as Statistics Canada (*The Daily Statistics Canada*, November 18, 1993, pp. 1–10) reaffirm that the male violence against women is there if the lessons that have been learned about its measurement are applied. In contrast, publication of flawed sexual assault estimates by international agencies are a cruel hoax for women. The low numbers invalidate women's experience, indicate a lack of commitment and concern for women's well-being, and fuel illusions that rape is a minor issue on which feminists are overly focused. As a result, rape activists are less able to speak authoritatively about the need for social changes or to command financial resources for intervention and prevention services.

However, it is very unlikely that a single large data collection can address the multiple questions that exist about rape prevalence among diverse groups. It is more reasonable to develop a strategy to allow smaller scale, specialized data gathering efforts to be cumulated into a comprehensive literature on rape prevalence cross-nationally. Achievement of such a goal rests on developing professional consensus around the following issues:

How will rape and consent be defined? Clearly, a single definition of rape with global currency is lacking. For example, the world is not of a single mind on the validity of the concept of marital rape. One solution to this dilemma is to use multiple items that query about experiences under various consent circumstances. Then individual items can be included or excluded as necessary to calculate local rates or to permit comparison across nations.

What questions will be used to identify rape? Much is already known about the kinds of questions that result in underdetection of rape, including single omnibus abuse items, items expressed in professional terms such as sexual assault, and items that are vague for the purpose of avoiding offense. Successful detection of rape depends on the use of multiple questions expressed in the most concrete and behaviorally specific language possible. However, the forms of rape that are commonly seen may vary across societies. Therefore, individual research teams may need to use qualitative methods to determine the forms of rape that are most characteristic in a given society and guide their choice of screening items accordingly. A common core of screening items that was standard across studies would allow accumulation into a coherent body of literature, while still permitting individual investigators the flexibility to add on specialized items of local relevance.

How will data be collected? Methods that are feasible in industrialized countries such as mailed or telephone surveys lack appropriateness in other settings. In-person data collection is an obvious alternative, but prevalence research demands large and representative samples. The assembly of such samples will require attention to sample planning as well as the commitment of financial resources.

How will confidentiality and rapport be established? Data collection must be completely confidential and conducted in total privacy. Otherwise, women may hesitate to reveal rape, particularly in societies where severe stigma attaches to the rape victim, and can even result in her being incarcerated or put to death. In addition, given the large proportion of rapes that are perpetrated by family members, questioning in front of others may place the woman who reveals rape at risk of retaliatory violence. Careful thought must be given to the selection of the culturally appropriate people to serve as interviewers, while at the same time developing procedures to ensure that interviewers can avoid work with kin or acquaintances.

How will the validity of the responses be demonstrated? There is no evidence that women inflate their reports of minor victimizations. Indeed, respondents are more likely to take a conservative approach in which only obvious incidents are labeled as abuse (Mullen et al. 1988). Some observers consider underdetection of rape to be a more serious problem than false reporting (Koss 1993). However, it is prudent to include reliability and validity checks into survey protocols to bolster the credibility of the data. This step is important because any data on rape are a powerful challenge to the patriarchal status quo and are likely to be received with scrutiny and skepticism.

DESCRIBING THE CONTEXT AND IMPACT OF RAPE

Participants at a recent meeting of the Population Council and the Pacific Institute for Women's Health concluded that a research agenda on sexual violence globally should be guided by several general principles: It should be across cultures, across continents, across the life span, and free from heterosexist bias. Currently, there are almost no scientific studies of rape prevalence or consequences in the nonindustrialized world. In redressing this deficit, it is necessary for world organizations to develop strategies to bring academics and activists together. Alone, activists may lack the training and support to carry out scientifically valid research; and academics may use sophisticated methods to ask the wrong questions. Collaborative research models are needed, models that may require researchers to respond to realities of sexual oppression that lie outside of their previous, perhaps privileged experience (e.g., Lykes 1989). Guided by their conclusions and principles, and recognizing the importance of credible research findings to the international women's movement to conceptualize women's rights as human rights, we emphasize the following areas of investigation for future research:

1. Context of Violence

Studies are needed to address the sociocultural context that shapes and supports gender-based sexual violence, including studies of sexual values, attitudes and scripts, and gender-linked sexual roles; influential sociocultural institutions and organizations and their mechanisms for influencing sexual violence; and economic and cultural practices that engender violence. Such studies are particularly needed to document the public nature of this issue.

2. Basic Epidemiologic Research

To document the societal impact of rape on health, prevalence estimates based in different healthcare settings are needed. Links between rape, other forms of violence, and other social problems (e.g., unwanted pregnancy) must be explored. Questions on gender-linked violence should be integrated into health and social surveys and ongoing research on AIDS, sexuality, and family planning.

3. Interpretations and Meanings

Popular myths about rape, its perpetrators and victims, and how such myths limit understanding of the destructive consequences of violence, must be documented cross-culturally. Although physical and emotional symptoms seen in the aftermath of rape may be similar across cultures, groups differ in the meanings attached to these symptoms and in the preferred methods for healing. Urgently needed are culturally sensitive portraits of violence and its effects from the point of view of its victims (Russo, Koss, and Goodman forthcoming).

4. Consequences of Rape

Studies of the consequences of rape need to be extended into settings where multiple sources of trauma are occurring, as well as studies of the cultural attitudes toward rape that shape the form of recovery and influence the extent to which recovery is even believed to be possible. Studies are needed on the psychological, social, somatic, and economic consequences of various forms of rape in diverse sociocultural contexts.

5. Processes that Maintain Violence

The major systems of criminal justice, law, media, and medical care play a role in maintaining rape by procedures that deny victimization, create obstacles to obtaining validation or care, and decontextualize injury and illness. Studies that delineate these processes are needed, including how laws are enforced, how victims are handled in systems (e.g., in the courts or in emergency rooms), how rape is reported by the media, and biases held by key decision-makers (e.g., police, judges, editors, physicians).

6. Intervention

Little is known about the social networks through which people are now dealing with sexual violence. This information is essential to formulate responses to sexual violence that are culturally appropriate. Undesirable medicalizing of the response to sexual violence can be avoided by understanding cultural patterns in healing the victim and addressing the perpetrator. In many countries, sexual violence is viewed as a community problem for which there must be a political response.

7. Prevention/Education

Informed approaches to intervention rest upon developing a theoretical and empirical understanding of the context of violence and the social processes that maintain violence. But in addition to developing a relevant knowledge base, it is necessary to disseminate that knowledge to women's groups, as well as others, so that the findings can be used to take effective action.

Many of these research avenues will pose formidable methodological and practical challenges. Yet, credible research on rape is urgently needed that explores its multiple forms in criminal context and documents its health consequences and public impact. Feminist psychologists who blend the identities of academic and activist have special roles to play in building bridges across disciplines, communities, and cultures so that the outcome of our efforts will reflect the reality of women's lives around the world, and will address real survival threats to women.

SECTION 3
Battering in Intimate Relationships

The story is compelling, and only too familiar. A Division I football player is sanctioned by his college judicial system for assaulting his former girlfriend by banging her head against a wall and dragging her down three flights of stairs. He is suspended for six games, but is reinstated in time to help score a big win in a championship game. When she does not play up to speed during the rest of the season, the victim, a basketball player, loses her athletic scholarship, although it is later reinstated due to public outrage. The abuser becomes one of the top selections in the National Football League draft, assured of a multimillion-dollar contract.

The case of the football player, running back Lawrence Phillips, contains many of the elements that make violence in intimate relationships so troubling. The young man has been rewarded throughout his life for the controlled and successful use of violence on the playing field. That violent behavior, so valued in one context, spills over into other areas of conflict, should be no surprise. The gendered system that values the violent and controlling behavior of men and devalues its victims, permeates the hypermasculine arena of sport, the corporate boardroom, political life, and the interpersonal relationships of men and women. The spillover effects the high incidence of male-on-male violence, as well as the abuse of women by men.

The violence that occurs in intimate relationships seems to contradict what we believe constitutes relationships built on love; yet our response as a society is ambivalent. We claim to abhor the violence, yet we rationalize it and often overlook it.

A Movement for Change

As was the case with rape, the impetus to address domestic violence came out of the women's movement of the 1960s and 1970s. The first refuge for battered women, Chiswick Women's Aid, opened in England in 1972. Local women, provided with an alternative to staying at home with a violent spouse, overwhelmed the facility. The need for such services was clear. In 1974 the first shelter for battered women in the United States opened in Minnesota, quickly followed by shelters in several other states (Dobash and Dobash 1987; Schecter 1982). In the 1970s, the battered women's movements in the United States and Britain focused on raising public awareness about domestic violence.

It was a decade of major achievements against the obdurate obstacles of tradition and apathy.

By the early 1980s, shelters in the United States were serving approximately 270,000 women and children annually. At any point in time in Britain, approximately 900 women were staying in 128 refuges (Dobash and Dobash 1987). Close on the heels of the British and U.S. movements, shelters were set up in Ireland, Canada, Australia, and several European countries (Women's Aid 1994). By the end of its first decade, the battered women's movements had reached their goal to "name the hidden and private violence in women's lives, declare it public, and provide safe havens and support" (Schecter 1982, 11).

Advocates working with victims of domestic violence soon realized that lasting change in social conditions would not occur without increased public education and legislative action. Beginning in the mid-1970s legislation was passed in Britain and the United States to provide legal remedies and shelter for battered women (Dobash and Dobash 1987).

Although the successes of the battered women's movements in victim support, raising awareness, and forcing legislative change have been impressive, of equal importance has been their influence on research and scholarship in domestic violence. Inspired by the battered women's movements, scholars have documented the widespread experience of abuse at the hands of intimate partners. The newness of the field, however, coupled with strongly held disciplinary and ideological perspectives, has lead to very heated controversies over methodology, research emphasis, and terminology (see Gelles and Loseke 1993; Murphy and O'Leary 1994; Dobash, Dobash, Wilson, and Daly 1992). The terms *battering, wife abuse, wife beating, spouse abuse, family violence,* and *domestic violence* are being applied inconsistently and with differing meanings, complicating discussion of the subject.

As a result, literature on the subject, while voluminous, has yet to coalesce into a widely held theory of domestic violence. The amount and frequency of domestic violence, as well as descriptive information about abusers and victims, remains tremendously underdeveloped.

Emerging Global Issues in Domestic Violence

Although current statistics on domestic violence may not reveal a complete picture, one widely quoted study found that in the United States, approximately 30 percent of couples have at least one episode of domestic violence over the course of the marriage (Straus 1991b). Studies in Austria, Poland, Chile, Korea, Kuwait, Nigeria, Vanuatu, and Uganda have found high rates of wife abuse (Carillo 1992). While there is some evidence that women are violent in relationships, it is almost always in self-defense. When the rate of injury is considered, "women's victimization is ten times greater than men's" (Gelles 1995).

Most of the research on domestic violence to date has originated in Western Europe, North America, Australia, and New Zealand. What little we do know from other cultures indicates that the forms domestic violence takes may be culture and society specific (Davies 1994).

Research from Papua New Guinea found that most wives in that country have been physically abused. As the first comprehensive research by a developing nation, the Papua New Guinea study points to a particularly difficult problem. The researchers found that men's violence "prevents or limits women's participation in development"

(Bradley 1994, 16). Through beatings and threats women are prevented from attending meetings, husbands force women to hand over their income, and women who are attempting to limit childbearing are forced to have sex at fertile times in their reproductive cycles. In fact, forced sex was cited as the primary cause of domestic violence in Papua New Guinea, where marital rape is allowed by law. Finally, fear of violence prevents women from attempting to advance their careers. In fact, programs for development may increase the likelihood of violence for women because they threaten male authority. While development programs may expose women to more violence, they may also undermine traditional systems that have offered women some protection in the past. Unlike the West, where domestic violence is hidden due to the silence of victims and the complicity of social institutions, in Papua New Guinea it is seen as "normal and therefore not a problem" (Bradley 1994, 20).

As countries around the world begin to grapple with the problem of domestic violence, the research from Papua New Guinea serves as a cautionary example. Although domestic violence is widespread, local responses must acknowledge the specific concerns of the culture in which they take place. Westerners, who have taken the lead in exposing the problem of domestic violence, must act with caution when suggesting policies outside their area of cultural and societal familiarity.

Dating Violence

In recent years, more attention has been focused on violence among young people in dating relationships. Approximately 28 percent of people who date have been involved in interpersonal violence as part of their dating experience (Sugarman and Hotaling 1991). Young women, like older women, stay involved in violent relationships for a number of reasons. Subject to tremendous pressure to conform, young women often feel that involvement in a dating relationship is necessary to fit in. A teenage woman may be flattered by a dating partner who demands her time and attention, and she may view violence or efforts to control her behavior as signs of concern and commitment. Her lack of experience negotiating affection and sexual behavior, along with typical adolescent rejection of adult assistance, further contribute to the danger of abusive dating relationships (see Levy 1991). For adolescent lesbians and gay men, fear of familial and social rejection may further contribute to the danger and isolation of abusive relationships.

A Legacy of Abuse

Although the results of domestic violence are devastating, public concern and official response have been muted for much of human history. During the Middle Ages in Europe, church law exerted a strong influence on behavior. Women were subject to the authority of men, who had the explicit support of church law to correct women's behavior through punishment. Punishment was justified by women's inferior status and supposed spiritual weakness, which opened them to the influence of the devil. The legacy of medieval law, which permitted the authorized abuse of women, continued through the eighteenth-century Napoleonic Code, which in turn influenced the laws of France, Switzerland, Italy, and Germany. In these countries men had absolute family power, including the use of violence against family members up to the point of murder (Davidson 1977).

Over the course of human history efforts to protect women from the abuse of male intimates have had limited success. Urbanization and its attendant close living quarters made acts of violence against wives widely visible in nineteenth-century England. Police records from that era indicate that wife abuse was very common, with insubordinate and nonsubmissive behavior frequently cited as cause by the abusers (Tomes 1978). John Stuart Mill's 1869 essay "The Subjection of Women" addressed the plight of battered women in England. His compelling concern for wives "against whom [a husband] can commit any atrocity except killing her, and, if tolerably cautious, can do that without much danger of the legal penalty" (Mill 1983, 57) helped to mobilize efforts to rewrite English law. By the late 1900s British common law made wife abuse illegal (Goldman 1978).

In colonial Massachusetts from 1640 to 1680, the Puritans "enacted the first laws anywhere in the world against wife beating" (Pleck 1989, 20). Family violence was thought to be a sin. Neighbors were expected to be watchful of each other's behavior and to interfere when necessary. There were, of course, limits to the Puritans' vigilance, and the records from that era include numerous cases of severe violence against wives (Pleck 1987; Eldridge, this volume).

In the mid-1800s in the United States "an ideal of an anger-free family" had developed in close association with industrialization (Stearns and Stearns 1986, 11). The new standards for family behavior focused on the family and home as a refuge from the outer world of work and strife. During the late 1800s efforts to address wife abuse were initiated as part of larger concerns about cruelty to children (Pleck 1989). This may have had some effect, because by the late 1800s it appears that wife beaters may have been "more restrained in their violence" (Pleck 1989, 100) and that fewer men beat their wives. Perhaps this resulted from changing views of the paternalistic responsibilities of men toward women (Peterson 1992). Conversely, the blurring of gender lines and dependency patterns as more women work for wages and control their own finances may contribute to apparent increases in abuse today (Peterson 1992). Paternalism may have offered women some protection from abuse in previous eras, but it certainly contributed to diminishing their power in all aspects of life.

Domestic Violence as a Legal Concern

We are currently in another period of ferment about wife abuse. In a review of the literature of attitudes about wife abuse, Irene Hanson Frieze and Angela Browne (1989) found that tolerance of violence against wives has decreased. People are less likely than in the past to voice approval of the appropriateness of wife abuse. The current period of reform is focused primarily on increasing the criminalization of domestic violence (Pleck 1989; Zimring 1989). Violence within intimate relationships has not always been viewed as criminal violence, and family privacy continues to serve as a rationale to avoid criminalizing wife abuse; thus, the effort to widen criminal law to include responses to wife abuse is an uphill struggle against the history of a narrow jurisprudence of the family that has seen fit to intervene only in cases of "the taking of life, parental incest, and the imminent threat to the life or health of a minor child" (Zimring 1989, 552).

Worldwide reports reveal that legal responses to wife abuse have been ineffective. A U.S. study found that suspects in violent offenses are treated more leniently by the court if they are related to their victims (Herzberger and Channels 1991). In Denver, Colorado, in 1982 the typical sentence for a batterer was a twenty-five-dollar fine, even when the injuries inflicted included brain damage and attempted strangulation (Crites 1987). In the United States, police continue to be reluctant to respond appropriately to domestic violence calls (Caputo 1991), and the characteristics of the abusers play a more central role than the level of the abuse in deciding police intervention (Gondolf 1988a; Dutton 1988). Police insensitivity to victims and lack of awareness of the dangers of domestic violence are perceived as endemic (Roberts 1984). The response of the police and courts in other countries is similar. Studies have found that domestic violence cases in Scotland are treated much less seriously by the courts than comparable nondomestic violence cases (Wasoff 1982). A study by English police found very low rates of serious charges in domestic violence cases (Edwards 1987).

Efforts to change police and court procedures have been undertaken in locales around the world and have met with some success. Due to the tremendous mobilization of the Brazilian women's movement, separate police stations dedicated to addressing crimes of violence against women and staffed by women were created in 1985 in direct response to lack of interest and follow-through from traditional police departments (Thomas 1994). In 1991, Brazil's highest court of appeal overturned a lower court's acceptance of the traditional "honor defense," which permitted a man to murder his wife if she had committed adultery.

The civil and criminal court systems process cases of violence against wives and cohabitees in accordance with a number of factors that influence police investigation, prosecution, and sentencing, including

> the physical severity and visibility of the injuries; . . . the degree to which women conform to or deviate from appropriate female roles of wife, mother, homemaker; . . . the degree to which women are seen as responsible; . . . the degree to which women are thought to have provoked their own demise either by: a) being sexually inappropriate [by having relationships with other men or being lesbian] b) being inappropriate in terms of gender, that is, bad mothers, bad cooks, bad housewives c) challenging either the gender assumptions of their expected roles or challenging male domination. (Edwards 1987, 158)

Two approaches have emerged in answer to the question of how to address wife abuse in the criminal justice system. The first approach stresses the criminal aspect of domestic violence and urges that it should be treated in the same manner as assaults from strangers. The second approach focuses on mediation and therapy to modify relationship dynamics (Connors 1994). These approaches overlap to the extent that many jurisdictions mandate some kind of treatment or therapy for abusers in addition to jail sentences. Neither approach has a long enough track record to claim success, although there is qualified support for both the criminal approach (Ford 1991; Fagan 1989) and, to a lesser degree, the therapeutic model (Saunders and Azar 1989; Tolman and Bhosley 1991; see also Gondolf 1988b). Others have strongly argued that making domestic violence a therapeutic issue ignores the structural conditions of patriarchal control and dominance (Dobash and Dobash 1992; Bowker 1993).

The social institutions that women turn to for assistance have often been insensitive, resistant, and hostile to their concerns. For members of minority communities in the United States, the responses of helping agencies are complicated by racism, which makes assistance even less likely; thus, for abused women of color, the criminal approach to domestic violence presents a dilemma. Because police have not historically been perceived as the allies of minority communities, it is difficult for many women of color to depend on them for assistance (Miller 1993). In addition, African American women who call attention to domestic violence in the Black community may face anger about perceived disloyalty to African American men (Richie 1985). Some African American women believe that abusive African American men are reacting to the deprivation they have experienced through racism. Racial justice, in this view, would eradicate battering in African American families. These beliefs present strong barriers against depending on the criminal justice system for protection and resolution. Concerns about racism may prevent some women from seeking help outside the family (Lockhart and White 1989).

The small amount of research in American Indian communities indicates a high rate of domestic violence (Bachman 1992). Extreme poverty, joblessness, rural isolation, and alcohol abuse may be contributing factors, especially when understood within the frame of cultural decimation. Violent American Indian men may have internalized the "qualities ascribed to them for centuries by the society around them" (Gunn Allen 1986). Domestic violence, in this context, is due in large part to colonization and the replacement of an egalitarian social structure with the patriarchal hierarchy promoted by missionary colonists.

Asian women, particularly recent immigrants, face tremendous barriers to legal remedies for domestic violence. For many, traditional values of family loyalty and honor combined with beliefs that hold women secondary to men may promote interpersonal violence and prevent women from seeking help. Problems of reporting to official institutions include language barriers, isolation, fear of deportation, and the cultural insensitivity of the service providers (Lai 1986).

Latina (women born south of the U.S.–Mexico border) and Hispanic (those whose language is Spanish) women represent a diverse group that encompasses a variety of ancestral lands, skin colors, religious beliefs, and socioeconomic classes. Valid statistical information on domestic violence in the Hispanic and Latina/o communities is sparse due in large part to cultural barriers that prevent access to services. Sharing of explicit information and the intrusive questioning of police and counselors may be experienced as highly inappropriate. Emphasis on modesty and indirect communication may prevent many women from sharing their concerns even within the family (Ginorio and Reno 1986). All of these issues are complicated by a dearth of services for those who are not fully comfortable communicating in English.

Battered lesbians and gay men face issues of prejudice and a lack of appropriate services. Shelter programs are often inhospitable to lesbians (Geraci 1986) and nonexistent for gay men. Homophobia is so pervasive that many lesbians and gay men never attempt to bring their abuse to the criminal justice system. The tremendous insensitivity toward gay victims of intimate violence is exemplified by the Jeffrey Dahmer case. When a young man, naked, bleeding, and incoherent, approached police officers on the street in Milwaukee in 1991, the officers, who assumed it was a lover's spat, and thus declined to intervene, returned him to Dahmer, who had drugged him and later murdered him.

Causes of Domestic Violence

According to feminist analysts, the power relations of patriarchy produce the cultural conditions that create domestic violence. Patriarchal power structures, combined with cultural advocacy of violence as an effective and desirable method of interpersonal dynamics, produces what Wayne Ewing has referred to as the "civic advocacy of [male] violence" (1982, 5). The abuse of female intimates is possible with the structural support of a system that maintains and reproduces male dominance and female submission (Radford 1987). According to this theory, the state, through its treatment of victims, is complicit in reinforcing passive acquiescence and conformity to narrow gender roles (Edwards 1987). The valuing of gender-stereotyped behaviors in victims produces a hierarchy of worthiness, which is also influenced by race, sexual behavior, and class. This dynamic produces categories of women who are "appropriate" victims. For example, if women are held accountable for the maintenance of relationships and the care of children, yet prevented from having access to the same financial resources available to (White) men, their ability to escape a violent relationship is seriously compromised. The political discourse of the late twentieth century has centered around strong defense of an idealized family. Beliefs in the sanctity of the family, which protect it from public scrutiny, serve to permit the abuses of women by men to whom they are tied by family relationships.

Feminists understand domestic violence as a logical outgrowth of the imbalance of power between men and women coupled with beliefs in the impropriety of public intervention in "private matters." Some scholars point to the family as a site where many forms of violence occur within a privatized hierarchical structure that gives some family members the authority to wield power over others (Pagelow 1989). In order to take a strong stance against domestic violence, "wife abuse must be judged so morally intolerable as to override usual preferences for family privacy" (Loseke 1992).

Others see natural selection in the structure of family relations. They believe that anatomical and physiological differences between men and women create divergent reproductive strategies (see the discussion of sociobiological causes for rape in section 2) that lead females to prefer males of higher social status. This disparity in social status contributes to male social dominance and female victimization (Burgess and Draper 1989). Those who argue against this perspective point out that a natural science paradigm cannot adequately explain "a human context laden phenomenon such as violence" (Hoff 1990).

Psychopathological models focus on individual characteristics as the cause of domestic violence. Some psychopathological explanations focus on the psychology of the offender, while others find that violence against women stems from the psychological problems or deficiencies of the victims. These theories view violence in men as a result of dysfunctional communication patterns evidenced by poor anger control and often complicated by stress and drug and alcohol abuse. Many violent men, according to this theory, were themselves abused by their own families. The most dangerous of abusers may be violent to people outside their families as well. Abused women are understood to suffer from dependent or self-defeating personality disorders that encourage violence either through passive hostility, masochism, or low self-esteem. Recently, a great deal of criticism has been leveled at diagnostic labels for battered women. Empirical support for correlating battered women and personality disorders has not been convincing, and many view the behavior of abused women as the result rather than the cause of battering.

Effects of Domestic Violence

Our current understanding of the range of behaviors that comprise domestic violence includes slapping, biting, kicking, punching, throwing objects, confining, denying care (food or medication), abuse of pets and property, sexual abuse, stabbing, shooting, choking, threatening, insulting, and degrading.

Despite the humorous treatment of domestic violence in popular culture (i.e., the ubiquitous wife who threatens her husband with a rolling pin or frying pan), studies continue to find that the results are very serious. According to the National Crime Survey, assaults against spouses accounted for 12 percent of all assaults that caused serious injury. Of assaults that required medical care, 16 percent were caused by spouses. In a study by Lewis Okun (1986) of shelter residents, on average women residents had experienced more than sixty-five assaults per year. Two-thirds of the women had been "extensively beaten up or worse," with injuries including fractures, dislocations, ruptured eardrums, lacerations, and stab and bullet wounds. More than two-thirds of the victims were prevented by their abusers from receiving medical attention for their injuries. A Brazilian study found that serious physical injury occurred in more than 40 percent of reported incidents of domestic violence (Thomas 1994). A study of women in shelters found that half those interviewed had received head injuries, 13 percent had broken bones, and 10 percent had been hospitalized. More than 40 percent of these women had been abused with weapons, and more than two-thirds had their lives threatened verbally (Gondolf and Fisher 1988). In fact, the killing of one spouse by the other accounts for approximately 25 percent of homicides in the United States, about 50 percent in Canada, and 66 percent in Denmark (Straus 1991b). Another study found that unmarried couples have experienced a rise in murder rates while there has been a decrease in lethal violence between married couples (Browne and Williams 1993). Women are most at risk to kill or be killed when they attempt to report the abuse or leave an abusive relationship (Browne 1987). Others have found that battering may increase during pregnancy (Gelles 1975), thus contributing to the incidence of low-birth-weight infants (U.S. Senate Committee on the Judiciary 1990) and birth defects (Chiles 1988).

Even for those who are able to seek medical attention, a positive outcome is not assured. Doctors and nurses in the emergency room often fail to address clear symptoms of abuse (Warshaw 1989; Stark and Flitcraft 1982), treating the wounds without addressing the victimization. Even psychiatric emergency room personnel have been found to "underinvestigate victimization [and] minimize its importance" (Gondolf 1990, 175).

"Learned helplessness," a term first used by psychologist Lenore Walker, describes the result of women's becoming psychologically conditioned to the experience of abuse over a period of time. Walker (1993) asserts that women in battering relationships learn that there is nothing they can do to stop the violence, so they fail to take action to help themselves. This theory also explains why some battered women lash out, even killing their abusers after years of seemingly tolerating the violence. Because such women see no way to end the violence, when they finally react, it is out of a sense of utter desperation. Critics of this theory point out that it does not acknowledge the many strategies women use to attempt to escape or end abusive relationships, and the woefully inadequate responses of systems of assistance.

Contributions to This Section

The selections that follow address historical, societal, and personal aspects of domestic violence. Read together, these works provide a foundation for comprehending the contemporary intransigence of domestic violence and facilitate a wider understanding of the problem.

In his previously unpublished essay "Nothing New under the Sun: Spouse Abuse in Colonial America," Larry D. Eldridge searches the historical record to ascertain what has remained constant and what has changed in the behavior of abusive spouses and the official response to that behavior. The author makes apparent the connection between the early American effort to reconcile the family and current judicial policy.

In "Violence against Women," R. Emerson Dobash and Russell P. Dobash present an overview of current social conditions and their effect on the incidence of and solutions to domestic violence. This excerpt from their book *Women, Violence and Social Change* includes testimony from women around the world on the nature of domestic violence, the range of injuries experienced, the effect on women's physical and emotional state, and the sources of conflict that preceded the violence. The authors provide a cautionary vision: without dramatic and fundamental changes in gender relations, we will continue to experience a legacy of violence remarkably unchanged over hundreds of years.

bell hooks problematizes the term "battered woman" in "Violence in Intimate Relationships: A Feminist Perspective." In hooks's view, the term emphasizes an extreme aspect of male violence against women and thus eclipses the mild physical abuse that is normalized in intimate relationships. The term "battered woman" implies an ongoing dynamic of abuse that may not apply to the less severe and isolated incidents many women experience, and may be rejected by women thus labeled.

The state of knowledge about domestic violence in same-sex relationships is the subject of Claire M. Renzetti's new essay "Violence in Lesbian and Gay Relationships." Renzetti points out the difficulties in garnering attention for a topic that has been marginalized and trivialized. In her own research, the author found parallels as well as significant differences between heterosexual and homosexual victims of battering. Most significantly, a context of misogyny and heterosexism contributes to our lack of knowledge about the true prevalence of abuse in lesbian and gay relationships: as long as homophobia prevents many lesbians and gay men from revealing their sexual identities, it will be difficult to develop empirical data.

Terri Whittaker's "Violence, Gender, and Elder Abuse: Toward a Feminist Analysis and Practice" addresses the abuse of elderly women by elderly men. Whittaker finds that the current orthodoxy, in which overgeneralized explanations of elder abuse contribute to victim blaming, masks the gendered nature of most elder abuse. Researchers further obscure the central role of gender through an overriding concern with family preservation and a tendency to shift the focus of research away from primarily female victims to perpetrators and interpersonal dynamics without acknowledging gender.

Suggestions for Further Reading

Cynthia Gillespie, *Justifiable Homicide: Battered Women, Self-Defense, and the Law* (Columbus: Ohio State University Press, 1989).

Dee Graham with Edna Rawlings and Roberta Rigsby, *Loving to Survive: Sexual Terror, Men's Violence, and Women's Lives* (New York: New York University Press, 1994).

Marsali Hansen and Michèle Harway (eds.), *Battering and Family Therapy: A Feminist Perspective* (Newbury Park, CA: Sage, 1993).

Ann Jones, *Next Time She'll Be Dead: Battering and How to Stop It* (Boston: Beacon Press, 1994).

Barrie Levy (ed.), *Dating Violence: Young Women in Danger* (Seattle: Seal Press, 1991).

Ann Petry, "Like a Winding Sheet," in Charles L. James (ed.), *From the Roots: Short Stories by Black Americans* (New York: Dodd, Mead, 1970).

Elizabeth Pleck, *Domestic Tyranny: The Making of American Social Policy against Family Violence from Colonial Times to the Present* (New York: Oxford University Press, 1987).

To Judge Faolain, Dead Long Enough: A Summons

LINDA McCARRISTON

Your Honor, when my mother stood
before you, with her routine
domestic plea, after weeks
of waiting for speech to return
to her body, with her homemade
forties hairdo, her face purple still
under pancake, her jaw off just a little,
her *holy of holies* healing,
her breasts wrung, her heart
the bursting heart of someone
snagged among rocks deep
in a sharkpool—no, not "someone,"

but a woman there, snagged
with her babies, *by* them,
in one of hope's pedestrian
brutal turns—when, in the tones
of parlors overlooking the harbor,
you admonished that, for the sake
of the family, the wife
must take the husband back to her bed,
what you willed not to see before you
was a woman risen clean to the surface,
a woman who, with one arm flailing,
held up with the other her actual

burdens of flesh. When you clamped
to her leg the chain of *justice,*

you ferried us back down to *the law,*
the black ice eye, the maw, the mako
that circles the kitchen table nightly.
What did you make of the words
she told you, not to have heard her,
not to have seen her there? Almost-
forgiveable ignorance, you were not
the fist, the boot, or the blade,
but the jaded, corrective ear and eye
at the limits of her world. Now

He took part in the blade / boot / fist.

I will you to see her as she was, to ride
your own words back into light: I call
your spirit home again, divesting you
of robe and bench, the fine white hand
and half-lit Irish eye. Tonight, put on
a body in the trailer down the road
where your father, when he can't
get it up, makes love to your mother
with a rifle. Let your name be
Eva-Mary. Let your hour of birth
be dawn. Let your life be long
and common, and your flesh endure.

16

Nothing New under the Sun: Spouse Abuse in Colonial America

LARRY D. ELDRIDGE

As public awareness of domestic violence grows, and with it concern and the search for solutions, historical perspective on the problem becomes increasingly important. Historical perspective helps us distinguish that which is endemic from that which is peculiar to the sociopolitical context of our time. By revealing persistent elements, it can also reduce our frustration with current authorities' apparent inability to effectively address the problem. Moreover, it helps us identify those areas where improvement has been made and helps us focus on how that happened over time, so that we can more profitably pursue solutions. The first step in that process is to understand spouse abuse in the past, so we can recognize how it has changed since. That is the primary focus of this chapter. Here I explore spouse abuse in seventeenth-century America, considering in turn the nature of the offense, its causes, and the responses of victims and authorities.

Spouse abuse took myriad forms in the seventeenth-century colonies, as it does now. My primary concern here is with physical violence, although desertion, neglect, and verbal abuse deserve some attention because of the essential context they provide. Most who endured blows did so within a milieu of domestic suffering. Neglect and desertion constituted especially important forms of abuse on the Atlantic frontier of the seventeenth century, for women there had far fewer avenues of redress and support than they do today.

Sometimes "abuse" involved simple neglect in one form or another. In 1673 Massachusetts officials ordered James Harris to post a £5 bond and find two sureties for his future good behavior, and in addition ordered that he either be whipped with "ten stripes" or pay a fine of £1 for "neglecting and refusing to provide for" his wife and children. Sometimes neglect was combined with freeloading. In 1683, Sarah Harris petitioned Maryland authorities a second time for help. She complained because her husband remained away from home most of the year, returning only in "the dead of winter, and then comes to your petitioner and stays until he hath eaten up all your petitioner's and children's maintenance which she all the year provides for the keeping of them." Instead of providing for her, Sarah told authorities, her husband "abuses her and her children." The previous order that he provide maintenance for her and her five children had no effect. Now Sarah would be happy enough to do this herself if officials would just force Thomas "not to trouble or molest her." The Maryland Council ordered that she be helped "with all convenient speed."[1]

Sometimes men deserted their wives entirely. The cases of Ann Stewart and Sarah Winslow well illustrate the horrors such a situation could produce. In 1692, Ann Stewart petitioned North Carolina authorities for help. When she married John Stewart, she explained, she brought into the marriage "a considerable estate." Yet he had "squandered and made away all the estate so that she is altogether without a maintenance but what she is assisted with by her children." Along the way, she lost one of her legs, and had been left "a criple." But that was not the worst of it. Her husband had not only squandered her estate, but had run up debts as well. In her miserable condition, and only with the help of her children, Ann had been scraping out a subsistence. Now her husband's creditors were trying to "lay claim to it for payment of their debts." She begged the court to "please provide to the contrary" and save her. What the judges did is not recorded.[2]

Sarah Winslow's case was even more tragic. In New Hampshire during the winter of 1683–84, her home caught fire and she was badly burned. According to witnesses, Sarah "laid in a very sad condition for twenty days, her skin being as hard as pork, corruption being under, so that it stank. There was no enduring the scent." She lost all the fingers from one hand, "and the hand like to be cut off," and the other was "shrank up by the burn." Sarah had "not one farthing to support her." Her own words are preserved in her petition to the court for "clemency and relief." She was "under great affliction," Sarah told the court, "by an accident which happened unto me this last winter past, being almost burned to death by fire, and now very ill by means of sickness, and my former wounds breaking out, and a cancer in my breast, which I fear will be my death." She was "very poor," she added, "having nothing wherewith to sustain myself, my husband being gone I know not where."[3]

Verbal abuse of spouses, if generally less endangering than neglect or desertion, was common in the early colonies. Bay Colony judges tried Henry Flood in January 1673/74 for abusing his wife "in ill words calling her whore and cursing her." Flood had to post a £12 bond to be of good behavior until the next county court. In 1634 Evarardus Bogardus, a New Netherland minister, was criticized for verbal abuse. "Scarcely a person in the entire land have you spared," an official noted, "not even your own wife." Sometimes words went beyond ridicule and became directly threatening. Hubertus Mattown appeared before a Maine court in 1681 for saying he would poison his wife. In 1686, the same court sentenced Francis Herlow to spend an hour in the stocks on a cold January morning "for swearing he would cut his wife's throat." In 1679, Roger Michaels's wife complained to a Virginia magistrate "that her husband had threatened to maim and kill her." He was jailed until he posted a bond to keep the peace.[4]

Spouse abuse thus took a variety of forms, and each of them was important. But what concerns us most here is physical abuse. Women sometimes came before the colonial courts for domestic violence. Mary Latham "did frequently abuse her husband [an old man]," John Winthrop recounted in 1644, "setting a knife to his breast and threatening to kill him, calling him an old rogue and cuckold." Massachusetts authorities eventually executed her for adultery. In 1693/94, New Jersey officials worked to reconcile Mary and Thomas Peachee. She "abused and scandalized" her husband, who in turn put her out of the house. In 1680, according to Griffin Jones, Robert Lawrence's "wife call[ed] her husband a bald-pated old rogue" and "struck him with her fist." He fled to Jones's house and remained there "nearly a week because . . . he was afraid to go home." Sometimes such abuse extended even to death. In 1692, for example, Abigale Kemble committed "a horid murder upon the body of one Richard Kemble," her Maryland husband. She then fled to Virginia with William Luffman. The governor of Maryland sent a formal request that the two be returned for trial. The Virginia Council agreed, so long as security was first provided for the payment of all debts the two had run up in Princess Anne County.[5]

Though women sometimes physically abused their husbands, much more often it was the other way around. Catrina Matthisen complained to New York authorities in 1667/ 68 that "she is no longer able to keep house with her husband on account of his greatly abusing her every day by pushing and beating and chasing her and her children out of the house, and further by threats to kill her." In 1673, Henry Bodg appeared before Maine's York County Court "for beating his wife grossly." Though Elizabeth had made the complaint, she failed to appear at the trial. Henry conceded only "that accidentally he cut his wife's hand," insisting that he "intended no further hurt to her." The judges dismissed the case after admonishing him. The Pennsylvania Council imprisoned John Richardson in 1690 pending a full investigation after he beat his wife so badly "that it is much feared he may be her death."[6]

On April 17, 1656, Maryland's Provincial Court heard a very disturbing case. A midwife had come to Francis Brooke's home to help his wife with a difficult birth. The child was born dead, witnesses testified, and "it was all bruises and the blood black in it." The midwife asked Mrs. Brooke "how the child came so bruised," and it came out that in an angry outburst a few weeks before, her husband had grabbed "a pair of tongs and did beat her with the great end." The midwife took the dead child in her arms and confronted Francis Brooke, telling him that even if he "[e]scaped in this world, yet in the world to come he should answer for it before a judge that useth no partiality." We may imagine the scene. The angry midwife. The pitiful child in her arms. The mournful wife recovering from the delivery, still in her bed. The glowering husband. He retorted that his wife "fell out of a peach tree," then turned on her and demanded whether this was not so, "and she said yes." Though Francis Brooke went to trial over the matter, what finally happened to him went unrecorded.[7]

Sometimes men beat their wives severely enough to kill them but escaped the full force of the law. Such was the case of John Richardson, who in 1669 went on trial in Maryland for murdering his wife, Mary. According to the presentment, John severely beat Mary "with a certain tobacco stick to the value of one penny sterling," whereupon she "received a mortal blow." The jury decided that John did not really intend to kill Mary, so they acquitted him of murder, declaring the death to have been accidental— "by misadventure." In discussing this case, Raphael Semmes observed what we might: "It is difficult to understand how beating a woman to death with a tobacco stick can be called homicide 'by misadventure.' "[8]

The causes of abuse, as they can be gleaned from the colonial records, were varied. Sometimes men were simply violent and abusive. Thomas Russell is a good example. In 1681, his wife, Mary, complained to Massachusetts authorities after "he came home late, beat her unmercifully, kicked her about the house and struck her violently upon the head." He had also "threatened to cut her throat or burn her," and Benjamin Parmeter often "had seen her bloody from her husband's abuse." Russell had previously "nearly strangled" his own daughter in a rage one Sabbath night, and beat a neighbor with a cudgel when he tried to intervene. There were other incidents as well. Six neighbors—all women—testified that Thomas Russell "had frightened them many times in the night, threatening them with a gun or pistols like a mad man." He once "threw Remember White into a ditch, holding a great stake over her, and saying he would knock her down if she meddled with his dog." She told him that he was "a murderous wretch," adding, "thou dost not care if thou killest a man." Russell replied that he "would as soon kill a man as let him alone and he might kill her sometime." Another witness noted that Russell "frequently threatened that whoever had Thomas Cauley's land should never enjoy it peaceably, for he would cut down the fence." Because of that, the land could not be sold.[9]

One might expect the wife's provocation to be commonly noted as a mitigating factor in wife abuse cases. In fact, that was uncommon, though it did happen. Mary Neal testified before Massachusetts authorities in July 1674. On the road in front of her house, Neal "saw Jacob Pudeator strike his wife three or four times, throw her down and kick her." The judges punished Jacob "for striking and kicking his wife," but later "moderated" the sentence, observing that "the woman is of great provocation." Isabell, Jacob's wife, indeed had a history of trouble. She was repeatedly punished for drunkenness and abusive words. In 1669/70, she was fined "for drunkness, railing, and base words," for example, and again for the same in 1671. In 1676, she endured a public whipping of fifteen lashes "for drinking, unruly carriage, and abusing her husband and his goods."[10]

Jealousy related to sexual matters, from flirtation to adultery, often lay behind spouse abuse. On August 26, 1638, New Netherland authorities considered the complaint of Nanne Beecher against her husband after he beat her. What became of the case is unclear, but what brought it on is not. According to testimony, the two had attended a party, making "merry at the house of Claes Cornelisen." Nanne, "notwithstanding her husband's presence, fumbled at the front of the breetches of most all of those who were present." When her husband "requested her to go home with him," Nanne refused and "continued to act as before."[11]

A revealing incident occurred between Stephen and Abigale Willy in 1683 at their New Hampshire home. In the middle of the night, Stephen spread an alarm to look for a "rogue" he had seen leaving his house half dressed. Neighbors gathered and helped him search. They found no man, and though Stephen made his wife get out of bed and stand aside as they looked for the clothes left behind, none were found. Enraged, he "took up a chair and struck at his wife, and swore he would kill her." He bloodied Abigale's face before the others could stop him, then ran to the kitchen for a knife swearing "that he would stab his wife, if there were no more women alive." He was searching for the knife when the constable finally arrived and arrested him. Stephen admitted "that if his wife did take any notice of any man by laughing or talking, that he did believe that his wife loved other men better than she did himself." Abigale confirmed this. No one "dare countenance in any way of natural friendship" with her, she said, "but I must become the suffering subject of his insatiable jealousy." Stephen Willy had beaten his wife repeatedly over a period of years, even attacking her once with an axe and a hoe. The records do not preserve how authorities ultimately dealt with this tortured and torturing man.[12]

Sometimes couples just seemed unable to get along, and their violence and quarreling proved an irritant to their neighbors. One night "about Easter" in 1659, Clove Mace fled to his neighbors after his wife ran him out of their Maryland home. Bleeding, Clove told the neighbors that his wife and Robin Coop, apparently a boarder, "were both upon him." John Shancks and John Gee went to the Mace home in hopes of sorting out the trouble and restoring peace. After Shancks and Gee "knocked at the door asking how they did," Mrs. Mace replied that her husband "had abused Robin and her." When the two men asked her to "come to her husband" that night, she refused, but later agreed to come the next morning and "be friends with her husband." The couple had a history of troubles. Later testimony revealed, for example, that once "her husband threatened to beat her," to which she had answered "if he did she would cut his throat or poison him or make him away." If she could not do it herself, she added, she would get John Hart to help her "be revenged on him and beat him." At various times, one witness testified, "she drank healths to the confusion of her husband, and said she would shoe her horse round." The St. Clement's Manor court, which heard the initial testimony, "ordered that this business be transferred to the next county court according to law." What became of the matter is uncertain.[13]

Abuse often grew out of ordinary circumstances as varied as colonial life. Mary Pray, for example, lost her temper with her husband, Richard, on a winter evening in 1649. According to the record, he took "a letter she had gotten written for England." Later, unable to contain her anger, "at supper [she] threw a trencher at him and also a bone." Bay Colony authorities released her with an admonition.[14]

In-laws sometimes caused strife. When Elizabeth and Sylvester Stover appeared before Maine authorities in 1660 for the third time in five years, York County judges identified at least part of the problem. Elizabeth's mother lived with the couple, and stirred trouble between them. If Sylvester "shall make any just cause of complaint appear against Mis Norton, his mother in law, occasioning future differences between him and his wife," the judges ordered, "the said Mis Norton is then to be removed from the Stover's house, or sent to prison, if other means cannot prevent her therein."[15]

Among the most common causes of abuse was drunkenness. In 1671, Thomas Prince was fined an unspecified amount in Essex County, Massachusetts, "for being disguised with drink, it being the second or third conviction," and "was bound to appear at the next Ipswich court for abusing his wife." Prince appeared again for abusing Margaret in 1675. Mary Hadley and William Vincen testified to Prince's behavior. Mary "saw Thomas Prince so drunk at his house that he could not stand upon his legs, but abused his wife." Vincen added that "Thomas Prince had drunk too much these many years," and noted that on one recent occasion Thomas "came home drunk at midnight and used words not fit to be spoken." Sometimes drinking combined with other problems to bring on abuse. Thomas Smith, for example, spent some two years confined in Boston for "drunkness and madness" and "putting his wife and children in fear of their lives."[16]

Drunken abuse was not an exclusively male province. Mary Woods found herself in court after she "came home drunk one time . . . from a wedding and beat her husband and turned him out of doors." Her husband went to John Gatchell's and asked to stay the night, "for the devil was at home." Essex County authorities gave Hana Mason a choice of a fine or a whipping in 1678 for her drunkenness and abusive words, and for "offering to strike her husband," John, a brickmaker. In June 1670, she was fined "for being drunk, it being the second or third offense." In 1671, she appeared "for being drunk a third time." In 1674, the court noted a summons for her to appear for drunkenness. And on it went.[17]

The kinds and causes of spousal abuse were as varied in the seventeenth century as they are today. So were the responses of the victims and the courts. Women sought to protect themselves from abusive husbands in diverse ways. Some simply ran away to friends or family, or even to live alone, though that was rarely a realistic option on the early colonial frontier. In August 1675, after Margriet Phillipsen and her husband fought, she fled to her parents' home. Hoping for reconciliation, he sent a minister to persuade her "if possible by kind words to go with him to New York." In 1681, Anneke Schaets refused to go home to her husband, saying "she would prefer to be dead or imprisoned for life rather than live with him." When New York officials pressed her on the matter, it came out "that he beat and struck her, used abusive language to her, etc."[18]

Other women sought separations and divorces. There were many variations of this, but for our present purposes they can be treated as a group. Separations were typically for an indeterminate time, and the husband usually had to support his wife. That was partly out of humanity, but also to keep the woman from becoming a financial burden on the community. On November 28, 1676, Mary Jones petitioned the Maryland Provincial court, making the financial burden element explicit. Mary asked the court "to commiserate her deplorable condition" and "compel and order her husband to take such course and care for the maintenance of her and her child as the Court shall think meet." "Otherwise," Mary told the court, "she and her child must inevitably be chargeable to the county for their maintenance." The court granted the request, and made a specific list of what he had to provide her, including "yearly one winter suit, one summer suit, three pairs of shoes and stockings, three barrels of corn, three shifts of dowlas or lockerum and head linen convenient, and 300 pounds of meat." The court further ordered "that the child have the same allowance."[19]

Ann Middleton's case well illustrates the importance of such financial concerns to colonial authorities, even at the end of the century. In 1699, she petitioned the Westmorland County court in Virginia, "sufficiently showing to the court her deplorable condition." She "was reduced to extreme indigence and poverty," she explained, "by means of her said husband having spent and embezzled most part of his estate." Worse, that very estate "came to him by his intermarrying with her," and after he squandered it, "he had left her and absented himself and kept company with a base strumpet." The judges ordered Richard Middleton jailed until he posted sureties of 4,000 pounds of tobacco "to maintain his wife, and," the court added, "so protect the parish from her charge."[20]

Sometimes women sought divorces, not merely separations. In May 1675, Elizabeth Rogers left her abusive husband, John, and went to live with her father. She petitioned Connecticut authorities, seeking a divorce, but they equivocated. At last, on October 12, 1676, the General Court granted the petition as a matter of "compassion to the woman under so great distress and hazard." At this same time, 1675/76, Sarah Gibson petitioned Virginia authorities for permission to leave her husband, Simon, after he "did in a most violent manner beat and maim her." Several witnesses testified that she was "bruised and wounded in a very lamentable condition." The General Court allowed her to go to England as "she shall think best for her safety."[21]

Rather than leaving, legally or otherwise, some women remained at home and defended themselves as best they could, while others endured anguished lives of abuse without ever appearing in the court records. Some indication of that reality comes from the occasional case that did come to court, but only after the woman had quietly suffered years of torment. Rachel Davenport is a good illustration. In 1671 she finally petitioned New York authorities for relief, explaining "that for many years together she hath undergone a bitter and wearisome life by reason of her husband's inhumane usage, blows, and cruel carriages towards her."[22]

When women did seek the help of authorities, the most common official response was an attempt to reconcile the couple. That was at least partly due to the realities of life on the colonial frontier. Women left on their own had few options, especially if they had children to support. The Maryland case of Annicak Hanson and his wife helps make the point. He died unexpectedly in 1655, leaving her with "four small children" and pregnant, yet "having no estate left for maintenance of herself and children." In what must have been a heartrending decision, she gave up her children to other families who could provide for them.[23]

Authorities everywhere worked to get couples back together, but perhaps nowhere was this more common than in New York. The Claas case is a good illustration. In March of 1664/65, Dirk Claas found himself before a New York court. He "has driven away his wife," the records note, so that she "suffers great want and lies on straw without bed or bedding." The judges worked to get the couple back together, but ordered that if this could not be done, he would have to provide her a proper maintenance. Sometimes providing independent support for a separated wife proved too much for the husband. William Hallet and his wife received a "deed of separation" from New York authorities in 1674. He later requested that the deed "may be annulled" because he could not afford the £15 annual sum he had to pay her. Officials ordered that arbitrators try to reconcile the couple. After three assigned referees failed to reconcile Baefie Pieterse and her husband in 1679, Albany judges granted the couple "a separation of bed and board" and evenly divided the couple's possessions between them. "It is not possible" the court concluded, "for her to live any longer with him." [24]

Beyond reconciliation lay the matter of punishment of abusive husbands. Sometimes authorities did little to punish wife beaters. In 1668, for example, the Maine Court of Associates tried John Barret after he "offered several abuses to his wife by kicking her, etc." But, "he acknowledging his fault and promising amendment, this court thinketh meet to pass by and remit his fault for the time past." Interestingly, the words "promising amendment" were striken out in the original. Paying court costs, Barret escaped punishment. [25]

Many cases record no punishment, but that does not mean none was administered. Court records from the period often leave such information unrecorded. Even so, most reported spouse abusers did face some sort of punishment. Among those clearly punished, some endured stern admonishments from the bench. Susanna Bradt appeared before New York authorities in 1680/81 formally complaining "about her husband's godless life in drinking, clinking, beating and throwing, etc., so that she can no longer stand it." The court admonished him for "ill treatment of his wife," then released him "upon promise of improvement." In 1679, Elizabeth Waters complained to Bay Colony authorities about her husband's neglect and abuse. The court admonished William Waters "for his cruelty and unkindness to his wife," and ordered him to "forthwith provide suitable meat, drink, and apparrell." George Barlow and his wife came before Plymouth authorities in 1662 for fighting and "most ungodly living in contention one with the other." The court admonished them "to live otherwise." Ann Wampus appeared before the Suffolk County Court in Massachusetts "to answer for abusing and striking of her husband" in 1673. "The court upon giving her an admonition," the record tersely notes, "ordered her to pay fees of court and so discharged her." [26]

Beyond simple admonishments, colonial courts employed a variety of penalties against spouse abusers. Some offenders were fined. In 1665, New York authorities fined Jan Jansen van Amersfoort 200 guilders for cruelly beating his wife when she "was in the last stage of pregnancy." Connecticut's Particular Court fined John Brooks £2 in 1657/58 "for his inhumane carriage towards his wife." He also had to pay the witnesses against him two shillings a day for their trouble. William Smith paid an unspecified fine in 1672 when Bay Colony judges convicted him of "pushing his wife." New York's Suffolk County court fined Nathaniel Baker the unusually large sum of £20 in 1683 after he "struck or kicked" his wife. In 1663, Plymouth judges fined Ralph Earle £1 "for drawing his wife in an uncivil manner in the snow." Albany officials fined Peter Lassing 100 guilders in 1678/79 after he attacked his wife with a sword in their home and left her "bleeding from the nose and mouth." [27]

Women were not often fined because they rarely enjoyed the independent income to pay an amercement. Still, some women were fined, while others were allowed to choose between amercements and other penalties. Elizabeth Batson, for example, confessed to abusing her husband, Stephen, and falsely accusing him of incest in 1660. She could take twenty lashes, the Maine judges informed her, or she could pay a £5 fine and make two public acknowledgments of her guilt—one in court and the other in a town meeting. Shunning the post, she made the acknowledgments and paid the fine.[28]

Bonds and sureties to guarantee appropriate behavior were a common colonial penalty in spouse abuse cases, as in others. A bond was a pledge to forfeit a given sum if one misbehaved in the future. Sureties were others who pledged to forfeit bonds if an offender did not behave. Two Massachusetts cases offer good illustrations. In 1647, Richard Bidgood had already forfeited one bond, so authorities placed him under another—this one, of £20, to ensure his good behavior "to all men and women, but especially to his wife." Six months later, Bidgood was "discharged of his bond for good behavior," having acted properly in the intervening time. Such discharges upon good behavior were typical in all sorts of cases. When charged with beating his wife in 1680, Massachusetts authorities ordered William Fanning to find sureties willing to guarantee his good behavior pending trial, but he could not. The judges were going to keep him in jail, but "protesting that his hay would be lost if he were detained and his family deeply suffer, his own bond was accepted." Fanning "offered as security one-half of four acres of Indian corn," as well as a horse and five pigs.[29]

Colonial offenders also faced corporal punishment, something we have since abandoned. Public lashings were a staple, and women as well as men "kissed the whipping post," to use a seventeenth-century expression. Hugh Browne's wife was "severely whipped" in 1641 after Bay Colony authorities took a dim view of her "breaking [her husband's] head and threatening that she would kill him so that he is ever weary of his life." Richard Cowley stood convicted of "beating his wife, threatening of her, and other misdemeanors" in Suffolk County, Massachusetts, in 1677. The court ordered him to "be severely whipped with 20 stripes."[30]

Humiliation penalties, especially stocks and pillory, were also common. Thomas Wilson appeared before the Virginia General Court in 1626 and confessed that he "hath abused himself in drink and beaten his wife." He was placed in the stocks and fined £1. In 1671 Richard Marshall appeared before Plymouth judges "for abusing his wife by kicking her from a stool into the fire." The judges ordered him "to sit in the stocks during the pleasure of the court, which was accordingly done."[31]

Occasionally offenders were subjected to unusual punishments. Sometimes they were men. "Indian Sam" appeared before a Plymouth court in 1687 "for abusing and endeavoring to murder his squaw." He was whipped twenty lashes, then sold into slavery (probably to the West Indies). More often, offenders facing unusual penalties were women. In 1626 Margaret Jones railed at her husband and called him a "base rascal." Virginia authorities ordered her to be tied to the back of a boat and dragged up and down the James River. "For frequent laying hands on her husband to the danger of his life," in 1636/37 Massachusetts authorities ordered Dorothy Talbie "to be chained to a post," releasing her only briefly to attend church, then returning her, "until she repents." Maine officials made Sarah Morgan stand "with a gag in her mouth half an hour at Kittery at a public town meeting" for "striking her husband" in 1671. A paper with her offense written on it was placed "upon her forehead."[32]

Whatever punishment authorities ordered, they often remitted the order upon expectation of better behavior in the future, usually following a defendant's show of submission. Sometimes judges reduced an offender's penalty at the victim's request. Frances Hilton appeared before Maine authorities in 1655 "for railing at her husband and saying he went with John his bastard to his three half-penny whores and that he carried a cloak of profession for knavery." The court ordered her whipped twenty lashes, but upon her husband's request the sentence was remitted. Henry Renolds obtained the same clemency in 1648. A Bay Colony court ordered Renolds "to sit in the stocks one-half hour next lecture day, if the weather be seasonable, for beating his wife." But "at her request [he] was only fined."[33]

Offenders commonly suffered a combination of punishments when they came before the colonial courts. William Carpenter and James Hermon are good examples. In 1671, Massachusetts officials jailed Carpenter and ordered him "whipped with 15 stripes" for beating his wife. They also made him post a bond of £10 sterling. In 1669, a Maine court convicted James Hermon of "beating and abusing his wife" and ordered him to receive "ten stripes on the naked back and to stand bound in a sum of £20 for his good behavior until the next county court." Hermon had a history of hurting women. Two years later, he so scandalously abused his own daughter, Jane, that a Court of Associates took the unusual step of forcibly removing her from the home and apprenticing her as "a servant unto James Gibbines for the full term of eight years."[34]

There is much that is familiar in the nature of spousal abuse, its causes, and the responses of victims and authorities to it in colonial America. True enough, some forms of punishment sound strange to modern ears. Gags in mouths, public lashings, pillory and the like belong to a bygone age. Yet, then as now, verbal abuse, neglect, and desertion were mixed with physical attacks. Then as now, men were usually the offenders. Then as now, drunkenness and abusive personalities loomed large in the picture. Then as now, authorities worked to reconcile couples and punished wife beaters unevenly.

Still, in at least one area, things are different now. Women faced with violent husbands then had precious few options. If they were fortunate enough to have sympathetic friends or family nearby, they might find refuge there. If not, they could seek the court's help, but that was an uncertain course, and one likely to further enrage the husband exposed to public scrutiny. Today, as society and the courts become increasingly concerned with the problem of domestic violence, shelters are opening up and judges are intervening more actively. Moreover, expanding educational and economic opportunity in this century increasingly means that women today can more readily leave abusive relationships and make independent lives for themselves. This is no easy business to be sure, especially with children to support. But it constitutes much more protection and freedom than were available to women before, many of whom were faced, at best, with the daunting choice between married lives of pain and despair or single lives in abject poverty. In many ways an historical perspective on domestic violence pushes us to ponder the words of Ecclesiastes: "there is nothing new under the sun." But in women's expanding options, at least, we may see a glimmer of hope.

NOTES

1. For James Harris, see Colonial Society of Massachusetts, "Records of the Suffolk County Court, 1671–1680," *Collections* XXIX, XXX, 2 vols. (Boston, 1933), 1:307 (1673) (hereinafter cited as MA/SCC). For Sarah Harris, see William Hand Browne et al., eds., *Archives of Maryland,* 72 vols. to date (Baltimore: Maryland Historical Society, 1884–), 17:192 (1683) (hereinafter cited as MD/A).

2. For Ann Stewart, see Mattie Erma Edwards Parker, William S. Price, and Robert Cain, eds., *North Carolina Higher-Court Records, 1670–1696*, 5 vols. (Raleigh, N.C.: State Department of Archives and History, 1963–81), 1:383–84 (1692) (hereinafter cited as NC/HC). For similar North Carolina cases, see NC/HC-1:370 (1686), 371 (1687), and NC/HC-2:273–331 (1698–99).

3. For Sarah Winslow, see Nathaniel Bouton, ed., "Province Records and Court Papers from 1680 to 1692," New Hampshire Historical Society, *Collections*, vol. 8 (Concord: New Hampshire Historical Society, 1866), 207 (1684) (hereinafter cited as NH/CHS). For other examples, see H. R. McIlwaine, ed., *Minutes of the Council and General Court of Colonial Virginia, 1622–1632, 1670–1676, with Notes and Excerpts from Original Council and General Court Records, Into 1683, Now Lost* (Richmond: Virginia State Library, 1924), 113 (hereinafter cited as VA/GCR); Edmund B. O'Callaghan and Berthold Fernow, eds., *Documents Relative to the Colonial History of the State of New York; Procured in Holland, England and France by John Romeyn Brodhead, Esq., Agent*, 15 vols. (Albany, 1853–71), 4:719, 760, 841 (1700) (hereinafter cited as NY/DRCH); George F. Dow, ed., *Records and Files of the Quarterly Courts of Essex County, Massachusetts, 1636–1683*, 7 vols. (Salem, Mass.: Essex Institute, 1911–21), 1:59 (1641) (hereinafter cited as MA/ECC), *Minutes of the Provincial Council of Pennsylvania*, 3 vols. (Harrisburg, 1838–40), 1:442 (1694) (hereinafter cited as PA/PCR), PA/PCR-1:536 (1698); and Susie M. Ames, ed., *County Court Records of Accomack-Northampton, Virginia, 1632–1640* (Washington, D.C.: American Historical Association, 1954; reprint, Millwood, N.Y.: Kraus Reprint Company, 1975), 136 (1638/39). In that last case a Virginia man abandoned his pregnant wife in the winter of 1638/39. Before doing so, he sold all of her belongings and spent the money, leaving her "destitute of all manner of means." Not all desertion cases involved men abandoning their wives. In March of 1682/83, for example, Lydia Toe deserted her husband and moved in with John Carter. New Jersey authorities ordered the two "whipped on their naked bodies," and sent Lydia home. See H. Clay Reed and George J. Miller, eds., *The Burlington Court Book: A Record of Quaker Jurisprudence in West New Jersey, 1680–1709* (Washington, D.C.: American Historical Association, 1944), 18 (1682/83) (hereinafter cited as NJ/BCB).

4. For Henry Flood, see MA/SCC-1:410, 425 (1673/74). For Everardus Bogardus, see NY/DRCH-14:69 (1634). For Hubertus Mattown, see Charles T. Libby, Neal W. Allen, and Robert E. Moody, eds., *Province and Court Records of Maine, 1636–1692*, 4 vols. (Portland: Maine Historical Society, 1928–47), 4:110 (1681) (hereinafter cited as ME/PCR). For Francis Herlow, see ME/PCR-4:98, 110 (1697/98). For Roger Michaels, see Philip Alexander Bruce, *Institutional History of Virginia in the Seventeenth Century: An Inquiry into the Religious, Moral, Educational, Legal, Military, and Political Condition of the People, Based on Original and Contemporaneous Records*, 2 vols. (New York: G. P. Putnam's Sons, 1910), 1:480. Secondary sources often note such cases. For other examples, see Lyle Koehler, *A Search for Power: The "Weaker Sex" in Seventeenth-Century New England* (Urbana: University of Illinois Press, 1980), 144–45; Carl Holliday, *Women's Life in Colonial Days* (New York: Ungar, 1960), 289; and Roger Thompson, *Sex in Middlesex: Popular Mores in a Massachusetts County, 1649–1699* (Amherst: University of Massachusetts Press, 1986), 118.

5. For Mary Latham, see James Kendall Hosmer, ed., *[John] Winthrop's Journal: "History of New England," 1630–1649*, 2 vols. (New York: Barnes and Noble, 1946), 2:161–63 (1644) (hereinafter cited as MA/JWJ). For Mary and Thomas Peachee, see NJ/BCB: 163–4 (1693/94). For Robert Lawrence, see MA/ECC-8:102 (1680/81). For similar Massachusetts cases, see MA/SCC-1:116 (1672), 330 (1673). For Abigale Kemble, see H. R. McIlwaine, ed., *Executive Journals of the Council of Colonial Virginia, 1680–1721*, 3 vols. (Richmond: Davis Bottom, Superintendent of Public Printing, 1925–1927), 1:271 (1692).

6. For Catrina Matthisen, see Peter R. Christoph, Kenneth Scott, and Kenn Stryker-Rodda, eds., *New York Historical Manuscripts: Dutch, Kingston Papers*, 2 vols. (Baltimore: Genealogical Publishing Co., under the direction of the Holland Society of New York, 1976), 2:392 (1667/68) (hereinafter cited as NY/KP). For Henry Bodg, see ME/PCR-2:263 (1673). For John Richardson, see PA/PCR-1:337 (1690).

7. See MD/A-10:464–5, 466 (1656). For a similar case, see MA/ECC-2:36–38 (1657).

8. For John Richardson, see MD/A-57:599–600 (1669); and MD/A-51:346–48. For the Semmes quotation, see Raphael Semmes, *Crime and Punishment in Early Maryland* (Baltimore: Johns Hopkins University Press, 1938; reprint, Montclair, N.J.: Patterson Smith, 1970), 135. For some examples of attempted spousal murder, see David Thomas Konig, ed., *Plymouth [County] Court Records, 1686–1859*, 3 vols. to date (Wilmington, Del.: Michael Glazier, 1978), 1:194 (1687/ 88) (hereinafter cited as MA/PlyCo); Nathaniel B. Shurtleff, ed., *Records of the Governor and Company of Massachusetts Bay in New England, 1628–1686*, 5 vols. in 6 (Boston: William White, Printer to the Commonwealth, 1853–54), 1:334; and John Noble and John F. Cronin, eds., *Records of the Court of Assistants of the Colony of Massachusetts Bay, 1630–1692*, 3 vols. (Boston: County of Suffolk, 1901–28), 2:108 (1641). Lyle Koehler relates the case of Elaezer Parker, a Cambridge, Massachusetts, man. He got drunk and tried to stab his wife, but she was narrowly preserved by "a book in her bosom." See Koehler, *A Search for Power*, 139.

9. MA/ECC-8:104–05 (1681). Russell was regularly involved in violent incidents, and that same year was struck so hard "that his hearing had not come back as it was before." See MA/ ECC-8:65 (1681).

10. For Jacob Pudeator, see MA/ECC-5:377 (1674). For some of Isabelle's troubles, see MA/ ECC-4:214 (1670), 410 (1671), 6:193 (1676). For a similar example, see the Miller prosecution at ME/PCR-2:460 (1672). In 1672, Richard Miller appeared before Maine authorities "for several abusive speeches and behaviors towards his wife," Grace. After an investigation the judges admonished Grace, noting that she "hath given too much cause of suspicion of neglect of her family and want of industry therein, with other carriages which may administer jealousies to her husband."

11. NY/KP-1:54–57 (1638).

12. NH/CHS:141, 142–43, 147–48 (1683). For a similar case in Delaware, see Leon de Valinger, Jr., ed., *Court Records of Kent County, Delaware, 1680–1705* (Washington, D.C.: American Historical Association, 1959), 48–49, 69, 78 (1681). There Sarah Bartlet complained that her husband Nicholas "abused her in a gross and inhumane manner." Part of the problem, it seems, was that a servant girl "went out of her bed very cold" to see Bartlet, and "came after a while to bed again all in a sweat."

13. MD/A-53:628 (1659).

14. MA/ECC-1:184 (1649/50).

15. ME/PCR-2:92 (1660). The editor of these records, writing in 1931, added this commentary: "The perspicacity of the court's psychological analysis and the adequacy of their adoption of means to ends excites admiration in this day of dead-centered courts swarming with lawyers."

16. For Thomas Prince, see MA/ECC-4:441 (1671), 6:116 (1675). For Thomas Smith, see MA/ SCC-1:101–2 (1679).

17. For May Woods, see MA/ECC-4:108 (1668/69). For Hana Mason, see MA/ECC-4:274 (1670), 4:410 (1671), 5:374 (1674), 7:1 (1678).

18. For Margriet Phillipsen, see A. J. F. van Laer, ed., *Court Minutes of Albany, Rensselaerswyck, and Schenectady, 1668–1685*, 3 vols. (Albany: University Press of New York, 1926–1932), 2:9–11 (1675) (hereinafter cited as NY/ARS). For Anneke Schaets, see NY/ARS-2:133, 144–45, 148–51 (1681). In 1659, Mrs. Schotten petitioned New Netherland authorities to depart the colony "in the same wise and manner as Maria Wouters went from here." Schotten wanted to leave her husband behind, and made the request "without his knowledge." See NY/DRCH-2:103–4 (1659).

19. MD/A-66:315 (1676).

20. Manuscript Records of the Westmorland County Court, Virginia (Richmond: Virginia State Archives), June 28, 1699. For another Virginia example, see VA/GCR:520 (1679).

21. For Elizabeth Rogers, see Charles J. Hoadly and J. H. Trumbull, eds., *Public Records of the Colony of Connecticut, 1636–1776*, 15 vols. (Hartford, Conn.: Brown and Parsons, 1850–1890), 2:292 (1676) (hereinafter cited as CT/CR). For Sarah Gibson, see VA/GCR:452, 518 (1675/76). For other examples, see MD/A-15:321–22 (1680); William P. Palmer, ed., *Calendar of Virginia State Papers and Other Manuscripts, 1652–1781, preserved in the Capitol at Richmond* (Rich-

mond: R. F. Walker, Superintendent of Public Printing, 1875), 1:29 (1691); John Russell Bartlett, ed., *Records of the Colony of Rhode Island and Providence Plantations in New England, 1636–1792*, 10 vols. (Providence, R.I.: A. Crawford Greene and Brother, State Printers, 1856–65), 2:251; and Edmund Morgan's discussion of Mary Litchfield's 1684/85 petition on behalf of her abused daughter in *The Puritan Family: Religion and Domestic Relations in Seventeenth-Century New England* (New York: Harper and Row, 1944; revised edition, 1966), 38 n. 33.

22. Berthold Fernow, ed., *The Records of New Amsterdam from 1653 to 1674, anno domini*, 7 vols. (New York: The Knickerbocker Press, 1897), 6:309 (1671) (hereinafter cited as NY/NAR).

23. MD/A-54:28-29 (1655). In 1661, no less than seventeen widows in Jamaica petitioned London for help because of their "deplorable condition." See Noel W. Sainsbury et al., eds., *Calendar of State Papers, Colonial Series, Preserved in the State Paper Department of Her Majesty's Public Record Office* (London: Her Majesty's Stationary Office, 1860–1910), 5:36 (1661).

24. For Dirk Claas, see NY/NAR-5:202 (1664/65). For William Hallet, see NY/DRCH-2:717 (1674). For Baefie Pieterse, see NY/ARS-2:399–400 (1679).

25. ME/PCR-2:403 (1668). Years earlier, Robert Mendam was charged with beating his wife in Maine in 1647, but the prosecution was "lett fall." See ME/PCR-1:119 (1647).

26. For Susanna Bradt, see NY/ARS-3:70 (1680/81). For Elizabeth Waters, see MA/SCC-2:1063 (1679). For George Barlow, see Nathaniel B. Shurtleff and David Pulsifer, eds., *Records of the Colony of New Plymouth in New England, 1620–1692*, 12 vols. (Boston: William White, Printer to the Commonwealth, 1855–61), 4:10 (1662) (hereinafter cited as PLY/CR). For Ann Wampus, see MA/SCC-1:330 (1673).

27. Jan Janson van Amersfoort, see NY/KP-1:250–52 (1665). For John Brooks, see *Records of the Particular Court of Connecticut, 1639–1663*, Connecticut Historical Society *Collections* XXII (1928) (Hartford, 1928), 187 (1657/58). For William Smith, see MA/ECC-5:64 (1672). For Nathaniel Baker, see Edmund B. O'Callaghan, ed., *The Documentary History of New York; Arranged under the Direction of the Hon. Christopher Morgan, Secretary of State*, 4 vols. (Albany: Weed, Parsons and Co., Public Printers, 1849–51), 3:213 (1683). For Ralph Earle, see PLY/CR-4:47 (1663). For Peter Lassing, see NY/ARS-2:381 (1678/79). For other examples, see MA/ECC-1:414 (1656), MA/PlyCo-1:249 (1700/01).

28. ME/PCR-2:368–69 (1660).

29. For Richard Bidgood, see MA/ECC-1:128 (1647), 143 (1648). For William Fanning, see MA/ECC-382 (1680).

30. For Hugh Browne, see MA/ECC-1:25 (1641). For Richard Cowley, see MA/SCC-2:867 (1677). For contemporary use of the term "kissing the post," see VA/GCR:39 (1624).

31. For Thomas Wilson, see VA/GCR:108 (1626). For Richard Marshall, see PLY/CR-5:61 (1671). This was a form of humiliation well known in Europe at the time. After a Frenchman was put in the stocks in Boston in 1644, John Winthrop commented that "in France it is a most ignominious thing to be laid in the stocks." It was "most ignominious" in the English colonies, too. That is why it was used against offenders. See MA/JWJ-2:191–92 (1644).

32. For Indian Sam, see MA/PlyCo-1:194 (1687/88). For Margaret Jones, see VA/GCR:119 (1626). For Dorothy Talbie, see MA/ECC-1:6 (1636/37). For Sarah Morgan, see ME/PCR-2:224 (1671). For other examples of unusual punishments, see MA/ECC-6:387–88 (1677/78) and MA/ECC-5:147 (1672/73).

33. For Frances Hilton, see ME/PCR-2:43 (1655). For Henry Renolds, see MA/ECC-1:158 (1648/49). Sometimes men escaped punishment because their wives withdrew the complaints. For a typical example, see MA/ECC-8:104–5 (1681).

34. For William Carpenter, see MA/SCC-1:88 (1671/72). For James Hermon, see ME/PCR-2:412 (1669), 2:422 (1671).

17

Violence against Women

**R. EMERSON DOBASH AND
RUSSELL P. DOBASH**

For the women who have been physically abused in the home by the men with whom they live, the past two decades have seen both radical change and no change at all. The lives of some have been touched by an ever expanding, worldwide movement to support women who have been battered and to challenge male violence. Some legal and social institutions have begun to respond, while others remain in a nexus of traditional tolerance of male violence and indifference to those who suffer from such violence. This is a time marked by social change and resistance to change, by innovation and reassertion of tradition. Both the new and the old responses are used, challenged and defended by those with differing views about the nature of this problem and how best to confront it. The arena of change and challenge is alive with ideas and activity.

Increasingly, women who have been abused come forward for support in directly challenging the violence or organizing their escape from it. Although relatively few violent men are being confronted with the unacceptability of their violence and their responsibility for its elimination, the numbers are growing. The fact that this occurs at all is due almost solely to the efforts of the battered-women's movement in bringing the issue to public attention and organizing a pragmatic response to assisting women based on a wider philosophy of feminist inspired change. The story of the development of these innovative changes covers individual terror and personal triumph as well as institutional action and reaction. It is a story of one of the important social movements of our time. It is about deeply held cultural beliefs, entrenched patterns of response and the struggle to move away from supporting male violence and towards its rejection. It is a story that is at once personal and institutional, local and international, depressing and inspirational.

In many countries it is now well known that violence in the home is commonplace, that women are its usual victims and men its usual perpetrators.[1] It is also known that the family is filled with many different forms of violence and oppression, including physical, sexual and emotional, and that violence is perpetrated on young and old alike. It is the battered-women's movement, with the support of the media, who have put the issues of the physical and sexual abuse of women and girls firmly on the social agenda. The now familiar stories of personal pain and degradation fill out the statistics with

From *Women, Violence, and Social Change*, Routledge, 1992, pp. 1–14. Reprinted by permission.

human dimensions and make the social facts comprehensible. For some, familiarity with accounts of violence breeds indifference and inaction; for others they bring indignation and a call for action.

Although the stories may now be familiar, they still remain both painful and powerful. For women who have been attacked, there is a litany of abuses from repeated assaults to rape and murder. In the 1970s the stories at once described what were then unfamiliar accounts of abuse, and informed a disbelieving public of its widespread nature. Women's accounts revealed the nature of men's violence and the sources of conflict leading to attacks. They also described women's emotions and reactions as well as the inaction of social and legal institutions. The words of only a few of the millions of women who have been abused describe the nature of the violence ranging from slapping and shoving to brutal assaults and sometimes murder:

I have had glasses thrown at me. I have been kicked in the abdomen when I was visibly pregnant. I have been kicked off the bed and hit while lying on the floor—again, while I was pregnant. I have been whipped, kicked and thrown, picked up again and thrown down again. I have been punched and kicked in the head, chest, face, and abdomen more times than I can count.[2] (American woman)

It was punching, banging my head on walls. Kicking everything.[3] (Northern Irish woman)

He tried to strangle me last night. I was terrified. I did manage to get out of the house but I had to go back the next morning. You see it was Easter weekend and my two children were afraid the Easter Bunny wouldn't come if mummy and daddy were fighting.[4] (Canadian woman)

He once used a stick, he hit me once with a big fibreglass fishing pole, six foot long. And he just went woosh, he gave me such a wallop with that. I had a mark . . . right down my back. I thought my back had broke.[5] (Scottish woman)

He'd kick me or hit me on the back of the head (so it wouldn't show). He raped me once, then smashed me in the face.[6] (Northern Irish woman)

He used to bang my head against the wall or the floor. I finally left him when I thought he was trying to kill me.[7] (English woman)

The injuries inflicted during these attacks range from cuts and bruises to broken bones, miscarriages and permanent damage. Again, women from numerous countries recount similar incidents and report a full range of injuries:

I wasn't badly hurt. My ear was bruised and my hair was pulled out.[8]

Punching, I had my nose broken, ribs broken, two black eyes—he dragged me out of bed by the hair and pulled me along the ground. He smashed the door of my parent's house down when I was there.[9]

Each one got harder and harder . . . one time he hit me so hard on the back of the head he broke his own hand.[10]

The elbow was all lying open, the top of my legs was lying open . . . gashes all over.[11]

I had treatment for a fractured skull and I lost a child in a miscarriage due to violence.[12]

The effect upon women's physical and emotional state is frequently recorded:

> [The worst aspects of the experience of battering are]: Feeling so ill and tired after the beatings, and so useless, I couldn't face people with the marks on my body.[13]

> I was always terrified. My nerves were getting the better of me. . . . He knew this and I think he loved this.[14]

> The fear of not knowing what he would do—I feared for my life.[15]

> I remember the tension of becoming aware that I had to notice what I was saying all the time, to make sure I didn't offend him. I had become afraid of him.[16]

> Was he going to scare me all my life? Was he going to punch me in the head and knock me out and I'd die?[17]

The sources of conflict leading to violent events reveal a great deal about the nature of relations between men and women, demands and expectations of wives, the prerogatives and power of husbands, and cultural beliefs that support individual attitudes of marital inequality:

> I realized I was under terrible strain the whole time. . . . I'd go into a blind panic about what side the spoon had to be on. It was that sort of detail everyday.[18]

> There was too much grease on his breakfast plate and he threw his plate at me.[19]

> I had a poker thrown at me—just because his tea was too weak—he just takes it for granted, if you're married you'll have to accept it. It's part of being a wife.[20]

> And then he had his belt and I was whipped over the shoulders everywhere, on my face and everything. And this was to teach me not to argue with him.[21]

> He would stay out all night and become violent when questioned.[22]

The four main sources of conflict leading to violent attacks are men's possessiveness and jealousy, men's expectations concerning women's domestic work, men's sense of the right to punish "their" women for perceived wrongdoing, and the importance to men of maintaining or exercising their position of authority.[23] For many women, a sense of shame and responsibility, along with fear of reprisals, keeps them silent, sometimes for years. The U.S. National Crime survey of domestic violence cases from 1978 to 1982 found that 48 percent were not reported to the police (because it was viewed as a private matter or because of fear of reprisal).[24] An Irish woman who went to a refuge after twenty years of violence, explains her silence:

> I hid what was happening to me from everyone. I made excuses for my bruises and marks. I thought I should put up with it . . . accept my lot as being part of marriage. . . . I wanted to keep it hidden.[25]

It should be noted that in the same U.S. survey 52 percent of women did report the violence to the police because they hoped this would prevent further incidents.[26] The problem of women's reluctance to report men's violence is often exacerbated by social, medical and legal institutions whose actions reveal a powerful legacy of policies and practices that explicitly or implicitly accept or ignore male violence and/or blame the victim and make her responsible for its solution and elimination.[27]

By the late 1980s, public accounts had chipped away at persistent images of the violence as a problem confined to the working class, ethnic groups or the poor. The United States was rocked by revelations that John Fedders, one of President Reagan's high-ranking legal officials, had beaten his wife for eighteen years.[28] The image of the perfect marriage of a member of the Washington establishment was crushed in the account of a daily life of repeated attacks. Insult and further injustice were added to injury when the courts awarded him a percentage of the royalties from the book she wrote about the relationship on the grounds that she could not have written the book had he not made it possible by abusing her.[29]

Equally as sensational and as destructive of myths of middle-class immunity was the trial of a wealthy, Jewish, New York lawyer for the murder of his adopted daughter in what has been described as a vast inventory of abuse and intimidation also directed at his female partner, a well-educated, Jewish editor of children's books:

> The 6th Precinct officers were so shocked by Hedda's condition that they videotaped her, lumps of hair missing, clusters of small scabs on the bare scalp—were they cigarette burns? Deep ulcers on gangrenous legs. A bruise on the buttock the size of a football. Bruises on her back. A pulverised nose. Jaw broken in two places. Nine broken ribs, a cauliflower ear, a split lip . . . a ruptured spleen, removed in hospital, a broken knee, a bruised neck and innumerable black eyes—10 in one year—and after her arrest doctors discovered minor brain damage.[30]

The case became sensational not so much because of the violence itself but because it took place in an affluent home. Controversy increased when he was found guilty of manslaughter rather than murder because the use of cocaine may have meant he was not completely aware of his actions. There was even more controversy about the responsibility of a seriously abused woman for stopping her abuser from also abusing their child.[31] The case fuelled a new wave of interest in domestic violence in the United States, added some new dilemmas and brought a new twist to victim blaming.

With repeated male violence, death sometimes occurs. In one case, a retired vicar from the affluent south of England "bludgeoned his wife to death" over two hours when he had trouble with radio reception. At the end, his son, who lived in an adjoining house, heard him shout "Are you dead yet?" It was reported that the seventy-four-year-old vicar "was 'arrogant and self-centred with an explosive temper' and had previously beaten his eighty-five-year-old wife during their forty-six-year marriage."[32] The claim of diminished responsibility was used to reduce the charge from murder to manslaughter and the judge initially stated he intended to put the Reverend on three years probation to be spent in a Benedictine Abbey. The Abbot later decided the vicar was medically unsuited for their facility.[33]

Stories of death are more sensational and therefore more likely to be reported in the press, but they often reflect the final event following a history of male violence not deemed sufficiently important or dramatic to appear in print or in police statistics. The ultimate victim of domestic homicide may, of course, be either the woman or the man. When the woman dies, it is usually the final and most extreme form of violence at the hands of her male partner. When the man dies, it is rarely the final act in a relationship in which she has repeatedly beaten him. Instead, it is often an act of self-defence or a reaction to a history of the man's repeated attacks.[34] No matter who dies, the antecedent is often a history of repeated male violence, not of repeated female violence. This is a common pattern known in the United States at least since the 1950s[35] and one that continues today. The following Scottish case illustrates many features common to cases in which men kill wives and female partners:

> Mary Khelifati was murdered . . . by her violent husband. She had been rehoused [after a stay in a refuge] . . . , but her husband had traced her to her new address. By this stage, Mary was convinced that the end was near. Her solicitor had achieved everything possible on her behalf [an exclusion order and an interdict (injunction)] but the danger had not lessened. Khelifati stabbed Mary to death in front of their six year old daughter. At his trial . . . , the jury unanimously found him guilty of murder, and he was sentenced to life imprisonment. Press coverage of the trial focused on Khelifati's defence claim that Mary had said she would take the child abroad and he would never see her again. . . . No mention was made of his continual violence and threats towards Mary, nor of her attempts to escape from him. Even after her brutal death, Mary's life of hell was being trivialized and her suffering negated.[36]

Some abused women think about escaping violence by killing their male abuser or themselves, and some actually do so:

> And we had this great big carving knife downstairs and I used to go upstairs and stand there with it and think "If I stick it in him—will I get done for murder?" And sometimes if he threw me out I used to go and get three or four bottles of aspirins and go into a cafe and think "Get myself a couple of cups of tea—take all these and the problem's solved—all this will be finished with." But there was always [my son] to consider, I used to think if I leave [my son] with him what's he going to grow up like—twisted—like his dad.[37]

In their comprehensive and scholarly examination of homicide in many countries, Daly and Wilson strongly support the idea that it is men's sexual jealousy and possessiveness, or proprietary rights, that lead to spousal homicide, be it committed by the man or the woman. They conclude that:

> In every society for which we have been able to find a sample of spousal homicides, the story is basically the same: Most cases arise out of the husband's jealous, proprietary, violent responses to his wife's (real or imagined) infidelity or desertion.[38]

They cite evidence from industrial and primitive societies. In spousal homicides, sexual proprietariness (jealousy and attempts to stop a wife's desertion) was cited in 81 percent of cases in a 1955 study in Baltimore, Maryland,[39] while a 1980 study in Virginia noted this factor in nearly every case excluding those with diagnosed psychiatric disorders.[40] Peter Chimbos found a similar pattern in his 1978 Canadian study of convicted men and women.[41] Daly and Wilson note that:

> Men . . . strive to control women, albeit with variable success; women struggle to resist coercion and to maintain their choices. There is brinksmanship and risk of disaster in any such contest, and homicides by spouses of either sex may be considered the slips in this dangerous game.[42]

Chimbos notes that one of the most important single findings from his Canadian study is that spousal homicide "is rarely a sudden explosion in a blissful marriage" but is based on the situation at the time and on a history of quarrels, usually about sexual jealousy and possessiveness.[43] It was the "endpoint" in a series of conflicts, and 70 percent reported prior assaults.[44] He also found that apart from stabbing (38 percent) and firearms (30 percent), 32 percent of the killings he studied were the result of beating, always by men, who can use their body and strength as tools for killing.[45] In another study of spousal homicide in Florida, it was found that 73 percent of the women who killed reported that they had previously been beaten by their partner,[46] while in Totman's the rate was 93 percent.[47] Zimring and his colleagues have referred to this as the "female use of lethal counterforce."[48]

As stated earlier, the dynamics are usually very different when women kill their husband or male partner. It is usually a response to years of male violence and not a culmination of years of female violence. The following letter from a battered woman who killed her husband reveals some of these dynamics.

> I was used and abused, battered stupid and nearly strangled. I passed out, had hair torn out of my head. I was actually pulled along the street by my hair. I've had my ear stitched, my cheek bones fractured, my nose fractured, my jaw fractured. I still remember the doctor saying you must have a jaw like [a professional boxer].
>
> It was pure agony, life was hell. I often thought of taking the easy way out but I had a young son to consider and it was always him I thought about. I tried pills once and I actually had a knife on my hand to cut my wrists but I kept thinking about my son, he kept me sane. . . .
>
> I could write a book about my fifteen years of anguish because you see I killed my husband, not deliberately, it was an accident, but as the doctors said it was like the straw on the camel's back. I snapped. I took it until I could take no more and for that I got three years imprisonment.[49]

In every country where the issue of battering has now been recognized there are well-known cases of women in prison who have killed their male partners after years of his violent abuse. Some have become *causes célèbres* and are subsequently released. Others remain unknown and serve out sentences because they were first abused by their male partners and then failed by a society unwilling or unable to provide the necessary means of protection or escape.[50] In her historical and contemporary study of *Women Who Kill*, Ann Jones cites numerous such cases:

> Katherine Rohrich shot her husband four times as he slept, but only after she and her eleven children had endured years of battering, and only after she had been denied the help of local law-enforcement personnel several times. . . . [The judge] described [her] as a woman "pushed to the wall."[51]

> New Orleans district attorney's office in July 1978 dropped charges against Viola Williams, who shot her common-law husband, Harold Randolph, twice in the head and neck and eleven times in the back. Pretrial investigation determined that Randolph had beaten her for ten years, shoved her face into an anthill, and once pled guilty to a simple battery charge after clubbing her with a baseball bat; at the time she shot him, he was attacking her with a knife. She shot twice in self-defence, she said, and then eleven times more for what he had done to her. [The District Attorney acknowledged she had a] "valid self-defence claim. . . . I'm sorry the system didn't help her sooner. . . . We have evidence that she sought help many times."[52]

For Jones, "Homicide is a last resort, and it most often occurs when men simply will not quit."[53] Examples include:

[She] left her husband, but he kept tracking her down, raping and beating her; finally when he attacked her with a screwdriver, she shot him.[54]

[She] filed for divorce, but her husband kept coming back to beat her with a dog chain, pistol-whip her, and shoot at her. At last, after she had been hospitalized seven times, she shot him.[55]

. . . teaching submission, [he] made her watch him dig her grave, kill the family cat, and decapitate a pet horse. When she fled he brought her back with a gun held to her child's head.[56]

Angela Browne's study of battered women who kill is filled with similar accounts of women repeatedly beaten, abused, raped and terrorized before killing their abuser.[57] Jones notes that many case records show men following, harassing and beating their wives for years before they are themselves killed by the woman who had for so long been their victim. For Jones, it is misdirected to ask "why women stay" and more telling to address "Why don't men let them go?" [58]

With expanding awareness of the problem, thousands of accounts from across the world can be added to the British and North American voices above. The accounts reveal patterns strikingly similar across countries even as they reflect important and distinct cultural differences. In India and Bangladesh, for example, women are beaten and killed because of men's possessiveness and demands about women's domestic work, but also because of the price of a wife and the bereavement of a widow. Dowry deaths are common and sati, the burning of a widow upon the death of her husband, has been the subject of a vigorous, though not completely successful, women's campaign for abolition.[59] In urban Maharashtra and Greater Bombay, nearly a quarter of deaths among women between fifteen and forty-four years of age are due to "accidents" caused by burns.[60] The pattern is worst among the youngest women and reflects the problem of dowry deaths. Although the Dowry Prohibition Acts have been passed in both countries, the social custom of dowry is still practised.[61] Women are frequently beaten or killed when her family fails to meet payments or the husband or his family decide they want more than originally agreed.[62] Doused with cooking oil and set alight they become the victim of an "accident" in the kitchen. In Bangladesh they have also had to legislate against the practice known as acid throwing.[63] In both countries, women are often harassed and abused until they commit suicide.

In Papua, New Guinea, the Constitution guarantees equality for women and prohibits punishment that is cruel or violates human dignity. Many government officials strongly resisted these new laws and men still beat and kill their wives, sometimes in unfamiliar ways but usually for familiar reasons: [64]

A man in Gulf Province has been arrested for shooting his wife in the ribs with an arrow and inflicting a severe axe wound to her head. . . .[65]

A blind man was charged with murder for beating his wife to death with his cane on Independence Day. . . . He is alleged to have beaten up his wife after hearing stories that she was being unfaithful to him.[66]

In many African countries, women are triply abused within the family, the economy and the state: by husbands who beat them, by the ravages of war and as exploited workers who make up most of the farm labourers in agricultural economies.[67] Genital mutilation of women and girls in order to control their sexuality is also widely practised in many African countries.[68] In Latin American countries the image of the macho man continues and violence against women is perpetuated within that cultural context. For example, in Quito, Ecuador, over 80 percent of women interviewed in one study had been beaten by their partners, and such incidents make up 70 percent of all crimes reported to the police in Peru.[69] In 1986 and 1987, 18,000 cases of woman abuse were reported to the police in Sao Paulo, Brazil,[70] and a Women's Police Station was established in 1986 as part of an effort to combat violence against women.[71]

In Israel, with its emphasis on the importance of the family and the belief that violence has no place in Jewish society, wives are still beaten by husbands.[72] The fashion for stress-reducing "toys" in Japan in the late 1980s included an "I am sorry doll" who speaks only when spoken to, and begs "Please forgive me" and "Please don't hit me." There are three types: the company boss, the female police officer and the wife.[73] In Malaya, the stereotypes and myths about the abuse of wives are all too familiar:

Only poor and uneducated men batter their wives.
No one should interfere in the domestic affairs of man and wife.
Unhappy families are better than no families.
Alcohol causes battering.
She must have enjoyed it. Otherwise she'd leave.
Husbands have every right to do what they want with their wives.
Women who are beaten obviously deserve it.
Its just the odd domestic tiff.[74]

In response to this violence and to the unwillingness or inability of social, legal and medical agencies to act effectively to assist women after abuse, refuges and shelters have now been established throughout much of the world by activists who provide an immediate, pragmatic response to the problem. Usually against great odds, and often resourced primarily by women volunteers, refuges and shelters have opened in country after country forming a watershed in the response to this social problem. Countless women from all over the world speak of the importance of the refuge in their lives: the value of escaping from violence, the importance of mutual support and solidarity; the end of isolation; and support for self-reliance rather than continued dependence. An Israeli woman tells of the relief after thirty years of marital violence:

I had no family who could help me and I suffered great fear. He said he would kill me, and I believed him. I stayed to take care of the children and when the last one left home, somehow I got up the courage to come here. . . . I'm afraid to go out in the street. Every night I dream that he is coming to kill me. My daughter tells me she has the same dreams. If I hadn't had the centre to come to, I don't know what I would have done.[75]

From New Zealand, a fifty-two-year-old woman tells of the return to normal life after twenty years of violence:

At long last we were able to be normal loving human beings. My children and I could laugh and joke with one another out in the open. . . . Friends could visit me without me worrying about him coming in and being so rude and aggressive that they wouldn't come back again.[76]

Their British and North American counterparts also emphasize the importance of the refuge in changing their lives:

> You weren't there eight years ago when I needed a place to go with my baby. Thank God you're there now for those in need![77] (American woman)

> I used to be ashamed to talk about battering to people. I can really talk openly here because they've all been through the same thing.[78] (English woman)

> We all run it as a group, so we all take decisions. It's like a small community—we all help each other.[79] (English woman)

> A lot of women here give you courage. At first I asked, "Did I do the right thing? Is it me?" Now I say, "I don't have to take this. We, women, are in this together."[80] (American woman)

The beginning of the social movement dealing with violence against women, like most beginnings, was rather unspectacular and went without too much notice. But this changed quickly as refuge provision grew from local groups to national organization, and recognition of the problem became international. In 1972, the first refuge for battered women opened in Britain. Others were soon to follow throughout Britain[81] as well as in Europe, the United States, Canada and Australia[82] as activists travelled within and between countries, sharing ideas and providing support for opening new refuges.

The battered-women's movement has now extended throughout much of the world, providing shelter and working for social change. For example, in 1988 Welsh Women's Aid sponsored an international conference with delegates representing over forty countries.[83] The process of innovation and change evident in this worldwide movement is the focus here. While examples of the old ways, the old attitudes and beliefs and the old responses of agencies and social policies abound and indicate continued support for the abuse of wives and female partners, they offer no hope or useful direction for action. Hope and inspiration for positive action lay in the innovations, the breaks with the legacy of violence. It is here that present and future changes are being formed and reformed; here, that the nature of women's lives may be freed from the constant possibility that force might be unleashed against them as they conduct the business of daily life; here, that attention might productively turn in pursuit of an end to the centuries of protection and support for male violence and a beginning of the era of its rejection.

In pursuing an analysis of this change, we shall inevitably concentrate on innovations that reject violence and its foundations rather than on established patterns that support them. The intention is to examine change in progress and consider models for development that are challenging and innovative. But this should not be taken as an indication that innovations are the norm or that resistance to change is not strong. We shall also examine how innovations have been blocked and sometimes diverted as they have been implemented in a wider, less supportive social context. That is, how challenging ideals have sometimes been subverted, undermined and reshaped by legislation and institutional response.

This involves consideration of the internal dynamics of the movement: its resources and organization; the diversity of goals and tactics; and negotiations with the community, institutions of the state, policy makers, researchers, violent men and others. None of these facets are ossified but are themselves changing with time and circumstances. Thus, the task of characterizing a living movement while still in the process of development is inevitably more complex than charting one that has become a memory. The battered-women's movement has negotiated for social change within the wider context of the existing economic, political and social position of women in society, and the established philosophies, priorities and practices of existing institutions and agencies of the state. Notions about the nature of the problem, the most effective strategies and solutions, and who or what is in need of change vary and are themselves the subject of debate. The nature of social change, the dynamics of a social movement and the ideas and practices of feminism are all at work as the process of change stops and starts, moves forward and backward, and occasionally takes a step sideways.

Notes

1. R. E. Dobash and R. P. Dobash, *Violence against Wives*, New York. The Free Press and Macmillan Distributing, Brunel Road, Houndmills, Basingstoke, England, 1979. M. Daly and M. Wilson, *Homicide*, New York, Aldine De Gruyter, 1988.

2. D. Martin, *Battered Wives*, San Francisco, CA, Glide Publications, 1976, pp.1–2.

3. E. Evason, *Hidden Violence*, Belfast, Farset Co-operative Press, 1982, p. 27.

4. P. Kincaid, *The Omitted Reality*, Ontario, Canada, Learners Press, 1982, p. 23.

5. R. E. Dobash and R. P. Dobash, "The nature and antecedents of violent events," *British Journal of Criminology*, vol. 24, no. 3, July, 1984, pp. 269–88.

6. Evason, op. cit., p. 28.

7. L. Kelly, *Surviving Sexual Violence*, Oxford, Polity Press, 1988, p. 130.

8. R. E. Dobash, R. P. Dobash, C. Cavanagh and M. Wilson, "Wifebeating: The victims speak," *Victimology*, no. 2, vol. 3–4, 1977/78, pp. 608–22, p. 612.

9. Evason, op. cit., p. 28.

10. Kelly, op. cit., p. 130.

11. Dobash and Dobash, op. cit., 1984, p. 276.

12. Evanson, op. cit., p. 30.

13. Casey, op. cit., p. 26. See p. 19 for summary of forms of violence recorded in the survey of 127 women in refuges during 1986.

14. Dobash and Dobash, op. cit., 1979, p. 111.

15. M. Casey, *Domestic Violence against Women: The Women's Perspective*, Federation of Women's Refuges and Social and Organisational Psychology Research Unit, UCD, Dublin, 1987–88.

16. Kelly, op. cit., p. 127.

17. Ibid.

18. Kelly, op. cit., p. 130.

19. Dobash, Dobash, Cavanagh and Wilson, op. cit., p. 611.

20. J. Pahl (ed.), *Private Violence and Public Policy: The Needs of Battered Women and the Response of the Public Services*, London, Routledge, 1985, p. 77.

21. Dobash and Dobash, op. cit., 1979, p. 108.

22. Ibid.

23. Dobash and Dobash, op. cit., 1979, pp. 98–106; Dobash and Dobash, op. cit., 1984, pp. 272–4. See also Kelly, op. cit., p. 131; J. Edelson and Z. Eisikovits, "Men who batter women: A critical review of the evidence," *Journal of Family Issues*, vol. 6, no. 2, June, 1986, pp. 229–47; M. P. Brygger and J. L. Edleson, "The domestic abuse project: A multi-systems intervention in woman battering," Unpublished paper, Domestic Abuse Project, 2445 Park Ave South, Minneapolis, MN 55404, USA, 1986; Emerge, "Emerge: A men's counseling service on domestic violence," in Betsy Warrior (ed.), *Battered Women's Directory*, 8th edition, 46 Pleasant St., Cambridge, MA 02139,

1982, pp. 226–42; Raven (Rape, and violence end now), "Men working to end violence against women," in Betsy Warrior (ed.), *Battered Women's Directory*, 8th edition, 46 Pleasant St., Cambridge, MA 02139, 1982, pp. 243–46.

24. P. Langan and C. Innes, "Preventing domestic violence against women?" U.S. Dept. of Justice, Bureau of Justice Statistics, Special Report, Washington DC 20531, August, 1986, p. 1.

25. Casey, op. cit., p. 27.

26. Langan and Innes, op. cit., p. 1.

27. Dobash and Dobash, op. cit., 1979, pp. 31–74, 179–222; R. E. Dobash, R. P. Dobash and C. Cavanagh, "The contact between battered women and social and medical agencies," in Jan Pahl, op. cit., pp. 142–65; M. Homer, A. Leonard and P. Taylor, *Private Violence: Public Shame, a Report on the Circumstances of Women Leaving Domestic Violence in Cleveland*, Middlesbrough, Cleveland Refuge and Aid for Women and Children (CRAWC), c/o Cleveland Council for Voluntary Service, 47 Princes Road, Middlesbrough, Cleveland, England, 1984; M. Maynard, "The response of social workers to domestic violence," in J. Pahl, op. cit., pp. 125–41; T. Faragher, "The police response to violence against women in the home," in J. Pahl, op. cit., pp. 110–24.

28. M. McGrory, "A blow to battered wives," *The Boston Globe*, 21 October, 1987.

29. C. Fedders, *Shattered Dreams*, New York, Harper and Row, 1987.

30. B. Campbell, "The trial of terror" (The case of Joel Steinberg and Hedda Nussbaum), *Guardian*, Monday 2 January, 1989, p. 15.

31. J. Rosen, "Uproar over conviction in NY child abuse case," *Guardian*, 1 February, 1989.

32. *Guardian*, 18 February, 1989, p. 3.

33. Ibid., *Guardian*, 23 February, 1989, p. 16.

34. A. Jones, *Women Who Kill*, New York, Fawcett Columbine, 1980; A. Browne, *When Battered Women Kill*, New York, The Free Press, 1987; M. Daly and M. Wilson, *Homicide*, op. cit.

35. M. Wolfgang, *Patterns in Criminal Homicide*, New York, Wiley, 1958. Dobash and Dobash, op. cit., 1979, pp. 15–19.

36. N. Cutherbertson and L. Irving, "Death of a battered women: An examination of the circumstances surrounding the killing of Mary Khelifati by her estranged husband," Scottish Legal Action Group, 1985, p. 148.

37. Homer, Leonard and Taylor, op. cit., p. 4.

38. Daly and Wilson, op. cit., p. 202.

39. M. S. Guttmacher, "Criminal responsibility in certain homicide cases involving family members," in P. H. Hoch and J. Zubin (eds.), *Psychiatry and the Law*, New York, Grune and Stratton, 1955; also cited in Daly and Wilson, op. cit., p. 201.

40. R. C. Showalter, R. J. Bonnie and V. Roddy, "The spousal-homicide syndrome," *International Journal of Law and Psychiatry*, 3, 1980, pp. 117–41; also cited in Daly and Wilson, op. cit., p. 201.

41. P. Chimbos, *Marital Violence: A Study of Interspouse Homicide*, San Francisco, R&E Research Associates, 4843 Mission St., San Francisco, CA 94112, 1978.

42. Daly and Wilson, op. cit., p. 205.

43. Chimbos, op. cit., p. 67.

44. Ibid., p. 47.

45. Ibid., p. 61.

46. Bernard, Vera and Newman, 1982, cited in Browne, op. cit., 1987, p. 143, no. 1, p. 205.

47. Totman, 1978 cited in A. Browne, and R. Flewelling, "Women as victims or perpetrators of homicide," Paper presented at the American Society of Criminology Annual Meeting, Atlanta, 29 October–1 Nov., 1986, p. 12.

48. F. E. Zimring, S. K. Mukherjee and B. Van Winkle, "Intimate violence: A study of intersexual homicide in Chicago," *University of Chicago Law Review*, vol. 50, no. 2, 1983, pp. 910–30, cited in Browne and Flewelling, op. cit., p. 12.

49. Personal correspondence, 1988.

50. Jones, op. cit., Browne, op. cit., Daly and Wilson, op. cit.

51. Jones, ibid., p. 290.

52. Jones, ibid., p. 312.

53. Ibid., p. 298.

54. Ibid.

55. Ibid.

56. Ibid., pp. 298–99.

57. Browne, op. cit.

58. Jones, op. cit., p. 299.

59. R. Kumar, "Contemporary Indian feminism," *Feminist Review,* no. 33, Autumn, 1989, pp. 28–29.

60. M. Karkal, "How the other half dies in Bombay," *Economic and Political Weekly,* 24 August, 1985, p. 124.

61. L. Das, "Hindu family laws and manu's legacy," Paper presented at Women in Interfaith Dialogue Conference organized by World Council of Churches, Toronto, Canada, available from Women's Centre, Bombay, India, B/27 Clifton, Juhu Road, Bombay, India 400 049, June, 1988, p. 5; L. Das, "Violence against women, An Indian view," in Welsh Women's Aid, *Worldwide Action on Violence Against Women: A Report on the International Women's Conference in Cardiff,* October, 1988, c/o Welsh Women's Aid, 38/42 Crwys Road, Cardiff, Wales, UK, 1988; pp. 8–13, p. 8; Rokhsana Khondker, "Domestic violence and the law: Case studies from Bangladesh," in Welsh Women's Aid, *Worldwide Action on Violence Against Women: A Report on the International Women's Conference in Cardiff,* October, 1988, c/o Welsh Women's, Aid 38/42 Crwys Road, Cardiff, Wales, UK, 1988, pp. 8–13, p. 8; Rokhsana Khondker, "Domestic violence and the law: Case studies from Bangladesh," in Welsh Women's Aid, *Worldwide Action on Violence Against Women: A Report on the International Women's Conference in Cardiff,* October 1988, c/o Welsh Women's Aid, 38/42 Crwys Road, Cardiff, Wales, UK, 1988, pp. 35–37; L. Heise, "Crimes of gender," *World-Watch,* vol. 2, no. 2, March/April, 1989, pp. 12–21, pp. 14–15; Commonwealth Secretariat, *Confronting Violence: A Manual for Commonwealth Action,* Women and Development Programme, Human Resource Development Group, Commonwealth Secretariat, Marlborough House, Pall Mall, London SW1 5HX, 1987, pp. 140–42.

62. S. Maharaja, Women Equal Rights Group, D3, Akashdeep Apartment. Opp. Telephone Exchange, Ellisbridge, Ahmedabad-380 006, Bombay, India, 1983, p. 4.

63. Khondker, op. cit., p. 36.

64. Heise, op. cit., pp. 15–16; Women and Law Committee, "Wife-beating is a crime," public information leaflet no. 1, Women and Law Committee, P.O. Box 3439, Boroko, Papua New Guinea (ND, 1980s); C. Bradley, "How can we help rural beaten wives? Some suggestions from Papua New Guinea," in Welsh Women's Aid, op. cit., pp. 43–46.

65. C. Bradley, "Information and resource materials on domestic violence in Papua New Guinea," presented to the Welsh Women's Aid International Conference, October, 1988.

66. Ibid.

67. A. Magezi, "Violence in Uganda," in Welsh Women's Aid; op. cit., pp. 14–17; National Union of Eritrean Women, "Women's displacement in Eritrea," Unpublished paper presented at Welsh Women's Aid Conference International Conference, Cardiff, Wales, October, 1988.

68. Heise, op. cit., p. 19.

69. Ibid.

70. Ibid., p. 14.

71. B. Savl, in Welsh Women's Aid, op. cit., pp. 29–31, p. 29.

72. T. P. Halpern, "Working with battered women in Israel," *ALIYON,* Spring, 1980, pp. 22–23; Hazelton, 1977, estimates that 20 percent of Israeli women are beaten by their partners (cited in Halpern, p. 27).

73. *Guardian,* 1 June, 1988.

74. Women's Aid Organization (WAO), *Battered Women: A Self-help Guide,* P.O. Box 493, Jalan Sultan, 46760 Petaling Jaya, Malaya, 1987, pp. 20–23; C. S. Hong, "The Malaysian experience," in Welsh Women's Aid, op. cit., pp. 18–20.

75. S. Scan and C. Novis, "New home OK'd for the battered," *Jerusalem Post*, 27 November, 1987, no page.

76. (NCIWR) National Collective of Independent Women's Refuges, "Home is where the hurt is," NCIWR, P.O. Box 6386, Te Aro, Wellington, New Zealand, 1988, p. 1.

77. Martin, op. cit., p. 202.

78. V. Binney, G. Harkell and J. Nixon, *Leaving Violent Men*, Leeds, England, WAFE/DERT, 1981, p. 54. See also J. Pahl, *A Refuge for Battered Women: A Study of the Role of a Women's Centre*, London, Her Majesty's Stationery Office, 1978; Homer, Leonard and Taylor, op. cit.

79. Binney, Harkell and Nixon, ibid.

80. S. Schechter, *Women and Male Violence: The Visions and Struggles of the Battered Women's Movement*, Boston, South End Press, 1982, p. 60.

81. C. Charlton, "The first cow on Chiswick High Road," *Spare Rib*, 24, 1972, pp. 24–25; R. E. Dobash, and R. P. Dobash, "Love, honour and obey: Institutional ideologies and the struggle for battered women," *Contemporary Crisis*, 1, 1977, pp. 403–15, 403–4; Dobash and Dobash, op. cit., *Violence against Wives*, pp. 223–24; J. Sutton, "The growth of the British movement for battered women," *Victimology*, vol. 2, nos. 3–4, 1977–78, pp. 576–84; J. Hanmer, "Community action, Women's Aid and the women's liberation movement," in M. Mayo (ed.), *Women in the Community*, London, Routledge, 1977.

82. B. Warrior, *Battered Women's Directory*, 46 Pleasant St., Cambridge, MA 02139, USA, 1976; pp. 196–231; M. Karl, "Refuges in Europe," *Victimology*, vol. 2, nos. 3–4, 1977–78, pp. 657–66; no author, "Resources in the United States and Canada," *Victimology*, vol. 2, nos. 3–4, 1977–78, pp. 666–68; R. E. Dobash, "Violence against women—A worldwide view," Keynote address, Welsh Women's Aid International Conference, Cardiff, Wales, proceedings published as Report of the International Women's Aid Conference, Cardiff, Wales, Welsh Women's Aid, 38/42 Crwys Road, Cardiff, Wales, UK, 1988, pp. 21–26.

83. Welsh Women's Aid, op. cit., pp. 108–14.

18

Violence in Intimate Relationships: A Feminist Perspective

BELL HOOKS

We were on the freeway, going home from San Francisco. He was driving. We were arguing. He had told me repeatedly to shut up. I kept talking. He took his hand from the steering wheel and threw it back, hitting my mouth—my open mouth, blood gushed, and I felt an intense pain. I was no longer able to say any words, only to make whimpering, sobbing sounds as the blood dripped on my hands, on the handkerchief I held too tightly. He did not stop the car. He drove home. I watched him pack his suitcase. It was a holiday. He was going away to have fun. When he left I washed my mouth. My jaw was swollen and it was difficult for me to open it.

I called the dentist the next day and made an appointment. When the female voice asked what I needed to see the doctor about, I told her I had been hit in the mouth. Conscious of race, sex, and class issues, I wondered how I would be treated in this white doctor's office. My face was no longer swollen so there was nothing to identify me as a woman who had been hit, as a black woman with a bruised and swollen jaw. When the dentist asked me what had happened to my mouth, I described it calmly and succinctly. He made little jokes about how "we can't have someone doing this to us now, can we?" I said nothing. The damage was repaired. Through it all, he talked to me as if I were a child, someone he had to handle gingerly or otherwise I might become hysterical.

This is one way women who are hit by men and seek medical care are seen. People within patriarchal society imagine that women are hit because we are hysterical, because we are beyond reason. It is most often the person who is hitting that is beyond reason, who is hysterical, who has lost complete control over responses and actions.

Growing up, I had always thought that I would never allow any man to hit me and live. I would kill him. I had seen my father hit my mother once and I wanted to kill him. My mother said to me then, "You are too young to know, too young to understand." Being a mother in a culture that supports and promotes domination, a patriarchal, white-supremacist culture, she did not discuss how she felt or what she meant. Perhaps it would have been too difficult for her to speak about the confusion of being hit by someone you are intimate with, someone you love. In my case, I was hit by my companion at a time in life when a number of forces in the world outside our home had

From *Talking Back: Thinking Feminist, Thinking Black*. South End Press, 1989, pp. 84–91. Reprinted by permission.

already "hit" me, so to speak, made me painfully aware of my powerlessness, my marginality. It seemed then that I was confronting being black and female and without money in the worst possible ways. My world was spinning. I had already lost a sense of grounding and security. The memory of this experience has stayed with me as I have grown as a feminist, as I have thought deeply and read much on male violence against women, on adult violence against children.

In this essay, I do not intend to concentrate attention solely on male physical abuse of females. It is crucial that feminists call attention to physical abuse in all its forms. In particular, I want to discuss being physically abused in singular incidents by someone you love. Few people who are hit once by someone they love respond in the way they might to a singular physical assault by a stranger. Many children raised in households where hitting has been a normal response by primary caretakers react ambivalently to physical assaults as adults, especially if they are being hit by someone who cares for them and whom they care for. Often female parents use physical abuse as a means of control. There is continued need for feminist research that examines such violence. Alice Miller has done insightful work on the impact of hitting even though she is at times anti-feminist in her perspective. (Often in her work, mothers are blamed, as if their responsibility in parenting is greater than that of fathers.) Feminist discussions of violence against women should be expanded to include a recognition of the ways in which women use abusive physical force toward children not only to challenge the assumptions that women are likely to be nonviolent, but also to add to our understanding of why children who were hit growing up are often hit as adults or hit others.

Recently, I began a conversation with a group of black adults about hitting children. They all agreed that hitting was sometimes necessary. A professional black male in a southern family setting with two children commented on the way he punished his daughters. Sitting them down, he would first interrogate them about the situation or circumstance for which they were being punished. He said with great pride, "I want them to be able to understand fully why they are being punished." I responded by saying that "they will likely become women whom a lover will attack using the same procedure you who have loved them so well used and they will not know how to respond." He resisted the idea that his behavior would have any impact on their responses to violence as adult women. I pointed to case after case of women in intimate relationships with men (and sometimes women) who are subjected to the same form of interrogation and punishment they experienced as children, who accept their lover assuming an abusive, authoritarian role. Children who are the victims of physical abuse—whether one beating or repeated beatings, one violent push or several—whose wounds are inflicted by a loved one, experience an extreme sense of dislocation. The world one has most intimately known, in which one felt relatively safe and secure, has collapsed. Another world has come into being, one filled with terrors, where it is difficult to distinguish between a safe situation and a dangerous one, a gesture of love and a violent, uncaring gesture. There is a feeling of vulnerability, exposure, that never goes away, that lurks beneath the surface. I know. I was one of those children. Adults hit by loved ones usually experience similar sensations of dislocation, of loss, of new found terrors.

Many children who are hit have never known what it feels like to be cared for, loved without physical aggression or abusive pain. Hitting is such a widespread practice that any of us are lucky if we can go through life without having this experience. One undiscussed aspect of the reality of children who are hit finding themselves as adults in similar circumstances is that we often share with friends and lovers the framework of our childhood pains and this may determine how they respond to us in difficult situations. We share the ways we are wounded and expose vulnerable areas. Often, these revelations provide a detailed model for anyone who wishes to wound or hurt us. While the literature about physical abuse often points to the fact that children who are abused are likely to become abusers or be abused, there is no attention given to sharing woundedness in such a way that we let intimate others know exactly what can be done to hurt us, to make us feel as though we are caught in the destructive patterns we have struggled to break. When partners create scenarios of abuse similar, if not exactly the same, to those we have experienced in childhood, the wounded person is hurt not only by the physical pain but by the feeling of calculated betrayal. Betrayal. When we are physically hurt by loved ones, we feel betrayed. We can no longer trust that care can be sustained. We are wounded, damaged—hurt to our hearts.

Feminist work calling attention to male violence against women has helped create a climate where the issues of physical abuse by loved ones can be freely addressed, especially sexual abuse within families. Exploration of male violence against women by feminists and non-feminists shows a connection between childhood experience of being hit by loved ones and the later occurrence of violence in adult relationships. While there is much material available discussing physical abuse of women by men, usually extreme physical abuse, there is not much discussion of the impact that one incident of hitting may have on a person in an intimate relationship, or how the person who is hit recovers from that experience. Increasingly, in discussion with women about physical abuse in relationships, irrespective of sexual preference, I find that most of us have had the experience of being violently hit at least once. There is little discussion of how we are damaged by such experiences (especially if we have been hit as children), of the ways we cope and recover from this wounding. This is an important area for feminist research precisely because many cases of extreme physical abuse begin with an isolated incident of hitting. Attention must be given to understanding and stopping these isolated incidents if we are to eliminate the possibility that women will be at risk in intimate relationships.

Critically thinking about issues of physical abuse has led me to question the way our culture, the way we as feminist advocates focus on the issue of violence and physical abuse by loved ones. The focus has been on male violence against women and, in particular, male sexual abuse of children. Given the nature of patriarchy, it has been necessary for feminists to focus on extreme cases to make people confront the issue, and acknowledge it to be serious and relevant. Unfortunately, an exclusive focus on extreme cases can and does lead us to ignore the more frequent, more common, yet less extreme case of occasional hitting. Women are also less likely to acknowledge occasional hitting for fear that they will then be seen as someone who is in a bad relationship or someone whose life is out of control. Currently, the literature about male violence against women identifies the physically abused woman as a "battered woman." While it has been important to have an accessible terminology to draw attention to the issue of male violence against women, the terms used reflect biases because they call attention to only one type of violence in intimate relationships. The term "battered woman" is problematical. It is not a term that emerged from feminist work on male violence against women; it was already used by psychologists and sociologists in the literature on domestic violence. This label "battered woman" places primary emphasis on physical assaults that are continuous, repeated, and unrelenting. The focus is on extreme violence, with little effort to link these cases with the everyday acceptance within intimate relationships of physical abuse that is not extreme, that may not be repeated. Yet these lesser forms of physical abuse damage individuals psychologically and, if not properly addressed and recovered from, can set the stage for more extreme incidents.

Most importantly, the term "battered woman" is used as though it constitutes a separate and unique category of womanness, as though it is an identity, a mark that sets one apart rather than being simply a descriptive term. It is as though the experience of being repeatedly violently hit is the sole defining characteristic of a woman's identity and all other aspects of who she is and what her experience has been are submerged. When I was hit, I too used the popular phrases "batterer," "battered woman," "battering" even though I did not feel that these words adequately described being hit once. However, these were the terms that people would listen to, would see as important, significant (as if it is not really significant for an individual, and more importantly for a woman, to be hit once). My partner was angry to be labelled a batterer by me. He was reluctant to talk about the experience of hitting me precisely because he did not want to be labelled a batterer. I had hit him once (not as badly as he had hit me) and I did not think of myself as a batterer. For both of us, these terms were inadequate. Rather than enabling us to cope effectively and positively with a negative situation, they were part of all the mechanisms of denial; they made us want to avoid confronting what had happened. This is the case for many people who are hit and those who hit.

 Women who are hit once by men in their lives and women who are hit repeatedly do not want to be placed in the category of "battered woman" because it is a label that appears to strip us of dignity, to deny that there has been any integrity in the relationships we are in. A person physically assaulted by a stranger or a casual friend with whom they are not intimate may be hit once or repeatedly but they do not have to be placed into a category before doctors, lawyers, family, counselors, etc., take their problem seriously. Again, it must be stated that establishing categories and terminology has been part of the effort to draw public attention to the seriousness of male violence against women in intimate relationships. Even though the use of convenient labels and categories has made it easier to identify problems of physical abuse, it does not mean the terminology should not be critiqued from a feminist perspective and changed if necessary.

 Recently, I had an experience assisting a woman who had been brutally attacked by her husband (she never commented on whether this was the first incident or not), which caused me to reflect anew on the use of the term "battered woman." This young woman was not engaged in feminist thinking or aware that "battered woman" was a category. Her husband had tried to choke her to death. She managed to escape from him with only the clothes she was wearing. After she recovered from the trauma, she considered going back to this relationship. As a church-going woman, she believed that her marriage vows were sacred and that she should try to make the relationship work. In an effort to share my feeling that this could place her at great risk, I brought her Lenore Walker's *The Battered Woman* because it seemed to me that there was much that she was not revealing, that she felt alone, and that the experiences she would read about in the book would give her a sense that other women had experienced what she was going through. I hoped reading the book would give her the courage to confront the reality of her situation. Yet I found it difficult to share because I could see that her self-esteem had already been greatly attacked, that she had lost a sense of her worth and value, and that possibly this categorizing of her identity would add to the feeling that she should just forget, be silent (and certainly returning to a situation where one is likely to be abused is one way to mask the severity of the problem). Still I had to try. When I first gave her the book, it disappeared. An unidentified family member had thrown it away. They felt that she would be making a serious mistake if she began to see herself as an absolute victim which they felt the label "battered woman" implied. I stressed that she should ignore the labels and read the content. I believed the experience shared in this book helped give her the courage to be critical of her situation, to take constructive action.

Her response to the label "battered woman," as well as the responses of other women who have been victims of violence in intimate relationships, compelled me to critically explore further the use of this term. In conversation with many women, I found that it was seen as a stigmatizing label, one which victimized women seeking help felt themselves in no condition to critique. As in, "who cares what anybody is calling it—I just want to stop this pain." Within patriarchal society, women who are victimized by male violence have had to pay a price for breaking the silence and naming the problem. They have had to be seen as fallen women, who have failed in their "feminine" role to sensitize and civilize the beast in the man. A category like "battered woman" risks reinforcing this notion that the hurt woman, not only the rape victim, becomes a social pariah, set apart, marked forever by this experience.

A distinction must be made between having a terminology that enables women, and all victims of violent acts, to name the problem and categories of labeling that may inhibit that naming. When individuals are wounded, we are indeed often scarred, often damaged in ways that do set us apart from those who have not experienced a similar wounding, but an essential aspect of the recovery process is the healing of the wound, the removal of the scar. This is an empowering process that should not be diminished by labels that imply this wounding experience is the most significant aspect of identity.

As I have already stated, overemphasis on extreme cases of violent abuse may lead us to ignore the problem of occasional hitting, and it may make it difficult for women to talk about this problem. A critical issue that is not fully examined and written about in great detail by researchers who study and work with victims is the recovery process. There is a dearth of material discussing the recovery process of individuals who have been physically abused. In those cases where an individual is hit only once in an intimate relationship, however violently, there may be no recognition at all of the negative impact of this experience. There may be no conscious attempt by the victimized person to work at restoring her or his well-being, even if the person seeks therapeutic help, because the one incident may not be seen as serious or damaging. Alone and in isolation, the person who has been hit must struggle to regain broken trust—to forge some strategy of recovery. Individuals are often able to process an experience of being hit mentally that may not be processed emotionally. Many women I talked with felt that even after the incident was long forgotten, their bodies remain troubled. Instinctively, the person who has been hit may respond fearfully to any body movement on the part of a loved one that is similar to the posture used when pain was inflicted.

Being hit once by a partner can forever diminish sexual relationships if there has been no recovery process. Again there is little written about ways folks recover physically in their sexualities as loved ones who continue to be sexual with those who have hurt them. In most cases, sexual relationships are dramatically altered when hitting has occurred. The sexual realm may be the one space where the person who has been hit experiences again the sense of vulnerability, which may also arouse fear. This can lead either to an attempt to avoid sex or to unacknowledged sexual withdrawal wherein the person participates but is passive. I talked with women who had been hit by lovers who described sex as an ordeal, the one space where they confront their inability to trust a partner who has broken trust. One woman emphasized that to her, being hit was a "violation of her body space" and that she felt from then on she had to protect that space. This response, though a survival strategy, does not lead to healthy recovery.

Often, women who are hit in intimate relationships with male or female lovers feel as though we have lost an innocence that cannot be regained. Yet this very notion of innocence is connected to passive acceptance of concepts of romantic love under patriarchy which have served to mask problematic realities in relationships. The process of recovery must include a critique of this notion of innocence which is often linked to an unrealistic and fantastic vision of love and romance. It is only in letting go of the perfect, no-work, happily-ever-after union idea, that we can rid our psyches of the sense that we have failed in some way by not having such relationships. Those of us who never focussed on the negative impact of being hit as children find it necessary to reexamine the past in a therapeutic manner as part of our recovery process. Strategies that helped us survive as children may be detrimental for us to use in adult relationships.

Talking about being hit by loved ones with other women, both as children and as adults, I found that many of us had never really thought very much about our own relationship to violence. Many of us took pride in never feeling violent, never hitting. We had not thought deeply about our relationship to inflicting physical pain. Some of us expressed terror and awe when confronted with physical strength on the part of others. For us, the healing process included the need to learn how to use physical force constructively, to remove the terror—the dread. Despite the research that suggests children who are hit may become adults who hit—women hitting children, men hitting women and children—most of the women I talked with not only did not hit but were compulsive about not using physical force.

Overall the process by which women recover from the experience of being hit by loved ones is a complicated and multi-faceted one, an area where there must be much more feminist study and research. To many of us, feminists calling attention to the reality of violence in intimate relationships has not in and of itself compelled most people to take the issue seriously, and such violence seems to be daily on the increase. In this essay, I have raised issues that are not commonly talked about, even among folks who are particularly concerned about violence against women. I hope it will serve as a catalyst for further thought, that it will strengthen our efforts as feminist activists to create a world where domination and coercive abuse are never aspects of intimate relationships.

19

Violence in Lesbian and Gay Relationships

CLAIRE M. RENZETTI

When I first began to study partner abuse in same-sex relationships ten years ago, I was sometimes met with surprise, suspicion, and even amusement on the part of my colleagues, homosexual and straight. Many in the heterosexual academic community said that they didn't think abuse occurred in lesbian relationships, although after some reflection, they decided that it probably happened in butch-femme relationships and the batterer was the partner who "played the role of the man." Others expressed a kind of voyeuristic interest, although most did not see the topic as one worthy of serious scientific study. A number of lesbian and gay colleagues, who, unlike their straight peers, were aware of partner abuse in homosexual relationships, wondered why I, a straight woman, would study such a problem, and worried that my research would only fuel homophobic stereotypes and provide homophobes with an additional reason to denounce homosexuals.

Today, as I write this chapter, I can report that there have been important changes in professional attitudes toward partner abuse in same-sex relationships. For example, more research is being undertaken (see Hamberger and Renzetti 1996; Renzetti and Miley 1996), and attempts are being made to improve victim services (Margolies and Leeder 1995; Renzetti 1995; Renzetti and Miley 1996). At the same time, however, much remains the same as it was in 1985: homophobia is rampant; most battered lesbians and gay men do not receive the services they need; and the problem of same-sex partner abuse is not given the serious attention it deserves within the mainstream domestic violence movement. At a recent conference, for instance, a colleague highly regarded for his domestic violence research questioned the value of discussing lesbian battering because, as he put it, it just doesn't happen that often. Others have taken to (mis)using the data available on homosexual partner abuse to "prove" that feminist theories of domestic violence are "wrong" (e.g., Dutton 1994). If women do this to other women, they ask, then how can patriarchy be the cause?

My primary goal in this chapter is to provide an overview of what is currently known as a result of empirical research about violence in lesbian and gay relationships. Here I will focus on the issues of incidence and contributing factors.[1] What will become clear is that what we do know about same-sex domestic violence is far less than what we do *not* know. Consequently, we must be careful not to be too quick in drawing conclusions or making generalizations based on a small pool of data derived from limited samples.

However, we must also commit ourselves to learning more, and so I will also suggest various topics that warrant our attention in future research.

Same-Sex Domestic Violence: What It Is, How and When It Occurs

Homosexual partner abuse may be defined as a "pattern of violent [or] coercive behaviors whereby a lesbian [or gay man] seeks to control the thoughts, beliefs, or conduct of [an] intimate partner or to punish the intimate for resisting the perpetrator's control" (Hart 1986, 173). In light of this definition it should be clear that same-sex domestic violence is quite similar to heterosexual domestic violence. Yet, there are important ways in which same-sex domestic violence is unique.

In my research with battered lesbians (Renzetti 1992), I found that the most common forms of physical abuse reported were being pushed and shoved; being hit with open hands or fists; being scratched or hit in the face, breasts, or genitals; and having things thrown at them. The most common forms of psychological or emotional abuse were being threatened; being demeaned in front of friends, relatives, and strangers; having sleeping and eating habits disrupted; and having property damaged and destroyed. It also was not uncommon for the partners of these respondents to abuse others in the household (e.g., children or pets).

These findings, though notable in themselves, were overshadowed by two others that I consider even more significant. First, on the questionnaire to which these women responded, there was a list of sixteen different forms of physical abuse and seventeen different forms of psychological abuse. Although some of the most severe types of abuse listed (e.g., being stabbed or shot, having guns or knives inserted into one's vagina) were relatively rare, they did occur; in fact, every type of abuse listed was experienced by at least two participants in my study. Second, the list, despite its length, was not exhaustive; respondents described numerous additional forms of abuse (e.g., being physically restrained, being forced to sever all ties and contacts with relatives and friends, partners stealing their property). Abusers would sometimes hurt or threaten to hurt themselves, as a means to control or manipulate the respondents. In addition, abusers often tailored the abuse to the specific vulnerabilities of their partners (e.g., a diabetic was forced to eat sugar as "punishment" for "misbehavior"). These findings are not unique to abusive lesbian relationships; David Island and Patrick Letellier (1991) recount numerous equally disturbing examples from their discussions with gay male victims of domestic violence.

What these findings suggest is that it is not so much the form the abuse takes, but rather the motivation underlying the abuse that is important in understanding it. Research with battered heterosexual women points us in the same direction, and in listening to the stories of abused wives we hear the similarities between their abuse experiences and those of battered lesbians and gay men. In fact, one of the participants in my study (Renzetti 1992) told me that she was working in a battered women's shelter at the time her partner was abusing her, and it was in doing intake interviews with battered heterosexual women that she came to recognize herself as a battered woman.

Nevertheless, there are important differences between heterosexual domestic violence and same-sex domestic violence. As Suzanne Pharr (1986) has pointed out, battered heterosexual women experience violence in the context of misogynism, but battered lesbians and gay men experience violence in the context of a world that is both misogynistic *and homophobic.* Homophobia comes into play on several different levels, which I will consider at various points throughout the remainder of this chapter. Here, however, I wish to emphasize that homophobia may be used by an abuser as a weapon of control. More specifically, one form of abuse unique to same-sex relationships is the threat or practice of "outing," that is, threatening to reveal or actually revealing to others (e.g., relatives, employers, landlords) that an individual is lesbian or gay, when that individual wishes to conceal their sexual orientation. In our homophobic society, outing may result in abandonment by relatives and friends, the loss of a job, and a wide variety of other discriminatory behaviors, against which the victim has little or no legal recourse. In my research (Renzetti 1992), for instance, 21 percent of the respondents reported that their partners had threatened to out them. Several respondents stated that they quit their jobs before their partners carried through on the threat to out them at work, explaining that they felt if they left on their own and resolved their problems with their partners, they could find another job more easily than if they were outed, subsequently fired or laid off, and perhaps surreptitiously blacklisted by an employer.

AIDS also raises special issues for gay male victims of domestic violence. Although AIDS does not solely affect gay male relationships, gay men do constitute the largest percentage of people with AIDS. Island and Letellier (1991) express concern that the stress induced from the fear of contracting AIDS, from dealing with the disease if one has contracted it, or in trying to care for an infected partner is becoming an excuse for gay male domestic violence. Elsewhere, Letellier (1996) outlines how AIDS may impact gay male domestic violence, particularly by increasing the difficulty abuse victims have in trying to leave their batterers. For instance, an abuse victim who also has AIDS may be so dependent on his batterer for financial support and health care assistance that he decides it is better to remain in the relationship than to risk living alone. An abuse victim whose batterer has AIDS may feel tremendous guilt about leaving a dying partner with no one else to care for him. According to Letellier (1996), abusers actively reinforce these worries in their partners.

Despite the differences between same-sex and heterosexual battering, it has been argued that both occur at similar rates. It has been estimated that the incidence of domestic violence among heterosexual couples is anywhere from 12 percent to 33 percent, depending on the sample and how abuse is measured (Koss 1990; Straus 1993; Straus and Gelles 1990). Studies of abuse in lesbian and gay male relationships have found rates ranging from almost 11 percent to more than 73 percent (Island and Letellier 1991; Lie, Schilit, Bush, Montagne, and Reyes 1991); rates of verbal abuse have been reported as high as 95 percent (Kelly and Warshafsky 1987).[2] Not surprisingly, many commentators cite these figures as evidence that violence occurs at least as frequently in lesbian and gay relationships as it does in heterosexual relationships. My own work (Renzetti 1992) is often mistakenly cited in support of this claim (see, e.g., Harris and Cook 1994), when in fact my research is not a true prevalence study at all. None of the research so far on partner abuse in gay and lesbian relationships has been able to measure "true prevalence" because the studies have utilized self-selected rather than random samples. Indeed, it is doubtful that a true prevalence study of lesbian and gay partner abuse is possible as long as the stigma attached to homosexual relationships leads many lesbians and gay men to hide their sexual identities from others, including researchers. Instead, what my research and that of others (e.g., Island and Letellier 1991) does show is simply that partner abuse occurs in same-sex relationships; it is not so infrequent as to be anomalous; and once it does occur, it is like to reoccur and to become increasingly severe over time.

Explaining Same-Sex Partner Abuse

Little effort has been made to understand same-sex partner abuse beyond superimposing heterosexual models onto lesbian and gay relationships. For instance, research repeatedly shows that in Western societies masculinity is associated with aggression as well as dominating authority within intimate relationships. These norms of masculinity, not surprisingly, have been related to various forms of violent behavior among men, including domestic violence (Messerschmidt 1993). With increasing reports of same-sex domestic violence has come the popular stereotype that partner abuse occurs in homosexual relationships involving role-playing among the partners. Thus, it is assumed that the abuser is the masculine partner and the victim the feminine partner. However, researchers who have studied homosexual relationships report that role-playing does not characterize the majority of lesbian and gay couples. Instead, most find that role differentiation and expectations are quite diverse (Blumstein and Schwartz 1983; Tanner 1978). Moreover, research with victims of same-sex domestic violence shows that the abuser is not necessarily more "masculine" than the victim in terms of physical size, appearance, or mannerisms (Renzetti 1992).

The relatively few researchers who have studied domestically violent homosexual relationships have examined a number of other variables as possible contributing factors to the abuse. Again, however, most of these variables have been suggested by research with heterosexual couples, and the findings with regard to homosexual couples are equivocal at best. Consider, for example, the role of alcohol and drug abuse. In several studies of same-sex domestic violence, the use of alcohol and drugs has been found to be related to partner abuse in 33 percent to over 70 percent of the couples studied (Coleman 1990; Kelly and Warshafsky 1987; Schilit, Lie, and Montagne 1990). Others (e.g., Island and Letellier 1991; Renzetti 1992), however, report that although alcohol and drug use is often present in violent lesbian and gay relationships, it is neither a necessary nor a sufficient cause for partner abuse. Instead, the use of alcohol and drugs often serves as an excuse for or facilitator of abuse; much abuse occurs when batterers are not under the influence of drugs or alcohol, and alcohol and drug use may follow rather than precede battering incidents (see also Gelles 1993).

Similarly, research that has examined the role of previous exposure to domestic violence (usually in the batterer's and/or victim's family of origin) has produced inconsistent results.[3] Although Gwat-Yong Lie and coworkers (1991) found that lesbians who witnessed and/or experienced domestic violence in their families of origin were more likely than those who grew up in nonviolent families to be victimized as an adult and/or to abuse their own partners, others (Coleman 1990; Kelly and Warshafsky 1987; Renzetti 1992) have found no significant evidence showing the intergenerational transmission of violence in abusive lesbian and gay relationships.

Feminist analyses have emphasized the importance of understanding the role of patriarchal power in the etiology of domestic violence. Unfortunately, translating power into a measurable variable for empirical research has proved difficult because of the multifaceted nature of the construct. Power operates on different levels (individual, institutional, societal) and manifests itself in numerous ways. Traditionally, power in intimate relationships has been measured in terms of which partner has greatest decision-making authority, but this approach has been extensively criticized (see Renzetti and Curran 1995). More broadly, patriarchal power has been operationalized with measures such as the Status of Women Index, a state-by-state composite of economic, educational, political, and legal indicators of gender inequality (Yllö and Straus 1990).

In studies of both heterosexual and homosexual domestic violence, however, power operationalized in one or more of these ways has not been consistently strongly correlated with abuse.

With respect to heterosexual domestic violence, for example, Kersti Yllö and Murray Straus (1990) found a curvilinear relationship between patriarchal power and abuse: High rates of abuse were found in states in which women had relatively high status as well as in those states in which women's status was relatively low. Similarly, Michael Smith (1990b) reported that patriarchal beliefs and attitudes explained only 20 percent of the variance in rates of wife abuse in his Canadian study. At the micro-level, most studies of heterosexual couples have shown that the risk of wife abuse increases if the male partner considers himself to be less powerful in the relationship relative to his wife or if his perceives his power relative to his wife to be waning (Gondolf 1988a; Finkelhor, Gelles, Hotaling, and Straus 1983). In virtually all the empirical studies of partner abuse, power has been measured on the micro-level in terms of decision-making authority or the relative resources (i.e., money, education, status) that each partner brings to the relationship (Bologna, Waterman, and Dawson 1987; Coleman 1990; Kelly and Warshafsky 1987; Renzetti 1992). Although a few power measures in these studies were significantly correlated with the frequency and severity of partner abuse, most were not.

Nevertheless, the question of perceived power or powerlessness is not unrelated to the issue of partners' relative dependency on one another, which has been found to be strongly associated with abuse in both heterosexual and homosexual relationships. More specifically, research indicates that in heterosexual relationships, couples at greatest risk for violence were those in which husbands have high dependency (or affiliation) needs, but their wives seek relative autonomy and independence (Byrne, Arias, and O'Leary 1992). Although I know of no research that has examined empirically the role of partners' relative dependency in gay male relationships, my own research with battered lesbians produced findings consistent with those of Daniel Byrne and coworkers (1992): The greater the lesbian batterer's dependency *and* the greater the victim's desire to be independent, the more likely the batterer is to inflict more types of abuse with greater frequency. Batterers, both gay and straight, also have been found to have poor self-concepts and low self-esteem, which in turn are related to their dysfunctionally high dependency needs (Byrne 1996; Coleman 1990; Walker 1989).

Findings such as these have led some researchers to argue that social structural factors, such as patriarchy and gender inequality, are less important than individual personality factors in explaining partner abuse in both homosexual and heterosexual relationships (Dutton 1994; Letellier 1994; O'Leary 1993). More specifically, these researchers maintain that the primary causal factor of intimate violence is diagnosable psychopathology, which typically manifests as a personality disorder. The personality disorders most commonly associated with abusive behavior are borderline personality disorder, narcissism, antisocial behavior, and the aggressive-sadistic personality. The more frequent and severe the abuse, the greater the likelihood of psychopathology in the abuser (Dutton 1994).

D. G. Dutton (1994) cites an impressive list of studies that show that at least among heterosexual men who are court-referred or self-referred for clinical treatment as a result of wife assault, about 80 to 90 percent have a diagnosable psychological pathology. However, such data for gay and lesbian abusers are scarce, a fact that may be due in part to reluctance among some researchers in this area to begin labeling interactions in gay and lesbian relationships "sick" or "abnormal" given the negative ways homosexuality has been treated historically by most mainstream psychiatrists and psychologists. Nevertheless, V. E. Coleman (1994) reports that the lesbian batterers she sees in her clinical practice often exhibit personality disorders, especially borderline and narcissistic disorders (see also Island and Letellier 1991).

Coleman (1994), however, maintains that intimate violence, regardless of the sexual orientation of the couple involved, is best understood in terms of a multidimensional perspective that incorporates sociocultural variables with individual psychological factors. We can perhaps best see how social structural and psychological factors may intersect by considering the issue of internalized homophobia. Internalized homophobia occurs when gay men and lesbians accept heterosexual society's negative evaluations of them and incorporate these into their self-concepts. It is analogous to internalized racism, in which people of color accept white people's prejudices against them (Allport 1958; Margolies, Becker, and Jackson-Brewer 1987). In applying the phenomenon of internalized homophobia to same-sex domestic violence, James Shattuck (1992) asks: How might the experience of being gay or lesbian (that is, oppressed and alienated by heterosexual society, being forced to "live outside the rules") affect one's relational abilities with an intimate partner? Clinicians report that internalized homophobia causes homosexuals to experience lowered self-esteem, feelings of powerlessness, obsessive closeting of sexual orientation, denial of difference between themselves and heterosexuals, and self-destructive behavior such as substance abuse (Margolies et al. 1987; Nicoloff and Stiglitz 1987; Riddle and Sang 1978; Vargo 1987). It may also lead to aggression against members of one's own group, which could take the form of partner abuse (Shattuck 1992). Thus, societal homophobia (a social structural variable) generates internalized homophobia (a psychological variable), which, in turn, may lead to partner abuse in same-sex relationships.

Unfortunately, there is no research yet that tests the relationship between internalized homophobia and homosexual partner abuse. Such research first requires the development of a reliable and valid measure of internalized homophobia—a difficult task to say the least. In addition, researchers need to address the question of why some gay men and lesbians succumb to internalized homophobia while others do not, even though all live in a heterosexist, homophobic society. It may be the case that low self-esteem and perceived powerlessness are antecedents rather than consequences of internalized homophobia. Both, we have seen, are related to intimate violence in homosexual and heterosexual relationships. Perhaps, then, both are risk markers not only for partner abuse, but also for other dysfunctional outcomes, one of which may be internalized homophobia among gay men and lesbians.

Of course, teasing out the relationships among these and a host of other variables requires much more study utilizing more rigorous methodologies than what we have done to date. Moreover, in designing and implementing this research, there is an array of additional issues that merit serious consideration. I conclude this chapter by outlining some of them.

Research Challenges

Social scientists, it seems, delight in categorization. We develop dichotomies and typologies to classify the multitude of behaviors and other phenomena we observe. Importantly, domestic violence research has shown that to ask the questions, "Is a particular individual a batterer or not?" and "Is a particular individual a victim or not?" simply establishes false dichotomies. At the same time, we now know that neither batterers nor victims constitute a homogenous group (Gelles 1995). Why, then, are some of us so quick to dismiss social structural variables, such as patriarchy and gender inequality, in favor of individual psychological causes, if same-sex partner abuse at first glance does not appear to meet the criteria for our preconceived categories of "batterers" and "victims"? Knowing as we do that battering and victimization, as well as patriarchy and gender inequality, are highly complex constructs, why are we surprised when same-sex domestic violence does not always "look like" heterosexual domestic violence?

Our research on same-sex domestic violence to date has been guided by the research on heterosexual domestic violence because many of us have been trained to view scientific work according to what one of my undergraduate professors used to call the "pebble theory of knowledge." That is, each researcher, through her or his individual studies, builds on the work of other researchers, adding pebbles to the pile until eventually a "mountain of knowledge" accumulates and hopefully our questions are answered—we have discovered Truth. Thomas Kuhn (1970) referred to this process as "normal science." However, as Kuhn pointed out, it sometimes becomes necessary to strike out in a new direction, to start asking different questions, to begin building a new pile of pebbles if you will. I submit that this time has come in domestic violence research.

I am not taking this opportunity to volunteer to lead this scientific revolution; I've never had much of a sense of direction, and building is hardly one of my talents. However, I can share here a number of issues that have arisen in recent discussions with feminist colleagues, and these, in turn, may serve as the basis for innovative research questions.[4]

Feminist research by women of color has taught us that we cannot assume that everyone experiences an event similarly or gives the same meaning to a particular set of interactions. Instead, in attempting to understand a phenomenon such as domestic violence, we must take *intersectionality* into account (Crenshaw 1994). That is, we must consider how people who are differentially located in our society not only because of their sexual orientation, but also because of their race, gender, and social class, may experience a phenomenon differently and give different meanings to it. Those who are marginalized, who have been rendered "outsiders" or "the Other," often experience and define situations as problematic differently than those who are members of dominant groups (Collins 1986; Crenshaw 1994). Consequently, one of the major challenges for future domestic violence research is inclusivity: a careful examination of how racism, sexism, social class inequality, and homophobia may impact on both the causes and consequences of intimate violence. The goal is not to fit "others" into the dominant mold, but rather to come to a better understanding of the diversity of domestic violence experiences, the significance and meaning this violence has in the lives of different groups of people, and how this intersectionality affects outcomes, particularly institutional responses to domestic violence.

Achieving this understanding requires research that is not only inclusive, but also *contextualized*. Future domestic violence research must examine the meanings that specific behaviors have for the social actors involved in them. Research is now being done that provides analyses of heterosexual men's accounts of why they batter (e.g., Adams and Cayouette 1995; Barnett, Lee, and Thelen 1995; Eiskovits and Buchbinder 1995) and how heterosexual men's and women's accounts of their motivations for using violence differ (e.g., Barnett, Lee, and Thelen 1995). To date, however, I know of no research that undertakes an analysis of whether such accounts and motives vary by race, class, or sexual orientation as well. Victoria Burbank's work (1994a, 1994b) also shows that the meanings and motives underlying intimate violence vary among societies, thus also alerting us to the need for more cross-cultural research.

Of course, such work requires the use of diverse research methodologies. Innumerable scales and indices have been developed, with varying levels of reliability and validity, to measure an array of behaviors and affects, from the use of various types of abuse to relationship satisfaction and self-image. Nevertheless, such measures rarely if ever can place behavior and emotion in context. Nor can these measures effectively pick up on the often subtle, but no less important, differences in meanings that specific words or phrases have for members of different groups.[5] On pencil-and-paper measures and in artificial experimental settings, research participants rarely have the opportunity to ask for clarification of a term, to contextualize their responses, or even to simply to tell their stories. Our research designs, therefore, must make more use of interview, narrative, and ethnographic methods, and our research strategies must make room for genuine collaboration between researchers and participants. Fortuantely, domestic violence researchers do not have to "reinvent the wheel" for this undertaking; the feminist methodologies being utilized to study a wide variety of topics are available to guide us (see, e.g., Reinharz 1992; Maguire 1987).

It should be clear at this point that I consider many of the recent comparisons between same-sex domestic violence and heterosexual domestic violence to be overly simplistic and falsely framed. In short, many of us have been asking the wrong questions and looking in the wrong places for the answers. This is not to say, however, that same-sex domestic violence and heterosexual domestic violence should be studied separately, or that findings regarding one are irrelevant to the other. Rather, what I am proposing here is simply that we stop using a specific model of heterosexual domestic violence research—one that overlooks the intersectionality of social locating variables and decontextualizes behavior and emotion—as the central organizing paradigm of our work. Indeed, what I am advocating is that we turn this paradigm on its head: That we develop, as the foundation for our mountain of knowledge, findings from contextualized, collaborative studies of intimate violence among lesbian and gay couples, as well as couples from other marginalized groups and from differing cultures.

Will we come to recognize the value of such research? If we truly seek to understand domestic violence, we must.

NOTES

1. Space limitations preclude a discussion of services and treatment issues. For a discussion of these topics, see Margolies and Leeder 1995; Renzetti 1992; and Renzetti and Miley 1996.

2. For other incidence estimates, see Bologna, Waterman, and Dawson 1987; Brand and Kidd 1986; Coleman 1990; Lie and Gentlewarrior 1991; and Loulan 1987.

3. This should not be surprising, given that research with heterosexual couples has also generated confounding findings. Compare, for example, DeMaris 1990; Forsstrom-Cohn and Rosenbaum 1985; Kalmuss 1984; O'Leary 1993; and Straus, Gelles, and Steinmetz 1980.

4. I am indebted to my colleagues—Angela Browne, Walter DeKeseredy, Rebecca and Russell Dobash, Ann Goetting, Ed Gondolf, Demie Kurz, Beth Ritchie, Kersti Yllö, and many others—who attended the Wheaton College Conference on Feminism and Domestic Violence, June 22–25, 1995, for raising these issues and, through their provocative discussions, leading me to think carefully about how the issues relate to research on same-sex domestic violence, an area that I feel is well suited for exploring these issues empirically. Special thanks to Kersti Yllö for organizing the conference and providing me the opportunity to take part in it.

5. For example, I am reminded of a verbal exchange I had several years ago with a member of

the battered lesbians support group with whom I was working to develop a questionnaire. While trying to understand the woman's objection to my use of a particular word on the questionnaire I said, "Now, let's get this straight . . . " at which point she interrupted me and said, "That's what I mean: No matter how hard you try, we'll never get it *straight*." We shared a good laugh, but her point was well taken.

20

Violence, Gender, and Elder Abuse: Toward a Feminist Analysis and Practice

TERRI WHITTAKER

Introduction

The last twenty-five years have witnessed a mass of research and intervention targeted at child abuse and domestic violence. However, it is only fairly recently, in the context of rapid demographic change and growing anxiety about the family, that policy makers and academics have shown an interest in elder abuse (Phillipson 1993). Specifically, there has been an upswing in research emanating in the main from the USA which has focused on the modern phenomenon of elder abuse (Sengstock and Liang 1982; Phillips 1986; Godkin et al. 1989; Pillemer and Wolf 1986; Quinn and Tomita 1986; Eastman 1984; Pritchard 1992; Bennett and Kingston 1993; Decalmer and Glendenning 1993).

This new momentum in research interest has been dominated by professionals and "experts" from the field of "family violence" and by a health/welfare model of elder abuse. This approach locates causation within individuals or families and seeks to develop typologies or "profiles" of abusers/abused within various models of family violence in an attempt to make predictions about those most at risk of harm (Parton 1985). This selective claiming and framing of elder abuse as a product of interpersonal dynamics and/or of various forms of family violence is linked to significant theoretical, definitional and methodological problems which have led to wide ranging and contradictory findings (McCreadie 1991; Decalmer and Glendenning 1993). Nonetheless this "orthodoxy" looks set fair to achieve the status of "common sense" amongst those working in the area of elder abuse. Within the literature on elder abuse there is a curious lack of discussion about why it occurs and little reference to the complex social and political problems inherent in the construction and resolution of social problems.

One of the few consistent findings from the research literature on elder abuse is that the majority of "victims" of elder abuse are old women (McCreadie 1991, 21). This is especially so in relation to physical and/or sexual abuse (Pillemer and Wolf 1986; Holt 1993). However, there has been no systematic attempt to develop a feminist analysis of elder abuse which appears to have been screened out of the debate on the grounds that women have been found to abuse their elders too (Godkin et al. 1989; Pillemer and Wolf 1986; Pillemer and Suitor 1988). This paper represents an attempt to acquire and transform "orthodox" knowledge in an effort to illustrate the gendered nature of elder

From *Journal of Gender Studies* 4, no. 1 (1995):35–45. Reprinted by permission.

abuse and chart the beginnings of a feminist analysis. The need for more adequate theorizing about causation is identified particularly at the social structural level and in relation to the social and political construction of the "family," old age and masculinity.

Elder Abuse: Definitions, Prevalence, and Incidence

DEFINITIONS

The first stage in developing any adequate form of policy or practice amongst those involved in elder abuse necessitates reaching agreement on what it is, how common it is, why it happens and how best to respond to it.

McCreadie's (1991) review of available USA and UK research reveals that the process of reaching agreement about elder abuse is fraught with difficulties. It appears that professionals and academics have been heavily involved in debates about definitions, incidence and prevalence at the expense of adequate theorizing. The main problems seem to centre around which criteria to include or exclude in various definitions of abuse and around whether or not elder abuse is different from other forms of "family violence."

These difficulties have been attributed to differences in emphasis and perspective amongst investigators and a tendency to distinguish between typologies and conceptualizations of elder abuse and neglect. This "definitional disarray" and failure to reach consensus is a major thread throughout the published literature. There appears to be no attempt to include the victim's subjective experience of abuse as part of the definitional debate and virtually no attention is paid to issues of inequalities of power between victim and perpetrator other than to stress that old people are not children and that dependency exists as a two-way process within relationships between them and their abusers (Ogg and Bennett 1992).

PREVALENCE AND INCIDENCE OF ELDER ABUSE

The concern with numbers of old people who are abused appears to be another false trail. As yet we cannot say exactly how common elder abuse is. There has been no major study of the prevalence or incidence of elder abuse in Britain. Evidence from the USA indicates that 10 percent of elders supported by family members are at risk (Eastman and Sutton 1982, 12). In Britain, Ogg and Bennett (1992, 63) have translated American figures to arrive at an estimate of "eight elderly people who are subjected to abuse or inadequate care within a patient register of 200." Other investigators have commented upon the methodological problems pertaining to much of the American research relating to prevalence/incidence (Decalmer and Glendenning 1993, 12) while others point to difficulties inherent in the fact that much elder abuse is hidden and unreported (McPherson 1990, 360).

Hairsplitting discussions about what is elder abuse and how common it is, obscure the evidence that a significant number of old women are exposed to unacceptable forms of violence from adult men in particular and detracts from thinking about why it happens. Much more important than establishing an agreed definition or a prevalence rate is agreeing on a set of rules about what is permissible or not and ensuring that old people are protected as and when necessary and/or appropriate.

Victims and Perpetrators

Until recently, most research attention has been focused on the characteristics of the "victims" of elder abuse and on the production of a stereotypical picture of the nature of old age. The "classic" victim of elder abuse has been painted by various British, Canadian and American researchers (Horrocks 1988; Tomlin 1989; Bennett 1990) as:

1. Female aged over 75.
2. Living at home with adult carer/s.
3. Physically and/or mentally impaired.
4. Roleless. Lost previous roles as wife/mother/caregiver.
5. Isolated, fearful.

This profile of the "victim" of abuse has run parallel with liberal explanations of elder abuse concentrated on depicting a straight correlation between biological aging and dependency (Phillips 1986, 198). The situational or "carer stress" model in which elder abuse is persistently explained in these terms has had huge appeal for professionals who, while not condoning abuse as such, have been able to empathize with this picture of old age and the strain of caring. In so doing, there has been a tendency to downplay the gender significance of elder abuse and to look for victim-related sources of stress thereby falling into the "victim blaming" trap and colluding with various forms of institutionalized ageism and sexism (Traynor and Hasnip 1984).

Recently, a more complex picture of victims and perpetrators has begun to emerge which indicates that old men are also victims of elder abuse while women are also perpetrators. Though there is consistent agreement that the overwhelming majority of abusers are men and the majority of victims are old women, research does demonstrate that frail, vulnerable old men are also victims of abuse and that some of their abusers are women (Godkin et al. 1989; Pillemer and Wolf 1986; Pillemer and Suitor 1988).

Within newer research there is a suggestion of gender-specific differences in the forms and types of abuse which occur (Homer and Gilleard 1990; Holt 1993). Miller and Dodder (1989) separated physical abuse from neglect and discovered a statistically different sex bias in that men were more likely to physically abuse while women were more likely to neglect the old person in their care. They point to the high rates of reported neglect by women and stress that this may create the appearance of large numbers of female abusers when in fact the nature and extent of physical or sexual elder abuse by men is as yet unknown and there is much more resistance to disclosure of abuse of this type. Holt (1993) investigating ninety cases of elder abuse discovered a female to male victim ratio of 6:1 and that all but two abusers were male. Holt hypothesized that the common denominator between male and female victims of abuse was physical and mental frailty and their consequent vulnerability to abuse by those in positions of power and authority.

Orthodox research, underpinned by liberal notions of old age as dependency and a concern with preserving the "family" has generally failed to adequately examine the significance of gender as a centrally important feature of elder abuse. This may account for the shift in research focus away from the characteristics of predominantly female victims towards the characteristics and circumstances of perpetrators and a concern with the "dynamics" of their interpersonal relationships. In this context, the resistance to the idea that elder abuse is predominantly a male problem has been manifested in various forms including a focus on an increasing number of female abusers and the claim that women are also perpetrators of elder abuse. In this way, "experts" justify refusing to engage with feminist analysis and fail to recognise or acknowledge men's power in the world and in the family.

Women are of course quite capable of abusing power and trust or of exploiting old people to fulfil their own emotional and material needs. However, it seems they rarely resort to physical and/or sexual abuse. This does not imply that women are morally superior but suggests that if we refuse to consider gender-specific behaviours, we may lose important clues as to why elder abuse occurs.

The Perpetrators and Their Characteristics and Circumstances

In recent years, the focus of attention in elder abuse has shifted from "granny battering." New research has drawn on theories of family pathology to challenge the ideas of a close association between abuse and the physical and/or mental state of the "victim" suggesting that the characteristics and circumstances of the perpetrators may be more important risk indicators (Pillemer and Wolf 1986; Homer and Gilleard 1990). The notion of "inadequate care" which is underpinned by a model of a stressed and/or pathological abuser, has been introduced to facilitate this shift (Fulmer and O'Malley 1987). Various attempts have been made to identify the predisposing factors leading to abuse and researchers have emphasized the dependency of "carers" on victims and on drugs or alcohol as significant factors.

As a result, earlier ways of seeing and thinking about elder abuse as a form of "granny battering" have been dismissed. What is called "the initial stereotyped plot" (Bennett and Kingston 1993) is set aside in favour of a new orthodoxy in which it is held that elder abuse is much more complex, consisting of a varied set of characteristics and relationships which occur within the context of the relationship between the victim and the carer (Homer and Gilleard 1990).

From a feminist perspective there is some irony in the continued use of the word "carer" and the deliberate misuse of gender-neutral language to mask gender-specific behaviour. Language such as "carers," victims, perpetrators, abusers, and abused all serve to obscure the gender significance of data. This, together with information relating to the inadequate personality types of the "carers," forms the basis for "compassion" as opposed to "control" philosophies of assessment and intervention (Bennett and Kingston 1993). In this context, notions of family autonomy and support for "carers" dominate policy and practice formulations while legal and punitive modes of intervention are considered unhelpful (Newberger and Bourne 1977).

The Relationship between Elder Abuse and "Family" Violence

Recently, there has been a growing interest and concern among researchers in the nature and extent of the relationship between elder abuse and other forms of family violence. Elder abuse is said to occur in a context of family relations and therefore it is argued, more attention needs to be paid to the literature relating to child and spouse abuse (Pillemer and Suitor 1988). Some writers have argued that elder abuse should be seen as a part of the spectrum of domestic abuse which affects all ages (Department of

Health 1992) while others have sought to establish a special category for elder abuse and associated programmes of assessment and intervention (Finkelhor and Pillemer 1988).

The growing interest in domestic violence in general and child abuse and spouse abuse in particular looks set to dominate the discourse on elder abuse. However, as with early research and debates on child abuse the interest is confined to certain liberal and conservative theories of family violence which are often not made explicit. In this context, the growing interest in the "family" is not about making the gender significance of research data more explicit or about exposing the problems of sexual politics inherent in elder abuse. Instead, the research reflects a growing anxiety about the nature of the "family" and a concern to enshrine and safeguard "normal" family relationships.

Five major explanations rooted in theories of family violence are examined at various points in the research (Pillemer 1986). They are:

1. Pathology of abuser: intra-individual dynamics.
2. Cycle of violence: Violence transmitted between generations.
3. Dependency: of abused and/or abuser.
4. Isolation: limited social networks/denial of access.
5. External stress: unemployment, bereavement, inadequate community care, low income, poor housing.

Pillemer and Suitor (1988, 49) reviewing the literature associated with these themes argue:

> These factors may directly precipitate domestic violence against the elderly. That is *families* that have one of these characteristics may be at greater risk of elder abuse. (my italics)

What is crucial here is the focus on the "family" rather than particular individuals who may have abused or been abused. Indeed the literature is now beginning to be peppered with references to "abusive families" (Godkin et al. 1989) as "systems" or sets of interrelationships which are not functioning properly. Thus elder abuse becomes a *symptom* of what is wrong within the *family* and the personality traits and behaviour of both victims and abusers become fair game however widely they vary. Discussion of the complex gender issues and sexual politics inherent in the relationship between them is completely avoided and there is no attempt to explain why it is mostly men who abuse. Instead, we are prompted towards compassionate responses as we learn that "carers" have histories of psychosocial disorder, are addicted to drugs or alcohol and/or are dependent upon the predominantly frail and vulnerable old women they are "caring" for:

> Elders *(mostly women)* mistreated by spouses *(mostly male)* were more apt to suffer from physical abuse, to be in poorer emotional health and to be more dependent on them for companionship, financial resources, management and maintenance of property. The perpetrators were more likely to have both recent and long term medical complaints and to have experienced a recent decline in physical health. . . . They were also more likely to have a history of mental illness and alcoholism. (Wolf and Bergman 1989, 163; my italics)

Another twist to the tale of the "problem relative" (Pillemer & Finkelhor, 1989) lies in the notion of the "cycle of violence." Here, some commentators argue that elder abuse is directly related to the fact that perpetrators were themselves products of domestic violence which had become learned behaviour and normative for them (Fulmer and O'Malley 1987). The child abuse literature has shown how dangerous these ideas are and pointed to the way they feed myths about "pathological" families and fuel class and race stereotypes to the point where abusers have been known to tell their victims that abuse is quite normal (Nelson 1987, 48).

The idea that "perpetrators" abuse because they were themselves abused says nothing about the number of perpetrators who were abused in childhood who do not go on to abuse young or old women or about the number of women who were abused in childhood but have not married or had relationships with men who abused them at any point in their lifespan. There has been no attempt to describe or confirm a causal link between childhood or family abuse and adults who abuse old people yet it is important not to underestimate the strength of these ideas. Not only do they have a spurious liberal appeal by saying that individual men are not to blame, but they are also internalized by all of us and their effect is to prompt compassionate and therapeutic responses and to absolve the abuser of responsibility by inferring that *he* is a victim too!

From Anger to Analysis: Toward a Feminist Analysis of Elder Abuse

There is scope for growing anger as one reads the annals of academic enquiry into elder abuse. However, if we are to move from the suspicion of conspiracy toward a better understanding of why elder abuse occurs and to an adequate examination of the complex gender, social and political issues therein, we must move beyond rage and "problem families."

Ageing society is primarily a female society. It is well known that women generally outlive men and that ageism and sexism combine to produce a socially constructed dependency in old age in which the feminization of poverty is a key feature (Taylor and Ford 1983; Walker 1990; Glendenning 1987). These social processes are so pervasive that it is but a small step from here to accept as inevitable the discrimination and disadvantage which old women experience and to render them and their experiences invisible. MacDonald and Rich (1984) note that for older women, invisibility is symbolic of the process and politics of aging and point to the way this extends to the feminist movement which until recently has given very little thought to the position of older women in the family. Any adequate analysis of elder abuse must take account of the social structural position of old women in our society and how this relates to their position within the family and the resources they have at their disposal to resist abusive behaviours.

In this context, it is perhaps not so extraordinary that the high levels of severe physical abuse experienced by old women who rely on their "carers" for financial, practical and emotional support are explained by reference to demographics, longevity and variations in reporting elder abuse (Johnson et al. 1985; Pillemer and Wolf 1986). The sexual, social and economic politics which underpin their relationships with men within the "family" are not explored. Does this mean, as Schecter (1982) suggests, that we are indifferent to the pain and danger in old women's lives or that we prefer to hide behind principles of family autonomy and self-determination rather than get involved?

Feminist analysis starts with gender. In looking at why elders get abused we are not looking at some psychopathological abuser or dependent, provoking or controlling old woman who "initiates" abuse (Penhale 1993). Nor are we looking at problems of "inadequate caregiving" or even at "dysfunctional families." A feminist analysis will consider problematic sexual and adult—child politics and take account of the marginalization of old people in general and old women in particular within our society. In this context, elder abuse is not the product of a pathological family but of a patriarchal family in which men have access to and power over those less powerful and more vulnerable than themselves and regard them as their property. In so doing they are protected by societal norms which uphold the sanctity and privacy of "home" despite it being the prime site of women's oppression.

From this perspective, the references in the literature to the provoking and controlling characteristics and behaviours of "non-compliant" dependant victims (Steinmetz 1988; Homer and Gilleard 1990) "the caregiver is seen as being driven to a sense of helplessness, rage and frustration" (Decalmer and Glendenning 1993, 15) can be seen as attempts by old women to struggle against and resist the power and control of men and women in their lives. However these behaviours are more commonly seen as indicators of carer stress and used to explain and justify abusive behaviours and prompt compassionate responses which absolve the abuser from responsibility. Instead of problematizing the biology of old age and associated vulnerability and dependency, feminists consider the socially constructed aspects of dependency which women young and old experience (albeit differently) and look for answers to abuse in the cultural representation of masculinity, femininity and sexuality.

As yet the voices of "survivors" of elder abuse have not been heard above those of "experts" in the field so we know very little about the strategies or tactics employed by victims to resist or cope with abuse. The difficulties inherent in helping victims to talk and tell due to fear of stigma, institutionalization or physical and mental frailty can be overcome by validating the feelings and experiences of old women. Feil (1993) had developed techniques for communicating with vulnerable old people which may prove useful in this respect. However, there is an urgent need for feminists to test the transferability of knowledge and expertise relating to "disclosure" processes to the area of elder abuse (Kelly 1988). There is a need to build up a body of knowledge based on old women's experiences of abuse and to learn about what is helpful from this. Feminist policies for tackling abuse must therefore be concerned with advocacy and empowerment and with increasing the resources old women have available to them to empower themselves and help them resist male violence.

Feminist theory holds that abuse of women is just one part of a spectrum of male violence and that it is a mistake to separate off any particular manifestation or to see it as a special case. This is not to argue against the complexity of elder abuse or to suggest that feminist theory with its focus on gender, is the only dimension for analysis and theorizing about the phenomenon. It is, however, an argument against those who insist that elder abuse deserves a special category because of the dependency or vulnerability of victims or because of the difficulties inherent in locating responsibility due to the fact that old women are legally autonomous beings.

The argument about legal autonomy is a spurious one. Everything we know about male violence to women tells us that their legal status as adults offers little in the way of the protection women say they want from the men who abuse them (Kelly 1987). Equally, the argument for special categories and programmes due to the dependency and vulnerability of old people is at best misguided paternalism, and at worst another example of resistance to feminist analysis. While the orthodox insistence on separation of elder abuse from the spectrum of other forms of male violence remains unchallenged, thinking and theorizing about elder abuse will continue to be powerfully constrained and woefully inadequate. One of the lessons learned from child abuse work which is transferable is that the answer as to why the majority of abusers are male will not be found in studying their victims or in gender blind studies of their personal inadequacies or those of their families (Dobash and Dobash 1992).

From Analysis to Practice

A feminist challenge to orthodox practice with elder abuse will tackle notions of old women as burdensome, controlling and provoking individuals who initiate their own abuse by stressed-out carers within dysfunctional families; or as legally autonomous adults who cannot be protected because of their rights to say "no." No matter how scientifically and academically respectable orthodox thinking on elder abuse is, the first aim of feminist practice must be to develop and argue an alternative theory which recognizes abuse for what it is—a crime against the person. It is well known that the "family" is filled with many different forms of male violence and oppression and that violence is perpetrated on old and young alike (Dobash and Dobash 1992). Feminists must develop analyses of elder abuse which acknowledge the social and cultural construction of abuse and locate causation outside of the personality traits and characteristics of either abuser or abused. There is an urgent need for feminists to grasp the nettle with regard to elder abuse. The fact that they have yet to do so is a reflection not only of the powerfully constraining effects of orthodox thinking and the resistance to feminist analysis, but also of deeply entrenched ageism within the movement.

From a different analysis and meaning arise different policies and practice. It is apparent that the ideological and methodological debates within elder abuse are mirroring those which occurred in the child protection area and that elder abuse has been claimed by "experts" in family violence (Penhale 1993). It is thus not surprising that many agencies attempting to deal with elder abuse have looked for guidance to the experiences of the child abuse orthodoxy which, unlike elder abuse has been successfully challenged by feminist thinking and practice. However, child abuse procedures based on normative versions of the "family" are not, as various writers have noted, transferable wholesale to the area of elder abuse (Decalmer and Glendenning 1993; Penhale 1993). There is a need for much more research, debate and discussion before an adequate theory, policy or practice of elder abuse is articulated or implemented.

There is an urgent need therefore, for feminists to contest the hold by family violence "experts" on elder abuse terrain. Elder abuse has to be located within a feminist analysis of the "family" and dominant ideologies about old women and "dependency" within the family have to be challenged. Feminists have to press for changes at the policy level which will place more resources at the disposal of old women to enable them to resist various forms of abuse by "families" in old age. Some feminists have pointed to the feminization of poverty in old age and recognized economic independence as a crucial form of self care and empowerment for old women. This is certainly a crucial element in any successful preventative strategy (Groves 1983; Groves and Finch 1983).

Research has indicated that most "victims" of elder abuse want to remain in their own homes and families (Department of Health 1992) so moves to enable the exclusion of abusive men and to find alternative forms of "care" in the community would be important elements in a feminist policy/practice framework, as would the development of "safe places" for old women who need respite from abuse and do not want to be placed in a residential home. This is particularly challenging in the context of changes in community care legislation and policy which are forcing more and more old people to rely on already overstretched and underresourced systems of "family" or "informal" care. This can only increase the risk of abuse especially for the very old and frail who are predominantly women.

Various writers have pointed to the inadequate legal framework which exists in terms of elder abuse and to the need for balance between protection and intrusion upon adult status and autonomy (Griffiths et al. 1992). Feminists will be concerned with finding such a balance and ensuring that old women are not infantilized but do get the protection from abuse they need. This means working with a range of agencies to improve collaboration and coordination and arguing for forms of intervention which locate responsibility where it belongs and acknowledge the risks of abuse which old women are exposed to. The growing professionalization and medicalization of old age in general and elder abuse in particular should be treated with caution. A decade ago Parton (1985) pointed to how the health/welfare model of child abuse dominated research, policy and practice. This orientation locates the causes of elder abuse within "burnt out" or pathological "carers" and/or within dependant, controlling elders. It assumes that abuse occurs mainly in dysfunctional families and seeks to identify the "type" of individual that would harm their elders and/or the characteristics of the victim which may put them at greater risk. This focus on inadequate personality types or "profiles" of abused/abuser as risk indicators is highly problematic if a feminist analysis of elder abuse leads to the conclusion that it is a product of the social, political and cultural construction of the "family" old age, masculinity and sexuality.

The child abuse literature demonstrates the fact that therapeutic or compassionate philosophies of assessment of intervention which obscure the complex gender and power issues around abuse have done very little to reduce risk (Parton 1985). Feminists will be aware of the need to work for changes in theory, policy and practice in relation to elder abuse and to press for changes in the law which are appropriate. This means contesting orthodox notions of the "family" and the tendency to reduce domestic violence to "system" faults. The family is clearly not a monolithic structure which serves everyone's needs equally. The inequalities of power and the conflicts of interest and struggle for scarce resources within families have to be acknowledged. This is not an argument for no intervention but for wider and more adequate theorizing about causation.

What Is to Be Done about Abusers?

The literature on elder abuse has virtually nothing to say about abusers beyond the production of their psychosocial profiles as risk indicators. Whether the abuser is mentally ill, dependent on drugs or alcohol, prone to violence or isolated and unemployed, there is no discussion of the links between the abuse and wider social and political systems. In Britain at any rate, there is little or no real debate about the criminal aspects of elder abuse. Attempts by some lawyers to guide practitioners on how the law can be used to pursue criminal proceedings (Griffiths et al. 1992) appear to be widely ignored and there is an almost unspoken assumption, fuelled by compassionate philosophies of assessment and intervention, that the criminalization of elder abuse is inappropriate.

A feminist analysis and practice relating to elder abuse will have to question whether or not criminal proceedings are the most appropriate way of dealing with offences. Arguments against criminalization come from those who believe that abuse is a "family" matter; from those who believe it punishes and blames the victim still further;

from those who argue that labels such as "abuse" and associated proceedings prevent disclosure and from those who believe that prosecution and prison will not change the man, whereas therapy might. Feminists will argue that the decriminalization of elder abuse and the reluctance to consider "control" forms of assessment/intervention are misguided because it is giving a very clear message to society at large and men in particular that there is nothing very serious or wrong about abusing old women. It is also a way of supporting the idea that abusers are over stressed, pathetic, dependent or disturbed characters and certainly not responsible for their actions.

Elder abuse, like other forms of abuse, must be seen as a crime against the person. Anything else is unjust. While it is clear that prison is not successful at reforming anyone, to abandon it as a possibility is to collude with those who want to see elder abuse as a separate category of behaviour and abusers are not responsible for it. As long as the orthodoxy perpetuate the ideology of abusers being "driven" to it by provoking, controlling, non-compliant, burdensome, old women, abusers will internalize it for themselves and statutory workers will concur. The argument that involving the police only increases victims feelings of self-blame is an important one but experience of working with other survivors indicates that victims are ambivalent about their feelings and that one way of helping is for society to say quite clearly, "He is responsible" (Kelly 1987). What is clear is that arguments about what should be done should not come from denial and an inability to face up to and accept the reality and seriousness of elder abuse.

Until and unless the complex gender issues inherent in elder abuse are addressed as a product of dominant ideologies about the "family" about old age, masculinity and sexuality, there can be no adequate theory or practice. Attempting to begin the difficult task of posing an alternative explanation of elder abuse and thereby giving it a different meaning is an essential part of the wider political struggle towards real prevention and change. Feminists have a wealth of experience and knowledge to bring to the task at hand. Their expertise and commitment is needed urgently.

SECTION 4
Children and Gender Violence

The previous three sections have focused on sexual harassment, rape, and domestic violence, particularly as they are experienced by adults. In this section we explore how children encounter various forms of gender violence.

Children are linked to a gendered system of power through their historical social position as the property of fathers, as well as their own identity as male or female. Their rights to self-determination about work, sexual activity, bodily integrity, basic care, and life itself have been contested over time. Indeed, the nature of what constitutes child abuse continues to be debated.

In the past, children experienced infanticide, mutilation, abandonment, sexual exploitation, and dangerous labor conditions. We can see the legacy of these concerns today in the disproportionately high number of male children in some regions of China, due to female infanticide; the high rate of abortions of female fetuses in India (Narasimhan 1994); the ritualized mutilation of the sex organs of female children in some parts of Africa (Dorkenoo and Elworthy 1994) and, some would argue, the widespread acceptance of circumcision of male infants in the United States (see Ritter 1992); the proliferation of child prostitution worldwide; and the ready availability of child pornography, now enhanced through electronic technology. In fact, the ideal of a protected childhood is a relatively new concept that has not yet been successful across cultures and may be eroding for children who traditionally have been protected.

Indeed, violence toward children may be on the rise; in the United States, reports of child abuse have increased steadily from 1976 to the present (U.S. Department of Health and Human Services 1995). Reports indicate that battering of pregnant women is the major cause of birth defects (Chiles 1988) and one of the primary causes of low birth weight infants (U.S. Senate Committee on the Judiciary 1990). One study, conducted in an inner-city hospital, found that 10 percent of the children sampled had witnessed a stabbing or shooting by age six (Groves 1994). It is likely, given the high incidence of domestic violence witnessed by children, that a substantial number of the victims were mothers attacked by fathers. Estimates of the number of children in the United States who witness the abuse of their mothers each year range from 3.3 million (Carlson 1984) to 10 million (Straus 1991a). The battering of young women by their boyfriends is gaining recognition as a widespread problem (Brustin 1995), compounded by the increasingly deadly use of force by young men (Greenfeld and Zawitz 1995). Diana

E. H. Russell (1986) found that one in six women are incestuously abused by the age of eighteen, and one in eight by the age of fourteen. The highest risk group for rape in the United States continues to be females between the ages of sixteen and nineteen (Flowers 1994). Worldwide, children continue to be major victims of war, with girls facing the added risk of increasingly common sexual abuses associated with ethnic and regional disputes (UNICEF 1995).

Of course, a child's gender identity has much to do with how she or he reacts to and copes with violence. Boys are more likely to learn that male violence is normal behavior for men. Popular culture abounds with images of violent men as heroes: film and television characters, sports figures, rock and rap musicians all contribute to a generalized environment of male violence and female victimization as normal and acceptable. In a culture that glorifies violence and makes heroes of violent "winners," it is no wonder that many boys choose not to identify with the "losers." Girls continue to be bombarded with messages about their diminished social value relative to boys. Positions of strength and power in the real world are still dominated by men, and this is reflected in characterizations of women in popular culture. Women are still measured by their ability to attract the attention of men, and to refer to a male as a girl or woman is still a pejorative term implying incompetent performance (Segal 1990).

Children who watch television witness tremendous amounts of violence, much of it gendered in nature. Research continues to show that, especially for children, the boundaries between fantasy and reality are permeable, so that it is very difficult for them to ascertain what is a true account of human suffering and what is ostensibly a rendition of human suffering intended as entertainment. Since some scholars have found that the development of empathy is key to inhibiting violent behavior, it seems important to inspect the possible connections between media images of violence, how children process those images, cultural supports for aggression, and the increasing numbers of violent crimes committed by children, often against other children. There is a growing concern that these fictional and "entertaining" images may have a profound effect on attitudes and tolerance of violence. For children who have experienced violence at home, television may provide a "double dose effect" confirming their perception of the world as a dangerous and violent place where the rule of force is the norm (Jaffe, Wolfe, and Wilson, this volume). Recent findings indicate that experiences of cruelty and violence may alter the chemistry of a child's brain, which may in turn affect behavior, particularly in regard to aggression (Goleman 1995).

Forms of Gender Violence Experienced by Children: Child Witnesses

Although the last several decades have seen a tremendous increase in awareness of the occurrence of rape and domestic violence directed specifically against women, only recently have people started to ask where the children are when their mothers are being assaulted. It has become clear that only too frequently they are cowering in the next room, hiding in a closet, or attempting to intervene physically to stop the abuse (an action that may expose them to the full wrath of the abuser). One study found that children witnessed 11 percent of marital rapes (Russell 1990). The Los Angeles County Sheriff's Homicide Division estimates that 10 to 20 percent of homicides in their jurisdiction are witnessed by children and that a parent is most commonly the victim (Eth and Pynoos 1985).

Child witnesses of violence exhibit a wide range of emotions and behaviors related to their experience, including being overwhelmed, sleep disturbances, guilt, lack of trust in adult restraint, and aggressive, reckless, or self-destructive behavior. Even infants and toddlers exposed to violence have exhibited symptoms of anxiety, depression, and disruptive behavior (Zeanah 1994). Clinicians report that the symptoms exhibited by their child clients who have witnessed the abuse of a parent are consistent with post-traumatic stress disorder (Eth and Pynoos 1985; Arroyo and Eth 1995; Silvern, Karyl, and Landis 1995; Zeanah 1994). Whether children see it or hear it or witness only the aftermath, domestic violence is a terrifying and traumatic experience that profoundly affects the way they understand their world.

Concern about the devastating effects of witnessing abuse has prompted more than half of Canada's provinces to create laws that qualify some children who witness woman abuse for protection (Echlin and Marshall 1995). Currently there are no federal or state laws in the United States that categorize children who witness the abuse of their mothers as themselves victims of abuse. Lack of legislative attention to this issue has paved the way for potentially abusive custody arrangements, permitting batterers to use their children as pawns in "a power relationship with the children's mother, played out through the issues of custody and visitation" (McMahon and Pence 1995, 187). Men who batter their partners are more likely to seek custody (and less likely to pay child support) than men who are not abusive (Liss and Stahly 1993). Although the traumatic effects on children of witnessing their parents' abuse have been well documented, there is little real protection offered them and very little discussion about what needs to take place to change this on a structural level. In fact, the question of whether child witnesses of woman abuse are in fact themselves abused children is still being debated.

Child Physical Abuse

Statistics on the physical abuse of children indicate that women abuse children at an equal or somewhat higher rate than men do; however, when the relative amount of time that women and men spend with children is taken into consideration, it becomes apparent that men account for the majority of child physical abuse per hour of exposure. Studies also show that men are more likely to commit the more serious forms of child abuse, causing more devastating injuries (Hegar, Zuravin, Orme 1991). Fathers and mothers' boyfriends were found to be responsible for most child fatalities resulting from abuse (Alfaro 1987; Thompson and Wilson 1989). There also appears to be a strong correlation between households where men batter women and those in which child physical abuse occurs. According to Lee Bowker, Michelle Arbitell, and J. Richard McFerron (1988), the intentional abuse of children may be one of many strategies used by violent men to control their families. These researchers also found that the children of battered women are "very likely" to be victims of battering by the same men, and that the degree of severity of wife abuse was predictive of the severity of child abuse. Others have found that the "typical context for child abuse," whether perpetrated by the man or the woman, is one where the woman is also battered (Stark and Flitcraft 1988, 98). Despite statistical claims that women are the group primarily responsible for the physical abuse of children, a more complete understanding of the context and conditions under which physical child abuse takes place requires us to consider more carefully its gendered nature and the relational contexts in which it occurs.

Child Abductions

Estimates of the number of parental abductions of children run from 100,000 (Flowers 1994) to as high as 350,000 (Greif and Hegar 1993) per year in the United States. Parental kidnapping is associated with gender violence because it often occurs against a background of domestic violence or child sexual assault. Jeffrey Greif and Rebecca Hegar found that almost half of the parents who considered abducting their children were responding to a perceived need to protect the child from abuse by the other parent. Women who abduct their children are often attempting to escape violence aimed at themselves, while husbands who abduct their children are often using the kidnapping as one more act of abuse against their wives.

Child Sexual Abuse

Child sexual abuse has been a widely recognized social problem since the late 1970s, when women, encouraged by the attention that the women's movement had focused on rape, began to speak out about sexual abuses they had suffered as children, often at the hands of family members or trusted members of their communities. In turn, these personal testimonies sparked theorists and researchers to take a new look at an issue that had long been relegated to silence. In one of the first books to look squarely at the issue, *The Best Kept Secret*, Florence Rush (1980) placed contemporary child sexual abuse in a historical and cultural context. She found support for the early sexual use of children in both Talmudic and early canon law and pointed out that "the sexual abuse of children by adults has never been established as an irrefutable legal and moral violation and to this day remains a debatable polemic" (1980, 73).

Today we know that children are sexually exploited through a variety of means, including incest, molestation, rape, prostitution, and pornography; yet, due to the breadth of possible abuses, it is extremely difficult to develop comprehensive statistics on victimization. This difficulty in collecting reliable information is compounded by the nature of such abuse; children are not generally prepared to search outside the family for assistance (and the abuser is often a family member), nor are they prepared to discuss sexual matters within the family (if the abuser is not related). Some children feel complicit in their victimization; they may be threatened with dire consequences if they divulge the abuse, and thus collude in keeping a secret. Others trade one form of abuse for another; most child prostitutes, for instance, have escaped from homes where they were sexually abused.

Despite the limitations in our knowledge of childhood sexual abuse, we are able to form basic conclusions based on available information. Studies of incest victims and offenders have found that most incestuous abuse is committed by fathers against daughters, with increased reports of boy victims in recent years (Flowers 1994). Offenders are almost always male (Russell 1986; La Fontaine 1990). While incestuous reproduction has been effectively tabooed in the United States (reports are rare), incest without reproduction is widespread (Finkelhor 1984; Russell 1984). Child victims of incest suffer myriad consequences such as withdrawal, intense fears, sexual acting out (and thus higher risk for pregnancy, AIDS, and other sexually transmitted diseases), alcohol and drug abuse, suicidal thoughts, poor peer relationships, and eating disorders (La Fontaine 1990; Klein and Chao 1995).

It may be that the Western norm of familial privacy and discreet housing arrangements, coupled with a patriarchal family structure, permit incestuous abuse to flourish.

Without available research on incest from other parts of the world it is impossible to draw conclusions about the relative safety of children within their families in the various existent familial and social arrangements. Laws in the United States strongly favor the sanctity of the nuclear family, even to the extent that a policy of family reunification and preservation often mandates the return of incest victims to their victimizers (Berliner 1993).

Girls are also, by far, the most common victims of nonincestuous rape and molestation, although reports of boy victims have been increasing. Children who are sexually victimized by acquaintances and strangers may exhibit some of the same fears and self-destructive behaviors as incest victims. Some children are bribed or coerced into complicity with their abusers; others are forcibly assaulted. Men are the overwhelming majority of sexual offenders against nonrelated children. These men often make elaborate arrangements to be in frequent contact with children through babysitting, coaching, child-care, scouting, and similar activities.

Diana E. H. Russell and David Finkelhor developed a list of factors that may help to explain the gender gap among perpetrators. These factors include the fact that women are socialized to prefer older, larger, more powerful sexual partners, while men are socialized to prefer partners who are smaller, younger, and less powerful; that women overwhelmingly are less likely to initiate first sexual encounters, while men learn to initiate sexual contact and not to view resistance as an obstacle; that men seem to be more motivated than women to have multiple sexual partners and to sexualize relationships; that men appear to be more easily aroused, while women appear to rely on the nature of the relationship; that men may sexualize emotions (such as affection and intimacy) more than women do; that for men sexual opportunities are linked more to self-esteem than for women, which may make men more open to other sexual outlets when alternatives are not readily available; that women may be more protective of children because they are socialized for maternal responsibilities, while men generally have limited interaction with children; that women, who are more frequently sexually victimized, may be more cognizant of the possible harm to children of sexualizing a relationship than men would be; and that there exists a male subculture that condones sexual contact with children, while there is no equivalent support for women (Russell and Finkelhor in Russell 1984). In fact, numerous publications and organizations support the alteration of laws in the United States and the United Kingdom to permit adults to have sexual access to children of any age. One of the best known is the California-based René Guyon Society whose slogan is "Sex by year eight or else it's too late" (Flowers 1994, 75).

Advocates working on behalf of children perceive child prostitution and pornography to be mutually supporting in that they serve to sexualize and commodify children. Child pornography can be seen as an advertisement for the sexual use of children while prostitution supplies the promised goods. Child pornography is believed to be a multi-billion-dollar business (Flowers 1986) with distribution made easy through computer technology. In recent years the global economy has spurred free trade and travel between the United States and its poorer neighbor, Mexico. International electronic communications coupled with an expanding market for child pornography in the United States have put foreign children at higher risk. In addition to legitimate trade, highly organized rings of child abusers have filmed Mexican children engaged in sex acts for distribution in the United States (Preston 1996). Perhaps one of the saddest features of child prostitution and pornography is that the children featured are often runaways from homes where they were incestuously abused (Flowers 1994).

As potential sexual beings, children are subject to the sexual demands of predatory adults or other children, or to the commodification of their sexuality through child pornography and prostitution. Their lack of personal experience and knowledge about sexual matters within a cultural context of blatantly expressed sexuality (see Schur, this volume) compounds their confusion and increases their vulnerability. The sense that being sexual and acting sexual are inevitable and part of what it means to be adult may confuse children, who often model adult behavior and are not informed enough about the consequences of sexual activity to understand the potential outcome of the behaviors pressed upon them. Whatever the specific nature of the abuse, the tremendous number of child victims of sexual exploitation and abuse are an indictment of a society that professes great concern for children but fails to develop adequate protections. As long as adults, who hold all the power in relationship to children, have the authority of the state to uphold patriarchal tradition, children will continue to be victimized.

Children and Sexual Harassment

The experience of sexual harassment in schools and on the playground can serve as an introduction to expected gender roles. Starting in kindergarten girls are subjected to a barrage of verbal attacks on their abilities, their intelligence, their options, and their bodies, all intended to remind them that they have limits on their aspirations. Recent studies have found that sexual harassment occurs with relentless frequency in elementary and secondary schools (Sadker and Sadker 1994). Not only does the harassment make girls feel like second-class citizens, but it also has a chilling effect on their willingness to call attention to themselves by participating in class. Ultimately their reluctance may cause their school performance to suffer, and thereby create a real and lasting effect on their future options. Even the school playground is a site where gendered power roles are enacted with detrimental consequences for girls and boys (Thorne 1993).

In terms of its frequency, the numbers of people affected by it, and its widespread and damaging outcomes for girls and women, sexual harassment is probably the most virulent form of gender violence experienced by children. Adolescent girls, who rarely report harassment because of peer pressure and a desire to be independent, are perhaps most vulnerable. Boys are not immune, however; those who do not meet a standard of athleticism are harassed as "girls" through a combination of homophobic and misogynistic rituals.

Teens and Gender Violence

One-third of the victims of reported rapes are under age twenty. Sixteen- to nineteen-year-olds have the highest rate of victimization among women twelve to sixty-five years old, with African American teens being most at risk. Statistics most likely underestimate the percentage of young rape victims because victims under age twenty are less likely to report violent crimes (Flowers 1994).

Close to one-fourth of high school students experience physical violence in the context of a dating relationship (Sugarman and Hotaling 1991). Although it appears that both males and females are violent in adolescent dating relationships, young women are more likely than young men to experience fear and more damaging forms of violence (see Brustin 1995).

For girls, the average age of entry into prostitution in the United States is fourteen.

Boys may account for between one-third and one-half of child prostitutes. Virtually all customers are male (Flowers 1994). Child prostitution is highly correlated with depression, mental illness, past sexual and physical abuse, and rape (Flowers 1986). The tremendous increase in AIDS among adult prostitutes is also a concern for children, who are less likely than their adult counterparts to make use of preventive measures.

New concerns about teens and gender violence are coming into focus. Emerging research is connecting gender expectations and self-inflicted violence, particularly in two areas: the relationship of homosexuality to adolescent suicide; and of the cult of thinness to eating disorders. Internalized expectations about gender are strongly connected to self-destructive acts.

Contributions to This Section

The readings in this section urge us to challenge assumptions about children and gender violence. Together these articles argue for a more complex and nuanced understanding of the problems associated with children and gender violence.

In "Family Violence, Feminism, and Social Control," Linda Gordon uses the records of child protection workers to explore the tensions and contradictions between the needs and desires of clients (mostly poor women and children) and the interpretations and actions of social welfare workers and agencies. She describes a complex interaction that emphasizes conflict between men, women, children and the individuals and social institutions that define child abuse. Gordon's perspective has important implications for how we view the power and efficacy of the wives of violent men and their abused children and encourages us to look beyond the simple dichotomy of dominating abuser and helpless victim.

In "Who Stole Incest?" Louise Armstrong explores how incest has been interpreted as an illness rather than a crime of violence against women and children. Armstrong, one of the earliest voices to assert a feminist position on the sexual abuse of children (see 1978 book, *Kiss Daddy Goodnight*), finds that framing incest as a medical issue needing treatment, rather than a social issue demanding political solutions, has served to continue the silencing that has characterized attempts to focus attention on sexually abused children throughout history. The outcome is that child rape remains socially tolerated.

Carol-Ann Hooper, in "Child Sexual Abuse and the Regulation of Women: Variations on a Theme," considers how official policies dealing with child sexual abuse have marginalized the feminist definition of the problem as stemming from the social construction of masculinity. Hooper sees child sexual abuse as a location where male sexual control over women and children is acted out. Agencies reproduce the dominant discourse of women's responsibility for intrafamilial events through the control and restraint of women rather than the men who abuse. In the current climate of conservatism, child sexual abuse becomes visible through concerns about its meaning within the traditional (patriarchal) family.

In "Definition and Scope of the Problem: Historical Perspective on Children from Violent Homes," Pater Jaffe, David Wolfe, and Susan Kaye Wilson present us with an issue on the cusp of public awareness. The authors inform us of a social problem that has received very little attention and, as yet, has inspired minimal policy. There have been attempts in the past to bring the children of abusive fathers to public attention, notably as part of the effort to gain sympathy for temperance movements in England and the United States (see Sanchez-Eppler 1995). The current effort places the discourse within the realm of contemporary feminist thought on power within the family. Given the concerns addressed by the previous authors in this section regarding the shaping of the discourses of physically and sexually abused children, it will be interesting to look back in ten or twenty years to see what direction is taken by those concerned with developing policy to assist children from violent homes.

SUGGESTIONS FOR FURTHER READING

Dorothy Allison, *Bastard Out of Carolina* (New York: Dutton, 1992).

Louise Armstrong, *Rocking the Cradle of Sexual Politics: What Happened When Women Said Incest* (Reading, MA: Addison-Wesley, 1994).

David Finkelhor, *Child Sexual Abuse: New Theory and Research* (New York: Free Press, 1984).

Linda Gordon, *Heroes of Their Own Lives: The Politics and History of Family Violence* (New York: Viking, 1988).

Peter Jaffe, David Wolfe, and Susan Kaye Wilson, *Children of Battered Women* (Newbury Park, Calif: Sage, 1990).

Sue Lees, *Sugar and Spice: Sexuality and Adolescent Girls* (New York: Penguin, 1993).

Jeffrey Moussaieff Masson, *The Assault on Truth: Freud's Suppression of the Seduction Theory* (New York: Penguin, 1985).

Diana Russell, *The Secret Trauma: Incest in the Lives of Girls and Women* (New York: Basic Books, 1986).

The Second Photograph

MARGARET RANDALL

I have found another portrait.
You have me on your lap
flanked by my two grandmothers
both looking congenitally worried
as well they should.

You, on the other hand, seem vaguely crazed
as you certainly were,
your lips and eyes focused on different planes.

I have looked long and hard
at the hands in this picture.
Both women hide theirs, differently.
Yours, Grandpa, are loosely circled
about my three-year-old body.
Your right covers my left, your left
comes round my party-dressed buttocks,
your fingers strangely held as if in secret sign.

I am reading this into the image.
I am reading it because now, half a century later,
I understand why my eyes in the picture
take the camera head on, demanding answers.

Albuquerque, Spring 1986

From Margaret Randall's *Memory Says Yes* (Curbstone Press, 1988). Reprinted with permission of Curbstone Press. Distributed by Consortium.

21

Family Violence, Feminism, and Social Control

LINDA GORDON

In studying the history of family violence, I found myself also confronting the issue of social control, incarnated in the charitable "friendly visitors" and later professional child protection workers who composed the case records I was reading. At first I experienced these social control agents as intruding themselves unwanted into my research. My study was based on the records of Boston "child-saving" agencies, in which the oppressions of class, culture, and gender were immediately evident. The "clients" were mainly poor, Catholic, female immigrants. (It was not that women were responsible for most of the family violence but that they were more often involved with agencies for reasons we shall see below.) The social workers were exclusively well educated and male and overwhelmingly White Anglo-Saxon Protestant (WASP). These workers, authors of case records, were often disdainful, ignorant, and obtuse—at best, paternalistic—toward their clients.

Yet, ironically, these very biases created a useful discipline, showing that it was impossible to study family violence as an objective problem. Attempts at social control were part of the original definition and construction of family violence as a social issue. The very concept of family violence is a product of conflict and negotiation between people troubled by domestic violence and social control agents attempting to change their supposedly unruly and deviant behavior.

In this essay I want to argue not a defense of social control but a critique of its critiques and some thoughts about a better, feminist, framework. I would like to make my argument as it came to me, through studying child abuse and neglect. Nine years ago when I began to study the history of family violence, I assumed I would be focusing largely on wifebeating because that was the target of the contemporary feminist activism which had drawn my attention to the problem. I was surprised, however, to find that violence against children represented a more complex challenge to the task of envisioning feminist family policy and a feminist theory of social control.

Reprinted in part from *Feminist Studies* 12, no. 3 (fall 1986):453–78, by permission of the publisher, Feminist Studies, Inc., c/o Women's Studies Program, University of Maryland, College Park, MD 20742.

Social Control

Many historians of women and the family have inherited a critical view of social control, as an aspect of domination and the source of decline in family and individual autonomy. In situating ourselves with respect to this tradition, it may be useful to trace very briefly the history of the concept. "Social control" is a phrase usually attributed to the sociologist E. A. Ross. He used the phrase as the title of a collection of his essays in 1901, referring to the widest range of influence and regulation societies imposed upon individuals.[1] Building on a Hobbesian view of human individuals as naturally in conflict, Ross saw "social control" as inevitable. Moving beyond liberal individualism, however, he argued for social control in a more specific, American Progressive sense. Ross advocated the active, deliberate, expert guidance of human life not only as the source of human progress but also as the best replacement for older, familial, and communitarian forms of control, which he believed were disappearing in modern society.

Agencies attempting to control family violence are preeminent examples of the kind of expert social control institutions that were endorsed by Ross and other Progressive reformers. These agencies—the most typical were the Societies for the Prevention of Cruelty to Children (SPCCs)—were established in the 1870s in a decade of acute international alarm about child abuse. They began as punitive and moralistic "charitable" endeavors, characteristic of nineteenth-century elite moral purity reforms. These societies blamed the problem of family violence on the depravity, immorality, and drunkenness of individuals, which they often traced to the innate inferiority of the immigrants who constituted the great bulk of their targets. By the early twentieth century, the SPCCs took on a more ambitious task, hoping not merely to cure family pathology but also to reform family life and childraising. Describing the change slightly differently, in the nineteenth century, child protection agents saw themselves as paralegal, punishing specific offenses, protecting children from specific dangers; in the early twentieth century, they tried to supervise and direct the family lives of those considered deviant.

The view that intervention into the family has increased, and has become a characteristic feature of modern society, is now often associated with Talcott Parsons's writings of the late 1940s and 1950s. Parsons proposed the "transfer of functions" thesis, the notion that professionals had taken over many family functions (for example, education, childcare, therapy, and medical care). Parsons's was a liberal, optimistic view; he thought this professionalization a step forward, leaving the family free to devote more of its time and energy to affective relations. There was already a contrasting, far more pessimistic, interpretation, emanating from the Frankfurt school of German Marxists, who condemned the decline of family autonomy and even attributed to it, in part, the horrors of totalitarianism.

The latter tradition, critical of social control, has conditioned most of the historical writing about social control agencies and influences. Much of the earlier work in this mid-twentieth-century revival of women's history adopted this perspective on social control, substituting gender for class or national categories in the analysis of women's subordination. In the field of child saving in particular, the most influential historical work has adopted this perspective.[2] These critiques usually distinguished an "us" and a "them," oppressed and oppressor, in a dichotomous relation. They were usually functionalist: they tended to assume or argue that the social control practices in question served (were functional for) the material interests of a dominant group and hindered (were dysfunctional to) the interests of the subordinate. More recently, some women's historians have integrated class and gender into this model, arguing that the growth of the state in the last 150 years has increased individual rights for prosperous women but has only subjected poor women to ever greater control.[3] Alternatively, women's historians represent social control as half of a bargain in which material benefits—welfare benefits, for example—are given to those controlled in exchange for the surrender of power or autonomy.[4]

The development of women's history in the last decade has begun to correct some of the oversimplifications of this "anti-social-control" school of analysis. A revival of what might be called the Beardian tradition (after Mary Beard) recognizes women's activity—in this case, in constructing modern forms of social control.[5] Historians of social work or other social control institutions, however, have not participated in the rethinking of the paradigm of elite domination and plebeian victimization.[6]

The critique of the domination exercised by social work and human services bureaucracies and professionals is not wrong, but its incompleteness allows for some serious distortion. My own views derive from a study of the history of family violence and its social control in Boston from 1880 to 1960, using both the quantitative and qualitative analysis of case records from three leading child-saving agencies.[7] Looking at these records from the perspective of children and their primary caretakers (and abusers), women, reveals the impoverishment of the anti-social-control perspective sketched above and its inadequacy to the task of conceptualizing who is controlled and who is controlling in these family conflicts. A case history may suggest some of the complexities that have influenced my thinking.

In 1910 a Syrian family in Boston's South End, here called the Kashys, came to the attention of the Massachusetts Society for the Prevention of Cruelty to Children (MSPCC) because of the abuse of the mother's thirteen-year-old girl.[8] Mr. Kashy had just died of appendicitis. The family, like so many immigrants, had moved back and forth between Syria and the United States several times; two other children had been left in Syria with their paternal grandparents. In this country, in addition to the central "victim," whom I shall call Fatima, there was a six-year-old boy and a three-year-old girl, and Mrs. Kashy was pregnant. The complainant was the father's sister, and indeed all the paternal relatives were hostile to Mrs. Kashy. The MSPCC investigation substantiated their allegations: Mrs. Kashy hit Fatima with a stick and with chairs, bit her ear, kept her from school and overworked her, expecting her to do all the housework and to care for the younger children. When Fatima fell ill, her mother refused to let her go to the hospital. The hostility of the paternal relatives, however, focused not only on the mother's treatment of Fatima but mainly on her custody rights. It was their position that custody should have fallen to them after Mr. Kashy's death, arguing that "in Syria a woman's rights to the care of her chn [abbreviations in original] or the control of property is not recognized." In Syrian tradition, the paternal grandfather had rights to the children, and he had delegated this control to his son, the children's paternal uncle.

The paternal kin, then, had expected Mrs. Kashy to bow to their rights; certainly her difficult economic and social situation would make it understandable if she had. The complainant, the father's sister, was Mrs. Kashy's landlady and was thus in a position to make her life very difficult. Mrs. Kashy lived with her three children in one attic room without water; she had to go to the ground level and carry water up to her apartment. The relatives offered her no help after her bereavement and Mrs. Kashy was desperate; she was trying to earn a living by continuing her husband's peddling. She needed Fatima to keep the house and care for the children.

When Mrs. Kashy resisted their custody claims, the paternal relatives called in as a mediator a Syrian community leader, publisher of the *New Syria*, a Boston Arabic-language newspaper. Ultimately the case went to court, however, and here the relatives lost as their custody traditions conflicted with the new preference in the United States for women's custody. Fatima's wishes were of no help to the agency in sorting out this conflict, because throughout the struggle she was ambivalent: sometimes she begged to be kept away from her mother, yet when away, she begged to be returned to her mother. Ultimately, Mrs. Kashy won custody but no maternal help in supporting her children by herself. As in so many child abuse cases, it was the victim who was punished: Fatima was sent to the Gwynne Home, where—at least so her relatives believed—she was treated abusively.

If the story had stopped there one might be tempted to see Mrs. Kashy as relatively blameless, driven perhaps to episodes of harshness and temper by her difficult lot. But thirteen years later, in 1923, a "school visitor" brought the second daughter, now sixteen, to the MSPCC to complain of abuse by her mother and by her older, now married, sister Fatima. In the elapsed years, this second daughter had been sent back to Syria; perhaps Mrs. Kashy had had to give up her efforts to support her children. Returning to the United States eighteen months previously, the girl had arrived to find that her mother intended to marry her involuntarily to a boarder. The daughter displayed blood on her shirt which she said came from her mother's beatings. Interviewed by an MSPCC agent, Mrs. Kashy was now openly hostile and defiant, saying that she would beat her daughter as she liked.

In its very complexity, the Kashy case exemplifies certain generalizations central to my argument. One is that it is often difficult to identify a unique victim. It should not be surprising that the oppressed Mrs. Kashy was angry and violent, but feminist rhetoric about family violence has often avoided this complexity. Mrs. Kashy was the victim of her isolation, widowhood, single motherhood, and patriarchal, hostile in-laws; she also exploited and abused her daughter. Indeed, Mrs. Kashy's attitude to Fatima was patriarchal: she believed that children should serve parents and not vice versa. This aspect of patriarchal tradition served Mrs. Kashy. But, in other respects, the general interests of the oppressed group—here the Syrian immigrants—as expressed by its male, *petit bourgeois* leadership, were more inimical to Mrs. Kashy's (and other women's) aspirations and "rights" than those of the elite agency, the MSPCC. Furthermore, one can reasonably surmise that the daughters were also actors in this drama, resisting their mother's expectations as well as those of the male-dominated community, as New World ideas of children's rights coincided with aspirations entirely their own. None of the existing social control critiques can adequately conceptualize the complex struggles in the Kashy family, nor can they propose nonoppressive ways for Fatima's "rights" to be protected.

Feminism and Child Abuse

Feminist theory in general and women's history in particular have moved only slowly beyond the "victimization" paradigm that dominated the rebirth of feminist scholarship. The obstacles to perceiving and describing women's own power have been particularly great in issues relating to social policy and to family violence, because of the legacy of victim blaming. Defending women against male violence is so urgent that we fear women's loss of status as deserving, political "victims" if we acknowledge women's own aggressions. These complexities are at their greatest in the situation of mothers because they are simultaneously victims and victimizers, dependent and depended on, weak and powerful.

If feminist theory needs a new view of social control, thinking about child abuse virtually demands it. Child abuse cases reveal suffering that is incontrovertible, unnecessary, and remediable. However severe the biases of the social workers attempting to "save" the children and reform their parents—and I will have more to say about this later—one could not advocate a policy of inaction in regard to children chained to beds, left in filthy diapers for days, turned out in the cold. Children, unlike women, lack even the potential for social and economic independence. A beneficial social policy could at least partly address the problem of wifebeating by empowering women to leave abusive situations, enabling them to live in comfort and dignity without men, and encouraging them to espouse high standards in their expectations of treatment by others. It is not clear how one could empower children in analogous ways. If children are to have "rights" then some adults must be appointed and accepted, by other adults, to define and defend them.

Women, who do most of the labor of childcare, have the strongest emotional bonds to children, fought for and largely won rights to child custody over the last 150 years. Yet women are often the abusers and neglecters of children. Indeed, child abuse becomes the more interesting and challenging to feminists because in it we meet women's rage and abuses of power. Furthermore, child abuse is a gendered phenomenon, related to the oppression of women, whether women or men are the culprits, because it reflects the sexual division of the labor of reproduction. Because men spend, on the whole, so much less time with children than do women, what is remarkable is not that women are violent toward children but that men are responsible for nearly half of the child abuse. But women are always implicated because even when men are the culprits, women are usually the primary caretakers who have been, by definition, unable to protect the children. When protective organizations remove children or undertake supervision of their caretakers, women often suffer greatly, for their maternal work, trying as it may be, is usually the most pleasurable part of their lives.

Yet in the last two decades of intense publicity and scholarship about child abuse, the feminist contribution has been negligible. This silence is the more striking in contrast to the legacy of the first wave of feminism, particularly in the period 1880 to 1930, in which the women's rights movement was tightly connected to child welfare reform campaigns. By contrast, the second wave of feminism, a movement heavily influenced by younger and childless women, has spent relatively little energy on children's issues. Feminist scholars have studied the social organization of mothering in theory but not the actual experiences of childraising, and the movement as a whole has not significantly influenced child welfare debates or policies. When such issues emerge publicly, feminists too often assume that women's and children's interests always coincide. The facts of child abuse and neglect challenge this assumption as does the necessity sometimes of severing maternal custody in order to protect children.

Protecting Children

Child abuse was "discovered" as a social problem in the 1870s. Surely many children had been ill-treated by parents before this, but new social conditions created an increased sensitivity to the treatment of children and, possibly, actually worsened children's lot. Conditions of labor and family life under industrial capitalism may have made poverty, stress, and parental anger bear more heavily on children. The child abuse alarm also reflected growing class and cultural differences in beliefs about how children *should* be raised. The anti-cruelty-to-children movement grew out of an anti-corporal-punishment campaign, and both reflected a uniquely professional-class view that children could be disciplined by reason and with mildness. The SPCCs also grew from widespread fears among more privileged people about violence and "depravity" among the urban poor; in the United States, these fears were exacerbated by the fact that these poor were largely immigrants and Catholics, threatening the WASP domination of city culture and government.

On one level, my study of the case records of Boston child-saving agencies corroborated the anti-social-control critique: the work of the agencies did represent oppressive intervention into working-class families. The MSPCC attempted to enforce culturally specific norms of proper parenting that were not only alien to the cultural legacy of their "clients" but also flew in the face of many of the economic necessities of the clients' lives. Thus, MSPCC agents prosecuted cases in which cruelty to children was caused, in their view, by children's labor: girls doing housework and childcare, often staying home from school because their parents required it; girls and boys working in shops, peddling on the streets; boys working for organ grinders and lying about their ages to enlist in the navy. Before World War I, the enemies of the truant officers were usually parents, not children. To immigrants from peasant backgrounds it seemed irrational and blasphemous that adult women should work while able-bodied children remained idle. Similarly, the MSPCC was opposed to the common immigrant practice of leaving children unattended and allowing them to play and wander in the streets. Both violated the MSPCCs norm of domesticity for women and children; proper middle-class children in those days did not—at least not in the cities—play outside on their own.

The child savers were attempting to impose a new, middle-class urban style of mothering and fathering. Mothers were supposed to be tender and gentle and above all, to protect their children from immoral influences; the child savers considered yelling, rude language, or sexually explicit talk to be forms of cruelty to children. Fathers were to provide models of emotional containment, to be relatively uninvolved with children; their failure to provide adequate economic support was often interpreted as a character flaw, no matter what the evidence of widespread, structural unemployment.

MSPCC agents in practice and in rhetoric expressed disdain for immigrant cultures. They hated the garlic and olive oil smells of Italian cooking and considered this food unhealthy (overstimulating, aphrodisiac). The agents were unable to distinguish alcoholics and heavy drinkers from moderate wine and beer drinkers, and they believed that women who took spirits were degenerate and unfit as mothers. They associated many of these forms of depravity with Catholicism. Agents were also convinced of the subnormal intelligence of most non-WASP and especially non-English-speaking clients; indeed, the agents' comments and expectations in this early period were similar to social workers' views of black clients in the mid-twentieth century. These child welfare specialists were particularly befuddled by and disapproving of non-nuclear childraising patterns: children raised by grandmothers, complex households composed of children from several different marriages (or, worse, out-of-wedlock relationships), children sent temporarily to other households.

The peasant backgrounds of so many of the "hyphenated" Americans created a situation in which ethnic bias could not easily be separated from class bias. Class misunderstanding, moreover, took a form specific to urban capitalism: a failure to grasp the actual economic and physical circumstances of this immigrant proletariat and subproletariat. Unemployment was not yet understood to be a structural characteristic of industrial capitalism. Disease, overcrowding, crime, and—above all—dependence were also not understood to be part of the system, but, rather, were seen as personal failings.

This line of criticism, however, only partially uncovers the significance of child protection. Another dimension and a great deal more complexity are revealed by considering the feminist aspect of the movement. Much of the child welfare reform energy of the nineteenth century came from women and was organized by the "woman movement."[9] The campaign against corporal punishment, from which the anti-child-abuse movement grew, depended upon a critique of violence rooted in feminist thought and in women's reform activity. Women's reform influence, the "sentimentalizing" of the Calvinist traditions,[10] was largely responsible for the softening of childraising norms. The delegitimation of corporal punishment, noticeable among the prosperous classes by mid-century, was associated with exclusive female responsibility for childraising, with women's victories in child custody cases, even with women's criticisms of traditionally paternal discipline.[11]

Feminist thinking exerted an important influence on the agencies' original formulations of the problem of family violence. Most MSPCC spokesmen (and those who represented the agency in public were men) viewed men as aggressors and women and children, jointly, as blameless victims. However simplistic, this was a feminist attitude. It was also, of course, saturated with class and cultural elitism: these "brutal" and "depraved" men were of a different class and ethnicity than the MSPCC agents, and the language of victimization applied to women and children was also one of condescension. Nevertheless, despite the definition of the "crime" as cruelty to children, MSPCC agents soon included wifebeating in their agenda of reform.

Even more fundamentally, the very undertaking of child protection was a challenge to patriarchal relations. A pause to look at my definition of patriarchy is necessary here. In the 1970s a new definition of that term came into use, first proposed by Kate Millett but quickly adopted by the U.S. feminist movement: patriarchy became a synonym for male supremacy, for "sexism." I use the term in its earlier, historical, and more specific sense, referring to a family form in which fathers had control over all other family members—children, women, and servants. This concept of a patriarchal family is an abstraction, postulating common features among family forms that differed widely across geography and time. If there was a common material base supporting this patriarchal family norm (a question requiring a great deal more study before it can be answered decisively), it was an economic system in which the family was the unit of production. Most of the MSPCC's early clients came from peasant societies in which this kind of family economy prevailed. In these families, fathers maintained control not only over property and tools but also, above all, over the labor power of family members. Historical patriarchy defined a set of parent-child relations as much as it did relations between the sexes, for children rarely had opportunities for economic independence except by inheriting the family property, trade, or craft. In some ways mothers, too, benefited from patriarchal parent-child relations. Their authority over daughters and young sons was important when they lacked other kinds of authority and independence, and in old age they gained respect, help, and consideration from younger kinfolk.

The claim of an organization such as an SPCC to speak on behalf of children's rights, its claim to the license to intervene in parental treatment of children, was an attack on patriarchal power. At the same time, the new sensibility about children's rights and the concern about child abuse were symptoms of a weakening of patriarchal family expectations and realities that had already taken place, particularly during the eighteenth and early nineteenth centuries in the United States. In this weakening, father-child relations had changed more than husband-wife relations. Children had, for example, gained the power to arrange their own betrothals and marriages and to embark on wage work independent of their fathers' occupations (of course, children's options remained determined by class and cultural privileges or the lack of them, inherited from fathers). In contrast, however, wage labor and long-distance mobility often made women, on balance, more dependent on husbands for sustenance and less able to deploy kinfolk and neighbors to defend their interests against husbands.

Early child protection work did not, of course, envision a general liberation of children from arbitrary parental control or from the responsibility of filial obedience. On the contrary, the SPCCs aimed as much to reinforce a failing parental/paternal authority as to limit it. Indeed, the SPCC spokesmen often criticized excessive physical violence against children as a symptom of inadequate parental authority. Assaults on children were provoked by children's insubordination; in the interpretation of nineteenth-century child protectors, this showed that parental weakness, children's disobedience, and child abuse were mutually reinforcing. Furthermore, by the turn of the century, the SPCCs discovered that the majority of their cases concerned neglect, not assault, and neglect exemplified to them the problems created by the withdrawal, albeit not always conscious or deliberate, of parental supervision and authority (among the poor who formed the agency clientele there were many fathers who deserted and many more who were inadequate providers). Many neglect and abuse cases ended with *children* being punished, sent to reform schools on stubborn child charges.

In sum, the SPCCs sought to reconstruct the family along lines that altered the old patriarchy, already economically unviable, and to replace it with a modern version of male supremacy. The SPCCs' rhetoric about children's rights did not extend to a parallel articulation of women's rights; their condemnation of wifebeating did not include endorsement of the kind of marriage later called "companionate," implying equality between wife and husband. Their new family and childraising norms included the conviction that children's respect for parents needed to be inculcated ideologically, moralistically, and psychologically because it no longer rested on an economic dependence lasting beyond childhood. Fathers, now as wage laborers rather than as slaves, artisans, peasants, or entrepreneurs, were to have single-handed responsibility for economic support of their families; women and children should not contribute to the family economy, at least not monetarily. Children instead should spend full-time in learning cognitive lessons from professional teachers, psychological and moral lessons from the full-time attention of a mother. In turn, women should devote themselves to mothering and domesticity.

Feminism, Mothering, and Industrial Capitalism

This childraising program points to a larger irony—that the "modernization" of male domination, its adaptation to new economic and social conditions, was partly a result of the influence of the first wave of feminism. These first "feminists" rarely advocated full equality between women and men and never promoted the abolition of traditional gender relations or the sexual division of labor. Allowing for differences of emphasis, the program just defined constituted a feminist as well as a liberal family reform program in the 1870s. Indeed, organized feminism *was* in part such a liberal reform program, a program to adapt the family and the civil society to the new economic conditions of industrial capitalism, for consciously or not, feminists felt that these new conditions provided greater possibilities for the freedom and empowerment of women.

To recapitulate, child protection work was an integral part of the feminist as well as the bourgeois program for modernizing the family. Child saving had gender as well as class and ethnic content, but in none of these aspects did it simply or homogeneously represent the interests of a dominant group (or even of the composite group of WASP elite women, that hypothetical stratum on which it is fashionable to blame the limitations of feminist activity). The antipatriarchalism of the child protection agencies was an unstable product of several conflicting interests. Understanding this illuminates the influence of feminism on the development of a capitalist industrial culture even as feminists criticized the new privileges it bestowed on men and its degradation of women's traditional work. The relation of feminism to capitalism and industrialism is usually argued in dichotomous and reductionist fashion: either feminism is the expression of bourgeois woman's aspirations, an ultimate individualism that tears apart the remaining noninstrumental bonds in a capitalist society; *or,* feminism is inherently anticapitalist, deepening and extending the critique of domination to show its penetration even of personal life and the allegedly "natural." Although there is a little truth in both versions, at least one central aspect of feminism's significance for capitalism has been omitted in these formulations—its role in redefining family norms and particularly norms of mothering.

Changes in the conditions of motherhood in an industrializing society were an important part of the experiences that drew women to the postbellum feminist movement. For most women, and particularly for urban poor women, motherhood became more difficult in wage labor conditions. Mothers were more isolated from support networks of kin, and mothering furthered that isolation, often requiring that women remain out of public space. The potential dangers from which children needed protection multiplied, and the increasing cultural demands for a "psychological parenting" increased the potential for maternal "failure."[12] These changes affected women of all classes, while, at the same time, motherhood remained the central identity for women of all classes. Childbirth and childraising, the most universal parts of female experience, were the common referents—the metaphoric base of political language—by which feminist ideas were communicated.

As industrial capitalism changed the conditions of motherhood, so women began to redefine motherhood in ways that would influence the entire culture. They "used" motherhood simultaneously to increase their own status, to promote greater social expenditure on children, and to loosen their dependence on men, just as capitalists "used" motherhood as a form of unpaid labor. The working-class and even sub-working-class women of the child abuse case records drew "feminist" conclusions—that is, they diagnosed their problems in terms of male supremacy—in their efforts to improve their own conditions of mothering. In their experiences, men's greater power (economic and social), in combination with men's lesser sense of responsibility toward children, kept them from being as good at mothering as they wanted. They responded by trying to rid themselves of those forms of male domination that impinged most directly on their identity and work as mothers and on children's needs as they interpreted those needs.

But if child protection work may have represented *all* mothers' demands, it made *some* mothers—poor urban mothers—extremely vulnerable by calling into question the quality of their mothering, already made more problematic by urban wage labor living conditions, and by threatening them with the loss of their children. Poor women had less privacy and therefore less impunity in their deviance from the new childraising norms, but their poverty often led them to ask for help from relief agencies, therefore calling themselves to the attention of the child-saving networks. Yet poor women did not by any means figure only on the victim side, for they were also often enthusiastic about defending children's "rights" and correcting cruel or neglectful parents. Furthermore, they used an eclectic variety of arguments and devices to defend their control of their children. At times they mobilized liberal premises and rhetoric to escape from patriarchal households and to defend their custody rights; they were quick to learn the right language of the New World in which to criticize their husbands and relatives and to manipulate social workers to side with them against patriarchal controls of other family members. Yet at other times they called upon traditional relations when community and kinfolk could help them retain control or defend children. Poor women often denounced the "intervention" of outside social control agencies like the SPCCs but only when it suited them, and at other times they eagerly used and asked such agencies for help.

Let me offer another case history to illustrate this opportunistic and resourceful approach to social control agencies. An Italian immigrant family, which I will call the Amatos, were "clients" of the MSPCC from 1910 to 1916.[13] They had five young children from the current marriage and Mrs. Amato had three from a previous marriage, two of them still in Italy and one daughter in Boston. Mrs. Amato kept that daughter at home to do housework and look after the younger children while she earned money doing piece rate sewing at home. This got the family in trouble with a truant officer, and they were also accused, in court, of lying to Associated Charities (a consortium of private relief agencies), saying that the father had deserted them when he was in fact living at home. Furthermore, once while left alone, probably in the charge of a sibling, one of the younger children fell out of a window and had to be hospitalized. This incident provoked agency suspicions that the mother was negligent.

Despite her awareness of these suspicions against her, Mrs. Amato sought help from many different organizations, starting with those of the Italian immigrant community and then reaching out to elite social work agencies, reporting that her husband was a drunkard, a gambler, a nonsupporter, and a wifebeater. The MSPCC agents at first doubted her claims because Mr. Amato impressed them as a "good and sober man," and they blamed the neglect of the children on his wife's incompetence in managing the wages he gave her. The MSPCC ultimately became convinced of Mrs. Amato's story because of her repeated appearance with severe bruises and the corroboration of the husband's father, who was intimately involved in the family troubles and took responsibility for attempting to control his son. Once the father came to the house and gave his son "a warning and a couple of slaps," after which he improved for a while. Another time the father extracted from him a pledge not to beat his wife for two years!

Mrs. Amato wanted none of this. She begged the MSPCC agent to help her get a divorce; later she claimed that she had not dared take this step because her husband's relatives threatened to beat her if she tried it. Then Mrs. Amato's daughter (from her previous marriage) took action, coming independently to the MSPCC to bring an agent to the house to help her mother. As a result of this complaint, Mr. Amato was convicted of assault once and sentenced to six months. During that time Mrs. Amato survived by "a little work and ... Italian friends have helped her." Her husband returned, more violent than before: he went at her with an axe, beat the children so much on the head that their "eyes wabbled [*sic*]" permanently, and supported his family so poorly that the children went out begging. This case closed, like so many, without a resolution.

The Amatos' case will not support the usual anti-social-control interpretation of the relation between oppressed clients and social agencies. There was no unity among the client family and none among the professional intervenors. Furthermore, the intervenors were often dragged into the case and by individuals with conflicting points of view. Mrs. Amato and Mrs. Kashy were not atypical in their attempts to use "social control" agencies in their own interests. Clients frequently initiated agency intervention; even in family violence cases, where the stakes were high—losing one's children—the majority of complaints in this study came from parents or close relatives who believed that their own standards of childraising were being violated.[14]

In their sparring with social work agencies, clients did not usually or collectively win because the professionals had more resources. Usually no one decisively "won." Considering these cases collectively, professional social work overrode working-class or poor people's interests, but in specific cases the professionals did not always formulate definite goals, let alone achieve them. Indeed, the bewilderment of the social workers (something usually overlooked because most scholarship about social work is based on policy statements, not on actual case records) frequently enabled the clients to go some distance toward achieving their own goals.

The social control experience was not a simple two-sided trade-off in which the client sacrificed autonomy and control in return for some material help. Rather, the clients helped shape the nature of the social control itself. Formulating these criticisms about the inadequacy of simple anti-social-control explanations in some analytic order, I would make four general points.

First, the condemnation of agency intervention into the family, and the condemnation of social control itself as something automatically evil, usually assumes that there can be, and once was, an autonomous family. On the contrary, no family relations have been immune from social regulation.[15] Certainly the forms of social control I examine here are qualitatively and quantitatively different, based on regulation from "outside," by those without a legitimate claim to caring about local, individual values and traditions. Contrasting the experience of social control to a hypothetical era of autonomy, however, distorts both traditional and modern forms of social regulation.

The tendency to consider social control as unprecedented, invasive regulation is not only an academic mistake. It grew from nineteenth-century emotional and political responses to social change. Family autonomy became a symbol of patriarchy only in its era of decline (as in 1980s' New Right rhetoric). Family "autonomy" was an oppositional concept in the nineteenth century, expressing a liberal ideal of home as a private and caring space in contrast to the public realm of increasingly instrumental relations. This symbolic cluster surrounding the family contained both critical and legitimating responses to industrial capitalist society. But as urban society created more individual opportunities for women, the defense of family autonomy came to stand against women's autonomy in a conservative opposition to women's demands for individual freedoms. (The concept of family autonomy today, as it is manipulated in political discourse, mainly has the latter function, suggesting that women's individual rights to autonomous citizenship will make the family more vulnerable to outside intervention). The Amatos' pattern, a more patriarchal pattern, of turning to relatives, friends, and, when they could not help, Italian-American organizations (no doubt the closest analogue to a "community" in the New World), was not adequate to the urban problems they now encountered. Even the violent and defensive Mr. Amato did not question the right of his father, relatives, and friends to intervene forcibly, and Mrs. Amato did not appear shocked that her husband's relatives tried, perhaps successfully, to hold her forcibly in her marriage. Family autonomy was not an expectation of the Amatos.

Second, the social control explanation sees the flow of initiative going in only one direction: from top to bottom, from professionals to clients, from elite to subordinate. The power of this interpretation of social work comes from the large proportion of truth it holds and also from the influence of scholars of poor people's movements who have denounced elite attempts to blame "the victims." The case records show, however, that clients were not passive but, rather, active negotiators in a complex bargaining. Textbooks of casework recognize the intense interactions and relationships that develop between social worker and client. In the social work version of concern with counter-transference, textbooks often attempt to accustom the social worker to examining her or his participation in that relationship.[16] This sense of mutuality, power struggle, and intersubjectivity, however, has not penetrated historical accounts of social work/social control encounters.

Third, critics of social control often fail to recognize the active role of agency clients because they conceive of the family as a homogeneous unit. There is an intellectual reification here which expresses itself in sentence structure, particularly in academic language: "The family is in decline," "threats to the family," "the family responds to industrialization." Shorthand expressions attributing behavior to an aggregate such as the family would be harmless except that they often express particular cultural norms about what "the family" is and does, and they mask intrafamily differences and conflicts of interest. Usually "the family" becomes a representation of the interests of the family head, if it is a man, carrying an assumption that all family members share his interests. (Families without a married male head, such as single-parent or grandparent-headed families, are in the common usage broken, deformed, or incomplete families, and thus do not qualify for these assumptions regarding family unity). Among the clients in family violence cases, outrage over the intervention into the family was frequently anger over a territorial violation, a challenge to male authority; expressed differently, it was a reaction to the exposure to others of intrafamily conflict and of the family head's lack of control. Indeed, the interventions actually *were* more substantive, more invasive, when their purpose was to change the status quo than if they had been designed to reinforce it. The effect of social workers' involvement was often to change existing family power relations, usually in the interest of the weaker family members.

Social work interventions were often invited by family members; the inviters, however, were usually the weaker members of a family power structure, women and children. These invitations were made despite the fact, well known to clients, that women and children usually had the most to lose (despite fathers' frequent outrage at their loss of face) from MSPCC intervention because by far the most common outcome of agency action was not prosecution and jail sentences but the removal of children, an action fathers dreaded less than mothers. In the immigrant working-class neighborhoods of Boston the MSPCC became known as "the Cruelty," eloquently suggesting poor people's recognition and fear of its power. But these fears did not stop poor people from initiating contact with the organization. After the MSPCC had been in operation ten years, 60 percent of the complaints of known origin (excluding anonymous accusations) came from family members, the overwhelming majority of these from women with children following second. These requests for help came not only from victims but also from mothers distressed that they were not able to raise their children according to their own standards of good parenting. Women also maneuvered to bring child welfare agencies into family struggles on their sides. There was no Society for the Prevention of Cruelty to Women, but in fact women like Mrs. Amato were trying to turn the SPCC into just that. A frequent tactic of beaten, deserted, or unsupported wives was to report their husbands as child abusers; even when investigations found no evidence of child abuse, social workers came into their homes offering, at best, help in getting other things women wanted—such as support payments, separation and maintenance agreements, relief—and, at least, moral support to the women and condemnation of the men.[17]

A fourth problem is that simple social control explanations often imply that the clients' problems are only figments of social workers' biases. One culture's neglect may be another culture's norm, and in such cultural clashes, one group usually has more power than the other. In many immigrant families, for example, five-year-olds were expected to care for babies and toddlers; to middle-class reformers, five-year-olds left alone were neglected, and their infant charges deserted. Social control critiques are right to call attention to the power of experts not only to "treat" social deviance but also to define problems in the first place. But the power of labeling, the representation of poor people's behavior by experts whose status is defined through their critique of the problematic behavior of others, coexists with real family oppressions. In one case an immigrant father, who sexually molested his thirteen-year-old daughter, told a social worker that that was the way it was done in the old country. He was not only lying but also trying to manipulate a social worker, perhaps one he had recognized as guilt-ridden over her privileged role, using his own fictitious cultural relativism. His daughter's victimization by incest was not the result of oppression by professionals.

Feminism and Liberalism

The overall problem with virtually all existing critiques of social control is that they remain liberal and have in particular neglected what feminists have shown to be the limits of liberalism. Liberalism is commonly conceived as a political and economic theory without social content. In fact, liberal political and economic theory rests on assumptions about the sexual division of labor and on notions of citizens as heads of families.[18] The currently dominant left-wing tradition of anti-social-control critique, that of the Frankfurt school, merely restates these assumptions, identifying the sphere of the "private" as somehow natural, productive of strong egos and inner direction, in contrast to the sphere of the public as invasive, productive of conformity and passivity. If we reject the social premises of liberalism (and of Marx), that gender and the sexual division of labor are natural, then we can hardly maintain the premise that familial forms of social control are inherently benign and public forms are malignant.

Certainly class relations and domination are involved in social control. Child protection work developed and still functions in class society, and the critique of bureaucracies and professionalism has shown the inevitable deformation of attempts to "help" in a society of inequality, where only a few have the power to define what social order should be. But this critique of certain kinds of domination often serves to mask other kinds, particularly those between women and men and between adults and children. And it has predominantly been a critique that emphasizes domination as opposed to conflict.

Social work and, more generally, aspects of the welfare state have a unique bearing on gender conflicts. Women's subordination in the family, and their struggle against it, not only affected the construction of the welfare state but also the operations of social control bureaucracies. In fact, social control agencies such as the MSPCC, and more often, individual social workers, did sometimes help poor and working-class people. They aided the weaker against the stronger and not merely by rendering clients passive. Social work interventions rarely changed assailants' behavior, but they had a greater impact on victims. Ironically, the MSPCC thereby contributed more to help battered women, defined as outside its jurisdiction, than it did abused children. Industrial capitalist society gave women some opportunity to leave abusive men because they could earn their own livings. In these circumstances, even a tiny bit of material help, a mere hint as to how to "work" the relief agencies, could turn these women's aspirations for autonomy into reality. Women could sometimes get this help despite class and ethnic prejudices against them. Italian-American women might reap this benefit even from social workers who held derogatory views of Italians; single mothers might be able to get help in establishing independent households despite charity workers' suspicions of the immorality of their intentions. Just as in diplomacy the enemy of one's enemy may be *ipso facto* a friend, in these domestic dramas the enemy of one's oppressor could be an ally.

These immigrant clients—victims of racism, sexism, and poverty, perhaps occasional beneficiaries of child welfare work—were also part of the creation of modern child welfare standards and institutions. The welfare state was not a bargain in which the poor got material help by giving up control. The control itself was invented and structured out of these interactions. Because many of the MSPCC's early "interventions" were in fact invitations by family members, the latter were in some ways teaching the agents what were appropriate and enforceable standards of childcare. A more institutional example is the mothers' pension legislation developed in most of the United States between 1910 and 1920. As I have argued elsewhere, the feminist reformers who campaigned for that reform were influenced by the unending demands of single mothers, abounding in the records of child neglect, for support in raising their children without the benefit of men's wages.[19]

The entire Progressive era's child welfare reform package, the social program of the women's rights movement, and the reforms that accumulated to form the "welfare state" need to be reconceived as not only a campaign spearheaded by elites. They resulted also from a powerful if unsteady pressure for economic and domestic power from poor and working-class women. For them, social work agencies were a resource in their struggle to change the terms of their continuing, traditional, social control, which included but was not limited to the familial. The issues involved in an anti-family-violence campaign were fundamental to poor women: the right to immunity from physical attack at home, the power to protect their children from abuse, the right to keep their children—not merely the legal right to custody but the actual power to support their children—and the power to provide a standard of care for those children that met their own standards and aspirations. That family violence became a social problem at all, that charities and professional agencies were drawn into attempts to control it, were as much a product of the demands of those at the bottom as of those at the top.

Still, if these family and child welfare agencies contributed to women's options, they had a constricting impact too. I do not wish to discard the cumulative insights offered by many critiques of social control. The discrimination and victim blaming women encountered from professionals was considerable, the more so because they were proffered by those defined as "helping." Loss of control was an *experience*, articulated in many different ways by its victims, including those in these same case records. Often

328 I LINDA GORDON

the main beneficiaries of professionals' intervention hated them most, because in wrestling with them one rarely gets what one really wants but rather another interpretation of one's needs. An accurate view of the meanings of this "outside" intervention into the family must maintain in its analysis, as the women clients did in their strategic decisions, awareness of a tension between various forms of social control and the variety of factors that might contribute to improvements in personal life. This is a contradiction that women particularly face, and there is no easy resolution of it. There is no returning to an old or newly romanticized "community control" when the remnants of community rest on a patriarchal power structure hostile to women's aspirations. A feminist critique of social control must contain and wrestle with, not seek to eradicate, this tension.

NOTES

1. E. A. Ross, *Social Control* (New York, 1901).

2. A few examples follow: Anthony M. Platt, *The Child Savers: The Invention of Delinquency* (Chicago: University of Chicago Press, 1969); Barbara Ehrenreich and Deirdre English, *For Her Own Good: One Hundred and Fifty Years of the Experts' Advice to Women* (Garden City, N.Y.: Anchor/Doubleday: 1978); Christopher Lasch, *Haven in a Heartless World: The Family Besieged* (New York: Basic Books, 1977); and his *The Culture of Narcissism: American Life in an Age of Diminishing Expectations* (New York: Norton, 1979); Jacques Donzelot, *The Policing of Families*, trans. Hurley (New York: Pantheon, 1979); Barbara M. Brenzel, *Daughters of the State: A Social Portrait of the First Reform School for Girls in North America, 1856–1905* (Cambridge: MIT Press, 1983); Stuart Ewen, *Captains of Consciousness: Advertising and the Social Roots of the Consumer Culture* (New York: McGraw-Hill, 1976); Daniel T. Rodgers, *The Work Ethic in Industrial America, 1850–1920* (Chicago: University of Chicago Press, 1974); and Nigel Parton, *The Politics of Child Abuse* (New York: St. Martin's Press, 1985).

3. Eileen Boris and Peter Bardaglio, "The Transformation of Patriarchy: The Historic Role of the State," in *Families, Politics, and Public Policy: A Feminist Dialogue on Women and the State*, ed. Irene Diamond (New York: Longman, 1983), 70–93; Judith Areen, "Intervention between Parent and Child: A Reappraisal of the State's Role in Child Neglect and Abuse Cases," *Georgetown Law Journal* 63 (March 1975): 899–902; Mason P. Thomas, Jr., "Child Abuse and Neglect," pt. 1: "Historical Overview, Legal Matrix, and Social Perspectives," *North Carolina Law Review* 50 (February 1972): 299–303.

4. John H. Ehrenreich, *The Altruistic Imagination: A History of Social Work and Social Policy in the United States* (Ithaca: Cornell University Press, 1985).

5. Alice Kessler-Harris, *Out to Work: A History of Wage-Earning Women in the United States* (New York: Oxford University Press, 1982), esp. chap. 7; Gwendolyn Wright, *Moralism and the Modern Home: Domestic Architecture and Cultural Conflict in Chicago, 1873–1913* (Chicago: University of Chicago Press, 1980); Kathryn Sklar, "Hull House as a Community of Women in the 1890s," *Signs* 10 (Summer 1985); Susan Ware, *Beyond Suffrage: Women in the New Deal* (Cambridge: Harvard University Press, 1981).

6. Exceptions include Michael C. Grossberg, "Law and the Family in Nineteenth-Century America" (Ph.D. diss., Brandeis University, 1979); Boris and Bardaglio.

7. The agencies were the Boston Children's Service Association, the Massachusetts Society for the Prevention of Cruelty to Children, and the Judge Baker Guidance Center. A random sample of cases from every tenth year was coded and analyzed. A summary of the methodology and a sampling of findings can be found in my "Single Mothers and Child Neglect, 1880–1920," *American Quarterly* 37 (Summer 1985): 173–92.

8. Case code no. 2044.

9. In Boston the MSPCC was called into being largely by Kate Gannett Wells, a moral reformer, along with other members of the New England Women's Club and the Moral Education

Association. These women were united as much by class as by gender unity. Wells, for example, was an antisuffragist, yet in her club work she cooperated with suffrage militants such as Lucy Stone and Harriet Robinson, for they considered themselves all members of a larger, loosely defined but nonetheless coherent community of prosperous, respectable women reformers. This unity of class and gender purpose was organized feminism at this time. See New England Women's Club Papers, Schlesinger Library; MSPCC Correspondence Files, University of Massachusetts/Boston Archives, folder 1; Arthur Mann, *Yankee Reformers in the Urban Age* (Cambridge: Harvard University Press, 1954), 208.

10. Ann Douglas, *The Feminization of American Culture* (New York: Knopf, 1977).

11. For examples of the growing anti-corporal-punishment campaign, see Lyman Cobb, *The Evil Tendencies of Corporal Punishment as a Means of Moral Discipline in Families and School* (New York, 1847); Mrs. C. A. Hopkinson, *Hints for the Nursery* (Boston, 1863); Mary Blake, *Twenty-Six Hours a Day* (Boston: D. Lothrop, 1883); Bolton Hall, "Education by Assault and Battery," *Arena* 39 (June 1908): 466–67. For historical commentary, see N. Ray Hiner, "Children's Rights, Corporal Punishment, and Child Abuse: Changing American Attitudes, 1870–1920," *Bulletin of the Menninger Clinic* 43, no. 3 (1979): 233–48; Carl F. Kaestle, "Social Change, Discipline, and the Common School in Early Nineteenth-Century America," *Journal of Interdisciplinary History* 9 (Summer 1978): 1–17; Myra C. Glenn, "The Naval Reform Campaign against Flogging: A Case Study in Changing Attitudes toward Corporal Punishment, 1830–1850," *American Quarterly* 35 (Fall 1983): 408–25; Robert Elno McGlone, "Suffer the Children: The Emergence of Modern Middle-Class Family Life in America, 1820–1870" (Ph.D. diss., University of California at Los Angeles, 1971).

12. Nancy Chodorow and Susan Contratto, "The Fantasy of the Perfect Mother," in *Rethinking the Family: Some Feminist Questions,* ed. Barrie Thorne and Marilyn Yalom (New York: Longman, 1982); Joseph Goldstein, Anna Freud, and Albert J. Solnit, *Beyond the Best Interests of the Child* (New York: Free Press, 1973); and *Before the Best Interests of the Child* (New York: Free Press, 1979).

13. Case code no. 2042.

14. To this argument it could be responded that it is difficult to define what would be a parent's "own" standards of childraising. In heterogeneous urban situations, childraising patterns change rather quickly, and new patterns become normative. Certainly the child welfare agencies were part of a "modernization" (in the United States called Americanization) effort, attempting to present new family norms as objectively right. However, in the poor neighborhoods, poverty, crowding, and the structure of housing allowed very little privacy, and the largely immigrant clients resisted these attempts and retained autonomous family patterns, often for several generations. Moreover, my own clinical and research experience suggests that even "anomic" parents, or mothers, to be precise, tend to have extremely firm convictions about right and wrong childraising methods.

15. Nancy Cott, for example, has identified some of the processes of community involvement in family life in eighteenth-century Massachusetts, in her "Eighteenth-Century Family and Social Life Revealed in Massachusetts Divorce Records," *Journal of Social History* 10 (Fall 1976): 20–43; Ann Whitehead has described the informal regulation of marital relations that occurred in pub conversations in her "Sexual Antagonism in Herefordshire," in Diana Leonard Barker and Sheila Allen, *Dependence and Exploitation in Work and Marriage* (London: Longman, 1976), 169–203.

16. For example, see William Jordan, *The Social Worker in Family Situations* (London: Routledge & Kegan Paul, 1972); James W. Green, *Cultural Awareness in the Human Services* (Englewood Cliffs, N.J. Prentice-Hall, 1982); Alfred Kadushin, *Child Welfare Services* (New York: Macmillan, 1980), chap. 13.

17. Indeed, so widespread were these attempts to enmesh social workers in intrafamily feuds that they were responsible for a high proportion of the many unfounded complaints the MSPCC always met. Rejected men, then as now, often fought for the custody of children they did not really want as a means of hurting their wives. One way of doing this was to bring complaints

against their wives of cruel treatment of children, or the men charged wives with child neglect when their main desire was to force the women to live with them again. Embittered, deserted wives might arrange to have their husbands caught with other women.

18. Zillah Eisenstein, *The Radical Future of Liberal Feminism* (New York: Longman, 1981); Joan B. Landes, "Hegel's Conception of the Family," 125–44; and Mary Lyndon Shanley, "Marriage Contract and Social Contract in Seventeenth-Century English Political Thought," 80–95, both in Jean Bethke Elshtain, ed., *The Family in Political Thought* (Amherst: University of Massachusetts Press, 1982).

19. See my "Single Mothers and Child Neglect," *American Quarterly* 37 (Summer 1985): 173–92.

22

Who Stole Incest?

LOUISE ARMSTRONG

In 1978, when people asked what I'd written about, I'd say "incest." And they would then most often ask, "Oh? Are you a feminist?"

Now, when I say (with some reticence) that I have written about incest, people ask, "Oh? Are you a psychologist?"

Incest, the sexualization of children cast in Procrustean form, has been transmogrified—hijacked. From a political issue framed by feminists as one of male violence against women and children—a sexual offense on the part of men, for which we demanded accountability, and censure—incest has, in these years, been coopted and reformulated by the therapeutic ideology, as an illness in women, to be treated. In children, it is a prediction of illness to be treated.

In 1971, we spoke of what caused child sexual abuse and its role in socializing women, and training them for sexual submission.

By now, you will hear few speak of what causes incest. Most speak only of what incest causes: sleeplessness, lack of trust, sexual acting-out, timidity, aggression, destiny itself. Children raped by fathers and stepfathers are said to be doomed—to become depressed, dissociated, drug-addicted, suicidal . . .

The issue of incest is now one of illness.

It is not social, but medical.

The response is not a call for change, but a call for "treatment."

It is not that we were wrong. Far from it. We identified incest as something fathers and stepfathers had done throughout history and continued to do, not in spite of the fact that they knew it was wrong, but because they believed it was their right: *justifiable.*

And this is what the offenders said as well. ("It's natural; it's perfectly normal.") By 1980, men were helping our understanding still more, as academics and other professionals spoke to us as the "pro-incest lobby" of "positive incest." They told us that "children have the right to express themselves sexually, even with members of their own family." They told us that, in any case, "the rate of incidence is so high as to make prohibition absurd." They told us that incest could be *beneficial.*

Well, we knew it could be, too. And we knew who benefitted.

We knew that incest was not only the grotesque absurdity of men turning the full

From *On the Issues* 3, no. 4 (fall 1994):30–32. Reprinted by permission.

power of adult male sexuality against infants, toddlers and pre-teens. It was also a form of violence against women. Our fathers had helped us out here as well. ("This would kill your mother if she found out." "She's not good for anything anyway, the bitch.")

During the 1980s, we had further corroboration that incest was not confined to the rape of children, but among the many male violences against women. Children, we learned, were now being abused by fathers in retaliation for divorce. And they were being abused with far less finesse.

Yet by then what we knew, what could be seen from the evidence, had already been overridden, suppressed by male-protective forces. From the moment of our first speaking out, newfound experts on the rape of children had risen full-blown from the sea, pronouncing with the authority of mental health professionals, knowledge. The oddest thing was that even they knew that the rape of daughters was also violence against women. They said so. In their own language, of course, their own sort of way.

The mothers of incest victims, they pronounced, simply did not put out enough, weren't attractive enough, weren't nice enough to their men, they were rejecting or frigid (or sexually rapacious). This, they said, is what drives men to the beds of their five-year-olds, this "incest mother."

Well, this was not *exactly* the way we would have put it. But it meant these new experts saw what we did: That when men sexually assault their children, it is often driven by rage at women.

There was a subtle but serious distinction between the "pro-incest" folks and the new experts. The "pro-incesters" wanted incest legalized, where the new experts wanted it "de-criminalized." Legalized had the virtue of candor. But decriminalized won. That meant that as a matter of policy incest was subject to state intervention: civil, not criminal. An intervention that would target—not rapist fathers, but—"incest families." Civil statutes were now written that faulted the mother who "knew or should have known." Well, looked at generously, even that message was not so very different from ours: women should know that men feel at liberty to rape children.

One problem with their way of putting things was that in order to have "intra-familial child sexual abuse" for which the woman was equally (or more) culpable, you absolutely had to have this "incest mother" hanging around, in the picture, choosing her husband over her child, denying what the kid said . . . You had to have her, alive or dead ("sometimes the incest mother is absent from the home, or terminally ill").

So women who, discovering the abuse, left and tried to protect the child were simply not playing their role in the drama as now scripted. For this outrageous failure to read their lines as written (in a script essential to defraying male accountability), the mothers had to be viciously punished. And so these women, "vindictive, hysterical," lost custody of their children—to the alleged abusers. They were that dangerous. They threatened to expose the whole conceptual fraud. War on children and their mothers had been declared.

Another problem with the new experts' way of putting things was that in practice a policy of de-criminalization not only resulted in punishing women and children, it also diminished the import of adult survivors' testimony. It rendered individual survivors vulnerable to the newly emerging specialists in problem management—those in the therapeutic arena who, alone, assured survivors that what had happened to them mattered.

Alas, in this medicalized world, survivors' experience mattered in direct proportion to the degree of manifest illness. How sick you were proved how bad it was. Checklists offered expanding lists of expected symptoms, the display of which was said to be evidence of your past abuse.

Within this individualized universe, some individual survivors sought personal, rather than united political, action: they did battle against statutes of limitation and instigated lawsuits against alleged perpetrators. Making incest a pocketbook issue for offenders, of course, galvanized a spirited, quickly organized, political response. The oxymoronic False Memory Syndrome was born. War on adult survivors' credibility had been declared.

On both fronts of this war against children and mothers and against adult survivors—it was the other side that had the army and the medics. Individualization, medicalization had precluded political organization.

By now, friends-in-this-struggle would say, "Things are not going well."

To which I replied, "Things are going very well. Just not for us."

We have been re-silenced. Within the larger world. And within a world that is labeled feminist as well.

You cannot hear us anymore—those who spoke out early on and have spoken out since about incest as a licensed abuse of male power. Our voices have been drowned out by those who speak of incest as "gender neutral." Drowned out by those who speak of incest-as-illness—who would have us hear only that women survivors have been made fragile and helpless by the event in their childhood vaguely rendered by the word incest. Women are portrayed to us, in tones of great sympathy, as damaged, suffering from diminished capacity. And signs of damage in women, signs of diminished capacity—working backwards—are taken as "indicators" that they have been wounded by incest. Incest has become a metaphor for all the oppressions that feminism named.

What has happened in this brief fifteen years since feminists first spoke out on incest is the explicit exoneration of fathers, the implication of mothers—and the infantilization of women as survivors.

The personal is political. You may still hear the words, but you can no longer hear the meaning behind them. You cannot hear that the point of speaking out was to identify commonalities that, once identified, could lead to political action for change. We spoke out publicly to break a silence—when there was a silence to break. But speaking out was never meant to be all there was.

We endorsed help for individual women. But that was never meant to be all there was: the building of field hospitals to tend a predictably endless supply of wounded.

You cannot hear us anymore. Even though—in the tiniest tucky-holes of this country—you cannot any longer hear silence on the prevalence of incest, you cannot anywhere hear what all this talk of incest means. You can't hear that it is about a license that is historical. Or that, until recently, what silenced women was not reticence or shame, but intimidation. You can't hear that, as recently as 1978, the law in Texas, for instance, held the complaining child liable as an accomplice-witness, a "participant," an instigator. For all the loose talk of the "crime" of incest, you can't hear that this male abuse of power continues to be quasi-semi-more-or-less legal in this country. Or that where children and their protective mothers refuse to be silent—they will be silenced by the courts, and punished. And you cannot hear that these things are all connected, all part of the same weave. That the myth of the incest "triad," that the exclusive focus on victim pathology is all tailored to protect the male offender. You can't hear this even within most gatherings of feminists.

Even the incest stories you now hear are selective. The stories of children yanked into the child welfare system are unheard. The stories of those children placed under psychiatric surveillance, sometimes institutionalized, presumed according to mental health ideology to be at risk of emotional disturbance because their fathers raped them—are unheard. And yet we are everywhere told that we are, at last, *listening to the children.*

Nor do survivor's stories speak clearly of incest as male violence, nor of the deliberateness of that violence. Indeed, with the focus so heavily on illness, you can barely discern the fact of human agency: it is as though "incest" is on the order of a natural catastrophe—not rape by Daddy, who could just as easily have not done it.

What you can hear now is that we are, at last—fifteen years after women began publicly speaking out, ten years after the televising of the breakthrough documentary, "Something about Amelia," five years after every talk show in the nation has routinized the airing of incest stories—breaking the silence.

Women continue to speak out, but seldom in their own, authentic voices. Rather, their speech echoes that of therapists; they speak the language of mental health—of their disorders, and their path to healing. They speak of being in recovery—as though it were a geographical space. Their stories are absent context, without larger meaning.

In being framed as medical, incest has been rendered trivial.

Somehow, mental health ideology infiltrated and subverted feminist rationality. Once incest was re-formulated by treaters and healers, speaking out itself was transformed. Its meaning was changed. The personal became public, but not political. It was not the abuse of male power, but individual women and their symptoms who needed to change.

What we are speaking of here is not therapy, the private event. It is the therapeutic ideology—a way of seeing the world that enlarges the personal, with no agenda for the political. It is a belief system, a way of seeing the world that subverts the goals of feminism: it promotes the personal to the paramount, sells belonging in suffering, offers consolation that what afflicts you is not politically engineered, but an individual fate. When the therapeutic ideology triumphs—feminism loses.

Alas, it has proved very seductive. The therapeutic ideology infiltrated feminism through the issue of incest. It hijacked the issue from under feminism's nose. It pretended to feminism by hijacking feminist language.

Combining that language with mental health credo, it offered to survivors something it called *empowerment.* All women needed was the *courage* to cede their power to experts. The language promised *liberation;* spoke of the *struggle.* By the early 1990s, you no longer distinguish what survivors were calling the survivor movement from what everyone else was calling the recovery movement. And all of this in the name of feminism.

Speaking out—lopped free from all political foundation—was bankrupt. No more than confession. It was now said to be a "stage" in healing.

But who would dare challenge such things? To speak out on this is to seem to be making rude noises on an intensive care ward. Who among us is brutal enough to speak against healing?

We have been re-silenced.

Fathers and stepfathers continue to rape children. Children pay a high price for that. Their mothers pay a high price for that. The cost benefit analysis of incest remains the same. The fact of incest, the incidence of incest—routine, banal, non-exotic incest—is the sexualization of children in everyday reality: the expression of rage at women by wounding their children, in everyday reality.

Pictures in the media of children sexualized are signifiers of the licensed act. Images of women dressed as children, of children made up and photographed as little women, are signifiers, a warning of license.

As long as the act itself remains uncensured, and the aggressors remain publicly unchallenged as a collective force, by a collective force as long as feminist analysis and energy is submerged in and overridden by mental health doctrine, images of the sexualization of children are (to use the old incest cliche) the "tip of the iceberg."

The iceberg remains the socially tolerated act of child-rape by fathers.

23

Child Sexual Abuse and the Regulation of Women: Variations on a Theme

CAROL·ANN HOOPER

The current wave of recognition of child sexual abuse is not the first in the history of child-protection work. From the 1870s for roughly sixty years, intermittent anxieties emerged and attempts at legal reform were made, culminating in a specific campaign on sexual offences against children initiated by feminists in the 1930s. At the end of this period, however, the criminal justice system was still hopelessly ineffective, the campaign fizzled out, and a public silence ensued (broken briefly during the 1950s) until the 1970s, when feminists again brought the issue to public attention. In both the earlier period and the present one, a number of interest groups have promoted and laid claims to the issue, offering competing definitions. Feminist definitions locating the problem in the social construction of masculinity have commonly been marginalised from the policy agenda.

Child sexual abuse is itself a site of informal social control by men over women. As girls who are victimised themselves, as partners of abusive men and as mothers and primary carers of sexually abused children, the sexual abuse of children operates to restrict women's autonomy and control of their own lives. The responses of voluntary and statutory agencies to child sexual abuse have also been centrally concerned with the regulation of women, much more so than with the control of men who abuse. In the earlier period, it was the behaviour of sexually abused girls themselves that was most subject to surveillance, although often in the name of their future as mothers. Today, it is the mothers of sexually abused children whose behaviour is the prime concern of child protection agencies.

The shift from girls to their mothers is attributable to two main trends. First, increased attention through the present century first to children's physical needs and later to their psychological needs, within an ideological context which defines child welfare as women's private business, has generated redefinitions of motherhood which accord women increased responsibilities. Definitions of fatherhood have been much less implicated (if at all) by attention to child welfare, despite the evidence now available that men far outnumber women as sexual abusers of children and play a more or less equal role in physical abuse (Stark and Flitcraft 1988; Gordon 1988). Second, state

From *Regulating Womanhood: Historical Essays on Marriage, Motherhood and Sexuality,* C. Smart (ed.), Routledge, 1992, pp. 53–77. Reprinted by permission.

intervention in the home to protect children has gained greater (although by no means uncontested) acceptability. The voluntary activities of philanthropists and charitable organisations in the late-nineteenth century, to which contemporary child protection work owes its roots (Behlmer 1982; Ferguson 1990), have been replaced by a child-abuse management system which attempts to co-ordinate the activities of a wide range of professionals and statutory agencies. The combined effect of these trends has been to legitimate greater surveillance of mothers, alongside a still-limited commitment of resources to public services to contribute to the work and costs of childcare.

This chapter considers both periods of anxiety about child sexual abuse to illustrate the variety of ways in which women have been constructed in regulatory discourses. In the first period, I focus on how the construction of the problem changed, influenced by changing social anxieties and the strengths and orientations of social movements. In the later period, I discuss the alternative constructions of motherhood involved in contemporary discourses on child sexual abuse, and their influence on and resistance by mothers and social workers, the prime actors in the protection of children. In this section I draw on my contemporary study of mothers of sexually abused children, which involved interviews with both mothers and social workers (Hooper 1990).

The analysis of both periods is necessarily selective and the focus on girls in the early period and their mothers in the contemporary period to some extent schematic. The greater emphasis on protecting children today is certainly not unproblematic for girls who are sexually abused, and the control of their sexuality is clearly still an issue in medical, child protection and judicial discourse (see Mitra 1987; Kitzinger 1988). More-over, from its nineteenth-century beginnings, child protection work in England has sought where possible to enforce rather than replace parental responsibility for children and in doing so has reflected and perpetuated gendered definitions of proper parenting (Ferguson 1990). In child-protection practice, there has probably therefore been as much continuity as change. However, constructions of women are continually renegotiated in specific contexts and this chapter seeks to identify some sources of variability.

There has been some speculation recently that the current anxiety about child sexual abuse is not simply a product of changed social anxieties and political movements, but a response to a new and growing problem (see O'Hagan 1989; Gledhill et al. 1989). Before discussing the historical shifts in visibility and definitions therefore, it is worth reviewing briefly the available evidence on incidence.

On the Incidence of Child Sexual Abuse

It is difficult to unearth the history of a problem kept so invisible. The most reliable sources of evidence on historical trends are contemporary surveys of adults using age-stratified samples. These are limited in scope by the lifespan and age of those inter-viewed, and by problems of memory, but the evidence of two such surveys, both conducted in the USA, is instructive. Russell (1984) found that incestuous abuse, but not extrafamilial child sexual abuse, had increased over the years 1916 to 1961, although the peak occurred in 1956. It is possible however that memories of incestuous abuse were more deeply buried for older women, for whom the subject had been unspeakable for so much of their lives. Finkelhor et al.'s (1990) more recent survey found no consistent upward trend over time. Lower rates of abuse were reported by women aged over sixty but those born 1955–67 reported no higher level of abuse than their immedi-ate predecessors.

Both studies, however, suggest that the most significant fluctuations have coincided with war. Women born during the Second World War reported the highest levels of abuse in both surveys. Russell's analysis of period rates found that the incidence of incestuous abuse declined during both world wars, and increased immediately after. Extrafamilial child sexual abuse also declined during the Second World War and increased after, although in contrast it increased during the First World War. Although other fluctuations cannot be linked to war, these findings are illustrative of one of the many dilemmas child sexual abuse raises. Children tend to be safest from sexual abuse in the absence of men, but it is in part men's separation from children which makes them a threat when they return.

Since it is some years since any of those interviewed were children, these studies do not answer the question of whether child sexual abuse is currently increasing. It is highly likely, however, that the rapid increase during the 1980s in the number of cases of child sexual abuse on child protection registers[1] held by local authorities reflects increased reporting by members of the public, increased awareness and detection by professionals and/or increased use of the child protection register in the management of cases.

Nor do these studies reach back into the nineteenth century. Gordon's (1988) study of child protection records in Boston 1880–1960, however, found a consistent level of 10 percent of cases involving incest throughout the period, despite fluctuating levels of public awareness.

It seems safe to assume that whatever its exact incidence child sexual abuse is not a new problem. This should not be surprising, since the social conditions which support it have remained consistent—the construction of masculine sexuality as predatory and not requiring reciprocity, the eroticisation of dominance, and the lack of responsibility men have for childcare.

It is not in fact correct to say that child sexual abuse has been wholly invisible. Rather, it has at certain periods been partially visible, its definition as a problem mediated through other social anxieties about "the family," sexuality and reproduction. It is often these other concerns—with the "health of the race" in the 1900s, or with the "decline of the traditional family" in the 1980s, for example—that have shaped the dominant discourses.

1870s to 1930s: From Victims to Delinquents and Law to Medicine

Public awareness of what we would now call child sexual abuse arose in the 1870s in the context of concern about child prostitution. Shortly after, the National Society for the Prevention of Cruelty to Children (NSPCC), formed by philanthropic reformers in 1889, drew attention also to sexual abuse in the home. Up until the end of the First World War, it referred regularly (if euphemistically) to these in its annual reports, indicating that they were far more common than would easily be believed.[2] Other nineteenth-century reformers, too, encountered incestuous abuse, most notably during the investigation of housing conditions (Wohl 1978). Campaigns were waged by the social purity movement (primarily the National Vigilance Association [NVA]), by the NSPCC itself and by feminist groups, focusing initially on legal reforms to facilitate an effective response from the criminal justice system both to incestuous and extrafamilial abuse.

Some successes were achieved in these, and two major pieces of legislation concerning sexual assault were passed during this period. Neither was unproblematic. The Criminal Law Amendment Act 1885, which raised the age of consent for sexual intercourse from thirteen to sixteen, was supported by a range of groups brought together in a short-lived coalition. This Act could be and was used to prosecute men, including fathers, for sexual abuse. However, by portraying young prostitutes as sexually innocent, passive victims of individual evil men, the reformers had also paved the way for the increased surveillance of working-class girls and diverted attention from the economic reasons why many engaged in prostitution (Gorham 1978). The potential for "protection" to become control of female sexuality is a recurring theme in responses to child sexual abuse. The Punishment of Incest Act 1908, again supported by a range of groups, made incest a criminal, as opposed to an ecclesiastical, offence for the first time (Bailey and Blackburn 1979). Calls for legislation specific to incest had been made from the 1890s, suggesting the inclusion of assaults by men in positions of authority, including employers, schoolmasters and guardians under this label (*The Vigilance Record*, December 1895). The Act passed excluded even stepfathers, adopting consanguinity as the defining feature, after debates which were concerned far more with the regulation of sexuality than the protection of children. Further campaigns achieved amendments to the 1885 Act, including the raising of the age of consent for indecent assault from thirteen to sixteen (1922), the partial removal of "the defence of reasonable belief" (that the man had believed a girl was over the age of consent when she was not) (1922) and extending the time limit under which prosecutions could be brought, from three months (1885), to six months (1904), nine months (1922) and finally to twelve months in 1928.

However, when a government review was conducted in 1925, a number of further problems were noted with the law and its administration. The Report of the Departmental Committee on Sexual Offences against Young Persons (1925) noted that many cases were unreported, that many more, once reported, were sifted out before reaching court for lack of proof, and that for those that did reach court, the acquittal rate was unusually high. Its recommendations involved measures to ease the strain of the process on children (including the greater use of women as police, doctors and magistrates in such cases, and the quicker and less formal conducting of court proceedings) and changes to the rules of evidence (since in effect a higher level of proof was required for sexual offences than in most others, making convictions almost impossible). A recommendation was also made that the age of consent be raised to seventeen, although four members of the Committee dissented, three wanting no change and one wanting it raised to eighteen.

The report did not concern itself only with the criminal law. It made a range of recommendations on prevention, and also on changes to the civil law to facilitate the removal of children from their homes. However, it was the role of the criminal law that was the spark for action, since groups hoping to see these recommendations incorporated in the forthcoming Children's Bill were disappointed when it was published in 1932.[3] Resolutions were passed at various organisations' annual conferences, and the feminist Association of Moral and Social Hygiene, then led by Alison Neilans, a former active suffragist, held a small specific conference in November 1932. From this a Joint Committee on Sexual Offences against Children was established, representing fourteen national organisations (including AMSH itself, the NVA, the National Council of Women, the British Social Hygiene Council, the National Council of Mental Hygiene and the Howard League for Penal Reform, amongst others). Representatives of these groups met over the next three years, with the aim of agreeing a limited bill with a good chance of success around which to mobilise a campaign. They were not able to do so. They dissolved in 1935 having published a brief report and two leaflets[4] and little further campaigning occurred on the problem of child sexual abuse.

I am not suggesting that had they achieved further legal reforms, this would have solved the problem of child sexual abuse. The law was and is one of the ways in which patriarchal power is maintained and has rarely provided protection for women or girls from male violence, as feminists have frequently pointed out. Furthermore, many of the recommendations of the 1925 report, on which the campaign focused, did not require legislation. It is probably more important that the degree of disagreement within the campaigns, in which the significance of the criminal law was a key issue, weakened the commitment to any further action. The result, however, was that the major legislation passed in the wake of the government review, the Children and Young Persons Act 1933, focused on the control of juvenile delinquency (defined for girls in relation to their sexuality) and on the removal of children "in moral danger" or "beyond parental control" from their parents (identifying parental, primarily maternal, neglect as the problem). How did this reconstruction of the problem come about? And how, then, did the issue disappear from public attention effectively until the 1970s? Viewing the period of sixty years or so very broadly, two major shifts seem significant. First, social anxieties about the "health of the race" from the turn of the century resulted in an increasing significance attached to motherhood in the latter part of the period. Changing concepts of childhood and adolescence at the same time made the problem of defining abuse, represented by debates on the age of consent, increasingly contentious. Second, popular support for the social purity movement whose main focus had been legal reform had declined, the strength of the medical profession which offered a new alliance of science and morality in the discourse of social hygiene had increased, and the declining feminist movement increasingly sided with the latter rather than the former. The disputes that occurred in debates on child sexual abuse during the 1930s reflected these broader changes.

The growing influence of Freudian ideas in the inter-war years no doubt also played its part. Freud's volte-face which led him to attribute his women patients' accounts of sexual abuse to incestuous fantasy has been well documented elsewhere (Rush 1984; Masson 1985). But the reluctance to believe children's accounts, which was displayed by some (though not all) members of the Joint Committee, and to name the abuse of paternal power, was neither new, nor is it passed today.

THE HEALTH OF THE RACE AND THE RISE OF MATERNALISM

Around the turn of the century, the health of the population became a major national concern. Anxieties about the falling birth rate, high infant mortality, the poverty uncovered by Booth and Rowntree and the poor physical conditions of recruits to the Boer War combined in a rising fear that the nation's health was degenerating. This fear continued and increased during the war as deaths at the front increased, and the birth rate continued to fall. In response, childhood, motherhood and sex were all accorded new meanings. Child protection and child welfare reforms were facilitated by these concerns, since children were the raw material to be safeguarded in the name of national efficiency. Motherhood became defined as crucial to child health. High infant mortality and physical deterioration were attributed not to poverty but to ignorant motherhood, the solution seen as the education of working-class mothers better to fulfil their national duty as "guardians of the race" (Davin 1978; Bland 1982). Sex became the key to the question of population, both in its effects on the health of the individual (particularly via VD), and on the future of the population (via the association of VD with sterility, and the higher infant mortality of unmarried mothers) (Weeks 1989). At the same time, the notion of adolescence as a distinct period of development, and one of particular significance for the channeling of sexuality towards responsible parenthood, emerged.

These shifts influenced the way sexual abuse was constructed in a number of ways. First, concern focused often not on the victimised girl herself but on her potential offspring as the true victim. In the Commons debate on the Incest Bill 1908, the main argument put forward by Herbert Samuel, Home Office Under-Secretary, for criminalising incest was that "it might entail consequences of a disastrous kind on the offspring which sometimes followed from such intercourse, and from that point of view society had a special interest that should lead to steps being taken to put a stop to it" (*Hansard,* 26 June 1908, col. 284).

Second, and linked to this, the response to the victimised girl increasingly reflected concerns about her potential performance as a mother. The Royal Commission on the Care and Control of the Feeble-Minded which sat in 1908 heard evidence that "feeble-minded" girls were particularly vulnerable to sexual assault, that many had illegitimate children as a result, and that such children were likely to be "imbeciles, or degenerates, or criminals." Its response was to recommend the segregation of such girls in order to prevent them from reproducing themselves.[5]

The NVA, whose aim was to transform sexual behaviour towards a high standard of chastity in both men and women, increasingly adopted the new concern for the national stock in place of the moral language of vice and corruption it had previously used. Germany was criticised for allowing earlier marriage in order to counter the falling birth rate, since to "prematurely exploit young girlhood" would not pay off "from the racial point of view" (*The Vigilance Record,* October 1915: 79–80). In 1922 an article in the *Evening Standard* was cited approvingly, arguing against the use of the "reasonable cause to believe" defence as follows:

> (the law) should, in fact, regard adolescent women as at least as important as adolescent fish or breeding animals. It is an offence to shoot game in the close season, or to take fish below a certain size, and no "reasonable cause" can be pleaded. Why should there be a necessity for a big loophole regarding the age of consent? (*The Vigilance Record,* September 1922: 59)

Motherhood and promiscuity were constructed as separate routes by the social hygiene movement during this period, and the concern of the newly developing sex education was primarily to divert girls from "promiscuity" towards responsible and healthy motherhood (Bland 1982). Hence this concern with motherhood facilitated the shift of concern from abuse itself to its consequences (perceived through the lens of women as reproducers), since the diversion of girls from "promiscuity," from the risk of VD and from unmarried motherhood (all of which were for some girls the consequence of sexual abuse) became a high priority. It was considerably easier and less threatening to prevailing power structures to patrol and control girls in all these circumstances, sending them to homes for their reform, than effectively to counter the abuses of men in the home or on the street.

This concern to preserve girls for their future reproductive roles was one continued justification for those who sought the further raising of the age of consent. Debates on this issue were complex, however, and are not adequately represented as concerned solely with the repressive regulation of female sexuality sought by social purity or a feminist obsession with male vice. Feminists in the 1885 debates were sometimes drawn into an alliance with social purity in opposition to the attempts of upper-class men to preserve their unfettered access to working-class girls, losing sight temporarily of the risks of such legislation for the civil liberties of young women (Gorham 1978). Despite increasing recognition of the problems the age of consent brought, however, many continued to be ambivalent. While purity campaigners sought the protection of girls "from themselves," some feminists noted more their protection from exposure to the full rigours of the double standard (e.g., *The Vote*, 11 May 1912). The age of consent marked the dividing line around which the contradictions of women's responsibility for sexuality, both less and more responsible than men, polarised (Bland 1982). Below it girls were perceived as without responsibility, justifying (sometimes oppressive) protection. But above it, they bore responsibility not only for themselves but also for men, as illustrated by the prosecution of women for soliciting.

Later, the arguments of some feminists for raising the age of consent to eighteen were allied to the cause of sexual equality by calling for the raising of the age of criminal responsibility also to eighteen. This was justified by the new medicalised concept of adolescence as an inherently unstable time when neither boys nor girls were fit to decide for themselves.[6] The NVA had by the 1930s also bowed to the new definition of adolescence although they took a different, and in this instance less repressive, approach laying strong emphasis on distinguishing between assaults on young children, and what they referred to as "technical assaults" or "boy and girl cases" involving "foolish youths and precocious girls." The 1925 report was criticised for conflating the two quite different issues and the NVA consistently attempted to exclude the latter from campaigns. Divisions on this issue continued to emerge in the 1930s, although the Joint Committee agreed from the beginning to exclude the age of consent from their remit as too contentious. The Home Office had already indicated that further legislation on the issue would get nowhere.

The third way in which concerns with motherhood influenced the construction of sexual abuse was by the new responsibilities and powers accorded women as mothers. Concern with child health and the role of mothers in securing it brought a shift towards greater emphasis on women as mothers and a lesser emphasis on women as wives. The extended length of childhood further exaggerated the role of women as mothers. As women were accorded greater powers to influence their children, attention to their own victimisation declined. Feminist groups continued in the suffrage campaigns to draw attention to the victimisation of women as well as children,[7] and to the inequity of the responsibilities accorded mothers for children when they had few legal rights and limited access to resources. But while the link between delinquency and parental neglect was not new,[8] it was firmly established in the 1933 Act. Family breakdown and working mothers became the key culprits, both seen as the result of economic deprivation (League of Nations 1934). Many feminists by then felt the new responsibilities of motherhood offered potential for enhancing women's status in the home and pursued welfare reforms with this aim, simultaneously moving away from the earlier critique of sexual exploitation by men. Thus AMSH cited approvingly a reference to the causes of delinquency which commented "a home without a mother is only half a home" (*The Shield*, November 1934), and in the debates on child sexual abuse of the 1930s, a National Council of Women conference observed that "a great many problem cases would never have arisen if children had been brought up in the right knowledge" (*Scotsman*, 21 November 1933). Parent education was advocated as a preventive measure, as was the speeding up of slum clearance. The former in effect accorded mothers the responsibility for preventing sexual abuse. The latter implied that incestuous abuse was the product of overcrowded housing and did nothing to tackle the power of men within households.

SOCIAL PURITY, SOCIAL HYGIENE, AND FEMINISM

The weakening of the feminist critique of masculinity reflects another important shift, the relative decline of the social purity movement and the rise of social hygiene, alongside changing attitudes amongst feminists both to sex and to the law. During the late-nineteenth century, the social purity movement had mobilised a major campaign for moral reform and the suppression of vice. Their stress on criminal legislation as a means of achieving this reflected a then new perception of the state's capacity to transform sexual and moral behaviour (Mort 1987). The NVA, for example, claimed that in Ireland where incest was a criminal offence, it did not occur (*The Vigilance Record*, December 1895). In the suffrage campaigns many feminists shared this faith in the potential role of law, despite its current male bias. The Women's Freedom League made similarly wild claims for a legal system open to the beneficial influence of women (see, e.g., *The Vote*, 9 March 1912). Many (although not all) feminists had also shared social purity concerns with male lust and the double standard, campaigning for women's right to say no to unwanted sex.[9] However, by the 1930s popular support for social purity, with its explicitly moral language of sin, vice and degeneracy and adherence to criminal law as a deterrent had declined. The social hygiene movement on the other hand, which had emerged in the 1900s offering new scientific knowledges to the population debates, was well established, speaking an apparently more progressive language. Many of the same moral judgements were in fact reworked into the medical discourse of science, but social hygiene promoted a more positive image of sex with an emphasis on education and prevention as regulatory practices rather than suppression and punishment.

Many feminists by this time had moved to some degree away both from their earlier suspicion of the medical profession (derived from the involvement of the latter in the regulation of prostitution in the nineteenth century), and their faith in the efficacy of legal reform, recognising that the latter often resulted in greater surveillance of women. Increasingly, they also focused on women's right to sexual pleasure rather than on protection from sexual exploitation (Bland 1983). Hence, they allied themselves with the seemingly more progressive forces of social hygiene. Alison Neilans was an enthusiastic representative of this trend, calling for legislation on sexual assault that would "take people out of the category of criminals and put them into the category of mental invalids" (*Scotsman*, 21 November 1933). AMSH, in its calls for new legislation, focused entirely on the medical examination and treatment of offenders against children under thirteen. The medicalisation of sexual offences against young children that took place in this period was part of a broader trend occurring, although not without conflict, towards psychological explanations for crime and delinquency (Weeks 1989). Its basis in moral criteria is illustrated by the label adopted of "moral perversion" and by the claim made for the role of the medical profession by Dr. W. D. Fairbairn: "I submit that, since a child does not constitute a natural object of overt sexual behaviour on the part of an adult, such behaviour in itself constitutes a perverse act" (Fairbairn 1935, 15). Such elaborate claims for a disease model were not apparently inhibited by the fact that neither the cause nor the cure had yet been found.

Neither earlier feminists nor social-purity campaigners had been hesitant in naming the construction of normal male sexuality as a problem. The medical profession, however, relied on the concept of abnormality for its claims both to seek and to treat pathology, and feminists who dissented from this were increasingly marginalised. The receptiveness of feminists to the medical model was increased both by sympathy for men's suffering in the war, and increasing interest in the problem of persistent offenders, since the case was made that treating one offender successfully would prevent a series of further assaults. Broader ideas of prevention were drawn from social hygiene's image of sex as a healthy instinct in need of channelling towards socially approved goals. The 1925 report recommended sex education and the provision of facilities for healthy indoor and outdoor recreation as preventive measures, and in some later debates allowing earlier marriage was suggested. Feminist proposals for prevention also included sex education, along with talks to parents and improved housing.

Representatives of the medical profession claimed their analysis did not affect the issue of criminal responsibility. Purity campaigners, however, saw it as a direct challenge to their ideas, and one not to be taken lying down. While some members of the NVA shifted towards a medical discourse and officially it endorsed calls for medical examination and treatment, internally members were divided, and Frederick Sempkins, the current Secretary, waged a personal campaign against "throwing (the issue) over to the alienists." Medical treatment was to him both a soft option, and of limited relevance, since it mattered little what was done with convicted offenders when the main problem was the impossibility of gaining convictions in the first place. The latter point (still pertinent today) seems to have fallen on deaf ears, in part because feminists (and others) were preoccupied with resisting his punitive emphasis on the law as a deterrent and occasional advocacy of flogging, in part because of the intransigence of the legal profession when faced with any proposal which addressed the problem.

While the general public had received the 1925 report well (with the exception of the proposal to raise the age of consent to seventeen), the legal profession had not. They objected strongly and consistently to proposals for changes in legal procedure. The report was attacked for being "founded on the popular misconception that every prosecution is necessarily well-founded and every defence inevitably a speculative subterfuge" (*Law Journal*, 6 March 1926: 215). The recommendation for the greater involvement of women police and doctors in sexual offences received almost equal hostility, on the grounds that this would bias the system further against men. This latter argument resonates ironically with the arguments of the suffrage campaign. The Women's Freedom League for instance had claimed "it would be quite as intelligible to expect a Tory to legislate to a Liberal's satisfaction as to expect one sex to legislate fairly for another" (*The Vote*, 19 March 1910). Given the shared assumption of inevitable difference, and "sex antipathy" (*Law Journal*, 6 March 1926: 215), clearly the legal profession preferred the option of unfettered male bias. It was not uncommon for the intimidating nature of a court appearance for young girls to be deliberately increased by the exclusion of women magistrates and jury members from sexual assault cases (Report of the Departmental Committee on Sexual Offences against Young Persons 1925). While in the 1930s, Sempkins located one sympathetic judge, Judge Cecil Whiteley, willing to argue for changes in procedure including relaxation of corroboration rules, and a tribunal system of questioning,[10] even he appeared to give up on so controversial a subject, and the legal advisers to the Joint Committee dismissed proposals for any change to legal procedure out of hand.

The Joint Committee dissolved in 1935, having failed to resolve the conflicts between medical and legal definitions of child sexual abuse which were frequent during the 1920s and 1930s. Both the declining strength of feminism, and the shifts in its orientation, towards a focus on sexual pleasure more than danger, on economic rather than sexual exploitation, on education rather than legal reform and on strengthening women's maternal role, all contributed further to the loss of child sexual abuse as a public issue as the medical profession took it over in its claims to a new scientific discourse on sex.

The 1970s on: Women as Cause, Protection, and Control

There can be few people who are not aware of the rediscovery of child sexual abuse in the present. Initiated by feminist campaigns against male violence in the 1970s, child sexual abuse became a high-profile public issue during the late 1980s and remains one today. Contemporary social anxieties about sex and the family have influenced this, and child sexual abuse has been attributed both to the "sexual permissiveness" of the 1960s (O'Hagan 1989), and to the "decline of the traditional family" (Gledhill et al. 1989). Concerns about demographic changes, the increased divorce rate and proportion of lone-parent families, underlie anxiety that the extent of child sexual abuse revealed by research will lead to a further escalation in "fragmented (i.e., fatherless) families" (Fawcett 1989). At the same time, the relative rights and powers of children, parents and the different agencies and professional groups involved in child protection, to define what constitutes abuse, remain hotly contested. The ineffectiveness of the criminal justice system has continued, despite some changes facilitated by the existence of new technology as well as a considerably stronger child protection lobby.[11] The context of response by other agencies, however, has changed.

The medical profession's dominance over the fields of both child abuse and sexuality is now well established, reflected in policy debates if not necessarily in practice. Post-war developments in child care have attributed changed significance to family life, reflected in the acquisition of new duties by local authorities, first to return children from care to their families where possible (the Children Act 1948) and then to prevent their reception into care by helping families with children at home (the Children and Young Persons Act 1963). The idealised view of family life underlying these changes retracted a little after the battering to death of Maria Colwell by her stepfather in 1973 (after being returned home to her natural mother), and the Children Act 1975 made it easier to extricate children from their natural parents.[12] Further changes are enshrined in the Children Act 1989, implemented in 1991, which was influenced by a series of inquiries held during the 1980s, first involving three children who died at home at the hands of their fathers or stepfathers, for whom professionals were blamed for doing too little too late,[13] and later involving 121 children suspected of being sexually abused in Cleveland, for whom professionals were accused of doing too much too soon.[14] The Act attempts again to rework the balancing act, both increasing the grounds for state intervention to protect children and setting out a new framework for partnership with parents geared to the preservation and support of parental responsibilities. Despite these shifts, childcare work throughout has focused primarily on mothers, with child abuse defined as a problem of poor mothering but separation from mothers also defined as a key traumatic event to be avoided for children. Child sexual abuse as a problem for statutory agencies landed in this context. Consequently, the surveillance of girls in the previous period has been to some extent replaced (and certainly supplemented) by the increased surveillance of women as mothers of sexually abused children.

Feminist criticisms of mother-blaming in relation to child sexual abuse have focused primarily on "family dysfunction theory," a medical discourse preoccupied with causality, which, having shifted its focus from the individual to the family as unit, sought it in any deviation from androcentrically defined and historically specific norms (see, e.g., Nelson 1987; MacLeod and Saraga 1988). In the dominant versions of this, sexuality as the core feature of marriage and a construction of motherhood defined in relation to children's psychological and emotional needs (both developments of the post-war period) were enshrined, as was a functionalist model of the family which defined the sexual division of labour as natural. The result was the implication of women in the cause of abuse, via sexual estrangement from their partners, the unmet needs of their children, and/or their absence from the home (e.g., CIBA Foundation 1984), a model which has been roundly condemned by feminists, to some effect. However, the influence this model exerted over the social practices of agencies involved in child protection was never obvious, since social workers generally pay more attention to pragmatic concerns than theoretical explanations (Corby 1987) and their resources for therapeutic work are limited. In this section I want to consider first, what influence this discourse has had on social workers (the prime actors in the surveillance of women), and on mothers themselves (the prime actors in child protection), and second, to discuss the problems and potential of the child protection discourse which I would argue is more central for both groups. Finally, I discuss the construction of motherhood in contemporary judicial discourse. While there is overlap between the constructions of women in different discourses, there are also significant differences.

SOCIAL WORKERS, MOTHERS, AND MEDICAL DISCOURSE

Social workers draw on the available professional discourses alongside other sources of knowledge, from the wider community and their own experience, in their efforts to make sense of their work (Pithouse 1987). In my study, labels such as "a collusive wife," and "a dysfunctional family" were employed with little meaning in themselves as part of the process of distancing the worker from the client. Judgements such as "she knew" or "she disbelieved" were also made in relation to mothers of sexually abused children, despite evidence of far more complex processes involving doubt, uncertainty and ambivalence, as shorthand for "not doing enough." "Enough" however was often defined with the benefit of hindsight, and the label served the purpose primarily of attributing fault (Hooper 1990).

For social workers, "blaming" clients, by constructing them as a "particular sort of person" to whom it could be expected that awful things would happen, is one of the main ways in which they manage "occupational impotence" (Pithouse 1987). Where child sexual abuse is concerned the sources of occupational impotence are numerous: the tightrope social workers must walk between criticism for unwarranted intervention in the family on the one hand and failure to protect children on the other, difficulties of gaining direct access to children and to evidence of abuse, uncertainty about both the definition of abuse and often about the best solution, an inadequate knowledge base to predict accurately the risk to children that leaving them in the care of a particular adult involves, the relatively low status of social workers in the professional networks involved in child protection compared with the medical profession and police, the inadequacy of the criminal justice system, the lack of resources both for alternative accommodation for children and therapeutic work with individuals and families, and the reluctance of some individuals and families to participate in what services are offered.

The result is high levels of anxiety. As one social worker in my study put it, "My protectiveness to her is like an Aertex vest . . . total protection is a myth." Since mothers are the main alternative sources of child protection, it is they who bear the brunt of social workers' frustration in their talk of cases. Such talk does not translate in any direct way into practice. In order to gain access to the detailed personal information their work depends on, practitioners have to withhold judgement on the moral worth of their clients (Pithouse 1987). To blame them directly is counterproductive, and women confronted in the heat of a worker's anxiety with no consideration for their own feelings rarely confided in social workers again. In practice the expectations social workers set for mothers depended more on the alternatives they had available for children than on any theoretical model of child sexual abuse (Hooper 1990).

Mothers experienced the medical discourse in other ways than through their contact with agencies, however, through its influence on lay understandings of child sexual abuse, on which they also drew in order to make sense of their experience. Women who discover that their children have been sexually abused, especially by their own partner, face a situation of severe loss and confusion, in which many former assumptions about their worlds are overturned. In their search for meaning they are both vulnerable to and often resist available definitions of their roles.

Perhaps the most popular definition of mothers' roles in medical discourse is now the idea that there is a "cycle of abuse" between mothers and daughters. The thesis of "intergenerational transmission" is based on limited evidence but fits neatly within a family-systems perspective, legitimating professional intervention, and frequently making the abuser himself invisible. For mothers, "cycle of abuse" theories have a subjective appeal in the "why me? why her?" stage of coming to terms with loss, and one which carries strong risks, particularly where the guilt often felt in response to childhood sexual abuse is still unresolved. The following account illustrates this:

> I . . . thought to myself well maybe it was something that I did in my life, something bad, you know really bad that I'd done and she was being punished for it . . . all sorts of things went through my mind, I thought perhaps that it was because of when my father was abusing me, there were times when I actually enjoyed it.

While their own histories of abuse could cause extra distress, however, women also saw them positively as a resource, sometimes actively searching memory for experiences of their own that would help them understand those of their children.

Other components of the medical model also influenced women. The idea that abusers were "sick" diminished their responsibility, since illness is generally regarded as outside the individual's control, and not deserving of blame (see Cornwell 1984). It also implies the possibility of cure. To be an effective ally to a child requires attributing responsibility clearly to the offender, and those women who did so rejected such explanations, adopting an explicitly moral discourse involving conscious action ("He knew what he was doing") and personal responsibility ("old enough to know right from wrong"). Similarly, the idea that sexual problems in their own relationships might explain the abuser's actions both diminished his responsibility and could cause devastating guilt for mothers, unless it was accompanied by a clear sense of their own right to sexual autonomy.

CHILD-PROTECTION DISCOURSE

The medical discourse is not insignificant in its impact on either social workers or mothers. However, in their practice social work agencies draw more, I would argue, on a child-protection discourse which is preoccupied not with causality but with parental responsibility. A phrase reminiscent of the earliest and most misogynistic of advocates of family dysfunction, that mothers are crucial or central, recurs in child-protection discourse but for different reasons, that as primary carers, mothers are usually the key person in preventing further abuse and thus obviating the need to receive the child into care. The role and responsibility accorded mothers in this discourse raises more complex issues for feminists, at least if the need for some social control role on behalf of children is accepted (see Gordon 1986).

There are two main problems with the way in which parental responsibility is commonly attributed to women. First, the problem is that women are commonly accorded *sole* responsibility for the welfare of children (not that they bear *any* responsibility), and further, that they lack the resources to exercise it effectively. Motherhood is thus characterized by "powerless responsibility" (Rich 1977). The implicitly gendered assumptions that underlie discussion of parental responsibilities are illustrated by the argument of Bentovim and colleagues that "a parent who knows that the other parent is in a state of depression, anger or frustration and leaves that parent to care for the child . . . indicates a failure in sharing responsibility" (Bentovim et al., 1987, 29). This clearly means mothers leaving depressed fathers. If fathers who left depressed mothers to care for children were cause for state intervention, social services departments (SSDs) would be swamped.

Second, parents are commonly presented as an indivisible unit with identical interests, obscuring the conflicts between them. The Department of Health, for example, suggests that showing remorse and taking responsibility for abuse are positive indicators in the assessment of parents (DoH 1988). For a non-abusing mother in cases of child sexual abuse, the opposite is more likely to be the case. Despite evidence that the battering of women frequently precedes both physical and sexual child abuse (see Truesdell et al. 1986; Stark and Flitcraft 1988; Hooper 1990), this rarely merits a mention in the mainstream child-abuse literature or policy debate. While both women and children often seek help from agencies to control the more powerful members of the household, official discussion of the social control role of social work constructs it as one-way, between the state and the family as a unit, and in practice the burden commonly falls on women.

Consequently, women in my study who sought help when their children were sexually abused sometimes received little but surveillance of themselves in return. Where they had been victimised themselves, an approach to authority by social workers which failed to disaggregate parents was particularly counterproductive. Women used to resisting their partner's control and fighting to retain some of their own simply adopted similar strategies, focusing on "beating the system," when another authority stepped in to set rules for them. Children, too, already used to seeing their mothers powerless, are likely to have this perception reinforced in witnessing such encounters with professionals, increasing their own insecurity. The control role was not always unwelcome to mothers, but they wanted it used to back up their own efforts rather than turned against them. Their criticisms were of the failure of social workers to exercise authority at the appropriate time and with the appropriate person, and the tendency to accord them greater powers than they had to control abusive men themselves.

Despite these common problems, the discourse of child protection could be used to empower women, since local authorities and social workers have considerable discretion to negotiate their policies and practices within the broad framework set out by central government. Both mothers' and social workers' accounts of the child protection register illustrated this. All local authorities are required to hold a register, listing children who are known to have been abused or are thought to be at risk of abuse. There has been much confusion about the exact purpose of registers, and decisions to place children's names on them are often inconsistent (Corby 1987). It is generally assumed that they are stigmatising to parents, and suggestions have been made that they be scrapped. However, registration has variable meanings, both to social workers and mothers. Social workers did not perceive the decision simply as a bureaucratic one, but one made within the context of negotiating a complex set of relationships. Thus decisions were sometimes influenced by the message that registration might give to the mother (the possibility of either damaging an existing relationship of co-operation or of motivating an improved one), to the child (showing a complaint had been taken seriously), or to a new authority when a family was moving (attempting to ensure the allocation of a social worker). Some mothers certainly did experience registration as unjust, especially where the child had no further contact with the abuser, saying, for example, that it was like a criminal conviction against them. Others, however, did not, seeing it positively as giving either entitlement to priority help, or backing to exclude an abusive partner from the house.

Judicial Discourse

Judicial discourse involves further constructions of women whose children are sexually abused, as sources of domestic stress (primarily through the breakdown of sexual relationships), the financial dependants of men and agents of informal control, which are crucial to approaches to offenders. The Parole Board for 1968 advocated a welfare approach to incest offenders on the assumption that inadequate sexual relationships with their wives were at root (Bailey and McCabe 1979), implicitly endorsing men's right to sexual satisfaction within the family. Sentencing practice reinforces traditional family structures by its use both of sexual estrangement and a continuing marital relationship as mitigating factors. Thus, fathers are returned to the position of power in families which is at the root of incestuous abuse (Mitra 1987). The case for non-custodial sentences with conditions of treatment is also based to a large extent on the effects of family breakup and the loss of a breadwinner on "the family" (Glaser and Spencer 1990).

In this debate women are presented as naturally, or at least happily, dependent and hence invariably resistant to the prosecution of their husbands. In my study, however, while fear of losing a breadwinner was an issue for some women, inhibiting reporting, for others fear that no effective legal action would be taken was the more important factor increasing their sense of isolation and powerlessness in the family. The possibility of prosecution had both negative and positive meanings, the most important of the latter being the clear message it gave about the individual responsibility of the abuser, and an opportunity to discover their own capacity for independence. In practice, the effectiveness of non-custodial alternatives for offenders rests on the informal controls operated by the family (i.e. women) as well as court orders on treatment and residence (Wolf et al., 1988), although this role is often invisible in debates.

Concluding Remarks

I have aimed in this chapter to highlight some of the varying ways in which responsibilities have been attributed to women and girls in constructions of child sexual abuse, both at different periods of history and in competing discourses. Over the period considered, from the 1870s to the present, the greater recognition of children's needs alongside a recurring reluctance to consider collective or male responsibility for meeting them, has resulted in increased expectations of mothers. Women have gained rights as well as responsibilities over this period of course, to political citizenship, greater access to education and paid employment, divorce and a minimal level of welfare provision. While they are therefore somewhat less subject to the control of individual men in the household, their move into the public sphere has been accompanied by continued subordination within it (Walby 1990). Women's disadvantage in the labour market and responsibility for child care (before and after divorce) mean divorce carries a high risk of poverty. Yet "reasonable parental care," as expressed in the Children Act 1989, is defined according to expectations of "the average or reasonable parent," abstracted from social context, who must, if unable to meet their child's needs themselves, seek help from others who can (DoH 1989b). If women are to meet these expectations when a partner abuses their child, then the economic dependence which inhibits them both from stopping such abuse themselves and from seeking help must be addressed, and when they do seek help, services which meet their own needs and their children's must be available.

In conclusion, I want to comment briefly on the impact of feminist definitions of child sexual abuse on current policy. There are increasing attempts to sever family-systems thinking from its preoccupation with causality and its reactionary sexual politics, and to integrate it with feminist analyses (see, e.g., Masson and O'Byrne 1990). The DoH no longer attributes incestuous abuse to "distorted family relationships" (DHSS 1988) but cautiously accepts the need for further explanatory frameworks (DoH 1989a). At the same time as the claims of family therapists are being modified, however, wider social anxieties about "family breakdown" encourage resort to its practices. The danger is that the use of such practices will be driven more by the New Right's attempt to buttress the traditional family than any evidence of their effectiveness in preventing abuse, and attention diverted from alternative strategies to reduce the social and economic disadvantages that family breakdown brings for women and children.

The DoH has also adopted the concept of non-abusing parents (usually mothers), who "may need help to adjust to the changes in their lives" (DoH 1989a, 29), and the recommendation that abusing men should be excluded from the home in preference to removing children into care. Here, there is a danger that in the current political context, the changes for which feminists have campaigned may have perverse effects. Where SSDs are starved of resources and collective responsibility for child care is minimal, the designation of women as non-abusing parents may facilitate their definition simply as resources for their children rather than women with their own needs, and the exclusion of abusing men may increase women's responsibilities while depleting their resources. To turn such strategies to the empowerment of women and children demands their location within a broader programme of social change.

NOTES

1. The figures produced by the NSPCC, based on a sample of registers covering about 10 percent of the child population in England and Wales, show that the number of children on

registers more than doubled from 1983 to 1987, and the proportion of these who had been sexually abused increased from 5 percent in 1983 to 28 percent in 1987 (S. J. Creighton and P. Noyes, *Child Abuse Trends in England and Wales 1983–1987*, London: NSPCC, 1989).

2. NSPCC *Annual Reports* 1893–94, 1906–7, 1907–8, 1908–9, 1910–11, 1912–13, 1913–14, 1914–15 and 1918–19.

3. The Home Office had issued a circular in 1926 backing some of the recommended changes in police and court practice, but allowing discretion for varying local circumstances.

4. See *Report of the Joint Committee on Sexual Offences*, December 1935; *Sexual Offences against Young Persons: Memorandum for Magistrates*, December 1935; *Memorandum on "The Need for a Medical-Mental Examination of Persistent Sexual Offenders"* by Dr. Gillespie, December, 1935. These, the minutes of the Joint Committee and correspondence concerning it, on which this chapter draws, are located in the NVA archives, Fawcett Library, London.

5. See *Report of the Royal Commission on the Care and Control of the Feeble-Minded*, vol. VIII, London: HMSO, 1908: pp. 120–21.

6. Miss E. H. Kelly, a member of the 1925 Committee and of the National Council of Women, made this case. AMSH also claimed to have suggested it in 1918 (*The Shield*, Feb–Mar. 1926).

7. *The Vote*, for example, carried a column entitled variously "How Men Protect Women," "How Some Men Protect Women," and "The Protected Sex," which reported cases of violence against women and children and the paltry sentences which men commonly received for them.

8. Behlmer (1982) traces it back to 1816.

9. See Jeffreys (1982) for a review of these campaigns, and Bland (1983) for variations amongst Victorian feminists in attitudes to sex.

10. See discussion on "The Problem of the Moral Pervert," reported in *Journal of the Institute of Hygiene*, April 1933: 236–38.

11. The Criminal Justice Act 1988 introduced an experimental scheme allowing children to give evidence in the Crown Court through a live, closed-circuit television link. Further changes have recently been proposed using video-recorded interviews, which would allow children to give evidence before the trial, thus avoiding the distress caused by long delays (Pigot Committee, *Report of the Advisory Group on Video Evidence*, London: Home Office, 1989). The Children Act 1989 also enabled civil proceedings relating to children to admit hearsay evidence and the unsworn evidence of a child.

12. See MacLeod (1982) for a review of these changes and their implications.

13. See London Borough of Brent, *A Child in Trust: Report of the panel of inquiry investigating the circumstances surrounding the death of Jasmine Beckford*, 1985; London Borough of Greenwich, *A Child in Mind: Protection of Children in a Responsible Society*, The Report of the Commission of Inquiry into the circumstances surrounding the death of Kimberley Carlisle, 1987; and London Borough of Lambeth, *Whose Child? A Report of the Public Inquiry into the death of Tyra Henry*, 1987.

14. See Secretary of State for Social Services, *Report of the Inquiry into Child Abuse in Cleveland 1987*, London: HMSO, 1988.

24

Definition and Scope of the Problem

PETER JAFFE, DAVID WOLFE, AND SUSAN KAYE WILSON

Historical Perspective on Children from Violent Homes

The last two decades have been marked by a growing public awareness of wife assault or wife beating. The belief that all family life is safe and secure has been shattered by those who have pointed out the alarming frequency of various violent incidents in many North American families. This topic was once considered either a family secret or acceptable behavior within a patriarchal society. Extensive research by social scientists has suggested that family violence is widespread and is interwoven with the very fabric of society's attitudes and values (e.g., Gelles and Straus 1988). Now, graphic media coverage of celebrated cases and regular discussions on the most widely seen television programs are commonplace (Toufexis 1987).

A recent analysis by *Time* magazine on 464 Americans killed by guns in one ("typical") week (May 1–7, 1989) pointed out that the vast majority of homicide victims were murdered by family members:

> The pattern in these 464 deaths is depressingly clear: guns most often kill the people who own them or people whom the owners know well. Despite the outcry over street gangs and drug dealers, the week's homicides typically involve people who loved, or hated, each other—spouses, relatives, or close acquaintances. ("Seven Deadly Days," 1989, p. 11)

Although several important books were published on the topic of wife assault in the 1970s, very few researchers considered the impact of this behavior on the children who witness this violence. Most of the early literature in this field focused on the incidence of violence against women and the inadequate response of community agencies represented by the justice, health, and social service systems (Walker 1979). The needs of children in these families were rarely considered. Except when children were physically abused as well, they were considered by service providers to be part of the battered woman's responsibility and added to the complexity of finding safety, appropriate housing, and financial support.

Case studies of battered women and their families in the initial literature in this field often made indirect references to the children and began to suggest several areas of concern. These included the following beliefs:

- A boy who witnesses his father assaulting his mother is learning that violence is acceptable behavior that is an integral part of intimate relationships.
- A girl who witnesses her mother being assaulted by her father is learning about victimization and the extent to which men can utilize violence and fear to exert power and control over family members.
- Boys and girls who live with violence are experiencing significant emotional trauma. Rather than having a family that can offer security and nurturance for their positive development, these children experience fear, anxiety, confusion, anger, and the disruptions in lives that are the aftermath of violent episodes. More recently, these experiences and their consequences are being labeled by many child abuse specialists as emotional abuse or psychological maltreatment (e.g., Brassard, Germain, and Hart 1987).

When the concept of children witnessing their mother being assaulted is discussed, it is important to have some definition and frame of reference for the terms *assault* and *witness*. Defining *assault* is no simple task because, as Gelles and Straus (1988, 57) have succinctly pointed out,

> Twenty years of discussion, debate, and action have led us to conclude that there will never be an accepted or acceptable definition of abuse, because abuse is not a scientific or clinical term. Rather, it is a political concept. Abuse is essentially any act that is considered deviant or harmful by a group large enough or with sufficient political power to enforce the definition.

Recognizing this dilemma, we accept Dutton's (1988, 1) view that wife assault is any "physical act of aggression by a man against a woman with whom he is in an intimate relationship." In our view, this act may or may not be fully intended to cause injury or to maintain power and control. Although this work focuses on physical abuse of women, because of the concrete definitions sought by courts and shelter funders, it is acknowledged that emotional abuse that degrades and belittles women is an equally important area of study. The Conflict Tactics Scale developed by Straus and his colleagues has been utilized as the best available description for specific acts of verbal and physical aggression (Straus, Gelles, and Steinmetz 1980).

When this study refers to children witnessing violence directed at their mothers, a wide range of experiences is encompassed. Children may observe this violence directly by seeing their father (or another intimate partner of their mother) threaten or hit their mother. They may overhear this behavior from another part of their residence, such as their own bedroom. Children may be exposed to the results of this violence without hearing or seeing the commission of any aggressive act. For example, children may see the bruises or other injuries clearly visible on their mother or the emotional consequences of fear, hurt, and intimidation that may be very apparent to them. Less commonly, children may be exposed to isolated incidents of violence, although these cases are unlikely to come to the attention of police or other social service professionals. Thus the phrase *children of battered women* refers to children who have repeatedly witnessed severe acts of emotional and physical abuse directed at their mother by her intimate partner. In too many cases, these children have observed repeated acts of violence perpetrated by multiple partners throughout their entire childhood.

Witnessing wife assault can have a broad range of effects on children. As Carlson (1984) has indicated, the initial knowledge about the impact on children of witnessing wife assault was developed through several areas of literature, including the impact of parental conflict, retrospective accounts of battered women and their husbands, anecdotal reports, and early studies on shelters for battered women.

Literature on the impact of divorce and separation on children (see review in Emery 1982) suggested that the most significant stressor for children was the amount of conflict to which they were exposed. Even though it may be assumed that the most serious form of marital conflict involves physical and emotional abuse, the nature of such conflict was never detailed in these studies. Research focusing on childhood adjustment and the search for predictors of behavioral and emotional problems has also paralleled these findings on marital conflict. For example, researchers have identified a host of factors that usually include parental conflict and family dysfunction as predictors of child adjustment problems (Rutter 1979). Had Straus and his colleagues at the Family Violence Research Center at the University of New Hampshire been involved in this research, and more specific measures such as the Conflict Tactics Scale been utilized, parental conflict and family dysfunction would likely have emerged as significant components, or "by-products," of wife assault.

Retrospective accounts of battered women and their husbands often point out childhoods marked by witnessing their fathers' violence. Women who are battered often report that they came to expect violence in their marriage and saw very few options to end the violence (Roy 1977). Batterers themselves acknowledge the learning experiences in their childhood when their fathers taught them how to be men and how to be husbands.

These retrospective accounts have been validated in later research that indicates that the vast majority of batterers have witnessed this behavior in their families of origin and that the rate of wife beating is dramatically higher for sons of batterers compared with sons of nonviolent fathers (Straus et al. 1980). However, not all sons growing up in violent homes become batterers, and in fact many siblings of batterers may live peacefully in nonviolent marriages (Dobash and Dobash 1979). Retrospective studies of victims and batterers were a vital starting point in focusing on children in these families.

Anecdotal reports offered some vivid descriptions of children's experiences in a violent home. Even in the earliest books on the topic of wife assault, authors were cognizant of the plight of these children. For example, Davidson in his 1978 book *Conjugal Crime* captured this victimization:

> The witnessing children are the most pathetic victims of conjugal crime because their childhood conditioning will color their entire lives. All other input will be processed through the mire of the first marriage they ever saw and their earliest role models of husband and wife, father and mother. Daddy is cruel to mommy, who can't do anything to change it. No one seems to care, neither in the house nor out in society. The nightmare apparently is to be regarded as natural—or nonexistent—since it is neither acknowledged nor alleviated. To the child growing up in this environment, it seems as if all power is on the side of the wrongdoer. Nice people finish last. Perhaps wrong is right, after all. (Davidson 1978, 117)

The phenomenon of children witnessing violence covers a wide extreme, from listening to the violence from their bedrooms to being forced to watch their mother being abused by their father as a lesson in fear and control:

Oh yes, they've seen me be hit. He used to delight in lifting them up out their beds so they could watch. And this was 2 A.M. and he sat on the chair and told me everything he thought about me and he dragged the full three kids out of their beds and made them all sit. He lined them right up against the couch and told them all what I was. He says to them, "Now you see her, she's a whore." And he'd say to Chris, "See her, she's a cow." And the baby was only months old, and he'd say to him, "See her, she's no good. She's dirt. That's what women are. They're all dirt. There's your daddy been out working all day and that's no tea ready for him. See how rotten she is to your daddy." And all the children were dragged out of their beds for no reason at all. (Dobash and Dobash 1979, 151)

Early studies on shelters for battered women began to identify the needs of children who accompanied their mothers to safety. At least 70 percent of all battered women seeking shelter have children who accompany them, and 17 percent of the women bring along three or more children (MacLeod 1987). Shelter staff pointed out the fact that the most vulnerable clients they had were financially dependent battered women who were responsible for their children. In addition, the children presented themselves with a number of emotional and behavioral problems that required immediate attention. However, the times when the children needed their mothers the most as principal caretaker, the mothers were unavailable, as a result of their own overwhelming needs related to their victimization. Pizzey (1977) identified this concern, noting that battered women may become labeled as unfit mothers, and their children may experience the further disruption of being moved from a shelter to foster home placements.

Estimated Incidence of Children Who Witness Violence in the Family

Current studies suggest that at least one in ten women are abused every year by the man with whom they live (MacLeod 1987). Repeated, severe violence occurs in one in fourteen marriages (Dutton 1988). Estimates have pointed to the fact that approximately 3 million to 4 million American households and 500,000 Canadian households live with this violence every year (MacLeod 1987; Stark, Flitcraft, Zuckerman, Gray, and Frazier 1981). The extremes of this violence are demonstrated by the fact that women in North America are more likely to be killed by their partners than by anyone else. The magnitude of the problem in terms of a known war is captured by statistics that indicate that the United States lost 39,000 soldiers in the line of duty during the Vietnam War while during the same time period (1967–1973) 17,500 American women and children were killed by members of their families (Grusznski, Brink, and Edleson 1988). More women are abused by their husbands or boyfriends than are injured in car accidents, muggings, or rapes (Toufexis 1987).

Straus and his colleagues (1980) have completed the most detailed study of violence in American families through 2,143 family interviews. This research, which pioneered the development of the Conflict Tactics Scale, discovered a wide variety of emotional and physical abuse in the family. Although Straus found a high incidence of husband abuse as well, subsequent researchers have noted that much of this behavior is in self-defense and may not cause the same degree of injuries and hospitalization (Dutton 1988). From Straus's initial and more recent study of family violence, the type of actions and the frequency of their occurrence that children may observe are shown in Table 1.

Straus points out that children are often in the middle of this violence in a number of ways. Arguments about child-rearing practice and children's behavior are a major

TABLE 1. FREQUENCY OF HUSBAND TO WIFE VIOLENCE IN PREVIOUS
TWELVE-MONTH PERIOD

	Rate Per 1000 Wives	
Category	*1980*	*1988*
Threw something	28	28
Pushed, grabbed, shoved	107	93
Slapped	51	29
Kicked, bit, or punched	24	15
Hit or tried to hit with something	22	17
Beat up	11	8
Threatened with a knife or gun	4	4
Used a knife or gun	3	2

Source: Straus, M. A., Gelles, R. J., and Steinmetz, S. (1980). *Behind Closed Doors.* New York: Doubleday, Anchor Press: Gelles, R. J., and Straus, M. A. (1988). *Intimate Violence.* New York: Simon and Schuster.

precipitating crisis that leads to violent episodes. Although children are not the cause of the violence, many children blame themselves for the violence because of the sequence of events and the family's inability to examine the real underlying factors. As stated by the authors,

> Even though there is little difference in the amount of conflict over money, sex, housekeeping, children, or social activities, a disagreement on one of these may still cause more trouble than a disagreement on another. Sex and money are widely believed to be the issues which cause the most trouble. But our data show that neither of these provoked the most violence. Rather, it is conflict over children which is most likely to lead a couple to blows. The more often a couple disagree about things concerning their children, the higher the rate of violence. In fact, two-thirds of the couples who said they always disagree over the children had at least one violent incident during the year of our survey! Children are a tremendous source of pride and satisfaction. Parents feel intensely about their children and their children's welfare, probably more intensely than about anything else in the family. It follows that when things go wrong with the children—as they inevitably do at some time or other—there are equal depths of despair, anguish, and conflict. (Straus et al. 1980, 171–72)

Are children present during the violence? Carlson (1984) estimates (based on an average of two children in 55 percent of violent households) that at least 3.3 million children in the United States between the ages of three and seventeen years are yearly at risk of exposure to parental violence. From our own clinical experience, many parents minimize or deny the presence of children during incidents of wife assault by suggesting that the children were asleep or playing outside. However, from interviews with children, we find that almost all can describe detailed accounts of violent behavior that their mother or father never realized they had witnessed (see also Rosenberg 1984). Similarly, Bard (1970), in an evaluation of a police crisis intervention program in New York City, found that children were present in 41 percent of the "domestic disturbances" that led to a police intervention (an alarmingly high rate considering the likelihood that police become involved in a relatively small percentage of domestic assaults). A Toronto, Ontario, research project indicated that 68 percent of 2,910 wife assault cases had children present (Leighton 1989). Finally, Sinclair (1985), based on her clinical experience, has suggested that if children are in a violent family 80 percent of them will witness an episode of wife assault. What they witness may range from a fleeting moment of abusive language to a homicide. Extreme events will stay with them for a lifetime and may be relived through subsequent court hearings (Bowker, Arbittel, and McFerron 1988).

Many authors have also noted a significant overlap between wife assault and child abuse. There is reason to suspect that many children suffer from repeated exposure to violence, both as direct and as indirect victims. For example, retrospective accounts from women in shelters reveal that as many as 80 percent of the women recall witnessing their mother being assaulted by their father as well as being assaulted themselves (Gayford 1975). In a community sample of battered women who were not residing in crisis shelters, almost one-third indicated that they had witnessed violence and had been abused themselves (Kincaid 1982). Based on the histories and symptoms of battered women and their children in shelters, researchers estimate the extent of overlap between wife assault and child physical or sexual abuse to be approximately 30 percent to 40 percent (Hughes 1982; Straus et al. 1980).

Children may find themselves at risk for witnessing violence during significant periods of the family's history. Even before they are born, some children face the dangers of family violence. Gelles (1975) and others have indicated that pregnancy can be a critical period related to wife assault, with very serious consequences for women and children. Moore (1979) also reported that wife battering was most likely to occur within a family as soon as children became family members. Her research led her to suggest that wife battering, like child abuse, was associated with the early years or the teen years. Infants and toddlers were seen to add a significant stressor for the family and to leave women in the most vulnerable position in regard to battering. Other authors also point to the beginning of adolescence as a critical time in marital adjustment and violence (Langley and Levy 1977). In many instances, increased violence is precipitated by the very problems of adolescence (delinquency, running away) that may be associated with older children reacting to many years of witnessing their mother being assaulted by their father (Pizzey 1977).

Characteristics of Children and Families

Considerable research over the past decade has profiled battered women, their partners, and their children. Although consistent patterns of behavior have been described from observations of battered women and their families, what is often unclear is the extent to which certain personality and psychological factors precede or result from living with violence. Some of these descriptive factors are briefly discussed below.

Battered Women

Most studies of battered women involved those victims who sought refuge in a shelter after a serious incident of violence, which most likely represents a bias toward economic and social disadvantage. Yet, as recent studies have begun to examine a broader community sample of victims who had approached nonresidential services for legal and emotional counseling, researchers are discovering the existence of a wider range of psychological and social conditions among victims of all socioeconomic backgrounds than was previously acknowledged (Greaves, Heapy, and Wylie 1988).

Many battered women not only are coping with the present violence but are also struggling with the trauma of their personal histories. A significant percentage of battered women have childhoods marked by witnessing violence themselves or being physically and sexually abused. The impact of their current victimization is undoubtedly magnified by these previous experiences (Hughes 1982).

The Battered Woman's Syndrome (Walker 1979) is now well accepted by most professionals working in the field as well as by many courts who try to understand victims' behavior. The syndrome is marked by a victim's increasing sense of helplessness and hopelessness about finding safety and terminating the violence. These feelings are reinforced by a sense of isolation and poor self-esteem, fostered by the batterer. Over time, victims can begin to deny and minimize the extent of the violence and underestimate the lethality of the situation for themselves and their children (Browne 1987).

For the most part a victim's sense of isolation and being a prisoner in her own home is maintained by real economic and social factors that limit alternative solutions (Schechter and Gary 1988). This victimization has direct implications for a mother's effectiveness as a parent because the vast majority are principal caretakers for their children. Battered women's role as parents is radically demeaned through their victimization, because the dysfunction and disorganization offers little nurturance, support, structure, or supervision for children. In extreme cases children may themselves be abused or neglected by the mothers they depend on (Bowker et al. 1988). As pointed out earlier, the children's misbehavior and special needs are at a peak when their mother's ability to respond to them is at a low point.

Men Who Batter

As outlined previously, a very common factor associated with men battering their partners is witnessing violence in their own families of origin. Interviews with batterers consistently point to childhood experiences of exposure to wife assault and, in many histories, direct physical abuse by their fathers as well (Dutton 1988). Accordingly, violence is learned as the basis of power and control in the family.

Recent studies have suggested that men who batter may lack the verbal skills required to negotiate nonviolent conflict resolution and have poor impulse control and a rigid style of demanding and controlling behaviors. Of particular significance as well is the idea that many violent episodes have no clear external antecedents or may be a misinterpretation of the partner's behavior (Dutton 1988). For example, a woman's choice to obtain a part-time job or upgrade her education is interpreted to be an attempt to humiliate a husband by publicly suggesting he is unable to look after his dependent partner.

Batterers find ways to isolate their wives and children in order to decrease the likelihood of detection and assistance. In most families secrecy is an important value. Extreme jealousy can be apparent from the involvement of any "outsiders." Even a walk to the corner store is a threat to a husband who worries constantly that his wife may lose her prisoner status (Gelles 1987). Violence is the means of maintaining fear in all family members. Children may be asked to watch their mother's victimization as a lesson in control and what may happen to them if they disobey their father (Finkelhor, Gelles, Hotaling, and Straus 1983). Over time this experience is associated with the batterer's tone of voice and/or a facial expression and these cues alone can cause a high level of fear and intimidation.

Alcohol is present in almost half of all incidents of wife assault, although most researchers indicate a correlational rather than a causal relationship (Schechter and Gary 1988). Alcohol abuse by the batterer obviously compounds the family's disorganization and increases the number of crises that require police intervention. The batterer and his victim usually minimize the violent behavior and focus on the alcohol as the root cause of any family problem (Pagelow 1984). Continued alcohol abuse obviously leads to serious economic and social consequences for the family, which creates a greater need for the victim to look after the batterer. The children continue to cope with the violence in the context of further economic and social disadvantage.

THE CHILDREN

Children's responses to witnessing their mother being assaulted by their father will vary according to their age, sex, stage of development, and role in the family. Many other factors will play a role, such as the extent and frequency of the violence, repeated separations and moves, economic and social disadvantage, and special needs that a child may have independent of this violence (e.g., significant learning disabilities).

Infants who are raised in an environment of wife abuse may suffer serious, unintended consequences. Their basic needs for attachment to their mother may be significantly disrupted. Routines around sleeping and feeding may become far from normal. A mother living in fear of her husband may be unable to handle the stressful demands of an infant. Clearly, an infant will recognize this distance and lack of availability of his or her principal caretaker (Hart and Brassard 1987). Infants or young toddlers may also be injured in a violent episode by being "caught in the cross fire." They may accidentally be hit, pushed, or dropped during a violent outburst, or their mother may hold them for their own safety but discover that their father has no regard for their physical and emotional vulnerability.

Latency-age children look to their parents as significant role models. Boys and girls who witness violence quickly learn that violence is an appropriate way of resolving conflict in human relationships. Girls may learn that victimization is inevitable and no one can help change this pattern. Suffering in silence is reinforced. Children may attempt to practice what they have learned at home in the community through fights in the neighborhood or at school. Externalizing behavior problems will undermine their school adjustment and trigger consequences from the school system that aggravate the existing stressors in their home.

For latency-age children the consequences of exposure to wife assault may also lead to significant emotional difficulties. These children may live in shame in terms of the hidden violence and be embarrassed by the family secret. These feelings are often fluctuating with the idea that maybe someone will find out and rescue them (Davidson 1978). The children's experience undermines their sense of self-esteem and the confidence they have in the future. They may have few opportunities to develop outside the family because of their father's domination and control, which isolates them and keeps them from extracurricular activities. These children may also experience guilt out of a sense that perhaps they could prevent the violence. If only they were "better" children, their father would not get so upset and be violent toward their mother. They are often confused by the violence and have a divided sense of loyalty in wanting to protect their mother, but still respecting and fearing their father's right to control their family.

Many children live with fear and anxiety, waiting for the next violent episode. They feel no safety in their own home yet are too young to seek out or even want an alternative. They may spend most of their hours in school distracted and inattentive to the academic tasks before them. At night they remain alert for the early warning signs of more violence. Little peace or security is available for these children.

Adolescence is a time when children first develop intimate relationships outside their families and can practice the sex role and communication patterns they have learned. For some youngsters it is the beginning of violence within their own relationships in dating and early courtship. For adolescent girls it is a crucial turning point in which they may start to accept threats and violence from boyfriends who control them through this behavior. As one study puts it, "What really gets me down [in the transition house] is seeing the daughters of women we sheltered and counseled 10 years ago coming to us as battered wives. Even when their mothers got their 'heads together' and got away from the violence, their daughters are repeating the pattern" (MacLeod 1987, 33).

Many adolescents have lived with the violence in their families for many years, accompanied by physical and emotional abuse. One study of mothers in shelters reported that half of them had been battered for more than five years on a weekly basis and in some instances the battering was almost a daily occurrence (Layzer, Goodson, and deLange 1985). In seeking their independence and relief from the family distress and violence, adolescents realize that there may be an escape. Although their mother may be a prisoner, they recognize that there may be some hope in trying to spend more time away from the home even if it means running away (Davidson 1978). It is interesting to note that most interviews of runaway children and adolescents point to family conflict and exposure to violence as a major factor on the decision to run:

> With both wives and teenagers, independence is often an issue. For example, when wives and adolescents assert their autonomy and the authority figure reacts with anger, violence is always an implicit possibility, particularly in a culture such as our own that condones violence as an expression of concern and as a disciplinary tactic. The independence of the previously submissive, intimate loved one particularly threatens a personality that needs absolute compliance from its dependents in order to confirm its own validity. Many authority figures simply lose control of their impulses when a challenge becomes unbearable. Teenagers are notorious for their expertise at provoking anger in their parents. Like wives, they are thus more capable of precipitating their own abuse. This does not mean that wives and teenagers are really to blame, or that they are responsible for their own abuse. However, it means that they are integrally involved in a system of relating that does not work. They will need to learn new ways to respond, as will the aggressors. Without justifying abuse, we must note that the perpetrator is often a victim of circumstances. (Garbarino and Gillian 1980, 114)

Adolescents may confront their mothers with the fact that they cannot live with violence any more. Sadly, the mother was often staying with her husband to provide the children with the "stability" of a male-dominated household (Davidson 1978). Some adolescents begin to act out their anger and frustration in more dramatic ways that result in delinquencies and the interventions of the juvenile justice system (Grusznski et al. 1988). Some adolescent boys handle their frustration with the behavior that has been most clearly modeled for them by assaulting their mother or siblings (Straus et al. 1980, 104):

> Beaten wives we interviewed told us that their children began threatening them after seeing their fathers become violent. A child who sees his mother hit by his father comes to

view hitting as the thing to do—a means of getting what he wants. Some mothers of young children report that when they refuse to give their child candy or cookies, the child will indignantly retort: "You better give me some candy, or I'll get Daddy to hit you!" Later on, the child takes matters into his own hands. Our survey uncovered many women battered by both their husbands and their teen-age children.

While witnessing violence may lead some adolescents to run away or become involved in delinquent behavior, other adolescents may take on additional responsibilities to keep the peace and provide safety for their families. Older youngsters, especially girls and those with younger siblings, may take over parenting responsibility for most members of the household. They protect younger siblings during violent episodes and offer support or reassurance in the aftermath of the violent behavior. These adolescents may feel they cannot leave home because they have to protect their mother or find ways to calm their father's angry outbursts. Obviously these responsibilities are a heavy burden for young men and women who often carry this role into their early adult years.

Some of the characteristics of battered women, their husbands, and child witnesses to this violence have been outlined above. These characteristics are all interrelated. Obviously, a husband's domination and control through aggressive acts will create a number of physical and emotional adjustment problems for his wife. Children will be affected by what behaviors are modeled, by the trauma they are experiencing, and by the distress of their parents. The cruel irony for these children is that the very adults on whom they depend for safety and nurturance can offer neither safety nor nurturance (Van der Kolk, 1987).

Summary

This chapter has placed the study of children of battered women into a historical perspective by examining the literature's initial references to this population. Through the many tragic case histories of children who witness violence as well as the retrospective accounts of battered women and their partners, a terrifying portrait of fear and chaos emerges. Equally alarming are some of the estimates of the scope of the problem, which suggest that several million children in North America witness their mothers being abused. The potential consequences for these children in terms of their emotional and social development was outlined in this chapter.

PART III
Social Problems—Social Change

The last part of this book focuses on two very specific aspects of the contemporary discourse on gender violence. Each of the forms of violence addressed in part 2 have come to be recognized as social problems in most areas of the world, but only after immense intellectual scrutiny and political activism. The first section of this part studies pornography as a current example of a struggle for definition that has not been resolved, within either the general public or the feminist community. The process of defining various aspects of gender relations as problematic occupies a large space within current discussions of gender violence. The views articulated here represent art history, sociology, and legal theory. Another significant discussion revolves around identifying and prescribing the personal, political, and cultural requirements that might bring about positive social change. Section 2 presents a roundtable of articles that explore routes toward nonviolence in gender relations from the perspectives of philosophy, criminology, sociology, and feminist activism.

SECTION 1

Pornography and Violence: A Contested Social Problem

Most forms of gender violence are subject to contentious debate about how they are to be defined. As we have seen, standards for identifying sexual harassment vary greatly. Whether date rape is truly a form of rape provokes angry exchanges on college campuses across the country. Domestic violence experts debate over the extent of abuse and the major factors that contribute to it. Although controversy seems to lie at the heart of gender issues, there is now both legal and public acknowledgment that sexual harassment, rape, domestic violence, and child abuse are social problems that require remedies. These problems are underreported and frequently trivialized; nonetheless, there is growing public concern about their existence, and the laws that criminalize them are symbols of this awareness, even if they are not always effective in regulating violence. Some aspects of gender relations, however, have been questioned by the academic and activist communities, but have not been viewed as violence by the larger community. Examples include prostitution, forced sterilization, abortion prohibitions, and pornography. Prostitution and pornography are even passionately debated within the feminist community.

In this section, we present the pornography debate as an illustration of a contested arena in the realm of gender violence analysis. Pornography differs from the phenomena studied in part 2 precisely because community consensus has not emerged to define it either as violence or as a large-scale social problem. Prior to the emergence of the "sexual revolution" of the 1960s, advocacy against pornography was primarily the preserve of a small contingent of religious conservatives, given that pornography was neither as mainstream nor as available as it is today. Contemporary feminism emerged simultaneously with the sexual revolution, and some suggest that the real revolution was in the changed sexual attitudes and practices of women, not men (Ehrenreich, Hess, and Jacobs 1986). Historians of the pornography debate note that activists in the contemporary feminist movement initially embraced the use of pornography as a tool for the sexual liberation of women.

The dual threats of changing sexual mores and feminist politics were central themes in the crystallization of the New Religious Right in the United States in the late 1970s, which made pornography a central issue in the quest for a return to traditional morality. Ironically, during the same period pornography became the subject of radical feminist attack through the writings of Susan Brownmiller and Robin Morgan, the latter of whom generated the slogan "Pornography is the Theory, Rape is the Practice" (see Segal, this volume). This argument suggests that the sexual liberation movement, particularly in the form of pornography, actually produced more mechanisms to oppress women than to liberate them (Kappeler 1986). Still staunchly advocating equality under the law and personal freedom, however, much of the liberal feminist mainstream supported the rights of women and men to produce and consume pornography. The debate intensified throughout the 1980s and is still a hotly contested issue in feminist discourse, as well as in the larger cultural debate over sexuality and violence in the mass media.

As is the case with most contested social issues, both sides of the pornography debate operate in response to perceptions of threat. For those who advocate the criminalization of pornography, the perceived threat is of continued degradation and objectification of women and escalating gender violence. For those who would preserve the status quo, the primary threat is the loss of freedom, with additional concern that censorship and social control within the existing political context would fall most heavily upon traditionally marginalized groups, including gay men and lesbians and other "radical" women. Although it is important to understand the shared perceptions that forge competing perspectives on an issue such as pornography, sociological research on social problems shows that information control is perhaps the most crucial aspect of the definitional process. The ultimate outcome of the pornography debate will most likely depend upon which group of proponents can successfully control the flow of information. Both sides have articulate leadership, moral entrepreneurs for whom the issue is a passionate crusade (Becker 1963). Activists are mobilized on both sides of the issue, with academic experts and other influential people enlisted to legitimize the arguments that both sides present for public consumption.

The pornography debate is, however, emblematic of a much deeper definitional schism that undergirds most of the still contested areas in the larger discussion of gender in society. There is still a deep theoretical division over what constitutes oppression and liberation. In addition, there are differing opinions regarding the best route to social justice. These questions, as we shall see, are always simmering beneath the debates over singular issues such as pornography and prostitution.

Measuring the Effects of Pornography

There is no definitive research that finds pornography to be a direct cause of gender violence, and the imperfect methodologies and conflicting results of pornography research contribute to the lack of resolution of the debate. Currently, pornography research falls into three categories: experimental laboratory research, studies of the pornography consumption of convicted sex offenders, and aggregate social studies that measure rates of gender violence against circulation rates of pornographic magazines (Kimmel 1993). Results of research in the first two categories find some correlation between pornography consumption and violent attitudes and behaviors but have failed to establish causality. Findings of aggregate research are largely contradictory to the hypothesis that consumption of pornography escalates domestic violence and rape.

Laboratory research methodologies provide the primary source of direct measurements of the relationships among pornography, attitudes toward gender violence, and increased levels of male aggression against women. Social scientists studying the effects of pornography in the laboratory recognize that their studies are insufficient to gauge possible long-term effects of pornography upon behavior. They have nonetheless measured positive correlations between the viewing of some types of pornography and subsequent acceptance of rape myths and beliefs in positive victim outcomes, as well as observed agitation and aggressive responses to women (Malamuth and Check 1981; Donnerstein 1984; Donnerstein and Linz 1986). More than a decade of research has still not established causality, however, and the most recent research has distinguished between the effects of nonviolent pornography and those of aggressive pornography; moreover, it has found that media depiction of violence against women in nonsexual contexts produces responses similar to aggressive pornography, where the link between sex and violence is explicit (Donnerstein, Linz, and Penrod 1987). Men who are shown R-rated "slasher" films, for example, are more likely to exhibit hostility toward women than those who observe soft-core pornography. In fact, researchers have been unable to find strong correlations between the viewing of nonviolent pornography and violent behavioral outcomes.

Critics of laboratory research call into question the types of behaviors labeled aggressive by laboratory researchers, as well as their inability to make claims about the effects of pornography in the absence of reliable long-term measurements. Some sociologists have been particularly skeptical of any research findings that emerge from the study of artificial social conditions. They claim that laboratory conditions are a poor approximation of the social contexts of everyday life. Sociological research has been more likely to focus on studies that attempt to measure socialization effects, such as those comparing the pornography consumption patterns of sex criminals and batterers to those of "normal" men in the population. These studies are predicated upon the theory that men for whom pornography is a primary agent of socialization will be more likely to act out against women than those who view little or no pornography. Results of such studies have been decidedly mixed. Several studies have found a majority of rapists to be heavy users of pornography (Kimmel 1993); yet M. J. Goldstein's (1973) research comparing a control group of men to a mixed sample of rapists, gay men, and heavy consumers of pornography found that the control group had had more exposure to pornography during adolescence than the other men surveyed.

Aggregate studies are also inconclusive. Larry Baron (1990) found higher rape rates in the states with highest circulation of eight men's magazines, yet studies of rape in Denmark after pornography was legalized found a general decrease in sex crimes (Kutchinsky 1973). In some research, the circulation rates of outdoor magazines such as *American Rifleman* had a higher correlation with rape rates than did circulation rates of pornographic magazines (Kimmel 1993). Of course, it can be argued that circulation rates are not an accurate representation of the distribution of pornographic materials, particularly in the age of cable television and relatively uncontrolled dissemination of pornographic texts and images on the Internet.

The only possible conclusion that one can make from reviewing the research is that causality is extremely difficult to prove, and that neither pro-pornography nor anti-pornography camps can stake legitimacy claims based upon the findings of experts. Predictably, the debate has been rooted more deeply in ideological and theoretical discourse than in the empirical realm. The failure of social science to provide empirical proof of pornography's harm has also led to a general stagnation in the legal realm: prohibition of child pornography reflects a widespread cultural consensus and is legally upheld, while the lack of either cultural consensus or evidence of harm maintains a situational and arbitrary system of dealing with pornographic depictions of adults.

The Case against Pornography

Arguments against pornography originate from within three constituencies: religious conservatives, anti-pornography feminists, and pro-feminist men. There are distinct differences in definition and rationale, however, particularly between the religious conservative perspective and the feminist perspectives that inform the latter two groups. Among religious conservatives, any sexually explicit material constitutes pornography. Equating pornography with violence is not a core aspect of this analysis; the major problems that pornography poses for this group are its presentation of sex as recreational rather than procreational, and its frequent portrayals of nonmarital and nonheterosexual liaisons. Charles E. Cottle and his colleagues (this volume) found that religious conservatives view pornography as a threat to the moral development of children, traditional family values, and the moral fabric of society. Pornography from this perspective is a perversion of sexuality, which is most naturally and morally situated within the context of marital relationships.

The anti-pornography feminist stance posits that pornography is a form of sexual discrimination, and that it contributes to the violation of women's rights (Cottle et al. this volume). The major focus of this perspective is on the exploitative, degrading, and frequently racist nature of pornography, as differentiated from erotica—material that depicts consensual sex or explicit sexual imagery but does not objectify the subject, whether male or female. The distinction between pornography and erotica is clear: depictions of dominant-submissive sex, coerced sex, or images that dehumanize subjects are pornographic, and not depictions of sex per se.

The anti-pornography feminist perspective has been most passionately articulated in the theoretical and legal writings of Andrea Dworkin (1974, 1981) and Catherine MacKinnon (1993). From this viewpoint, pornography is violent in every sense of the word. By viewing pornography as simultaneously active and symbolic, the analysis developed by Dworkin and MacKinnon finds pornography dangerous to women. Given its representational exploitation and subordination of women, as well as the real harm done to individual women by men who derive their value systems from it, pornography should be seen as an accessory to the psychological and physical abuse of women. Pornographers, therefore, should be held accountable for the violation of women's civil rights that often accompanies the use of their materials. The legal protection of pornography as free speech under the provisions of the First Amendment provides pornography with a symbolic legitimacy that effectively silences women's attempts to define their own sexuality and subjectivity. Pornography is thus also conceptualized as a violation of women's right to free speech (see MacKinnon, this volume). Some feminist women of color have demonstrated that pornographic images of African American women frequently portray scenarios suggestive of slavery, and that women of color are generally presented in more dehumanized ways than White women in pornographic representations (Hill Collins, this volume).

The most recent voice to enter the chorus of pornography protesters is that of the pro-feminist male. Although there is as much variance in theoretical logic among pro-feminist male writers as among feminist women, a strong anti-pornography contingent has emerged that accepts the major premises of the anti-pornography feminist critique but expands the notions of harm and victimization to include men. John Stoltenberg, for example, suggests that aggressive pornography is a mechanism for maintaining systemic inequality through his use of the following analogy: pornography is to male supremacy as segregation is to white supremacy (1988, 454). Pornography imprisons the sexual experience of both men and women, a condition that is denied by those who would define pornography as a central manifestation of sexual liberation. The pro-feminist male anti-pornography response views all images of oppressive sexuality as problematic, regardless of who is portrayed in the material. This stance equally condemns aggressive pornographic images of same-sex partners and the sexualized inequality of heterosexual pornography.

The Case for Maintaining Pornography

There are a variety of pro-pornography perspectives, articulated through classic liberal prescriptions of freedom of self-expression and political autonomy. There is also a more radical stance that views certain forms of pornography as subversive and therefore politically expedient for some traditionally marginalized groups. A strong case for preserving the current cultural and legal norms that govern the production and use of pornography is articulated in sexual libertarian ideology. According to Steven Seidman (1992), sexual libertarianism was initially framed by participants in social movements for sexual liberalization and liberation in the 1960s and 1970s. Sex for this group is defined as beneficial and joyous; moreover, sexual expression in a variety of forms is connected to personal health, self-fulfillment, and social progress. The sexual libertarian stance toward pornography views the use of such material as a legitimate and culturally acceptable form of sexual expression.

Some liberal feminist analysts subscribe to a position similar to sexual libertarian ideology with respect to an individual's right to privacy and sexual freedom. There is also a more complex standpoint within liberal feminism that simultaneously rejects the objectification and exploitation of women represented in the predominance of pornography and supports the free speech and expression rights of producers and consumers of pornography. Research suggests that many liberal feminists are personally opposed to pornography, but view the resurgence of sexual repression and the potential for widespread censorship as potentially more problematic for society than the effects of pornography (Cowan 1992). The liberal feminist stance would preserve the legal status quo, while attempting to subvert the power of pornography through progressive gender socialization and the promotion of egalitarian relationships among men and women in cultural representations of sexuality and in daily life. A parallel argument is articulated in much pro-feminist analysis of pornography (see Kimmel 1990).

Independent of the liberal political perspective, some feminists argue that anti-pornography feminism has incorrectly portrayed pornography as the cause of gender violence rather than a symptom of misogyny and institutionalized sexism (Small 1985; Segal 1990; Segal, this volume). By defining pornography as the cause of gender violence, they argue, the anti-pornography feminists mute critiques of the larger political and economic conditions that contribute to gender violence; moreover, the predominantly male perpetrators of gender violence are provided with a cultural scapegoat that diminishes their personal responsibility for their actions.

Many lesbian critics of anti-pornography feminism suggest that censorship legislation would result in the banning of homoerotic images, regardless of their violent or nonviolent content. The range of self-defined lesbian erotica is wide, however, and includes some representations that would be classified as pornographic in the anti-pornography feminist definition of the term. Lesbian advocates of sado-masochism argue that it is mutual trust that characterizes and permits their sexual practice and its representations; such practice subverts the relationship of dominance and submission that characterizes sexual relationships constructed under the conditions of compulsory heterosexuality. As is the case in most contested areas of gender and sexuality, there is radicalism at either end of the continuum of ideas. While the condemnation of everything except marital sexual representations represents the far-right radical stance in the pornography debate, the case for gay and lesbian sado-masochistic pornography is often conceptualized as the endpoint on the radical left.

Pornography and the Law

Currently, obscenity law is the primary mode through which pornography is evaluated in the British and U.S. legal systems. In both countries, obscenity law is derived from interpretations of community morals and values (Segal 1990; Linz et al. 1995). Court decisions regarding obscenity, at least in the United States, have not required the presentation of empirical evidence of community values, although defendants have introduced expert testimony and public opinion polls to provide legitimacy for their actions (Linz et al. 1995). Daniel Linz and coworkers suggest that there are frequent discrepancies between court interpretations of community values and the empirical reality of public values, particularly in the case of violent materials. Their research in Tennessee suggests that although obscenity laws have historically been used to condemn sexual explicitness rather than sexual violence, it is the latter that a substantial constituency finds unacceptable.

Several attempts have been made to legislate the MacKinnon-Dworkin conceptualization of pornography as a violation of women's civil rights. Minneapolis and Indianapolis passed ordinances that would have allowed raped or battered women to sue pornographers for damage if connections could be made between a perpetrator's use of specific pornographic materials and the victim's abuse. Both ordinances were subsequently reversed upon appeal. In Canada, where free speech is defined less broadly than in the United States, the civil rights argument has held more sway. In February 1992, the Canadian Supreme Court ruled that obscenity should be defined by the harm it does to women's pursuit of equality, rather than by abstract community standards. Although this decision set a symbolic precedent and has certainly stimulated cultural reflection and scrutiny in Canada, the strong powers of provincial governments limit its regulatory capacity.

By and large, the persistence of the legal definition of pornography as a form of speech and the guarantee of speech provided under the First Amendment to the U.S. Constitution have set the stage for a legal stalemate between abolitionists and their opponents. Few Americans, even those who express a personal distaste for pornography, are prepared to challenge the slippery slope of free speech guarantees.

Ellen Levy (1993) believes the deep wedge that the pornography debate has driven into the feminist community is the manifestation of distinctly different stances toward justice between pro-pornography and anti-pornography feminists. Using Carol Gilligan's (1982) typology of adversarial and situational moralities, Levy suggests that the inability of feminists to resolve the pornography debate has less to do with attitudes toward censorship than with perceptions of justice. The liberal stance is consistent with the typically male moral-ethical system of determining justice through balancing the proposed regulation against the rights of individuals. In the case of pornography, the liberal opponents of anti-pornography legislation see the issue as a "choice between absolute free speech and censorship" (Levy 1993, 17). For anti-pornography feminists, the issue is not an either/or proposition but a complex situation in which the potential for harm should outweigh the preservation of a decidedly sexist legal system in which purportedly neutral justice is often skewed toward protecting the privilege of men. The theoretical logic of the anti-pornography stance is thus more consistent with the typically female "ethic of care" that Gilligan delineates in her work: "While an ethic of justice proceeds from the premise of equality—that everyone should be treated the same—an ethic of care rests on the premise of nonviolence—that no one should be hurt" (1982, 174). The correlations between Gilligan's typology and the bifurcated feminist response to pornography are not perfect, but this comparison illustrates the complexity of feminist politics and portends ill for a quick resolution to the pornography debate.

Contributions to This Section

The chapters in this section's compendium reflect the social construction of pornography in various forums. The authors explore the complexity of the pornography issue as it is mediated by artistic claims to legitimacy, sexual preference, race, and political ideologies in both historical and contemporary contexts. The solid theoretical logic of each demonstrates the tenacity of the various voices in this debate and illustrates why the public definition of pornography as either a form of violence or a social problem has been forestalled.

Art historian Linda Nead presents the debate as it is articulated by artists. She shows how the legitimacy of the female nude as an artistic form is preserved by juxtaposing "true art" against pornographic depictions of women. By portraying art as an existential experience and pornography as an incitement to action (read exploitation or violence) the artistic community has distanced itself from obscenity debates and cultural critiques of sexual exploitation through sexual representation. Nead, however, discusses the ways in which the female nude can be seen as emblematic of the properties of patriarchal culture.

Charles E. Cottle and colleagues present empirical evidence of the ideological variation across the three major parties to the pornography debate: religious conservatives, anti-pornography feminists, and liberal feminists. This article elaborates on the overview in this introduction by providing concrete examples of the viewpoints espoused by these constituencies. The analysis of ideological difference undertaken by the authors suggests that the partial agreement of conservatives and anti-pornography feminists over political solutions to the problem of pornography is not indicative of a forthcoming political coalition.

Patricia Hill Collins, in "Pornography and Black Women's Bodies," theorizes the pornographic treatment of African American women under slavery to be antecedent to the construction of contemporary pornographic images. Beyond their historical use as sexual objects by White men, Collins suggests, the animalistic portrayal of Black women in much contemporary pornography serves notice of the stratification among women in American and European societies, and particularly of the subordinate status of African American women.

In "Pornography, Civil Rights, and Speech," Catharine MacKinnon sets forth the primary theoretical argument of anti-pornography feminists. She presents the case for a legal stance against pornography, based on both the symbolic use of pornography to silence women and the notion of harm.

The response of pro-pornography feminists to the MacKinnon-Dworkin conceptualization of pornography is articulated by Lynne Segal. This response addresses the perceived danger to women's rights posed by the anti-pornography stance, particularly in its tendency to minimize persistent structural and interpersonal conditions that produce gender violence.

SUGGESTIONS FOR FURTHER READING

Kathleen Barry, *The Prostitution of Sexuality* (New York: New York University Press, 1995).

Andrea Dworkin, *Pornography: Men Possessing Women* (New York: Putnam, 1981).

Michael Kimmel (ed.), *Men Confront Pornography* (New York: Crown Publishers, 1990).

Daniel Linz and Neil M. Malamuth, *Pornography* (Newbury Park, Calif.: Sage, 1993).

Diana E. H. Russell (ed.), *Making Violence Sexy: Feminist Views on Pornography* (New York: Teachers College Press, 1993).

Lynne Segal and Mary McIntosh (eds.), *Sex Exposed: Sexuality and the Pornography Debate* (New Brunswick, N.J.: Rutgers University Press, 1993).

Nadine Strossen, *Defending Pornography: Free Speech, Sex, and the Fight for Women's Rights* (New York: Scribner's, 1995).

Philadelphia Story: September 1987

KATHLEEN O'TOOLE

Another set of bones in an attic, more
elaborate details of shackles and torture,
numbered female body parts, what
the neighbors saw and did not hear.

See the grainy photographs of victims.
Hear the shock in commentators' voices
repeating, one more time . . . The leering's in
the language, the lingering, live at 11:00.

Obligatory cries of outrage greet
each new scenario's atrocity revealed.
It's equal opportunity for mass murderers
this month, in one city. Yet the double digit

dead, these statistics, happen to be sisters.
My sisters the carrion here, as greedy vultures
circle—newspapier mâché with camera eyes—
under blood red, white and blue skies. Odd

glory in the city of filia, the repository
of constitutional pride, where you'll hear
no cry to stake the heart of this vampire.
Not while publicists' dollars stack up

around women's bodies. Seeing our own
likeness distorted, traded like soiled currency,
we circle the ring, attraction and spectator
both, trapped in this cynical circus.

25

The Female Nude: Pornography, Art, and Sexuality

LYNDA NEAD

> To my mind art exists in the realm of contemplation, and is bound by some sort of imaginative transposition. The moment art becomes an incentive to action it loses its true character. This is my objection to painting with a communist programme, and it would also apply to pornography.
>
> KENNETH CLARK, testimony to the Lord Longford committee on pornography

The evidence given by Kenneth Clark, one of the world's leading art historians, to Lord Longford's committee on pornography in Britain, in 1972 is just one fragment of a vast body of discourses that has been produced on the subject of pornography over the last few decades.[1] The Longford committee was a privately sponsored investigation that claimed to represent public opinion. Its report, published in the form of a mass-market paperback and launched in a blaze of publicity, fueled the pornography debate in Britain in the 1970s. From the seventies onward, feminists, moral crusaders, governments, and various other pressure groups have presented their views on the issue, with the result that pornography has become one of the most fiercely and publicly contested areas within contemporary cultural production.[2]

Perhaps one of the most disabling limitations of much of this public debate has been the attempt to look at pornography as a discrete realm of representation, cut off and clearly distinct from other forms of cultural production. This perspective is frequently attended by the view that the pornographic resides *in* the image, that it is a question of content rather than form, of production rather than consumption. Even when pornography is defined in terms of its circulation, as a matter of audience expectations, markets, and institutions, it is still separated off as though it exists in isolation and can be understood outside of its points of contact with the wider domain of cultural representation.

To suggest that pornography needs to be examined in relation to other forms of cultural production, however, is not to move toward the position that claims that *all* of patriarchal culture is therefore pornographic. It is simply to argue that we need to specify the ways in which pornography is defined and held in place. We need to get behind the commonsense notions of pornography in order to uncover the processes by which the term has been defined and the historical changes in the term's meaning. At any particular moment there is no one unified category of the pornographic but rather a struggle between several competing definitions of decency and indecency. As John Ellis has written, "These definitions will work within a context defined by several forces, the current form of the pornography industry and its particular attempts at

From *Signs: Journal of Women in Culture and Society* 15, no. 2 (1990):323–35, by University of Chicago. All rights reserved. Reprinted by permission.

legitimisation; the particular forms of the laws relating to obscenity and censorship; and the general mobilisation of various moral and philosophical positions and themes that characterise a particular social moment."[3] Ellis's comments begin to move the debate toward a model of the discursive formation of pornography; a formation that includes its operations as an industry, its forms of distribution and consumption, its visual codings, and its very status as the illicit.

One of the most significant ways in which pornography is historically defined is in relation to other forms of cultural production; we know the pornographic in terms of its difference, in terms of what it is not. The most commonplace opposition to pornography is art. If art is a reflection of the highest social values, then pornography is a symptom of a rotten society; if art stands for lasting, universal values, then pornography represents disposability, trash. Art is a sign of cleanliness and licit morality, whereas pornography symbolizes filth and the illicit. In this cultural system, aesthetic values readily communicate sexual and moral values. This is the basis of Kenneth Clark's testimony in which art and pornography are defined in terms of their effects on the spectator. Art is pacifying and contemplative, whereas communist painting and pornography incite the viewer to action and therefore cannot belong to the realm of high artistic culture.[4]

Although conventionally art and pornography are set up in this oppositional relationship, they can be seen instead as two terms within a greater signifying system that is continually being redefined and that includes other categories, such as obscenity, the erotic, and the sensual. All of these terms occupy particular sexual and cultural spaces; none of them can be understood in isolation since each depends on the other for its meaning. From this position we can begin to examine the changing historical relationships between the terms and the ways in which the boundaries between these categories have been and continue to be policed in order to maintain the aesthetic and the pornographic as a necessary ideological polarity in patriarchal society.

The Female Nude: Policing the Boundaries

It is often at the very edge of social categories that the work of definition takes place most energetically and that meaning is anchored most forcefully. For art history, the female nude is both at the center and at the margins of high culture. It is at the center because within art historical discourse paintings of the nude are seen as the visual culmination of Renaissance idealism and humanism. This authority is nevertheless always under threat, for the nude also stands at the edge of the art category, where it risks losing its respectability and spilling out and over into the pornographic. It is the vagueness and instability of such cultural definitions that make these marginal areas so open and precarious. Since pornography may be defined as any representation that achieves a certain degree of sexual explicitness, art has to be protected from being engulfed by pornography in order to maintain its position as the opposition to pornography. In other words, through a process of mutual definition, the two categories keep each other and the whole system in place. Categories such as the erotic and the sensual play an important role as middle terms in the system—defining what can or cannot be seen, differentiating allowable and illicit representations of the female body, and categorizing respectable and nonrespectable forms of cultural consumption.

Within the history of art, the female nude is not simply one subject among others, one form among many, it is *the* subject, *the* form. It is a paradigm of Western high culture with its network of contingent values: civilization, edification, and aesthetic pleasure. The female nude is also a sign of those other, more hidden properties of patriarchal culture, that is, possession, power, and subordination. The female nude works both as a sexual and a cultural category, but this is not simply a matter of content or some intrinsic meaning. The signification of the female nude cannot be separated from the historical discourses of culture, that is, the representation of the nude by critics and art historians. These texts do not simply analyze an already constituted area of cultural knowledge, rather, they actively define cultural knowledge. The nude is always organized into a particular cultural industry and thus circulates new definitions of class, gender, and morality. Moreover, representations of the female nude created by male artists testify not only to patriarchal understandings of female sexuality and femininity, but they also endorse certain definitions of male sexuality and masculinity.

In Britain in the 1970s, the discourse of critics and art historians was implicated in a radical redefinition of sexuality. In the art world, there were renewed efforts to pin down the female nude in high art so as to free it from debasing associations with the sexual. These efforts were countered by other attempts to implicate the images of high culture in the pornographic. In the 1980s context created by AIDS, political conservatism, and religious revivalism, the debate regarding sexuality and representation that took place in the 1970s has taken on a renewed significance. The boundaries between art and pornography continue to shift and to raise complex issues for feminist cultural and sexual politics.

The decade of the sixties in Britain was characterized by a series of legislative reforms in the sphere of moral and sexual conduct. Stuart Hall has described the general tendency of British national legislation in the 1960s as the shift toward "increased regulation coupled with selective privatisation through contract or consent."[5] The Sexual Offences Act of 1967 changed the laws on male homosexuality, decriminalizing private sexual relations between adult males. In the same year, the Abortion Act extended the grounds for a lawful termination of pregnancy, and the Family Planning Act introduced wider provision of contraceptives by local authorities. Other legislation made divorce more accessible (1969) and introduced the defense of literary merit into trials charging publications with obscenity (1959 and 1964). At the same time, modification of cinema and theater censorship allowed more explicit portrayals of sexuality in film and on the stage. This series of legislative reforms represents a shift in the style of moral regulation. Although collectively the British legislation shifted toward the general direction of a more relaxed, permissive moral code, the reforms of the sixties should be recognized as a revision of an older conservative moralism and an attempt to create a liberal form of morality at a moment when the main political and economic tendencies were also in the direction of a more libertarian form of capitalism.

Beginning in the late 1960s, the notion of permissiveness began to take on a particular symbolic importance. With signs of a breakdown in the old order, a growing sense of social crisis gave way, by the early 1970s, to a generalized moral panic—a moral backlash against the permissive legislation of the 1960s. On the Left, the women's movement and the emerging gay liberation movement challenged the extent of the liberalism of the reforms, while on the Right, there was a revival of moral traditionalism, led, with evangelical fervor, by individuals such as Malcolm Muggeridge, Mary Whitehouse, and Lord Longford. According to this new authoritarian morality, the sixties legislation had been the final nail in the coffin of traditional values and Christian morality. The faction's leaders called for a return to family values and retrenchment behind the institutions of law and order.[6] The focus for this moral panic was the issue of pornography. Obscene and blasphemous material was seen to be the source of social and moral decay, undermining the family and corrupting both the public and the private spheres. As Jeffrey Weeks has commented, pornography became for the moral crusaders of the 1970s what prostitution had been for the social puritans of the 1880s—a symbol of decay and social breakdown.[7]

The new moralism of the 1970s focused on the image and the word. In the early 1970s there was a cluster of prosecutions for obscenity: the National Viewers and Listeners Association organized a popular campaign against immorality in broadcasting, and in 1972 Lord Longford published his report on pornography. The Longford report concluded that exposure to pornography adversely affected social behavior and morality. The state, it seemed, could not be relied on to maintain sexual standards, and the report cited the Danish and American situations as examples of the state either failing to cohere and reflect public attitudes or adopting a radically libertarian position.[8] The most important point to be made about all these tactics is that moral regulation in the 1970s took the form of the regulation of *representations* of sexuality as opposed to regulation of sexual behavior. Indeed, representation was at the center of discourses on sexuality during the period.

In the context of this public debate, cultural classification became particularly significant, and the differentiation of terms such as the erotic and the obscene took on a heightened importance. The aesthetic had to be distinguished from the titillating; art had to be sealed off from pornography.

Historically, high culture has provided a space for a viable form of sexual representation: that which is aestheticized, contained, and allowed. In the 1970s this site had to be reinforced and shored up. The differences between paintings of the female nude and "pin-ups," glamour photography, soft- and hard-core porn had to be redefined. During this period the British Library cataloged the 1976 edition of Kenneth Clark's high art survey, *The Nude*, in the general stacks but relegated Arthur Goldsmith's *The Nude in Photography* and Michael Busselle's *Nude and Glamour Photography* to the special locked cases.[9] The special cases are reserved for books that are prone to theft or damage and that include commercial or titillating representations of sex, in other words, books that are regarded as an incitement to action rather than contemplative reading. In the 1970s, photographs of the female nude clearly were seen to fall within these guidelines; but the images included in Clark's text escaped the contaminating associations of pornography and could be consulted without fearful consequences to either the book or the reader. In this way the classifications of the British Library map on to the conventional opposition of high and low culture, of fine art versus mass media.

Within traditional aesthetics, the painting has a peculiar status. Valued as an authentic and unique object, the singular product of a special act of creativity, the painting is, as Victor Burgin writes, "part holy relic, part gilt-edged security."[10] In contrast, the material and cultural value of the photograph is reduced by its reproducibility, and the photograph carries none of the connotations of human agency and cultural dignity. Unlike the connoisseur of high art, the consumer of photographic art does not possess a unique object, and within the polarity of high and low art, the photograph is devalued as the product of mass technology, popular and vulgar.

Thus, paintings of the female nude such as those illustrated in Clark's book were set apart physically as well as symbolically from photographic images of the female nude. With obscenity as the focus of sexual regulation, high art had to be maintained as an edifying, moral, and privileged form of cultural consumption. Emphasis was placed on the nude as an ideal form that embodies perfection, universality, and unity. These conventions were in opposition to the codes and functions of pornography—fragmentation, particularity, titillation. Above all else, paintings of the female nude had to be closed off from any associations with commercialism or sexual arousal. Refusing the connotation of commodity, the discourse of high art retreated into a vocabulary of contemplation and aesthetic response. As Kenneth Clark explained to the Longford committee:

> In a picture like Correggio's *Dänae* the sexual feelings have been transformed, and although we undoubtedly enjoy it all the more because of its sensuality, we are still in the realm of contemplation. The pornographic wall-paintings in Pompeii are documentaries and have nothing to do with art. There are one or two doubtful cases—a small picture of copulation by Géricault and a Rodin bronze of the same subject. Although each of these is a true work of art, I personally feel that the subject comes between me and complete aesthetic enjoyment. It is like too strong a flavour added to a dish. There remains the extraordinary example of Rembrandt's etching of a couple on a bed, where I do not find the subject at all disturbing because it is seen entirely in human terms and is not intended to promote action. But it is, I believe, unique, and only Rembrandt could have done it.[11]

In the end, Clark comes up with an extremely personal and idiosyncratic set of distinctions. Indeed, it is the very obscurity of his criteria that is most striking. His definition rests on a precarious differentiation between a *sensuality* that can be incorporated within aesthetic contemplation and a *sexuality* that disrupts this response and becomes an incitement to behavior. Sensuality thus performs an essential role, signifying a form of sexual representation that remains within the permissible limits of art.

But other art historians during the 1970s did not seek to keep high art as a discrete, desexualized category. In fact, they deliberately sought to break open and redefine the category's boundaries and to address directly the representation of the sexual within paintings of the female nude. Far from being a separate plane of activity, art, they claimed, participates in the social definition of male and female sexuality. Three of these texts, all of which were produced outside of the mainstream of art history, reveal the competing definitions that were thrown up by the issue of cultural representation and sexuality during this period.

John Berger's *Ways of Seeing*, first published in 1972, established a fundamental distinction between female nakedness and nudity. Whereas the nude is always subjected to pictorial conventions, "To be naked," he writes, "is to be oneself."[12] In this framework, Berger juxtaposes European oil paintings with photographs from soft porn magazines, identifying the same range of poses, gestures, and looks in both mediums. The particularity of the medium and cultural form is not important. What matters is the repertoire of conventions that *all* nudes are believed to deploy, irrespective of historical or cultural specificity. But according to Berger there are a few valuable exceptions to the voyeurism that is constructed through the European high art tradition.

> They are no longer nudes—they break the norms of the art-form; they are paintings of loved women, more or less naked. Among the hundreds of thousands of nudes which make up the tradition there are perhaps a hundred of these exceptions. In each case the painter's personal vision of the particular women he is painting is so strong that it makes no allowance for the spectator. . . . The spectator can witness their relationship—but he can do no more; he is forced to recognise himself as the outsider he is. He cannot deceive himself into believing that she is naked for him. He cannot turn her into a nude.[13]

Berger's evocation of the hundred or so exceptions to the tradition of the female nude in European art assumes that the relationship between the male artist and the female model, a heterosexual relationship, is inherently natural and good. Power, for Berger, is constituted as public. Private relationships lie outside the domain of power; love transforms the *nude* into a *naked woman* and prevents the male spectator, the outsider, from turning the female figure into a voyeuristic spectacle. This interpretation, of course, is entirely based on a naive, humanist faith in the honesty and equality of private heterosexual relationships. It also assumes a familiarity with artistic biography; the spectator needs to know the nature of the relationship between a particular artist and his model in order to make this reading of the picture. Significantly, both Berger and Lord Clark, in his statement to the Longford committee, invoke paintings by Rembrandt as unique representations of sex. Great artists, apparently, produce exceptional images regardless of subject-matter, and cultural value is thus a safe index of moral worth.

Linda Nochlin's feminist essay, "Eroticism and Female Imagery in Nineteenth-Century Art," also published in 1972, represents one voice from the women's movement, which during this period addressed the construction of patriarchy in high culture.[14] Nochlin shares Berger's analysis of the female nude as a patriarchal image for male consumption, but she goes much further, rejecting the idea of the personal erotic imagery of individual male artists in favor of a social basis for the sexual definitions established in images of the female nude. She also points to the absence of any public imagery for women's desires and calls for an available language to express women's erotic needs. This call for female erotica was part of a much wider demand by members of the women's movement during the early 1970s. Unfortunately, Nochlin's argument was recast by the publisher's dust jacket to once again present female erotica from a male perspective. "The book is superbly illustrated and combines the pleasures of a rich catalogue of esoteric erotica, with the satisfaction of a penetrating and original study."

Another effort to redefine sexuality and sexual pleasure in relation to the visual arts can be seen in Peter Webb's *The Erotic Arts*, first published in 1975. The book is a paradigm of the sexual libertarianism that emerged in the late 1960s and continued into the 1970s, particularly within certain sections of the gay liberation movement. For Webb, sexual freedom was synonymous with social freedom, and sexual liberation was the first step toward social revolution. Webb challenged directly the antipornography lobby and obscenity trials of the early 1970s, which set up liberation in opposition to the authoritarian morality of censorship. Webb, however, was also keen to isolate a category of erotic art from that of pornography. "Pornography is related to obscenity rather than erotica and this is a vital distinction. Although some people may find a pornographic picture erotic, most people associate eroticism with love, rather than sex alone, and love has little or no part to play in pornography. . . . Eroticism, therefore, has none of the pejorative associations of pornography; it concerns something vital to us, the passion of love. Erotic art is art on a sexual theme related specifically to emotions rather than merely actions, and sexual depictions which are justifiable on aesthetic grounds."[15] Webb assumes an essentialist model of human sexuality, conceiving of it as a driving, instinctive force that must find expression through either legitimate or illegitimate channels. In his attempt to distinguish erotic art and pornography, he relies on a familiar set of oppositions: love versus sex, aesthetic value versus bad art, and feeling or emotion versus action. Again, as with the arguments of Clark and Berger, there is a juggling of aesthetic and moral criteria in order to justify one category of representation and to invalidate another.[16]

The Female Nude and Sexual Metaphor

In the three examples considered above, the authors directly address the issue of sexual definition in cultural representation, but they do so from different political and moral standpoints. In the mainstream of art history, however, the approach is more indirect; sex has to be implicit rather than explicit in order to keep the art/contemplation coupling intact and to maintain the conventional polarity of art and pornography. Within traditional aesthetics, the language of connoisseurship has developed as an expression of aesthetic judgment, taste, and value. The way language is mobilized in discussions of paintings of the female nude allows us to assess the role of sexual metaphor in recent art criticism.

As cultural commodities, oil paintings have been relished by critics and art historians, and the practice of applying paint to canvas has been charged with sexual connotations. Light caresses form, shapes become voluptuous, color is sensuous, and the paint itself is luxuriously physical. This representation of artistic production supports the dominant stereotype of the male artist as productive, active, controlling, a man whose sexuality is channeled through his brush, who finds expression and satisfaction through the act of painting.[17] The artist transmutes matter into form. The canvas is the empty but receptive surface, empty of meaning—naked—until it is inscribed and given meaning by him. Surface texture is thus charged with significance; the marks on the canvas are essential traces of human agency, evidence of art, and also signs of sexual virility, a kind of masculine identity.

These phallic and sexual metaphors take on an astonishing resonance when the painting is of a female nude. The artist transmutes matter into the form of the female body—the nude, ideal, perfect, the object of contemplation and delectation. Within the discourse of art history, sex is written into descriptions of paint, surface, and form. The category of art does not permit a sexuality that is an obvious or provocative element, but such sexuality *can* be articulated in the discussion of a particular painting's handling and style. The sexual, then, is distanced from the subject represented on the canvas and is defined instead through the metaphorical language of connoisseurship. Lawrence Gowing, for example, describes a small female figure in a Matisse interior as "abandon(-ing) herself to the colour."[18] In *Nude Painting*, Michael Jacobs refers to Titian's *Nymph and Shepherd*, in which "the dynamics of flesh and blood are revealed in their rawest state, all distracting movement, colour and meaning are stripped away by the rigorous harshness of the artist's late style."[19] And Malcolm Cormack describes a Veronese in which "the whole is a riot of the senses where the sensuous mode of expression emphasises the theme."[20]

However, the issue of the representation of the female nude is not simply a question of the male artist or viewer imposing order on and controlling the canvas or the female body. There is another relationship at stake. The mythology of artistic genius proposes a model of masculinity and male sexuality that is free-ranging, unbounded, needing to be contained within forms.[21] Woman and femininity provide that cultural frame; woman controls and regulates the impetuous and individualistic brush. In a review of an exhibition of impressionist drawings at the Ashmolean in Oxford, the art critic William Feaver considered the representation of the female nude. "A Renoir drawing 'Nude Woman Seen from the Back,' in red chalk with touches of white, illustrates more clearly than any painting the Impressionist concept of untrammelled instinct: Renoir's caress, Monet's spontaneity. But drawing was the basis. Without it Renoir would have been incoherent."[22] Just what is invoked by "the Impressionist concept of untrammelled instinct"? What are we to make of "Renoir's caress" and "Monet's spontaneity"? Artists and lovers, paintings and sex are collapsed into each other. Masculinity is defined as the site of unregulated instinct, potentially anarchic and incoherent. But the discipline of drawing and the form of the female nude—high culture and femininity—give order to this incoherence; together they civilize and tame the wild expressiveness of male sexuality.

Thus, pictures of the female nude are not *about* female sexuality in any simplistic way; they also testify to a particular cultural definition of male sexuality and are part of a wider debate around representation and cultural value. The female nude is both a cultural and a sexual category; it is part of a cultural industry whose languages and institutions propose specific definitions of gender and sexuality and particular forms of knowledge and pleasure.

The relationship between art and pornography as illustrated by the British discourse explored here begins to reveal the ways in which cultural and aesthetic designations are mapped onto the moral and sexual values of Western patriarchal culture generally. To date, the popular debate about pornography in both Britain and America has focused on a limited and rather too familiar set of issues. At the center is the issue of legal censorship. Debate about censorship has become polarized between those who advocate state intervention to ban pornographic material and those who invoke the right of individual freedom of choice, particularly as it is reflected by the private consumption of pornography as opposed to its public display. Supporters of state intervention argue that at issue is the safety of women, that pornographic representations incite violence against women. Yet, social investigation, empirical research, statistics, and personal testimony have been used both to endorse and to refute the links between pornography and acts of sexual violence.[23] Besides the ambiguities concerning these investigations and their conclusions, some of the social effects of pornography, such as women's fear, embarrassment, and anger, cannot be measured and accounted for in any straightforward way.

The parallels between the poles of this debate and the poles of the pornography/art debate are striking. Both debates focus on the impetus to action as a criterion for classification of images of the female nude. Art critics argue over the merits of sensual or erotic images, and those who would either regulate or deregulate pornography argue over the implications of a patriarchal representation of female and male sexuality. These parallels suggest that the relationship between representation and reality, image and action, is not going to be resolved by tugging empirical data backward and forward between positions. Rather, the meanings of eroticism and obscenity, sensuality and sexuality, art and pornography change over time, their boundaries shaped by the forms and institutions of culture and society. Thus, censorship is only a provisional strategy by which to "contain" patriarchal culture; it is a categorization that reflects pornography's present definition as outside the norm, as deviant, hidden culture. Only by continuing to examine the complexity with which such categorizations as pornography and art map out broad cultural notions of the licit and the illicit and societal notions of male and female sexuality will we come to a more subtle understanding of the implications of images of the female nude.

NOTES

1. Quoted in Lord Longford, *Pornography: The Longford Report* (London: Coronet, 1972), 99–100.

2. The published material on pornography is extensive so it is difficult to extract a handful of texts that accurately represent the debate. A very useful selection of British feminist writings is

reprinted in Rosemary Betterton, ed., *Looking On: Images of Femininity in the Visual Arts and Media* (London and New York: Pandora, 1987), 143–202.

3. John Ellis, "Photography/Pornography/Art/Pornography," *Screen* 21, no. 1 (Spring 1980): 81–108, quote on 83.

4. It is Kant's theory of the self-contained aesthetic experience that is at the bottom of all this, but in Clark's usage it becomes simplified and popularized, an accessible formula for cultural definition (see Immanuel Kant, *Critique of Aesthetic Judgement*, trans. J. C. Meredith [Oxford: Clarendon, 1911]).

5. Stuart Hall, "Reformism and the Legislation of Consent," in *Permissiveness and Control: The Fate of the Sixties Legislation*, ed. National Deviancy Conference (London: Macmillan, 1980), 1–43, quote on 18.

6. See Jeffrey Weeks, *Sex, Politics and Society: The Regulation of Sexuality since 1800* (London and New York: Longman, 1981), 273–88, on which this discussion of seventies moralism is based.

7. Ibid., 280.

8. See Longford, pt. 1, chap. 7. Longford discusses the American congressional "Report of the Commission on Obscenity and Pornography, September 1970" (Washington, D.C.: Government Printing Office, September 30, 1970), which rejected any clear correlation between pornography and acts of sexual violence and advocated a liberalizing of sex education in order to foster "healthy" sexual development. The report resulted in a split between members of the commission and was rejected by the Senate and president.

9. Kenneth Clark, *The Nude* (Harmondsworth: Penguin, 1976); Arthur Goldsmith, *The Nude in Photography* (London: Octopus, 1976); Michael Busselle, *Nude and Glamour Photography* (London: Macdonald, 1981).

10. Victor Burgin, *The End of Art Theory: Criticism and Postmodernity* (London: Macmillan, 1986), 42.

11. Quoted in Longford (n. 1 above), 100.

12. John Berger, *Ways of Seeing* (London: BBC & Penguin, 1972), 54.

13. Ibid., 57.

14. Linda Nochlin, "Eroticism and Female Imagery in Nineteenth-Century Art," in *Woman as Sex Object: Studies in Erotic Art, 1730–1970*, ed. Thomas B. Hess and Linda Nochlin (London and New York: Allen Lane, 1972), 8–15. For a detailed discussion of this collection of essays, see Lise Vogel, "Fine Arts and Feminism: The Awakening Conscience," *Feminist Studies* 2, no. 1 (1974): 3–37.

15. Peter Webb, *The Erotic Arts* (London: Secker & Warburg, 1975), 2.

16. Interestingly, both Webb and Berger argue that Oriental art offers honest and frank representations of sex as opposed to the repressed and unhealthy sexuality of Western bourgeois art. In this way, they support the racist mythology of the unrestrained sexuality of non-European races and perpetuate the particular art historical version of the ideology of primitivism.

17. For an important discussion of the metaphor of penis-as-paintbrush, see Carol Duncan, "The Esthetics of Power in Modern Erotic Art," *Heresies*, no. 1 (January 1977), 46–50.

18. Lawrence Gowing, *Matisse* (London: Thames & Hudson, 1979), 63.

19. Michael Jacobs, *Nude Painting* (Oxford: Phaidon, 1979), 24.

20. Malcolm Cormack, *The Nude in Western Art* (Oxford: Phaidon, 1976), 25.

21. On the mythology of male artistic genius, see G. Pollock, "Artists, Media, Mythologies: Genius, Madness and Art History," *Screen* 21, no. 3 (1980): 57–96.

22. William Feaver, *The Observer* (March 25, 1986), 25.

23. In the social sciences there have been many publications on the relationship between exposure to images and resulting action. Recently, the publication in Britain of the Minneapolis public hearings on pornography (1983) has endorsed the link between the use of pornographic material and acts of sexual violence; see *Pornography and Sexual Violence: Evidence of the Links: The Complete Transcript of Public Hearings on Ordinances to Add Pornography as Discrimination against Women: Minneapolis City Council, Government Operations Committee, December 12 and 13, 1983* (London: Everywoman, 1988).

26

Conflicting Ideologies and the Politics of Pornography

CHARLES E. COTTLE, PATRICIA SEARLES, RONALD J. BERGER, AND BETH ANN PIERCE

Pornography has emerged in recent years as one of the most hotly contested social issues, and one that has divided the feminist community in the United States (Berger et al. forthcoming). Radical feminists and religious fundamentalists have decried the harm caused by pornography and have proposed various, though differing, political and legal remedies. The U.S. Attorney General's Commission on Pornography (1986) called for increased prosecutions under existing obscenity law, as well as the passage of new laws against pornography (Douglas 1986; Vance 1986). Civil libertarians within and outside the feminist community in the United States have challenged this political agenda, charged the antipornography movement with advocating censorship, and warned of the negative consequences of increased governmental involvement in this issue (see Burstyn 1985; Durham 1986; McCormack 1985a).

The aim of this study was to provide an empirically based analysis of different ideological positions on pornography that are prevalent in the public domain in the United States. In this article we used the term *ideology* to refer to the taken-for-granted and shared symbolic systems used by individuals to make sense of their world and from which their social action is informed and directed. This usage does not carry with it the negative connotations of false consciousness, and it is not concerned with the truth or falsity of a given point of view, although some ideologies may dominate others through their institutionalization in ongoing social, political, and legal practices (Althusser 1971; Hunt 1985; Sumner 1979).

The study used Q-methodology. Respondents sorted a sample of opinion statements on definitions of pornography, personal reactions to it, its causes and effects, and social policy recommendations. Factor analysis was used to identify distinct clusters of individuals who share common subjectively defined points of view on pornography. The three positions that emerged from the analysis were labeled Religious-Conservative, Liberal, and Antipornography Feminist. In this article, we examine the logical and ethical structures of these points of view and their political and legal implications. We conclude that the viewpoints are too incompatible to sustain stable and effective political alignments among the adherents.

From *Gender and Society* 3, no. 3 (1989):303–33 (edited), copyright © 1989 by Sage Publications, Inc. Reprinted by permission of Sage Publications, Inc. Tables deleted in this volume may be found in the original.

Survey Research on Pornography

Despite political, academic, and media reliance on surveys to gauge the public's perception of pornography (Smith 1987), the data are insufficient and at times contradictory. In 1985, *Newsweek* published a U.S. national survey on pornography conducted by the Gallup polling organization. About three-quarters of the respondents agreed that "sexually explicit material denigrates women and leads some people to sexual violence," and about two-thirds were in favor of banning "magazines, movies and video cassettes that feature sexual violence" (p. 58). At the same time, a majority expressed an acceptance of nonviolent pornography in contemporary society. For example, four-fifths opposed banning "magazines that show nudity," two-fifths opposed banning the showing of X-rated movies in theaters, and two-thirds opposed banning the "sale or rental of X-rated video cassettes for home viewing" (p. 60). Although about half said they believed that sexually explicit magazines, movies, and books "provide information about sex" and "can help improve the sex lives of some couples," two-thirds were concerned that such materials lead "to a breakdown of public morals" (p. 60).

Similarly, in the 1986 General Social Survey, a majority of respondents agreed with statements asserting that pornography has positive effects (e.g., that it "provide[s] information about sex" or "an outlet for bottled-up impulses"), and a majority also agreed with statements claiming it has negative effects (e.g., that it causes a "breakdown of morals" or leads "people to commit rape"; Davis and Smith 1986). Although about one-quarter of the respondents said they had "seen an X-rated movie in the last year," a majority believed that there "should be laws against the distribution of pornography." Our own cross-tabular analysis of the GSS data indicated that women were less likely than men to say they had seen an X-rated movie, and more likely to agree that pornography has negative effects and to disagree that it has positive effects.

The public's ambivalence toward pornography is also evident in a 1986 survey conducted for *Time* by Yankelovich Clancy Shulman. For example, only 38 percent of those polled said they believed that "sexually explicit movies, magazines or books have 'harmful effects upon people'." Yet between 54 and 65 percent of the respondents agreed that the same materials "lead people to be more sexually promiscuous," "encourage people to consider women as sex objects," "lead to a breakdown of social morals," "lead people to commit rape," and "lead people to commit acts of sexual violence" (p. 22). The survey also found that women were much more concerned about pornography than men.

Studies with more specialized concerns that go beyond the polling of respondents reach similar conclusions. For example, Bart et al. (1985) surveyed patrons of the antipornography film *Not a Love Story* and found that women were "significantly more negative toward pornography than men," and that they experienced "greater attitude and belief changes from the film" (p. 307). Their factor analysis of the survey items revealed that men evaluated pornography along different dimensions than women did. For instance, women's affirmation of a pluralistic society tolerant of pornography was more contingent than men's on whether they believed pornography causes harm to women.

In a survey conducted in Madison, Wisconsin, Thompson et al. (1986) found that women tended to react more negatively to pornography than men did and that "older women, who tend to have less exposure to pornography, are the strongest advocates of government regulation" (p. 2). Perceived negative effects of pornography were "by far the largest predictor of attitudes toward regulation." Although "no clear 'community' standard was evident," about two-thirds of the respondents believed that pornographic materials deserve constitutional protection (p. 2). In a survey conducted in the Atlanta metropolitan area, Herrman and Bordner (1983) also found no clear community standard, but men, blacks, and younger, more educated, less religious, and less morally rigid respondents had more tolerant and favorable personal attitudes toward pornography (also see Wood and Hughes 1984).

Finally, Kirkpatrick and Zurcher (1983) surveyed feminist activists, who tended to be highly educated, middle class, nonreligious, and young. They found that 37 percent distinguished between pornography and erotica, with 66 percent believing that pornography caused violence and 40 percent believing that the primary goal of feminist antipornography organizations was to educate people about pornography and violence against women. In addition, 49 percent felt that the producers of pornography were "profiteers out to make easy money" (p. 19).

Q-Methodology and the Pornography Q-Sort

Q-method provides information about the ways in which opinions on an issue fit together in a coherent and holistic fashion. Q-sorting is a modified rank-order technique that allows the empirical representation or reconstruction of perspectives concerning any given topic of interest (Brown 1980; Stephenson 1953). Its emphasis is on subjectivity and the individual's viewpoint as he or she understands it (Brown 1980, 321). Subjects are presented with a representative sample of the universe of discourse on some issue in the form of opinion statements, and are requested to rank-order these statements from most agreement to most disagreement. If the statements presented to subjects are truly a representative sample of opinion on the matter under investigation, the rank-order operations performed by each subject result in a model of his or her point of view.

In Q-method, factor analysis is used to interpret the data, treating individual opinion statements as observations and subjects as variables. Thus, instead of representing clusters of similar responses, factors in Q-method identify clusters of like-minded respondents; that is, each factor represents the commonality of responses that operationally define an attitude or ideological position of a group of people. Once clusters of respondents are identified, factor scoring is used to ascertain the relative importance and valence of the Q-sort statements that form each perspective. Q-method provides an in-depth analysis of the structure of perspectives, ideologies, or world views. "Estimates of the proportions of the population holding various views are not made, nor is it assumed that all points of view are captured in a single study" (Fried 1988, 141).

In Q-method, *population* refers to the entire range of existing opinions on a particular topic, and *sample* refers to a subset of statements that are selected theoretically to reflect these opinions (Brown 1980). In this study, 85 subjects sorted a sample of 86 opinion statements from "most like my point of view" (+5) to "most unlike my point of view" (−5) according to the following quasi-normal, "forced-choice" distribution.

	(Most Unlike My Point of View)									(Most Like My Point of View)	
Value	−5	−4	−3	−2	−1	0	+1	+2	+3	+4	+5
Number of Statements	4	6	8	9	10	12	10	9	8	6	4 (n = 86)

Subjects who found this distribution too confining were allowed to vary their distribution of rank-order statements, since it makes little difference statistically if respondents do not follow the forced distribution precisely (Brown 1980, 201–3; Cottle and McKeown 1980).

The statement sample (see Appendix in original publication) was derived from a wide range of popular and academic writings on pornography,[1] as well as from informal exploratory interviews. An initial pool of 140 statements was winnowed to the final 86 in an attempt to obtain a manageable sample and to provide representation of markedly disparate points of view (e.g., liberal, conservative, religious, feminist). In Q-method, an effort is made to select statements that, in ethnomethodological terms, adhere as closely as possible to the way people actually talk about an issue (Brown 1980, 190). Thus Q-statements sometimes include what the external observer might consider contradictory components.

The selection of subjects in Q-method is not random but theoretical. An attempt is made to administer the Q-sort to persons from diverse sectors of society who might be expected to hold different points of view on a particular topic. Whether the variation in views occurs as expected is an empirical matter to be determined by the statistical analysis (Brown 1980, p. 194). Thus in Q-method, "large numbers of persons are nowhere at issue since differences are among factor types," rather than social categories such as class, gender, and political identification (p. 175). "All that is required are enough subjects to establish the existence of a factor for purposes of comparing one factor with another" (p. 192). Q-method does not make claims about the distribution of the discovered points of view throughout the general population.

Subjects for this study were chosen on the basis of characteristics we felt germane to different points of view concerning pornography. The literature survey and exploratory interviews suggested that variations in gender, occupation, education, political and religious orientation, sexual preference, age, and race were related to different points of view on pornography. Subjects with the range of relevant characteristics were obtained through community contacts in three major urban areas and several smaller cities in southern Wisconsin. Each community contact completed the Q-sort and helped obtain additional subjects who met our demographic requirements. In order to avoid an exclusively regional group of subjects, Q-sorts were also mailed to contact persons in other states, who, on the basis of a priori characteristics, were expected to hold varying points of view on pornography. Of the 85 subjects who participated in the study, 12 were from out of state.

Logical and Ethical Structures of the Three Positions

RELIGIOUS CONSERVATIVE

Adherents of the religious-conservative view in this study emphasized the dangers that pornography poses to the moral development of children, traditional family values, and the moral fabric of society, with these concerns embedded in a religious orientation.

Their agreement and disagreement with the 86 statements indicated that they believe that "pornography interferes with the healthy moral development of children," and that society should "take steps to prevent children from being exposed" to it. They were concerned that "pornography teaches young people that sex is just a physical act rather than an integral part of a meaningful emotional relationship," and they feared that pornography will lead "young people to experiment with sex before marriage" and increase the rate of teenage pregnancy, adult promiscuity, and adultery. In short, Religious-Conservatives felt that pornography is undermining the traditional family unit and "the moral fabric of society," and that "we do no one a service by taking the attitude that what others do is their own concern and not that of their neighbor."

Their position was that sexual relations should remain within the boundaries of heterosexual marriage. They expressed an abhorrence of gay and lesbian sex and a belief that pornography portrays abnormal behavior as normal. They agreed that

> pornography is like heroin and cocaine. People who use it keep coming back for more and more—to get new sexual highs. What was shocking and disgusting becomes commonplace. The creation of pain and the degradation of others become trivial matters.

Although the Religious-Conservative position here was that "pornography is an obsession with sex and the perversion of it," sex was not viewed as "dirty"—"after all, God created sex and pronounced his creation good." While it may seem counterintuitive to suggest that religious-conservatives believe that sex for its own sake is good, as some fundamentalists have denied the legitimacy of sex for pleasure (Davis 1983), our data indicate that contemporary religious-conservatives may value *marital* sex. Ehrenreich et al. (1986, 135) observe that, to some extent, "the sexual revolution has penetrated even the self-enclosed world of right-wing fundamentalism," and that sex books and manuals for Christian audiences have become increasingly popular (see LaHaye and LaHaye 1976; Morgan 1973). Pornography, however, was differentiated from healthy sex and viewed as the perversion rather than the "celebration of sexuality," as well as "a sin and an offense against God."

Religious-Conservatives in this study did not believe that pornography plays "a healthy role in providing an outlet for sexual urges," that it prevents rape by giving people "a way to harmlessly act out their sexual fantasies," or that it provides useful information about sex. To them, pornography was not "simply a diversion" or mere "entertainment." They disagreed that "there is no substantial evidence that pornography promotes or encourages rape and other forms of sexual violence."

Their position focused on the potential harm of pornography to children and traditional morality, not to women. Their concern for women was strongest when the statements paired women with children:

> Those people who fail to see the harms done by pornography are like the tobacco companies who continue to say that smoking does not cause cancer. They defend pornography as freedom of speech and at the same time deny the injuries done by pornography to real women and children.

> Freedom of speech and freedom of press are among the most important rights granted by the U.S. Constitution. But the Constitution was never intended to protect the rights of pornographers who encourage the exploitation and dehumanization of women and children.

> Pornography lures many unsuspecting people into its web. Both children and adults are forced into making pornographic films against their will.

At the policy level, this group favored enforcing "the criminal laws which are often violated in the production of pornography," and strongly opposed "making the production, distribution, and possession of all types of pornography completely legal." Although they appeared somewhat willing to "tolerate some types of pornography," as long as action is taken against the "hard-core" variety, they were, of all three groups, the least opposed to censorship.

ANTIPORNOGRAPHY FEMINIST

The Antipornography Feminist position in this study focused on the role pornography plays in maintaining and perpetuating "women's inferior social status." This group strongly endorsed the view that pornography "leads to the violation of [women's] personal rights," and that it is "a form of sexual discrimination" that differentially harms women. The harm of pornography was seen by them to include "dehumanization, sexual exploitation, forced prostitution, and physical injury. It . . . diminishes women's opportunities for equal employment, education, and freedom of movement." Antipornography Feminists in this study believed that pornography "exists because of the economic interests that profit from the exploitation of women," and that "we need fundamental social changes in the way society treats women."

They also thought pornography "degrading to both men and women" and harmful to both women (or adults) *and children.* However, they did not strongly believe that "pornography interferes with the healthy moral development of children" or resonate with statements that focused only on the protection of children.

Antipornography Feminists in this study, like the Religious-Conservatives, felt that "pornography teaches young people that sex is just a physical act"; however, only the Antipornography Feminists believed that pornography purports to teach "that what [men] see in magazines and films accurately reflects what women are really like" and "that violence is a normal and necessary part of sexual arousal." They felt that women are portrayed in pornography as sexually insatiable, desirous of male dominance, and even masochistic. Antipornography Feminists were more concerned that pornography teaches that violence is normal, whereas Religious-Conservatives were more concerned that pornography teaches that sexual perversion is normal. Antipornography Feminists did not express the antigay sentiments of Religious-Conservatives or the concern that "pornography is destroying the family and the moral fabric of society." Antipornography Feminists did not conceptualize pornography as "sin," and responded negatively to statements indicating a religious-based opposition to pornography. Unlike Religious-Conservatives, they felt that "pornography should not be confused with obscenity. The fundamental issue in pornography is the control and exploitation of women by men . . . [whereas obscenity] concerns questions of what is immoral, tasteless, and just plain dirty."

Points of similarity were rejection of the view that pornography is a "celebration of sexuality," simply "entertainment," useful "information about sex," or a healthy "outlet for sexual urges." Both groups disagreed that there is no evidence that pornography "encourages rape."

Antipornography Feminists in this study were more emotionally affected by and personally concerned about the pornography issue than were the Religious-Conservatives, perhaps because they focused on its concrete harm to women rather than on its abstract harm to the moral fabric of society. Their average scores on the following statements indicate the differences in emotional responses (the Antipornography Feminist scores are given first):

When I see pornographic images I feel pain and sadness.

Pornographic images offend me and make me angry.

I understand some people are concerned about pornography, but it's just not an issue that concerns me very much.

Antipornography feminists in this study did not believe that "all types of pornography" should be "completely legal" and advocated direct personal involvement in antipornography strategies:

> The best way to oppose pornography is through direct action such as civil disobedience, demonstrations, boycotts, education, petitions, and legal action.

They did not express any serious reservations about censorship, although they did not believe civil rights laws giving women the right "to sue the producers and distributors of pornography" constituted censorship.

Antipornography Feminists, in comparison to Religious-Conservatives, emphasized the distinction between pornography and erotica:

> I consider pornography and erotica to be two different things. Pornography combines sex and violence, and portrays women as objects to be used for the sexual pleasure of men. Erotica, in contrast, expresses love, affection, and mutuality in sexual relationships.

> We need to make distinctions between various kinds of sexually oriented materials such as violent hard-core pornography, soft-core pornography, erotica, sex education materials, and so forth. Only in this way can we make intelligent decisions about these materials.

Because Antipornography Feminists focused on the concrete harms produced by pornography, they were more supportive of sexually explicit materials that involve depictions of consensual, nonexploitive relations and of materials designed for sex education. However, they did not accept the view of some feminists (see English 1980) that "flood[ing] the market with erotica" will reduce the public's consumption of the materials that feminists find objectionable.

Antipornography Feminists were less likely than Religious-Conservatives to make a distinction between "hard-core pornography and mainstream men's magazines such as *Playboy* and *Penthouse*." Because they focused more on the pervasiveness of sexism in society, Antipornography Feminists were more likely to find the objectification of women in these popular men's magazines offensive.

Liberal

The liberals in this study made the question of pornography's definition central in their perspective:

> It's impossible to find a definition of pornography that everyone will agree with. Definitions of pornography are determined by individual tastes and preferences. What one person finds unappealing and even offensive, another person might find erotic and artistic.

While they emphasized the need to distinguish between "violent hard-core pornography, soft-core pornography, erotica, [and] sex education materials," they did not strongly resonate with the pornography-erotica distinction. Of the three groups, only the Liberals indicated a strong enjoyment of some pornography, especially now that they could watch it on cable TV and VCRs in the privacy of their own homes:

> There are different kinds of pornography. Some of it is crude and offensive. Some of it is violent and offensive. And some pornography is not offensive at all. This last type is often erotic and appealing.

They were the most likely to distinguish between "hard-core pornography and mainstream men's magazines," believing that some men's magazines contain "good articles" as well as "beautiful" nudes that are "tastefully photographed." They disagreed with those who do not "understand how anyone can get sexually excited by looking at pictures of naked people," and they believed that "there is no reason why I should have to defend my enjoyment of pornography. After all, sexual arousal is its own best self-defense."

They believed that people who want to ban pornography and sexually explicit materials are "too moralistic. In their self-righteous wisdom they have decided what the rest of us should see and read." They also thought that "we're overdoing it with all this concern about pornography," and that "we're going back to the days of the Puritan ethic and sexual repression. We should be more open and relaxed about nudity and sexuality."

The Liberals defended the right to produce and consume pornography, basing their argument on the necessity to maintain First Amendment freedoms:

> I oppose the censorship of pornography. Our First Amendment freedoms of free speech and free press must be preserved, even if some publications offend some people. The price of living in a free society is putting up with points of view you don't like.

> I am opposed to the censorship of pornography or any sexually explicit materials. If we remove hard-core magazines from bookstore shelves, *Playboy* and *Penthouse* will follow. After that, *Glamour* and *Cosmopolitan* will be found obscene by some politically influential group. Where does censorship stop?

Although they believed "it won't do any good to try to censor or ban pornography because . . . it will just go underground," they did express a respect for the legal status quo, agreeing with the *Miller v. California* U.S. Supreme Court decision on obscenity:

> As the U.S. Supreme Court has said, different communities should be allowed to enforce their own standards regarding pornography. The majority should decide if pornography should be available.

They expressed mild support for a rating scheme for "printed materials" and appeared willing to prohibit the "public display" of pornography. Insofar as they are "against the types of pornography that involve children," they also expressed implicit agreement with the *New York v. Ferber* decision that allows the banning of child pornography (458 U.S. 747 1982) because they believed that "society must take steps to prevent children from being exposed to pornography." However, they felt strongly that "as long as children are not involved, . . . adults should be allowed to see or participate in pornography." This protective stance toward children suggests an underlying concern that pornography may have some harmful effects, but with regard to adult pornography, this concern did not override First Amendment priorities or a desire to have access to pornography. If there *are* risks involved, adults are assumed to have the maturity to make responsible decisions for themselves. Further evidence of this tension is seen in this group's agreement with the following statements:

> I really don't know what the effects of pornography are. If I was convinced that it was harmful, I would want to do something about it.

> It's hard to know what to do with pornography because the right to privacy and the right to protection seem to be in conflict. We want both freedom and security, but seem to have to choose between them. It's a hard decision.

In general, the Liberals did not see pornography as harmful. They felt "there is no substantial evidence that pornography promotes ... sexual violence," and they disagreed that pornography harms women, trivializes degradation and normalizes the abnormal, undermines the traditional family unit and the moral fabric of society, constitutes "a sin and an offense against God," or has "an effect on how we relate sexually to others." They rejected the notion that pornography is addicting, and in fact felt that "a little exposure to pornography is harmless and satisfies people's curiosity. After awhile, you just become bored with it." In their view, pornography may even be "beneficial because it helps to reduce sexual inhibitions and increase one's willingness to try new sexual experiences ... [It may] help improve the sex lives of many couples." They did make a strong distinction between violent, hard-core and soft-core pornography, and while they felt pornography does not negatively affect most men, they suspected it might "make men who have angry or hostile feelings toward women more likely to treat women aggressively."

Overall, Liberals did not express any negative personal or emotional response to pornography; it did not offend or anger them, elicit a pained or sad response, or make them feel vulnerable, self-conscious, sexually inadequate, cheap or dissatisfied with themselves, or guilty. They acknowledged the appeal of some pornography, and strongly rejected the notion that "people who regularly look at pornographic magazines or watch pornographic movies are just plain sick" or that they are wallowing in sin. They expressed mild disagreement with the view that "nowadays we have so much pornography because men feel less powerful than they used to," and that "men need pornography because they have difficulty relating to real women."

Views on Pornography and Political-Legal Implications

The three positions on pornography suggested different views of human nature and sexuality with particular political-legal implications. Concerned about the human propensity to sin, Religious-Conservatives believed that only in the context of the watchful and caring community can the individual find safety from moral peril, and that even the Christian family is not safe from the corrupting influence of pornography. They therefore opposed the proliferation of pornography, though for different reasons than those of Antipornography Feminists, and advocated that the criminal law be used against the production of pornography.

While Antipornography Feminists shared some of the Religious-Conservatives' concerns about the dangers of untrammeled individual freedom, their substantial agreement about the harms of pornography belied a fundamental disagreement about the nature of sexuality itself. Religious-Conservatives viewed pornography as the perversion of a naturally good sexuality realized only through heterosexual marriage. Antipornography Feminists, in contrast, implied that sexuality is socially constructed and learned rather than natural. They focused not on perversion but on pornography's pernicious socializing influence: It teaches that violence is a normal part of sexual arousal and that what men see in magazines and films are what women are really like. Although Religious-Conservatives appeared to adopt a socialization model when expressing concern about children's moral development and adults' commitment to family-centered sex, they did not believe that pornography conditions men's conception of women and women's sexuality. For them, pornography may promote sexual obsession and tempt men to have illicit sex, but they did not feel that men acquired a "pornographic" view of women.

Thus Antipornography Feminists were more concerned about sexism and the sexual objectification of women and more strongly advocated changes in the way society treats women. They focused on pornography's discriminatory effects and role in maintaining women's inferior social status. In contrast, the social and political agenda of Religious-Conservatives aims to preserve the traditional nuclear family, an institution that feminists generally believe reinforces women's subordinate status and oppresses sexual minorities. These different concerns were reflected in different conceptions of pornography. Antipornography Feminists asserted a distinction between pornography and obscenity that Religious-Conservatives did not make. For the former, pornography is sexually explicit material that creates and reinforces gender-based power differentials, while obscenity focuses on representations of sex that are often perceived as immoral and in bad taste, but that may not be pornographic. Religious-Conservatives, in contrast, tended to equate the concepts of pornography and obscenity, and consequently deemed materials pornographic that are nonproblematic from a feminist perspective (e.g., depictions of consensual homosexual activity). It follows that the Antipornography Feminists have reason to heed warnings that Religious-Conservatives desire to censor some sex education materials, other materials deemed sexually liberating for women, and erotic imagery not considered offensive or pornographic (see Burstyn 1985; Duggan et al. 1985; Rich 1985).

The distinction between pornography and obscenity made by Antipornography Feminists suggests agreement with the critique of traditional legal approaches that has been advanced by feminists such as Catharine MacKinnon (1984) and Andrea Dworkin (1985). According to MacKinnon and Dworkin, criminal law approaches, including obscenity law, have not been effective in eliminating pornography. Obscenity law in particular is aimed not at protecting individuals from harm, but at maintaining the "purity" of the community. Thus while Antipornography Feminists in this study, like Religious-Conservatives, supported enforcement of criminal laws against pornography, they were more willing to expand remedies to include civil action and direct confrontation.

Because Antipornography Feminists viewed pornography as a form of sexual discrimination and violation of the personal rights of women, they refused to endorse the majority rule implied by the Miller decision. Presumably, for them, the fundamental rights of women overrode considerations of majority rule. Similarly, while Antipornography Feminists considered First Amendment freedoms important, they did not believe these freedoms were intended to protect pornographers. With their personal and empathic involvement in this issue, they were acutely concerned about the concrete harm to real people, and only then about the abstract obligation to respect First Amendment liberties.

The Liberals, in contrast, granted priority to First Amendment freedoms of speech and press over most concerns about pornography. Traditionally, liberals have favored an expanded sphere of freedom for individuals and have held that individuals can independently assess and rationally pursue their self-interests (Jaggar 1983). Since pornography may be a vehicle for the gratification of sexual self-interests, the only justifiable restrictions on the consumption of pornography are those invoked by the necessity to avoid doing harm to others (see Mill 1961). In this study, Liberals felt that if there were harmful consequences, restrictions on the production and distribution of some pornographic materials might be allowed. In the case of children, restrictions might even be encouraged. But in the absence of evidence of harm and consensus about the types of sexually explicit materials that should be restricted, they thought community standards or consumer demand should prevail. Thus Liberals appeared to be willing to tolerate some commercialization of sexuality. They viewed human sexuality as naturally good, a feature of existence to be enjoyed, and were more concerned about the harm of sexual repression than about the harm of pornography.

The Liberals' willingness to endorse community standards and child pornography restrictions suggests acceptance of obscenity law as it has been defined by U.S. Supreme Court rulings. For the time being, the liberal position has become the status quo, and much pornography, including violent pornography, has been allowed to flourish under prevailing law (MacKinnon 1984). However, if Religious-Conservatives were to be successful in changing community standards and gaining control of the state law enforcement apparatus, the community standards provision of the Miller decision would work against the Liberals.

Conclusion

Ideologies are symbolic systems used by individuals to make sense of their world and to guide their social action. Most important, ideologies are *shared* cognitive structures. In this study, 79 of the 85 subjects' views correlated significantly with the views of others. Considering the number of ways these statements could have been rank-ordered, it is noteworthy that subjects operating independently reproduced similar Q-sorts in such a consistent manner.

This pattern of response raises the larger issue of the relationships among ideology, human subjectivity, and social structure. From the perspective of methodological individualism (see Alexander 1982), one might argue that the 85 subjects acted independently to generate the three positions on pornography. Yet from a structuralist perspective, ideology exists as an element of culture, and the positions on pornography exist independently of the specific individuals performing the Q-sort. Ideology, in addition to its other functions, provides the interface between individuals and ongoing institutionalized social practices. To the extent that subjects in this study made "choices," these choices were constituents of readily available systems of shared symbolic meaning.

In structural terms, the subjects in our study gave voice to current conflicts between social institutions and practices. Religious-Conservatives felt that traditional family values and the sanctity of marital sex were threatened by the commercialization of sexuality and access to variety tolerated by Liberals. Antipornography Feminists, like Liberals, did not want to rule out some varieties of sexuality that the Religious-Conservatives condemned (e.g., gay and lesbian sex and other nonmarital sex), but they differed over whether pornography demeans, objectifies, and threatens women and conveys misinformation about female sexuality. Antipornography Feminists could not accept the values of Liberals who minimized the harm of pornography and emphasized the individual's right to access, as long as it met the local community's standards of approval.

Although feminist and religious antipornography activists desire some community control over pornography to protect people from its harmful consequences, the significant differences between these two groups make political coalitions tenuous and conflictual. In promoting antipornography politics, feminists face the danger of facilitating the religious-conservative's establishment of a broader antifeminist social agenda. On the other hand, an alignment of anticensorship feminists with nonfeminist anticensorship forces minimizes women's particular sexual vulnerability.

Note

1. See Barry 1979; Bart 1985a, 1986; Blakely 1985; Burstyn 1985; Diamond 1980; Durham 1986; Dworkin 1985; English 1980; Gray 1982; *Harper's* 1984; Hughes 1970; Lederer 1980; MacKinnon 1984; Minnery 1986; *Newsweek* 1985; Soble 1986; Squire 1985.

27

Pornography and Black Women's Bodies

PATRICIA HILL COLLINS

> For centuries the black woman has served as the primary pornographic "outlet" for white men in Europe and America. We need only think of the black women used as breeders, raped for the pleasure and profit of their owners. We need only think of the license the "master" of the slave women enjoyed. But, most telling of all, we need only study the old slave societies of the South to note the sadistic treatment—at the hands of white "gentlemen"—of "beautiful young quadroons and octoroons" who became increasingly (and were deliberately bred to become) indistinguishable from white women, and were the more highly prized as slave mistresses because of this. (Walker 1981, 42)

Alice Walker's description of the rape of enslaved African women for the "pleasure and profit of their owners" encapsulates several elements of contemporary pornography. First, Black women were used as sex objects for the pleasure of white men. This objectification of African-American women parallels the portrayal of women in pornography as sex objects whose sexuality is available for men (McNall 1983). Exploiting Black women as breeders objectified them as less than human because only animals can be bred against their will. In contemporary pornography women are objectified through being portrayed as pieces of meat, as sexual animals awaiting conquest. Second, African-American women were raped, a form of sexual violence. Violence is typically an implicit or explicit theme in pornography. Moreover, the rape of Black women linked sexuality and violence, another characteristic feature of pornography (Eisenstein 1983). Third, rape and other forms of sexual violence act to strip victims of their will to resist and make them passive and submissive to the will of the rapist. Female passivity, the fact that women have things done to them, is a theme repeated over and over in contemporary pornography (McNall 1983). Fourth, the profitability of Black women's sexual exploitation for white "gentlemen" parallels pornography's financially lucrative benefits for pornographers (Eisenstein 1983). Finally, the actual breeding of "quadroons and octoroons" not only reinforces the themes of Black women's passivity, objectification, and malleability to male control but reveals pornography's grounding in racism and sexism. The fates of both Black and white women were intertwined in this breeding process. The ideal African-American woman as a pornographic object was indistinguishable from white women and thus approximated the images of beauty, asexuality, and chastity forced on white women. But inside was a highly sexual whore, a "slave mistress" ready to cater to her owner's pleasure.[1]

Contemporary pornography consists of a series of icons or representations that focus

From *Making Violence Sexy: Feminist Views on Pornography*, D. E. H. Russell (ed.), Teacher's College Press, 1993, pp. 97–103. Reprinted by permission.

the viewer's attention on the relationship between the portrayed individual and the general qualities ascribed to that class of individuals. Pornographic images are iconographic in that they represent realities in a manner determined by the historical position of the observers, their relationship to their own time, and to the history of the conventions which they employ (Gilman 1985). The treatment of Black women's bodies in nineteenth-century Europe and the United States may be the foundation upon which contemporary pornography as the representation of women's objectification, domination, and control is based. Icons about the sexuality of Black women's bodies emerged in these contexts. Moreover, as race/gender-specific representations, these icons have implications for the treatment of both African-American and white women in contemporary pornography.

I suggest that African-American women were not included in pornography as an afterthought, but instead, form a key pillar on which contemporary pornography itself rests. As Alice Walker points out, "the more ancient roots of modern pornography are to be found in the almost always pornographic treatment of black women who, from the moment they entered slavery . . . were subjected to rape as the 'logical' convergence of sex and violence. Conquest, in short" (1981, 42).

One key feature about the treatment of Black women in the nineteenth century was how their bodies were objects of display. In the antebellum American South white men did not have to look at pornographic pictures of women because they could become voyeurs of Black women on the auction block. A chilling example of this objectification of the Black female body is provided by the exhibition, in early nineteenth-century Europe, of Sarah Bartmann, the so-called Hottentot Venus. Her display formed one of the original icons for Black female sexuality. An African woman, Sarah Bartmann was often exhibited at fashionable parties in Paris, generally wearing little clothing, to provide entertainment. To her audience she represented deviant sexuality. At the time European audiences thought that Africans had deviant sexual practices and searched for physiological differences, such as enlarged penises and malformed female genitalia, as indications of this deviant sexuality. Sarah Bartmann's exhibition stimulated these racist and sexist beliefs. After her death in 1815, she was dissected. Her genitalia and buttocks remain on display in Paris (Gilman 1985).

Sander Gilman explains the impact that Sarah Bartmann's exhibition had on Victorian audiences:

> It is important to note that Sarah Bartmann was exhibited not to show her genitalia—but rather to present another anomaly which the European audience . . . found riveting. This was the steatopygia, or protruding buttocks, the other physical characteristic of the Hottentot female which captured the eye of early European travelers. . . . The figure of Sarah Bartmann was reduced to her sexual parts. The audience which had paid to see her buttocks and had fantasized about the uniqueness of her genitalia when she was alive could, after death and dissection, examine both. (1985, p. 213)

In this passage Gilman unwittingly describes how Bartmann was used as a pornographic object similar to how women are represented in contemporary pornography. She was reduced to her sexual parts, and these parts came to represent a dominant icon applied to Black women throughout the nineteenth century. Moreover, the fact that Sarah Bartmann was both African and a woman underscores the importance of gender in maintaining notions of racial purity. In this case Bartmann symbolized Blacks as a "race." Thus the creation of the icon applied to Black women demonstrates that notions of gender, race, and sexuality were linked in overarching structures of political domination and economic exploitation.

The process illustrated by the pornographic treatment of the bodies of enslaved African women and of women like Sarah Bartmann has developed into a full-scale industry encompassing all women objectified differently by racial/ethnic category. Contemporary portrayals of Black women in pornography represent the continuation of the historical treatment of their actual bodies. African-American women are usually depicted in a situation of bondage and slavery, typically in a submissive posture, and often with two white men. As Bell observes, "this setting reminds us of all the trappings of slavery: chains, whips, neck braces, wrist clasps" (1987, 59). White women and women of color have different pornographic images applied to them. The image of Black women in pornography is almost consistently one featuring them breaking from chains. The image of Asian women in pornography is almost consistently one of being tortured (Bell 1987, 161).

The pornographic treatment of Black women's bodies challenges the prevailing feminist assumption that since pornography primarily affects white women, racism has been grafted onto pornography. African-American women's experiences suggest that Black women were not added into a preexisting pornography, but rather that pornography itself must be reconceptualized as an example of the interlocking nature of race, gender, and class oppression. At the heart of both racism and sexism are notions of biological determinism claiming that people of African descent and women possess immutable biological characteristics marking their inferiority to elite white women (Gould 1981; Fausto-Sterling 1989; Halpin 1989). In pornography these racist and sexist beliefs are sexualized. Moreover, for African-American women pornography has not been timeless and universal but was tied to Black women's experiences with the European colonization of Africa and with American slavery. Pornography emerged within a specific system of social class relationships.

This linking of views of the body, social constructions of race and gender, and conceptualizations of sexuality that inform Black women's treatment as pornographic objects promises to have significant implications for how we assess contemporary pornography. Moreover, examining how pornography has been central to the race, gender, and class oppression of African-American women offers new routes for understanding the dynamics of power as domination.

Investigating racial patterns in pornography offers one route for such an analysis. Black women have often claimed that images of white women's sexuality were intertwined with the controlling image of the sexually denigrated Black woman: "In the United States, the fear and fascination of female sexuality was projected onto black women; the passionless lady arose in symbiosis with the primitively sexual slave" (Hall 1983, 333). Comparable linkages exist in pornography (Gardner 1980). Alice Walker provides a fictional account of a Black man's growing awareness of the different ways that African-American and white women are objectified in pornography: "What he has refused to see—because to see it would reveal yet another area in which he is unable to protect or defend black women—is that where white women are depicted in pornography as 'objects,' black women are depicted as animals. Where white women are depicted as human bodies if not beings, black women are depicted as shit" (Walker 1981, 52).

Walker's distinction between "objects" and "animals" is crucial in untangling gender, race, and class dynamics in pornography. Within the mind/body, culture/nature, male/female oppositional dichotomies in Western social thought, objects occupy an uncertain interim position. As objects white women become creations of culture—in this case, the mind of white men—using the materials of nature—in this case, uncontrolled female sexuality. In contrast, as animals Black women receive no such redeeming dose of culture and remain open to the type of exploitation visited on nature overall. Race becomes the distinguishing feature in determining the type of objectification women will encounter. Whiteness as symbolic of both civilization and culture is used to separate objects from animals.

The alleged superiority of men to women is not the only hierarchical relationship that has been linked to the putative superiority of the mind to the body. Certain "races" of people have been defined as being more bodylike, more animalike, and less godlike than others (Spelman 1982, 52). Race and gender oppression may both revolve around the same axis of disdain for the body; both portray the sexuality of subordinate groups as animalistic and therefore deviant. Biological notions of race and gender prevalent in the early nineteenth century which fostered the animalistic icon of Black female sexuality were joined by the appearance of a racist biology incorporating the concept of degeneracy (Foucault 1980). Africans and women were both perceived as embodied entities, and Blacks were seen as degenerate. Fear of and disdain for the body thus formed a key element in both sexist and racist thinking (Spelman 1982).

While the sexual and racial dimensions of being treated like an animal are important, the economic foundation underlying this treatment is critical. Animals can be economically exploited, worked, sold, killed, and consumed. As "mules," African-American women become susceptible to such treatment. The political economy of pornography also merits careful attention. Pornography is pivotal in mediating contradictions in changing societies (McNall 1983). It is no accident that racist biology, religious justifications for slavery and women's subordination, and other explanations for nineteenth-century racism and sexism arose during a period of profound political and economic change. Symbolic means of domination become particularly important in mediating contradictions in changing political economies. The exhibition of Sarah Bartmann and Black women on the auction block were not benign intellectual exercises—these practices defended real material and political interests. Current transformations in international capitalism require similar ideological justifications. Where does pornography fit in these current transformations? This question awaits a comprehensive Afrocentric feminist analysis.

Publicly exhibiting Black women may have been central to objectifying Black women as animals and to creating the icon of Black women as animals. Yi-Fu Tuan (1984) offers an innovative argument about similarities in efforts to control nature—especially plant life—the domestication of animals, and the domination of certain groups of humans. Tuan suggests that displaying humans alongside animals implies that such humans are more like monkeys and bears than they are like "normal" people. This same juxtaposition leads spectators to view the captive animals in a special way. Animals require definitions of being like humans, only more openly carnal and sexual, an aspect of animals that forms a major source of attraction for visitors to modern zoos. In discussing the popularity of monkeys in zoos, Tuan notes: "Some visitors are especially attracted by the easy sexual behavior of the monkeys. Voyeurism is forbidden except when applied to subhumans" (1984, 82). Tuan's analysis suggests that the public display of Sarah Bartmann and of the countless enslaved African women on the auction blocks of the antebellum American South—especially in proximity to animals—fostered their image as animalistic.

This linking of Black women and animals is evident in nineteenth-century scientific literature. The equation of women, Blacks, and animals is revealed in the following description of an African woman published in an 1878 anthropology text:

She had a way of pouting her lips exactly like what we have observed in the orangutan. Her movements had something abrupt and fantastical about them, reminding one of those of the ape. Her ear was like that of many apes.... These are animal characters. I have never seen a human head more like an ape than that of this woman. (Halpin 1989, 287)

In a climate such as this, it is not surprising that one prominent European physician even stated that Black women's "animallike sexual appetite went so far as to lead black women to copulate with apes" (Gilman 1985, 212).

The treatment of all women in contemporary pornography has strong ties to the portrayal of Black women as animals. In pornography women become nonpeople and are often represented as the sum of their fragmented body parts. Scott McNall observes:

This fragmentation of women relates to the predominance of rear-entry position photographs.... All of these kinds of photographs reduce the woman to her reproductive system, and, furthermore, make her open, willing, and available—not in control.... The other thing rear-entry position photographs tell us about women is that they are animals. They are animals because they are the same as dogs—bitches in heat who can't control themselves. (McNall 1983, 197–98)

This linking of animals and white women within pornography becomes feasible when grounded in the earlier denigration of Black women as animals.

Developing a comprehensive analysis of the race, gender, and class dynamics of pornography offers possibilities for change. Those Black feminist intellectuals investigating sexual politics imply that the situation is much more complicated than that advanced by some prominent white feminists (see, e.g., Dworkin 1981) in which "men oppress women" because they are men. Such approaches implicitly assume biologically deterministic views of sex, gender, and sexuality and offer few possibilities for change. In contrast, Afrocentric feminist analyses routinely provide for human agency and its corresponding empowerment and for the responsiveness of social structures to human action. In the short story "Coming Apart," Alice Walker describes one Black man's growing realization that his enjoyment of pornography, whether of white women as "objects" or Black women as "animals," degraded him:

He begins to feel sick. For he realizes that he has bought some of the advertisements about women, black and white. And further, inevitably, he has bought the advertisements about himself. In pornography the black man is portrayed as being capable of fucking anything ... even a piece of shit. He is defined solely by the size, readiness and unselectivity of his cock. (Walker 1981, 52)

Walker conceptualizes pornography as a race/gender system that entraps everyone. But by exploring an African-American *man's* struggle for a self-defined standpoint on pornography, Walker suggests that a changed consciousness is essential to social change. If a Black man can understand how pornography affects him, then other groups enmeshed in the same system are equally capable of similar shifts in consciousness and action.

Note

1. Offering a similar argument about the relationship between race and masculinity, Paul Hoch (1979) suggests that the ideal white man is a hero who upholds honor. But inside lurks a "Black beast" of violence and sexuality, traits that the white hero deflects onto men of color.

28

Pornography, Civil Rights, and Speech

CATHARINE MACKINNON

There is a belief that this is a society in which women and men are basically equals. Room for marginal corrections is conceded, flaws are known to exist, attempts are made to correct what are conceived as occasional lapses from the basic condition of sex equality. Sex discrimination law has concentrated most of its focus on these occasional lapses. It is difficult to overestimate the extent to which this belief in equality is an article of faith for most people, including most women, who wish to live in self-respect in an internal universe, even (perhaps especially) if not in the world. It is also partly an expression of natural law thinking: if we are inalienably equal, we can't "really" be degraded.

This is a world in which it is worth trying. In this world of presumptive equality, people make money based on their training or abilities or diligence or qualifications. They are employed and advanced on the basis of merit. In this world of just deserts, if someone is abused, it is thought to violate the basic rules of the community. If it doesn't, victims are seen to have done something they could have chosen to do differently, by exercise of will or better judgment. Maybe such people have placed themselves in a situation of vulnerability to physical abuse. Maybe they have done something provocative. Or maybe they were just unusually unlucky. In such a world, if such a person has an experience, there are words for it. When they speak and say it, they are listened to. If they write about it, they will be published. If certain experiences are never spoken about, if certain people or issues are seldom heard from, it is supposed that silence has been chosen. The law, including much of the law of sex discrimination and the First Amendment, operates largely within the realm of these beliefs.

Feminism is the discovery that women do not live in this world, that the person occupying this realm is a man, so much more a man if he is white and wealthy. This world of potential credibility, authority, security, and just rewards, recognition of one's identity and capacity, is a world that some people do inhabit as a condition of birth, with variations among them. It is not a basic condition accorded humanity in this society, but a prerogative of status, a privilege, among other things, of gender.

I call this a discovery because it has not been an assumption. Feminism is the first

From *Harvard Civil Rights—Civil Liberties Law Review* 20, no. 1 (1985):1–17. Reprinted by permission.

theory, the first practice, the first movement, to take seriously the situation of all women from the point of view of all women, both on our situation and on social life as a whole. The discovery has therefore been made that the implicit social content of humanism, as well as the standpoint from which legal method has been designed and injuries have been defined, has not been women's standpoint. Defining feminism in a way that connects epistemology with power as the politics of women's point of view, this discovery can be summed up by saying that women live in another world: specifically, a world of *not* equality, a world of inequality.

Looking at the world from this point of view, a whole shadow world of previously invisible silent abuse has been discerned. Rape, battery, sexual harassment, forced prostitution, and the sexual abuse of children emerge as common and systematic. We find that rape happens to women in all contexts, from the family, including rape of girls and babies, to students and women in the workplace, on the streets, at home, in their own bedrooms by men they do not know and by men they do know, by men they are married to, men they have had a social conversation with, and, least often, men they have never seen before. Overwhelmingly, rape is something that men do or attempt to do to women (44 percent of American women according to a recent study) at some point in our lives. Sexual harassment of women by men is common in workplaces and educational institutions. Based on reports in one study of the federal workforce, up to 85 percent of women will experience it, many in physical forms. Between a quarter and a third of women are battered in their homes by men. Thirty-eight percent of little girls are sexually molested inside or outside the family. Until women listened to women, this world of sexual abuse was *not spoken* of. It was the unspeakable. What I am saying is, if you *are* the tree falling in the epistemological forest, your demise doesn't make a sound if no one is listening. Women did not "report" these events, and overwhelmingly do not today, because no one is listening, because no one believes us. This silence does not mean nothing happened, and it does not mean consent. It is the silence of women of which Adrienne Rich has written, "Do not confuse it with any kind of absence."

Believing women who say we are sexually violated has been a radical departure, both methodologically and legally. The extent and nature of rape, marital rape, and sexual harassment itself, were discovered in this way. Domestic battery as a syndrome, almost a habit, was discovered through refusing to believe that when a woman is assaulted by a man to whom she is connected, that it is not an assault. The sexual abuse of children was uncovered, Freud notwithstanding, by believing that children were not making up all this sexual abuse. Now what is striking is that when each discovery is made, and somehow made real in the world, the response has been: it happens to men too. If women are hurt, men are hurt. If women are raped, men are raped. If women are sexually harassed, men are sexually harassed. If women are battered, men are battered. Symmetry must be reasserted. Neutrality must be reclaimed. Equality must be reestablished.

The only areas where the available evidence supports this, where anything like what happens to women also happens to men, involve children—little boys are sexually abused—and prison. The liberty of prisoners is restricted, their freedom restrained, their humanity systematically diminished, their bodies and emotions confined, defined, and regulated. If paid at all, they are paid starvation wages. They can be tortured at will, and it is passed off as discipline or as means to a just end. They become compliant. They can be raped at will, at any moment, and nothing will be done about it. When they scream, nobody hears. To be a prisoner means to be defined as a member of a group for whom the rules of what can be done to you, of what is seen as abuse of you, are reduced as part of the definition of your status. To be a woman is that kind of definition and has that kind of meaning.

Men *are* damaged by sexism. (By men I mean the status of masculinity that is accorded to males on the basis of their biology but is not itself biological.) But whatever the damage of sexism to men, the condition of being a man is not defined as subordinate to women by force. Looking at the facts of the abuses of women all at once, you see that a woman is socially defined as a person who, whether or not she is or has been, can be treated in these ways by men at any time, and little, if anything, will be done about it. This is what it means when feminists say that maleness is a form of power and femaleness is a form of powerlessness.

In this context, all of this "men too" stuff means that people don't really believe that the things I have just said are true, though there really is little question about their empirical accuracy. The data are extremely simple, like women's pay figure of fifty-nine cents on the dollar. People don't really seem to believe that either. Yet there is no question of its empirical validity. This is the workplace story: what women do is seen as not worth much, or what is not worth much is seen as something for women to do. *Women* are seen as not worth much, is the thing. Now why are these basic realities of the subordination of women to men, for example, that only 7.8 percent of women have never been sexually assaulted, not effectively believed, not perceived as real in the face of all this evidence? Why don't *women* believe our own experiences? In the face of all this evidence, especially of systematic sexual abuse—subjection to violence with impunity is one extreme expression, although not the only expression, of a degraded status— the view that basically the sexes are equal in this society remains unchallenged and unchanged. The day I got this was the day I understood its real message, its real coherence: *This is equality for us.*

I could describe this, but I couldn't explain it until I started studying a lot of pornography. In pornography, there it is, in one place, all of the abuses that women had to struggle so long even to begin to articulate, all the *unspeakable* abuse: the rape, the battery, the sexual harassment, the prostitution, and the sexual abuse of children. Only in the pornography it is called something else: sex, sex, sex, sex, and sex, respectively. Pornography sexualizes rape, battery, sexual harassment, prostitution, and child sexual abuse; it thereby celebrates, promotes, authorizes, and legitimizes them. More generally, it eroticizes the dominance and submission that is the dynamic common to them all. It makes hierarchy sexy and calls that "the truth about sex" or just a mirror of reality. Through this process pornography constructs what a woman is as what men want from sex. This is what the pornography means.

Pornography constructs what a woman is in terms of its view of what men want sexually, such that acts of rape, battery, sexual harassment, prostitution, and sexual abuse of children become acts of sexual equality. Pornography's world of equality is a harmonious and balanced place. Men and women are perfectly complementary and perfectly bipolar. Women's desire to be fucked by men is equal to men's desire to fuck women. All the ways men love to take and violate women, women love to be taken and violated. The women who most love this are most men's equals, the most liberated; the most participatory child is the most grown-up, the most equal to an adult. Their consent merely expresses or ratifies these preexisting facts.

The content of pornography is one thing. There, women substantively desire dispossession and cruelty. We desperately want to be bound, battered, tortured, humiliated, and killed. Or, to be fair to the soft core, merely taken and used. This is erotic to the male point of view. Subjection itself, with self-determination ecstatically relinquished, is the content of women's sexual desire and desirability. Women are there to be violated and possessed, men to violate and possess us, either on screen or by camera or pen on behalf of the consumer. On a simple descriptive level, the inequality of hierarchy, of which gender is the primary one, seems necessary for sexual arousal to work. Other added inequalities identify various pornographic genres or sub-themes, although they are always added through gender: age, disability, homosexuality, animals, objects, race (including anti-Semitism), and so on. Gender is never irrelevant.

What pornography *does* goes beyond its content: it eroticizes hierarchy, it sexualizes inequality. It makes dominance and submission into sex. Inequality is its central dynamic; the illusion of freedom coming together with the reality of force is central to its working. Perhaps because this is a bourgeois culture, the victim must look free, appear to be freely acting. Choice is how she got there. Willing is what she is when she is being equal. It seems equally important that then and there she actually be forced and that forcing be communicated on some level, even if only through still photos of her in postures of receptivity and access, available for penetration. Pornography in this view is a form of forced sex, a practice of sexual politics, an institution of gender inequality.

From this perspective, pornography is neither harmless fantasy nor a corrupt and confused misrepresentation of an otherwise natural and healthy sexual situation. It institutionalizes the sexuality of male supremacy, fusing the erotization of dominance and submission with the social construction of male and female. To the extent that gender is sexual, pornography is part of constituting the meaning of that sexuality. Men treat women as who they see women as being. Pornography constructs who that is. Men's power over women means that the way men see women defines who women can be. Pornography is that way. Pornography is not imagery in some relation to a reality elsewhere constructed. It is not a distortion, reflection, projection, expression, fantasy, representation, or symbol either. It is a sexual reality.

In Andrea Dworkin's definitive work, *Pornography: Men Possessing Women*, sexuality itself is a social construct gendered to the ground. Male dominance here is not an artificial overlay upon an underlying inalterable substratum of uncorrupted essential sexual being. Dworkin presents a sexual theory of gender inequality of which pornography is a constitutive practice. The way pornography produces its meaning constructs and defines men and women as such. Gender has no basis in anything other than the social reality its hegemony constructs. Gender is what gender means. The process that gives sexuality its male supremacist meaning is the same process through which gender inequality becomes socially real.

In this approach, the experience of the (overwhelmingly) male audiences who consume pornography is therefore not fantasy or simulation or catharsis but sexual reality, the level of reality on which sex itself largely operates. Understanding this dimension of the problem does not require noticing that pornography models are real women to whom, in most cases, something real is being done; nor does it even require inquiring into the systematic infliction of pornography and its sexuality upon women, although it helps. What matters is the way in which the pornography itself provides what those who consume it want. Pornography *participates* in its audience's eroticism through creating an accessible sexual object, the possession and consumption of which *is* male sexuality, as socially constructed; to be consumed and possessed as which, *is* female sexuality, as socially constructed; pornography is a process that constructs it that way.

The object world is constructed according to how it looks with respect to its possible uses. Pornography defines women by how we look according to how we can be sexually used. Pornography codes how to look at women, so you know what you can do with one when you see one. Gender is an assignment made visually, both originally and in everyday life. A sex object is defined on the basis of its looks, in terms of its usability for sexual pleasure, such that both the looking—the quality of the gaze, including its point of view—and the definition according to use become eroticized as part of the sex itself. This is what the feminist concept "sex object" means. In this sense, sex in life is no less mediated than it is in art. Men have sex with their image of a woman. It is not that life and art imitate each other; in this sexuality, they *are* each other.

To give a set of rough epistemological translations, to defend pornography as consistent with the equality of the sexes is to defend the subordination of women to men as sexual equality. What in the pornographic view is love and romance looks a great deal like hatred and torture to the feminist. Pleasure and eroticism become violation. Desire appears as lust for dominance and submission. The vulnerability of women's projected sexual availability, that acting we are allowed (that is, asking to be acted upon), is victimization. Play conforms to scripted roles. Fantasy expresses ideology, is not exempt from it. Admiration of natural physical beauty becomes objectification. Harmlessness becomes harm. Pornography is a harm of male supremacy made difficult to see because of its pervasiveness, potency, and principally, because of its success in making the world a pornographic place. Specifically, its harm cannot be discerned, and will not be addressed, if viewed and approached neutrally, because it *is* so much of "what is." In other words, to the extent pornography succeeds in constructing social reality, it becomes invisible as harm. If we live in a world that pornography creates through the power of men in a male-dominated situation, the issue is not what the harm of pornography is, but how that harm is to become visible.

Obscenity law provides a very different analysis and conception of the problem of pornography. In 1973 the legal definition of obscenity became that which the average person, applying contemporary community standards, would find that, taken as a whole, appeals to the prurient interest; that which depicts or describes in a patently offensive way—you feel like you're a cop reading someone's *Miranda* rights—sexual conduct specifically defined by the applicable state law; and that which, taken as a whole, lacks serious literary, artistic, political or scientific value. Feminism doubts whether the average person gender-neutral exists; has more questions about the content and process of defining what community standards are than it does about deviations from them; wonders why prurience counts but powerlessness does not and why sensibilities are better protected from offense than women are from exploitation; defines sexuality, and thus its violation and expropriation, more broadly than does state law; and questions why a body of law that has not in practice been able to tell rape from intercourse should, without further guidance, be entrusted with telling pornography from anything less. Taking the work "as a whole" ignores that which the victims of pornography have long known: legitimate settings diminish the perception of injury done to those whose trivialization and objectification they contextualize. Besides, and this is a heavy one, if a woman is subjected, why should it matter that the work has other value? Maybe what redeems the work's value is what enhances its injury to women, not to mention that existing standards of literature, art, science, and politics, examined in a feminist light, are remarkably consonant with pornography's mode, meaning, and message. And finally—first and foremost, actually—although the subject of these materials is overwhelmingly women, their contents almost entirely made up of women's bodies, our invisibility has been such, our equation as a sex *with* sex has been such, that the law of obscenity has never even considered pornography a women's issue.

Obscenity, in this light, is a moral idea, an idea about judgments of good and bad. Pornography, by contrast, is a political practice, a practice of power and powerlessness. Obscenity is ideational and abstract; pornography is concrete and substantive. The two concepts represent two entirely different things. Nudity, excess of candor, arousal or excitement, prurient appeal, illegality of the acts depicted, and unnaturalness or perversion are all qualities that bother obscenity law when sex is depicted or portrayed. Sex forced on real women so that it can be sold at a profit and forced on other real women; women's bodies trussed and maimed and raped and made into things to be hurt and obtained and accessed, and this presented as the nature of women in a way that is acted on and acted out, over and over; the coercion that is visible and the coercion that has become invisible—this and more bothers feminists about pornography. Obscenity as such probably does little harm. Pornography is integral to attitudes and behaviors of violence and discrimination that define the treatment and status of half the population.

At the request of the city of Minneapolis, Andrea Dworkin and I conceived and designed a local human rights ordinance in accordance with our approach to the pornography issue. We define pornography as a practice of sex discrimination, a violation of women's civil rights, the opposite of sexual equality. Its point is to hold those who profit from and benefit from that injury accountable to those who are injured. It means that women's injury—our damage, our pain, our enforced inferiority—should outweigh their pleasure and their profits, or sex equality is meaningless.

We define pornography as the graphic sexually explicit subordination of women through pictures or words that also includes women dehumanized as sexual objects, things, or commodities; enjoying pain or humiliation or rape; being tied up, cut up, mutilated, bruised, or physically hurt; in postures of sexual submission or servility or display; reduced to body parts, penetrated by objects or animals, or presented in scenarios of degradation, injury, torture; shown as filthy or inferior; bleeding, bruised, or hurt in a context that makes these conditions sexual. Erotica, defined by distinction as not this, might be sexually explicit materials premised on equality. We also provide that the use of men, children, or transsexuals in the place of women is pornography. The definition is substantive in that it is sex-specific, but it covers everyone in a sex-specific way, so is gender neutral in overall design. . . .

This law aspires to guarantee women's rights consistent with the First Amendment by making visible a conflict of rights between the equality guaranteed to all women and what, in some legal sense, is now the freedom of the pornographers to make and sell, and their consumers to have access to, the materials this ordinance defines. Judicial resolution of this conflict, if the judges do for women what they have done for others, is likely to entail a balancing of the rights of women arguing that our lives and opportunities, including our freedom of speech and action, are constrained by—and in many cases flatly precluded by, in and through—pornography, against those who argue that the pornography is harmless, or harmful only in part but not in the whole of the definition; or that it is more important to preserve the pornography than it is to prevent or remedy whatever harm it does.

In predicting how a court would balance these interests, it is important to understand that this ordinance cannot now be said to be either conclusively legal or illegal under existing law or precedent, although I think the weight of authority is on our side. This ordinance enunciates a new form of the previously recognized governmental interest in sex equality. Many laws make sex equality a governmental interest. Our law is designed to further the equality of the sexes, to help make sex equality real. Pornography is a practice of discrimination on the basis of sex, on one level because of its role in creating and maintaining sex as a basis for discrimination. It harms many women one at a time and helps keep all women in an inferior status by defining our subordination as our sexuality and equating that with our gender. It is also sex discrimination because its victims, including men, are selected for victimization on the basis of their gender. But for their sex, they would not be so treated.

The harm of pornography, broadly speaking, is the harm of the civil inequality of the sexes made invisible as harm because it has become accepted as the sex difference. Consider this analogy with race: if you see Black people as different, there is no harm to segregation; it is merely a recognition of that difference. To neutral principles, separate but equal was equal. The injury of racial separation to Blacks arises "solely because [they] choose to put that construction upon it." Epistemologically translated: how you see it is not the way it is. Similarly, if you see women as just different, even or especially if you don't know that you do, subordination will not look like subordination at all, much less like harm. It will merely look like an appropriate recognition of the sex difference.

Pornography does treat the sexes differently, so the case for sex differentiation can be made here. But men as a group do not tend to be (although some individuals may be) treated the way women are treated in pornography. As a social group, men are not hurt by pornography the way women as a social group are. Their social status is not defined as *less* by it. So the major argument does not turn on mistaken differentiation, particularly since the treatment of women according to pornography's dictates makes it all too often accurate. The salient quality of a distinction between the top and the bottom in a hierarchy is not difference, although top is certainly different from bottom; it is power. So the major argument is: subordinate but equal is not equal.

Particularly since this is a new legal theory, a new law, and "new" facts, perhaps the situation of women it newly exposes deserves to be considered on its own terms. Why do the problems of 53 percent of the population have to look like somebody else's problems before they can be recognized as existing? Then, too, they can't be addressed if they do look like other people's problems, about which something might have to be done if something is done about these. This construction of the situation truly deserves inquiry. Limiting the justification for this law to the situation of the sexes would serve to limit the precedential value of a favorable ruling.

Its particularity to one side, the *approach* to the injury is supported by a whole array of prior decisions that have justified exceptions to First Amendment guarantees when something that matters is seen to be directly at stake. What unites many cases in which speech interests are raised and implicated but not, on balance, protected, is harm, harm that counts. In some existing exceptions, the definitions are much more open-ended than ours. In some the sanctions are more severe, or potentially more so. For instance, ours is a civil law; most others, although not all, are criminal. Almost no other exceptions show as many people directly affected. Evidence of harm in other cases tends to be vastly less concrete and more conjectural, which is not to say that there is necessarily less of it. None of the previous cases addresses a problem of this scope or magnitude—for instance, an eight-billion-dollar-a-year industry. Nor do other cases address an abuse that has such widespread legitimacy. Courts have seen harm in other cases. The question is, will they see it here, especially given that the pornographers got there first. I will confine myself here to arguing from cases on harm to people, on the supposition that, the pornographers notwithstanding, women are not flags. . . .

To reach the magnitude of this problem on the scale it exists, our law makes trafficking in pornography—production, sale, exhibition, or distribution—actionable. Under the obscenity rubric, much legal and psychological scholarship has centered on a search for the elusive link between harm and pornography defined as obscenity. Although they were not very clear on what obscenity was, it was its harm they truly could not find. They looked high and low—in the mind of the male consumer, in society or in its "moral fabric," in correlations between variations in levels of antisocial acts and liberalization of obscenity laws. The only harm they have found has been harm to "the social interest in order and morality." Until recently, no one looked very persistently for harm to women, particularly harm to women through men. The rather obvious fact that the sexes *relate* has been overlooked in the inquiry into the male consumer and his mind. The pornography doesn't just drop out of the sky, go into his head, and stop there. Specifically, men rape, batter, prostitute, molest, and sexually harass women. Under conditions of inequality, they also hire, fire, promote, and grade women, decide how much or whether we are worth paying and for what, define and approve and disapprove of women in ways that count, that determine our lives.

If women are not just born to be sexually used, the fact that we are seen and treated as though that is what we are born for becomes something in need of explanation. If we see that men relate to women in a pattern of who they see women as being, and that forms a pattern of inequality, it becomes important to ask where that view came from or, minimally, how it is perpetuated or escalated. Asking this requires asking different questions about pornography than the ones obscenity law made salient.

Now I'm going to talk about causality in its narrowest sense. Recent experimental research on pornography shows that the materials covered by our definition cause measurable harm to women through increasing men's attitudes and behaviors of discrimination in both violent and nonviolent forms. Exposure to some of the pornography in our definition increases the immediately subsequent willingness of normal men to aggress against women under laboratory conditions. It makes normal men more closely resemble convicted rapists attitudinally, although as a group they don't look all that different from them to start with. Exposure to pornography also significantly increases attitudinal measures known to correlate with rape and self-reports of aggressive acts, measures such as hostility toward women, propensity to rape, condoning rape, and predicting that one would rape or force sex on a woman if one knew one would not get caught. On this latter measure, by the way, about a third of all men predict that they would rape, and half would force sex on a woman.

As to that pornography covered by our definition in which normal research subjects seldom perceive violence, long-term exposure still makes them see women as more worthless, trivial, nonhuman, and objectlike, that is, the way those who are discriminated against are seen by those who discriminate against them. Crucially, all pornography by our definition acts dynamically over time to diminish the consumer's ability to distinguish sex from violence. The materials work behaviorally to diminish the capacity of men (but not women) to perceive that an account of a rape is an account of a rape. The so-called sex-only materials, those in which subjects perceive no force, also increase perceptions that a rape victim is worthless and decrease the perception that she was harmed. The overall direction of current research suggests that the more expressly violent materials accomplish with less exposure what the less overtly violent—that is, the so-called sex-only materials—accomplish over the longer term. Women are rendered fit for use and targeted for abuse. The only thing that the research cannot document is which individual women will be next on the list. (This cannot be documented experimentally because of ethics constraints on the researchers—constraints that do not operate in life.) Although the targeting is systematic on the basis of sex, for individuals it is random. They are selected on a roulette basis. Pornography can no longer be said to be just a mirror. It does not just reflect the world or some people's perceptions. It *moves* them. It increases attitudes that are lived out, circumscribing the status of half the population.

What the experimental data predict will happen actually does happen in women's real lives. You know, it's fairly frustrating that women have known for some time that these things do happen. As Ed Donnerstein, an experimental researcher in this area, often puts it, "We just quantify the obvious." It is women, primarily, to whom the research results have been the obvious, because we live them. But not until a laboratory study predicts that these things *will* happen do people begin to believe you when you say they *did* happen to you. There is no—*not any*—inconsistency between the patterns the laboratory studies predict and the data on what actually happens to real women. Show me an abuse of women in society, I'll show it to you made sex in the pornography. If you want to know who is being hurt in this society, go see what is being done and to whom in pornography and then go look for them other places in the world. You will find them being hurt in just that way. We did in our hearings.

In our hearings women spoke, to my knowledge for the first time in history in public, about the damage pornography does to them. We learned that pornography is used to break women, to train women to sexual submission, to season women, to terrorize women, and to silence their dissent. It is this that has previously been termed "having no effect." The way men inflict on women the sex they experience through the pornography gives women no choice about seeing the pornography or doing the sex. Asked if anyone ever tried to inflict unwanted sex acts on them that they knew came from pornography, 10 percent of women in a recent random study said yes. Among married women, 24 percent said yes. That is a lot of women. A lot more don't know. Some of those who do testified in Minneapolis. One wife said of her ex-husband, "He would read from the pornography like a textbook, like a journal. In fact when he asked me to be bound, when he finally convinced me to do it, he read in the magazine how to tie the knots." Another woman said of her boyfriend, "[H]e went to this party, saw pornography, got an erection, got me . . . to inflict his erection on. . . . There is a direct causal relationship there." One woman, who said her husband had rape and bondage magazines all over the house, discovered two suitcases full of Barbie dolls with rope tied on their arms and legs and with tape across their mouths. Now think about the silence of women. She said, "He used to tie me up and he tried those things on me." A therapist in private practice reported:

> Presently or recently I have worked with clients who have been sodomized by broom handles, forced to have sex with over 20 dogs in the back seat of their car, tied up and then electrocuted on their genitals. These are children, [all] in the ages of 14 to 18, all of whom [have been directly affected by pornography,] [e]ither where the perpetrator has read the manuals and manuscripts at night and used these as recipe books by day or had the pornography present at the time of the sexual violence.[1]

One woman, testifying that all the women in a group of exprostitutes were brought into prostitution as children through pornography, characterized their collective experience: "[I]n my experience there was not one situation where a client was not using pornography while he was using me or that he had not just watched pornography or that it was verbally referred to and directed me to pornography." "Men," she continued, "witness the abuse of women in pornography constantly and if they can't engage in that behavior with their wives, girl friends or children, they force a whore to do it."

Men also testified about how pornography hurts them. One young gay man who had seen *Playboy* and *Penthouse* as a child said of such heterosexual pornography: "It was one of the places I learned about sex and it showed me that sex was violence. What I saw there was a specific relationship between men and women. . . . [T]he woman was to be used, objectified, humiliated and hurt; the man was in a superior position, a position to be violent. In pornography I learned that what it meant to be sexual with a man or to be loved by a man was to accept his violence." For this reason, when he was battered by his first lover, which he described as "one of the most profoundly destructive experiences of my life," he accepted it.

Pornography also hurts men's capacity to relate to women. One young man spoke about this in a way that connects pornography—not the prohibition on pornography—with fascism. He spoke of his struggle to repudiate the thrill of dominance, of his difficulty finding connection with a woman to whom he is close. He said: "My point is that if women in a society filled by pornography must be wary for their physical selves, a man, even a man of good intentions, must be wary for his mind. . . . I do not want to be a mechanical, goose-stepping follower of the Playboy bunny, because that is what I think it is. . . . [T]hese are the experiments a master race perpetuates on those slated for extinction." The woman he lives with is Jewish. There was a very brutal rape near their house. She was afraid; she tried to joke. It didn't work. "She was still afraid. And just as a well-meaning German was afraid in 1933, I am also very much afraid."

Pornography stimulates and reinforces, it does not cathect or mirror, the connection between one-sided freely available sexual access to women and masculine sexual excitement and sexual satisfaction. The catharsis hypothesis is fantasy. The fantasy theory is fantasy. Reality is: pornography conditions male orgasm to female subordination. It tells men what sex means, what a real woman is, and codes them together in a way that is behaviorally reinforcing. This is a real five-dollar sentence, but I'm going to say it anyway: pornography is a set of hermeneutical equivalences that work on the epistemological level. Substantively, pornography defines the meaning of what a woman is seen to be by connecting access to her sexuality with masculinity through orgasm. What pornography means *is* what it does.

So far, opposition to our ordinance centers on the trafficking provision. This means not only that it is difficult to comprehend a group injury in a liberal culture—that what it *means* to be a woman is defined by this and that it is an injury for all women, even if not for all women equally. It is not only that the pornography has got to be accessible, which is the bottom line of virtually every objection to this law. It is also that power, as I said, is when you say something, it is taken for reality. If you talk about rape, it will be agreed that rape is awful. But rape is a conclusion. If a victim describes the facts of a rape, maybe she was asking for it or enjoyed it or at least consented to it, or the man might have thought she did, or maybe she had had sex before. It is now agreed that there is something wrong with sexual harassment. But describe what happened to you, and it may be trivial or personal or paranoid, or maybe you should have worn a bra that day. People are against discrimination. But describe the situation of a real woman, and they are not so sure she wasn't just unqualified. In law, all these disjunctions between women's perspective on our injuries and the standards we have to meet go under dignified legal rubrics like burden of proof, credibility, defenses, elements of the crime, and so on. These standards all contain a definition of what a woman is in terms of what sex is and the low value placed on us through it. They reduce injuries done to us to authentic expressions of who we are. Our silence is written all over them. So is the pornography.

We have as yet encountered comparatively little objection to the coercion, force, or assault provisions of our ordinance. I think that's partly because the people who make and approve laws may not yet see what they do as that. They *know* they use the pornography as we have described it in this law, and our law defines that, the reality of pornography, as a harm to women. If they suspect that they might on occasion engage in or benefit from coercion or force or assault, they may think that the victims won't be able to prove it—and they're right. Women who charge men with sexual abuse are not believed. The pornographic view of them is: they want it; they all want it. When women bring charges of sexual assault, motives such as venality or sexual repression must be invented, because we cannot really have been hurt. Under the trafficking provision, women's lack of credibility cannot be relied upon to negate the harm. There's no woman's story to destroy, no credibility-based decision on what happened. The hearings establish the harm. The definition sets the standard. The grounds of reality definition are authoritatively shifted. Pornography is bigotry, *period*. We are now—the world pornography has decisively defined—having to meet the burden of proving, once and for all, for all of the rape and torture and battery, all of the sexual harassment, all of the child sexual abuse, all of the forced prostitution, *all* of it that the pornography is part of and that is part of the pornography, that the harm *does happen* and that when it happens it looks like this. Which may be why all this evidence never seems to be enough.

It is worth considering what evidence has been enough when other harms involving other purported speech interests have been allowed to be legislated against. By comparison to our trafficking provision, analytically similar restrictions have been allowed under the First Amendment, with a legislative basis far less massive, detailed, concrete, and conclusive. Our statutory language is more ordinary, objective, and precise and covers a harm far narrower than the legislative record substantiates. Under *Miller*, obscenity was allowed to be made criminal in the name of the "danger of offending the sensibilities of unwilling recipients or exposure to juveniles." Under our law, we have direct evidence of harm, not just a conjectural danger, that unwilling women in considerable numbers are not simply offended in their sensibilities, but are violated in their persons and restricted in their options. Obscenity law also suggests that the applicable standard for legal adequacy in measuring such connections may not be statistical certainty. The Supreme Court has said that it is not their job to resolve empirical uncertainties that underlie state obscenity legislation. Rather, it is for them to determine whether a legislature could reasonably have determined that a connection might exist between the prohibited material and harm of a kind in which the state has legitimate interest. Equality should be such an area. The Supreme Court recently recognized that prevention of sexual exploitation and abuse of children is, in their words, "a governmental objective of surpassing importance." This might also be the case for sexual exploitation and abuse of women, although I think a civil remedy is initially more appropriate to the goal of empowering adult women than a criminal prohibition would be.

Other rubrics provide further support for the argument that this law is narrowly tailored to further a legitimate governmental interest consistent with the goals underlying the First Amendment. Exceptions to the First Amendment—you may have gathered from this—exist. The reason they exist is that the harm done by some speech outweighs its expressive value, if any. In our law a legislature recognizes that pornography, as defined and made actionable, undermines sex equality. One can say—and I have—that pornography is a causal factor in violations of women; one can also say that women will be violated so long as pornography exists; but one can also say simply that pornography violates women. Perhaps this is what the woman had in mind who testified at our hearings that for her the question is not just whether pornography causes violent acts to be perpetrated against some women. "Porn is already a violent act against women. It is our mothers, our daughters, our sisters, and our wives that are for sale for pocket change at the newsstands in this country." *Chaplinsky v. New Hampshire* recognized the ability to restrict as "fighting words" speech which, "by [its] very utterance inflicts injury." Perhaps the only reason that pornography has not been "fighting words"—in the sense of words that by their utterance tend to incite immediate breach of the peace—is that women have seldom fought back, yet.

Some concerns that are close to those of this ordinance underlie group libel laws, although the differences are equally important. In group libel law, as Justice Frankfurter's opinion in *Beauharnais* illustrates, it has been understood that an individual's treatment and alternatives in life may depend as much on the reputation of the group to which that person belongs as on their own merit. Not even a partial analogy can be made to group libel doctrine without examining the point made by Justice Brandeis and recently underlined by Larry Tribe: would more speech, rather than less, remedy the harm? In the end, the answer may be yes, but not under the abstract system of free speech, which only enhances the power of the pornographers while doing nothing substantively to guarantee the free speech of women, for which we need civil equality. The situation in which women presently find ourselves with respect to the pornography is one in which more *pornography* is inconsistent with rectifying or even counterbalancing its damage through speech, because so long as the pornography exists in the way it does there *will not be more speech by women*. Pornography strips and devastates women of credibility, from our accounts of sexual assault to our everyday reality of sexual subordination. We are stripped of authority and reduced and devalidated and silenced. Silenced here means that the purposes of the First Amendment, premised upon conditions presumed and promoted by protecting free speech, do not pertain to women because they are not our conditions. Consider them: individual self-fulfillment—how does pornography promote our individual self-fulfillment? How does sexual inequality even permit it? Even if she can form words, who listens to a woman with a penis in her mouth? Facilitating consensus—to the extent pornography does so, it does so one-sided by silencing protest over the injustice of sexual subordination. Participation in civic life—central to Professor Meiklejohn's theory—how does pornography enhance women's participation in civic life? Anyone who cannot walk down the street or even lie down in her own bed without keeping her eyes cast down and her body clenched against assault is unlikely to have much to say about the issues of the day, still less will she become Tolstoy. Facilitating change—*this law* facilitates the change that existing First Amendment theory had been used to throttle. Any system of freedom of expression that does not address a problem where the free speech of men silences the free speech of women, a real conflict between speech interests as well as between people, is not serious about securing freedom of expression in this country.

For those of you who still think pornography is only an idea, consider the possibility that obscenity law got one thing right. Pornography is more actlike than thoughtlike. The fact that pornography, in a feminist view, furthers the idea of the sexual inferiority of women, which is a political idea, doesn't make the pornography itself into a political idea. One can express the idea a practice embodies. That does not make the practice into an idea. Segregation expresses the idea of the inferiority of one group to another on the basis of race. That does not make segregation an idea. A sign that says "Whites Only" is only words. Is it therefore protected by the First Amendment? Is it not an act, a practice, of segregation because what it means is inseparable from what it does? *Law* is only words.

The issue here is whether the fact that words and pictures are the central link in the cycle of abuse will immunize that entire cycle, about which we cannot do anything without doing something about the pornography. As Justice Stewart said in *Ginsburg*, "When expression occurs in a setting where the capacity to make a choice is absent, government regulation of that expression may coexist with and *even implement* First Amendment guarantees." I would even go so far as to say that the pattern of evidence we have closely approaches Justice Douglas' requirement that "freedom of expression can be suppressed if, and to the extent that, it is so closely brigaded with illegal action as to be an inseparable part of it." Those of you who have been trying to separate the acts from the speech—that's an act, that's an act, there's a law against that act, regulate that act, don't touch the speech—notice here that the illegality of the acts involved doesn't mean that the speech that is "brigaded with" it *cannot* be regulated. This is when it *can* be.

I take one of two penultimate points from Andrea Dworkin, who has often said that pornography is not speech for women, it is the silence of women. Remember the mouth taped, the woman gagged, "Smile, I can get a lot of money for that." The smile is not her expression, it is her silence. It is not her expression not because it didn't happen, but because it *did* happen. The screams of the women in pornography are silence, like the screams of Kitty Genovese, whose plight was misinterpreted by some onlookers as a lovers' quarrel. The flat expressionless voice of the woman in the New Bedford gang rape, testifying, is silence. She was raped as men cheered and watched, as they do in and with the pornography. When women resist and men say, "Like this, you stupid bitch, here is how to do it" and shove their faces into the pornography, this "truth of sex" is the silence of women. When they say, "If you love me, you'll try," the enjoyment we fake, the enjoyment we learn is silence. Women who submit because there is more dignity in it than in losing the fight over and over live in silence. Having to sleep with your publisher or director to get access to what men call speech is silence. Being humiliated on the basis of your appearance, whether by approval or disapproval, because you have to look a certain way for a certain job, whether you get the job or not, is silence. The absence of a woman's voice, everywhere that it cannot be heard, is silence. And anyone who thinks that what women say in pornography is women's speech—the "Fuck me, do it to me, harder," all of that—has never heard the sound of a woman's voice.

The most basic assumption underlying First Amendment adjudication is that, socially, speech is free. The First Amendment says Congress shall not abridge the freedom of speech. Free speech, get it, *exists*. Those who wrote the First Amendment *had* speech—they wrote the Constitution. *Their* problem was to keep it free from the only power that realistically threatened it: the federal government. They designed the First Amendment to prevent government from constraining that which, if unconstrained by government, was free, meaning *accessible to them*. At the same time, we can't tell much about the intent of the framers with regard to the question of women's speech, because I don't think we crossed their minds. It is consistent with this analysis that their posture toward freedom of speech tends to presuppose that whole segments of the population are not systematically silenced socially, prior to government action. If everyone's power were equal to theirs, if this were a nonhierarchical society, that might make sense. But the place of pornography in the inequality of the sexes makes the assumption of equal power untrue.

This is a hard question. It involves risks. Classically, opposition to censorship has involved keeping government off the backs of people. Our law is about getting some people off the backs of other people. The risks that it will be misused have to be measured against the risks of the status quo. Women will never have that dignity, security, compensation that is the promise of equality so long as the pornography exists as it does now. The situation of women suggests that the urgent issue of our freedom of speech is not primarily the avoidance of state intervention as such, but getting affirmative access to speech for those to whom it has been denied.

NOTE

1. *Public Hearings on Ordinances to Add Pornography as Discrimination Against Women*, Committee on Governmental Operations, City Council, Minneapolis MN, December 12–13, 1983.

29

Pornography and Violence: What the "Experts" Really Say

LYNNE SEGAL

It is now conventional wisdom that there is overwhelming scientific evidence linking pornography with sexual violence. The link "is considerably stronger than that for cigarette smoking and cancer," *Everywoman* announces in its introduction to the transcript of the public hearings organized by Minneapolis City Council in 1983 to collect the latest evidence on pornography and sexual violence in support of proposals for new legislation against pornography, the Minneapolis Ordinance. (*Everywoman* 1988, 5) "I doubt that anybody disputes the data," the psychologist Edward Donnerstein, a leading figure in pornography research, breezily announces at these same hearings. (*Everywoman* 1988, 22) Well, anybody except himself, perhaps, and his fellow researchers, who, in their more scholarly writing, not only confess that their research on possible links between pornography and violence has been misunderstood and misused, but add that whether their laboratory experiments tell us anything at all "about real-world aggression, such as rape, is still a matter for considerable debate" (Donnerstein et al. 1987, 174). That debate, however, has not so much been opened up as closed down by much of the recent writing and activity around pornography.

This is not so surprising. Accompanying an ever greater and more chilling awareness of the extent and horror of men's violence against women and children, much of it sexual violence, pornography is becoming one of the most fiercely contested moral issues of our time—conceptually and politically. Traditionally defined as sexually explicit, and therefore obscene or lewd words or images intended to provoke sexual excitement, the term was first used in the 1860s to describe the photography of prostitutes. Today, however, there is immense disagreement over both its definition and its significance—such disagreement flowing inevitably from the contrasting political positions which exist around pornography. Before analysing the psychological research on the effects of pornography, therefore, we need to be clear about the competing political and moral arguments which feed into the debates.

The Politics of Pornography

It has become customary to separate out three distinct positions on pornography: *liberal, moral right* and *feminist.* The liberal position, manifest in the North American

From *Feminist Review,* no. 36 (1990):29–41. Reprinted by permission of the author.

Presidential Commission on pornography of 1970 or, in a more qualified way, in the parallel British *Williams Report* of 1979, offers a nonevaluative definition of pornography, as sexually explicit material designed for sexual arousal. It argues that there is no scientific evidence for pornography causing harm in society, and therefore no sound reasons for banning it. While pornography may offend many women and men, it brings harmless pleasure to others. The *Williams Report* aimed to limit the public display of pornography to protect those who might find it offensive. (We shall look into the justifications, if any, for such tolerance in a moment.)

The position of the moral right, of Mary Whitehouse and the Festival of Light, is outlined in the *Longford Report* of 1972, and defines pornography as representations of sex or violence removed from their proper social context, or "a symptom of preoccupation with sex which is unrelated to its purpose" (Longford 1972, 205). It sees pornography as a threat to traditional family values, arguing that sex exists for procreation and should be confined to marriage. In line with this approach, censorship in Britain during the 1950s and early 1960s was mainly directed towards nudity and premarital and extramarital sex. The moral right has also always sought to suppress information on birth control, abortion and sex education in schools. It has demanded rigid censorship of sexually explicit material designed for recreational consumption, particularly of so called "perverse" and homosexual imagery, claiming that it threatens family life and creates general social and moral decay.

This position has strengthened throughout the more conservative climate of the 1980s, assisted by sexual panics around AIDS. Under the Thatcher Government there has been an ever increasing, though piecemeal, tightening up of censorship legislation in line with moral conservatism. For example, the Local Government (Miscellaneous Provisions) Act of 1982, which provided guidelines to councils for controlling the licensing of "sex establishments" and their cinematic materials, replaced the *Williams Report's* emphasis on harm with condemnation of material intended to stimulate "sexual activity" or "acts of force or restraint which are associated with sexual activity" or that which portrays "genital organs or urinary or excretory functions." Two years later, the Video Recordings Act went further, again with stipulations not just against violence, but against explicit sexual images of genitalia, excretory functions and acts of sex (Merck 1988). The moral right, however, is the position least interested in whether psychological research offers evidence of links between pornography and violence, claiming as a fact of common sense that imagery or writing designed primarily for titillation is offensive and bound to contribute to sexual decadence and sex crimes.

Finally, there is the feminist critique of the sexism and exploitation of women represented in most pornographic material—which is also frequently racist. It is from *within* this position, however, that some of the most passionate battles have been waged in recent years. It is widely thought that feminists have uniformly understood pornography as offensive to women and an incitement to violence against them. And certainly, all feminists have seen the standard images of pornography as promoting and strengthening sexist images of women. In its heterosexual versions, reducing women to flesh—or bits of flesh—it celebrates the idea of men's insatiable sexual appetite and women's ubiquitous sexual availability. Defined and consumed by men, standard pornography would seem to mock feminist attempts to express a more women-centred sexuality.

In the 1970s, however, few feminists sought legal restrictions on pornography. The state and judiciary were seen as essentially patriarchal, and obscenity laws were known to have always served to suppress the work of those fighting for women's own control of their fertility and sexuality. Objecting to all forms of sexist representations, feminists set out to subvert a whole cultural landscape which, whether selling carpet sweepers, collecting census information or uncovering women's crotches, placed women as the subordinate sex. Representatively, Ruth Wallsgrove, then working for *Spare Rib*, declared in 1977, "I believe we should not agitate for more laws against pornography, but should rather stand up together and say what we feel about it, and what we feel about our own sexuality, and force men to re-examine their own attitudes to sex and women implicit in their consumption of porn" (Wallsgrove 1977, 65).

In Britain, however, a more single-minded focus on pornography as the root of male violence and therefore of male domination was becoming evident in feminist writings from the close of the 1970s. "Pornography" was redefined by many feminists as material which inevitably depicts violence against women, and is in itself the enactment of violence against women. It had been the popular writing of Susan Brownmiller (1975) and Robin Morgan (1978) in the mid-1970s which first made a definitive connection between pornography and male violence, generating the slogan: "Pornography is the Theory, Rape is the Practice." More recently, following through this logic to draft model legislation—the Minneapolis Ordinance—which would allow any individual to use the courts to ban pornographic material, U.S. feminists Andrea Dworkin and Catherine MacKinnon define pornography as "a systematic practice of exploitation and subordination based on sex that differentially harms women" (Chester and Dickey 1988, 258). Dworkin's *Pornography: Men Possessing Women* remains undoubtedly the single most influential feminist text on pornography. Here she argues that pornography is the ideology behind all forms of female oppression, indeed all forms of exploitation, murder and brutality throughout human history. Women can never be liberated until all pornography is banned (Dworkin 1981).

And yet, despite the growth and strength of the Western feminist antipornography movement during the 1980s, particularly in the United States and in Britain (where we have seen the emergence of the Campaign Against Pornography and a similar Campaign Against Pornography and Censorship), some feminists, myself included (represented in Britain by Feminists Against Censorship), passionately reject Dworkin's analysis, and its related feminist practice. They see it as a complete mistake to reduce the dominance of sexism and misogyny in our culture to sexuality and its representations. They believe men's cultural contempt for and sexualization of women long pre-dated the growth of commercial pornography, and is a product of the relative powerlessness of women as a sex. Narrowing the focus on women's subordination to pornography, they argue, downplays the sexism and misogyny at work within all of our most respectable social institutions and practices, whether judicial, legal, familial, occupational, religious, scientific or cultural.

More dangerously (in today's conservative political climate), they fear that the evolving exploration by women of their own sexuality and pleasure is put at risk by forming alliances with—instead of combating—the conservative antipornography crusade (alliances which Dworkin and MacKinnon have unhesitatingly pursued in the U.S. despite being opposed by some of the most well-established feminist writers and groups working and campaigning around women's sexuality, like Adrienne Rich and the Boston Women's Health Group Collective). Blanket condemnation of pornography, they stress, discourages women from facing up to their own sexual fears and infantile fantasies, which are by no means free from the guilt, anxiety, shame, contradiction, as well as the eroticization of power on display in men's pornographic productions. What women need, according to feminists opposed to antipornography crusades, is not more censorship but more sexually explicit material produced by and for women, more open and honest discussion of all sexual issues, alongside the struggle against women's general subordinate economic and social status.

Early Research on Pornography and Its Effects

So these are currently the *four* (rather than three) distinct political positions on pornography. Which one, if any, does psychological research support? Interestingly, the liberal arguments behind the relaxations on censorship which occurred in the U.S. and Britain in the 1970s were based almost entirely upon psychological research, or what was seen as scientific evidence. There had been little systematic study of the effects of pornography before the U.S. Commission on Obscenity and Pornography of 1970, which was set up partly in order to undertake new research, as well as to report on existing research. The studies conducted at this time, each and every one of them, supported the view that pornography had no harmful effects on its consumers.

There can be few things more contested, even from within its own theoretical framework, than the relevance of the controlled and contrived social psychological experiment in the laboratory to human action in the world at large. However, it was and is from such research that many of the conclusions of policy-makers and campaigners around pornography have been and are still drawn. Considering the impact of pornographic material on sexual arousal and behaviour, the studies of the 1970s reported that a large proportion of adult males and females did find sexually explicit material arousing; men tended to appear more aroused by films and photographs, women by written material. Heterosexual people were more aroused by heterosexual material, and homosexual males by homosexual material. Despite repeated exposure to slides showing highly "deviant" sexual activity, subjects showed no tendency to copy such practices, that is, there were no changes in subjects' own customary sexual practices. (Those happily enjoying missionary sex remained untempted by titillating representations of its alternatives!) Those with less guilt, and more liberal attitudes around sexuality, found pornographic material more arousing. The greater the exposure to sexually arousing material, however, the less the arousal. And the greater the exposure to such material, the more liberal and tolerant of it consumers became. These studies thus reported *no* antisocial changes in sexual behaviour after short- or long-term exposure to sexually explicit material (Lamberth 1970; Davis and Braucht 1970; Mann et al. 1970; Kutchinsky 1973; and Mosher 1970). At this time, only one study was done on the effects of exposure to erotica on aggressive behaviour (willingness of a person to administer electric shock to another person). This study by Tannenbaum found that exposure to highly arousing erotica did lead to increased shock levels being administered to another person (the experimenter's stooge or "confederate") who had earlier angered the subject (in Donnerstein et al. 1987). However, illustrating the ambiguity of the experimental data, Tannenbaum found that the same material also led to more *positive* behaviour towards the stooge, if the previous interaction had been friendly.

Other studies undertaken by this Commission also supported the liberal position on pornography. Those investigating the connections between pornography and sex crimes in the U.S., for example, reported no correlation between pornographic consumption and juvenile crimes in general, while studies of convicted rapists found them to have had *less* exposure to pornography during adolescence, and also less recent exposure to pornography than the control group (Goldstein et al. 1970; Johnson et al. 1970). (Interestingly, and tellingly for later reports to the Minneapolis hearings from people working with sex offenders, the rapists themselves were nevertheless inclined to claim that pornography was connected with their crime.) The empirical research by Kutchin-sky (1973) from Copenhagen in Denmark, which had removed all legal prohibitions between 1967 and 1969, similarly reported a *negative* correlation between access to pornography and sex crimes. The quite significant reductions in sex-crimes reported over that same period convinced the Committee that access to pornography did not increase the rate of sexual crimes. Subsequent work (Kant and Goldstein 1978) also confirmed that sex offenders had less exposure to pornography, both as teenagers and as adults. (Although it does not invalidate these findings, we do, however, need to take into account the problem that rape is very often not reported and rapists—especially if they are white and apparently "respectable"—very often escape conviction. This means that the rapists who are reported and successfully convicted are only a minority of rapists, and may be an atypical minority.)

The psychological and sociological research of the late sixties and early seventies which, by and large, concluded that there was no connection between pornographic consumption and either change in sexual practices or an increase in sexual violence, however, was always rejected as irrelevant by the moral right in both the U.S. and Britain. (As U.S. newspaper columnist James Kilpatrick declared [in Donnerstein et al. 1987, 1]: "Common sense is a better guide than laboratory experiments; and common sense tells us pornography is bound to contribute to sexual crime. . . . It seems ludicrous to argue 'bad' books do not promote bad behaviour." No wonder there is so much bad behaviour around!) More significantly, in terms of subsequent research, these studies were conducted just before the emergence of the feminist critique of pornography: in the beginning stressing its significance as part of our culture of sexism and misogyny; later, for some, stressing its role in directly causing violence against women, in being in itself violence against women. On the latter view, pornography becomes *the* source of myths about women's sexuality, teaching men that women enjoy being raped or sexually coerced. This feminist critique has helped to spark off the new psychological research which is currently being used by those seeking new legal restrictions around pornography.

Updating the Research on Pornography

Whereas in the 1960s and early 1970s studies of pornography had been concerned to look at the effects of pornography, seen as sexually explicit material, on men's sexual or antisocial behaviour, by the late seventies the emphasis has shifted to the more specific study of men's violence against women. Feminists could indeed rightly claim it as a victory, as Mandy Merck (unpublished) suggests, that whereas once the concern about pornography was primarily over its effects upon those who consume it, today the concern has shifted to its effects upon those represented by it. Another reason for the shift in concern, however, was the assumption, encouraged by feminist writing like that of Dworkin, that pornography had become more violent. In fact, although this was repeated throughout the Minneapolis Commission, there is little evidence of this. One study (Malamuth and Spinner 1980) found that violent images in *Playboy* and *Penthouse* had increased from 1 percent to 5 percent between 1973 and 1977. But a more recent U.S. study (Scott 1985) on such imagery in *Playboy* between 1954 and 1983 found a *decline* from 1977, with well under 1 percent of material containing violent imagery. Nor was there any increase in violent sexual imagery in adult videos, in another U.S. study covering the years 1979–1983 (Donnerstein et al., 1987). However, while it may be a myth that violent imagery in pornography has in fact been increasing, experiments on its possible effects have undoubtedly been increasing. The best summary of this newer research can be found in Donnerstein, Linz and Penrod, *The Question of Pornography: Research Findings and Policy Implications* (1987).

In this book, the authors distinguish different types of pornography in order to detect its effects. First of all, they report a multitude of laboratory experiments following exposure to *nonviolent* pornographic material. Here, like the earlier research of the 1970s, they fail to find any increase in men's aggressive, or general antisocial behaviour—either towards other men or against women. Indeed some of the experiments suggested that exposure to nonviolent pornography increases subjects' sociability and decreases their level of aggression, measured, for example, by their willingness to reward a confederate of the experimenter (with money) after such exposure, and their failure to increase their aggressiveness when angered after viewing erotica. Nor did exposure to this type of pornography alter subject attitudes towards rape.

Next, they look at the research on what they define as nonviolent but degrading images of women (depictions of women as sexually promiscuous and insatiable, even in the face of men's callousness and contempt). For example, Check in 1985 showed male subjects a film clip of a woman doctor being verbally abused and sexually harassed by a male, who, once she catches sight of his penis, is desperately eager for, and enjoys, instant sex. Following such exposure, Check claimed subjects were more likely to say that they might commit rape—if they could get away with it. Linz, on the other hand, also in 1985, found that subjects watching a similar film narrative, *Debbie Does Dallas*, but seeing it in its entirety rather than in brief excerpts, exhibited no significant increase in their acceptance of calloused attitudes about rape, nor any increased likelihood to view women as sexual objects or to condone the actions of rapists and judge the victim of rape narratives as more responsible for their own assault (in Donnerstein et al. 1987). Donnerstein, Linz and Penrod therefore argue that no definite conclusions can be drawn about nonviolent but degrading images of women.

Their main concern, however, is to explore the effects of violent pornography. Here they conclude, drawing on their own research and that of Malamuth, Check, and others, that exposure to violent pornography (for example depictions of rape) does increase sexual arousal in some men, especially if the victim is shown as "enjoying" the rape. And a few subjects, those who say that they might commit a rape if they could get away with it, show the same arousal, even when the victim is seen to be suffering. Some researchers suggest, therefore, that arousal to sadistic material might provide a good predictor of men's proclivity to rape. (Quite what would be said about women's frequent arousal to masochistic and rape fantasies is not clear, given women's rather low levels of known rape behaviour. But we are in the laboratory here, where troublesome knowledge can be safely ignored as unscientific.)

The main finding which Donnerstein, Linz and Penrod wish to emphasize is that exposure to aggressive pornography does not only *titillate* men (though in fact the main finding from their research was that the great majority of men *dislike* sadistic pornography), but also that it *can*, in some cases, in certain circumstances, alter certain men's attitudes and behaviour towards women. That is, it can produce more calloused attitudes towards women and greater acceptance of rape myths which downplay or dismiss the significance of rape. Thus, Malamuth and Donnerstein report that exposing male college students to sexually violent films in which a woman is raped but also portrayed as "enjoying" it causes subjects, who have also been provoked by insults from a female "confederate" of the experimenter, to score higher on a Rape Acceptance Scale

(Donnerstein et al. 1987). From other experiments which asked men if they might commit rape if guaranteed they would not be caught, Malamuth and Check suggested that the negative effects they reported from exposure to violent pornography may only occur if men are already predisposed to consider sexual violence towards women. Donnerstein, Linz and Penrod therefore conclude that the calloused attitudes to rape, which may in certain cases follow exposure to violent pornography in certain men, may not so much be *caused* by the exposure to pornography, as strengthened by it (1987).

They further suggest, from experiments using imagery which is not sexually explicit but involves violence against women, that it is the violence, rather than the sexual explicitness, which is mainly responsible for any increase in aggressiveness and more calloused attitudes in men following exposure to violent pornography. And this in turn means, as they indicate, that material which is not pornographic at all—from soap operas to popular commercially released films—but which contains violence against women, may be more of a problem than most pornography. Their aim is, of course, as they say, to emphasize the need to educate consumers about the effects of sexual violence and violence in general in the media.

Psychologists Fall Out over Experimental Research

There are problems, however, even with the limited conclusions Donnerstein, Linz and Penrod draw from their survey of recent research—some of which the authors themselves admit. Indeed they now, rather disingenuously, criticize the uses to which their research has been put by Dworkin and MacKinnon in submissions to the U.S. Meese Commission on Pornography of 1986, attempting to enact new sorts of antipornography legislation, like the Minneapolis Ordinance: "It seems to us that the legal recommendations made by the commission for strengthening obscenity laws do not follow from the data" (Donnerstein et al. 1987, 178). (This is interpreted by *Everywoman* and the antipornography campaigners as evidence that Donnerstein has "changed sides and now works for the pornography publishers and producers"! *Everywoman* 1988, 5).

The problems with the psychological research, as many others have noted, derive first of all from the intrinsic weaknesses of all laboratory experiments in social psychology. The highly artificial conditions in which psychologists produce their results may not involve behaviour which is in any way generalizable. So, for instance, the tests of arousal have been criticized by Canadian psychologist Thelma McCormack because the subjects' own reports of sexual arousal may be unreliable, and the apparatus used to measure tumescense (expansion of the penis) may itself stimulate arousal (McCormack 1985b). There is the additional problem of the failure of these researchers even to consider the complex question of the relationship between fantasy and reality, between psychic arousal and behaviour. They assume some direct causal relation between arousal to sado-masochistic fantasy and the seeking out of such engagements in reality, when we know for instance from the surveys of Nancy Friday, Shere Hite and Thelma McCormack (if not our own experience), that such fantasy is commonly used by both women and men to enhance sexual arousal—particularly masochistic fantasy (Friday 1973; Hite 1976; McCormack 1985b). It would be absurd to suggest that most of us therefore condone the existence of rape, let alone that we desire to be raped. So arousal to sexual fantasy would seem, contrary to the expectations of these psychologists, to be a very poor predictor of behaviour.

Similarly, the measures for increases in violent behaviour following exposure to violent pornography produced in the laboratory may also have little correspondence with subjects actual likelihood to resort to real violence outside it. The measure used is most often the subject's willingness to act in complicity with the experimenter in apparently delivering an electric shock to the experimenter's "confederate" for failure in some task, usually after having, as well, been provoked in some way by this same confederate. But the validity of this test of aggressive behaviour would depend upon the laboratory behaviour having the same *meaning* for the subject as aggression in other situations—which seems most unlikely. (Even Donnerstein, Linz and Penrod now admit, as I have already indicated, that laboratory "aggression" may be unrepresentative of aggressive behaviour outside the laboratory.) There is also the danger, as in all psychological experiments, that subjects may "wise up to the game," attempting to guess and confirm the experimenter's hypotheses—this is the now well-known "experimenter demand effect." The extremely simplified and totally artificial nature of these experiments would seem to cast doubt on their usefulness in considering the shifting and complex meanings attached to events and behaviour in real life. Donnerstein, Linz and Penrod (1987), for example, report that if, following exposure to rape narratives where the victim was depicted as "enjoying" the rape, experimenters debriefed the subjects afterwards by pointing out that of course rape was always a terrible thing, then not only did subjects *not* show increased acceptance of rape myths or greater callousness towards women, but instead they displayed greater sensitivity about sexist material and a heightened *rejection* of rape myths. This effect, moreover, continued even many months after the original exposure to violent pornography followed by the debriefing.

As I have already mentioned, it is also the case—perhaps surprisingly—that the main findings of these recent experiments around men's reaction to depictions of sexual cruelty is one of anxiety and depression, or revulsion rather than of arousal (whether self-report or tumescence is the data being recorded). And in the small number of cases where arousal to sexual violence *is* reported, Donnerstein and Malamuth themselves now admit that they are not quite sure how to interpret their positive finding (Donnerstein et al. 1987). The psychologist Sherif points out, for example, that these experimenters always assume that any male arousal must occur through the subject's identification with the male aggressor, when of course it could be that the subject was identifying with the female victim (Sherif 1980). For all these reasons, it is less than clear that the recent experiments on violent pornography can establish that access to such material does in fact cause greater violence against women. The most any of the experiments can claim, as U.S. psychiatrist Martha Kirkpatrick succinctly summarizes, "is an extremely weak effect in a very few people under carefully controlled clinical settings" (quoted in Donnerstein et al. 1987, 10). Indeed, Donnerstein and his colleagues confess: "To date, no one has conducted a study that examines adults who have been exposed to media violence for prolonged periods outside the laboratory in order to determine if there is an increase in aggressive behaviour" (1987, 65).

However, although it is not really possible to demonstrate a causal relationship between the consumption of violent pornography and men's violence against women, we can certainly claim that such material is a significant part of the general sexist, racist and misogynist climate and culture of our times. It is therefore legitimate and necessary to engage in criticism of it. But in objecting to sexism, racism and misogyny, should we not tackle *all* sexist and racist representations of women, rather than reduce these to the explicitly sexual and call upon what are probably spurious connections between pornography and violent behaviour? We are ubiquitously surrounded by images which confirm women as passive, fetishized objects for male consumption, and which work to deny weakness, passivity or any type of "femininity" in men. Pornography is far from unique in its endorsement of myths of women's desire for the brute. They abound in more "respectable" discourses and images (whether expressed in the popular writing of psychological scholars and therapists like Anthony Storr (1970), or consumed daily in the massive romantic fiction market, this time a multimillion-dollar industry produced by women for women).

As I argue in *Is the Future Female? Troubled Thoughts on Contemporary Feminism* (1987) and *Slow Motion: Changing Masculinities, Changing Men* (1990), if the feminist rejection of pornography is to be more than the projection and denial of our own anxiety and confusion about sex, we need to look more critically upon, and create our own alternatives of, all forms of representation and media production. The offensive codes and meanings of pornography—if less overt—are nevertheless clearly present in them all. (This has been neatly illustrated in Coward 1982.) Feminist campaigns focused solely upon pornography cannot pursue this wider goal. Indeed, insofar as they seek increased legal restrictions upon explicitly sexual representations, they are likely to distort and undermine such objectives, strengthening the moral right which would seek to ban feminist, lesbian and gay erotica. (Dworkin herself, like many feminist antipornography campaigners, is adamant that "erotica simply means pornography for intellectuals," and has no intention of condoning, let alone encouraging, women's own production of erotica.)

Antipornography campaigns—feminist or not—will mobilize today as they invariably did before, centuries of guilt and anxiety around sex, as well as lifetimes of confusion and contradiction in our personal experiences of sexual arousal and activity. In contrast, campaigns which get to the heart of men's violence and sadism towards women must draw upon the widest possible resources to empower all women to embrace only those types of sexual encounters they choose, and to explore openly all the interests and pleasures, as well as the problems, which titillate and/or trouble them. We will get little help from the "experts," or any of their psychological research, here.

SECTION 2

Changing Our Minds: Toward Nonviolence in Gender Relations

In previous sections we have explored the roots and the context of gender violence as well as the various forms that comprise its practice. We used pornography as one example of the contested nature of gender violence. Though there is no consensus as to the complete range of phenomena that constitute gender violence, that should not preclude our investigation of change. In this closing section, we address the possibility of change toward a future of nonviolence in gender relations.

Making Change Possible

What will it take to diminish or end gender violence? Perhaps if we learn the lessons of the history of gender violence, and how such violence relates to political and social structures, we can choose to create alternative institutional and interpersonal patterns. Even then, we will need to understand how gendered social structures of inequality contribute to gendered expectations and social scripts, which in turn contain the blueprint for violence. First, we must work to make the invisible visible. We must understand how gender operates as a hidden system that supports and reproduces inequities and abuses. As long as gender exists as a system of "omnipresent yet partly hidden plans" (Griffin 1992) we will be ignorant of its excesses and dangers. We must inspect how masculinities and femininities are constructed and parse out the results of building rigidly defined systems of identity. The ceremonies that shape manhood from boyhood should come under scrutiny; the voices of men who have resisted or been excluded could serve as possible guides. Women's voices, which express the experience of patriarchy from the vantage point of its margins, must be placed at the center. We must understand how the oppositional nature of gendered identity places actual people in opposition to each other; how a discourse and practice of male/female disparity makes us unknowable, strange, and other as gendered beings, and how that otherness contributes to violence. At the same time we must continue to explore the specificity of maleness and femaleness; to understand how difference is practiced in the lives of men and women, and how to move beyond conceptions of otherness fraught with hostility and fear.

We need to scrutinize socialization practices that force a dichotomization of the "male" and "female" qualities embodied by men and women, as well as to analyze the role of our group identity as men and women. As we begin to understand the coerced nature of dichotomous gender systems, their effect on the individual's propensity for aggression and passivity will become clearer. While it is imperative that we work to restructure systems that uphold and maintain gender violence, global solutions cannot take place without the action of individuals; and no individual can take responsibility for altering an entire system. We need to start from the parameters of our lives and search for the contributions we can make from there. Each small change will contribute to solutions.

Our relationship to violence must be acknowledged and understood. Violence is advocated in our culture as "the normal, appropriate and necessary behavior of power and control" (Ewing 1982, 7), and its practice is gendered. Through the advocacy of violence as an effective form of behavior, men are permitted to abuse women and other men. This is true whether they take advantage of that permission or not.

Because changes in gender relations will take many forms and be precipitated by many causes, each of us must become familiar with how the interpersonal and the institutional connect. While we are no doubt endowed with will and the ability to choose action, we are at the same time influenced in our desires and our choices by the traditions of the past, the shape of contemporary institutions such as religion, education, and family, and the expectations attendant on our biological sex. Although change can develop in each of these areas, the most far-reaching and effective changes will combine both the personal and the institutional.

Signs of Change

The Violence Against Women Act, signed into law in 1994, is the first U.S. federal law to address gender-based crimes through $1.6 billion in support for police, prosecution, and victim services. Authored by Senator Joseph Biden of Delaware, the Violence Against Women Act acknowledges the need for comprehensive governmental response to supplement laws at the local level. The new federal law provides additional protections for victims of violence, including the provision that states must reciprocally honor civil protection orders limiting contact between abusers and victims. Perhaps the most far-reaching aspect of the new law is that it recognizes violence against women as gender-bias crime, acknowledging that acts of violence against women discriminate against women as a class.

The international dialogue among women has become an important factor in forcing governments to pay attention to problems to which they have, both overtly and covertly, contributed. Gender violence occupied a significant position on the agenda at the 1995 Global Conference on Women in Beijing, China. Topics ranging from control of reproductive capacity to domestic violence to rape and sexual abuse within the context of war were addressed as urgent issues concerning women from all over the world. The conference resolutions are beginning to force governments around the world to acknowledge and reform policies and practices that have supported gender violence. For example, following the conference in Beijing, the United Nations Development Fund for Women (UNIFEM) launched an international campaign calling on governments to devise national plans of action to eradicate violence against women. The UNIFEM initiative calls on the United Nations to make additional financial resources available to a Special Rapporteur on Violence Against Women, a position which can monitor the actions of governments worldwide. By 1996 the impetus of the Beijing conference sparked several follow-up events, including a satellite conference under the auspices of

President Clinton to discuss the U.S. plans to implement the Beijing Platform for Action and meetings of five Arab nations (Jordan, Palestine, Lebanon, Syria, and Yemen) to develop regional plans of action.

In the summer of 1996 the International Criminal Tribunal in the Hague, responsible for investigating Bosnian war crimes, announced several indictments for rape. For the first time in history sexual assaults are to be treated separately as war crimes. Organized rape in time of war is now understood to be a crime against humanity (Simons 1996).

At the same time that events such as the Global Conference on Women, the implementation of the Violence Against Women Act, and the International Criminal Tribunal's recognition of rape as a war crime inspire hope for the future, we should recognize that, due to increased public scrutiny, much sexual violence and exploitation has been forced underground. There is evidence that abuses that were once practiced openly and with impunity are now done more subtly. The conditions that encourage and support gender violence are entrenched, and efforts to alter them face tremendous resistance. Piecemeal solutions may correct—or appear to correct—specific problems, but they will not effectively change the social context that permits the abuses to flourish. We can be heartened when influential institutions, such as the American Medical Association, acknowledge that sexual assault and domestic violence imperil the physical and emotional well-being of Americans; yet we must be wary of how such a position will be interpreted in policy and practice (American Medical Association 1995, 1992).

Like any book, this one has been limited by space constraints to what we see as the most virulent and established forms of gender violence. We would like to encourage the reader to use this book as a starting point. If we are to work towards ending gender violence, it is not enough simply to inform ourselves about the facts and occurrences of gender violence, or about the historical, philosophical, cultural, and interpersonal conditions that encourage and permit it. We must go on to learn about the conditions that make gender violence *impossible.*

Contributions to This Section

The chapters that follow comprise a few of the many voices that have offered visions and plans for a more peaceful future. The suggestions presented by the authors range from research strategies and policy initiatives to altered forms of language and new patterns of conciousness. It is our intention that these voices not stand alone. We envision strands of a web that connect the disparate views, which, woven together, comprise in their substance and the interstices between them a greater understanding of how we can end gender violence.

In "Beyond the Masculine Mystique," Myriam Miedzian challenges us to utilize the knowledge and means at our disposal to end increasing male violence. The author points to a number of current social conditions that encourage the development of a culture of violence expressed through a tough and unyielding masculinity. Despite her despair about the expanding effects of a culture of violence, Miedzian offers a compelling blueprint for change. With a foundation of shared knowledge between disciplines, the author makes claims about the development of human behavior that point to a tremendous capacity for empathy, nurturance, and altruism. The potential for developing and encouraging these human characteristics, according to Miedzian, can be used to reshape policies and practices aimed at stemming the rising tide of male violence.

Christine Alder explores the connections between economic and political conditions and the occurrence of violence. In "Violence, Gender, and Social Change," Alder exhorts us to explore the effects of technological advancement on the structure of the labor market and its relation to social class and race. She points out that although it has been recognized for some time that violent crime is committed almost exclusively by men, researchers have not adequately focused on the shaping of maleness or masculinity. She also claims that violence is strongly correlated with economic deprivation and marginality, which in turn is compounded by racial inequality.

Alder claims that where one form of violence is legitimated, other forms will be tolerated. To reduce violent crimes against women, Alder asserts, we must address social inequalities and the practices of groups that have traditionally been protected from criminal prosecution.

In her newly revised article, "Violence against Women or Family Violence? Current Debates and Future Directions," Demie Kurz reminds us that the answers to the questions we ask about gender violence are shaped by the questions themselves. The author cautions us to build research on an understanding of the norms and practices of male dominance. She suggests that through an understanding of male/female dynamics and family power structures within a context of dominance, we will be able to develop policies that truly address the needs of abused women. Development of a cross-cultural body of knowledge, Kurz asserts, will allow us to comprehend the various practices of male dominance and violence, and will provide us with useful models as we attempt to develop more equitable relations between men and women.

In "Pornography and the Alienation of Male Sexuality," Harry Brod argues that pornography has a detrimental effect on male sexuality. The author asserts that while patriarchy clearly operates to the advantage of men over women, one of its contradictions as an oppressive system is that it also disadvantages the group it privileges. By raising awareness of the damage that pornography does to both women and men, Brod hopes to engage men to work against it.

Brod's conclusions produce an array of possibilities. He suggests that we look to laws regarding business ethics, rather than the traditional free speech or civil liberties arenas, to argue for restrictions to pornography. If pornography was viewed as a consumer product, civil litigation for consumer safety could become an effective tool in curbing sexually exploitative material. At the very least, Brod argues for an approach that emphasizes the personal advantages to men of applying a feminist analysis to their own lives and experiences. This, he feels, will motivate men to work in cooperation with feminist women against the dangers of pornography.

In his article "The Reality of Linguistic Violence against Women," William Gay argues that sexist language contributes to a cultural practice of gender violence. The author places sexist language within a concept of violence as an instrument in achieving power and control over others. Gay perceives language as contributing to sexism, racism, and heterosexism; it does harm through perpetuating systems of oppression. Gay asserts that feminist criticism has exposed connections between sexist use of language and oppression and has offered alternative models that contribute to an effort to reduce cultural violence. In Gay's view, changing our use of sexist language precedes a change of consciousness, ultimately leading to a reduction in violence.

In "Action," Elizabeth Ward's focus on "Father–Daughter" rape encompasses not only incest, but all sexual abuses of female children that are made possible under a patriarchal social system. Ward sees imagination as the catalyst for a future free of gender violence. Change is a process that begins with conceptualization followed by creative action. Each change will make possible new concepts for change as yet unimaginable.

Ward's agenda for envisioning and creating a future free of sexual violence begins with the healing power and strength of women's shared identity. Ward rejects the false neutrality of objectivity and calls instead for passionate validation of women's experiences as a foundation for policies that are not rooted in the patriarchal status quo. The author claims that rape ideology will be destroyed through a revolutionary process in which naming will enable the birth of new concepts. Women will claim their rights from a new position of conceptualizing their experience, and men will have a new means to reflect on and comprehend their actions.

These voices contribute to the search for an answer to the riddle of gender violence. It is likely that there are many answers, or at least many parts to the answer. It is too simplistic to imagine that there is only one possible resolution to such a multifaceted and complex problem. Indeed, it is the thesis of this book that we must understand the works of many people, across many disciplines, in order to comprehend the nature and scope of gender violence, as well as its resolutions.

Suggestions for Further Reading

Emilie Buchwald, Pamela R. Fletcher, and Martha Ross, *Transforming a Rape Culture* (Minneapolis: Milkweed Editions, 1993).

Rus Ervin Funk, *Stopping Rape: A Challenge for Men* (Philadelphia: New Society Publishers, 1993).

Charlotte Perkins Gilman, *Herland* (New York: Pantheon, 1979).

Susan Griffin, *A Chorus of Stones* (New York: Doubleday, 1992).

Marge Piercy, *Woman on the Edge of Time* (New York: Knopf, 1976).

Lynn Segal, *Slow Motion: Changing Masculinities, Changing Men* (New Brunswick, NJ: Rutgers University Press, 1990).

Margaret Schuler (ed.), *Freedom from Violence: Women's Strategies from around the World* (New York: UNICEF, 1992).

John Stoltenberg, *Refusing to Be a Man: Essays on Sex and Justice* (Portland OR: Breitenbush Books, 1989).

30

Beyond the Masculine Mystique

MYRIAM MIEDZIAN

Between 1960 and 1995 homicide rates have more than doubled in the U.S. In recent years the violence has become increasingly haphazard, senseless, and committed by younger and younger perpetrators—between 1985 and 1995 there has been an increase of over 200 percent in the arrest of fifteen-year-old boys alone for murder. Between late July and mid-October 1990, eight children fourteen years old or younger were killed by random gunfire in New York City. "Your Sneakers or Your Life" is the title of the cover story on the May 13, 1990, issue of *Sports Illustrated.* The article describes how an increasing number of boys mug or murder their peers in order to get a pair of expensive sneakers or a coveted jacket bearing sports insignia. In Dallas, Texas, when ten current and former high school athletes were sentenced to prison for armed robbery, it turned out that their motives included "extra money for prom night" and "trips to an amusement park, food and athletic shoes." [1]

One would think that in light of this further escalation, every effort would be made to socialize boys so as to decrease violence. But this is not the case.

The atavistic values of the masculine mystique continue to be reinforced in most areas of entertainment, as well as in some sports.

Not only are fathers not being encouraged to play a major role in nurturant child-rearing, thus denying their sons nonviolent, caring masculine role models, but many boys are being deprived of adequate mothering. Most working mothers must conform to a marketplace designed for men with homemaker wives. This leaves millions of children unattended and emotionally deprived—a good breeding ground for anger and violence. Inadequate day care compounds the situation. Divorce leaves many women impoverished and makes child-rearing even more difficult for them. In the last forty years there has been a sixfold increase in the percentage of women giving birth who are unmarried. Very little is being done to change this or to encourage divorced or unmarried fathers to remain involved with and financially responsible for their children. With all due respect to *The Cosby Show* and a few other exceptions, the primary images of manhood projected by the media and reinforced by toy manufacturers have nothing to do with being a loving, nurturant father.

The increase in children deprived of fathering, the crisis in child care, and the creation of a culture of violence have gone hand in hand with a breakdown of moral values that emphasized personal and social responsibility, caring for and respecting others. While these values were seen as operating mainly in the personal realm—women guarded them and transmitted them to children while men went out into the "dog eat dog" world to earn a living—they did have some tempering effect on the world of men. Bribery and money scandals are nothing new, but they have reached new heights in recent years both on Wall Street and in government.

Prep school boys and high school football players who go on robbery sprees when they need some extra money are a recent phenomenon, as are high school boys who kill a classmate to see what it feels like.

Men who value money and power above all think nothing of hiring six-year-olds to help them sell drugs, or machine-gunning their rivals in drug wars that often take the lives of innocent bystanders as well.

The situation is aggravated by the ready availability of almost any weapon imaginable to boys and men who are raised to be violent. With two hundred million guns and seventy million gun owners in the United States, our current situation is analogous to making matches easily available to known pyromaniacs. This availability of weapons is facilitated by many men who seem to experience any form of gun control as emasculating.

Our government continues to misappropriate billions in taxpayers' money for military use. According to Robert Costello, the Pentagon's top procurement official in the late 1980s, 20 to 30 percent of defense expenditures for procurement of weapons and armed forces operations and purchasing "could be saved through the application of fundamental changes in procurement practices and . . . quality management principles."[2] In 1989, former Secretary of Defense Robert McNamara estimated that our annual military budget could be cut in half without any threat to our national security. At the same time, our national security is *genuinely* threatened by internal violence, drug use, and illiteracy. Programs geared toward helping children are regularly rejected for lack of funds, yet a small fraction of our close to three-hundred-billion-dollar annual military budget would help us begin to raise physically and mentally healthy, well-educated children who would genuinely be able to say no to drugs and to violence. This neglect goes hand in hand with the lack of recognition of the enormous importance of child-rearing as reflected in the $4.55 an hour earned by day-care center employees in 1987. Child-care workers earn less than parking-lot attendants or animal caretakers.

Everywhere there is homophobia, the fear that if we don't raise boys who are tough and tearless, they will be gay or at the very least wimpish. There is an abysmal failure of the imagination here, as if our choice were between John Wayne and Mr. Milquetoast. It is as if we cannot imagine boys and men who are strong, courageous, curious, and adventurous without being violent and obsessed with domination and power.

Instead of moving beyond an outdated and dangerous concept of masculinity, our society has encouraged the escalation of the masculine mystique's violent content. We have come a long way from the 1950s when the pressure to prove manhood tended to take the form of going to a hooker at age sixteen or seventeen, bragging about "scoring" with girls, making the football team, or "borrowing" mom or dad's car for a joy ride. In Harlem, according to Claude Brown's autobiography, *Manchild in the Promised Land*, it often meant more, perhaps stealing and conning, but not the random, senseless assault or murder of the 1970s and 80s.

More than any other group, African-American males are negatively affected by the values of the masculine mystique. Men at the bottom of the social hierarchy, without other outlets for achieving dominance and power, are the most likely to prove manhood through violence. This tendency has been exacerbated in the last few decades by the enormous increase in African-American teenage girls having babies. Our inner cities are now filled with millions of fatherless boys who are extremely susceptible to "hyper-masculinity" and the values of the masculine mystique. Since the mid to late eighties, an increasing number of teenage girls and women in ghetto areas have become addicted to cheap and readily available drugs. Their sons, often born addicted and then emotionally and physically neglected or battered, are at an even greater risk for violence than the other boys. The mass media furnish them with endless images of violent males.

While poor, fatherless boys are especially likely to be affected, these images influence boys of all races and social classes who are entertained by sociopathic and sadistic role models such as slasher film "heroes" Freddy Krueger and Jason, as well as Rambo. Freddy Krueger even has a fan club; children proudly wear T-shirts portraying their favorite sadistic sociopath. Behavior that would have been unthinkably repugnant twenty-five years ago is now seen over and over again on the screen.

A teacher at a good junior high school in a middle- to upper-middle-class suburb recently told me how disturbed she was by her students' reaction to a social studies classroom discussion about alleged cannibalism in Jamestown, Virginia, in the early seventeenth century; a few students had seen a film on TV that depicted it as having taken place during a time of intense starvation. "They—especially the boys—weren't horrified or repelled at all, they were excited by it and wanted to get all the details. Were the people cooked or raw? How did they cut them up?"

I was not surprised by her story. It makes sense that boys who grow up surrounded by the gore of slasher films, the xenophobia of professional wrestling, the rapist lyrics of some heavy metal and rap groups, not to mention the endless violence on TV and in toys, will become so desensitized that nothing becomes unthinkable in terms of gore and violence.

Is there really something unmanly about a boy or young man who is repelled by luridly violent films, who does not enjoy breaking bones and rupturing muscles—his own or others'—whether it be in the school yard, on the street, or on the football field? Is there really something unmanly in choosing to seek adventure by biking cross-country, going white water rafting, fighting forest fires, or volunteering for the Peace Corps in South America or Africa? We desperately need new heroes and new myths for our boys—heroes whose sense of adventure, courage, and strength are linked with caring, empathy, and altruism.

Women have much to gain from such a change. The present definition of masculinity leads many of them to admire and reinforce just those traits that are conducive to rape, wife abuse, child abuse, and murder.

There is the fear that if boys and girls are raised more alike, if boys are encouraged to play house and push baby carriages and make believe they are daddies, then we will obliterate all but the obvious physiological differences between men and women. Similar fears were expressed in the nineteenth century when women began to enter universities and wanted the vote. Today's women are not just like men, nor is there any reason to believe that if we cease raising boys by the values of the masculine mystique they will become just like girls. In fact, recent brain research suggests that there may well be differences in the male and female brain which will ensure some emotional, cognitive, and behavioral variance between males and females as a group, under any conditions.

As we approach the twenty-first century, we face a choice. We can begin to control violent behavior, both on a national and international level, or we can continue to let it control and perhaps ultimately destroy us. We have enough knowledge to be able to significantly decrease violence, which is not to say that our knowledge is definitive or that we don't have much to learn. Just as the work of research physicians ensures progress in the control of physical diseases, continued research in the social and biological sciences could ensure progress in the control of the social disease of violence.

As of now we can, with some assurance, make the following assertions:

1. The traditional "either/or" debate between nature and nurture with respect to violence is simple-minded and obsolete. Human behavior grows out of a complex interaction between a biologically given potential and environmental factors. If human beings had no biological potential for violence, it could never develop regardless of external conditions. On the other hand, the environment plays an all-important role in encouraging or discouraging this potential.

Equally simplistic is the notion that any *one* factor will *necessarily* cause an individual to act violently. Any serious study of violence — or of any other aspect of human conduct — is limited to researching and analyzing significant, *not universal,* correlations between behaviors.

2. The behavior of human beings is extremely malleable. Anthropological studies reveal the enormous variability of human behavior and values in different cultures. Studies in psychology and sociology show us how early childhood experiences, family, peer groups, and culture mold the individual. History reveals that radical changes have taken place within a given culture in a very short period of time: extremely violent groups have become peaceful, and vice versa.

We have the clearest example of the malleability of human beings within our own country. Boys raised in Hutterite communities start out just the same as other American boys. They have their conflicts and brawls. The community has its share of boys who suffer from attention deficit disorder and/or learning disabilities, and they are especially difficult to deal with. But Hutterite boys are raised to value community, charity, love, and nonviolence. Parents and teachers are intent on helping them resolve their quarrels nonviolently. Toy guns are not allowed. Play with make-believe guns is discouraged. Hutterite children's TV viewing is limited to carefully chosen videocassettes. Child-rearing is a focal point of community life. Fathers spend large amounts of time with their children.

Ian Winter, who is the principal at the Hutterian Brethren community school in Rifton, New York, tells me that physical fights do very rarely break out among thirteen- or fourteen-year-old boys. But by the time they are sixteen, the boys have learned to resolve their conflicts nonviolently. Domestic violence and criminal behavior are unheard of.

Benjamin Zablocki, professor of sociology at Rutgers and author of *The Joyful Community,* a study of the Hutterite Brethren, confirmed, in an interview, that violence is virtually unheard of among them.

3. Human beings, especially men, have a significant potential for violent behavior. A few of the twentieth-century manifestations of this potential have been two world wars that took tens of millions of lives, genocides of Armenians and Jews, the slaughter by their fellow countrymen of millions of Russian peasants and Cambodians. As I write, human beings all over the world are being beaten, tortured, and killed. This suggests that *if we are to significantly and lastingly decrease violence, it can only be done through an ongoing relentless effort. For short of widespread genetic mutations, the potential for violence, bigotry, and xenophobia will always be with us.*

We must acknowledge fully that many normal, otherwise decent people are capable of committing, either directly or indirectly, the most cruel and violent acts. Only if we do so will we be able to recognize and act on the enormous importance of encouraging empathy and discouraging xenophobia and bigotry in our children, and of teaching them the true courage and integrity of standing up for humane, altruistic, moral convictions and feelings regardless of external pressures or monetary rewards.

If we take these steps, if they become an integral part of early child-rearing, and a mandatory part of our educational system, then we may begin to move away from what political philosopher Hannah Arendt refers to as "the banality of evil."

In her book *Eichmann in Jerusalem*, Arendt concluded that Nazi henchman Adolf Eichmann, who shared responsibility for the deaths of millions of Jews, was "normal." Again and again Eichmann explained to the Israeli court that put him on trial that he was only doing his duty. Arendt writes that Eichmann suffered from a "lack of imagination." He *"never realized what he was doing* . . . It was sheer thoughtlessness . . . that predisposed him to become one of the greatest criminals of that period."[3] She comments that "such remoteness from reality and such thoughtlessness can wreak more havoc than all the evil instincts taken together . . ."[4]

In a study of Greek military policemen who served as torturers during the period from 1967 to 1974, when Greece was ruled by a right-wing military regime, researchers found no evidence of any abusiveness, sadism, or authoritarianism in these men's previous histories. When interviewed, the men were all leading normal lives. The researchers are convinced that certain kinds of training can lead "decent people to commit acts, often over long periods of time, that otherwise would be unthinkable for them. Similar techniques can be found in military training all over the world."[5]

These findings and Arendt's analysis of Eichmann are borne out by Stanley Milgram's study on obedience. A majority of Milgram's subjects continued to give what they thought were increasingly high electric shocks to a "victim" even after the victim screamed in pain, and in spite of the fact that they were free to disobey the psychologist's orders. Many more subjects disobeyed when the victim was in the same room than when the victim could only be heard but not seen.

We do not need to look at laboratory studies, or at studies of torturers or people like Adolf Eichmann, to become aware of any of this.

John Floyd is a friend of mine, a perfectly decent, nice guy. Yet when he served in Vietnam, John enjoyed the excitement and feeling of power of dropping bombs on Vietnamese and Laotians whom he thought of as "Commie enemies" and could not see from the height of his plane. It was only after his trip to Hiroshima that he began to realize what he had done.

When I interviewed former Secretary of Defense Robert McNamara I found him to be a thoughtful, appealing man, deeply concerned about the danger of nuclear destruction, and about the plight of poor African-Americans. Several former friends of McNamara's have corroborated my positive impression. Some of them are still shocked at the thought that Robert McNamara shares major responsibility for the *unnecessary* deaths of over a million Americans and Vietnamese.

Neither Floyd nor McNamara seems to have thought of the people whose lives they took as anything but abstractions. As a result, they were devoid of empathy or, as Hannah Arendt put it, they suffered from a "lack of imagination."

The enormous human potential for emotional detachment, denial, and lack of empathy is increased further by modern technology. Millions can now be killed without any direct contact between perpetrators and victims. This makes it even easier for decent men raised on the values of the masculine mystique to commit horrendous acts of violence.

Boys suffering from attention deficit disorder with hyperactivity, learning disability, mental retardation, extra y chromosome, and Asperger's syndrome will always require special attention and services, since many of them are even more prone than the rest of the population to engage in violent behavior. We must develop techniques for discouraging violence in them from the earliest age. The demise of the masculine mystique would ensure that the tendency on the part of some of them to reckless and violent behavior would in no way be admired and emulated by their peers. Instead it would be viewed as immature and problematic.

While many normal men can be recruited to participate in mass murder, it is nevertheless worth investigating whether inordinate numbers of men belonging to groups such as the Nazi brownshirts, the Haitian Tonton Macoute death squads, and the Ku Klux Klan suffered from some of these disabilities as children. More generally we need more research to determine the psychological profiles and backgrounds of the men who start and seek out these groups. Understanding will help us in taking the proper preventive measures.

4. *Human beings, male and female, have a significant potential for empathy and altruism.* According to recent studies, shortly after they have reached the age of one, virtually all children begin to have some level of understanding of other people's experiences and attempt to help or comfort the person who is in distress. From age one and a half to age two, there is a great increase in altruistic behavior. As children get older there is more variation in their behavior. Researchers have found that in older children the degree of empathy and altruism is linked to maternal and paternal behavior. Nurturant involvement in child-rearing on the part of fathers is linked to increased and enduring empathy in their children. Studies of mothers and children indicate that when mothers are themselves empathic, when they make their children aware emotionally of how hurtful behavior affects others, when they establish principled moral prohibitions against hurting others, then children will tend to be empathic and altruistic.[6]

Among adults, these empathic, altruistic tendencies manifest themselves in a variety of ways.

During World War II, in Le Chambon, a small French town near Switzerland, villagers, led by their Protestant minister and his wife, risked their lives to hide Jews from the Nazis. As a result, thousands of people were saved.

In the United States, Americans with low incomes, for whom the tax deduction incentive is not a factor, give a larger percentage of their hard-earned incomes to charity than do wealthy Americans.

It is not at all unusual for human beings to spontaneously jump into a river or in front of a car to save the life of a complete stranger, often at great personal risk.

The upshot of all this is that we can, if we want to, decrease violence. Human beings are born with a vast array of often conflicting potential behaviors. The environment they grow up in determines which of these behaviors will become dominant in their lives. It is nothing short of tragic that while the results of research findings are used regularly to prevent physical illness, the findings of the social sciences are rarely used in preventive programs. Changes in hygiene, the creation of vaccines, and more recently recommendations for dietary changes play a major role in preventing illness and saving lives. But *there are analogous measures that could be taken to prevent the social disease of violence.*

American boys must be protected from a culture of violence that exploits their worst tendencies by reinforcing and amplifying the atavistic values of the masculine mystique. Our country was not created so that future generations could maximize profit at any cost. It was created with humanistic, egalitarian, and altruistic goals. We must put our enormous resources and talents to the task of creating a children's culture that is consistent with these goals.

NOTES

1. The *New York Times,* September 24, 1989.
2. Costello, interview with the author, 1990.
3. Hannah Arendt, *Eichmann in Jerusalem,* 287–88.
4. Ibid., 288.
5. Janice T. Gibson and Mika Haritos-Fatouros, "The Education of a Torturer," *Psychology Today,* November 1986, 57.
6. See Carolyn Zahn-Waxler and Marian Radke-Yarrow, "The Development of Altruism: Alternative Research Strategies," in *The Development of Prosocial Behavior,* edited by Nancy Eisenberg. In the same volume, see Martin L. Hoffman, "Development of Prosocial Behavior: Empathy and Guilt." See also Radke-Yarrow and Zahn-Waxler, "The Role of Familial Factors in the Development of Prosocial Behavior: Research Findings and Questions," in *Development of Antisocial and Prosocial Behavior,* edited by D. Olweus, J. Block, and M. Radke-Yarrow.

31

Violence, Gender, and Social Change

CHRISTINE ALDER

Introduction

Discussions of violence in society frequently focus on the violent crimes recorded in criminal justice statistics—assault, robbery and homicide. These crimes are most often intra-racial and intra-class: the offenders and the victims are among the economically oppressed members of our society. These offences are the cause of much human suffering and personal disaster and thus warrant careful investigation. However, there are many different forms of violence in our society, some of which are often taken for granted: in the home, parents hit their children; on the playing field, sportsmen assault each other. Other forms of violence are of increasing public interest and concern, but they may not be treated as criminal matters: at work, industrial "accidents" occur; in our communities, dangerous chemicals are dumped; our governments turn a blind eye to the practices of some police officers; and our governments are responsible for the mass violence of war. We shall give some consideration to each of these forms of violence. The objective is to review briefly the implications of some major social changes for both the occurrence of violence and its possible reduction.

Women's Liberation

Women's emancipation or liberation has been one of the more popular and recurring themes in recent discussions of the implications of social change for violent crime (Smart 1976, 70–76). The work of Freda Adler (1975), *Sisters in Crime*, provides an example of this thesis, which essentially proceeds as follows: women are committing more violent crime; violent crime is masculine; women are becoming more masculine as a consequence of women's liberation.

Naffine (1987) provides a summary of the now extensive literature and research that has been generated in response to Adler's argument. More detailed analyses of data reveal that women have not been significantly more involved in violent crime in recent times. Female crimes remain predominantly the types of property offence consistent with traditional female role expectations (shop-lifting, fraud and petty theft). Further, female offenders are most often not the middle class women involved in the recent

From *International Social Science Journal* 44, no. 2. (1992):267–76. Reprinted by permission.

women's movement. In fact one study of young women found that those with more liberated views were less likely to be delinquent. Naffine concludes that, rather than the liberation of women, the social change more likely to have had an impact on increases in female property crime is the "feminization of poverty."

Masculinity

Across time and cultures, violent crime is overwhelmingly perpetrated by relatively young, economically marginalized, males (Wolfgang and Ferracuti 1967; Daly and Wilson 1988). Frequently, as indicated in homicide research, the violence is male to male (Polk and Ranson 1991; Daly and Wilson 1988; Wallace 1986). Research in countries such as Australia and the United States indicates that somewhat more than three-quarters of all homicide offenders, and two-thirds of all homicide victims, are male (Wallace 1986; Wolfgang and Ferracuti 1967).

In recent years feminist research, in particular, has also drawn attention to male violence towards women. These forms of violence frequently occur in "private," in the home, and police and other criminal justice agencies have been reluctant to define such violence as "criminal" or to respond to such "family" matters. Consequently, a good deal of violence against women is never recorded in official statistics (Hanmer, Radford, and Stanko 1989). Research in a number of different nations has revealed an extensive problem of domestic violence and a reluctance by formal agencies to deal with the problem (Dobash and Dobash 1992, ch. 1). Thus, despite the recent achievements of the refuge movements in many countries and their efforts to bring about social change (Dobash and Dobash 1992), the extent of male violence continues to be underestimated in official accounts.

While violence has been recognized as a predominantly male phenomenon, the maleness or the masculinity of the perpetrator has not been a focus of research. While a range of social characteristics of violent offenders have been analysed (their age, class, education, religion, race), their gender has been virtually ignored (Allen 1988, 16).

Recognizing the "maleness" of violent crime, feminist researchers have recently argued that male violence against women is an expression of male power and is used by men to reproduce and maintain their relative status and authority over women. Support for this argument is provided by an analysis of the main sources of conflict which result in male violence towards women: possessiveness and jealousy, expectations regarding women's domestic work, a sense of the right to punish "their" women for wrong-doing, and the importance of maintaining or exercising authority (Dobash and Dobash 1992, 4).

Analyses of male violence point out that the social construction of masculinity entails assumptions of power, and that both masculinity and power are linked to aggression and violence. Thus male to male confrontations are also confirmations of masculinity: a means of testing and establishing power in relation to other men (Messerschmidt 1986; Daly and Wilson 1988).

Morgan (1987) warns, however, against stereotyping constructions of masculinity on the basis of those presumed to be working class. He points out that constructions of both masculinity and violence are in fact variable and diffuse; there are different masculinities and some violence is legitimated while some is not. For example, he notes that even within groups which encourage violence, in some circumstances a man who can control his violence may be held in higher regard than one who engages in indiscriminate violence. That is, in some male groups the control of violence is as much an expression of masculinity as engaging in violence. Further analysis of the various constructions of masculinity and their relationship to violent behaviour, Morgan argues, will facilitate the identification of ways to alter some violent processes.

Since at present there is very little research in this area it is not possible to discuss in detail changes or variations in the construction of masculinity and violence and the relationship between these across time or place. However in many cultures masculinity and power are linked to the ability to protect and materially support a family. Masculine identity is closely related to a man's work and occupational duties outside the home (Messerschmidt 1986, 42). The relationship between economic status and violence has been the object of extensive research and it is in this arena that the consequences of social, in particular economic changes, for violent crime are most evident.

Inequality and Economic Change

In his discussion of crime in America, Currie comments that "there is an accumulated fund of sophisticated research linking serious crime with social and economic inequality" (Currie 1985, 146). While some studies have found a relationship between poverty and crime, others indicate that income inequality (the degree of relative poverty) is a better determinant of crime than absolute poverty (see Belknap 1989 for a review of these studies). Braithwaite and Braithwaite (1980) concluded from their study of homicide rates in thirty-one nations that higher homicide rates were related to the range of measures of economic inequality, including the gap between the rich and the average wage earner, the disparities in income between workers in different sectors of industry and the percentage of gross national product spent on social security.

Criminal violence has been found to be strongly related to economic inequalities, particularly when those inequalities are based on race. In their research on this topic in the United States, Blau and Blau (1982) used the following independent variables: percentage black, percentage poor, income inequality and racial socio-economic inequality. In interpreting their findings, Blau and Blau argue that "aggressive acts of violence seem to result not so much from lack of advantages as from being taken advantage of, not from absolute but from relative deprivation" (Blau and Blau 1982, 126).

Such findings suggest that economic changes which entail increasing economic inequality will consequently mean increasing rates of crime, including violent crime. Braithwaite (1979, 230) argues that there are "reasonable theoretical grounds" and "substantial empirical evidence" to suggest that a redistribution of wealth and power would diminish crime.

Those who are sceptical about a link between economic status and crime argue that the relationship, observed in official crime statistics, is an artifact of race and class bias in criminal justice practice. While not denying that such bias exists, the strength of the relationship would seem to be beyond that which could be explained simply in terms of bias (Braithwaite 1979, 32–46; Currie 1985).

Changes in unemployment rates are particularly illuminating when considering the plight of young people. Unemployment or labour force participation rates have frequently been used in studies of economic influences on crime. Studies in the U.S. have found that unemployment rates are positively related to rates of violent crime (e.g., Kau and Rubin 1975). Similarly Bechdolt (1975) concluded that the unemployment rate was a significant and strong predictor of both violent and property crime rates. From a review of sixty-three such studies, Chiricos (1987) concluded that there was sufficient evidence of a link between unemployment and crime to remove the "consensus of doubt" in criminology about this topic.

In refining the analysis of the relationship between unemployment and crime, it has been argued that, the development of social commitments requires more than simply having "a job." The importance and the value of work is not simply that it provides a material benefit, but that it also enables people to participate in society, to feel that they have something to contribute. Work which does not allow a person to experience a sense of worth is less likely to encourage the development of a commitment to society and thus a protection against a person's engaging in crime. Feelings of "purposefulness" and "alienation" can be produced by either not having a job, or by having a "shit" job, that is, a job with no future, a job which has little social value, which does not contribute to self-worth. It can be anticipated that young people in this marginalized position will be more likely than other youth to engage in criminal behaviour, including violence.

Recent changes in the structure of the labour market, such as economic specialization and technological expansion, have meant a marked decline in the jobs available to young people. For the present argument, there are two important aspects of these job losses. One, the losses are concentrated at the bottom of the social class structure. It is young people who are attempting to enter the labour force without qualifications, skills or experience who are feeling the greatest pressure, since it is the unskilled and semi-skilled work that is most likely to be replaced. Two, what the resultant unemployment means for many young people is not temporary unemployment, but a closing off of entry into work. Thus, a large proportion of young unemployed people have been so for a long period, and will remain so (Polk 1984; Duster 1987).

In many of the technologically developed countries there is a growing number of "new marginal youth" (Polk 1984) or what some have referred to as the urban "underclass" (Duster 1987). Due to racism, in countries such as the U.S. and the U.K. it is the black youths who are the hardest hit by this marginalization. In some of the Western European nations, the underclass population may be concentrated among the children of the guest-workers or other recent migrants. These are young people who are not simply out of work, they are often so far out they have ceased to look for it (Currie 1985, 117). Such young people who cannot see the opportunity to work in either the present or the future, have little incentive to abide by the rules of a society which has abandoned them. It is suggested that the growth of this new underclass population has implications in terms of the participation of young men in street violence. This becomes apparent when we look more closely at the nature of violent crime.

Four scenarios of lethal, masculine violence have been identified in a recent study of homicide (Polk and Ranson 1991). First, there was homicide in situations of sexual intimacy where the male violence was an ultimate attempt to control the behaviour of the female sexual partner. Second, homicide developed from a confrontation between males (a "status contest"); a fight which spilled over into lethal violence. Third, homicide was observed as a consequence of another crime, such as robbery. Fourth, the homicide took place between friends, where the violence was used as a means of conflict resolution between men whose exceptional marginality meant that conventional dispute resolution procedures were unavailable. Male-to-male violence, such as found in the last three forms of homicide, account for over half of all homicides (Wallace 1986). Further, these forms of violence are almost exclusively underclass or working-class male phenomena (Polk and Ranson 1991).

Economic changes which increase economic marginality are likely to have as a spin-off effect an increase in the forms of masculine violence closely tied to such marginality. Evidence suggests, in fact, that while homicide rates are generally more stable than other forms of crime, upward movements in the rate are a consequence of homicides taking place between males (put another way, the rate of domestic homicides tends to be more stable over time). Further, other research indicates that it is particularly homicides of strangers that are increasing in recent years (Daly and Wilson 1988), and such homicides arise almost exclusively either from masculine confrontations or out of the commission of other crimes, both of which are events most commonly involving underclass or lower class males (Polk and Ranson 1991).

It was the Finnish criminologist Veli Verkko (1951) who was one of the first to observe that the variability in homicide rates is largely due to variations which occur in patterns of homicide between males. To examine these findings further, Daly and Wilson (1988) reviewed data from Iceland, Denmark, Australia, Canada, Brazil and the United States and concluded that "the most variable component of the homicide rate between industrial nations and between years is that perpetrated by (and, to a lesser degree upon) . . . disadvantaged young men. . . . Where rates of homicide are high, the proportion of cases that involve such young men is high" (Daly and Wilson 1988, 285).

These findings indicate that an understanding of the implications of economic change for violence entails consideration of the interactions between masculinity and economic status.

In societies where masculine identity is tied to work and economic independence, young men without this source of confirmation of their masculinity will do so in other ways. Violence may be used by young men in such a situation to establish a sense of power and dominance, or as a form of resistance or anger at their relative deprivation. Greenberg (1978) argues that for some young men the cultural expectations for men are contradicted by the structural constraints on male status attainment which are imposed by the larger economic and political order. The resultant masculine status anxiety may result in some young men turning to whatever means are at their disposal to establish their masculinity. Thus, Greenberg (1978, 65) argues, attempts to dominate women and other forms of interpersonal violence may produce the sense of potency not available to these young men in other spheres of life.

In conclusion, then, we may say that while there may be a number of benefits which result from the movement of national economies into a post-industrial phase, one important consequence consists of the structural changes which close off opportunities for young people at the lower end of the economic spectrum to enter into viable work careers. The resultant building up of a new underclass population increases the potential for particular forms of male violence.

Corporate Violence

A quite different source of violence resulting from social change concerns the behaviour of large multinational corporations. Increasingly, the world is a global marketplace in which large corporations compete with each other for resources, labour, markets and profits. There are many potential benefits of multinational corporate activity as nations, especially in the underdeveloped world, come to experience new products, new sources of economic support, or expanded markets for their products. Unfortunately, these multinational organizations also have a capacity for large scale injury and death.

The search for cheaper labour, combined with the flight of capital from many developed countries, has meant a shift of various forms of productive activity into the less developed nations of the world. In these newly developing nations, the international companies may find it possible to engage in forms of production which, because of their danger, would be forbidden in the countries where the corporate headquarters are located. Huge stocks of used motor car batteries are shipped from the United States to countries in Asia where in the process of breaking them down for salvage, workers are directly exposed to concentrations of lead that would not be permitted in the United States. A recent report observed that a chlorine and caustic-soda corporation in Latin America, controlled by an overseas company, continued to discharge poisonous mercury into local waters, and instead of paying $650,000 for a pollution control system, declared a $3 million dollar dividend for its shareholders. This action was justified because it "would best protect the interests of shareholders in light of the unsettled political climate" of the country involved. One of the best known examples, of course, would be the tragedy of Bhopal where thousands died as a result of deadly gases released as the result of an accident in a Union Carbide plant (Mokhiber 1989).

Consumers as well as workers have been victims of such corporate behaviour. Nowhere is this better illustrated than in the pharamaceutical industry (Braithwaite 1984). Major drug companies have distributed drugs (e.g., Depo-Provera or clioquinol) in the third world which have been banned by the more stringent drug regulations of the developed countries. The Dalkon Shield, an intra-uterine device, was sold for years in other countries after it had been banned in the United States. Pesticides which are either banned or severely restricted in Europe or North America, such as heptachlor, chlordane, endrin and others are "routinely sold" in other parts of the globe (Mokhiber 1989). One dangerous chemical, the pesticide leptophos, was exported to such developing countries as Colombia, Egypt and Indonesia, but was never registered by the environmental protection agency of the developed country where the manufacturing was carried out. This pesticide causes delayed but lasting nervous system damage to humans, and was blamed for the deaths of several farmers and hundreds of farm animals in Egypt. Only when the workers at the production plant began to display symptoms of severe neurological damage was the manufacture of the pesticide halted (Mokhiber 1989, 187).

Clearly these are acts of violence which present us with the issue of whether they should also be treated as criminal acts. Both legal scholars and legal practitioners are increasingly putting the case that these are criminal actions. New criminal laws in California focus on the employers, company executives and the companies themselves, who knowingly allow life threatening faults to workers or consumers to go uncorrected. The Ford Motor Company was charged with criminal homicide in a court in Indiana for deaths which resulted when the company knowingly allowed a motor car with a serious fault to remain, uncorrected, on the road. The result, however, was an acquittal. New laws in the Netherlands have expanded the grounds whereby companies can be charged with criminal homicide when company negligence results in death.

Examples of corporate activities such as these clearly pose a significant threat to the citizens of many countries of the world. In fact, quite often the threat is much greater than that posed by the violence of more traditionally defined criminal behaviour. However, in general such violence has not been responded to with the same level of gravity of sanction that is reserved for the violent acts committed by less powerful members of our society. Our failure to confront this expanding source of violence in the world, to some extent legitimizes it.

The Legitimation of Violence

The approval and practice of violence are more pervasive than is generally acknowledged. This becomes most apparent in studies of wife battering. In Australia, one in five adults condones the use of physical force by one spouse against another (Public Policy Research Centre 1988). In the United States, one investigation found that one-fifth of all Americans approved of slapping one's spouse on appropriate occasions. Approval of this practice increased with income and education. Public opinion polls in the United States also show widespread support for violence committed by police (Archer and Gartner 1984, 63).

These sorts of research findings indicate that in society in general some violence is accepted, normalized and even legitimized. In fact, Morgan (1987, 182) points out, in some cases the legitimation process may be so effective that the violence is not recognized, for example corporal punishment in schools or at home. The extent to which violence is legitimated in a society is thought to affect the incidence of unlegitimated violence, or violent crime.

In their study of the homicide rates in fifty nations after a period of war, Archer and Gartner (1984) found support for what they referred to as the "legitimation of violence model." The model suggested that the social approval of killing, or the legitimation of violence during the war period produced a lasting reduction of inhibitions against the taking of human life. Most of the combatant nations, in contrast to the noncombatant nations in the study, had substantial postwar increases in their homicide rates. Further, "the increases were pervasive and occurred after both large and small wars, with several types of homicide indicators, in victorious as well as defeated nations, in nations with improved postwar economies and nations with worsened economies, among both men and women offenders, and among several age groups" (Archer and Gartner 1984, 96).

Archer and Gartner conclude that when acts of violence occur, and more particularly when at least some such acts seem to be socially acceptable or even lauded, as in wartime, then general attitudes toward the use of violence shift in the direction of acceptance, and thresholds for resorting to violence fall.

This research supports the obvious, although often ignored, proposition that the extent to which we condone and allow any violence in our society will affect the rate of violent crime. If we are concerned to reduce the incidence of violent crime, then the process of social change will require that we address those norms, values and structures which legitimate and glorify other forms of violence in our society.

Social Change and Violence

While the present discussion has been concerned mainly with identifying some of the ways that developmental changes in the social, economic and political conditions of nations influence patterns of violence, it also needs to be recognized that planned social change may have important effects as well. One of the clearest examples of such effects can be found in the influence of feminists' discussions of domestic violence. In a recent book, *Women, Violence and Social Change*, for example, Dobash and Dobash (1992) document and evaluate the efforts of the battered-women's movement. In general the goals of this movement are to provide "safety, shelter and autonomy for abused women" and to work towards the elimination of violence against women. The refuges established by this movement provide not only a haven for women and children, but they are also a visible and concrete challenge to the legacy of indifference to male violence against women (Dobash and Dobash 1992). This movement has also challenged both the discourse about violence against women and the criminal justice system. It thereby constitutes a vital element of efforts to bring about the social changes necessary to address the issue of male violence in society.

While the battered-women's movement has achieved a great deal, it alone cannot accomplish the breadth of social change required to respond to violence. The complexity of the nature of violence means that the necessary social changes should also be diverse and wide ranging. However it is clearly social changes that are required; violence will not be controlled through individually based strategies. It is apparent from the preceding review of the literature that the reduction of violent crimes will be made more possible by a reduction in the inequalities of wealth and power in society. Overall, to change the levels of violence, we will have to change the structured inequalities of race, class and sex.

Conclusions

Social change can take many forms, and have a variety of consequences, some of which are beneficial, while some result in harm. Nowhere is this clearer than in the lessons now being learned about technological development. With the gifts of technology we have controlled famine, brought devastating diseases under control, and brought to masses of people the benefits of markedly increased standards of living. Even the most developed nations, however, have experienced the mixed blessings of technological developments.

It is in some of the most advanced cities of the world that we encounter the persistent problems of communities of underclass residents, including distinctively masculine patterns of confrontational and predatory violence. Both developed and underdeveloped countries have been threatened by ecological disasters caused by corporations, and have seen their citizens suffer the violence which results from inadequate controls over consumer products ranging from dangerous motor cars, life-threatening medical preparations, or ruinous pesticides.

What recent experiences concerned with domestic violence have demonstrated, however, is that some forms of planned social change can begin to influence not only the shape of the violence, but also how people come to view it. Human intelligence, informed debate, and collective action, in other words, can serve to bring at least some forms of violence under community control.

32

Violence against Women or Family Violence? Current Debates and Future Directions

DEMIE KURZ

In recent years, due to the efforts of the battered women's movement and other reformers, much more public attention has been focused on the physical abuse of women at the hands of male partners (Dobash and Dobash 1992). The problems of "woman abuse" or "wife abuse" are now recognized as widespread and as having serious consequences. Advocates for battered women in many professions and organizations have worked to make legal, medical, and social service agencies more responsive to battered women (American Medical Association 1992; Dobash and Dobash 1992; Jones 1994; Koss 1990; Novello et al. 1992).

Despite increased recognition of the problem of male violence toward women, however, much of the research on violence in intimate relationships focuses not on woman abuse, but on "spouse abuse" or "partner abuse." Many researchers have argued that we should focus our attention on "family violence," and that adult family members are equally violent toward each other (Straus 1993). Thus, those who are interested in researching the question of wife abuse find instead data on "spouse abuse," which claims that men are victims of violence equally with women (Kurz 1993).

What lies behind this confusing discrepancy between the widely perceived view that women are the targets of violence at the hands of male partners, and the view held by some researchers that violence against women is really a "family violence" problem? It is not often recognized that differences in language reflect two sharply different views among researchers concerning the nature of violence in intimate relationships, particularly the question of whether women are violent toward men. In this chapter I will examine these two different perspectives on the issue of violence against women.

One group of social scientists adopts what has been called the "violence against women" perspective (Dobash and Dobash 1992) and argues that women are the victims of violence in relationships with men (Daly and Wilson 1988; Ellis and DeKeseredy 1996; Dobash and Dobash 1992; Kurz 1995; Loseke 1992; Saunders 1988; Stanko 1987; Yllö and Bograd 1988; Yllö 1993). Among these researchers, those who identify with the feminist tradition claim that, historically, the law has promoted women's subordination and condoned husbands' use of force in marriage. The other group of social scientists are the "family violence" researchers (Brinkerhoff and Lupri 1988; Gelles 1993; Gelles and Cornell 1985; Gelles and Straus 1988; McNeely and Mann 1990; McNeely and Robinson-Stimpson 1987; Shupe, Stacey, and Hazelwood 1987; Stets

1990; Straus 1993; Straus and Gelles 1990), who argue that the real problem is "spouse abuse" and "family violence." These researchers believe that women, as well as men, are violent, and some claim that women "initiate and carry out physical assaults on their partner as often as men" (Straus 1993, 67).

This debate over men's and women's use of violence has significant consequences for popular and academic conceptions of battered women, as well as for social policy. How a problem is framed determines the amount of concern that is generated and the solutions that are proposed for that problem. Research findings influence whether the media and the public take battered women seriously, or whether they view them as equally blameworthy partners in "family violence." Violence-against-women researchers fear that framing the problem as "spouse abuse" will lead to decreased funding for shelters, a diversion of resources to "battered men," and increased arrest of women in "domestic disputes" under mandatory arrest policies. More generally, violence-against-women researchers fear that the discourse of "spouse abuse" obscures the cause of violence against women—inequality and male dominance.

I argue that the violence against women point of view best explains the nature and the extent of violence between men and women in intimate relationships. Violence-against-women researchers argue that violence between intimates takes place within a context of inequality between men and women in marriage, while family violence proponents promote a gender-neutral view of power in intimate relationships. I will compare the evidence and theories presented by the proponents of each perspective, and I will argue that the family violence view is based on false assumptions about the nature of marriage and of equality between men and women.

A Violence against Women Perspective

Researchers who take a violence against women perspective argue that overwhelmingly it is women, not men, who are the victims of violence. They support their point of view with official crime statistics, data from the criminal justice system and hospitals, interviews with victims of battering and batterers, and historical evidence. As Dobash and Dobash (1992, 265) note, data from victimization surveys, court statistics, and police files in North America and Canada indicate that women are the victims of male violence in 90 to 95 percent of assaults within a family context. A number of researchers have examined National Crime Survey data and found that wives were the victims of violence at the hands of their husbands in the overwhelming majority of cases. In his analysis of National Crime Survey data, Schwartz (1987) found that only 4 percent of men claimed to be victims of violence at the hands of their wives. In the remaining 96 percent of cases, wives claimed to be the victims of violence at the hands of their husbands. Other researchers who have analyzed National Crime Survey data have reported similar findings (McLeod 1984; Gaquin 1977/78). In their study of police records in Scotland, Dobash and Dobash (1979) found that when gender was known, women were targets in 94 percent and offenders in 3 percent of cases. Other studies based on data from the criminal justice system show similar results (Kincaid 1982; Quarm and Schwartz 1985).

Data on injury patterns confirm that it is women, not men, who sustain injuries in conflicts between males and females in intimate relationships. Brush (1990), in an analysis of NSFH (National Survey of Families and Households) data, found that women were significantly more likely to be injured than men in disputes involving violent tactics. Berk and his colleagues (1983), based on their examination of police records, concluded that in 95 percent of cases it is the woman who is injured and that, even when both partners are injured, the woman's injuries are nearly three times as severe as the man's. Data from hospitals (JAMA 1990; Kurz 1990; McLeer and Anwar 1989; Stark and Flitcraft 1996) show women to be overwhelmingly the injured party. These data lead violence-against-women researchers to reject the concept of "spouse abuse," the idea that women are equally as violent as men.

Data from divorcing couples also provide evidence that women are more frequently the targets of violence than men. In their study of 362 separating husbands and wives, Ellis and Stuckless (1993) report that more than 40 percent of separating wives and 17 percent of separating husbands state that they were injured by their partners at some time during the relationship. In a random sample of divorced women with children from Philadelphia County, Kurz (1995) found that 70 percent of women reported experiencing violence at least once during their marriage, 54 percent two to three times, and 37 percent more than two to three times, findings similar to those found in other studies (Fields 1978; Parker and Schumacher 1977).

Researchers have also reported high rates of abuse after separation. Indeed, most surveys of post-separation abuse report more violence after separation than during relationships (Wilson and Daly 1993). Further, during separation women are not only at greater risk of injury, they are also at greater risk of death. Data gathered in Canada; New South Wales, Australia; and Chicago demonstrate that women are much more likely to be killed by their husbands after separating from them than when they are still living with them (Wilson and Daly 1993). These wives are at significantly high risk within the first two months of leaving a relationship (Wilson and Daly 1993; Schwartz 1987). Data indicate that separated and divorced women are also at increased risk of rape (Bowker 1981; Solicitor General of Canada 1985; U.S. Department of Justice 1987).

Researchers who take a violence against women perspective claim that the use of violence by men to control female intimates has long been condoned by major social institutions. The first law in the United States to recognize a husband's right to control his wife with physical force was an 1824 ruling by the Supreme Court of Mississippi permitting the husband "to exercise the right of moderate chastisement in cases of great emergency" (quoted in Browne 1987, 166). This and similar rulings in Maryland and Massachusetts were based on English common law, which gave a husband the right of "correction" of his wife, although he was supposed to use it in moderation.

> In 1871 wife beating was made illegal in Alabama. The court stated: The privilege, ancient though it be, to beat her with a stick, to pull her hair, choke her, spit in her face or kick her about the floor, or to inflict upon her like indignities, is not now acknowledged by our law. . . . [T]he wife is entitled to the same protection of the law that the husband can invoke for himself. (Quoted in Browne 1987, 167)

A North Carolina court made a similar decision in 1874, but limited the kinds of cases in which the court should intervene:

> If no permanent injury has been inflicted, nor malice, cruelty nor dangerous violence shown by the husband, it is better to draw the curtain, shut out the public gaze, and leave the parties to forget and forgive. (Quoted in Browne 1987, 167)

Until recent legal reforms were enacted, the "curtain rule" was widely used by the legal system to justify its nonintervention in wife-abuse cases.

The law and the nature of marriage have changed dramatically since the early twentieth century; however, violence-against-women researchers claim that these institutions continue to condone violence against women. New laws have criminalized battering, but we do not know whether these laws will be enforced (Buzawa and Buzawa 1996; Kurz 1992). One study suggests that even police who receive training in how to respond to battering cases as crimes may continue to view battered women as unfortunate victims of personal and social problems such as poverty and, in the absence of strong police department support, view arrests as low priority and not part of their "real" work (Ferraro 1989). To the extent that these laws are not taken seriously, the legal system will continue to treat battering as an individual problem, rather than as criminal behavior.

As for marriage, violence-against-women researchers, particularly those who are feminists, argue that it still institutionalizes the control of wives by husbands through the structure of husband-wife roles. As long as women are responsible for domestic work, child care, and emotional and psychological support, and men's primary identity is that of provider and revolves around employment, the husband has the more important status and also controls the majority of decisions in the family (Kurz 1995). It is through such a system, coupled with the acceptance of physical force as a means of control, that, in the words of the Dobashes (1979), the wife becomes an "appropriate victim" of physical and psychological abuse. Feminists argue further that the use of violence for control in marriage is perpetuated not only through norms about a man's rights in marriage, but also through women's continued economic dependence on their husbands, which makes it difficult to leave a violent relationship. This dependence is increased by the lack of adequate child care and job training, which would enable women to get jobs with which they could support themselves.

Citing interview data from men and women that demonstrate that battering incidents occur when husbands try to make their wives comply with their wishes, violence-against-women researchers believe that men still use violence as a way to control female partners. Based on data from interviews with 109 battered women, Dobash and Dobash (1979) demonstrate how batterers, over the course of their marriages, increasingly control wives through intimidation and isolation, findings confirmed by other interview studies (Kurz 1995; Pagelow 1981; Walker 1984). Violence, therefore, is just one of a variety of controls that men try to exercise over female partners; others are anger and psychological abuse (Dobash and Dobash 1992; Mederos 1987; Yllö 1993). Interviews with batterers (Adams 1988; Dobash and Dobash 1979; Ptacek 1988) show that men believe they are justified in their use of violence, particularly when their wives do not conform to the ideal of "good wife."

Finally, violence-against-women researchers demonstrate that a variety of institutions, in addition to the law and the family, condone male dominance and reinforce battering on an ongoing, everyday basis. Some have demonstrated how this occurs through the labeling and processing of abused women by front-line workers who have the most contact with these women. Stark and Flitcraft (1996) have argued that due to patriarchal medical ideologies and practices, health care practitioners have failed to recognize battering and instead label battered women as having psychological or psychosomatic problems. These researchers claim that the actions of health care workers serve to perpetuate battering relationships and argue that the medical system duplicates and reinforces the patriarchal structure of the family. Kurz (1990) has documented how individual staff in emergency rooms come to define battered women not as "true medical cases," but as "social" ones, and feel they make extra work and trouble for medical practitioners. Battered women who do not look like "typical victims" are frequently not recognized as battered and are sent back home, without any recognition of or attention to their battering.

Other studies address the issue of how violence against women is taught and reinforced in institutions such as the military (Russell 1989) and sports (Messner 1989). Sanday (1990) and others (Martin and Hummer, 1989) have studied the ways in which fraternity practices and rituals, in promoting loyalty to a brotherhood of men, legitimate gang rape and other types of violence against women. Kanin (1984) suggests that the college date rapists he studied came from a more highly sexualized subculture than men who did not commit date rape.

The Family Violence Perspective and Its Critics

In stark contrast to violence-against-women researchers, family-violence researchers focus on what they see as the problem of "spouse abuse" on women's as well as men's use of violence. They claim that women as well as men are perpetrators of physical violence (McNeeley and Mann 1990; McNeely and Robinson-Simpson 1987; Steinmetz and Lucca 1988), and some claim that women are as violent within the family as men (Shupe, Stacey, and Hazelwood 1987; Stets and Straus 1990; Straus 1993; Straus and Gelles 1986). In this section, I argue that when researchers claim that women are as violent as men, they do so on the basis of faulty data and assumptions about gender and the family.

Family-violence researchers typically base their claims about women's use of violence on data collected using the Conflict Tactics Scales (CTS) (Straus 1979), instruments that require respondents to identify conflict tactics they have used in the previous year. These range from nonviolent tactics (calm discussion) to the most violent tactics (use of a knife or gun). Using this scale, family-violence researchers (Straus 1993; Straus and Gelles 1986; Straus et al. 1980) find similar percentages of husbands and wives using violent tactics. On the basis of these data, some family-violence researchers conclude that "husband battering" is a serious problem and even that there is a "battered husband syndrome" (Steinmetz and Lucca 1988; Steinmetz 1977/78, 1988). Findings based on the CTS have been replicated by a number of researchers here and abroad (Brinkerhoff and Lupri 1988; Nisonoff and Bitman 1979; Stets 1990), including for dating relationships (Arias et al. 1987; DeMaris 1987; Lane and Gwartney-Gibbs 1985).

Findings from the 1985 National Family Violence Survey (NFVS), based on women's responses to the Conflict Tactics Scales, show that both wife and husband were violent in 48.6 percent of cases, the husband only was violent in 25.9 percent of cases, and the wife only was violent in 25.5 percent of cases (Straus 1993). Straus concludes from these data that "regardless of whether the analysis is based on all assaults, or is focused on dangerous assaults, about as many women as men attacked a spouse who had *not* hit them during the one year referent period." Citing other studies that show the same results, he concludes that these figures are "inconsistent with the 'self-defense' explanation for the high rate of domestic assault by women" (1993, 74).

Violence-against-women researchers (Berk et al. 1983; Dobash et al. 1992; Saunders 1989; Stark and Flitcraft 1996; Yllö 1993) argue that the data showing that women are as violent as men, particularly data based on the Conflict Tactics Scales, are misleading and flawed. These researchers believe that the validity of the scales is undermined because the continuum of violence in the scales is so broad that it fails to discriminate among different kinds of violence (Dobash and Dobash 1979, 1992; Stark and Flitcraft

1985). For example, the CTS contains an item "bit, kicked, or hit with a fist." Thus, a woman who bites is equated with a man who kicks or hits with a fist. Another item, "hit or tried to hit with an object," which is counted as severe violence, is similarly ambiguous. Further, critics argue, the scale does not take self-defense into account.

In support of their position, violence-against-women researchers also point to the findings of studies in which women were asked about their use of violence. For example, Saunders (1988) found that in the vast majority of cases, women attributed their use of violent tactics to self-defense and fighting back. Emery et al. (1989), in an interview study based on a small sample of women who were victims of dating violence, found that most women spoke of self-defense. Some women also spoke of using violence in frustration and anger at being dominated by their partners and in retaliation for their partners' violent behavior.

Further, violence-against-women researchers point out that the CTS focuses narrowly on counting acts of violence. Such a focus draws attention away from related patterns of control and abuse in relationships, including psychological abuse and sexual abuse, and does not address other means of nonviolent intimidation and domination including verbal abuse, the use of suicide threats, or the use of violence against property, pets, children, or other relatives. Similarly, the conception of violence as a "conflict tactic" fails to convey the connection between the use of violence and the exercise of power. Ylö (1993, 53) argues that violence is better conceptualized as a "tactic of coercive control to maintain the husband's power."

In addition to their view that women commit as many violent acts as men, family-violence researchers claim that women initiate violence as frequently as men. They draw this conclusion on the basis of responses to a question in the National Family Violence Survey about who initiated conflicts in the relationship. The NFVS, based on the CTS, found that in the case of wives who were involved in "violent relationships," 53 percent reported that they hit first, while their partners initiated the violence in 42 percent of cases (Straus 1993, 74). These findings have led family-violence researchers to a new focus on women's use of violence (Straus 1993). Even though husbands use more serious types of violence, these researchers now claim that violence by women against their husbands must be considered a serious problem.

Let us briefly examine the logic of the family-violence position that women initiate violence as often as men. Straus (1993, 79) turns our attention to occasions when a woman slaps a man. He refers to a "typical case" in which a woman uses acts of violence because a man who is acting like a "cad" has done something offensive to her: "Let us assume that most of the assaults by women are the 'slap the cad' genre and are not intended to, and only rarely cause physical injury." He then focuses on the woman's "assaults" and goes on to argue that a woman who "slaps the cad" is in effect provoking her partner by providing him with a justification for hitting:

> Such morally correct slapping acts out and reinforces the traditional tolerance of assault in marriage. The moral justification of assault implicit when a woman slaps or throws something at a partner for something outrageous reinforces the moral justification for slapping her when *she* is doing something outrageous, being obstinate, nasty, or "not listening to reason" as he sees it.

After claiming that assaults by wives are one of the "causes" of assaults by husbands, he concludes with a stern warning that all women must forsake violence:

One of the many steps needed for primary prevention of assaults on wives is for women to forsake even "harmless" physical attacks on male partners and children. Women must insist on non-violence by their sisters, just as they rightfully insist on it by men.

In a few sentences, Straus proceeds from women's defensive behavior to a focus on women as provoking the violence. What is wrong with this logic? Although eliminating violence should be a high-priority goal for all men, women, and children, this reframing of the issue puts the blame and responsibility for the violence on the woman. Targeting women's behavior removes the focus from what men might be doing to women. What does it mean that he is acting like a "cad"? Does this refer to unwanted sexual advances, the belittling of a woman, verbal intimidation, drunken frenzy? Who is responsible here? Focusing on the woman's behavior provides support for typical excuses and justifications by batterers, such as "she provoked me to do this" (Ptacek 1988).

Another problem with asking a single question about who initiated the violence is that it does not focus on the meaning and context of female violence against male partners. For example, there were no questions asked about women's motives for striking first. We know that male physical and sexual violence against women is often preceded by name-calling and other types of psychological abuse (Browne 1987), and that women may view these behaviors as early warning signs of violence and hit first in hopes of preventing their partners from using violence (Saunders 1989). Hanmer and Saunders (1984) have noted that many women hit first because of a "well-founded fear" of being beaten or raped by their husbands or male intimates. Thus, even when women do initiate violence, it may very well be an act of self-defense.

In my view, there are many reasons why it would be better if we all could be nonviolent—it may well be true that violence provokes more violence. However, we must understand the power dynamics behind the use of violence in particular types of relationships; we must examine who feels entitled to use violence and why. The violence against women perspective addresses these critical questions about the context of violence.

A brief examination of the theoretical perspective of family-violence researchers shows the faulty assumptions that guide their interpretation of the data. As one would expect from their findings, as well as their use of the terms "family violence" and "spouse abuse," family-violence researchers take a family systems approach to analyzing husbands' and wives' use of violence. They believe that the origins of the problem of violence lie in the nature of the family, not in the relationship between husband and wife (Gelles and Straus 1988; Straus 1993), and that violence affects all family relationships. According to Straus, Gelles, and Steinmetz (1980, 44):

> A fundamental solution to the problem of wife-beating has to go beyond a concern with how to control assaulting husbands. It seems as if violence is built into the very structure of the society and family system itself. . . . (Wife-beating) is only one aspect of the general pattern of family violence, which includes parent-child violence, child-to-child violence, and wife-to-husband violence.

Family-violence researchers (Gelles and Cornell 1985; Gelles and Straus 1988) believe that violence in the contemporary American family is caused by a variety of social-structural factors, including stresses from difficult working conditions, unemployment, financial insecurity, and health problems. They also believe that husbands and wives are affected by wider social norms condoning violence as a means of solving conflict, and they see evidence of the cultural acceptance of violence in television programming, folklore, and fairy tales (Straus 1980), and in surveys showing widespread public acceptance of violence. Straus and his colleagues also cite sexism as a factor in family violence; while they believe men and women are equally violent, they believe women are more victimized by family violence because of "the greater physical, financial, and emotional injury suffered by women" (Straus 1993).

Proponents of the family violence perspective make some important points about the prevalence of violence in American society; however, from a violence against women perspective, the family violence view is seriously flawed. Although cultural norms of violence and stressful living conditions may influence individuals' use of violence, these wider cultural norms and social conditions are mediated by the norms of particular institutions. In the case of marriage, norms promoting male dominance in heterosexual relationships and males' right to use force have a direct influence on how people behave in marriage.

Family-violence researchers do acknowledge male dominance when they argue that sexism is an important factor in domestic violence and that women are the ones who are most seriously hurt in battering relationships. However, from the perspective of a violence-against-women researcher, sexism is not just "a" factor in domestic violence. Rather, gender is one of the fundamental organizing principles of society. It is a social relation that enters into and partially constitutes all other social relations and activities, and pervades the entire social context in which a person lives. Thus, violence-against-women researchers criticize family-violence researchers for equating "spouse abuse," elder abuse, and child abuse, because women become just one of a number of victims. Violence-against-women researchers believe that wife abuse should be compared to related types of violence against women such as rape, marital rape, sexual harassment, and incest (Wardell et al. 1983), all of which are also products of male dominance.

Violence-against-women researchers believe that family-violence researchers disregard the influence of gender on marriage and heterosexual relationships and see power in the family as a gender-neutral phenomenon. Family-violence researchers claim that "violence is used by the most powerful family member as a means of legitimizing his or her dominant position" (Straus et al. 1980, 193) and believe that power can as easily be held by a wife as by a husband. According to violence-against-women researchers, this view of the exercise of power as gender-neutral misrepresents the nature of marriage as a partnership of equals. As discussed above, marriage has been and still is structured so that husbands have more power than wives. Men are the primary wage earners and women, as those responsible for childrearing and household work, do not typically have the same bargaining power as their husbands. Thus power is not gender-neutral; it is structured into the institution of marriage in such a way that women are disadvantaged.

The basic assumptions of the family violence and violence against women approaches to domestic violence are irreconcilable. Further, each group has voiced strong disagreements with the other. Family-violence researchers argue that the legitimate sociological approach to the issue of violence in the family should be a "multicausal" one and believe that violence against women perspectives, particularly those identified as feminist, are biased by a single-minded focus on gender (Straus 1991). Further, family-violence researchers criticize feminist work as "political" (Gelles 1983; Straus 1991) and charge that they have been harrassed for studying violent women (Gelles and Straus 1988, 106; Straus 1991). They believe that findings about women's violence have been "suppressed" because they are not "politically correct" (Straus 1993). Such statements posit a conspiracy of feminists to keep the "truth" from being known, rather than an understanding that different theories and methods lead to different conclusions.

Violence-against-women researchers fear that the family-violence approach will reinforce existing popular conceptions that women cause their own victimization by provoking their male partners. They fear that such views will lead to policy outcomes that are harmful to women. Family-violence researchers acknowledge that their research has been used to provide testimony against battered women in court cases and to minimize the need for shelters (Straus and Gelles 1986, 471; Gelles and Straus 1988, 90); however, they argue that this is less "costly" than the "denial and suppression" of violence by women (Straus and Gelles 1986, 471). The question is, costly for whom?

Further, these researchers are concerned that if funders come to believe that family violence is a "mutual" occurrence between "spouses," or that there is a "battered husband syndrome," there will be decreased support for shelters for battered women. Violence-against-women researchers also fear a diversion of resources to shelters for "battered men." Straus's work has been cited to provide evidence that women assault men (Lewin 1992, 12). Men's rights groups cite the "battered husband syndrome" when lobbying for custody and child support issues from a men's rights perspective (Ansberry 1988; Fathers for Equal Rights Organization 1988; McNeely and Robinson-Simpson 1987).

Violence-against-women researchers also fear that the family-violence perspective will reinforce the individualist bias in the field of counseling—that counselors will focus on clients' individual and personal problems without identifying the inequality between men and women that provides the context for battering (Adams 1988). They disagree with those family-violence researchers who argue that violence is caused primarily by frustration, poor social skills, or inability to control anger (Hotaling, Straus, and Lincoln 1990; Shupe, Stacey, and Hazelwood 1987; Steinmetz 1986). Finally, violence-against-women researchers worry that a belief in "spouse abuse" or a "battered husband syndrome" will encourage police who operate under mandatory arrest statutes to arrest women in "domestic disputes."

Conclusion

In this chapter I have argued that research that promotes a gender-neutral view of "family violence" misrepresents the nature of violence against women. Women are typically the victims, not the perpetrators, of violence in intimate relationships. A violence against women perspective much more accurately explains the nature of violence in intimate relationships. It is norms and practices of male dominance that promote the use of violence by men toward female intimates. The proponents of the family violence perspective, in arguing that women are violent toward men, disregard gender and its determining role in structuring marital and other heterosexual relationships. Existing data on the use of conflict tactics and acts of violence must be interpreted in the context of power differences in male-female relationships. Abstracted from their context, data on who initiates and uses violence promote faulty conclusions. Fortunately, some have begun to develop new ways of measuring the use of violence and control that take into account how gender shapes the exercise of power in heterosexual relationships (Yllö 1990).

One important direction for future research is to demonstrate how male dominance produces male violence against women on an ongoing, everyday basis (Hood 1989). One way to do this is to devote greater attention to the study of the major institutions in which males learn violence, such as the military (Russell 1989), sports (Messner 1992), and fraternities (Martin and Hummer 1993; Sanday 1991). Another is to investigate how major institutions, through their ideologies and practices, define the abuse of women by male intimates and respond to women who have experienced abuse. Researchers should focus both on institutionwide policies and practices and on the labeling and processing of abused women by front-line workers who have the most contact with abused women. In studying the institutional response to violence, it would be profitable to compare responses to the range of violence against women, including rape, marital rape, sexual harassment, and incest (Stanko 1985; Wardell et al. 1983).

One institution that is central in the labeling and processing of woman battering is the legal system. Traditionally, the legal system has defined woman battering as a private, family matter and has been instrumental in enforcing its privatization. Although new laws have criminalized woman battering, the critical question is whether these laws will be enforced. If these laws are not taken seriously, the legal system will continue to treat the problem of woman battering as an individual one and return battered women to the private sphere.

Another institution that is key in the identification of abuse is the health care system. We must analyze how current medical ideologies (Stark and Flitcraft 1996) and practices (Kurz 1990) ignore the problem of battering, or redefine it as a problem caused by women's own individual problems and therefore outside the purview of the health care system. We must also analyze how medical language and discourse render the problem of battering invisible. In a study of the medical records of women who had been physically abused, Warshaw (1993) found that physicians, through their use of disembodied language that focused on injuries caused by nameless forces, obscured the fact that women had been abused. Lamb (1991, 1995) found that when newspaper writers and even scholars write about physical abuse, they use vague language that fails to specify who is responsible for the abuse.

We need a major reexamination of those norms of male-female intimates and family relationships that promote and condone violence. One approach would be to place the study of woman battering in the context of other strategies of power and control in male-female relationships. Mederos (1987) suggests that there is a continuum of strategies that husbands use to control wives, from anger to emotional abuse to physical violence.

We would also profit from an understanding of women's responses to violence and their control strategies in intimate relationships. There are strong indications that men and women see violent acts differently (Adams 1988). Some argue that women minimize and rationalize the violence done to them (Greenblat 1983). Several studies (Dobash and Dobash 1979; Ferraro and Johnson 1983; Mills 1985) have documented a progression in women's outlook from an initial view of the violence as an aberrant, occasional event to a view of the violence as a serious problem. Mills (1985) describes how the women she interviewed minimized the problematic aspects of their husband's violence by ignoring it and focusing on the positive aspects of their relationship with their husband or by justifying their husband's behavior as beyond his control. As the violence in these relationships increased, however, the women became increasingly anxious. But women's perceptions that something is wrong must be validated by someone outside the situation in order for them to define the situation as one in which they are victims of physical abuse.

In the case of men, some argue that batterers have either a set of explanations by which they deny their abusive behavior or a set of rationalizations by which they legitimize their violent behavior (Okun 1986; Ptacek 1988). Understanding these control strategies would provide a greater understanding of power in marriage, of the origins of violence, and of the possibilities of reducing male violence toward female intimates.

A focus on power in the family also provides an opportunity to examine changes in rates of violence along with changes in family power. For example, it is widely accepted that when wives work, they increase their power in the family (Collins 1988; Scanzoni 1982). Does male violence against women increase or decrease as a result of this shift in power? Does it make a difference whether the wife works with mostly women or mostly men?

Finally, it would be very useful to have cross-cultural data on rates of violence and variations in institutional responses to violence. In a cross-cultural study of rape, Sanday (this volume) found that a combination of economic and cultural factors contributes to variations in rates of rape. In societies in which women are included in religious and cultural institutions and in which women's economic and reproductive contributions are recognized, there is less violence and rape against women. Cross-cultural data would provide useful information on the relative importance of a variety of factors influencing all the forms of violence against women: norms and practices of male domination, norms of violence, cultural production, and economic and family systems.

33

Pornography and the Alienation of Male Sexuality

HARRY BROD

This chapter is intended as a contribution to an ongoing discussion. It aims to augment, not refute or replace, what numerous commentators have said about pornography's role in the social construction of sexuality. I have several principal aims in this chapter. My primary focus is to examine pornography's model of male sexuality. Furthermore, in the discussion of pornography's role in the social construction of sexuality, I wish to place more emphasis than is common on the social construction of pornography. As I hope to show, these are related questions. One reason I focus on the image of male sexuality in pornography is that I believe this aspect of the topic has been relatively neglected. In making this my topic here, I do not mean to suggest that this is the most essential part of the picture. Indeed, I am clear it is not. It seems clear enough to me that the main focus of discussion about the effects of pornography is and should be the harmful effects of pornography on women, its principal victims. Yet, there is much of significance which needs to be said about pornography's representation, or perhaps I should more accurately say misrepresentation, of male sexuality. My focus shall be on what is usually conceived of as "normal" male sexuality, which for my purposes I take to be consensual, non-violent heterosexuality, as these terms are conventionally understood. I am aware of analyses which argue that this statement assumes distinctions which are at least highly problematic, if not outright false, which argue that this "normal" sexuality is itself coercive, both as compulsory heterosexuality and as containing implicit or explicit coercion and violence. My purpose is not to take issue with these analyses, but simply to present an analysis of neglected aspects of the links between mainstream male sexuality and pornography. I would argue that the aspect of the relation between male sexuality and pornography usually discussed, pornography's incitement to greater extremes of violence against women, presupposes such a connection with the more accepted mainstream. Without such a link, pornography's messages would be rejected by, rather than assimilated into, male culture. My intention is to supply this usually missing link.

My analysis proceeds from both feminist and Marxist theory. These are often taken to be theories which speak from the point of view of the oppressed, in advocacy for their interests. That they indeed are, but they are also more than that. For each claims

From *Social Theory and Practice* 14, no. 3 (1988):265–84. Reprinted by permission.

not simply to speak for the oppressed in a partisan way, but also to speak a truth about the social whole, a truth perhaps spoken in the name of the oppressed, but a truth objectively valid for the whole. That is to say, Marxism is a theory which analyzes the ruling class as well as the proletariat, and feminism is a theory which analyzes men as well as women. It is not simply that Marxism is concerned with class, and feminism with gender, both being united by common concerns having to do with power. Just as Marxism understands class as power, rather than simply understanding class differences as differences of income, lifestyle, or opportunities, so the distinctive contribution of feminism is its understanding of gender as power, rather than simply as sex role differentiation. Neither class nor gender should be reified into being understood as fixed entities, which then differentially distribute power and its rewards. Rather, they are categories continually constituted in ongoing contestations over power. The violence endemic to both systems cannot be understood as externalized manifestations of some natural inner biological or psychological drives existing prior to the social order, but must be seen as emerging in and from the relations of power which constitute social structures. Just as capitalist exploitation is caused not by capitalists' excess greed but rather by the structural imperatives under which capitalism functions, so men's violence is not the manifestation of some inner male essence, but rather evidence of the bitterness and depth of the struggles through which genders are forged.[1]

For my purposes here, to identify this as a socialist feminist analysis is not, in the first instance, to proclaim allegiance to any particular set of doctrinal propositions, though I am confident that those I subscribe to would be included in any roundup of the usual suspects, but rather to articulate a methodological commitment to make questions of power central to questions of gender, and to understand gendered power in relation to economic power, and as historically, materially structured.[2] If one can understand the most intimate aspects of the lives of the dominant group in these terms, areas which would usually be taken to be the farthest afield from where one might expect these categories to be applicable, then I believe one has gone a long way toward validating claims of the power of socialist feminist theory to comprehend the totality of our social world. This is my intention here. I consider the analysis of male sexuality I shall be presenting part of a wider socialist feminist analysis of patriarchal capitalist masculinity, an analysis I have begun to develop elsewhere.[3]

As shall be abundantly clear, I do not take a "sexual liberationist" perspective on pornography. I am aware that many individuals, particularly various sexual minorities, make this claim on pornography's behalf. I do not minimize or negate their personal experiences. In the context of our society's severe sexual repressiveness, pornography may indeed have a liberating function for certain individuals. But I do not believe an attitude of approval for pornography follows from this. Numerous drugs and devices which have greatly helped individual women have also been medical and social catastrophes—the one does not negate the other.

I shall be claiming that pornography has a negative impact on men's own sexuality. This is a claim that an aspect of an oppressive system, patriarchy, operates, at least in part, to the disadvantage of the group it privileges, men. This claim does not deny that the overall effect of the system is to operate in men's advantage, nor does it deny that the same aspect of the system under consideration, that is, male sexuality and pornography under patriarchy, might not also contribute to the expansion and maintenance of male power even as it also works to men's disadvantage. Indeed, I shall be arguing precisely for such complementarity. I am simply highlighting one of the "contradictions" in the system. My reasons for doing so are in the first instance simply analytic:

to, as I said, bring to the fore relatively neglected aspects of the issue. Further, I also have political motivations for emphasizing this perspective. I view raising consciousness of the prices of male power as part of a strategy through which one could at least potentially mobilize men against pornography's destructive effects on both women and men.

It will aid the following discussion if I ask readers to call to mind a classic text in which it is argued that, among many other things, a system of domination also damages the dominant group, and prevents them from realizing their full humanity. The argument is that the dominant group is "alienated" in specific and identifiable ways. The text I have in mind is Marx's "Economic and Philosophic Manuscripts of 1844." Just as capitalists as well as workers are alienated under capitalism according to Marxist theory (in a certain restricted sense, even more so), so men, I shall argue, and in particular male modes of sexuality, are also alienated under patriarchy. In the interests of keeping this paper a manageable length, I shall here assume rather than articulate a working familiarity with Marx's concept of alienation, the process whereby one becomes a stranger to oneself and one's own powers come to be powers over and against one. Since later in the paper I make use of some of Marx's more economistic concepts, I should however simply note that I see more continuity than rupture between Marx's earlier, more philosophical writings and his later, more economic ones.[4] While much of this paper presents an analysis of men's consciousness, I should make clear that while alienation may register in one's consciousness (as I argue it does), I follow Marx in viewing alienation not primarily as a psychological state dependent on the individual's sensibilities or consciousness but as a condition inevitably caused by living within a system of alienation. I should also note that I consider what follows an appropriation, not a systematic interpretation, of some of Marx's concepts.

Alienated pornographic male sexuality can be understood as having two dimensions, what I call the objectification of the body and the loss of subjectivity. I shall consider each in greater detail, describing various aspects of pornographic male sexuality under each heading in a way which I hope brings out how they may be conceptualized in Marx's terms. Rather than then redoing the analysis in Marx's terms, I shall then simply cite Marx briefly to indicate the contours of such a translation.

Objectification of the Body

In terms of both its manifest image of and its effects on male sexuality, that is, in both intrinsic and consequentialist terms, pornography restricts male sensuality in favor of a genital, performance oriented male sexuality. Men become sexual acrobats endowed with oversized and overused organs which are, as the chapter title of a fine book on male sexuality describes, "The Fantasy Model of Sex: Two Feet Long, Hard as Steel, and Can Go All Night."[5] To speak non-euphemistically, using penile performance as an index of male strength and potency directly contradicts biological facts. There is no muscle tissue in the penis. Its erection when aroused results simply from increased blood flow to the area. All social mythology aside, the male erection is physiologically nothing more than localized high blood pressure. Yet this particular form of hypertension has attained mythic significance. Not only does this focusing of sexual attention on one organ increase male performance anxieties, but it also desensitizes other areas of the body from becoming what might otherwise be sources of pleasure. A colleague once told me that her favorite line in a lecture on male sexuality I used to give in a course I regularly taught was my declaration that the basic male sex organ is not the penis, but the skin.

The predominant image of women in pornography presents women as always sexually ready, willing, able, and eager. The necessary corollary to pornography's myth of female perpetual availability is its myth of male perpetual readiness. Just as the former fuels male misogyny when real-life women fail to perform to pornographic standards, so do men's failures to similarly perform fuel male insecurities. Furthermore, I would argue that this diminishes pleasure. Relating to one's body as a performance machine produces a split consciousness wherein part of one's attention is watching the machine, looking for flaws in its performance, even while one is supposedly immersed in the midst of sensual pleasure. This produces a self-distancing self-consciousness which mechanizes sex and reduces pleasure. (This is a problem perpetuated by numerous sexual self-help manuals, which treat sex as a matter of individual technique for fine-tuning the machine rather than as human interaction. I would add that men's sexual partners are also affected by this, as they can often intuit when they are being subjected to rote manipulation.)

Loss of Subjectivity

In the terms of discourse of what it understands to be "free" sex, pornographic sex comes "free" of the demands of emotional intimacy or commitment. It is commonly said as a generalization that women tend to connect sex with emotional intimacy more than men do. Without romantically blurring female sexuality into soft focus, if what is meant is how each gender consciously thinks or speaks of sex, I think this view is fair enough. But I find it takes what men say about sex, that it doesn't mean as much or the same thing to them, too much at face value. I would argue that men do feel similar needs for intimacy, but are trained to deny them, and are encouraged further to see physical affection and intimacy primarily if not exclusively in sexual terms. This leads to the familiar syndrome wherein, as one man put it:

> Although what most men want is physical affection, what they end up thinking they want is to be laid by a Playboy bunny.[6]

This puts a strain on male sexuality. Looking to sex to fulfill what are really non-sexual needs, men end up disappointed and frustrated. Sometimes they feel an unfilled void, and blame it on their or their partner's inadequate sexual performance. At other times they feel a discomfitting urgency or neediness to their sexuality, leading in some cases to what are increasingly recognized as sexual addiction disorders (therapists are here not talking about the traditional "perversions," but behaviors such as what is coming to be called a "Don Juan Syndrome," an obsessive pursuit of sexual "conquests"). A confession that sex is vastly overrated often lies beneath male sexual bravado. I would argue that sex seems overrated because men look to sex for the fulfillment of nonsexual emotional needs, a quest doomed to failure. Part of the reason for this failure is the priority of quantity over quality of sex which comes with sexuality's commodification. As human needs become subservient to market desires, the ground is laid for an increasing multiplication of desires to be exploited and filled by marketable commodities.[7]

For the most part the female in pornography is not one the man has yet to "conquer," but one already presented to him for the "taking." The female is primarily there as sex object, not sexual subject. Or, if she is not completely objectified, since men do want to be desired themselves, hers is at least a subjugated subjectivity. But one needs another independent subject, not an object or a captured subjectivity, if one either wants one's own prowess validated, or if one simply desires human interaction. Men functioning in the pornographic mode of male sexuality, in which men dominate women, are denied satisfaction of these human desires.[8] Denied recognition in the sexual interaction itself, they look to gain this recognition in wider social recognition of their "conquest."

To the pornographic mind, then, women become trophies awarded to the victor. For women to serve this purpose of achieving male social validation, a woman "conquered" by one must be a woman deemed desirable by others. Hence pornography both produces and reproduces uniform standards of female beauty. Male desires and tastes must be channeled into a single mode, with allowance for minor variations which obscure the fundamentally monolithic nature of the mold. Men's own subjectivity becomes masked to them, as historically and culturally specific and varying standards of beauty are made to appear natural and given. The ease with which men reach quick agreement on what makes a woman "attractive," evidenced in such things as the "1–10" rating scale of male banter and the reports of a computer program's success in predicting which of the contestants would be crowned "Miss America," demonstrates how deeply such standards have been internalized, and consequently the extent to which men are dominated by desires not authentically their own.

Lest anyone think that the analysis above is simply a philosopher's ruminations, too far removed from the actual experiences of most men, let me just offer one recent instantiation, from among many known to me, and even more, I am sure, I do not know. The following is from the *New York Times Magazine*'s "About Men" weekly column. In an article titled "Couch Dancing," the author describes his reactions to being taken to a place, a sort of cocktail bar, where women "clad only in the skimpiest of bikini underpants" would "dance" for a small group of men for a few minutes for about twenty-five or thirty dollars, men who "sat immobile, drinks in hand, glassy-eyed, tapping their feet to the disco music that throbbed through the room."

> Men are supposed to like this kind of thing, and there is a quite natural part of each of us that does. But there is another part of us—of me, at least—that is not grateful for the traditional male sexual programming, not proud of the results. By a certain age, most modern men have been so surfeited with images of unattainably beautiful women in preposterous contexts that we risk losing the capacity to respond to the ordinarily beautiful women we love in our bedrooms. There have been too many times when I have guiltily resorted to impersonal fantasy because the genuine love I felt for a woman wasn't enough to convert feeling into performance. And in those sorry, secret moments, I have resented deeply my lifelong indoctrination into the esthetic of the centerfold.[9]

Alienation and Crisis

I believe that all of the above can be translated without great difficulty into a conceptual framework paralleling Marx's analysis of the alienation experienced by capitalists. The essential points are captured in two sentences from Marx's manuscripts:

1. *All* the physical and intellectual senses have been replaced by the simple alienation of *all* these senses; the sense of *having*.[10]
2. The wealthy man is at the same time one who *needs* a complex of human manifestations of life, and whose own self-realization exists as an inner necessity, a need.[11]

Both sentences speak to a loss of human interaction and self-realization. The first articulates how desires for conquest and control prevent input from the world. The second presents an alternative conception wherein wealth is measured by abilities for self-expression, rather than possession. Here Marx expresses his conceptualization of the state of alienation as a loss of sensuous fulfillment, poorly replaced by a pride of possession, and a lack of self-consciousness and hence actualization of one's own real desires and abilities. One could recast the preceding analysis of pornographic male sexuality through these categories. In Marx's own analysis, these are more properly conceived of as the results of alienation, rather than the process of alienation itself. This process is at its basis a process of inversion, a reversal of the subject-object relationship, in which one's active powers become estranged from one, and return to dominate one as an external force. It is this aspect which I believe is most useful in understanding the alienation of male sexuality of which pornography is part and parcel. How is it that men's power turns against them, so that pornography, in and by which men dominate women, comes to dominate men themselves?

To answer this question I shall find it useful to have recourse to two other concepts central to Marxism, the concept of "crisis" in the system and the concept of "imperialism."[12] Marx's conception of the economic crisis of capitalism is often misunderstood as a prophecy of a cataclysmic doomsday scenario for the death of capitalism. Under this interpretation, some look for a single event, perhaps like a stock market crash, to precipitate capitalism's demise. But such events are for Marx at most triggering events, particular crises, which can shake the system, if at all, only because of the far more important underlying structural general crisis of capitalism. This general crisis is increasingly capitalism's ordinary state, not an extraordinary occurrence. It is manifest in the ongoing fiscal crisis of the state as well as recurring crises of legitimacy, and results from basic contradictory tensions within capitalism. One way of expressing these tensions is to see them as a conflict between the classic laissez-faire capitalist market mode, wherein capitalists are free to run their own affairs as individuals, and the increasing inability of the capitalist class to run an increasingly complex system without centralized management. The result of this tension is that the state increasingly becomes a managerial committee for the capitalist class, and is increasingly called upon to perform functions previously left to individuals. As entrepreneurial and laissez-faire capitalism give way to corporate capitalism and the welfare state, the power of capitalism becomes increasingly depersonalized, increasingly reft from the hands of individual capitalists and collectivized, so that capitalists themselves come more and more under the domination of impersonal market forces no longer under their direct control.

To move now to the relevance of the above, there is currently a good deal of talk about a perceived crisis of masculinity, in which men are said to be confused by contradictory imperatives given them in the wake of the women's movement. Though the male ego feels uniquely beleaguered today, in fact such talk regularly surfaces in our culture—the 1890s in the United States, for example, was another period in which the air was full of a "crisis of masculinity" caused by the rise of the "New Woman" and other factors.[13] Now, I wish to put forward the hypothesis that these particular "crises" of masculinity are but surface manifestations of a much deeper and broader phenomenon which I call the "general crisis of patriarchy," paralleling Marx's general crisis of capitalism. Taking a very broad view, this crisis results from the increasing depersonalization of patriarchal power which occurs with the development of patriarchy from its pre-capitalist phase, where power really was often directly exercised by individual patriarchs, to its late capitalist phase where men collectively exercise power over women, but are themselves as individuals increasingly under the domination of those same patriarchal powers.[14] I would stress that the sense of there being a "crisis" of masculinity arises not from the decrease or increase in patriarchal power as such. Patriarchal imperatives for men to retain power over women remain in force throughout. But there is a shift in the mode of that power's exercise, and the sense of crisis results from the simultaneous promulgation throughout society of two conflicting modes of patriarchal power, the earlier more personal form and the later more institutional form. The crisis results from the incompatibility of the two conflicting ideals of masculinity embraced by the different forms of patriarchy, the increasing conflicts between behavioral and attitudinal norms in the political/economic and the personal/familial spheres.

From Patriarchy to Fratriarchy

To engage for a moment in even broader speculation than that which I have so far permitted myself, I believe that much of the culture, law, and philosophy of the nineteenth century in particular can be reinterpreted as marking a decisive turn in this transition. I believe the passing of personal patriarchal power and its transformation into institutional patriarchal power in this period of the interrelated consolidation of corporate capitalism is evidenced in such phenomena as the rise of what one scholar has termed "judicial patriarchy," the new social regulation of masculinity through the courts and social welfare agencies, which through new support laws, poor laws, desertion laws and other changes transformed what were previously personal obligations into legal duties, as well as in the "Death of God" phenomenon and its aftermath.[15] That is to say, I believe the loss of the personal exercise of patriarchal power and its diffusion through the institutions of society is strongly implicated in the death of God the Father and the secularization of culture in the nineteenth century, as well as the modern and postmodern problem of grounding authority and values.

I would like to tentatively and preliminarily propose a new concept to reflect this shift in the nature of patriarchy caused by the deindividualization and collectivization of male power. Rather than speak simply of advanced capitalist patriarchy, the rule of the *fathers*, I suggest we speak of fratriarchy, the rule of the *brothers*. For the moment, I propose this concept more as a metaphor than as a sharply defined analytical tool, much as the concept of patriarchy was used when first popularized. I believe this concept better captures what I would argue is one of the key issues in conceptualizing contemporary masculinities, the disjunction between the facts of public male power and the feelings of individual male powerlessness. As opposed to the patriarch, who embodied many levels and kinds of authority in his single person, the brothers stand in uneasy relationships with each other, engaged in sibling rivalry while trying to keep the power of the family of man as a whole intact. I note that one of the consequences of the shift from patriarchy to fratriarchy is that some people become nostalgic for the authority of the benevolent patriarch, who if he was doing his job right at least prevented one of the great dangers of fratriarchy, fratricide, the brothers' killing each other. Furthermore, fratriarchy is an intragenerational concept, whereas patriarchy is intergenerational. Patriarchy, as a father-to-son transmission of authority, more directly inculcates traditional historically grounded authority, whereas the dimension of temporal continuity is rendered more problematic in fratriarchy's brother-to-brother relationships. I believe this helps capture the problematic nature of modern historical consciousness as it emerged from the nineteenth century, what I would argue is the most significant single philosophical theme of that century. If taken in Freudian directions, the concept of fratriarchy also speaks to the brothers' collusion to repress awareness of the violence which lies at the foundations of society.

To return to the present discussion, the debate over whether pornography reflects men's power or powerlessness, as taken up recently by Alan Soble in his book *Pornography: Marxism, Feminism, and the Future of Sexuality*, can be resolved if one makes a distinction such as I have proposed between personal and institutional male power. Soble cites men's use of pornographic fantasy as compensation for their powerlessness in the real world to argue that "pornography is therefore not so much an expression of male power as it is an expression of their lack of power."[16] In contrast, I would argue that by differentiating levels of power one should more accurately say that pornography is both an expression of men's public power and an expression of their lack of personal power. The argument of this paper is that pornography's image of male sexuality works to the detriment of men personally even as its image of female sexuality enhances the powers of patriarchy. It expresses the power of alienated sexuality, or, as one could equally well say, the alienated power of sexuality.

With this understanding, one can reconcile the two dominant but otherwise irreconcilable images of the straight male consumer of pornography: on the one hand the powerful rapist, using pornography to consummate his sexual violence, and on the other hand the shy recluse, using it to consummate his masturbatory fantasies. Both images have their degree of validity, and I believe it is a distinctive virtue of the analysis presented here that one can understand not only the merits of each depiction, but their interconnection.

Embodiment and Erotica

In the more reductionist and determinist strains of Marxism, pornography as ideology would be relegated to the superstructure of capitalism. I would like to suggest another conceptualization: that pornography is not part of patriarchal capitalism's superstructure, but part of its infrastructure. Its commodification of the body and interpersonal relationships paves the way for the ever more penetrating ingression of capitalist market relations into the deepest reaches of the individual's psychological makeup. The feminist slogan that "The Personal is Political" emerges at a particular historical moment, and should be understood not simply as an imperative declaration that what has previously been seen solely as personal should now be viewed politically, but also as a response to the real increasing politicization of personal life.

This aspect can be illuminated through the Marxist concept of imperialism. The classical Marxist analysis of imperialism argues that it is primarily motivated by two factors: exploitation of natural resources and extension of the market. In this vein, pornography should be understood as imperialism of the body. The greater public proliferation of pornography, from the "soft-core" pornography of much commercial advertising to the greater availability of "hard-core" pornography, proclaims the greater colonization of the body by the market.[17] The increasing use of the male body as a sex symbol in contemporary culture is evidence of advanced capitalism's increasing use of new styles of masculinity to promote images of men as consumers as well as producers.[18] Today's debates over the "real" meaning of masculinity can be understood in large part as a struggle between those espousing the "new man" style of masculinity more suited to advanced corporate, consumerist patriarchal capitalism and those who wish to return to an idealized version of "traditional" masculinity suited to a more production-oriented, entrepreneurial patriarchal capitalism.[19]

In a more theoretical context, one can see that part of the reason the pornography debate has been so divisive, placing on different sides of the question people who usually find themselves allies, is that discussions between civil libertarians and feminists have often been at cross purposes. Here one can begin to relate political theory not to political practice, but to metaphysical theory. The classical civil liberties perspective on the issue remains deeply embedded in a male theoretical discourse on the meaning of sexuality. The connection between the domination of nature and the domination of women has been argued from many Marxist and feminist points of view.[20] The pivot of this connection is the masculine overlay of the mind-body dualism onto the male-female dichotomy. Within this framework, morality par excellence consists in the masculinized mind restraining the feminized body, with sexual desires seen as the crucial test for these powers of restraint. From this point of view, the question of the morality of pornography is primarily the quantitative question of how much sexual display is allowed, with full civil libertarians opting to uphold the extreme end of this continuum, arguing that no sexual expression should be repressed. But the crucial question, for at least the very important strain of feminist theory which rejects these dualisms which frame the debate for the malestream mainstream, is not *how much* sexuality is displayed but rather *how* sexuality is displayed. These theories speak not of mind-body dualism, but of mind/body wholism, where the body is seen not as the limitation or barrier for the expression of the free moral self, but rather as the most immediate and intimate vehicle for the expression of that self. The question of sexual morality here is not that of restraining or releasing sexual desires as they are forced on the spiritual self by the temptations of the body, but that of constructing spirited and liberating sexual relationships with and through one's own and others' bodies. Here sexual freedom is not the classical liberal freedom *from* external restraint, but the more radical freedom *to* construct authentically expressive sexualities.

I have argued throughout this paper that pornography is a vehicle for the imposition of socially constructed sexuality, not a means for the expression of autonomously self-determined sexuality. (I would add that in contrasting imposed and authentic sexualities I am not endorsing a sexual essentialism, but simply carving out a space for more personal freedom.) Pornography is inherently about commercialized sex, about the eroticization of power and the power of eroticization. One can look to the term's etymology for confirmation of this point. It comes from the classical Greek "*pornographos*, meaning 'writing (sketching) of harlots,'" sometimes women captured in war.[21] Any distinction between pornography and erotica remains problematic, and cannot be drawn with absolute precision. Yet I believe some such distinction can and must be made. I would place the two terms not in absolute opposition, but at two ends of a continuum, with gray areas of necessity remaining between them. The gradations along the continuum are marked not by the explicitness of the portrayal of sexuality or the body, nor by the assertiveness vs. passivity of persons, nor by any categorization of sexual acts or activities, but by the extent to which autonomous personhood is attributed to the person or persons portrayed. Erotica portrays sexual subjects, manifesting their personhood in and through their bodies. Pornography depicts sex objects, persons reduced to their bodies. While the erotic nude presents the more pristine sexual body before the social persona is adopted through donning one's clothing, the pornographic nude portrays a body whose clothing has been more or less forcibly removed, where the absence of that clothing remains the most forceful presence in the image. Society's objectification remains present, indeed emphasized, in pornography, in a way in which it does not in erotica. Erotica, as sexual art, expresses a self, whereas pornography, as sexual commodity, markets one. The latter "works" because the operation it performs on women's bodies resonates with the "pornographizing" the male gaze does to women in other areas of society.[22] These distinctions remain problematic, to say the least, in their application, and disagreement in particular cases will no doubt remain. Much more work needs to be done before one would with any reasonable confidence distinguish authentic from imposed, personal from commercial, sexuality. Yet I believe this is the crucial question, and I believe these concepts correctly indicate the proper categories of analysis. Assuming a full definition of freedom as including autonomy and self-determination, pornography is therefore incompatible with real freedom.

Conclusions

It has often been noted that while socialist feminism is currently a major component of the array of feminisms one finds in academic feminism and women's studies, it is far less influential on the playing fields of practical politics.[23] While an analysis of male sexuality may seem an unlikely source to further socialist feminism's practical political agenda, I hope this paper's demonstration of the interconnections between intimate personal experiences and large-scale historical and social structures, especially in what may have initially seemed unlikely places, may serve as a useful methodological model for other investigations.

In one sense, this chapter hopes to further the development of socialist feminist theory via a return to Hegel, especially the Hegel of the *Phenomenology*. Not only is Hegel's master-servant dialectic the *sine qua non* for the use of the concept of alienation in this paper, but the inspiration for a mode of analysis, which is true to the experimental consciousness of social actors while at the same time delimiting that consciousness by showing its partiality and placing it in a broader context, is rooted in Hegel's *Phenomenology*. It is not a coincidence that the major wave of socialist feminist theory and practice in the late 60s and early 70s coincided with a wave of Marxist interest in Hegel, and that current signs of a new feminist interest in Hegel coincide with signs of the resurgence of radical politics in the United States.[24] Analogous to the conception of socialist feminism I articulated in the Introduction to this chapter, my conception of Hegelianism defines Hegelianism as method rather than doctrine.[25] In some sense, contemporary Marxism and feminism can already be said to be rooted in Hegel, in the case of Marxism through Marx himself, and in the case of feminism through Beauvoir's *The Second Sex*. A more explicitly Hegelian influenced socialist feminism would embody a theory and practice emphasizing the following themes: the dialectic between individual consciousness and social structure, a thoroughly historical epistemology, a non-dualistic metaphysics, an understanding of gender, class, and other differences as being constituted through interaction rather than consisting of isolated "roles," the priority of political over moralistic or economistic theory, a probing of the relations between state power and cultural hegemony, a program for reaching unity through difference rather than through sameness, a tolerance of if not preference for ambiguity and contradiction, and an orientation toward process over end product.[26]

I would like to conclude with some remarks on the practical import of this analysis. First of all, if the analysis of the relationship between pornography and consumerism and the argument about pornography leading to violence are correct, then a different conceptualization of the debate over the ethics of the feminist anti-pornography movement emerges. If one accepts, as I do, the idea that this movement is not against sex, but against sexual abuse, then the campaign against pornography is essentially not a call for censorship but a consumer campaign for product safety. The proper context for the debate over its practices is then not issues of free speech or civil liberties, but issues of business ethics. Or rather, this is the conclusion I reach remaining focused on pornography and male sexuality. But we should remember the broader context I alluded to at the beginning of this chapter, the question of pornography's effects on women. In that context, women are not the consumers of pornography, but the consumed. Rather than invoking the consumer movement, perhaps we should then look to environmental protection as a model.[27] Following this line of reasoning, one could in principle then perhaps develop under the tort law of product liability an argument to accomplish much of the regulation of sexually explicit material some are now trying to achieve through legislative means, perhaps developing a new definition of "safe" sexual material.

Finally, for most of us, most of our daily practice as academics consists of teaching rather than writing or reading in our fields. If one accepts the analysis I have presented, a central if not primary concern for us should therefore be how to integrate this analysis into our classrooms. I close by suggesting that we use this analysis and others like it from the emerging field of men's studies to demonstrate to the men in our classes the direct relevance of feminist analysis to their own lives, at the most intimate and personal levels, and that we look for ways to demonstrate to men that feminism can be personally empowering and liberating for them without glossing over, and in fact emphasizing, the corresponding truth that this will also require the surrender of male privilege.[28]

NOTES

1. I am indebted for this formulation to Tim Carrigan, Bob Connell, and John Lee, "Toward a New Sociology of Masculinity," in Harry Brod, ed., *The Making of Masculinities: The New Men's Studies* (Boston: Allen & Unwin, 1987).

2. For the *locus classicus* of the redefinition of Marxism as method rather than doctrine, see Georg Lukács, *History and Class Consciousness: Studies in Marxist Dialectics*, trans. Rodney Livingstone (Cambridge, MA: MIT Press, 1972).

3. See my Introduction to Brod, *The Making of Masculinities*. For other recent books by men I consider to be engaged in essentially the same or a kindred project, see Jeff Hearn, *The Gender of Oppression: Men, Masculinity, and the Critique of Marxism* (New York: St. Martin's Press, 1987) and R. W. Connell, *Gender and Power* (Stanford, CA: Stanford University Press, 1987), particularly the concept of "hegemonic masculinity," also used in Carrigan, Connell, and Lee, "Toward A New Sociology of Masculinity." Needless to say, none of this work would be conceivable without the pioneering work of many women in women's studies.

4. For book-length treatments of Marx's concept of alienation, see István Mészáros, *Marx's Theory of Alienation* (New York: Harper & Row, 1972), and Bertell Ollman, *Alienation: Marx's Conception of Man in Capitalist Society* (Cambridge: Cambridge University Press, 1971).

5. Bernie Zilbergeld, *Male Sexuality: A Guide to Sexual Fulfillment* (Boston: Little, Brown and Company, 1978).

6. Michael Betzold, "How Pornography Shackles Men and Oppresses Women," in *For Men against Sexism: A Book of Readings*, ed. Jon Snodgrass. (Albion, CA: Times Change Press, 1977), p. 46.

7. I am grateful to Lenore Langsdorf and Paula Rothenberg for independently suggesting to me how this point would fit into my analysis.

8. See Jessica Benjamin, "The Bonds of Love: Rational Violence and Erotic Domination," *Feminist Studies* 6 (1980): 144–74.

9. Keith McWalter, "Couch Dancing," *New York Times Magazine*, December 6, 1987, p. 138.

10. Karl Marx, "Economic and Philosophic Manuscripts: Third Manuscript," in *Early Writings*, ed. and trans. T. B. Bottomore (New York: McGraw-Hill, 1964), pp. 159–60.

11. Marx., pp. 164–65.

12. An earlier version of portions of the following argument appears in my article "Eros Thanatized: Pornography and Male Sexuality" with a "1988 Postscript," forthcoming in Michael Kimmel, ed., *Men Confronting Pornography* (New York: Crown, 1989). The article originally appeared (without the postscript) in *Humanities in Society* 7 (1984) pp. 47–63.

13. See the essays by myself and Michael Kimmel in Brod, *The Making of Masculinities*.

14. Compare Carol Brown on the shift from private to public patriarchy: "Mothers, Fathers, and Children: From Private to Public Patriarchy" in Lydia Sargent, ed., *Women and Revolution* (Boston: South End Press, 1981).

15. According to Martha May in her paper " 'An Obligation on Every Man': Masculine Breadwinning and the Law in Nineteenth Century New York," presented at the American Historical Association, Chicago, Illinois, 1987, from which I learned of these changes, the term "judicial patriarchy" is taken from historian Michael Grossberg *Governing the Hearth: Law and the Family in Nineteen Century America* (Chapel Hill: University of North Carolina Press, 1985) and "Crossing Boundaries: Nineteenth Century Domestic Relations Law and the Merger of Family and Legal History," *American Bar Foundation Research Journal* (1985): 799–847.

16. Alan Soble, *Pornography: Marxism, Feminism, and the Future of Sexuality* (New Haven: Yale University Press, 1986), p. 82. I agree with much of Soble's analysis of male sexuality in capitalism, and note the similarities between much of what he says about "dismemberment" and consumerism and my analysis here.

17. See John D'Emilio and Estelle B. Freedman, *Intimate Matters: A History of Sexuality in America* (New York: Harper & Row, 1988).

18. See Barbara Ehrenreich, *The Hearts of Men: American Dreams and the Flight from Commitment* (New York: Anchor-Doubleday, 1983); and Wolfgang Fritz Haug, *Critique of Commodity Aesthetics: Appearance, Sexuality, and Advertising in Capitalist Society*, trans. Robert Bock (Minneapolis: University of Minnesota Press, 1986).

19. See my "Work Clothes and Leisure Suits: The Class Basis and Bias of the Men's Movement," originally in *Changing Men* 11 (1983) 10–12 and 38–40, reprint forthcoming in *Men's Lives: Readings in the Sociology of Men and Masculinity*, ed. Michael Kimmel and Michael Messner (New York: Macmillan, 1989).

20. This features prominently in the work of the Frankfurt school as well as contemporary ecofeminist theorists.

21. Rosemarie Tong, "Feminism, Pornography and Censorship," *Social Theory and Practice* 8 (1982): 1–17.

22. I learned to use "pornographize" as a verb in this way from Timothy Beneke's "Introduction" to his *Men on Rape* (New York: St. Martin's Press, 1982).

23. See the series of ten articles on "Socialist-Feminism Today" in *Socialist Review* 73–79 (1984–1985).

24. For the most recent feminist re-examinations of Hegel, see Heidi M. Raven, "Has Hegel Anything to Say to Feminists?", *The Owl of Minerva* 19 (1988) 149–68. Patricia Jagentowicz Mills, *Women, Nature, and Psyche* (New Haven: Yale University Press, 1987); and Susan M. Easton, "Hegel and Feminism," in David Lamb, ed., *Hegel and Modern Philosophy* (London: Croom Helm, 1987). Hegel enters contemporary radical legal thought primarily through the Critical Legal Studies movement. Especially relevant here is the work of Drucilla Cornell, for example, "Taking Hegel Seriously: Reflections on Beyond Objectivism and Relativism," *Cardozo Law Review* 7 (1985): 139; "Convention and Critique," *Cardozo Law Review* 7 (1986): 679; "Two Lectures on the Normative Dimensions of Community in the Law," *Tennessee Law Review* 54 (1987); 327; "Toward a Modern/Postmodern Reconstruction of Ethics," *University of Pennsylvania Law Review* 133 (1985): 291. See also papers from the Conference on "Hegel and Legal Theory," March 1988 at the Cardozo Law School of Yeshiva University, New York City, forthcoming in a special issue of the *Cardozo Law Review*. For signs of radical resurgence in the United States, I would cite such phenomena as the Jackson candidacy and the 1988 National Student Convention. Jefferson Morley writes: "The most fundamental idea shared by popular

movements East and West is the principle of 'civil society.' " Jefferson Morley, "On 'Civil Society,' " *The Nation*, May 7, 1988, p. 630.

25. I believe this is true to Hegel's own conception of Hegelianism, for Hegel put the Logic at the core of his system, and at the center of the Logic stands the transfiguration and transvaluation of form and content.

26. Much of the feminist critique of the philosophical mainstream echoes earlier critiques of the mainstream made in the name of "process thought." See *Feminism and Process Thought: The Harvard Divinity School/Claremont Center for Process Studies Symposium Papers*, ed. Sheila Greeve Davaney (Lewiston, NY: Edwin Mellen Press, 1981).

27. I am indebted to John Stoltenberg for this point.

28. I attempt to articulate this perspective principally in the following: *The Making of Masculinities*, Introduction and "The Case for Men's Studies;" *A Mensch among Men: Explorations in Jewish Masculinity* (Freedom, CA: Crossing Press, 1988), especially the Introduction; and "Why Is This 'Men's Studies' Different from All Other Men's Studies?,' " *Journal of the National Association for Women Deans, Administrators, and Counselors* 49 (1986): pp. 44–49. See also generally the small men's movement magazines *Changing Men: Issues in Gender, Sex and Politics* (306 North Brooks St., Madison, WI 53715), *brother: The Newsletter of the National Organization for Changing Men* (1402 Greenfield Ave., #1, Los Angeles, CA 90025), and *Men's Studies Review* (Box 32, Harriman, TN 37748).

34

The Reality of Linguistic Violence against Women

WILLIAM C. GAY

The Concept of Linguistic Violence

Hannah Arendt says that "violence is nothing more than the most flagrant manifestation of power."[1] Given this definition, one might expect that violence takes many forms. Numerous writers have, in fact, applied the concept of violence to more than direct bodily harm. Within philosophy, Newton Garver, for example, has developed a typology of violence that includes overt and covert forms, as well as personal and institutional forms.[2] In Garver's terms, what I call linguistic violence would be an example of covert institutional violence—assuming language is an institution and that its harm is more psychological than physical.

In this introductory section, I will respond to the position that denies the reality of linguistic violence and further clarify what I mean by linguistic violence. Then, in the next section, I will focus on sexist language as a particularly pervasive and pernicious form of linguistic violence. Finally, in my concluding section, I will rely on feminist criticisms of sexist language to sketch how efforts to supplant linguistic violence against women contribute to a broader practice of linguistic nonviolence.

Is linguistic violence real? Does it make sense to refer to the covert institutional violence of language? Thomas Platt answers both of these questions in the negative in his criticisms of such a broad concept of violence. Characterizing Garver's and others' usage of violence as polemic, Platt raises three main objections. His initial criticism is that such writers draw from the condemnatory nature of the term "violence." Platt claims that the "moral dubiousness" of various practices is independent of whether they are characterized as violent. More specifically, he stresses that "as the range of things denoted by a term expands, its descriptive force contracts."[3] Platt's objection, however, can divert us from the recognition that even a term that is polemic or condemnatory can have descriptive aspects. For example, to call an act "murder" is both condemnatory and descriptive in that one is also implying that someone has been killed.

Platt's second objection reduces to a minimalist ethic the moral perspective of those who extend the application of violence. He contends that violence is neither the only nor the most common form of immoral behavior. He goes on to state:

The contemporary tendency to extend the notion of violence assumes that it is the necessary condition for justifiably designating an action or practice as immoral. This assumption in turn seems to arise from our marked tendency to adopt an entirely negative . . . 'minimalist ethic'. Such a morality equates immoral behaviour with harmful behaviour, thus reducing one's moral obligations to a single obligation; the duty of non-maleficence.[4]

Platt is correct that some people can adopt a minimalist ethics that reduces moral obligation to non-maleficence. Nevertheless, even though people can equate immorality with harm, many people who oppose harm also affirm other moral principles. In other words, one can regard harm as a sufficient condition for moral condemnation, rather than a necessary one.

Platt's third objection is that such expanded usage may increase the level of violence. He suggests that claims that others are acting in violent ways can be used to justify counterviolence and can lead to increased social sanctions. Such a development, he says, could "increase the amount of real violence in the world rather than decrease it, while at the same time decreasing the amount of personal freedom in the world by extending the realm of behaviours justifiably subject to social control."[5] In response, I would simply note that just as I can be more than an ethical minimalist, I can also choose nonviolent responses to violence—regardless of how far I extend the term "violence."

Beyond these responses to the supposed pitfalls of extending the concept of violence, I wish to suggest an even broader view. I define *violentism* as the belief that violence— overt and covert, personal and institutional—is and perhaps should be used to achieve goals. Further, I contend that global culture has been and probably long will be one of violentism. But how does language do violence? How does language hurt or harm us? Rejecting the theory of etymological oppression, Stephanie Ross argues that "the ancient roots of ordinary English words cannot—by themselves—make those words oppressive."[6] Nevertheless, she contends, "Words can hurt, and one way they do is by conveying denigrating or demeaning attitudes."[7] To support her view, Ross utilizes Joel Feinberg's contention that hurt is a species of harm and that victims are necessarily aware of hurts. (For example, while assault is a hurt, undetected burglary is a harm.) Ross presents the distinction between offense and oppression as parallel to Feinberg's distinction between hurt and harm. As she puts it, "One can be oppressed unknowingly but offense requires (logically or conceptually) the awareness and acknowledgment of its victim."[8] So, language in general can perpetuate the harm of a system of oppression, regardless of whether individuals consciously experience the hurt of its offenses against them. The issue is whether such linguistic violence is an unavoidable consequence of the institution of language or whether through conscious effort it can be eliminated.

The concept of linguistic alienation can be traced back to Karl Marx,[9] but the most extensive and persuasive effort to develop this concept has been carried out by Ferruccio Rossi-Landi.[10] Arguing that speaking is a type of work, he explores the analogies between linguistics and economics. Because words can be marketed, language can function as capital with huge profits being reaped by the elite groups that control the means of linguistic production. Those portions of language that are treated like private property result in linguistic alienation for the masses.

Ranjit Chatterjee has made available to the English reader Rossi-Landi's radical interpretation of Ludwig Wittgenstein. Chatterjee cleverly, though sexistly, subtitles her essay "A Philosopher's Meaning Is His Use in the Culture."[11] Chatterjee claims that for Wittgenstein *philosophy is a struggle against the fascination of language.*"[12] Her conclusion is that for a Rossi-Landian Wittgensteinian:

the end of linguistic alienation, of human beings being charmed and fascinated by a fetish object, comes when language ceases to be idle, but paradoxically, language ceases being idle by going to work on itself, against itself. Just as the philosopher-fly can only leave the trap of the fly-bottle by the forgotten route of entry, every user of language can reach the end of linguistic alienation only by a thorough understanding—and rejection—of the hold of the fetish object. This is the connection with negative thought Rossi-Landi detected in Wittgenstein. By this connection, the reason for Wittgenstein's anti-theoretical posture, his noble inability to found a school, becomes clear. The founding of a school that would expound doctrines in the medium of words would simply represent the failure of the critique of language. Methodological minimalism in philosophy has as its consequence maximalism in the medium of deeds.[13]

I will try to take this recommendation of methodological minimalism to heart. As a consequence, I will follow Wittgenstein's advice. In other words, I will suggest that we look at how language is used.[14] Specifically, I will look at the diverse ways in which linguistic violence is practiced. In this sense, I will use Wittgenstein as a facilitator for applied philosophy.[15] Also, in the spirit of Rossi-Landi, I will not only describe these uses but also will criticize them.

From the perspective I have just sketched, I see certain tasks as unnecessary and others as crucial. On the one hand, the effort to provide a thorough causal explanation or a detailed theoretical framework is unnecessary. So, I am not going to argue for a primordial, monocausal root of linguistic violence, and I am not going to develop an extensive theory of linguistic violence. On the other hand, efforts to identify and eliminate linguistic violence are crucial. For this reason, I turn now to efforts to identify and eliminate the violence of sexist language.

The Violence of Sexist Language

Linguistic violence occurs across a continuum that stretches from subtle forms such as children's jokes to grievous forms such as totalitarian and genocidal language.[16] This continuum contains numerous abusive forms, such as racist, sexist, and heterosexist discourse. David Burgest, for example, notes how racist language serves to justify and rationalize the formation of groups for purposes of isolation.[17] As is now widely acknowledged, sexist language, along with racist language, pervades the history of discourse.[18] Another arena in which abusive language abounds is in the derogatory terminology used to describe gay and lesbian lifestyles. The long-standing and often physically violent reinforcement of the heterosexism of established discourse often makes an open discussion of sexual orientation quite difficult.[19]

My focus here is on the violence of sexist language, particularly as exposed by feminist scholars.[20] Some of these scholars have come to see the interesting way in which patriarchal language reverses nature. Specifically, Deborah Tannen observes that while in most languages the female form is "marked" (i.e., carries endings that mark a term as feminine), biologists have shown that, genetically, males are the marked gender.[21] In fact, in species that produce individuals who work but do not reproduce, such as worker bees, the workers are sterile females, which, since they have no reason to be one sex or the other, default to female.[22]

We know this reversal has occurred, but what is its status? Is it now an ineradicable feature of language or can sexist and other violent discourse be eliminated? Arthur Brittan and Mary Maynard contend that "language itself does not determine the oppression."[23] They continue, "Sexism is not defined by sexist language, it is sexism which gives sexist language its potency. The labelling . . . only has consequences if . . . supported by the possibility of force, violence, or other sanctions."[24] Finally, regarding the supposed inferiority and deficiency of women's language, they note, "Women's language is inferior when compared to that of males, which is already assumed to be the important yardstick and the superior form."[25]

As Deborah Cameron puts it, "Sexist language teaches us what those who use it and disseminate it think women's place ought to be: second-class citizens, neither seen nor heard, eternal sex-objects and personifications of evil."[26] In this way, sexist language is violent. Cameron refers to "violent speaking and writing and to violent-centric language"[27] and notes, "A whole vocabulary exists denigrating the talk of women who do not conform to male ideas of femininity: nag, bitch, strident. More terms trivialise interaction between women: girls' talk, gossip, chitchat, mothers' meeting."[28]

My aim in this section has not been to enumerate in detail instances of sexist language and how it does violence to women. Likewise, I have not even suggested a typology or scale in relation to sexist language. All I have tried to do in this section is connect some feminist analyses of sexist language with the broader concept of linguistic violence. More important, given this connection, is the issue of what can be done to eliminate linguistic violence against women. I now turn to this issue in my final section. And, again, I will rely on feminist writings to suggest how the abusive use of linguistic violence might be reduced and replaced with an emancipatory practice of linguistic nonviolence.

Feminist Responses to Linguistic Violence against Women

Feminism provides several role models for those wishing to supplant linguistic violence against women and other linguistically abused groups in society. These models include both methods for empirical research and recommendations of political action. On the empirical level, feminism has exposed many practices of oppressive language. This exposure has been radical in the sense of going to the roots of our linguistic usage. On the political level, after uncovering the sexist roots of many forms of linguistic violence, feminism has attempted to supplant them. These suggestions for political action rely on an affirmation of linguistic voluntarism.

In this final section, I wish to provide a few illustrations from feminist criticisms of sexist language that focus on supplanting linguistic violence against women. In particular, I will note how these efforts explicitly reject the view of linguistic determinism, that is, the view that speakers cannot change their sign system. Then, I will end this section by connecting feminist models and others that aim to reduce linguistic violence to the broader cultural context within which the various forms of violence occur.

In *Gender Voices*, David Graddol and Joan Swann provide a helpful feminist model for supplanting linguistic violence. Going beyond the type of linguistic determinism reflected in the poststructuralist view that "discourse is the 'site of struggle' and a cause of oppression," they claim "language both helps construct sexual inequality and reflects its existence in society."[29] It is not so much that language determines thought, but that, for practical purposes, it makes some rows much easier to hoe and makes others require arduous and often unappreciated labor.

Deborah Cameron is one of the most influential feminist writers on language. Her book *Feminism and Linguistic Theory* is particularly insightful, especially in refuting the type of determinist view to which Graddol and Swann refer. Cameron begins by noting how Mary Daly and Julia Kristeva have argued that since "language is part of patriarchy," we need a radical theory of language.[30] However, she is concerned that feminist linguistics avoid linguistic determinism. In her view, several leading feminists have fallen into this trap. In particular, she refers to the "dominant and muted" model of Shirley and Edwin Ardener, the "man made language" theory of Dale Spender, and the psychoanalytic model developed in the wake of Jacques Lacan. Cameron contends, "All three approaches display some degree of linguistic determinism." [31]

In looking for an alternative, she turns to Kristeva for an initial opening into the purported closure of linguistic determinism.[32] Based on her reading of Kristeva, Cameron makes several assertions that go beyond the mere rejection of linguistic determinism. Her aim is to affirm a voluntarist view of language that empowers women. In developing her argument, Cameron contends that: (1) "linguistic determinism is a myth"; (2) "male control over meaning is an impossibility"; and (3) "there is no reason in principle why language cannot express the experience of women to the same extent that it expresses the experience of men." [33]

In addressing the pervasiveness of what I term the reality of linguistic violence against women, Cameron notes:

> The institutions that regulate language use in our own society, and indeed those of most societies, are deliberately oppressive to women. . . . But *the* language, the institution, the apparatus of ritual, value judgement and so on, does not belong to everyone equally. It can be controlled by a small elite.[34]

In other words, she is suggesting that the problem is not in the structure of language but in the control over language.

In a feminist counterpart to Rossi-Landi, Cameron asks several of the questions that need to be raised in relation to discourse: "*What* are the registers that men control, *how* do they gain and keep control of those registers, and *why* does male control constitute a disadvantage for women?" [35] Her answers to these questions suggest that, through various forms of violence, men established numerous everyday linguistic conventions to augment their power over women.

Nevertheless, Cameron refuses to give language a privileged status in the construction of our "personalities." Language makes an important contribution to our sense of identity, but it is neither the only nor the greatest influence in shaping our self-understanding. In this regard, Cameron notes the equal or even greater influence of "socio-familial relations," "the division of labour and economic organisation that regulates societies," "the physical environment," and even "individual genetic make-up." [36]

In her rejection of the view that language itself precipitates disadvantage and oppression, Cameron makes one additional point that needs to be stressed. If language itself were the culprit, then we could provide "compensatory" education to underprivileged children and assertiveness training to women; in other words, those with privilege need not give up anything and society need not admit that its institutions "disadvantage the poor, the black and the female just because they are poor, or black, or female." [37] The aim is not to socialize women and other disenfranchised groups into the linguistic practices of the power elite. Instead, the aim is the transformation of language and of the social relations on which it rests.

As I mentioned at the outset of this final section, I wish to close by noting the broader context into which the struggle against linguistic violence needs to be placed. Replacing sexist and other violent language with more neutral or positive forms of linguistic expression is part of a larger project of reducing cultural violence. Graddol and Swann note:

472 | WILLIAM C. GAY

When compared with larger social and ideological struggles, linguistic reform may seem quite a trivial concern. A preoccupation with women's economic, social and physical oppression is one thing. A concern to replace *fireman* with *firefighter* can all too easily bring on ridicule—terms such as *personhole cover* are part of the stock armoury of those opposed to this sort of linguistic intervention. There is also the danger that effective change at this level is won when an institution adopts the word *chair* rather than *chairman* even though all 'chairs' remain male.[38]

In relation to this broader concern, Cameron has observed, "Silence is a symbol of oppression, while liberation is speaking out, making contact."[39]

The view of Cameron and others that we need to address alienation and oppression on more than one level parallels the distinction that Marx makes between formal and material equality.[40] Changing language is like changing the law; it affects the form but not the substance; it may be necessary, but it is not sufficient. Along with linguistic transformation, cultural transformation is equally important. In other words, to expose and eliminate sexist language will not end violence against women.

Sexist language is a symptom of deeper cultural violence. Nevertheless, when we realize the important connection between language and consciousness, we can also see how changing our language can lead to not only changed thought but also changed action. Thus, the feminist critique of sexist language is simultaneously a contribution to the practice of linguistic nonviolence and to the quest for societies in which human emancipation, dignity, and respect are not restricted on the basis of such irrelevant factors as gender, race, or sexual orientation.

NOTES

1. Hannah Arendt, *On Violence* (New York: Harcourt, Brace, and World, 1970), 35.

2. Newton Garver, "What Violence Is," *The Nation* 209, June 24, 1968, 817–22.

3. Thomas Platt, "The Concept of Violence as Descriptive and Polemic," *International Social Science Journal* 44, no. 2 (May 1992):188.

4. Ibid., 189.

5. Ibid., 190.

6. Stephanie Ross, "How Words Hurt: Attitude, Metaphor, and Oppression" in *Sexist Language: A Modern Philosophical Analysis,* ed. Mary Vetterling-Braggin (Littlefield, Adams, and Co., 1981), 195.

7. Ibid., 195.

8. Ibid., 197.

9. Cf. Richard W. Wilkie, "Karl Marx on Rhetoric," *Philosophy and Rhetoric* 9, no. 3 (1976), where he notes (on p. 237), "Language symbol alienation, that is, the estrangement of human beings from their concepts and ideas as expressed in words, appears to Marx to be the case of language symbols having lost or distorted their *human referent.* People, therefore, having lost such referential meaning in their language, will have *lost or lost control of their own consciousness as well,* since . . . language 'produces' consciousness."

10. Ferruccio Rossi-Landi, *Linguistics and Economics* (The Hague: Mouton, 1977); *Language as Work and Trade: A Semiotic Homology for Linguistics and Economics,* trans. Martha Adams et al. (South Hadley, MA: Bergin and Garvey Publishers, 1983); "On Linguistic Money," *Philosophy and Social Criticism* 7 (1980):346–72; "Ideas for the Study of Linguistic Alienation," *Social Praxis* 3, nos. 1–2 (1975):77–92. I have used his work in my essay "Nuclear Discourse and Linguistic Alienation," *Journal of Social Philosophy* 18, no. 2 (Summer 1987):42–49.

11. Ranjit Chatterjee, "Rossi-Landi's Wittgenstein: 'A Philosopher's Meaning Is His Use in the Culture,' " *Semiotica* 84, nos. 3/4 (1991):275–83.

12. Ibid., 278.

13. Ibid., 280–81.

14. Ludwig Wittgenstein, *Philosophical Investigations,* trans. G. E. M: Anscombe, 3d ed. (New York: Macmillan, 1958).

15. I develop this view in my article "From Wittgenstein to Applied Philosophy," *International Journal of Applied Philosophy* 9, no. 1 (Summer/Fall 1994):15–20.

16. I elaborate on this continuum in "Linguistic Violence," Presidential Address, Sixth Annual Conference of Concerned Philosophers for Peace, Hamline University and Macalester College, St. Paul, MN, October 9, 1993. This address will appear in *Institutional Violence,* eds. Deane Curtin and Bob Litke (Amsterdam: Rodopi Press, forthcoming).

17. David R. Burgest, "The Racist Use of the English Language," *Black Scholar,* September 1973, 44.

18. Cf. Luce Irigaray, "The Language of Man," trans. Erin G. Carlston, *Cultural Critique* 13 (Fall 1989):191–202.

19. For a response within the gay and lesbian communities, see Stephen O. Murray, "The Art of Gay Insulting," *Anthropological Linguistics* 21, no. 5 (May 1979):211–23.

20. Cf. Jean Bethke Elshtain, "Feminist Discourse and Its Discontents: Language, Power, and Meaning," *Signs: Journal of Women in Culture and Society* 7, no. 3 (1982):603–21.

21. Deborah Tannen, "Marked for Life," *St. Petersburg Times,* July 18, 1993, D1 and D5. Here she cites the work of biologist Ralph Fasold who has shown that "while two X chromosomes make a female, two Y chromosomes make nothing. Like the linguistic markers s, es or ess, the Y chromosome doesn't 'mean' anything unless it is attached to a root form—an X chromosome."

22. Ibid., D1.

23. Arthur Brittan and Mary Maynard, *Sexism, Racism and Oppression* (Oxford: Basil Blackwell, 1984), 19–20.

24. Ibid., 20.

25. Ibid., 164.

26. Deborah Cameron, *Feminism and Linguistic Theory* (New York: St. Martin's Press, 1985), 91.

27. Ibid., 4.

28. Ibid., 155.

29. David Graddol and Joan Swann, *Gender Voices* (Cambridge, MA: Basil Blackwell, 1989), 164; cf. "Sex Differences in Language, Speech, and Nonverbal Communication: An Annotated Bibliography," compiled by Nancy Henley and Barrie Thorne, in *Language and Sex: Difference and Dominance,* ed. Barrie Thorne and Nancy Henley (Rowley, MA: Newbury House Publishers, 1975), 204–305.

30. Cameron, *Feminism and Linguistic Theory,* 1 and 3.

31. Ibid., 92–93.

32. Ibid., 125–26.

33. Ibid., 143–44.

34. Ibid., 145.

35. Ibid., 146.

36. Ibid., 169–70.

37. Ibid., 171.

38. Graddol and Swann, *Gender Voices,* 195.

39. Cameron, *Feminism and Linguistic Theory,* 5.

40. Karl Marx, "On the Jewish Question," *The Marx-Engels Reader,* ed. Robert C. Tucker, 2d ed. (New York: W. W. Norton, 1978), esp. pp. 30–36.

35

Action

ELIZABETH WARD

The stories of women's lives
do not appear in magazines
even when they seem to

The stories of women's lives
are etched in the shadow
of a young girl's brown eyes

The stories of women's lives
are seared in the muscle
at the corners of their mouths

The stories of women's lives
weep down from the moon
in huge silver drops

carrying the siren sounds of
the stories of women's lives.

i dream
    a world beyond rape

i dream
    a world where the very bodies
    that we live in
    do not incite violence against us

> *i dream*
> > *a world where we can walk the streets*
> > *or country roads, on the darkest nights,*
> > *lit only by the stars*
> > *and our own freedom to move*

Dreaming is useful in envisaging where we want to go, because it helps us to get there. Such dreaming, however, grows out of an awareness of how we have been constructed and abused by patriarchy. The aim of this chapter is to help end the silence, lift the blinds, on the subject of Father–Daughter rape. As well as encouraging dreaming, I wish to emphasise the need for action. Action to change things in the world makes new dreaming possible.

The Speaking of Women

Women everywhere need to start talking about Father–Daughter rape. We need to talk with each other about our experiences of it, our fear of it, our confusions about it, our anger that is touched by it, and any other reactions that we have to it. We need to dredge our memories, the multiplicity of layers through which we know things, in search of our own experiences of growing up as a girl-child. We need to remember, see and understand that for girl-children there are constant messages being received about the power that men have over women. Girl-children are the receptors, as only children can be, of a multifarious network of visual, auditory and vibrationary signals about the sexual role they are expected to play in order to please men/the Father/the seat of power. Like a clean wind blowing away fog, this process of women remembering and asking and talking and validating the truth about Father–Daughter rape is the only way in which the depths of silence and blindness that have crippled most victims are going to be lifted. As Adrienne Rich has written:

> One of the most powerful social and political catalysts of the past decade has been the speaking of women with other women, the telling of our secrets, the comparing of wounds and the sharing of words. This hearing and saying of women has been able to break many a silence and taboo; literally to transform forever the way we see.[1]

Transforming the way we see, seeing this patriarchal world and how it is structured, is both a painful and an exhilarating experience. It is painful because it means confronting the depths of the limitation, humiliation and abuse that women and children suffer within patriarchy; it is exhilarating because new thoughts, new perceptions, visions of a truly humane society become possible.

Father–Daughter rape, Son–Mother rape, Brother–Sister rape: these are rape in its most intimate (family) form. Rape is about hatred. Male supremacist hatred of such proportions has been endured within the private sphere of the family by individual women for too long. As women begin to speak of these most intimate atrocities, the face, the very being of our society will change.

Mothers and Daughters

As the Daughters and Mothers emerge from the shades of silenced anger, they will find each other, form groups, speak and share through the quietest night hours, and emerge into the light of day transformed by the knowledge that they each, in their aloneness, were victims, but that in their togetherness they can vision a new world into being: our world, beyond rape. Mothers will tell their Daughters, the Daughters will tell each other, on and on down the line, that some things are not to be borne.

The Daughter–Mother tie reveals a particularised form of the power that resides within the speaking of women with each other. We have seen that for the Mothers "the eyes not seeing what the heart cannot hold"[2] has locked them off from their Daughters behind a barrier of blindness and broken hearts. When the Daughters and Mothers break through this barrier, the scales of patriarchal vision fall from their eyes and their broken hearts are mended by the love that women share—a special kind of love which occurs as women begin to acknowledge their shared identity, in suffering and in change.

The particular poignancy of Mothers and Daughters re-finding each other as sisters derives from the patriarchal injunction which blames Mothers for everything and anything—thereby depreciating Motherhood, while at the same time insisting that it is Woman's highest vocation. Daughters learn of this depreciation of Mothers, much as they breathe air: it is integral to patriarchal social forms. Daughters, nearly always, do not want to be Mothers *in the same way:* every Daughter determines to do it differently from how her Mother did it, to do it better. But the fulcrum of patriarchal reproduction is that she has to do it: be a Mother or a Non-Mother, either way trapped in the linguistic and social imperative that a woman be defined in terms of her relationship to Mothering.

Thus Daughters reject their Mothers—and at the same time they long for them. They long for a Mother who will show them how to get out of the trap, how to be independent, whole, herself. We long for an acknowledgment of what could be possible between Mothers and Daughters.

> Mothers and daughters have always exchanged with each other—beyond the verbally transmitted lore of female survival—a knowledge that is subliminal, subversive, preverbal: the knowledge floating between two alike bodies, one of which has spent nine months inside the other.[3]

The knowledge floating between two alike bodies . . . While this knowledge can be felt between any two women, it is most strongly experienced between Mothers and Daughters: one woman has created another, one's body is the same as that of the being who created it. They have known each other most intimately, in what must surely be the most intimate form of knowing experienced within the human condition: one woman created by another.

This knowing is the area that is being touched, like butterfly wings caressing (beautiful and fragile), when Mothers and Daughters speak truly, each to each.

Protection, Care, and Change

As the Daughters and Mothers, supported by other women, indentify what has been done to them, they will, hopefully, be involved in, even initiate, changes as to the type of protection and care which are needed. Ideally, after themselves being healed as far as is possible in the miasma of horror from which they are emerging, many of these girl-children and women will become involved in supportive networks and sheltered environments which they themselves will (help) establish and operate.

The social welfare model of care which is currently the only widely available form of institutional help needs to be publicly examined and contrasted with the self-help, grass-roots validation model being offered by rape crisis centres and women's refuges. The social welfare system must undergo an internal revolution in terms of knowledge and attitudes, if it is to be capable of even partially providing the kind of care needed by the victims of Father–Daughter rape. Instead of waiting rooms, medical examinations, welfare interviews, disconnected counselling sessions and the stated or implicit moral imperatives which accompany such impersonal types of "care," we need intense and complex systems of involvement in the ongoing process each Daughter and Mother needs to navigate in order to (re-)find a sense of integrity and belief in herself. The welfare system needs, most of all, to change its primary focus from that of family 'welder' (trying to get the family back together at all costs), to that of care and protection for the Daughter and understanding for the Mother.

Part of this process will include exposing the misuse of Freud's theory of infantile sexuality. It has been used as a blatant and outrageous form of invalidation of Father–Daughter rape. Quite apart from the vicious cruelty inflicted on individual victims by this myth, it has functioned to deepen the invisibility of Father–Daughter rape on a macro-social level. Functioning within the same cultural mode, the Fathers of the social sciences have diddled with the facts of Father–Daughter rape so as to further obscure reality. The academic interpreters of people's behaviour are just as guilty as the Fathers insofar as they purport to be "objective" when they are in fact operating from their own subjectivity. Eschewing passionless objectivity which is, by definition, rooted in the status quo, we need to direct our passionate attention to the validation of our own senses: to believe that the worst we see and feel really is happening; and to determine what we want to do about it. In this process we will find ways to name and reject the so-called objectivity of the social scientists who have manipulated our thoughts and feelings, misnaming the reality of Father–Daughter rape.

Mothers and Daughters will also have the most pertinent input into the immediately needed reforms of the law. In every state, territory and nation, laws must be brought into existence which recognise the commonness of Father–Daughter rape, and address themselves primarily to protecting the Daughters from the now current processes of minute cross-examination and the need for evidence of corroboration, as well as the myriad effects of "normal" rape cases.

Laws nearly always follow, rather than lead, public opinion and mainstream values. Thus the multi-faceted process of women talking, of naming, of mass publicity, of educating the silent majority, of convincing those who make and enforce laws, of involving those who deliver welfare systems and medical care, is still the first step, from which the rest will flow.

The Liberation of Women

The particular means by which women are kept dependent (on men) and oppressed as people, must be eradicated so that Daughters no longer find themselves with Mothers who cannot see, who cannot say No.

For women to rise out of their subordinate status, they must have economic independence. This means that the struggles for non-sexist education, non-sexist job definitions, the right to work, the right to a decent income as workers or Mothers, and truly equal pay are part of the struggle to end Father–Daughter rape.

Women must also have control of their own bodies. This means that the struggles for truly safe contraception, the right to sterilisation, the right to abortion on demand, the right to full and truthful sex education, the right to sexual partners of their choice, the right to childbirth-methods determined by the mother, and the right to full and honest information in medical matters are part of the struggle to end Father–Daughter rape.

Women must also be able to live their lives free of personal violence: the kind of personal violence which occurs because women are subordinate. This means that the struggles to eliminate wife-bashing, marital rape, street harassment, and sexual harassment on the job are part of the struggle to end Father–Daughter rape.

Ultimately, women will only be a liberated species when male supremacy ends. This means that any struggle which opposes the expression of male supremacy—expressions such as sexist advertising, pornography, the patriarchal nuclear family, rape in warfare and the use of nuclear energy and armaments—are part of the struggle to end Father–Daughter rape.

Sex and Sexuality Information

We must expand the embryonic attempts to educate girl-children, and society generally, about female sexuality, and about rape. The repression of information about female sexuality is clearly linked to rape in that the traditional view of women as sexually passive feeds straight into the myths about rape. Girl-children will only begin to be able to protect themselves when they (a) value their own bodies, and (b) know that they may be sexually approached by a man they know and trust.

We must teach girl-children about their own sexuality, as a base from which they can love and value their own bodies. We must teach our Daughters to recognise the experience of pleasure for what it is: their own precious bodily reactions, rather than an emotional response implying consent. We must teach them that they can and must say No to *anyone* who touches them against their will. We must teach them to exert as much control over their own bodies as is possible; and we must teach it to them as early as possible, along with walking and talking.

This mode of social-sex education, growing out of women talking together and thereby discovering what it is that girl-children need to know, is the first way in which girl-children are going to be empowered to say No. Social attitudes and availability of information which will allow them a sense of physical, emotional and sexual integrity are the obverse of the current practice of conditioned passivity based on fear induced through purposely manipulated ignorance. The very least we can ask for girl-children is a fighting chance to protect themselves by giving them as much information as we can.

The Patriarchal Family

The Daughters should *never* be forced, or even encouraged, to live again with the Father who has been raping them. This is the crux, and the crunch, of the change that needs to be wrought immediately. As Judith Herman points out:

> Men cannot be expected to overcome their abusive tendencies or to develop their nurturant capacities overnight, and it makes no sense to expose children to the unsupervised care of men whose interest in them may be ambivalent at best, and perverse at worst. Women are going to have to be the teachers and the protectors for some time to come.[4]

Only an end to the patriarchal nuclear family, only a new kind of family based on complete sharing of matriarchal skills and values will bring about an end to Father–Daughter rape.

The value system of male supremacist society holds the family to be inviolable, except under the most extraordinary circumstances. It will be argued (and it is true) that there are no ideal places for the Daughters to be removed to on a long-term basis: too often, the family is all there is. Rather than shrugging in resigned acceptance at this truism and turning away in despair, we must set about creating crisis shelters specifically for Daughter-victims, and creating or finding other living arrangements where they can live on a long-term basis. If we face the fact that most raped Daughters do *not* want to live with the person that has raped them, and believe that they should not have to, then we will find alternatives.

Naming Blame

The best "alternative," of course, is the removal of the Fathers. They, after all, *are* the problem. The patriarchal power of the courts, of counsellors, of the police and the welfare system ensures that this solution is not widely possible yet. But there will come a day, not far off, when women make this utterly reasonable demand.

The Father-offenders must be named, isolated, punished. This would only be a reversal of what happens now in many instances, where the victims are the ones who feel, and are, punished. The Fathers must be named as rapists of girl-children. It must be made *socially impossible* for them to get away with it. Ostracism, public ignominy, and a complete ban on access to girl-children seems a small amount to ask in the face of the damage, suffering and pain these men have inflicted. Therapy, "curing," counselling for individual Fathers are all very well for those who wish to deliver such services: the real problem is the social sanction of their behaviour. They must *not* be forgiven: what they have done is unforgivable.

The Power of Naming

In the development of the feminist movement, women have seized the power of naming. This is a revolutionary power because in naming (describing) what is being done to us (and inevitably to children and men as well), we are also naming what must change. The act of naming creates a new world view. The power of naming resides in the fact that we name what we see from the basis of our own experience: within and outside patriarchal culture, simultaneously.

We are finding forms of expression which convey the reality of Father–Daughter rape; we are finding forms of expression which reject male supremacist language—that language which presumes to tell us what is happening to us and how we feel about it. Father–Daughter rape can no longer be called "interference," "molestation," "fooling around with" or "incest." The feelings and reactions of the Daughters must be named, described, accepted. The confusion and angst of the Mothers must be named, described, accepted. The totality of rape ideology and its integration into sex-role conditioning must be named, described, eradicated. This revolution of women naming is already under way and it is a revolution which will, one day, bring about an end to rape in all its manifestations.

We, the Mothers and Daughters, are seeing now through our own eyes. We do not forgive the Fathers. It will be said that we are uncaring; that we hate men; that we are creating a state of war. I say that the war has been declared and waged by men since the first act of rape. Whatever the reasons for men's hatred of women, we ourselves are changing the structure of the battle. We are resisting; we are strategically withdrawing;

we are naming the hitherto unnameable. In doing these things *for our own sakes,* the corollary is that the Fathers have access to space in which to look at themselves: to hear what they have done, to see what they have done. The prognosis of changed behaviour on the far side of the battlefield is not promising: all types of rape statistics are rising at an alarming rate. But for us, the Mothers and Daughters, there is no going back.

> To dream a world into being
> is regarded by many as insanely
> impractical.
>
> *We know there is a world*
> *without rape and this world is*
> *in our minds.*
>
> As we struggle across the plains
> towards the mountains of freedom
> *we know*
>
> what to take with us and
> what to leave behind. Travelling
> light
>
> *we know* when to speak or be
> dumb (eyes glazed with the matt
> of our knowing)
>
> *we know* when to run, or to lie
> in the sun. We know when to run
> from danger
>
> and circle and weave and return
> from behind, clearing the plains
> of the canker.
>
> And the plains will rise up,
> the mountains sink down
> when we dream
>
> this world into being.

A day in the future dawns still and grey. Overcast and quiet. An unremarkable day.

A small grey woman, sleeping alone, wakes in her bedsitter. Remembering. Being eight years old, sleeping alone in the small room off the verandah at the back of the weatherboard house. Remembers how she taught herself to slip into the wall, from where she watched through a crack in the woodwork when her father came to her bed.

Watched the large red roughened hands lift up the little girl's nightgown, part her legs, touch her softest tissues. While the other large red roughened hand moved to the front of his own pants, grasped at the strange red thing which she knew was hot and sticky.

But this time, this remembering, she did not stay in the wall until it was all over, to creep out and slip inside the little girl when he went away. This time she came charging out of the wall, kicking, punching and shouting, threw herself on the man, her father, with every cell in her body fighting.

The small grey woman watched this remembering with wonder. She felt a smile lifting her lips.

In the mountains, a fifteen-year-old girl-woman woke to the still grey day. A strand of her long black hair lay across her face. It reminded her of the night and the silent visitor who had come again to her bed. As he had been doing every week or so since she was eleven.

Her hand rose to move the hair; but it stayed, half raised to her face. The hair was speaking to her fingers: Today you will tell. Today you will speak. Today you can be strong. Today, you will stop being lonely.

A young married woman rose that day and did the things she normally did. She saw her husband off to work, dropped her daughter off at preschool and set out to drive to work. As she turned the first corner, the memories came again, especially the one about the first time. She found she was no longer driving to work; she was going across town to her friend's place. I have to tell you something, she said, as she sat down at the kitchen table.

She found herself speaking, telling of how her grandfather used to stick his fingers up the leg of her pants and feel her.

It first happened when I was five. I'd loved him up till then: a lovely soft, cuddly old man who cradled me in his lap and told me stories.

But that day, after my father came into the room and it all stopped happening and I started to breathe again, my grandfather's eyes met mine. I hadn't seen those eyes of grandfather's before. That was when I knew that what had happened was really as awful as it felt. You will never speak of this, they said—and in the same movement, he slid his eyes blandly round to my father and chuckled about the idiosyncrasies of an elderly old man sitting in the dusk with his princess!

I remember I ran out to the kitchen and stood near the stove to get warm because my heart was thumping so loud. My mother didn't see my eyes, or hear my heart, even though I stood there and watched her make the whole meal and then serve it. In my mind I was screaming, telling her. And saying that I didn't want to be with grandpa any more.

But I didn't say. I never have till now. But my mind has done that for years and years. Remembered. And screamed.

And as the twenty-four hours of that still, grey day rolled their gently inexorable way round the globe, all the women woke in turn, reliving their rememberings, and one by one they arose with a new new smile on their faces, and one by one they spoke. And the sound of their speakings drowned out all the other sounds in the world that day: the machines and the factories and the cars and newsreaders and doctors and priests and politicians and all the learned men were silent, because the noise of the women speaking filled up all the space. And any little places left in the silences that occurred amid the speakings and cryings and laughings of women, were filled by the noise of children playing.

Notes

1. A. Rich, *On Lies, Secrets and Silence,* Virago, London, 1979, pp. 259–60.
2. T. Morrison, *Sula,* Bantam, New York, 1975, p. 67.
3. A. Rich, *Of Woman Born,* Virago, London, 1977, p. 220.
4. J. Herman, *Father–Daughter Incest,* Harvard University Press, Cambridge, 1982, p. 217.

Bibliography

Abrahamsen, D. 1960. *The Psychology of Crime.* New York: Columbia University Press.

Acker, Joan. 1990. "Hierarchies, Jobs, Bodies: A Theory of Gendered Organization." *Gender & Society* 4, no. 2:139–58.

Adams, D. 1988. "Treatment Models of Men Who Batter." In K. Ylló and M. Bograd (eds.) *Feminist Perspectives on Wife Abuse.* Newbury Park, CA: Sage.

Adams, D., and S. Cayouette. 1995. "Abuser Excuse Making and Complicity: A Reciprocal Influence." Paper presented at the Fourth International Family Violence Research Conference, July, Durham, NH.

Adams, J. W., J. L. Kottke, and J. S. Padgitt. 1983. "Sexual Harassment of University Students." *Journal of College Student Personnel* 23:484–99.

Adler, Freda. 1975. *Sisters in Crime.* New York: McGraw-Hill.

Ageton, S. S. 1983. *Sexual Assault among Adolescents.* Lexington, MA: D. C. Heath.

Agger, I. 1989. "Sexual Torture of Political Prisoners: An Overview." *Journal of Traumatic Stress* 2:305–18.

Alexander, Jeffrey C. 1982. *Positivism, Presuppositions, and Current Controversies: Theoretical Logic in Socioloy.* Vol. 1. Berkeley: University of California Press.

Alfaro, J. D. 1987. "Studying Child Maltreatment Fatalities: A Synthesis of Nine Projects." New York: Human Resources Division.

Allen, J. 1988. "The 'Masculinity' of Criminality and Criminology: Integrating Some Impasses." In Mark Findlay and Russell Hogg (eds.) *Understanding Crime and Criminal Justice.* Sydney: Law Book Company.

Alliance Against Sexual Coercion. 1981. *Fighting Sexual Harassment: An Advocacy Handbook.* Boston: Alyson.

Allport, G. 1958. *The Nature of Prejudice.* New York: Doubleday.

Althusser, Louis. 1971. *Lenin and Philosophy.* New York: Monthly Review Press.

American Medical Association. 1992. *Diagnostic and Treatment Guidelines on Family Violence.* Chicago: American Medical Association.

———. 1995. *Strategies for the Treatment and Prevention of Sexual Assault.* Chicago: American Medical Association.

American Medical Association Council on Ethical and Judicial Affairs. 1992. "Physicians and Domestic Violence: Ethical Considerations." *Journal of the American Medical Association,* 267, no. 23:3190–93. Chicago: American Medical Association.

American Psychiatric Association. 1987. *The Diagnostic and Statistical Manual of Mental Disorders III.* Washington, DC: American Psychiatric Association.

————. 1994. *Diagnostic and Statistical Manual of Mental Disorders IV.* Washington, DC: American Psychiatric Association.

Amir, Menachem. 1971. *Patterns in Forcible Rape.* Chicago: University of Chicago Press.

Amnesty International. 1992. *Rape and Sexual Abuse: Torture and Ill-Treatment of Women in Detention.* New York: Amnesty International.

Andenaes, J. 1966. "The General Prevention Effects of Punishment." *Pennsylvania Law Review* 114:949–83.

Andersen, Margaret L. 1993 [1988]. *Thinking about Women: Sociological Perspectives on Sex and Gender.* New York: Macmillan.

Angier, Natalie. 1995. "Sexual Harassment: Why Even Bees Do It." *New York Times,* October 10, p. C1.

Anonymous. 1991. "Sexual Harassment: A Female Counseling Student's Experience." *Journal of Counseling and Development* 69:502–5.

Ansberry, C. 1988. "Calling Sexes Equal in Domestic Violence, Article Stirs Clash among Rights Groups." *Wall Street Journal,* May 5.

Archavanitkui, K., and A. Pramualratana. 1990. "Factors Affecting Women's Health in Thailand." Paper presented at the Population Council Workshop on Women's Health in Southeast Asia, October, Jakarta.

Archer, D., and R. Gartner. 1984. *Violence and Crime in Cross-National Perspective.* New Haven: Yale University Press.

Ardrey, R. 1966. *The Territorial Imperative.* New York: Dell.

Arendt, Hannah. 1977. *Eichmann in Jerusalem: A Report on the Banality of Evil.* New York: Penguin.

Arias, I., M. Samios, and K. D. O'Leary. 1987. "Prevalence and Correlates of Physical Aggression during Courtship." *Journal of Interpersonal Violence* 2:82–90.

Armstrong, Louise. 1978. *Kiss Daddy Goodnight.* New York: Hawthorne.

Arnold, M. H. 1989. "The Life of a Citizen in the Hands of a Woman: Sexual Assault in New York City, 1790–1820," in K. Peiss and C. Simmons (eds.), *Passion and Power: Sexuality in History.* Philadelphia: Temple University Press.

Arroyo, William, and Spencer Eth. 1995. "Assessment following Violence-Witnessing Trauma," in Einat Peled, Peter Jaffe, and Jeffrey Edleson (eds.), *Ending the Cycle of Violence: Community Responses to Children of Battered Women.* Thousand Oaks, CA: Sage.

Asbury, Jo-Ellen. 1987. "African-American Women in Violent Relationships: An Exploration of Cultural Differences." In R. L. Hampton (ed.), *Violence in the Black Family.* Lexington, MA: Lexington Books.

Asia Watch. 1992. *Burma: Rape, Forced Labor, and Religious Persecution in Northern Arakan.* Washington, DC: Asia Watch.

Association of American Colleges. 1978. *The Problem of Rape on Campus.* Washington, DC: Project on the Status and Education of Women.

Attorney General's Commission on Pornography. 1986. *Final Report.* Washington, DC: U.S. Department of Justice.

Attorney General's Task Force on Family Violence. 1984. *Final Report.* Washington, DC: U.S. Department of Justice.

Avendano, C., and J. Vergara. 1992. *La Violencia Sexual en Chile, Dimensiones: Colectiva, Cultural y Politica.* Santiago, Chile: Servicio Nacional de la Mujer.

Babcock, B., A. Freedman, D. Norton, and S. Ross. 1975. *Sex Discrimination and the Law.* Boston: Little, Brown.

Bachman, Ronet. 1992. *Death and Violence on the Reservation.* New York: Auburn House.

Bailey, V., and S. Blackburn. 1979. "The Punishment of Incest Act 1908: A Case Study of Law Creation." *Criminal Law Review* (November):708–18.

Bailey, V., and S. McCabe. 1979. "Reforming the Law of Incest." *Criminal Law Review* (December):749–64.

Bandy, N. 1989. "Relationships between Male and Female Employees at Southern Illinois University." Ph.D. diss., College of Education, Southern Illinois University, Carbondale.

Banwell, S. S. 1990. *Law, Status of Women, and Family Planning in Sub-Saharan Africa: A Suggestion for Action.* Nairobi: Pathfinder Fund.

Baraka, Amina. 1983. "Soweto Song." In Amiri Baraka and Amina Baraka (eds.), *Confirmation.* New York: Quill.

Bard, M. 1970. "Role of Law Enforcement in the Helping System," in J. Monahan (ed.), *Community Mental Health and the Criminal Justice System.* Elmsford, NY: Pergamon.

Barnett, O. W., C. Y. Lee, and R. E. Thelen. 1995. "Gender Differences in Forms, Outcomes and Attributions for Interpartner Aggression." Paper presented at the Fourth International Family Violence Research Conference, July, Durham, NH.

Baron, L., and M. A. Straus. 1989. *Four Theories of Rape in American Society: A State-Level Analysis.* New Haven: Yale University Press.

Baron, L., M. A. Straus, and D. Jaffe. 1988. "Legitimate Violence, Violent Attitudes, and Rape: A Test of the Cultural Spillover Theory." In R. A. Prentky and V. L. Quinsey (eds.), *Human Sexual Aggression: Current Perspectives.* New York: New York Academy of Sciences.

Baron, Larry. 1990. "Pornography and Gender Equality: An Empirical Analysis." *Journal of Sex Research* 27, no. 3.

Barry, Kathleen. 1979. *Female Sexual Slavery.* New York: New York University Press.

Bart, Pauline B. 1985a "Pornography: Institutionalizing Woman-Hating and Eroticizing Dominance and Submission for Fun and Profit." *Justice Quarterly* 2:283–92.

———. 1985b. *Stopping Rape: Successful Survival Strategies.* Elmsford, NY: Pergamon.

———. 1986. "Pornography: Hating Women and Institutionalizing Dominance and Submission for Fun and Profit: Response to Alexis M. Durham III." *Justice Quarterly* 3:103–5.

Bart, P. B., R. L. Blumberg, T. Tombs, and F. Behan. "The Cross-Societal Study of Rape: Some Methodological Problems and Results." Paper presented at the Groves Conference International Workshop on Changing Sex Roles in Family and Society, Dubrovnik, Yugoslavia.

Bart, Pauline B., Linda Freeman, and Peter Kimball. "The Different Worlds of Women and Men: Attitudes toward Pornography and Responses to *Not A Love Story*—A Film about Pornography." *Women's Studies International Forum* 8:307–22.

Beattie, V. *Analysis of the Results of a Survey on Sexual Violence in the UK.* Cambridge, UK: Women's Forum (unpublished manuscript).

Bechdolt, B. V. 1975. "Cross-Sectional Analysis of Socioeconomic Determinants of Urban Crime." *Review of Social Economy* 33:132–40.

Becker, D., E. Lira, M. I. Castillo, E. Ganez, and J. Kovalskys. 1990. "Therapy with Victims of Political Repression in Chile: The Challenge of Social Reparation." *Journal of Social Issues* 46:133–49.

Becker, H. S. 1963. *The Outsiders: Studies in the Sociology of Deviance.* New York: Free Press.

Beebe, D. K. 1991. "Emergency Management of the Adult Female Rape Victim." *American Family Physician* 43:2041–46.

Behlmer, G. K. 1982. *Child Abuse and Moral Reform in England 1870–1908.* Stanford: Stanford University Press.

Belknap, J. 1989. "The Economics-Crime Link." *Criminal Justice Absracts,* March, 157.

Bell, Laurie (ed.). 1987. *Good Girls/Bad Girls: Feminists and Sex Trade Workers Face to Face.* Toronto: Seal Press.

Ben Baraka, M. 1993. "Defloration in Algeria: A Case Study of Force during Sexual Initiation." Paper presented at the United Nations Population Council Meeting, Sexual Coercion and Women's Reproductive Health, jointly sponsored by the Population Council and the Pacific Institute for Women's Health, November, New York.

Benedict, Helen. 1992. *Virgin or Vamp: How the Press Covers Sex Crimes.* New York: Oxford University Press.

Beneke, T. 1982. *Men on Rape: What They Have to Say about Sexual Violence.* New York: St. Martin's Press.

Beneria, L., and M. Roldan. 1987. *The Crossroads of Class and Gender.* Chicago: University of Chicago Press.

Benjamin, J. 1983. "Master and Slave: The Fantasy of Erotic Domination." In A. Snitow, C. Santsell, and S. Thomas (eds.), *Powers of Desire: The Politics of Sexuality.* New York: Monthly Review Press.

Bennett, G. 1990. "Stuffing Emphasis from Abused to Abuser." *Geriatric Medicine,* May.

Bennett, G., and P. Kingston. 1993. *Elder Abuse: Concepts, Theories and Interventions.* London: Chapman Hall.

Benson, D. J., and G. E. Thomson. 1982. "Sexual Harassment on a University Campus: The Confluence of Authority Relations, Sexual Interest, and Gender Stratification." *Social Problems* 29:236–51.

Bentovim, A., A. Elton, and M. Tranter. 1987. "Prognosis for Rehabilitation after Abuse." *Adoption and Fostering* 11, no. 1:26–31.

Berger, John. 1972. *Ways of Seeing.* London: BBC and Penguin.

Berger, R. J., and P. Searles. 1985. "Victim-Offender Interaction in Rape: Victimological, Situational, and Feminist Perspectives." *Women's Studies Quarterly* 13:9–15.

Berger, R. J., P. Searles, and C. E. Cottle. Forthcoming. "A Camp Divided: Feminists on Pornography." In G. Miller and J. Holstein (eds.), *Perspectives on Social Problems.* Greenwich, CT: JAI.

Berger, V. 1977. "Man's Trial, Woman's Tribulation: Rape Cases in the Courtroom." *Columbia Law Review* 77:1–101.

Berk, R., S. F. Berk, D. Loseke, and D. Rauma. 1983. "Mutual Combat and Other Family Violence Myths." In D. Finkelhor et al. (eds.), *The Dark Side of Families: Current Family Violence Research.* Beverly Hills, CA: Sage.

Berk, S. F. 1985. *The Gender Factory: The Apportionment of Work in American Households.* New York: Plenum Press.

Berliner, Lucy. 1993. "Is Family Preservation in the Best Interest of Children?" *Journal of Interpersonal Violence* 8, no. 4:556–62.

Bernard, Cheryl, and Edit Schlaffer. 1983. "The Man in the Street: Why He Harasses." In Laurel Richardson and Verta Taylor (eds.), *Feminist Frontiers: Rethinking Sex, Gender and Society.* New York: Random House.

Bernard, Jesse. 1982. *The Future of Marriage.* New Haven: Yale University Press.

Biaggio, M. K., D. Watts, and A. Brownell. 1990. "Addressing Sexual Harassment: Strategies for Prevention and Change." In M. A. Paludi (ed.), *Ivory Power: Sexual Harassment on Campus.* Albany: State University of New York Press.

Bielby, W., and J. N. Baron. 1986. "A Woman's Place Is with Other Women: Sex Segregation within Organizations." In Barbara Reskin (ed.), *Sex Segregation in the Workplace: Trends, Explanations, Remedies.* Washington, DC: National Academy Press.

Blakely, Mary Kay. 1985. "Is One Woman's Sexuality Another Woman's Pornography?" *Ms.,* April.

Bland, L. 1982. " 'Guardians of the Race' or 'Vampires upon the Nation's Health?' Female Sexuality and Its Regulation in Early Twentieth-Century Britain." In E. Whitelegg, M. Arnot, E. Bartels, V. Beechey, L. Birke, S. Himmelweit, D. Leonard, S. Ruehl, and M. A. Speakman (eds.), *The Changing Experience of Women.* Oxford: Basil Blackwell.

Blanguernon, C. 1955. *Le Hogger (The Hogger).* Paris: B. Arthaud. (Translated from the French for the Human Relations Area Files by Thomas Turner.)

Blatt, D. 1992. "Recognizing Rape as a Method of Torture." *New York University Review of Law and Social Change* 19:821–65.

Blau, F. D., and A. E. Winkler. 1989. "Women in the Labor Force: An Overview." In Jo Freeman (ed.), *Women: A Feminist Perspective.* Palo Alto, CA: Mayfield.

Blau, J., and P. Blau. 1982. "The Cost of Inequality: Metropolitan Structure and Violent Crime." *American Sociological Review* 47:114–29.

Blumstein, P., and P. Schwartz. 1983. *American Couples.* New York: William Morrow.

Bohmer, C., and A. Parrot. 1993. *Sexual Assault on Campus: The Problem and the Solution.* New York: Lexington Books.

Bologna, M. J., C. K. Waterman, and L. J. Dawson. 1987. "Violence in Gay Male and Lesbian Relationships: Implications for Practitioners and Policy Makers." Paper presented at the Third National Conference for Family Violence Researchers, July, Durham, NH.

Bourque, Linda Brookover. 1989. *Defining Rape.* Chapel Hill, NC: Duke University Press.

Bowen, D. J., L. Carscadden, K. Beighle, and I. Fleming. 1992. "Post-Traumatic Stress Disorder among Salvadoran Women: Empirical Evidence and Description of Treatment." *Women & Therapy* 13:267–80.

Bowker, Lee. 1981. "Women as Victims: An Examination of the Results of L.E.A.A.'s National Crime Survey Program." *Women and Crime in America* 158:164–65.

———. 1993. "A Battered Woman's Problems Are Social, Not Psychological." In Richard Gelles and Donileen Loseke (eds.), *Current Controversies on Family Violence*. Newbury Park, CA: Sage Publications.

Bowker, Lee, with Michelle Arbitell and J. Richard McFerron. 1988. "On the Relationship between Wife Beating and Child Abuse." In Kersti Yllö and Michele Bograd (eds.), *Feminist Perspectives on Wife Abuse*. Newbury Park, CA: Sage Publications.

Box, S. 1983. *Power, Crime, and Mystification*. London: Tavistock.

Boyer, D., and D. Fine. 1992. "Sexual Abuse as a Factor in Adolescent Pregnancy and Child Maltreatment." *Family Planning Perspectives* 23:4–10.

Bradley, Christine. 1990. "Why Male Violence against Women Is a Development Issue: Reflections from Papua, New Guinea." UNIFEM Occasional Paper. New York: United Nations Fund for Women. Reprinted in M. Davies (ed.), *Women and Violence*. London: Zed Books, 1994.

Braithwaite, J. 1979. *Inequality: Crime and Public Policy*. London: Routledge and Kegan Paul.

———. 1984. *Corporate Crime in the Pharmaceutical Industry*. London: Routledge and Kegan Paul.

Braithwaite, J., and V. Braithwaite. 1980. "The Effects of Income Inequality and Social Democracy on Homicide." *British Journal of Criminology* 20:45–53.

Brand, P. A., and A. H. Kidd. 1986. "Frequency of Physical Aggression in Heterosexual and Female Homosexual Dyads." *Psychological Reports* 59:1307–13.

Brassard, M. R., R. Germain, and S. N. Hart. 1987. "The Challenge: To Better Understand and Combat Psychological Maltreatment of Children and Youth." In M. R. Brassard, R. Germain, and S. N. Hart (eds.), *Psychological Maltreatment of Children and Youth*. New York: Pergamon.

Brent, Linda. 1973. *Incidents in the Life of a Slave Girl*. San Diego: Harvest/Harcourt Brace Jovanovich.

Brinkerhoff, M. and E. Lupri. 1988. "Interspousal Violence." *Canadian Journal of Sociology* 13:407–34.

Broude, G. J., and S. J. Greene. 1976. "Cross-Cultural Codes on Twenty Sexual Practices." *Ethnology* 15:409–29.

Brown, L. S. 1988. "Female Managers in the U.S. and in Europe." In Nancy J. Adler and Dafna N. Izraeli (eds.), *Women in Management Worldwide*. Armonk, NY: M. E. Sharpe.

———. 1991. "Psychological Evaluation of Victims of Sexual Harassment." National Conference to Promote Men and Women Working Together Productively, March, Bellevue, WA.

Brown, S. R. 1980. *Political Subjectivity: Applications of Q Methodology in Political Science*. New Haven: Yale University Press.

Browne, Angela. 1987. *When Battered Women Kill*. New York: Free Press.

Browne, Angela, and K. Williams. 1993. "Gender, Intimacy and Lethal Violence: Trends from 1976 through 1987." *Gender & Society* 7:78–98.

Brownmiller, S. 1975. *Against Our Will: Men, Women and Rape*. New York: Simon and Schuster.

Brush, Lisa D. 1990. "Violent Acts and Injurious Outcomes in Married Couples: Methodological Issues in the National Survey of Families and Households." *Gender & Society* 4:56–67.

Brustin, Stacy. 1995. "Legal Responses to Teen Dating Violence." *Family Law Quarterly* 20, no. 2 (summer):331–56.

Bryson, Norman. 1986. "Two Narratives of Rape in the Visual Arts: Lucretia and the Sabine Women." In Sylvana Tomaselli and Roy Porter (eds.), *Rape*. Oxford: Basil Blackwell.

Bunch, Charlotte. 1991. "Women's Rights as Human Rights: Toward a Re-Vision of Human

Rights." In Charlotte Bunch (ed.), *Gender Violence: A Development and Human Rights Issue*. New Brunswick, NJ: Center for Women's Global Leadership.

Bunster, X. 1986. "Surviving beyond Fear: Women and Torture in Latin America." In J. Nash and H. Safa (eds.), *Women and Change in Latin America*. South Hadley, MA: Bergin and Garvey.

Burbank, V. K. 1994a. *Fighting Women: Anger and Aggression in Aboriginal Australia*. Berkeley: University of California Press.

———. 1994b. "Cross-Cultural Perspectives on Aggression in Women and Girls: An Introduction." *Sex Roles* 30:167–76.

Bureau of National Affairs. 1987. *Sexual Harassment: Employer Policies and Problems*. Washington, DC: U.S. Government Printing Office.

Burgess, Ann Wolbert, and Lynda L. Holmstrom. 1974. "The Rape Trauma Syndrome." *American Journal of Psychiatry* 131:981–86.

Burgess, Robert, and Patricia Draper. 1989. "The Explanation of Family Violence: The Role of Biological, Behavioral and Cultural Selection." In Lloyd Ohlin and Michael Tonry (eds.), *Family Violence*. Chicago: University of Chicago Press.

Burgin, Victor. 1986. *The End of Art Theory: Criticism and Postmodernity*. London: Macmillan.

Burkhart, Barry R., and Annette L. Stanton. 1988. "Sexual Aggression in Acquaintance Relationships." In Gordon W. Russell (ed.), *Violence in Intimate Relationships*. New York: PMA Publishing Corp.

Burnam, M. A., J. A. Stein, J. M. Golding, S. B. Sorenson, A. B. Forsythe, and C. A. Telles. 1988. "Sexual Assault and Mental Disorders in a Community Population." *Journal of Consulting and Clinical Psychology* 56:843–50.

Burstyn, Varda (ed.). 1985. *Women against Censorship*. Vancouver: Douglas and McIntyre.

Burt, Martha R. 1980. "Cultural Myths and Supports for Rape." *Journal of Personality and Social Psychology* 38:217–30.

Burt, M. R., and R. S. Albin. 1981. "Rape Myths, Rape Definitions, and Probability of Conviction." *Journal of Applied Social Psychology* 11:212–30.

Busselle, Michael. 1981. *Nude and Glamour Photography*. London: Macdonald.

Buzawa, E. S., and C. G. Buzawa. 1996. *Domestic Violence: The Criminal Justice Response*. Newbury Park, CA: Sage.

Byrne, C., I. Arias, and D. K. O'Leary. 1992. "Autonomy as a Predictor of Marital Violence." Poster presented at the Annual Meeting of the Advancement of Behavior Therapy, November, Boston.

Byrne, D. 1996. "Clinical Models for the Treatment of Gay Male Perpetrators of Domestic Violence." In C. Renzetti and C. H. Miley (eds.), *Violence in Gay and Lesbian Domestic Partnerships*. New York: Harrington Park.

Campbell, Jacquelyn C. 1989. "Women's Responses to Sexual Abuse in Intimate Relationships." *Health Care for Women International* 8.

CAMVAC. 1985. *Carpeta de Información Basica para la Atención Solidaria y Feminista a Mujeres Violadas*. Mexico City: Centro de Apoyo a Mujeres Violadas.

Cancian, Francesca M. 1989. "Love and the Rise of Capitalism." In Barbara J. Risman and Pepper Schwartz (eds.), *Gender in Intimate Relationships*. Belmont, CA: Wadsworth.

Cann, A., L. G. Calhoun, J. W. Selby, and H. E. King (eds.). 1981. "Rape." *Journal of Social Issues* 37, no. 4 (Whole Issue).

Caputi, Jane, and Diana E. H. Russell. 1990. "Femicide: Speaking the Unspeakable." *Ms.* 1, no. 2.

Caputo, Richard. 1991. "Police Classification of Domestic-Violence Calls: An Assessment of Program Impact." In Dean Knudsen and JoAnn Miller (eds.), *Abused and Battered: Social and Legal Responses to Family Violence*. Hawthorne, NY: Aldine de Gruyter.

Carby, Hazel V. 1987. *Reconstructing Womanhood*. Oxford: Oxford University Press.

Carillo, Roxanna. 1992. *Battered Dreams: Violence against Women as an Obstacle to Development*. New York: UNIFEM.

Carlson, B. E. 1984. "Children's Observations of Interparental Violence." In A. R. Roberts (ed.), *Battered Women and Their Families.* New York: Springer.

Carothers, C., and P. Crull. 1984. "Contrasting Sexual Harassment in Female and Male Dominated Occupations." In K. Brodkin-Sachs and D. Remy (eds.), *My Troubles Are Going to Have Trouble with Me.* New Brunswick, NJ: Rutgers University Press.

Carpetas Basica. 1991. Mexico City: Procurador de Justicia del Distrito Federal de Mexico.

Chapman, J. R., and M. Gates (eds.). 1978. *The Victimization of Women.* Beverly Hills, CA: Sage.

Check, James V. P., and N. M. Malamuth. 1983. "Sex Role Stereotyping and Reactions to Depictions of Stranger versus Acquaintance Rape." *Journal of Personality and Social Psychology* 45:344–56.

Check, James V. P., Barbara Elias, and Susan A. Barton. 1988. "Hostility toward Men in Female Victims of Male Sexual Aggression." In Gordon W. Russell (ed.), *Violence in Intimate Relationships.* New York: PMA Publishing Corp.

Chester, G., and J. Dickey (eds.). 1988. *Feminism and Censorship: The Current Debate.* London: Prism Press.

Chiles, Lawton. 1988. "Death before Life: The Tragedy of Infant Mortality." In *Report of the National Commission to Prevent Infant Mortality.* Washington, DC: U.S. Government Printing Office.

Chiricos, T. 1987. "Rates of Crime and Unemployment: An Analysis of Aggregate Research Evidence." *Social Problems* 34:187–212.

Chodorow, Nancy. 1978. *The Reproduction of Mothering: Psychoanalysis and the Sociology of Gender.* Berkeley: University of California Press.

CIBA Foundation. 1984. *Child Sexual Abuse within the Family.* London: Tavistock.

Clark, Kenneth. 1976. *The Nude.* Harmondsworth: Penguin.

Clark, L. M. G. 1983. "Liberalism and Pornography." In D. Copp and S. Wendell (eds.), *Pornography and Censorship.* Buffalo: Prometheus.

Clatterbaugh, K. *Contemporary Perspectives on Masculinity.* Boulder, CO: Westview Press.

Cockburn, C. 1983. *Brothers: Male Dominance and Technological Change.* London: Pluto Press.

———. 1985. *Machinery of Dominance: Women, Men and Technical Know-How.* London: Pluto Press.

Coleman, V. E. 1990. "Violence between Lesbian Couples: A Between Groups Comparison." Ph.D. diss. Ann Arbor, MI: University Microfilms International.

———. 1994. "Lesbian Battering: The Relationship between Personality and the Perpetration of Violence." *Violence and Victims* 9:139–52.

Coles, F. S. 1986. "Forced to Quit: Sexual Harassment Complaints and Agency Response." *Sex Roles* 14:81–95.

Collins, E. G. C., and T. B. Blodgett. 1981. "Sexual Harassment: Some See It, Some Won't." *Harvard Business Review* 59 (March/April):77–95.

Collins, Patricia Hill. 1986. "Learning from the Outsider within: The Sociological Significance of Black Feminist Thought." *Social Problems* 33, no. 6:S14–S32.

Collins, Randall. 1988. *Sociology of Marriage and the Family.* Chicago: Nelson-Hall.

Collinson, D. L., and M. Collinson. 1989. "Sexuality in the Workplace: The Domination of Men's Sexuality." In J. Hearn, D. L. Sheppard, P. Tancred-Sheriff, and G. Burrell (eds.), *The Sexuality of Organization.* London: Sage.

Connell, R. W. 1987. *Gender and Power.* Stanford: Stanford University Press.

———. 1991. "Live Fast and Die Young: The Construction of Masculinity among Young Working-Class Men on the Margin of the Labor Market." *Australian and New Zealand Journal of Sociology* 27, no. 2:141–71.

———. 1995. "Masculinity, Violence, and War." Reprinted in M. S. Kimmel and M. A. Messner (eds.), *Men's Lives.* New York: Allyn and Bacon.

Connors, Jane. 1994. "Government Measures to Confront Violence against Women." In M. Davies (ed.), *Women and Violence.* London: Zed Books.

Consumers Association of Penang. 1988. *Rape in Malaysia*. Penang, Malaysia: Consumer Association on Penang.

Coomaraswamy, R. 1992. "Of Kali Born: Women, Violence, and the Law." In M. Schuler (ed.), *Freedom from Violence: Women's Strategies from around the World*. New York: UNIFEM Widbooks.

Corby, B. 1987. *Working with Child Abuse: Social Work Practice and the Child Abuse System*. Milton Keynes: Open University Press.

Cormack, Malcolm. 1976. *The Nude in Western Art*. Oxford: Phaidon.

Cornwell, J. 1984. *Hard-Earned Lives: Accounts of Health and Illness from East London*. London: Tavistock Publications.

Cortez, Jayne. 1983. "Rape." In Amiri Baraka and Amina Baraka (eds.), *Confirmation*. New York: Quill.

Cottle, C., and B. McKeown. 1980. "The Forced-Free Distinction in Q-Technique: A Note on Unused Categories in the Q-Sort Continuum." *Operant Subjectivity*, January, 58–63.

Council on Scientific Affairs. 1992. "Violence against Women: Relevance for Medical Practitioners." *Journal of the American Medical Association* 267:3184–89.

COVAC. 1990. *Evaluación de proyecto para Educación, Capacitación, y Atención a Mujeres y Menores de Edad en Materia de Violencia Sexual, Enero a Diciembre 1990*. Mexico City: Asociación Mexicana contra la Violencia a las Mujeres.

Cowan, G. 1992. "Feminist Attitudes toward Pornography Control." *Psychology of Women Quarterly* 16:165–77.

Coward, R. 1982. "Sexual Violence and Sexuality." *Feminist Review*, no. 11 (summer).

Crenshaw, K. W. 1994. "Mapping the Margins: Intersectionality, Identity Politics, and Violence against Women of Color." In M. A. Fineman and R. Mykitiuk (eds.), *The Public Nature of Private Violence*. New York: Routledge.

Crites, Laura L. 1987. "Wife Abuse: The Judicial Record." In Laura L. Crites and Winifred L. Hepperle (eds.), *Women, the Courts, and Equality*. Newbury Park, CA: Sage.

Crull, P. 1982. "Stress Effects of Sexual Harassment on the Job: Implications for Counseling." *American Journal of Orthopsychiatry* 52:539–44.

Culbertson, A. L., P. Rosenfeld, S. Booth-Kewley, and P. Magnusson. 1992. *Assessment of Sexual Harassment in the Navy: Results of the 1989 Navy-Wide Survey*. TR-92-11. San Diego: Navy Personnel Research and Development Center.

Currie, E. 1985. *Confronting Crime: An American Challenge*. New York: Pantheon.

Curry, T. J. 1991. "Fraternal Bonding in the Locker Room: A Profeminist Analysis of Talk about Competition and Women." *Sociology of Sport Journal* 8:119–35.

Daly, M., and M. Wilson. 1988. *Homicide*. New York: Aldine De Gruyter.

Davidson, T. 1978. *Conjugal Crime: Understanding and Changing the Wife Beating Pattern*. New York: Hawthorn.

Davies, Miranda. 1994. "Understanding the Problem." From the United Nations' resource manual *Strategies for Contronting Domestic Violence*. Reprinted in Miranda Davies (ed.), *Women and Violence*. London: Zed Books.

Davin, A. 1978. "Imperialism and Motherhood." *History Workshop* 5:9–65.

Davis, Angela. 1971. "Reflections on the Black Woman's Role in the Community of Slaves." *The Black Scholar* 3, no. 4:3–15.

————. 1983. *Women, Race and Class*. New York: Vintage Books.

Davis, J. A., and T. W. Smith. 1986. *General Social Surveys: Cumulative Codebook*. Chicago: National Opinion Research Center, University of Chicago.

Davis, K. E., and N. Braught. 1970. "Exposure to Pornography, Character, and Sexual Deviance." In *Technical Reports of the Commission on Obscenity and Pornography, vol. 7*. Washington, D.C.: U.S. Government Printing Office.

Davis, M. 1983. *Smut: Erotic Reality/Obscene Ideology*. Chicago: University of Chicago Press.

Decalmer, P., and F. Glendenning. 1993. *The Mistreatment of Elderly People*. London: Sage.

Deckard, B. S. 1983. *The Woman's Movement: Political, Socioeconomic, and Psychological Issues.* New York: Harper & Row.

DeKeseredy, W., and R. Hinch. 1991. *Woman Abuse: Sociological Perspectives.* Lewiston, NY: Thompson Educational.

DeKeseredy, W., and K. Kelly. 1993. "The Incidence and Prevalence of Woman Abuse in Canadian University and College Dating Relationships." *Canadian Journal of Sociology* 18:137–59.

De la Luz Lima, Maria. 1992. "Reforms in the Criminal Justice System." In *Violence against Women: Addressing a Global Problem.*" Transcript of the Ford Foundation Women's Program Forum. New York: Ford Foundation.

Del Tufo, Alisa. 1995. *Domestic Violence for Beginners.* New York: Writers and Readers Publishing.

DeMaris, A. 1987. "The Efficacy of a Spouse Abuse Model in Accounting for Courtship Violence." *Journal of Family Issues* 8:291–305.

———. 1990. "The Dynamics of Generational Transfer of Courtship Violence: A Biracial Exploration." *Journal of Marriage and the Family* 52:219–73.

D'Emilio, John, and Estelle B. Freedman. 1988. *Intimate Matters: A History of Sexuality in America.* New York: Harper & Row.

Department of Health. 1988. *Protecting Children: A Guide for Social Workers Undertaking a Comprehensive Assessment.* London: HMSO.

———. 1989a. *Working with Child Sexual Abuse: Guidelines for Training Social Services Staff.* Child Care Training Support Programme. London: HMSO.

———. 1989b. *An Introduction to the Children Act 1989.* London: HMSO.

Department of Health and Social Security. 1988. *Working Together: A Guide to Arrangements for Inter-Agency Co-operation for the Protection of Children from Abuse.* London: HMSO.

Department of Health Social Service Inspectorate. 1992. *Confronting Elder Abuse: An SSI London Region Survey.* London: HMSO.

Deutsch, H. 1944. *The Psychology of Women.* Vol. 1. New York: Grune and Stratton.

Diamond, I. 1980. "Pornography and Repression: A Reconsideration." *Signs: Journal of Women in Culture and Society* 5:686–701.

DiTomaso, N. 1989. "Sexuality in the Workplace: Discrimination and Harassment." In J. Hearn, D. L. Sheppard, P. Tancred-Sheriff, and G. Burrell (eds.), *The Sexuality of Organization.* London: Sage.

Dixon-Mueller, R. 1992. "Pais conta 337 Mulheres Agredidas por Dia." *Folha de San Paulo,* November 29.

Dobash, R. Emerson, and Russell P. Dobash. 1979. *Violence against Wives: A Case against the Patriarchy.* New York: Free Press.

———. 1984. "The Nature and Antecedents of Violent Events." *British Journal of Criminology* 24, no. 3:269–88.

———. 1987. "The Response of the British and American Women's Movements to Violence against Women." In Jalna Hanmer and Mary Maynard (eds.), *Women, Violence and Social Control.* Atlantic Highlands, NJ: Humanities Press International.

———. 1992. *Women, Violence and Social Change.* London: Routledge.

Dobash, Russell P., R. Emerson Dobash, Margo Wilson, and Martin Daly. 1992. "The Myth of Sexual Symmetry in Marital Violence." *Social Problems* 39, no. 1:71–91.

Donaldson, M. 1987. "Labouring Men: Love, Sex and Strife." *Australian and New Zealand Journal of Sociology* 23, no. 2:164–84.

Donnerstein, E. 1984. "Pornography: Its Effect on Violence against Women." In N. Malamuth and E. Donnerstien (eds.), *Pornography and Sexual Aggression.* Orlando, FL: Academic Press.

Donnerstein, E., and D. Linz. 1986. "Mass Media Sexual Violence and Male Viewers: Current Theory and Research." *American Behavioral Scientist* 29, no. 5:601–18.

Donnerstein, E., E. Linz, and S. Penrod. 1987. *The Question of Pornography: The Research Findings and Policy Implications.* London: Collier Macmillan.

Dorkenoo, Efua, and Scilla Elworthy. 1994. "Female Genital Mutilation." In Miranda Davies (ed.), *Women and Violence.* Atlantic Highlands, NJ: Zed Books.

Dorsey, J. O. 1884. *Omaha Sociology.* Smithsonian Institution, Bureau of Ethnology, Third Annual Report, 1881–82. Washington, DC: U.S. Government Printing Office.

Douglas, C. A. 1986. "Pornography: The Meese Report." *Off Our Backs* 4 (August–September).

Duggan, L., N. Hunter, and C. S. Vance. 1985. "False Premises: Feminist Antipornography Legislation in the U.S." In V. Burstyn (ed.), *Women against Censorship.* Vancouver: Douglas and McIntyre.

Duncan, Carol. 1977. "The Esthetics of Power in Modern Erotic Art." *Heresies* 1 (January):46–50.

Dunn, S. F., and V. J. Gilchrist. 1993. "Sexual Assault." *Primary Care* 20:359–73.

Dunwoody-Miller, V., and B. A. Gutek. 1985. *S.H.E. Project Report: Sexual Harassment in the State Workforce: Results of a Survey.* Sacramento: Sexual Harassment in Employment Project of the California Commission on the Status of Women.

Durham, A. M., III. 1986. "Pornography, Social Harm, and Legal Control: Observations on Bart." *Justice Quarterly* 3:95–102.

Duster, T. 1987. "Crime, Youth Unemployment and the Black Urban Underclass." *Crime and Delinquency* 30:300–316.

Dutton, D. G. 1988. *The Domestic Assault of Women: Psychological and Criminal Justice Perspectives.* Toronto: Allyn and Bacon.

———. 1994. "Patriarchy and Wife Assault: The Ecological Fallacy." *Violence and Victims* 9:167–82.

Dworkin, Andrea. 1974. *Woman Hating.* New York: Penguin.

———. 1981. *Pornography: Men Possessing Women.* London: Women's Press.

———. 1985. "Against the Male Flood: Censorship, Pornography, and Equality." *Harvard Women's Law Journal* 8:1–30.

Dziech, Billie Wright, and Linda Weiner. 1990. *The Lecherous Professor: Sexual Harassment on Campus.* Chicago: University of Illinois Press.

Eastman, M. 1984. *Old Age Abuse.* Mitcham: Age Concern England.

Eastman, M., and M. Sutton. 1982. "Granny Battering." *Geriatric Medicine,* November, 11–15.

Echlin, Carole, and Larry Marshall. 1995. "Child Protection Services for Children of Battered Women: Practice and Controversy." In Einat Peled, Peter Jaffe, and Jeffrey Edleson (eds.), *Ending the Cycle of Violence: Community Responses to Children of Battered Women.* Thousand Oaks, CA: Sage.

Economic and Social Council. 1992. *Report to the Working Group on Violence against Women.* Vienna: United Nations, E CN.6 WG.21 1992 L.3.

Edleson, J. L., Zvi Eisikovits, and E. Guttman. 1986. "Men Who Batter Women: A Critical Review of Evidence." *Journal of Family Issues* 6, no. 2:229–47.

Edwards, Alison. "Rape, Racism, and the White Women's Movement: An Answer to Susan Brownmiller." Chicago: Sojourner Truth Organization.

Edwards, Susan. 1987. " 'Provoking Her Own Demise': From Common Assault to Homicide." In Jalna Hanmer and Mary Maynard (eds.), *Women, Violence and Social Control.* Atlantic Highlands, NJ: Humanities Press International.

Ehrenreich, Barbara. 1983. *The Hearts of Men.* New York: Doubleday.

———. 1984. "A Feminist's View of the New Man." *New York Times Magazine,* May 20, 36–48.

———. 1989. *Fear of Falling.* New York: Pantheon.

Ehrenreich, Barbara, E. Hess, and G. Jacobs. 1986. *Re-Making Love: The Feminization of Sex.* New York: Doubleday.

Eisenhart, R. W. 1975. "You Can't Hack It Little Girl: A Discussion of the Covert Psychological Agenda of Modern Combat Training." *Journal of Social Issues* 31, no. 4:13–23.

Eisenstein, Hester. 1983. *Contemporary Feminist Thought.* Boston: G. K. Hall.

Eisikovits, Z., and E. Buchbinder. "Talking Violent: A Phenomenological Study of Metaphors Violence Men Use." Paper presented at the Fourth International Family Violence Research Conference, July 1995, Durham, NH.

Ellis, D., and W. S. DeKeseredy. 1996. *The Wrong Stuff: An Introduction to the Sociological Study of Deviance.* Toronto: Allyn and Bacon.

Ellis, D., and N. Stuckless. 1993. *Hitting and Splitting: Predatory Pre-Separation Abuse among Separating Spouses.* Mediation Pilot Project Report no. 7. Submitted to the Attorney General of Ontario.

Ellis, John. 1980. "Photography/Pornography/Art/Pornography." *Screen* 21, no. 1 (spring):81–108.

Ellis, Lee. 1989. *Theories of Rape: Inquiries into the Causes of Sexual Aggression.* New York: Hemisphere Publishing Corp.

Elwin, V. 1947. *The Muria and Their Ghotul.* Bombay: Geoffrey Cumberlege/Oxford University Press.

Emery, B., S. Lloyd, and A. Castleton. 1989. "Why Women Hit: A Feminist Perspective." Paper presented at the National Conference on Family Relations, New Orleans.

Emery, R. E. 1982. "Interparental Conflict and the Children of Discord and Divorce." *Psychological Bulletin* 92:310–30.

English, D. 1980. "The Politics of Porn: Can Feminists Walk the Line?" *Mother Jones* 5:20–23, 43–50.

Erdland, P. A. 1914. *Die Marshall-insulaner (The Marshall Islanders).* Münster: Anthropos Bibliothek Ethnological Monographs, 2(1). (Translated by Richard Neuse for Human Relations Area Files.)

Ericksen, K. P. 1994. "Recommendations to the Women's Health Advisory Committee on Women's Reproductive Health and Disease." Paper prepared for the American Psychological Association Conference on Psychosocial and Behavioral Factors in Women's Health, May, Washington, DC.

Estrich, Susan. 1987. *Real Rape.* Cambridge, MA: Harvard University Press.

Eth, Spencer, and Robert Pynoos. 1985. *Post-Traumatic Stress Disorder in Children.* Washington, DC: American Psychiatric Press.

Evans-Pritchard, E. E. 1971. *The Azande.* Oxford: Oxford University Press.

Everywoman. 1988. *Pornography and Sexual Violence: Evidence of Links.* London: Everywoman.

Ewing, Wayne. 1982. "The Civic Advocacy of Violence." *M* (spring):5–7, 22.

Fagan, Jeffrey. 1989. "Cessation of Family Violence: Deterrence and Dissuasion." In Lloyd Ohlin and Michael Tonry (eds.), *Family Violence.* Chicago: University of Chicago Press.

Fairbairn, W. R. D. 1935. "Medico-Psychological Aspects of the Problem of Child Assault." *Mental Hygiene* (April):1–16.

Farley, L. 1978. *Sexual Shakedown: The Sexual Harassment of Women on the Job.* New York: McGraw-Hill.

Fathers for Equal Rights Organization, Inc. 1988. *Father's Review* 1 (February).

Fausto-Sterling, Anne. 1989. "Life in the XO Corral." *Women's Studies International Forum* 12, no. 3:319–31.

Fauveau, V., and T. Blanchet. "Epidemiology and Cause of Deaths among Women in Rural Bangladesh." *International Journal of Epidemiology* 18:139–45.

Fawcett, J. 1989. "Breaking the Habit: The Need for a Comprehensive Long Term Treatment for Sexually Abusing Families." In *The Treatment of Child Sexual Abuse.* NSPCC, Occasional Paper Series no. 7. London: NSPCC.

Federal Bureau of Investigation. 1993. *Uniform Crime Reports.* Washington, DC: U.S. Government Printing Office.

Feil, N. 1993. *The Validation Breakthrough.* Baltimore: Health Professions Press.

Feldman, Hannah J. L. 1993. "More Than Confessional: Testimonial and the Subject of Rape." In Monica Chau, Hannah J. L. Feldman, Jennifer Kabat, and Hannah Kruse (eds.), *The Subject of Rape.* New York: Whitney Museum of American Art.

Feltey, K. M., J. J. Ainslie, and A. Geib. 1991. "Sexual Coercion Attitudes among High School Students: The Influence of Gender and Rape Education." *Youth & Society* 23:229–50.

Fenstermaker, S. 1989. "Acquaintance Rape on Campus: Responsibility and Attributions of Crime." In Maureen A. Pirog-Good and Jan E. Stets (eds.), *Violence in Dating Relationships.* New York: Praeger.

Ferguson, H. 1990. "Rethinking Child Protection Practices: A Case for History." In The Violence against Children Study Group: (eds.), *Taking Child Abuse Seriously.* London: Unwin Hyman.

Ferguson, K. E. 1984. *The Feminist Case against Bureaucracy.* Philadelphia: Temple University Press.

Ferraro, Kathleen J. 1988. "An Existential Approach to Battering." In G. T. Hotaling, D. Finkelhor, J. T. Kirkpatrick, and M. Straus (eds.), *Family Abuse and Its Consequences.* Newbury Park, CA: Sage.

———. 1989. "Policing Woman Battering." *Social Problems* 36 (1989):61–74.

Fields, M. D. 1978. "Wife-Beating: Facts and Figures." *Victimology* 2, nos. 3–4:643–47.

Fine, G. A. 1986. "The Dirty Play of Little Boys." *Society* 24, no. 1:63–67.

Finkelhor, David. 1979. *Sexually Victimized Children.* New York: Free Press.

———. (ed.). 1984. *Child Sexual Abuse: New Theory and Research.* New York: Free Press.

———. 1986. *A Sourcebook on Child Sexual Abuse.* Beverly Hills, CA: Sage.

———. 1987. "The Sexual Abuse of Children: Current Research Reviewed." *Psychiatric Annals* 17:233–41.

Finkelhor, D., R. J. Gelles, G. T. Hotaling, and M. A. Straus, (eds.). 1983. *The Dark Side of Families: Current Family Violence Research.* Beverly Hills, CA: Sage.

Finkelhor, D., G. T. Hotaling, I. A. Lewis, and C. Smith. 1990. "Sexual Abuse in a National Survey of Adult Men and Women: Prevalence, Characteristics and Risk Factors." *Child Abuse and Neglect* 14:19–28.

Finkelhor, D., and K. A. Pillemer. 1988. "Elder Abuse: Its Relation to Other Forms of Domestic Violence." In G. T. Hotaling, D. Finklehor, J. T. Kirkpatrick, and M. A. Strauss (eds.), *Family Abuse and Its Consequences: New Directions in Research.* Beverly Hills, CA: Sage.

Finkelhor, David, and Kersti Yllö. 1985. *License to Rape: Sexual Abuse of Wives.* New York: Free Press.

Fitzgerald, L. F. 1982. *Sexual Harassment in Higher Education: Concepts and Issues.* Washington, DC: National Education Association.

Fitzgerald, L. F., and K. F. Brock. 1992. *Women's Responses to Victimization: Validation of an Objective Inventory to Assess Strategies for Responding to Sexual Harassment.* Unpublished manuscript, Department of Psychology, University of Illinois, Champaign.

Fitzgerald, L., Y. Gold, M. Ormerod, and L. M. Weitzman. 1987. "The Lecherous Professor: A Study in Power Relations." Paper presented at the Midwestern Society for Feminist Studies, May, Akron, OH.

Fitzgerald, L. F., and S. L. Schullman. 1993. "Sexual Harassment: A Research Analysis and Agenda for the 1990s." *Journal of Vocational Behavior* 42:5–27.

Fitzgerald, L. F., S. L. Schullman, N. Bailey, M. Richards, J. Swecker, Y. Gold, A. J. Ormerod, and L. M. Weitzman. 1990. "The Incidence and Dimensions of Sexual Harassment in Academia and the Workplace." *Journal of Vocational Behavior* 32:152–75.

Flowers, Ronald Barri. 1986. *Children and Criminality: The Child as Victim and Perpetrator.* New York: Greenwood Press.

———. 1994. *The Victimization and Exploitation of Women and Children: A Study of Physical, Mental, and Sexual Maltreatment in the United States.* Jefferson, NC: McFarland.

Foa, E. B., B. O. Rothbaum, and G. S. Steketee. 1993. "Treatment of Rape Victims." *Journal of Interpersonal Violence* 8:256–76.

Folch-Lyon, E., I. Macorra, and S. B. Schearer. 1981. "Focus Group and Survey Research on Family Planning in Mexico." *Studies in Family Planning* 12:409–32.

Ford, David. 1991. "Preventing and Provoking Wife Battery through Criminal Sanctioning: A

Look at the Risks." In Dean Knudsen and JoAnn Miller (eds.), *Abused and Battered: Social and Legal Responses to Family Violence.* Hawthorne, NY: Aldine de Gruyter.

Forrester, John. 1986. "Rape, Seduction and Psychoanalysis." In Sylvana Tomaselli and Roy Porter (eds.), *Rape.* Oxford: Basil Blackwell.

Forsstrom-Cohn, B., and A. Rosenbaum. 1985. "The Effects of Parental Marital Violence on Young Adults: An Exploratory Investigation." *Journal of Marriage and the Family* 47:467–72.

Fort, A. 1989. "Investigating the Social Context of Fertility and Family Planning: A Qualitative Study in Peru." *International Family Planning Perspectives* 15:88–94.

Foucault, Michel. 1980a. *History of Sexuality.* New York: Vintage Books.

———. 1980b. *Power/Knowledge: Selected Interviews and Other Writings, 1972–1977.* Edited by Colin Gordon, New York: Pantheon.

Freedman, E. B. 1981. *Their Sisters' Keepers: Women's Prison Reform in America, 1893–1930.* Ann Arbor: University of Michigan Press.

———. 1989. "Uncontrolled Desires: The Response to the Sexual Psychopath, 1920–1960." In K. Peiss and C. Simmons (eds.), *Passion and Power: Sexuality in History.* Philadelphia: Temple University Press.

Freeman, Jo. 1984. "The Women's Liberation Movement: Its Origins, Structure, Activities, and Ideas." In J. Freeman (ed.), *Women: A Feminist Perspective.* Mountain View, CA: Mayfield Publishing Co.

Freeman-Longo, R. E., and R. V. Wall. 1986. "Changing a Lifetime of Sexual Crime." *Psychology Today,* March, 58–64.

Friday, N. 1973. *My Secret Garden.* New York: Trident.

Fried, A. 1988. "Abortion Politics as Symbolic Politics: An Investigation into Belief Systems." *Social Science Quarterly* 69:137–54.

Friedan, B. 1963. *The Feminine Mystique.* New York: Dell.

Friedman, A. R. 1992. "Rape and Domestic Violence: The Experience of Refugee Women." *Women & Therapy* 13:65–78.

Frieze, Irene Hanson. 1983. "Investigating the Causes and Consequences of Marital Rape." *Signs: Journal of Women in Culture and Society* 8, no. 3:532–53.

Frieze, Irene Hanson, and Angela Browne. 1989. "Violence in Marriage." In Lloyd Ohlin and Michael Tonry (eds.), *Family Violence.* Chicago: University of Chicago Press.

Fulmer, T., and T. A. O'Malley. 1987. *Inadequate Care of the Elderly.* New York: Springer.

Funk, Rus Ervin. 1993. *Stopping Rape: A Challenge for Men.* Philadelphia: New Society Publishers.

Game, A., and R. Pringle. 1984. *Gender at Work.* Boston: Allen and Unwin.

Gaquin, D. A. 1977/78 "Spouse Abuse: Data from the National Crime Survey." *Victimology* 2:632–43.

Garbarino, J., and G. Gillian. 1980. *Understanding Abusive Families.* Toronto: Lexington.

Gardner, Carol Brooks. 1995. *Passing By: Gender and Public Harassment.* Berkeley: University of California Press.

Gardner, T. A. 1980. "Racism in Pornography and the Women's Movement." In L. Lederer (ed.), *Take Back the Night: Women and Pornography.* New York: Morrow.

Gavey, N. 1991. "Sexual Victimization Prevalence among New Zealand University Students." *Journal of Consulting and Clinical Psychology* 59:464–66.

Gayford, J. J. 1975. "Wife Battering: A Preliminary Survey of 100 Cases." *British Medical Journal* 1:194–97.

Gelles, Richard J. 1975. "Violence and Pregnancy: A Note on the Extent of the Problem and Needed Services." *Family Coordinator* 24:81–86.

———. 1987. *The Violent Home.* Newbury Park, CA: Sage.

———. 1993. "Alcohol and Other Drugs Are Associated with Violence—They Are Not Its Cause." In R. J. Gelles and D. R. Loseke (eds.), *Current Conroversies in Family Violence.* Newbury Park, CA: Sage.

———. 1995. "Violence, Abuse, and Homicide: A Continuum of Violence or Distinctive Behaviors." Paper presented at the Fourth International Family Violence Research Conference, July, Durham, NH.

Gelles, Richard, and C. Cornell. 1985. *Intimate Violence in Families.* Beverly Hills, CA: Sage.

Gelles, Richard, and Donileen Loseke (eds.). 1993. *Current Controversies on Family Violence.* Newbury Park, CA: Sage.

Gelles, Richard, and Murray Straus. 1988. *Intimate Violence.* New York: Simon and Schuster.

Genovese, Eugene D. 1974. *Roll, Jordan, Roll: The World the Slaves Made.* New York: Pantheon.

George, A. 1993. "Coercive Sex within Consensual Unions: A Case Study from Bombay." Paper presented at the United Nations Population Council meeting on Sexual Coercion and Women's Reproductive Health, jointly sponsored by the Population Council and the Pacific Institute for Women's Health, November, New York.

Geraci, Linda. 1986. "Making Shelters Safe for Lesbians." In Kerry Lobel (ed.), *Naming the Violence: Speaking Out about Lesbian Battering.* Seattle: Seal Press.

Gibson, J. T., and Mika Haritos-Fatouros. 1986. "The Education of a Torturer." *Psychology Today,* November.

Giller, J. E. 1992. "War, Women, and Rape." Thesis presented to the School of Oriental and African Studies, University of London.

Gillespie, Cynthia. 1989. *Justifiable Homicide: Battered Women, Self-Defense, and the Law.* Columbus: Ohio State University Press.

Gilligan, Carol. 1982. *In a Different Voice: Psychological Theory and Women's Development.* Cambridge: Harvard University Press.

Gilman, Sander L. 1985. "Black Bodies, White Bodies: Toward an Iconography of Female Sexuality in Late Nineteenth-Century Art, Medicine, and Literature." *Critical Inquiry* 12, no. 1:205–43.

Ginorio, Angela, and Jane Reno. 1986. "Violence in the Lives of Latina Women." In Maryviolet Burns, (ed.), *The Speaking Profits Us: Violence in the Lives of Women of Color.* Seattle: Center for the Prevention of Sexual and Domestic Violence.

Glaser, D., and J. R. Spencer. 1990. "Sentencing, Children's Evidence and Children's Trauma." *Criminal Law Review* (June):371–82.

Gledhill, A., et al. 1989. *Who Cares? Children at Risk and Social Services.* London: Centre for Policy Studies.

Glendenning, C. 1987. "Impoverishing Women." In Alan Walker and Carol Walker (eds.), *The Growing Divide.* London: CPAG.

Godkin, M. A., R. S. Wolf, and K. A. Pillemer. 1989. "A Case-Comparison Analysis of Elder Abuse and Neglect." *International Journal of Aging and Human Development* 28, no. 3:207–25.

Goldberg-Ambrose, Carole. 1992. "Unfinished Business in Rape Law Reform." *Journal of Social Issues* 48, no. 1:173–85.

Goldfeld, A. E., R. F. Mollica, B. H. Pesavento, and S. V. Farone. 1988. "The Physical and Psychological Sequelae of Torture." *Journal of the American Medical Association* 259:2725–29.

Golding, J. M. 1994. "Sexual Assault History and Physical Health in Randomly Selected Los Angeles Women." *Health Psychology* 13:130–38.

Golding, J. M., J. A. Stein, J. M. Siegel, M. A. Burnam, and S. B. Sorenson. 1988. "Sexual Assault History and Use of Health and Mental Health Services." *American Journal of Community Psychology* 16:625–44.

Goldman, P. 1978. "Violence against Women in the Family." Unpublished master's thesis, McGill University, Faculty of Law.

Goldsmith, Arthur. 1976. *The Nude in Photography.* London: Octopus.

Goldstein, M. J. 1973. "Exposure to Erotic Stimuli and Sexual Deviance." *Journal of Social Issues* 29:197–219.

Goldstein, M. J. et al. 1970. "Exposure to Pornography and Sexual Behavior in Deviant and

Normal Groups." In *Technical Reports of the Commission on Obscenity and Pornography.* Vol. 7. Washington, DC: U.S. Government Printing Office.

Goleman, Daniel. 1995. "Early Violence Leaves Its Mark on the Brain." *New York Times,* October 3, C1.

Gondolf, Edward W. 1988a. *Research on Men Who Batter: An Overview, Bibliography and Resource Guide.* Bradenton, FL: Human Services Institute.

———. 1988b. "The State of the Debate: A Review Essay on Woman Battering." *Response* 11, no. 3:3–8.

———. 1990. *Psychiatric Response to Family Violence: Identifying and Confronting Neglected Danger.* Lexington, MA: Lexington Books.

Gondolf, Edward, with Ellen Fisher. 1988. *Battered Women as Survivors: An Alternative to Treating Learned Helplessness.* Lexington, MA: Lexington Books.

Goodman, Ellen. 1987. "My Equal Rights Winners." *Boston Globe,* August 25, p. 13.

Goodman, L. A., M. P. Koss, and N. F. Russo. 1993a. "Violence against Women: Physical and Mental Health Effects. Part I. Research Findings." *Applied and Preventive Psychology: Current Scientific Perspectives* 2:79–89.

———. 1993b. "Violence against Women: Physical and Mental Health Effects. Part II. Conceptualizing Post-Traumatic Stress." *Applied and Preventive Psychology: Current Scientific Perspectives* 2:123–30.

Goolkasian, Gail A. 1986. *Confronting Domestic Violence: The Role of the Criminal Court Judges.* U.S. Department of Justice, National Institute of Justice. Washington, DC: U.S. Government Printing Office.

Gordon, L. 1988. *Heroes of Their Own Lives: The Politics and History of Family Violence* New York: Viking.

Gordon, Margaret T., and Stephanie Riger. 1989. *The Female Fear.* New York: Free Press.

Gorham, D. 1978. "The 'Maiden Tribute of Modern Babylon' Reexamined: Child Prostitution and the Idea of Childhood in Late Victorian England." *Victorian Studies* 21, no. 3:353–87.

Gould, Stephen Jay. 1981. *The Mismeasure of Man.* New York: W. W. Norton.

Graitcer, P. L. and Z. Youssef (eds.). 1993. *Injury in Egypt: An Analysis of Injuries as a Health Problem.* Jointly published by USAID and the Ministry of Health, Cairo, Egypt.

Grauerholz, E. 1989. "Sexual Harassment of Women Professors by Students: Exploring the Dynamics of Power, Authority, and Gender in a University Setting." *Sex Roles* 21:789–801.

Gray, S. 1987. "Sharing the Shop Floor." In Michael Kaufman (ed.), *Beyond Patriarchy.* New York: Oxford University Press.

Gray, S. H. 1982. "Exposure to Pornography and Aggression toward Women: The Case of the Angry Male." *Social Problems* 29:387–98.

Greaves, L., N. Heapy, and A. Wylie. 1988. "Reassessing the Profile and Needs of Battered Women." *Canadian Journal of Community Mental Health* 7:39–51.

Greenberg, D. 1978. "Delinquency and the Age Structure of Society." In A. Pearl, D. Grant, and E. Wenk (eds.), *The Value of Youth.* Davis, CA: Responsible Action.

Greenblat, C. S. 1983. "A Hit Is a Hit Is a Hit . . . Or Is It? Approval and Tolerance of the Use of Physical Force by Spouses." In David Finkelhor, et al. (eds.), *The Dark Side of Families: Current Family Violence Research.* Beverly Hills, CA: Sage.

Greenfeld, Lawrence, and Marianne Zawitz. 1995. *Weapons Offenses and Offenders.* Bureau of Justice Statistics Selected Findings NCJ-155284.

Greif, Jeffrey, and Rebecca Hegar. 1993. *When Parents Kidnap.* New York: Free Press.

Greschner, D. 1985. Review of *Women against Censorship,* edited by Varda Burstyn. *Resources for Feminist Research* 13:66–67.

Griffin, Susan. 1971. "Rape: The All-American Crime." *Ramparts* 10:26–35.

———. 1992. *A Chorus of Stones.* New York: Doubleday.

Griffiths, A., G. Roberts, and J. Williams. 1992. *Sharpening the Instrument: The Law and Older People.* Stoke on Trent: British Association of Service to the Elderly.

Gross, J. 1993. "Where 'Boys Will Be Boys' and Adults Are Befuddled." *New York Times*, March 29.

Groth, A. (with H. Birnbaum). 1979. *Men Who Rape: The Psychology of the Offender.* New York: Plenum.

Groves, Betsy McAlister. 1994. "Interventions with Parents and Caregivers in the Community: Lessons from the Child Witness to Violence Project." In Joy Asofsky and Emily Fenichel (eds.), *Hurt Healing Hope: Caring for Infants and Toddlers in Violent Environments.* Arlington, VA: Zero to Three/National Center for Clinical Infant Programs, Inc.

Groves, D. 1983. "Members and Survivors: Women and Retirement Pensions Legislation." In J. Lewis (ed.), *Women's Welfare, Women's Rights.* London: Croom Helm.

Groves, D. and J. Finch. 1983. "Natural Selection: Perspectives on Entitlement to the Invalid Care Allowance." In D. Groves and J. Finch (eds.), *A Labour of Love: Women, Work and Caring.* London: Routledge and Kegan Paul.

Gruber, J. E., and L. Bjorn. 1982. "Blue-Collar Blues: The Sexual Harassment of Women Autoworkers." *Work and Occupations* 9:271–98.

———. 1986. "Women's Responses to Sexual Harassment: An Analysis of Sociocultural, Organizational, and Personal Resource Models." *Social Science Quarterly* 67, no. 4:814–26.

Grusznski, R. J., J. C. Brink, and J. L. Edleson. 1988. "Support and Education Groups for Children of Battered Women." *Child Welfare* 67, no. 5:431–44.

Gunn Allen, Paula. 1986. "Violence and the American Indian Women." In Maryviolet Burns (ed.), *The Speaking Profits Us: Violence in the Lives of Women of Color.* Seattle: Center for the Prevention of Sexual and Domestic Violence.

Gutek, Barbara A. 1981. "Experiences of Sexual Harassment: Results from a Representative Survey." Paper presented at the annual meeting of the American Psychological Association, Los Angeles.

———. 1985. *Sex and the Workplace: Impact of Sexual Behavior and Harassment on Women, Men, and Organizations.* San Francisco: Jossey-Bass.

———. Forthcoming. "Responses to Sexual Harassment." In S. Oskamp and M. Costanzo (eds.), *Gender Issues in Social Psychology: The Claremont Symposium on Applied Social Psychology.* Newbury Park, CA: Sage.

Gutek, B. A., and V. Dunwoody. 1988. "Understanding Sex and the Workplace." In A. H. Stromberg, L. Larwood, and B. A. Gutek (eds.), *Women and Work: An Annual Review.* Vol. 2. Newbury Park, CA: Sage.

Gutek, B. A., and B. Morasch. 1982. "Sex Ratios, Sex-Role Spillover, and Sexual Harassment of Women at Work." *Journal of Social Issues* 38, no. 4:55–74.

Gutek, B. A., C. Y. Nakamura, M. Gahart, I. Handschumacher, and D. Russell. 1980. "Sexuality in the Workplace." *Basic and Applied Social Psychology* 1:255–65.

Hall, J. D. 1983. "The Mind That Burns in Each Body: Women, Rape, and Racial Violence." In A. Snitow, C. Stansell, and S. Thompson (eds.), *Powers of Desire: The Politics of Sexuality.* New York: Monthly Review Press.

Hall, R. M., and B. R. Sandler. 1982. *The Classroom Climate: A Chilly One for Women?* Washington, DC: Project on the Status and Education of Women.

Hall, Ruth. 1985. *Ask Any Woman: A London Inquiry into Rape and Sexual Assault.* Bristol, Eng.: Falling Wall Press.

Hall, Ruth, Selma James, and Judit Kertesz. 1984. *The Rapist Who Pays the Rent.* Bristol, Eng: Falling Wall Press.

Hall, Stuart. 1980. "Reformism and the Legislation of Consent." In National Deviancy Conference (ed.), *Permissiveness and Control: the Fate of the Sixties Legislation.* London: Macmillan.

Hallowell, A. I. 1955. *Culture and Experience.* Philadelphia: University of Pennsylvania Press.

Halpin, Zuleyma Tang. 1989. "Scientific Objectivity and the Concept of the 'the Other'." *Women's Studies International Forum* 12, no. 3:285–94.

Hamberger, L. K., and C. M. Renzetti (eds.). 1996. *Domestic Partner Abuse: Expanding Paradigms for Understanding and Intervention.* New York: Springer.

Hamilton, J. A., S. W. Alagna, L. S. King, and C. Lloyd. 1987. "The Emotional Consequences of Gender-Based Abuse in the Workplace: New Counseling Programs for Sex Discrimination." *Women and Therapy* 6:155–82.

Hamilton, J. A., and J. L. Dolkart. 1991. "Legal Reform in the Area of Sexual Harassment: Contributions from Social Sciences." Paper presented at the National Conference to Promote Men and Women Working Productively Together, March, Bellevue, WA.

Handwerker, W. P. 1991. "Gender Power Difference May Be STD Risk Factors for the Next Generation." Paper presented at the ninetieth annual meeting of the American Anthropological Association, November, Chicago.

Hanmer, J., J. Radford, and E. A. Stanko. 1989. *Women, Policing and Male Violence: International Perspectives.* London: Routledge.

Hanmer, J., and S. Saunders. 1984. *Well-Founded Fear: A Community Study of Violence to Women.* London: Hutchinson.

Hanson, R. K. 1990. "The Psychological Impact of Sexual Assault on Women and Children: A Review." *Annals of Sex Research* 3:187–232.

Harlow, Carolyn Wolf. 1991. *Female Victims of Violent Crime.* Washington, DC: U.S. Department of Justice.

Harper, F. E. W. 1969. "Bury Me in a Free Land." In W. H. Robinson (ed.), *Early Black American Poets.* Iowa: W. C. Brown.

Harper's. 1984. "Forum: The Place of Pornography." November, p. 31.

Harris, M. 1977. *Cannibals and Kings.* New York: Vintage/Random House.

Harris, R. J., and C. A. Cook. 1994. "Attributions about Spouse Abuse: It Matters Who the Batterers and Victims Are." *Sex Roles* 30:553–65.

Harris, R. N., and R. W. Bologh. 1985. "The Dark Side of Love: Blue and White Collar Wife Abuse." *Victimology* 10:242–52.

Hart, B. 1986. "Lesbian Battering: An Examination." In K. Lobel (ed.), *Naming the Violence.* Seattle: Seal Press.

Hart, S. N., and M. R. Brassard. 1987. "A Major Threat to Children's Mental Health: Psychological Maltreatment." *American Psychologist* 42:160–65.

Hartmann, H. 1981. "The Unhappy Marriage of Marxism and Feminism: Towards a More Progressive Union." In L. Sargent (ed.), *Women and Revolution.* Boston: South End Press.

Harway, Michele. 1993. "Battered Women: Characteristics and Causes." In Marsali Hansen and Michele Harway (eds.), *Battering and Family Therapy: A Feminist Perspective.* Newbury Park, CA: Sage.

Harway, Michele, and Marsali Hansen. 1993. "An Overview of Domestic Violence." In Marsali Hansen and Michele Harway (eds.), *Battering and Family Therapy: A Feminist Perspective.* Newbury Park, CA: Sage.

Hearn, J. 1985. "Men's Sexuality at Work." In A. Metcalf and M. Humphries (eds.), *The Sexuality of Men.* London: Pluto Press.

Hearn, J., and W. Parkin. 1987. *Sex at Work.* New York: St. Martin's Press.

Hegar, R. L., S. J. Zuravin, and J. G. Orme. 1991. *Factors Predicting Severity of Child Abuse Injury: A Review of the Literature.* Unpublished Manuscript, School of Social Work, University of Maryland at Baltimore.

Heise, L. 1991. "When Women Are Prey." *Washington Post,* December 13, C1–C3.

———. 1993a. "Status of Existing Knowledge." Paper presented at the Population Council meeting on Sexual Coercion and Women's Reproductive Health, jointly sponsored by the Population Council and the Pacific Institute for Women's Health, November, New York.

———. 1993b. "Violence against Women and Reproductive Health: Where Are the Intersections?" *Journal of Law, Medicine, and Ethics* 21:76–86.

Heise, L., J. Pitanguy, and A. Germain. 1993. *Violence against Women: The Hidden Health Burden.* Washington, D.C.: World Bank.

Hemming, H. 1985. "Women in a Man's World: Sexual Harassment." *Human Relations* 38:67–79.

Hendricks-Mathews, M. K. 1993. "Survivors of Abuse: Health Care Issues." *Primary Care* 20:391–406.

Hennenberger, M., and M. Marriott. 1993. "For Some, Youthful Courting Has Become a Game of Abuse." *New York Times,* July 7.

Herman, Judith. 1982. *Father-Daughter Incest.* Cambridge: Harvard University Press.

Herrman, M. S., and D. C. Bordner. 1983. "Attitudes toward Pornography in a Southern Community." *Criminology* 21:349–74.

Herzberger, Sharon, and Noreen Channels. 1991. "Criminal Justice Processing of Violent and Nonviolent Offenders: The Effects of Familial Relationship to the Victim." In Dean Knudsen and JoAnn Miller (eds.), *Abused and Battered: Social and Legal Responses to Family Violence.* Hawthorne, NY: Aldine de Gruyter.

Hindelang, M. J. 1981. "Variations in Sex-Race-Age Specific Incidence of Offending." *American Sociological Review* 46:461–74.

Hite, S. 1976. *The Hite Report.* New York: Dell.

Hoch, Paul. 1979. *White Hero Black Beast: Racism, Sexism and the Mask of Masculinity.* London: Pluto Press.

Hochschild, Arlie. 1989. *The Second Shift.* New York: Viking.

———. 1992. "The Second Shift: Employed Women Are Putting in Another Day of Work at Home." In M. S. Kimmel and M. A. Messner (eds.), *Men's Lives.* New York: Macmillan.

Hocking, E. D. 1989. "Miscare—A Form of Abuse in the Elderly." *Update,* May 15, 2411–19.

Hoebel, E. A. 1960. *The Cheyennes.* New York: Holt, Rinehart and Winston.

Hoff, Lu Anne. 1990. *Battered Women as Survivors.* London: Routledge.

Hoffman, R. 1986. "Rape and the College Athlete: Part One." *Philadelphia Daily News,* March 17.

Högbacka, R., I. Kandolin, E. Haavio-Mannila, and K. Kauppinen-Toropainen. 1987. *Sexual Harassment in the Workplace: Result of a Survey of Finns.* Ministry of Social Affairs and Health, Equality Publications, Series E: Abstracts 1/1987. Helsinki: Valtion Painatuskeskus.

Holroyd, J. C., and A. M. Brodsky. 1977. "Psychologists' Attitudes and Practices regarding Erotic and Nonerotic Contact with Patients." *American Psychologist* 32:843–49.

Holt, M. 1993. "Elder Sexual Abuse in Britain: Preliminary Findings." *Journal of Elder Abuse and Neglect* 5, no. 2.

Homer, A., and C. Gilleard. 1990. "Abuse of Elderly People by Their Carers." *British Medical Journal* 301:1359–62.

Hood, Jane. 1989. "Why Our Society Is Rape-Prone." *New York Times,* May 16, p. 23.

hooks, bell. 1989. "Whose Pussy Is This: A Feminist Comment." *Talking Back.* Boston: South End Press.

———. 1994. "Sexism and Misogyny: Who Takes the Rap?" *Z Magazine* 7 no. 2:26–29.

Hooper, C. A. 1990. "A Study of Mothers' Responses to Child Sexual Abuse by Another Family Member." Unpublished Ph.D. thesis, University of London.

Hope, Akua Lezli. 1983. "Lament." In Amira Baraka and Amina Baraka (eds.), *Confirmation.* New York: Quill.

Hopkins, P. 1978. *Contending Forces.* Carbondale: Southern Illinois University Press.

Hopper, Columbus, and Johnny Moore. 1990. "Women in Outlaw Motorcycle Gangs." *Journal of Contemporary Ethnography* 18, no. 4:368–87.

Horrocks, P. 1988. "Elderly People: Abused and Forgotten." *Health Service Journal,* September 22.

Hotaling, G., M. Straus, and A. Lincoln. 1990. "Intrafamily Violence and Crime outside the Family." In M. Straus and R. Gelles (eds.), *Physical Violence in American Families.* New Brunswick, NJ: Transaction Publishers.

Hughes, D. A. (ed.). 1970. *Perspectives on Pornography*. New York: St. Martin's Press.

Hughes, H. M. 1982. "Brief Interventions with Children in a Battered Women's Shelter: A Model Preventive Program." *Family Relations* 31:495–502.

Hughes, Jean O., and Bernice R. Sandler. 1986. *In Case of Sexual Harassment: A Guide for Women Students*. Washington, DC: Association of American Colleges.

Hughes, Jean O., and Bernice R. Sandler. 1988. *Peer Harassment: Hassles for Women on Campus*. Washington, DC: Association of American Colleges.

Human Rights Watch. 1992a. *Double Jeopardy: Police Abuse of Women in Pakistan*. New York: Human Rights Watch.

Human Rights Watch. 1992b. *Rape and Mistreatment of Asian Maids [Kuwait]*. New York: Human Rights Watch.

Human Rights Watch. 1992c. *Untold Terror: Violence against Women [in Peru]*. New York: Human Rights Watch.

Human Rights Watch. 1993a. *Rape in Kashmir*. New York: Human Rights Watch.

Human Rights Watch. 1993b. *War Crimes in Bosnia-Hercegovina: Volume II*. New York: Human Rights Watch.

Human Rights Watch. 1993c. *Widespread Rape of Somali Women Refugees in NE Kenya*. New York: Human Rights Watch.

Hunt, A. 1985. "The Ideology of Law: Advances and Problems in Recent Applictions of the Concept of Ideology to the Analysis of Law." *Law and Society Review* 19:11–37.

Hursch, C. J. 1977. *The Trouble with Rape*. Chicago: Nelson-Hall.

Island, D., and P. Letellier. 1991. *Men Who Beat the Men Who Love Them*. New York: Harrington Park.

Jaggar, A. M. 1983. *Feminist Politics and Human Nature*. Totowa, NJ: Rowman and Allanheld.

Jahangi, A., and H. Jalani. 1990. *The Hudood Ordinance: A Divine Sanction?* Lahore, Pakistan: Rhodas Books.

Jensen, I., and B. A. Gutek. 1982. "Attributions and Assignment of Responsibility for Sexual Harassment." *Journal of Social Issues* 38:121–36.

Jensvold, M. F. 1991. "Assessing the Psychological and Physical Harm to Sexual Harassment Victims." Paper presented at the National Conference to Promote Men and Women Working Productively Together, March, Bellevue, WA.

Johnson, A. G. 1980. "On the Prevalence of Rape in the United States." *Signs: Journal of Women in Culture and Society* 6:136–46.

Johnson, T. F., J. G. O'Brien, and M. F. Hudson. 1985. *Elder Abuse: An Annotated Bibliography*. Westport, CT: Greenwood Press.

Johnson, W. T. et al. 1970. "Sex Offenders Experience with Erotica." *Technical Reports of the Commission on Obscenity and Pornography*. Vol. 7. Washington, DC: U.S. Government Printing Office.

Jones, A. 1994. *Next Time, She'll Be Dead: Battering and How to Stop It*. Boston: Beacon Press.

Jones, Gayle. 1975. *Corregidora*. Boston: Beacon Press.

Jordan, June. 1978. "Against the Wall." In *Civil Wars*. Boston: Beacon Press.

———. 1980a. "Rape Is Not a Poem." In *Passion: New Poems, 1977–1980*. Boston: Beacon Press.

———. 1980b. "The Rationale, or She Drove Me Crazy." In *Passion: New Poems, 1977–1980*. Boston: Beacon Press.

Jordon, W. 1968. *White over Black: American Attitudes toward the Negro*. Williamsburg, VA: University of North Carolina Press.

Journal of the American Medical Association. 1990. "Domestic Violence Intervention Calls for More Than Treating Injuries." *Journal of the American Medical Association* 264, no. 8:939.

Jozsa, B., and M. Jozsa. 1980. "Dirty Books, Dirty Films, and Dirty Data." In L. Lederer (ed.), *Take Back the Night: Women on Pornography*. New York: Morrow.

Kalmuss, D. S. 1984. "The Intergenerational Transmission of Marital Aggression." *Journal of Marriage and the Family* 46:11–19.

Kanarian, M., and K. Quina-Holland. 1981. "Attributions about Rape." Paper presented at the Eastern Psychological Association Meeting, April, New York.

Kandaloof, E. 1991. "Services at Haifa Rape Crisis Center." Paper presented at Leading the Way Out: A Global Conference to End Violence against Women, sponsored by the Global Fund for Women, May, Menlo Park, California.

Kanin, Eugene J. 1967. "Reference Groups and Sex Conduct Norm Violations." *Sociological Quarterly* 8:495–504.

———. 1984. "Date Rape: Unofficial Criminals and Victims." *Victimology* 9:95–108.

———. 1985. "Date Rapists: Differential Socialization and Relative Deprivation." *Archives of Sexual Behavior* 14:219–31.

Kanin, Eugene J., and Stanley J. Parcell. 1977. "Sexual Aggression: A Second Look at the Offended Female." *Archives of Sexual Behavior* 6:67–76.

Kant, H. S., and M. J. Goldstein. 1978. "Pornography and Its Effects." in D. Savitz and J. Johnson (eds.), *Crime in Society.* New York: Wiley.

Kant, Immanuel. 1911. *Critique of Aesthetic Judgement.* Trans. J. C. Meredith. Oxford: Clarendon.

Kanter, R. M. 1977. *Men and Women of the Corporation.* New York: Basic Books.

Kappeler, Susanne. 1986. *The Pornography of Representation.* Minneapolis: University of Minnesota Press.

Katz, J. 1988. *Seductions of Crime: Moral and Sensual Attractions in Doing Evil.* New York: Basic Books.

Kau, J. B., and R. Rubin. 1975. "New Estimates of the Determinants of Urban Crime." *Annals of Regional Science* 9:68–76.

Kelly, E. E., and L. Warshafsky. 1987. "Partner Abuse in Gay Male and Lesbian Couples." Paper presented at the Third National Conference for Family Violence Researchers, July, Durham, NH.

Kelly, L. 1987. "The Continuum of Sexual Violence." In J. Hanmer and M. Maynard (eds.), *Women, Violence and Social Control.* London: Macmillan.

———. 1988. *Surviving Sexual Violence.* Minneapolis: University of Minnesota Press.

Kilpatrick, D. G. 1992. "Treatment and Counseling Needs of Women Veterans Who Were Raped, Otherwise Sexually Assaulted, or Sexually Harassed during Military Service." Testimony before U.S. Senate Committee on Veteran's Affairs, June 30.

Kilpatrick, D. G., B. E. Saunders, L. J. Veronen, C. L. Best, and J. M. Von. 1987. "Criminal Victimization: Lifetime Prevalence, Reporting to Police, and Psychological Impact." *Crime and Delinquency* 33:479–89.

Kimerling, R., and K. S. Calhoun. 1994. "Somatic Symptoms, Social Support, and Treatment Seeking among Sexual Assault Victims." *Journal of Consulting and Clinical Psychology* 62:333–40.

Kimmel, Michael S. 1993. "Does Pornography Cause Rape?" *Violence Update* 3, no. 10:2–8.

———. (ed.). 1990. *Men Confront Pornography.* New York: Crown Publishers.

Kincaid, D. L. 1991. "Family Planning and the Empowerment of Women in Bangladesh." Paper presented at the annual meeting of the American Public Health Association, November 13, Atlanta.

Kincaid, P. J. 1982. *The Omitted Reality: Husband–Wife Violence in Ontario and Policy Implications for Education.* Concord, Ont.: Belsten.

King, H. E., and C. Webb. 1981. "Rape Crisis Centers: Progress and Problems." *Journal of Social Issues* 37, no. 4:93–104.

Kirkpatrick, R. G., and L. A. Zurcher. 1983. "Women against Pornography: Feminist Anti-Pornography Crusades in American Society." *International Journal of Sociology and Social Policy* 3:1–30.

Kisekka, M., and B. Otesanya. 1988. "Sexually Transmitted Disease as a Gender Issue: Examples from Nigeria and Uganda." Paper given at the AFARD/AAWORD Third General Assembly on the African Crisis and the Women's Vision of the Way Out, August, Dakar, Senegal.

Kitzinger, J. 1988. "Defending Innocence: Ideologies of Childhood." *Feminist Review* 28:77–87.

Klein, Hugh, and Betty Chao. 1995. "Sexual Abuse during Childhood and Adolescence as Predictors of HIV-Related Sexual Risk during Adulthood among Female Sexual Partners of Injection Drug Users." *Violence against Women* 1, no. 1 (March):55–76.

Klingbeil, K. S., and V. D. Boyd. 1984. "Emergency Room Intervention: Detection, Assessment, and Treatment." In A. R. Roberts (ed.), *Battered Women and Their Families*. New York: Springer.

Koehler, L. 1980. *A Search for Power: The "Weaker Sex" in Seventeenth-Century New England*. Urbana: University of Illinois Press.

Kolbert, Elizabeth. "Sexual Harassment at Work Is Pervasive, Survey Suggests." *New York Times*, Oct. 11, 1991, p. 1, A17.

Komter, A. 1989. "Hidden Power in Marriage." *Gender & Society* 3, no. 2:187–216.

Korean Sexual Violence Relief Center. 1991. *Informational Booklet of the Korean Sexual Violence Relief Center*. Seoul, Korea: Korean Sexual Violence Relief Center.

Koss, M. P. 1990. "Changed Lives: The Psychological Impact of Sexual Harassment." In M. A. Paludi (ed.), *Ivory Power: Sexual Harassment on Campus*. Albany: State University of New York Press.

———. 1993. "Detecting the Scope of Rape: A Review of Prevelence Research Methods." *Journal of Interpersonal Violence* 8:98–122.

Koss, M. P., Thomas E. Dinero, and Cynthia A. Seibel. 1988. "Stranger and Acquaintance Rape." *Psychology of Women Quarterly* 12:1–24.

Koss, M. P., C. A. Gidycz, and N. Wisniewski. 1987. "The Scope of Rape: Incidence and Prevalence of Sexual Aggression and Victimization in a National Sample of Higher Education Students." *Journal of Consulting and Clinical Psychology* 55:162–70.

Koss, M. P., L. A. Goodman, A. Browne, L. Fitzgerald, G. P. Keita, and N. Russo. 1994. *No Safe Haven: Male Violence against Women at Home, at Work, and in the Community*. Washington, DC: American Psychological Association.

Koss, M. P., and M. R. Harvey. 1991. *The Rape Victim: Clinical and Community Interventions*. Newbury Park, CA: Sage.

Koss, M. P., and L. Heslet. 1992. "Somatic Consequences of Violence Against Women." *Archives of Family Medicine* 1:53–59.

Koss, M. P., P. G. Koss, and W. J. Woodruff. 1991. "Deleterious Effects of Criminal Victimization on Women's Health and Medical Utilization." *Archives of Internal Medicine* 151:342–57.

Koss, M. P., K. E. Leonard, D. A. Beezley, and C. J. Oros. 1985. "Non-Stranger Sexual Aggression: A Discriminant Analysis of the Psychological Characteristics of Undetected Offenders." *Sex Roles* 12:981–92.

Koss, M. P., W. J. Woodruff, and P. G. Koss. 1991. "Criminal Victimization among Primary Care Medical Patients: Prevalence, Incidence, and Physician Usage." *Behavioral Sciences and the Law* 9:85–96.

Kressel, G. 1981. "Sororicide/Filiacide: Homicide for Family Honour." *Current Anthropology* 22:141–58.

Kuhn, Thomas S. 1970. *The Structure of Scientific Revolutions*. Chicago: University of Chicago Press.

Kurz, Demie. 1990. "Interventions with Battered Women in Health Care Settings." *Victims and Violence* 5, no. 4 (winter):243–56.

———. 1992. "Battering and the Criminal Justice System: A Feminist View." In E. Buzawa and C. Buzawa (eds.), *Domestic Violence: The Criminal Justice Response*. Westport, CT: Auburn House.

———. 1993. "Physical Assaults by Husbands: A Major Social Problem." In Richard Gelles and Donileen Loseke (eds.), *Current Controversies on Family Violence*. Newbury Park, CA: Sage.

———. 1995. *For Richer, for Poorer: Mothers Confront Divorce*. New York: Routledge.

Kutchinsky, B. 1973. "The Effect of Easy Availability of Pornography on the Incidence of Sex Crimes: The Danish Experience." *Journal of Social Issues* 29:163–81.

La Fontaine, Jean. 1990. *Child Sexual Abuse.* Cambridge: Polity Press.

LaFree, Gary D. 1989. *Rape and Criminal Justice: The Social Construction of Assault.* Belmont, CA: Wadsworth.

Lagae, C. R. Les Azande ou Niam-Niam. 1926. *Bibliothèque-Congo.* Vol. 18. Brussels: Vromant. English translation published by Human Relations Area Files, New Haven, CT.

LaHaye, T., and B. LaHaye. 1976. *The Act of Marriage: The Beauty of Sexual Love.* Grand Rapids, MI: Zondervan.

Lai, Tracy A. 1986. "Asian Women: Resisting the Violence." In Maryviolet Burns (ed.), *The Speaking Profits Us: Violence in the Lives of Women of Color.* Seattle: Center for the Prevention of Sexual and Domestic Violence.

Lamb, S. 1991. "Acts without Agents: An Analysis of Linguistic Avoidance in Journal Articles on Men Who Batter Women." *American Journal of Orthopsychiatry* 61, no. 2:250–57.

———. 1995. "Blaming the Perpetrator: Language That Distorts Reality in Newspaper Articles on Men Battering Women." *Psychology of Women Quarterly* 19:209–20.

Lambert, H. E. 1956. *Kikuyu Social and Political Institutions.* London: Oxford University Press.

Lamberth, J. 1970. "The Effect of Erotic Stimuli on Sex Arousal, Evaluative Responses, and Subsequent Behavior." In *Technical Reports of the Commission on Obscenity and Pornography.* Vol. 8. Washington, DC: U.S. Government Printing Office.

Lane, K. E. and P. A. Gwartney-Gibbs. 1985. "Violence in the Context of Dating and Sex." *Journal of Family Issues* 6:45–59.

Langan, Patrick A. and Christopher Innes. 1986. "Preventing Domestic Violence against Women." Washington, DC: U.S. Department of Justice Bureau of Justice Statistics.

Langley, R., and R. C. Levy. 1977. *Wife Beating: The Silent Crisis.* New York: E. P. Dutton.

LaPin, D. 1992. "Assessing Psychological Needs of Refugee Women and Children Using Rapid Field Techniques." Paper presented at the 120th Annual Meeting of the American Public Health Association, November, Washington, DC.

Layzer, J. I., B. D. Goodson, and C. deLange. 1985. "Children in Shelters." *Response* 9, no. 2:2–5.

Lazarus, R. S. 1991. "Cognition and Motivation in Emotion." *American Psychologist* 46:352–67.

League of Nations. 1934. "Child Welfare Committee Enquiry into the Question of Children in Moral and Social Danger." Geneva.

Lederer, L. (ed.). 1980. *Take Back the Night: Women on Pornography.* New York: Morrow.

Leighton, B. 1989. *Spousal Abuse in Metropolitan Toronto: Research Report on the Response of the Criminal Justice System.* Report No. 1989-02. Ottawa: Solicitor General of Canada.

Lerner, Gerda. 1986. *The Creation of Patriarchy.* New York: Oxford University Press.

Letellier, P. 1994. "Gay and Bisexual Domestic Violence Victimization: Challenges to Feminist Theory and Responses to Violence." *Violence and Victims* 9:95–106.

———. 1996. "Twin Epidemics: Domestic Violence and HIV Infection among Gay and Bisexual Men." In C. M. Renzetti and C. H. Miley (eds.), *Violence in Gay and Lesbian Domestic Partnerships.* New York: Harrington Park.

Levine, M. P. 1979. "Employment Discrimination against Gay Men." *International Review of Modern Sociology* 9:151–63.

Le Vine, R. A. 1959. "Gusii Sex Offenses: A Study in Social Control." *American Anthropologist* 61:965–90.

Levinson, D. 1989. *Violence in Cross-Cultural Perspective.* Newbury Park, CA: Sage.

Levi-Strauss, Claude. 1969. *The Elementary Structures of Kinship.* Boston: Beacon Press.

Levy, Barrie. 1991. *Dating Violence: Young Women in Danger.* Seattle: Seal Press.

Levy, Ellen. 1993. "She Just Doesn't Understand: The Feminist Face-Off on Pornography Legislation." *On the Issues,* Fall, 17–20.

Lewin, Miriam. 1985. "Unwanted Intercourse: The Difficulty of Saying No." *Psychology of Women Quarterly* 9:184–92.

Lewin, Tamar. 1991. "Law on Sex Harassment Is Recent and Evolving." *New York Times,* October 8, p. A22.

———. 1992. "Battered Men Sounding Equal Rights Battle Cry." *New York Times,* April 20, p. 12.

Lewis, Claude. 1988. "Date Rape Is OK, Grade Schoolers Say." *Philadelphia Inquirer,* May 4.

Lie, G., and S. Gentlewarrior. 1991. "Intimate Violence in Lesbian Relationships: Discussion of Survey Findings and Practice Implications." *Journal of Social Service Research* 15:41–59.

Lie, G., R. Schilit, I. Bush, M. Montagne, and L. Reyes. 1991. "Lesbians in Currently Aggressive Relationships: How Frequently Do They Report Aggressive Past Relationships?" *Violence and Victims* 6:121–35.

Lincoln, Abbey. (Aminata Moseka). 1983. "On Being High." In Amiri Baraka and Amina Baraka (eds.), *Confirmation.* New York: Quill.

Lindemann, B. S. 1984. " 'To Ravish and Carnally Know': Rape in Eighteenth-Century Massachusetts." *Signs: Journal of Women in Culture and Society* 10:63–82.

Lindsey, K. 1977. "Sexual Harassment on the Job and How to Stop It." *Ms.,* November, pp. 47–51, 74–78.

Linz, D., E. Donnerstein, B. J. Shafer, K. C. Land, P. L. McCall, and A. C. Graesser. 1995. "Discrepancies between the Legal Code and Community Standards for Sex and Violence: An Empirical Challenge to Traditional Assumptions in Obscenity Law." *Law and Society Review* 29:127–68.

Lippert, J. 1977. "Sexuality as Consumption." In J. Snodgrass (ed.), *For Men against Sexism.* Albion, CA: Times Change Press.

Liskin, I. 1981. "Periodic Abstinence: How Well Do New Approaches Work?" *Population Reports Series.* Vol. 1, no. 3. Baltimore: Population Information Program, Johns Hopkins University.

Liss, Marsha B., and Geraldine Butts Stahly. 1993. "Domestic Violence and Child Custody." In Marsali Hansen and Michele Harway (eds.), *Battering and Family Therapy: A Feminist Perspective.* Newbury Park, CA: Sage.

Lockhart, Lettie, and Barbara White. 1989. "Understanding Marital Violence in the Black Community." *Journal of Interpersonal Violence* 4., no. 4 (December):421–36.

Loh, W. D. 1981. "Q: What Has Reform of Rape Legislation Wrought? A: Truth in Criminal Labelling." *Journal of Social Issues* 37, no. 4:28–52.

Longford, Lord. 1972. *Pornography: The Longford Report.* London: Coronet.

Longino, H. E. 1980. "Pornography, Oppression and Freedom: A Closer Look." In L. Lederer (ed.), *Take Back the Night: Women on Pornography.* New York: Morrow.

Lorenz, K. 1966. *On Aggression.* London: Methuen.

Loseke, Donileen. 1992. *The Battered Woman and Shelters: The Social Construction of Wife Abuse.* Albany: State University of New York Press.

Lott, B., M. E. Reilly, and D. R. Howard. 1982. "Sexual Assault and Harassment: A Campus Community Case Study." *Signs: Journal of Women in Culture and Society* 8:296–319.

Loulan, J. 1987. *Lesbian Passion.* San Francisco: Spinsters/Aunt Lute.

Loy, P. H., and L. P. Stewart. 1984. "The Extent and Effects of Sexual Harassment of Working Women." *Sociological Focus* 17:31–43.

Lunde, I., and J. Ortmann. 1990. "Prevalence and Sequelae of Sexual Torture." *Lancet* 336:289–91.

Lurigio, A. J., and P. A. Resick. 1990. "Healing the Psychological Wounds of Criminal Victimization: Predicting Postcrime Distress and Recovery." In A. J. Lurigio, W. G. Skogan, and R. C. Davis (eds.), *Victims of Crime: Problems, Policies, and Programs.* Newbury Park, CA: Sage.

Lykes, M. B. 1989. "Dialogue with Guatemalan Indian Women: Critical Perspectives on Constructing Collaborative Research." In R. Unger (ed.), *Representations: Social Constructions of Gender.* Amityville, NY: Baywood.

Lykes, M. B., M. M. Brabeck, T. Ferns, and A. Radan. 1993. "Human Rights and Mental Health among Latin American Women in Situations of State-Sponsored Violence." *Psychology of Women Quarterly* 17:525–44.

MacDonald, B., and C. Rich. 1984. *Look Me in the Eye.* London: Women's Press.

MacDonald, J. M. 1971. *Rape: Offenders and Their Victims.* Springfield, IL: Charles C. Thomas.

MacKinnon, Catharine A. 1979. *Sexual Harassment of Working Women: A Case of Sex Discrimination.* New Haven: Yale University Press.

―――. 1983. "Feminism, Marxism, Method and the State: Toward Feminist Jurisprudence." *Signs: Journal of Women in Culture and Society* 8 (1983):635–658.

―――. 1984. "Not A Moral Issue." *Yale Law and Policy Review* 2:321–345.

―――. 1993. *Only Words.* Cambridge: Harvard University Press.

MacLeod, L. 1987. *Battered But Not Beaten . . . Preventing Wife Battering in Canada.* Ottawa: Canadian Advisory Council on the Status of Women.

MacLeod, M., and E. Saraga. 1988. "Challenging the Orthodoxy: Towards a Feminist Theory and Practice." *Feminist Review* 28:16–55.

Maguire, P. 1987. *Doing Participatory Research: A Feminist Approach.* Amherst: Center for International Education, School of Education, University of Massachusetts.

Mahoney, E. R. 1981. "Male Sexual Access Rights." In *Advocating for Victims of Sexual Assualt: A Training and Resource Manual.* Tacoma, WA: Pierce County Rape Relief.

Maiskii, I. 1921. *Sovremennaia Mongolia (Contemporary Mongolia).* Irkutsk: Gosudarstvennoe Izdatel'stvo, Irkutskoe Otedelenie. (Translated from the Russian for Human Relations Area Files by Mrs. Dayton and J. Kunitz.)

Majors, Richard. 1986. "Cool Pose: The Proud Signature of Black Survival." *Changing Men* 17:5–6.

Majors, Richard, and J. M. Billson. 1992. *Cool Pose: The Dilemmas of Black Manhood in America.* New York: Macmillan.

Malamuth, Neil M. 1981. "Rape Proclivity among Males." *Journal of Social Issues* 37:138–57.

―――. 1983. "Factors Associated with Rape as Predictors of Laboratory Aggression against Women." *Journal of Personality and Social Psychology* 45:432–42.

―――. 1986. "Predictors of Naturalistic Sexual Aggression." *Journal of Personality and Social Psychology* 50:953–62.

Malamuth, Neil M., and J. Briere. 1986. "Sexual Violence in the Media: Indirect Effects on Aggression against Women." *Journal of Social Issues* 42, no. 3:75–92.

Malamuth, Neil M., and J. V. P. Check. 1983. "Sexual Arousal to Rape Depictions: Individual Differences." *Journal of Abnormal Psychology* 92:436–46.

Malamuth, Neil M., and E. Spinner. 1980. "A Longitudinal Content Analysis of Sexual Violence in the Best-Selling Erotica Magazines." *Journal of Sex Research* 16.

Malcolm X. 1965. *The Autobiography of Malcom X.* New York: Grove Press.

Malette, Louise, and Marie Chalouh. 1991. *The Montreal Massacre.* Translated by Marlene Wildeman. Charlottetown, Prince Edward Island: Gynergy Books.

Malinowski, B. 1929. *The Sexual Life of Savages in North-western Melanesia.* London: G. Routledge & Sons.

Mann, J. et al. 1970. "Effects of Erotic Films on Sexual Behavior of Married Couples." *Technical Reports of the Commission on Obscenity and Pornography.* Vol. 8. Washington, DC: U. S. Government Printing Office.

Mansfield, P. K., P. B. Koch, J. Henderson, J. R. Vicary, M. Cohn, and E. W. Young. 1991. "The Job Climate for Women in Traditionally Male Blue Collar Occupations." *Sex Roles* 25:63–79.

Margolies, L., M. Becker, and K. Jackson-Brewer. 1987. "Internalized Homophobia: Identifying and Treating the Oppressor within." In Boston Lesbian Psychologies Collective (eds.), *Lesbian Psychologies.* Urbana: University of Illinois Press.

Margolies, L., and E. Leeder. 1995. "Violence at the Door: Treatment of Lesbian Batterers." *Violence against Women* 1:139–57.

Margolin, D. 1972. "Rape: The Facts." *Women: A Journal of Liberation* 3:19–22.

Margolin, L., M. Miller, and P. B. Moran. 1989. "When a Kiss Is Not Just a Kiss: Relating Violations of Consent in Kissing to Rape Myth Acceptance." *Sex Roles* 20:231–43.

Martin, Patricia Y., and Robert A. Hummer. 1989. "Fraternities and Rape on Campus." *Gender & Society* 3:457–73.

Martin, S. 1978. "Sexual Politics in the Workplace: The Interactional World of Policewomen." *Symbolic Interaction* 1:55–60.

———. 1980. *Breaking and Entering: Policewomen on Patrol.* Berkeley: University of California Press.

Martin-Baró, I. 1988. "La violencia politica y la guerra como causa del trauma psicosocial en El Salvador [political violence and war as causes of psychosocial trauma in El Salvador]." *Revista de Psicologia de El Salvador* 28:123–41.

Marx, Karl. 1978. "The German Ideology: Part I." In Robert C. Tucker (ed.), *The Marx-Engels Reader.* New York: W. W. Norton.

Masson, H., and P. O'Bryne. 1990. "The Family Systems Approach: A Help or a Hindrance?" In The Violence Against Children Study Group (eds.), *Taking Child Abuse Seriously.* London: Unwin Hyman.

Masson, J. M. 1985. *The Assault on Truth: Freud's Suppression of the Seduction Theory.* Harmondsworth: Penguin.

Mathur, K. 1992. "Bhateri Rape Case: Backlash and Protest." *Economic and Political Weekly,* October 10, pp. 2221–24.

Maybury-Lewis, D. 1967. *Akwe-Shavante Society.* Oxford: Clarendon Press.

McCann, I. L., D. K. Sakheim, and D. J. Abrahamson. 1988. "Trauma and Victimization: A Model of Psychological Adaptation." *Counseling Psychologist* 6:531–94.

McCormack, A. 1985. "The Sexual Harassment of Students by Teachers: The Case of Students in Science." *Sex Roles* 13:21–32.

McCormack, T. 1985a. "Feminism and the First Amendment." *Justice Quarterly* 2:271–82.

———. 1985b. "Making Sense of the Research on Pornography." In Varda Burstyn (ed.), *Women against Censorship.* Vancouver: Douglas and McIntyre.

McCreadie, C. 1991. *Elder Abuse: An Exploratory Study.* London: Age Concern (Institute of Gerontology, King's College).

McGrath, E., G. P. Keita, B. R. Strickland, and N. F. Russo. 1990. *Women and Depression: Risk Factors and Treatment Issues.* Washington, DC: American Psychological Association.

McLeer, S., and R. Anwar. 1989. "A Study of Battered Women Presenting in an Emergency Department." *American Journal of Public Health* 79:65–66.

McLeod, M. 1984. "Women against Men: An Examination of Domestic Violence Based on an Analysis of Official Data and National Victimization Data." *Justice Quarterly* 1:171–93.

McMahon, Martha, and Ellen Pence. 1995. "Doing More Harm Than Good? Some Cautions on Visitation Centers." In Einat Peled, Peter Jaffe, and Jeffrey Edleson (eds.), *Ending the Cycle of Violence: Community Responses to Children of Battered Women.* Thousand Oaks, CA: Sage.

McNall, Scott G. 1983. "Pornography: The Structure of Domination and the Mode of Reproduction." In Scott McNall (ed.), *Current Perspectives in Social Theory.* Vol. 4. Greenwich, CT: JAI Press.

McNeely, R. L., and CoraMae Richey Mann. 1990. "Domestic Violence Is a Human Issue." *Journal of Interpersonal Violence* 5, no. 1:129–32.

McNeely, R. L., and G. Robinson-Simpson. 1987. "The Truth about Domestic Violence: A Falsely Framed Issue." *Social Work* 32:485–90.

McPherson, B. 1990. *Aging as a Social Process.* Toronto: Butterworths.

Mead, Margaret. 1932. *The Changing Culture of an Indian Tribe.* New York: Columbia University Press.

———. 1935. *Sex and Temperament in Three Primitive Societies.* New York: Morrow.

Mederos, F. 1987. "Theorizing Continuities and Discontinuities between 'Normal' Men and Abusive Men." Paper presented at the Third National Family Violence Research Conference, University of New Hampshire, Durham, NH.

Merck, M. 1988. "Television and Censorship: Some Notes for Feminists." In G. Chester and J. Dickey (eds.), *Feminism and Censorship: The Current Debate*. London: Prism Press.

Messerschmidt, J. 1986. *Capitalism, Patriarchy and Crime: Toward a Socialist Feminist Criminology*. Totowa, NJ: Rowman and Littlefield.

———. 1993. *Masculinities and Crime: Critique and Reconceptualization of Theory*. Lanham, MD: Rowman and Littlefield.

Messner, M. 1989. "Masculinities and Athletic Careers." *Gender & Society* 3, no. 3:71–88.

Messner, Michael A., and Donald A. Sabo. 1994. *Sex, Violence and Power in Sports*. Freedom, CA: Crossing Press.

Meyer, M. C. 1981. *Sexual Harassment of Working Women*. New Haven: Yale University Press.

Meyerding, J. 1977. "Early Sexual Experience and Prostitution." *American Journal of Psychiatry* 134:1381–85.

Miceli, M. P., and J. P. Near. 1988. "Individual and Situational Correlates of Whistle-Blowing." *Personnel Psychology* 41:267–81.

Miedzian, M. 1993. "An Overview of Sex and Aggression in Popular Discourse." Paper presented at the Population Council meeting on Sexual Coercion and Women's Reproductive Health, jointly sponsored by the Population Council and the Pacific Institute for Women's Health, November, New York.

Mill, J. S. 1961. "On Liberty." In M. Cohen (ed.), *The Philosophy of John Stuart Mill*. New York: Modern Library.

———. 1988. "The Subjection of Women." In Donald Dutton (ed.), *The Domestic Assault of Women: Psychological and Criminal Justice Perspectives*. Newton, MA: Allyn and Bacon.

Miller, Eleanor. 1986. *Street Woman*. Philadelphia: Temple University Press.

Miller, R. B., and R. A. Dodder. 1989. "The Abused-Abuser Dyad: Elder Abuse in the State of Florida." In S. R. Ingman and R. Filinson (eds.), *Elder Abuse: Practice and Policy*. New York: Human Sciences Press.

Miller, Susan. 1993. "Arrest Policies for Domestic Violence and Their Implications for Battered Women." In Roslyn Muraskin and Ted Alleman (eds.), *It's a Crime: Women and Justice*. Englewood Cliffs, NJ: Regents/Prentice-Hall.

Millet, Kate. 1970. *Sexual Politics*. New York: Doubleday.

Mills, Trudy. 1985. "The Assault on the Self: Stages on Coping with Battering Husbands." *Qualitative Sociology* 8:103–23.

Milner, Christina, and Richard Milner. 1972. *Black Players: The Secret World of Black Pimps*. Boston: Little, Brown.

Minneapolis City Council, Government Operations Committee. 1988. *Pornography and Sexual Violence: Evidence of the Links: The Complete Transcript of Public Hearings on Ordinances to Add Pornography as Discrimination against Women: Minneapolis City Council, Government Operations Committee, December 12 and 13, 1983*. London: Everywoman.

Minnery, T. 1986. "Pornography: The Human Tragedy." *Christianity Today*, March 7, p. 7.

Minturn, L., M. Grosse, and S. Haider. 1969. "Cultural Patterning of Sexual Beliefs and Behavior." *Ethnology* 8:301–18.

Mitra, C. 1987. "Judicial Discourse in Father–Daughter Incest Appeal Cases." *International Journal of the Sociology of Law* 15, no. 2:121–48.

Mokhiber, R. 1989. *Corporate Crime and Violence: Big Business Power and the Abuse of the Public Trust*. San Francisco: Sierra Club Books.

Mollica, R. 1986. "Cambodian Refugee Women at Risk." Paper presented at the annual meeting of the American Psychological Association, August, Washington, DC.

Mollica, R., and L. Son. 1989. "Cultural Dimensions in the Evaluation and Treatment of Sexual Trauma: An Overview." *Psychiatric Clinics of North America* 12:363–79.

Mollica, R., G. Wyshak, and J. Lavelle. 1987. "The Psychological Impact of War Trauma and Torture on Southeast Asian Refugees." *American Journal of Psychiatry* 144:1557–71.

Moore, D. M. 1979. *Battered Women*. Beverly Hills, CA: Sage.

Morgan, D. H. J. 1987. "Masculinity and Violence." In J. Hanmer and M. Maynard (eds.), *Women, Violence and Social Control*. London: Macmillan.

Morgan, M. 1973. *The Total Woman*. Old Tappan, NJ: Fleming H. Revell.

Morgan, R. 1978. *Going Too Far*. New York: Random House.

———. 1980. "Theory and Practice: Pornography and Rape." In L. Lederer (ed.), *Take Back the Night: Women and Pornography*. New York: Morrow.

Morrison, Toni. 1970. *The Bluest Eye*. New York: Washington Square.

———. 1975. *Sula*. New York: Bantam.

Mort, F. 1987. *Dangerous Sexualities: Medico-Moral Politics in England since 1830*. London: Routledge & Kegan Paul.

Mosher, D. 1970. "Sex Callousness towards Women." *Technical Reports of the Commission on Obscenity and Pornography*. Vol. 7. Washington, DC: U.S. Government Printing Office.

Muehlenhard, C. L., and M. A. Linton. 1987. "Date Rape and Aggression in Dating Situations: Incidence and Risk Factors." *Journal of Counseling Psychology* 34:186–96.

Mullen, P. E., S. E. Romans-Clarkson, V. A. Walton, and P. G. Herbison. 1988. "Impact of Sexual and Physical Abuse on Women's Mental Health." *Lancet* 1:841.

Murdock, G. P., and D. R. White. 1969. "Standard Cross-Cultural Sample." *Ethnology* 8:329–69.

Murphy, Christopher, and K. Daniel O'Leary. 1994. "Research Paradigms, Values and Spouse Abuse." *Journal of Interpersonal Violence* 9, no. 2, (June):207–23.

Murphy, J. 1931. "Dependency in Old Age." *Annals of the American Academy of Political and Social Science* 154:38–41.

Murphy, Y., and R. Murphy. 1974. *Women of the Forest*. New York: Columbia University Press.

Mydans, S. 1993. "High School Gang Accused of Raping for Points." *New York Times*, March 20.

Naffine, N. 1987. *Female Crime: The Construction of Women in Criminology*. Sydney: Allen and Unwin.

Narasimhan, Sakuntala. 1994. "India: From Sati to Sex Determination Tests." In Miranda Davies (ed.), *Women and Violence*. Atlantic Highlands, NJ: Zed Books.

National Victims Center. 1992. *Rape in America: A Report to the Nation*. Prepared by the National Victims Center and the Crime Victims Research and Treatment Center, New York.

Near, J. P., and M. P. Miceli. 1987. "Whistle-Blowers in Organizations: Dissidents or Reformers?" In L. L. Cummings and B. M. Staw (eds.), *Research in Organizational Behavior*. Vol. 9. Greenwich, CT: JAI.

Nelson, S. 1987. *Incest: Fact and Myth*. Edinburgh: Stramullion.

Newberger, E. H., and R. Bourne. 1977. "The Medicalisation and Legalisation of Child Abuse." In J. M. Eekelaar and S. N. Katz (eds.), *Family Violence: An International and Interdisciplinary Study*. London: Butterworths.

Newsweek. 1985. "The War on Pornography." March 18, p. 53.

NFD Journal. 1989. "Study Finds Children Consuming Pornography." In Franklin Mark Osanka and Sara Lee Johann (eds.), *Sourcebook on Pornography*. Lexington, MA: Lexington Books.

Nicoloff, L. K., and E. A. Stiglitz. 1987. "Lesbian Alcoholism Etiology, Treatment and Recovery." In Boston Lesbian Psychologies Collective (eds.), *Lesbian Psychologies*. Urbana: University of Illinois Press.

Nisonoff, L., and I. Bitman. 1979. "Spouse Abuse: Incidence and Relationship to Selected Demographic Variables." *Victimology* 4:131–40.

Nochlin, Linda. 1972. "Eroticism and Female Imagery in Nineteenth-Century Art." In Thomas B. Hess and Linda Nochlin (eds.), Woman as Sex Object: Studies in Erotic Art, 1730–1970. London and New York: Allen Lane.

Norris, F. H. 1992. "Epidemiology of Trauma: Frequency and Impact of Different Potentially Traumatic Events on Different Demographic Groups." *Journal of Consulting and Clinical Psychology* 60:4409–18.

Northrup, D. 1992. "Sexual Harassment in Public Places and at Work: A National Survey of Canadian Women." Technical documentation, York University, Institute for Social Research, North York, Ontario, Canada.

Novello, Anthony, Mark Rosenberg, Linda Saltzman, and John Shosky. 1992. "From the Surgeon General, U.S. Public Health Service." *Journal of the American Medical Association,* June 17.

O'Farrell, B., and S. L. Harlan. 1982. "Craftworkers and Clerks: The Effects of Male Co-Worker Hostility on Women's Satisfaction with Non-Traditional Jobs." *Social Problems* 29:252–64.

O'Hagan K. 1989. *Working with Child Sexual Abuse.* Milton Keynes: Open University Press.

O'Leary, K. D. 1993. "Through a Psychological Lens: Personality Traits, Personality Disorders, and Levels of Violence." In R. J. Gelles and D. R. Loseke (eds.), *Current Controversies on Family Violence.* Newbury Park, CA: Sage.

Ogg, J., and G. Bennett. 1992. "Screening for Elder Abuse in the Community." *Geriatric Medicine,* February, pp. 63–67.

Ohlin, Lloyd, and Michael Tonry. 1989. "Family Violence in Perspective." In Lloyd Ohlin and Michael Tonry (eds.), *Family Violence.* Chicago: University of Chicago Press.

Okun, Lewis. 1986. *Woman Abuse: Facts Replacing Myths.* Albany: State University of New York Press.

Padavic, Irene, and Barbara F. Reskin. 1990. "Men's Behavior and Women's Interest in Blue Collar Jobs." *Social Problems* 37:613–28.

Pagelow, Mildred. 1981. *Woman-Battering: Victims and Their Experiences.* Beverly Hills, CA: Sage.

———. 1984. *Family Violence.* Toronto: Praeger.

———. 1989. "The Incidence and Prevalence of Criminal Abuse of Other Family Members." In Lloyd Ohlin and Michael Tonry (eds.), *Family Violence.* Chicago: University of Chicago Press.

Pahl, J. 1992. "Money and Power in Marriage." In P. Abbott and C. Wallace (eds.), *Gender, Power, and Sexuality.* London: Macmillan.

Paone, D., W. Chavkin, I. Willets, P. Friedman, and D. Des Jarlais. 1992. "The Impact of Sexual Abuse: Implications for Drug Treatment." *Journal of Women's Health* 1:149–53.

Parker, B., and D. Schumacher. 1977. "The Battered Wife Syndrome and Violence in the Nuclear Family of Origin: A Controlled Pilot Study." *American Journal of Public Health* 67, no. 8:760–61.

Parrot, Andrea, and Laurie Bechofer. 1991. *Acquaintance Rape: The Hidden Crime.* New York: John Wiley and Sons.

Parton, N. 1985. *The Politics of Child Abuse.* London: Macmillan.

Penhale, B. 1993. "The Abuse of Elderly People: Considerations for Practice." *British Journal of Social Work* 23, no. 2:95–112.

Perez, A. M. 1990. *Aproximación diagnostica a las Violaciones de Mujeres en los Distritos de Panama y San Miguelito.* Centrao Para el Desarrollo de la Mujer, Universidad de Panama.

Petchesky, R. 1984. *Abortion and Woman's Choice.* New York: Longman.

Peters, L. 1990. "A Student's Experience." *Initiatives* 52:17–21.

Peterson, David. 1992. "Wife Beating: An American Tradition." *Journal of Interdisciplinary History* 23, no. 1 (summer):97–118.

Petry, Ann. 1946. *The Street.* Boston: Beacon Press.

Pharr, Suzanne. 1986. "Two Workshops on Homophobia." In K. Lobel (ed.), *Naming the Violence.* Seattle: Seal Press.

Phillips, L. R. 1986. "Theoretical Explanations of Elder Abuse." In K. A. Pillemer and R. S. Wolf (eds.), *Elder Abuse: Conflict in the Family.* Dover, MA: Auburn House.

Phillipson, C. 1993. "Abuse of Older People: Sociological Perspectives." In P. Decalmer and F. Glendenning (eds.), *The Mistreatment of Elderly People.* London: Sage.

Pillemer, K. A. 1986. "Risk Factors in Elder Abuse: Results from a Case-Control Study." In K. A. Pillemer and R. S. Wolf (eds.), *Elder Abuse: Conflict in the Family.* Dover, MA: Auburn House.

Pillemer, K. A., and D. Finkelhor. 1989. "Causes of Elder Abuse: Caregiver Stress versus Problem Relatives." *American Journal of Orthopsychiatry* 59, no. 2:179–87.

Pillemer, K. A., and J. Suitor. 1988. "Elder Abuse." In V. Van Hasselt, R. Morrison, A. Belack, and M. Hensen (eds.), *Handbook of Family Violence*. New York: Plenum Press.

Pillemer, K. A., and R. S. Wolf (eds.). 1986. *Elder Abuse: Conflict in the Family*. Dover, MA: Auburn House.

Pithouse, A. 1987. *Social Work: The Social Organization of an Invisible Trade*. Avebury: Aldershot.

Pizzey, E. 1977. *Scream Quietly or the Neighbors Will Hear*. Short Hills, NJ: Ridley Enslow.

Pleck, Elizabeth. 1987. *Domestic Tyranny*. New York: Oxford University Press.

———. 1989. "Criminal Approaches to Family Violence, 1640–1980." In Lloyd Ohlin and Michael Tonry (eds.), *Family Violence*. Chicago: University of Chicago Press.

———. 1990. "Rape and the Politics of Race, 1865–1910." Working Paper 213, Wellesley College Center for Research on Women.

Pleck, Elizabeth H., and Joseph H. Pleck. 1980. *The American Male*. Englewood Cliffs, NJ: Prentice-Hall.

Pleck, Joseph H. 1980. "Men's Power with Women, Other Men, and Society: A Men's Movement Analysis." In Elizabeth H. Pleck and Joseph H. Pleck (eds.), *The American Male*. Englewood Cliffs, NJ: Prentice-Hall.

———. 1981. *The Myth of Masculinity*. Cambridge: MIT Press.

Polk, K. 1984. "The New Marginal Youth." *Crime and Delinquency* 30:462–80.

Polk, K., and D. Ranson. 1991. "Patterns of Homicide in Victoria." In D. Chappell, P. Grabosky, and H. Strang (eds.), *Australian Violence: Contemporary Perspectives*. Canberra: Australian Institute of Criminology.

Pollock, G. 1980. "Artists, Media, Mythologies: Genius, Madness and Art History." *Screen* 21, no. 3:57–96.

Porter, Roy. 1986. "Rape—Does It Have a Historical Meaning?" In Sylvana Tomaselli and Roy Porter (eds.), *Rape*. New York: Basil Blackwell.

Portugal, A. M. 1988. "Cronica de una violación provocada?" Revisa Mujer Fempress Contraviolencia. Santiago, Chile: FEMPRESS-ILET.

Powell, G. N. 1988. *Women and Men in Management*. Newbury Park, CA: Sage.

Preston, Julia. 1996. "Acapulco's Smut Ring: The Children Remember." *New York Times*, August 9, pp. A1, A12.

Pringle, Rosemary. 1988. *Secretaries Talk: Sexuality, Power and Work*. New York: Verso.

———. 1989. "Bureaucracy, Rationality and Sexuality: The Case of Secretaries." In J. Hearn, D. L. Sheppard, P. Tancred-Sheriff, and G. Burrel (eds.), *The Sexuality of Organization*. Newbury Park, CA: Sage.

Pritchard, J. 1992. *The Abuse of Elderly People: A Handbook for Professionals*. London: Jessica Kingsley.

Ptacek, J. 1988. "Why Do Men Batter Their Wives?" In K. Ylló and M. Bograd (eds.), *Feminist Perspectives on Wife Abuse*. Newbury Park, CA: Sage.

Public Policy Research Centre. 1988. *Domestic Violence Attitude Survey*. Conducted for the Office of the Status of Women, Department of the Prime Minister and Cabinet, Canberra, Australia.

Quarm, D., and M. Schwartz. 1985. "Domestic Violence in Criminal Court." In C. Schweber and C. Feinman (eds.), *Criminal Justice Politics and Women: The Aftermath of Legally Mandated Change*. New York: Haworth.

Quina, K., and N. L. Carlson. 1989. *Rape, Incest, and Sexual Harassment: A Guide for Helping Survivors*. New York: Praeger.

Quina, K., N. Carlson, and H. Temple. 1984. *Sexual Harassment and Assault: Myths and Reality*. Kingston: University of Rhode Island. (Contact Women's Studies Program, URI, Kingston, RI 02881).

Quinn, M. J., and S. K. Tomita. 1986. *Elder Abuse and Neglect: Causes, Diagnosis and Intervention Strategies*. New York: Springer.

Rabinowitz, V. C. 1990. "Coping with Sexual Harassment." In M. A. Paludi (ed.), *Ivory Power: Sexual Harassment on Campus*. Albany: State University of New York Press.

Radford, Jill. 1987. "Policing Male Violence—Policing Women." In Jalna Hanmer and Mary Maynard (eds.), *Women, Violence and Social Control*. Atlantic Highlands, NJ: Humanities Press International.

Ragins, B. R., and T. A. Scandura. 1992. "Antecedents and Consequences of Sexual Harassment." Paper presented at the Society for Industrial/Organizational Psychology Conference, May, Montreal.

Rando, T. 1984. *Loss and Grief*. Lexington, MA: Lexington Books.

Rattray, R. S. 1923. *Ashanti*. Oxford: Clarendon Press.

———. 1927. *Religion and Art in Ashanti*. Oxford: Clarendon Press.

Read, D. 1989. "(De)constructing Pornography: Feminisms in Conflict." In K. Peiss and C. Simmons (eds.), *Passion and Power: Sexuality in History*. Philadelphia: Temple University Press.

Reilly, M. E., B. Lott, and S. M. Gallogly. 1986. "Sexual Harassment of University Students." *Sex Roles* 15:333–58.

Reinharz, S. 1992. *Feminist Methods in Social Research*. New York: Oxford University Press.

Renzetti, Claire M. 1992. *Violent Betrayal: Partner Abuse in Lesbian Relationships*. Newbury Park, CA: Sage.

———. 1995. *Information Packet on Lesbian Battering*. Harrisburg, PA: National Resource Center on Domestic Violence.

Renzetti, C. M., and D. J. Curran. 1995. *Women, Men and Society: The Sociology of Gender*. Boston: Allyn and Bacon.

Renzetti, C. M., and C. H. Miley. 1996. *Violence in Gay and Lesbian Domestic Partnerships*. New York: Harrington Park.

Report of the Departmental Committee on Sexual Offences against Young Persons. 1925. London: HMSO.

Resick, P. A. 1987. "Psychological Effects of Victimization: Implications for the Criminal Justice System." *Crime and Delinquency* 33:468–78.

———. 1990. "Victims of Sexual Assault." In A. J. Lurigio, W. G. Skogan, and R. C. Davis (eds.), *Victims of Crime: Problems, Policies, and Programs*. Newbury Park, CA: Sage.

———. 1993. "The Psychological Impact of Rape." *Journal of Interpersonal Violence* 8:223–56.

Reskin, B., and P. Roos. 1987. "Status Hierarchies and Sex Segregation." In C. Bose and G. Spitze (eds.), *Ingredients for Women's Employment Policy*. Albany: State University of New York Press.

Rhode, Deborah L. 1989. *Justice and Gender: Sex Discrimination and the Law*. Cambridge: Harvard University Press.

Rich, Adrienne. 1977. *Of Woman Born*. London: Virago.

———. 1979. *On Lies, Secrets, and Silence*. London: Virago.

———. 1985. "We Don't Have to Come Apart over Pornography." *Off Our Backs*, July.

Richie, Beth. 1985. "Battered Black Women: A Challenge for the Black Community." *The Black Scholar*, March/April, pp. 40–44.

Riddle, D. I., and B. Sang. 1978. "Psychotherapy with Lesbians." *Journal of Social Issues* 34:84–100.

Riger, S., and M. T. Gordon. 1981. "The Fear of Rape: A Study in Social Control." *Journal of Social Issues* 37, no. 4:71–92.

Ritchie, B. 1995. "The Story of Gender Entrapment: The Intersection of Racism, Gender Violence and Crime." Paper presented at the Wheaton College Conference on Feminism and Domestic Violence, June, Norton, Massachusetts.

Ritter, Thomas. 1992. *Say No to Circumcision*. Aptos, CA: Hourglass Book Publishing.

Roberts, Albert. 1984. "Police Intervention." In Albert Roberts (ed.), *Battered Women and Their Families: Intervention Strategies and Treatment Programs*. New York: Springer.

————. 1993. "Women: Victims of Sexual Assault and Violence." In Roslyn Muraskin and Ted Alleman (eds.), *It's a Crime: Women and Justice.* Englewood Cliffs, NJ: Prentice-Hall.

Rogers, L. C. 1984. "Sexual Victimization: Social and Psychological Effects on College Women." Ph.D. diss., Auburn University, Alabama.

Roiphe, Katie. 1993. *The Morning After: Sex, Fear, and Feminism on Campus.* Boston: Little, Brown.

Romenesko, K., and E. M. Miller. 1989. "The Second Step in Double Jeopardy: Appropriating the Labor of Female Street Hustlers." *Crime and Delinquency* 35, no. 1:109–35.

Rompiendo el Silencio. 1992. *La Boletina,* October/November. Managua, Nicaragua: Puntos de Encuentro.

Rosas, M. I. 1992. "Violencia Sexual y Politica Criminal." *CLADEM Informativo,* no. 6. Lima, Peru.

Rosen, R. 1982. *The Lost Sisterhood: Prostitution in America: 1900–1918.* Baltimore: Johns Hopkins University Press.

Rosenberg, M. S. 1984. "Inter-Generational Family Violence: A Critique and Implications for Witnessing Children." Paper presented at the ninety-second annual convention of the American Psychological Association, Toronto.

Rosenfeld, A. H. 1985. "Discovering and Dealing with Deviant Sex." (Report on work of Abel, Becker, and Mittleman.) *Psychology Today,* April, pp. 8–10.

Roth, S., and L. Lebowitz. 1988. "The Experience of Sexual Trauma." *Journal of Traumatic Stress* 5:455–75.

Rothbaum, B. O., E. B. Foa, D. S. Riggs, T. Murdock, and W. Walsh. 1992. "A Prospective Examination of Post-Traumatic Stress Disorder in Rape Victims." *Journal of Traumatic Stress* 5:455–75.

Rowe, M. 1981. "Dealing with Sexual Harassment." *Harvard Business Review* 59 (May/June):42–46.

Roy, M. 1977. *Battered Women: A Psychological Study of Domestic Violence.* New York: Van Nostrand.

Rozée, P. D. 1993. "Forbidden or Forgiven? Rape in Cross-Cultural Perspective." *Psychology of Women Quarterly* 17:499–514.

Rozée, P. D., and G. B. Van Boemel. 1989. "The Psychological Effects of War Trauma and Abuse on Older Cambodian Refugee Women." *Women & Therapy* 8:23–50.

Rubin, Gayle. 1976. "The Traffic in Women: Notes on the Political Economy of Sex." In Rayna Rapp Reiter (ed.), *Toward an Anthropology of Women.* New York: Monthly Review Press.

Rush, Florence. 1980. *The Best Kept Secret: Sexual Abuse of Children.* New York: McGraw-Hill.

Russell, D. E. H. 1975. *The Politics of Rape: The Victim's Perspective.* New York: Stein and Day.

————. 1982a. "The Prevalence and Incidence of Forcible Rape and Attempted Rape of Females." *Victimology: An International Journal* 7:81–93.

————. 1982b. *Rape in Marriage.* New York: Macmillan.

————. 1984. *Sexual Exploitation: Rape, Child Sexual Abuse, and Workplace Harassment.* Newbury Park, CA: Sage.

————. 1986. *The Secret Trauma: Incest in the Lives of Girls and Women.* New York: Basic Books, Inc.

————. 1989. "Sexism, Violence, and the Nuclear Mentality." In Diana Russell (ed.), *Exposing Nuclear Phallocies.* New York: Plenum.

————. 1990. *Rape in Marriage,* 2d ed. Bloomington, IN: Indiana University Press.

Russo, N. F., M. P. Koss, and L. Goodman. Forthcoming. "Male Violence against Women: A Global Health and Development Issue." In L. L. Adler and F. L. Denmark (eds.), *Violence and the Prevention of Violence.* New York: Greenwood.

Rutter, M. 1979. "Protective Factors in Children's Responses to Stress and Disadvantage." In M. W. Kent and J. E. Rolf (eds.), *Primary Prevention of Psychopathology.* Vol. 3, *Promoting*

Social Competence and Coping in Children. Hanover, N.H.: University Press of New England.

Sadker, Myra, and David Sadker. 1994. *Failing at Fairness: How America's Schools Cheat Girls.* New York: Charles Scribner's Sons.

Safran, C. 1976. "What Men Do to Women on the Job: A Shocking Look at Sexual Harassment." *Redbook* 149, November, pp. 217–24.

Salisbury, J., A. B. Ginorio, H. Remick, and D. M. Stringer. 1986. "Counseling Victims of Sexual Harassment." *Psychotherapy* 23:316–24.

Sanchez, Sonia. 1981. "Memorial." In Erlene Stetson (ed.), *Black Sister.* Bloomington: Indiana University Press.

Sanchez-Eppler, Karen. 1995. "Temperance in the Bed of a Child: Incest and the Social Order in Nineteenth Century America." *American Quarterly* 47, no. 1 (March):1–33.

Sanday, Peggy Reeves. 1981a. *Female Power and Male Dominance: On the Origins of Sexual Inequality.* New York: Cambridge University Press.

———. 1981b. "The Socio-Cultural Context of Rape: A Cross-Cultural Study." *Journal of Social Issues* 37 (1981):5–27.

———. 1986. "Rape and the Silencing of the Feminine." In Sylvana Tomaselli and Roy Porter (eds.), *Rape.* New York: Basil Blackwell.

———. 1990. *Fraternity Gang Rape: Sex, Brotherhood, and Privilege on Campus.* New York: New York University Press.

———. 1993. "Men in Groups: A Cross-Cultural Look at Gang Rape." Paper presented at the Population Council meeting on Sexual Coercion and Women's Reproductive Health, jointly sponsored by the Population Council and the Pacific Institute for Women's Health, November, New York.

Saunders, B. E. 1992. "Sexual Harassment of Women in the Workplace: Results from the National Women's Study." Presentation of the Eighth Annual NC SC Labor Law Seminar, October 23, Asheville, NC.

Saunders, D. 1988. "Wife Abuse, Husband Abuse, or Mutual Combat?" In K. Yllö and M. Bograd (eds.), *Feminist Perspectives on Wife Abuse.* Newbury Park, CA: Sage.

———. 1989. "Who Hits First and Who Hurts Most? Evidence for the Greater Victimization of Women in Intimate Relationships." Paper presented at the American Society of Criminology, Reno, NV.

Saunders, Daniel, and Sandra Azar. 1989. "Treatment Programs for Family Violence." In Lloyd Ohlin and Michael Tonry (eds.), *Family Violence.* Chicago: University of Chicago Press.

Savitz, D., and J. Johnson (eds.). 1978. *Crime in Society.* New York: Wiley.

Scanzoni, John. 1982. *Sexual Bargaining.* Chicago: University of Chicago Press.

Schafran, Lynn Hecht. 1987. "Documenting Gender Bias in the Courts: The Task Force Approach." *Judicature* 70:280, 283–84.

Schecter, Susan. 1982. *Women and Male Violence: The Visions and Struggles of the Battered Women's Movement.* Boston: South End Press.

Schechter, Susan, and L. T. Gary. 1988. "A Framework for Understanding and Empowering Battered Women." In M. Straus (ed.), *Abuse and Victimization across the Life Span.* Baltimore: Johns Hopkins University Press.

Schilit, R., G. Lie, and M. Montagne. 1990. "Substance Use as a Correlate of Violence in Intimate Lesbian Relationships." *Journal of Homosexuality* 19:51–65.

Schneider, B. E. 1982. "Consciousness about Sexual Harassment among Heterosexual and Lesbian Women Workers." *Journal of Social Issues* 38:75–98.

———. 1991. "Put Up and Shut Up: Workplace Sexual Assaults." *Gender & Society* 5, no. 4:533–48.

Schuler, M. 1992. "Violence against Women: An International Perspective." In M. Schuler (ed.), *Freedom from Violence? Women's Strategies from around the World.* New York: UNIFEM WIDBOOKS.

Schur, E. L. 1988. *The Americanization of Sex*. Philadelphia: Temple University Press.

Schwartz, M. D. 1987. "Gender and Injury in Spousal Assault." *Sociological Focus* 20:61–75.

Schweber, Claudine, and Clarice Feinman (eds.). 1985. *Criminal Justice Politics and Women: The Aftermath of Legally Mandated Change*. New York: Haworth Press.

Schwendinger, J. R., and H. Schwendinger. 1983. *Rape and Inequality*. Beverly Hills, CA: Sage.

Scott, D. A. 1985. "Pornography and Its Effects on Family, Community, and Culture." *Family Policy Insights* 4, no. 2 (March).

Scully, Diana. 1990. *Understanding Sexual Violence: A Study of Convicted Rapists*. Boston: Unwin Hyman.

Scully, Diana, and Joseph Marolla. 1985. "Riding the Bull at Gilley's: Convicted Rapists Describe the Rewards of Rape." *Social Problems* 32:251–63.

Searles, P., and R. J. Berger. 1987. "The Current Status of Rape Reform Legislation: An Examination of State Statutes." *Women's Rights Law Reporter* 10:25–43.

Segal, Lynn. 1987. *Is the Future Female: Troubled Thoughts on Contemporary Feminism*. London: Virago.

———. 1990. *Slow Motion: Changing Masculinities, Changing Men*. New Brunswick, NJ: Rutgers University Press.

———. 1993. "False Promises—Anti-Pornography Feminism." In Ralph Miliband and Leo Penitch (eds.), *Socialist Register*. London: Merlin Press.

Seidman, Steven. 1992. *Embattled Eros: Sexual Politics and Ethics in Contemporary America*. New York: Routledge.

Sengstock, M. C., and J. Liang. 1982. *Identifying and Characterising Elder Abuse*. Unpublished manuscript, Wayne State University.

Shaheed, Farida. 1994. "The Experience in Pakistan." In Miranda Davies (ed.), *Women and Violence*. London: Zed Books.

Shamim, I. 1985. "Kidnapped, Raped, Killed: Recent Trends in Bangladesh." Paper presented at the International Conference on Families in the Face of Urbanization, December, New Delhi.

Shange, Ntozake. 1979. "Is Not So Good to Be Born a Girl." *The Black Scholar* 10:28–30.

Shattuck, J. 1992. "Organizing Domestic Violence Offender Services: Building Coalitions." Paper presented at the fourteenth National Lesbian and Gay Health Conference, July, Los Angeles, CA.

Sheffield, Carole. 1987. "Sexual Terrorism: The Social Control of Women." In B. B. Hess and M. Marx Feree (eds.), *Analyzing Gender: A Handbook of Social Science Research*. Beverly Hills, CA: Sage.

———. 1989. "The Invisible Intruder: Women's Experiences of Obscene Phone Calls." *Gender & Society* 3, no. 4:483–88.

Sheldon, Ann. 1972. "Rape: The Solution." *Women: A Journal of Liberation* 3:23.

Sheperd, J. 1992. "Post-Traumatic Stress Disorder in Vietnamese Women." *Women & Therapy* 13:281–96.

Sheppard, D. 1989. "Organizations, Power, and Sexuality: The Image and Self-Image of Women Managers." In J. Hearn, D. L. Sheppard, P. Tancred-Sheriff, and G. Burrell (eds.), *The Sexuality of Organization*. London: Sage.

Sherif, C. W. 1980. "Comment on Ethical Issues in Malamuth, Heim and Feshbach's 'Sexual Responsiveness of College Students to Rape Depictions: Inhibitory and Disinhibitory Effects'." *Journal of Personality and Social Psychology* 38, no. 3.

Shim, Y. 1992. "Sexual Violence against Women in Korea: A Victimization Survey of Seoul Women." Paper presented at the Conference on International Perspectives: Crime, Justice and Public Order, June 21–27, St. Petersburg, Russia.

Shupe, A., W. Stacey, and R. Hazelwood. 1987. *Violent Men, Violent Couples: The Dynamics of Domestic Violence*. Lexington, MA: Lexington Books.

Silverman, D. 1976–77. "Sexual Harassment: Working Women's Dilemma." *Quest: A Feminist Quarterly* 3:15–24.

Silvern, Louise, Jane Karyl, and Toby Landis. 1995. "Individual Psychotherapy for the Traumatized Children of Abused Women." In Einat Peled, Peter Jaffe, and Jeffrey Edleson (eds.), *Ending the Cycle of Violence: Community Responses to Children of Battered Women.* Thousand Oaks, CA: Sage.

Simons, Marlise. 1996. "For the First Time, Court Defines Rape as War Crime." *New York Times,* June 28, pp. A1, A6.

Sinclair, D. 1985. *Understanding Wife Assault: A Training Manual for Counselors and Advocates.* Toronto: Ontario Government Bookstore.

Slim, Iceberg. 1967. *Pimp: The Story of My Life.* Los Angeles: Holloway House.

Small, Fred. 1985. "Pornography and Censorship." In Michael S. Kimmel (ed.), *Men Confront Pornography.* New York: Crown Publishers.

Smart, C. 1976. *Women, Crime and Criminology.* London: Routledge and Kegan Paul.

Smith, M. 1990a. "Patriarchal Ideology and Wife Beating: A Test of a Feminist Hypothesis." *Violence and Victims* 5:257–73.

———. 1990b. "Sociodemographic Risk Factors in Wife Abuse: Results from a Survey of Toronto Women." *Canadian Journal of Sociology* 15, no. 1:39–58.

Smith, T. W. 1987. "The Use of Public Opinion Data by the Attorney General's Commission on Pornography." *Public Opinion Quarterly* 51:249–67.

Soble, A. 1986. *Pornography: Marxism, Feminism, and the Future of Sexuality.* New Haven: Yale University Press.

Sogbetun, A. O., K. O. Alausa, and A. O. Osoba. 1977. "Sexually Transmitted Disease in Ibadan, Nigeria." *British Journal of Venereal Disease* 53:158.

Sokoloff, N. J. 1980. *Between Money and Love.* New York: Praeger.

Solicitor General of Canada. 1985. *Canadian Urban Victimization Survey: Female Victims of Crime, 4.* Ottawa: Research and Statistics Group and Communication Division, Solicitor General.

Spelman, Elizabeth V. 1982. "Theories of Race and Gender: The Erasure of Black Women." *Quest* 5, no. 4:36–62.

Spencer, B., and F. J. Gillen. 1927. *The Arunta.* 2 Vols. London: Macmillan.

Squire, S. 1985. "How Women Are Changing Porn Films." *Glamour,* November.

Stanko, Elizabeth A. 1985. *Intimate Intrusions: Women's Experiences of Male Violence.* London: Routledge and Kegan Paul.

———. 1987. "Typical Violence, Normal Precaution: Men, Women and Interpersonal Violence in the U.S., England, Wales and Scotland." In J. Hanmer and M. Maynard (eds.), *Women, Violence and Social Control.* London: Macmillan.

———. 1990. *Everyday Violence: How Women and Men Experience Physical and Sexual Danger.* London: Pandora.

Stansell, C. 1986. *City of Women: Sex and Class in New York, 1789–1860.* New York: Knopf.

Stark, Evan, and Anne Flitcraft. 1982. "Medical Therapy as Repression: The Case of the Battered Woman." *Health and Medicine,* summer/fall, pp. 29–32.

———. 1985. "Woman Battering, Child Abuse and Social Heredity: What is the Relationship?" In N. Johnson (ed.), *Marital Violence.* London: Routledge and Kegan Paul.

———. 1988. "Women and Children at Risk: A Feminist Perspective on Child Abuse." *International Journal of Health Services* 18, no. 1:97–118.

———. 1996. *Women at Risk: Domestic Violence and Women's Health.* Newbury Park, CA: Sage.

Stark, E., A. Flitcraft, D. Zucherman, A. J. Grey, and W. Frazier. 1981. "Wife Abuse in the Medical Setting: An Introduction for Health Personnel." *Domestic Violence, Monograph Series* 1 (April):1–54.

Statistics Canada. 1993. "The Violence against Women Survey Highlights." *Daily Statistics Canada,* November 18, pp. 1–10.

Stearns, P. 1986. "Old Age Family Conflict: The Perspective of the Past." In K. A. Pillemer and R. S. Wolf (eds.), *Elder Abuse: Conflict in the Family.* Dover, MA: Auburn House.

Stearns, Carol, and Peter Stearns. 1986. *Anger: The Struggle for Emotional Control in America's History.* Chicago: University of Chicago Press.

Stein, Nan. 1995. "Sexual Harassment in School: The Public Performance of Gendered Violence." *Harvard Educational Review* 65:145–62.

Steinmetz, F. K. 1988. *Duty Bound: Elder Abuse and Family Care.* Beverly Hills, CA: Sage.

Steinmetz, S. 1986. "Family Violence: Past, Present, and Future." In M. Sussman and S. Steinmetz (eds.), *Handbook of Marriage and the Family.* New York: Plenum.

Steinmetz, S., and J. Lucca. 1988. "Husband Battering." In V. Van Hasselt, R. Morrison, A. Bellack, and M. Hersen (eds.), *Handbook of Family Violence.* New York: Plenum Press.

Stephenson, W. 1953. *The Study of Behavior: Q-Technique and Its Methodology.* Chicago: University of Chicago Press.

Stets, Jan E. 1990. "Verbal and Physical Aggression in Marriage." *Journal of Marriage and the Family* 52:501–14.

Stets, Jan E., and Murray A. Straus. 1989. "The Marriage License as a Hitting License: A Comparison of Assaults in Dating, Cohabitation and Married Couples." In M. A. Pirog-Good and Jan E. Stets (eds.), *Violence in Dating Relationships.* New York: Praeger.

———. 1990. "Gender Differences in Reporting Marital Violence and Its Medical and Psychological Consequences." In M. A. Straus and R. J. Gelles (eds.), *Physical Violence in American Families.* New Brunswick, NJ: Transaction.

Stoller, R. J. 1979. *Sexual Excitement.* New York: Pantheon Books.

Stoltenberg, John. 1989. "Pornography and Freedom." In M. Kimmel and M. Mesner (eds.), *Men's Lives.* New York: Macmillan.

Storr, A. 1970. *Human Aggression.* Harmondsworth: Penguin.

Stout, D. B. 1947. *San Blas Cura Acculturation.* New York: Viking Fund Publications in Anthropology.

Straus, Murray A. 1979. "Measuring Intrafamily Conflict and Violence: The Conflict Tactics (CT) Scales." *Journal of Marriage and the Family* 41:75–88.

Straus, Murray A. 1991a. "Children as Witnesses to Marital Violence: A Risk Factor for Lifelong Problems among Nationally Representative Sample of American Men and Women." Paper presented at the Ross Roundtable on Children and Violence, Washington, DC.

———. 1991b. "New Theory and Old Canards about Family Violence Research." *Social Problems* 38, no. 2:180–97.

———. 1991c. "Physical Violence in American Families: Incidence, Rates, Causes, and Trends." In Dean Knudsen and JoAnn Miller (eds.), *Abused and Battered: Social and Legal Responses to Family Violence.* Hawthorne, NY: Aldine de Gruyter.

———. 1993. "Physical Assaults by Wives: A Major Social Problem." In R. Gelles and D. Loseke (eds.), *Current Controversies on Family Violence.* Newbury Park, CA: Sage.

Straus, Murray, and R. Gelles. 1986. "Societal Change and Change in Family Violence from 1975 to 1985 as Revealed by Two National Surveys." *Journal of Marriage and the Family* 48:465–79.

———. 1990. "How Violent Are American Families: Estimates for the National Family Violence Resurvey and Other Studies." In M. Straus and R. Gelles (eds.), *Physical Violence in American Families.* New Brunswick, NJ: Transaction Press.

Straus, Murray A., R. J. Gelles, & S. Steinmetz. 1980. *Behind Closed Doors.* New York: Doubleday, Anchor.

Sugarman, David, and Gerald Hotaling. 1991. "Dating Violence: A Review of Contextual and Risk Factors." In Barrie Levy (ed.), *Dating Violence: Young Women in Danger.* Seattle: Seal Press.

Sumner, C. 1979. *Reading Ideologies: An Investigation into the Marxist Theory of Ideology and Law.* London: Academic Press.

Sumrall, Amber Coverdale, and Dena Taylor. 1992. *Sexual Harassment: Women Speak Out.* Freedom, CA: Crossing Press.

Swiss, S., and J. E. Giller. 1993. "Rape as a Crime of War: A Medical Perspective." *Journal of the American Medical Association* 270, no. 5:612–15.

Tancred-Sheriff, Peta. 1989. "Gender, Sexuality and the Labour Process." In J. Hearn, D. L. Sheppard, P. Tancred-Sheriff, and G. Burrell (eds.), *The Sexuality of Organization*. London: Sage.

Tangri, S., M. Burt, and L. Johnson. 1982. "Sexual Harassment at Work: Three Explanatory Models." *Journal of Social Issues* 38:33–54.

Tanner, D. 1978. *The Lesbian Couple*. Lexington, MA: D. C. Heath.

Taylor, N. (ed.). 1986. *All in a Day's Work. A Report on Anti-Lesbian Discrimination in Employment and Unemployment in London*. London: Lesbian Employment Rights.

Taylor, R., and G. Ford. 1983. "Inequalities in Old Age." *Aging and Society* 3:183–208.

Taylor, Verta, and Nicole C. Raeburn. 1995. "Identity Politics as High-Risk Activism: Career Consequences for Lesbian, Gay, and Bisexual Sociologists." *Social Problems* 42:252–73.

Temkin, Jennifer. 1986. "Women, Rape and Law Reform." In Sylvana Tomaselli and Roy Porter (eds.), *Rape*. Oxford: Basil Blackwell.

Terpstra, D. E., and D. D. Baker. 1988. "Outcomes of Sexual Harassment Charges." *Academy of Management Journal* 31:185–94.

———. 1992. "Outcomes of Federal Court Decisions on Sexual Harassment." *Academy of Management Journal* 35:181–90.

Themas, D. 1993. "Rape in Refugee and Conflict Situations." Paper presented at the United Nations Population Council meeting on Sexual Coercion and Women's Reproductive Health, jointly sponsored by the Population Council and the Pacific Institute for Women's Health, November, New York.

Thomas, Dorothy. 1994. "In Search of Solutions: Women's Police Stations in Brazil." In M. Davies (ed.), *Women and Violence*. London: Zed Books.

Thomas, K. 1978. *Religion and the Decline of Magic*. Harmondsworth: Penguin.

Thompson, F. 1973. "Testimony: The Memphis Riot 1865." In Gerda Lerner (ed.), *Black Women in White America*. New York: Vintage Books.

Thompson, L., and D. Wilson. 1989. *Report on Child Fatalities Related to Child Abuse and Neglect*. Olympia, Wash.: Department of Health and Human Services, Division of Children and Family Services.

Thompson, M. E., H. Oshagan, and S. Chaffee. 1986. *Pornography: A "Liberal" Dilemma*. Unpublished manuscript, University of Wisconsin-Madison.

Thorne, Barrie. 1993. *Gender Play: Girls and Boys at School*. New Brunswick, NJ: Rutgers University Press.

Tieger, Todd. 1981. "Self-Rated Likelihood of Raping and the Social Perception of Rape." *Journal of Research in Personality* 15:147–58.

Tiger, L. 1969. *Men in Groups*. New York: Random House.

Time. 1986. "Pornography: A Poll." July 21, p. 22.

Time. 1989. "Seven Deadly Days." July 17, p. 11.

Tolman, Richard, and Gauri Bhosley. 1991. "The Outcome of Participation in a Shelter-Sponsored Program for Men Who Batter." In Dean Knudsen and JoAnn Miller (eds.), *Abused and Battered: Social and Legal Responses to Family Violence*. Hawthorne, NY: Aldine de Gruyter.

Tolson, A. 1977. *The Limits of Masculinity*. New York: Harper and Row.

Tomaselli, Sylvana, and Roy Porter (eds.). 1986. *Rape*. Oxford: Basil Blackwell.

Tomes, Nancy. 1978. "A 'Torrent of Abuse': Crimes of Violence between Working-Class Men and Women in London, 1840–1875." *Journal of Social History* 11:328–45.

Tomlin, S. 1989. *Abuse of Elderly People: An Unnecessary and Preventable Problem*. London: British Geriatrics Society.

Tong, R. 1984. *Women, Sex, and the Law*. Totowa, NJ: Rowman and Allanheld.

Toubia, N. 1993. *Female Genital Mutilation: A Call For Global Action*. New York: Women, Ink.

Toufexis, A. 1987. "Home Is Where the Hurt Is: Wife Beating among the Well-to-Do Is No Longer a Secret." *Time*, December 21, p. 68.

Traynor, J., and J. Hasnip. 1984. "Sometimes She Makes Me Want to Hit Her." *Community Care*, August, pp. 22–24.

Treguear, T. L., and C. Carro. 1991. *Ninas Madres: Recuento de una Experiencia*. San Jose, Costa Rica: PROCAL.

Truesdell, D. J., J. S. McNeil, and J. P. Deschner. 1986. "Incidence of Wife Abuse in Incestuous Families." *Social Work* (March–April):138–40.

Tuan, Yi-Fu. 1984. *Dominance and Affection: The Making of Pets*. New Haven: Yale University Press.

Turnbull, C. 1965. *Wayward Servants*. New York: Natural History Press.

UNICEF. 1995. *State of the World's Children 1996*. New York: UNICEF.

United Nations. 1993. *Rape and the Abuse of Women in the Territory of Former Yugoslavia*. U.N. document E/CN.4/1993/L.21. Geneva, Switzerland: United Nations.

U.S. Congress. 1972. "Report of the Commission on Obscenity and Pornography, September 1970." In Lord Longford (ed.), *Pornography: The Longford Report*. London: Coronet.

U.S. Department of Health and Human Services, National Center on Child Abuse and Neglect. 1995. *Child Maltreatment 1993: Reports from the States to the National Center on Child Abuse and Neglect*. Washington, DC: U.S. Government Printing Office.

United States Department of Justice. 1987. *Violent Crime by Strangers and Non-Strangers*. Special Report (January).

———. 1988. *Uniform Crime Reports for the United States*. Washington, DC: U.S. Government Printing Office.

———. 1991. *Crime in the United States: Uniform Crime Reports, 1990*. Washington, DC: U.S. Government Printing Office.

———. 1992. *Criminal Victimization in the United States, 1990*. Washington, DC: U.S. Government Printing Office.

U.S. House of Representatives. 1980. *Hearings on Sexual Harassment in the Federal Government*. Committee on the Post Office and Civil Service, Subcommittee on Investigations. Washington, DC: U.S. Government Printing Office.

U.S. Merit Systems Protection Board. 1981. *Sexual Harassment in the Federal Workplace: Is It a Problem?* Washington, DC: U.S. Government Printing Office.

———. 1987. *Sexual Harassment in the Federal Workplace: An Update*. Washington, DC: U.S. Government Printing Office.

U.S. Senate Committee on the Judiciary, Hearings on Women and Violence. 1990. "Ten Facts about Violence Against Women."

Van Boemel, G. B. and P. D. Rozée. 1992. "Treatment for Psychosomatic Blindness among Cambodian Refugee Women." *Women & Therapy* 13:239–66.

Van der Kolk, B. A. 1987. "The Psychological Consequences of Overwhelming Life Experiences." In B. A. Van der Kolk (ed.), *Psychological Trauma*. Washington, DC: American Psychiatric Press.

van Dijk, J., and P. Mayhew. 1993. "Criminal Victimization in the Industrial World: Key Findings of the 1989 and 1992 International Crime Surveys." In A. Alvassi del Frate, U. Zvekic, and J. van Dijk (eds.), *Understanding Crime: Experiences of Crime and Crime Control*. U.N. publication E-93, III, N.2. Rome: United Nations International Crime and Justice Institute.

Vance, C. S. 1984. "Pleasure and Danger: Toward a Politics of Sexuality." In C. Vance (ed.), *Pleasure and Danger: Exploring Female Sexuality*. Boston: Routledge and Kegan Paul.

———. 1986. "The Meese Commission on the Road." *The Nation*, August.

Vargo, S. 1987. "The Effects of Women's Socialization on Lesbian Couples." In Lesbian Psychologies Collective (eds.), *Lesbian Psychologies*. Urbana: University of Illinois Press.

Verkko, Veli. 1951. *Homicides and Suicides in Finland and Their Dependence on National Character*. Copenhagen: G. E. C. Gads Forlag.

Victor, C. 1991. *Health and Health Care in Later Life.* Milton Keynes: Open University Press.

Vogel, Lise. 1974. "Fine Arts and Feminism: The Awakening Conscience." *Feminist Studies* 2, no. 1:3–37.

Walby, S. 1986. *Patriarchy at Work: Patriarchal and Capitalist Relations in Employment.* Minneapolis: University of Minnesota Press.

———. 1989. "Theorizing Patriarchy." *Sociology* 23, no. 2:213–34.

———. 1990. "From Private to Public Patriarchy: The Periodisation of British History." *Women's Studies International Forum* 13, nos. 1 and 2:91–104.

Walker, A. 1990. "Poverty and Inequality in Old Age." In J. Bond and P. Coleman (eds.), *Ageing and Society.* London: Sage.

Walker, Alice. 1981. "Coming Apart." In *You Can't Keep a Good Woman Down.* New York: Harcourt Brace Jovanovich.

———. 1982. *The Color Purple.* New York: Harcourt Brace Jovanovich.

———. 1989. "Trying to See My Sister." In *Living by the Word.* New York: Harcourt Brace Jovanovich.

Walker, Lenore E. 1977–78. "Battered Women and Learned Helplessness." *Victimology* 2, no. 4:525–34.

———. 1979. *The Battered Woman.* New York: Harper & Row.

———. 1984. *The Battered Woman Syndrome.* New York: Springer.

———. 1989. *Terrifying Love.* New York: Harper Perennial.

———. 1993. "Legal Self-Defense for Battered Women." In Marsali Hansen and Michele Harway (eds.), *Battering and Family Therapy: A Feminist Perspective.* Newbury Park, CA: Sage.

Walker, Margaret. 1967. *Jubilee.* New York: Bantam.

Wallace, A. 1986. *Homicide: The Social Reality.* Sydney: New South Wales Bureau of Crime Statistics and Research.

Wallsgrove, R. 1977. "Pornography: Between the Devil and the True Blue White House." *Spare Rib* 65 (December).

Walsh, C. 1990. "FARE: Fraternity Acquaintance Rape Education." Paper presented at the Southeastern Psychological Association meeting, April, Atlanta, Georgia.

Wardell, L., C. Gillespie, and A. Leffler. 1983. "Science and Violence against Women." In D. Finkelhor et al. (eds.), *The Dark Side of Families: Current Family Violence Research.* Beverly Hills, CA: Sage.

Warr, M. 1985. "Fear of Rape among Urban Women." *Social Problems* 32:239–50.

Warshaw, Carole. 1989. "Limitations of the Medical Model in the Care of Battered Women." *Gender & Society* 3, no. 4 (December):506–17.

———. 1993. "Limitations of the Medical Model in the Care of Battered Women." In P. B. Bart and E. G. Moran (eds.), *Violence against Women: The Bloody Footprints.* Newbury Park, CA: Sage.

Warshaw, Robin. 1988. *I Never Called It Rape: The Ms. Report on Recognizing, Fighting, and Surviving Date and Acquaintance Rape.* New York: Harper & Row.

Wasoff, F. 1982. "Legal Protection from Wifebeating: The Processing of Domestic Assaults by Scottish Prosecutors and Criminal Courts." *International Journal of the Sociology of Law* 10:187–204.

Watt, D., and M. Fuerst. 1992. *1993 Tremeear's Criminal Code.* Scarborough, Ont.: Carswell.

Webb, Peter. 1975. *The Erotic Arts.* London: Secker and Warburg.

Weeks, Jeffrey. 1981. *Sex, Politics and Society: The Regulation of Sexuality Since 1800.* London and New York: Longman.

———. 1989. *Sex, Politics and Society.* 2d ed. London: Longman.

Weis, Joseph. 1989. "Family Violence Research Methodology and Design." In Lloyd Ohlin and Michael Tonry (eds.), *Family Violence.* Chicago: University of Chicago Press.

Weis, Kurt, and Sandra S. Borges. 1973. "Victimology and Rape: The Case of the Legitimate Victim." *Issues in Criminology* 8:71–115.

West, C., and D. Zimmerman. 1987. "Doing Gender." *Gender & Society* 1, no. 2:125–51.

West, D. 1982. *The Living Is Easy.* New York: Feminist Press.

Williams, Joyce E. 1984. "Secondary Victimization: Confronting Public Attitudes about Rape." *Victimology: An International Journal* 9:66–81.

Williams, K. B., and R. R. Cyr. 1992. "Escalating Commitment to a Relationship: The Sexual Harassment Trap." *Sex Roles* 27:47–72.

Willis, P. E. 1978. *Profane Culture.* London: Routledge & Kegan Paul.

———. 1979. "Shop Floor Culture, Masculinity and the Wage Form." In J. Clarke, C. Critcher, and R. Johnson (eds.), *Working Class Culture.* London: Hutchinson.

Wilson, M., and M. Daly. 1993. "Spousal Homicide Risk and Estrangement." *Violence and Victims* 8:3–15.

Winfield, I., L. K. George, M. Schwartz, and D. G. Blazer. 1990. "Sexual Assault and Psychiatric Disorders among a Community Sample of Women." *American Journal of Psychiatry* 147:335–41.

Wise, S., and S. Stanley. 1987. *Georgie Porgie: Sexual Harassment in Everyday Life.* London: Pandora.

Wohl, A. S. 1978. "Sex and the Single Room: Incest among the Victorian Working Classes." In A. S. Wohl (ed.), *The Victorian Family.* London: Croom Helm.

Wolf, R., and S. Bergman (eds.). 1989. *Stress, Conflict and the Abuse of the Elderly.* Jerusalem: Brookdale Institute.

Wolf, S. C., J. R. Conte, and M. Engel-Meinig. 1988. "Assessment and Treatment of Sex Offenders in a Community Setting." In L. Walker (ed.), *Handbook on Sexual Abuse of Children.* New York: Springer.

Wolfgang, M., and F. Ferracuti. 1967. *The Subculture of Violence: Towards an Integrated Theory in Criminology.* London: Tavistock Publications.

Wolshok, M. 1981. *Blue-Collar Women: Pioneers on the Male Frontier.* Garden City, NJ: Anchor Books.

Women's Aid. 1994. "Domestic Violence: The Northern Ireland Response." In M. Davies (ed.), *Women and Violence.* London: Zed Books.

Women's Legal Defense Fund. 1991. *Sexual Harassment in the Worlplace.* Washington, DC: Women's Legal Defense Fund.

Wood, M., and M. Hughes. 1984. "The Moral Basis of Moral Reform: Status Discontent vs. Culture and Socialization as Explanations of Anti-Pornography Social Movement Adherence." *American Sociological Review* 49:86–99.

Working Women's Institute. 1975. *Speak-Out on Sexual Harassment.* Ithaca, NY: Working Women's Institute.

———. 1979. *The Impact of Sexual Harassment on the Job: A Profile of the Experiences of 92 Women.* New York: Working Women's Institute Research Series, Report no. 2.

World Bank. 1993. *World Development Report 1993: Investing in Health.* New York: Oxford University Press.

Worth, D. 1989. "Sexual Decision-Making and AIDS: Why Condom Promotion among Vulnerable Women Is Likely to Fail." *Studies in Family Planning* 20:297–307.

Wyatt, G. E. 1988. "The Relationship between Child Sexual Abuse and Adolescent Sexual Functioning in Afro-American and White American Women." *Annals of the New York Academy of Sciences* 528:111–22.

———. 1993. "Lessons from Jamaica." Paper presented at the Population Council meeting on Sexual Coercion and Women's Reproductive Health, jointly sponsored by the Population Council and the Pacific Institute for Women's Health, November, New York.

Wyatt, G. E., D. Guthrie, and C. M. Notgrass. 1992. "Differential Effects of Women's Child Sexual Abuse and Subsequent Sexual Revictimization." *Journal of Consulting and Clinical Psychology* 60:167–73.

Ylö, K. 1990. "Domestic Violence: Conflict Tactic or Coercive Control?" Paper presented at the Family Violence Seminar, Boston Children's Hospital, March.

———. 1993. "Through a Feminist Lens: Gender, Power, and Violence." In R. Gelles and D. Loseke (eds.), *Current Controversies on Family Violence*. Newbury Park, CA: Sage.

Yllö, K., and M. Bograd (eds.). 1988. *Feminist Perspectives on Wife Abuse*. Newbury Park, CA: Sage.

Yllö, K., and M. Straus. 1990. "Patriarchy and Violence against Wives: The Impact of Structural and Normative Factors." In M. A. Straus and R. J. Gelles (eds.), *Physical Violence in American Families*. New Brunswick NJ: Transaction Publishers.

Yoder, Janice D. 1991. "Rethinking Tokenism: Looking Beyond Numbers." *Gender & Society* 5:178–92.

Zalk, S. R. 1990. "Men in the Academy: A Psychological Profile of Harassment." In M. A. Paludi (ed.), *Ivory Power: Sexual Harassment on Campus*. Albany: State University of New York Press.

Zeanah, Charles. 1994. "The Assessment of Treatment of Infants and Toddlers Exposed to Violence." In Joy Asofsky and Emily Fenichel (eds.), *Hurt Healing Hope: Caring for Infants and Toddlers in Violent Environments*. Arlington, VA: Zero to Three/National Center for Clinical Infant Programs, Inc.

Zierler, S., L. Feingold, D. Laufer, P. Velentgas, S. B. Kantorwitz-Gordon, and K. Mayer. 1991. "Adult Survivors of Childhood Sexual Abuse and Subsequent Risk of HIV Infection." *American Journal of Public Health* 81:572–75.

Zimmer, Lynn. 1988. "Tokenism and Women in the Workplace: The Limits of Gender-Neutral Theory." *Social Problems* 35:64–77.

Zimring, Franklin. 1989. "Toward a Jurisprudence of Family Violence." In Lloyd Ohlin and Michael Tonry (eds.), *Family Violence*. Chicago: University of Chicago Press.

Zorza, Joan. 1991. "Women Battering: A Major Cause of Homelessness." *Clearinghouse Review* 24, no. 4 (Special Issue):421–29.

Index